MOON

W9-BPK-485

NORWAY

DAVID NIKEL

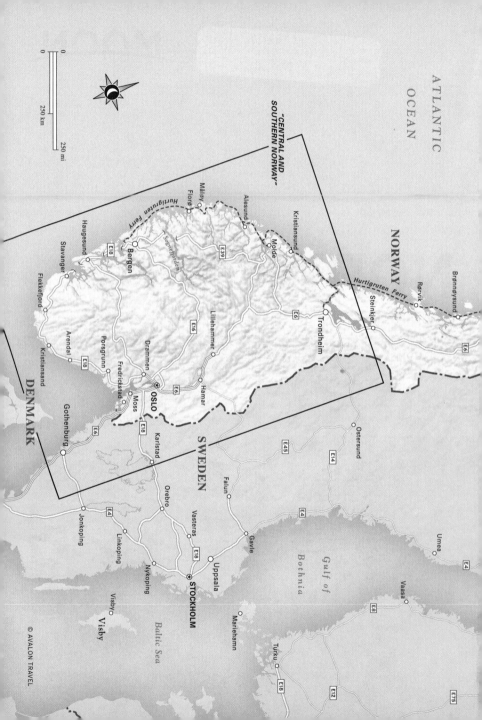

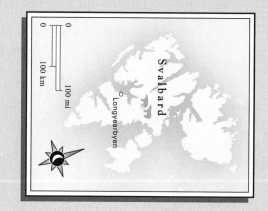

Svalbard

Longyearbyen

0
0
100 km
100 mi

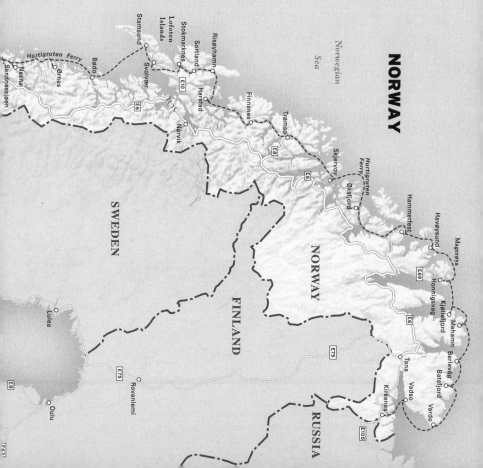

NORWAY

Norwegian
Sea

SWEDEN

FINLAND

NORWAY

RUSSIA

Hurtigruten Ferry

Stamsund
Lofoten
Islands
Stokmarknes
Sortland
Risøyhamn
Bodø
Ørnes
Nesna
Sandnessjøen
Svolvær
Harstad
Narvik
Finnsnes
Tromsø
Skjervøy
Øksfjord
Hammerfest
Havøysund
Magerøya
Honningsvåg
Kjøllefjord
Mehamn
Berlevåg
Båtsfjord
Vardø
Vadsø
Tana
Kirkenes
Rovaniemi
Oulu
Luleå

Hurtigruten
Ferry

E10
E6
E8
E6
E69
E6
E75
E105
E75
E8

Contents

DISCOVER
Norway

From the dancing aurora borealis and dramatic Lofoten islands in the north to the majesty of the western fjords and imposing mountainous terrain throughout, Norway in its natural form needs no enhancement. As you sail down a fjord between steep cliffs with sea eagles swooping above your head, you'll soon realize very little has changed since the time of the Vikings.

While many destinations build theme parks and other artificial attractions to draw in the crowds, Norway has never needed to do that. But the authorities are working to improve infrastructure, building new highways, tunnels, bridges, and lookout points to enhance the very best of what nature has to offer and make Norway easier to visit than ever before.

Norway's cities are full of international influence, and you'll find modern architecture alongside historical landmarks. Nowhere is this contrast more evident than Oslo, where the sparkling Oslo Opera House shares the waterfront with the medieval Akershus Fortress. Strike up a conversation (Norwegians speak great English) to discover the contemporary side of Scandinavia.

Norway strikes a magical balance between history, modernity, and natural beauty. There's no need to embellish what is astounding unadorned.

Clockwise from top left: Ålesund; modern buildings in Oslo; boat trip on a fjord; Oslo's Opera House; Vigeland Sculpture Park; the Royal Route near the Hjørundfjord.

10 TOP EXPERIENCES

1 **Geirangerfjord:** The pick of Norway's many spectacular fjords, Geiranger is renowned for its steep cliffs, tall slender waterfalls, and photo opportunities galore (page 179).

2 **Scenic Railways:**
The **Bergen
Line** (page 139) soars
over mountains while
the **Flåm Railway**
(pictured, page 187)
descends through a
lush valley to a fjord's
edge, offering two
of the world's most
spectacular rail trips.

>>>

3 **Preikestolen
Cliff:** The hike to
this flat cubed cliff,
which overlooks the
glistening Lysefjord,
is one of Norway's
most popular treks
(page 120).

>>>

4 **Atlantic Road:** This captivating eight-kilometer (five-mile) stretch of highway skips over an archipelago of islets and skerries (page 245).

^ ^ ^

5 **Art Nouveau Ålesund:** The perfect base for a trip to the Geirangerfjord, Ålesund was rebuilt in the fanciful art nouveau style after a devastating fire in 1904 (page 167).

>>>

6   Røros: A living museum high in the mountains, this former copper-mining town remains vibrant, focusing today on sustainable local food (page 225).

7 **Vigeland Sculpture Park:** This park within a park features hundreds of stone, bronze, and wrought-iron sculptures, the life's work of Gustav Vigeland (page 54).

>>>

8 **The Lofoten Road Trip:** This Arctic archipelago is home to diverse wildlife and picturesque fishing villages, surrounded by the most dramatic scenery that Norway has to offer (page 263).

>>>

9 **Northern Lights:** The chance to see the mystical aurora borealis dance across the sky draws visitors to the High North (page 303).

10 **Hurtigruten Ferry:** Running up and down the coast, the ferry serves a dual purpose as an informal cruise through stunning scenery and a vital service for tiny coastal communities (page 23).

If You Have . . .

- **ONE WEEK:** Visit Oslo, Bergen, and the fjords in between. Taking the Oslo to Bergen railway (the Bergen Line) is the best way to make the most of your time.

- **TWO WEEKS:** Extend your time in the fjord region to include a road trip to Ålesund and a few nights around the Geirangerfjord and

Trollstigen mountain pass. Alternatively, head to historic Trondheim.

- **THREE WEEKS:** Sail up the coast on the Hurtigruten ferry from Bergen, Ålesund, or Trondheim, and choose to stop at the stunning Lofoten islands, lively Tromsø, or Honningsvåg, from where the iconic North Cape is only a short bus ride away.

Planning Your Trip

Where to Go

Oslo

Norway's capital has an expanding list of **arts, culture, and music events.** The **rejuvenated waterfront** features a mix of old and new architecture, including the striking **Oslo Opera House.** Surrounded by water and forest, Oslo offers more outdoor experiences than any other city of its size. In the summer there is awesome **hiking, biking,** and **boating,** while in the winter you are never more than 20 minutes from a **cross-country skiing** trail. Beyond Oslo, historic **Fredrikstad** and sporty **Lillehammer** are both worthy of a day trip.

Southern Norway

Thousands of cruise ship passengers flock to **Stavanger** for its **street art** and proximity to world-famous sights such as the **Preikestolen** cliff, yet the rest of southern Norway is left for locals to enjoy. While temperatures can never be guaranteed, **Kristiansand** is known as Norway's summer city for good reason. The family-friendly **Kristiansand Dyreparken** and **idyllic coastal villages** make for a great alternative summer vacation, especially with children.

Bergen and the Fjords

The fjord region unfurls itself along Norway's west coast and two of the biggest fjords, **Hardangerfjord** and **Sognefjord,** are within easy reach of **Bergen.** Norway's second city, laid-back Bergen is the perfect base for a fjord safari, but take at least a couple of days to explore the city itself. Discover the city's Hanseatic past and ride the **Fløibanen Funicular** railway to the top of Mount Fløyen to fully appreciate the spectacular natural setting. Art nouveau **Ålesund** is a great base for a trip to the world-famous **Geirangerfjord.**

Trondheim and Central Norway

Hemmed in by mountain ranges, the Atlantic coast, and the Swedish border, lush valleys cut through central Norway, providing an **ever-changing landscape.** Viking capital **Trondheim** is a popular cruise stop that has a lot to offer visitors, from the imposing **Nidaros Cathedral** to the interactive contemporary music museum **Rockheim.** The hair-raising **Trollstigen mountain pass** and the island-hopping **Atlantic Road** make once-in-a-life-time road trips. Norway's heartland is the perfect

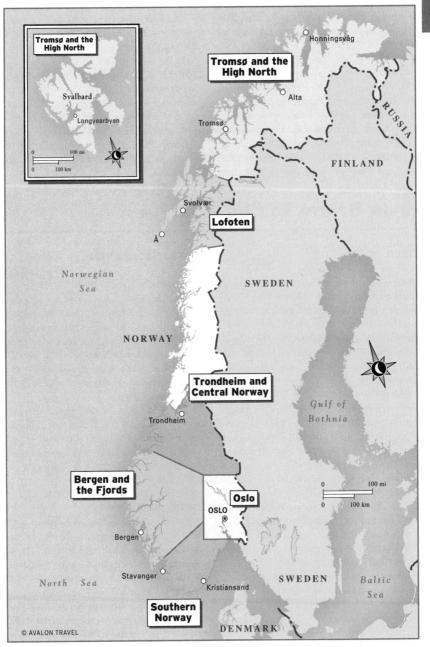

Tromsø and the
High North

Svalbard

Longyearbyen

0   100 mi
0   100 km

Honningsvåg

Tromsø and the
High North

Alta

Tromsø

RUSSIA

FINLAND

Svolvær

Lofoten

Å

Norwegian
Sea

SWEDEN

NORWAY

Trondheim and
Central Norway

Gulf of
Bothnia

Trondheim

Bergen and
the Fjords

Oslo

OSLO

0   100 mi
0   100 km

Bergen

Stavanger

SWEDEN

Baltic
Sea

North Sea

Kristiansand

Southern
Norway

DENMARK

© AVALON TRAVEL

destination for outdoor enthusiasts, from **fishing** and **kayaking** in the rivers to **hiking** in the many national parks.

Lofoten

The photogenic Lofoten archipelago shows Norway at its **most dramatic.** Surprisingly mild considering their location north of the Arctic Circle, the **islands** are known for their rugged **mountains,** sheltered **bays,** picturesque **fishing villages,** and even **beaches.** You could spend your entire vacation traveling across Lofoten by car or bicycle. The region is a **nature lover's dream.** Moose, sea eagles, otters, and colorful puffins are commonplace.

Tromsø and the High North

The **northern lights** give the Norwegian Arctic a magnetic pull. Yet the High North has much more to offer in both summer and winter. Explore **Sami culture,** see prehistoric rock carvings at **Alta,** watch the midnight sun at the **North Cape,** or take a **dogsled ride** across fresh untouched snow.

Know Before You Go

When to Go

In search of the surprisingly warm Scandinavian summer, most travelers head to the Norwegian fjords **June-August. High season** for tourism, this is the busiest time but also with the most diverse range of accommodations. **July** is the **Norwegian holiday month,** and it can be difficult to find accommodations in rural areas during that time; however, bargains can often be scored in cities.

A **vastly underrated** time is the spring. **February-April,** there is snow on the ground but the polar nights are long gone. Days are bright if crisp, and it's the best time for skiing. There are still possibilities for northern lights hunting, yet there are very few tourists. The spectacular Lofoten islands are at their most beautiful this time of year. The weather in **May** is usually pleasant, but be aware of the many **public holidays,** most notably Constitution Day on May 17, when services for tourists are limited.

September-November is the **rainy season** but also popular for **northern lights** hunting. The dreary months of **November-January** are **best avoided.** Although the streets are brightened by festive lights, services for travelers are limited during the Christmas and New Year period, and thick clouds often prevent a light show overhead.

Passports and Visas

Visitors entering the country are allowed to stay for up to **90 days.**

Although Norway is not part of the European Union, it is a participant in the **Schengen Agreement,** which allows **passport-free travel** between member countries. If arriving from a fellow Schengen country (which includes most, but not all, EU members), there are no passport checks, but the 90-day period applies to the entire Schengen Area.

For citizens of the United States, Canada, United Kingdom, South Africa, New Zealand, and Australia and residents of the vast majority of European and Latin American countries, **visas** are **not required** to enter Norway at the time of writing.

Transportation

Most travelers arrive in Norway by **plane,** and almost all long-haul international flights into Norway arrive in **Oslo.** It's also possible to fly to regional airports, including Bergen, Trondheim, and Stavanger, from European destinations such as London, Amsterdam, and Copenhagen.

Travel to **Bergen and the fjords** is best done by the remarkable **train** journey or a **rental car,** depending on how much time you have. Those heading to the **Arctic** need an additional plane

The Hurtigruten Coastal Cruise

The Hurtigruten takes almost two weeks to travel from Bergen to Kirkenes and back.

Norway is increasing in popularity as a cruise destination. Consider a much more intimate homegrown cruising experience.

The fleet of 13 Hurtigruten ships travel the length of the Norwegian coastline from Bergen to Kirkenes by the Russian border. In a tradition stretching back to 1893, the ships call at big cities and tiny remote communities, delivering goods and providing a vital transport link to local residents.

Unlike luxury cruise liners, the Hurtigruten ships are working ships with basic yet comfortable facilities for travelers. There's no black tie required for dinner. Passage can also be booked between any two points on the route, combining a mini-cruise with an excellent transportation option between cities such as Bergen, Ålesund, and Trondheim for those without a car.

Highlights of the full 13-day round-trip cruise from Bergen to Kirkenes include:

- An opportunity to see the **northern lights** (fall through spring) away from the light pollution of built-up areas.

- Local **seasonal menus** devised based on the ingredients picked up at ports along the route.

- A unique perspective on the dramatic **Lofoten islands** and parts of **Arctic Norway** that few other travelers get to see.

- **Walking tours** around the thriving cities of Bergen, Ålesund, Trondheim, and Tromsø, interspersed with relaxing sailings down the world-famous **Geirangerfjord** (summer only) and **Trollfjord.**

Get more information and tickets at www.hurtigruten.com.

journey and a rental car to make the most of the experience.

A popular alternative is to explore Norway's **coastline** either by rental car or by the **Hurtigruten ferry,** which sails almost the entire length of the country between Bergen and the Russian border. Either use the ship as a relaxing cruise with time to explore the major cities on foot, or as a ferry to move between some of Norway's coastal highlights including Bergen, Ålesund, Trondheim, Lofoten, and Tromsø.

Best of Norway

The most efficient way to see the best of Norway is to combine the modern capital Oslo, historical trading port Bergen, and the western fjords into your itinerary—and you can see it all by **rail** and **ferry**.

Most travelers without their own transport follow the self-guided Norway in a Nutshell itineraries from Fjord Tours (see pages 131 and 146 for more information). Although these packages offer convenience and good value, they are often crowded during the high season and can feel rushed. Use the one-day pre-set itinerary as a base for your own plan, but extend the trip to take in extra sights along the way, spend more time in two of Norway's most vibrant cities, and most importantly relax rather than rush through the fjords.

Day 1: Oslo

Spend the morning admiring the life's work of Gustav Vigeland at the **Vigeland Sculpture Park** before museum hopping in the afternoon. The Bygdøy peninsula is home to the maritime-themed **Viking Ship Museum, Fram Museum,** and the **Kon-Tiki Museum.** Alternatively, check out Edvard Munch's famous painting *The Scream* at the vast **National Gallery** downtown. Stay in one of the emerging budget hotel brands close to Oslo Central Station in preparation for an early start.

Day 2: A Railway Enthusiast's Dream

Take two of the world's best-known railroad journeys in the same day. Travel on the **Bergen Line** from Oslo to Myrdal before taking the remarkable **Flåm Railway,** which twists and turns its way from mountain plateau to fjord level through the lush Flåm valley in less than one hour. Learn how the railroad was built at the **Flåm** village museum, before enjoying a delicious meal of local food and matching craft beer at the

Vigeland Sculpture Park in Oslo

Bergen

Viking-themed **Flåmsbrygga** brewpub, run by local craft brewery Ægir. Stay overnight in a cabin overlooking the fjord.

Day 3: Cruise the Nærøyfjord

Enjoy a light lunch from the on-board café on the two-hour cruise from Flåm to Gudvangen, which takes you past picturesque fjordside villages and along the UNESCO-listed **Nærøyfjord.** Return to Flåm on the same ferry, or save time and money and return on the bus. Rent a **kayak** for the afternoon for a much more intimate experience with the fjords, or take a **hike** along the railroad. Stay a second night in Flåm.

Day 4: Bergen

Take the fast ferry to **Bergen** to ride the length of the epic **Sognefjord,** one of the world's longest and deepest fjords. Alternatively, return to Myrdal on the Flåm Railway to travel to Bergen along the remainder of the Bergen Line.

Orient yourself with a ride up the **Fløibanen Funicular.** Enjoy the view with a snack or meal in the hilltop restaurant, or take a hike along one of the myriad marked trails. Stay the night in Bergen and enjoy an evening stroll along the historic **Bryggen** wharf.

Days 5-7: Optional Extras

Extend your journey by returning to Oslo and taking the Dovre Line railway to **Trondheim.** Watch out for mainland Europe's only musk oxen in the **Dovrefjell-Sunndalsfjella National Park.** Explore the history of Norway, including an archaeological museum and the Crown Regalia at Nidaros Cathedral, before taking a stroll along the cobbled streets and sidewalk cafés of Trondheim's Bakklandet neighborhood. Spend the night in Trondheim and return to Oslo via the morning train to **Røros,** which allows you four hours to enjoy lunch in a traditional setting and explore the unique former copper mining town.

The Norwegian fjords were created thousands of years ago during the last Ice Age, when glaciers (which used to completely cover the country) cut deep valleys into the bedrock through abrasion. Most fjords are deeper than the adjacent sea.

The Norwegian word "fjord" actually has a wider meaning than in English and is used to refer to any long, narrow body of water. For example, the Oslofjord is simply a channel created by a geological rift, and it lacks the steep sides that characterize the famous fjords in the west.

Due to the excellent fishing opportunities combined with the protection from the storms of the Atlantic, many small farming communities grew up along the shorelines and at the innermost ends of the fjords. Although most of the cliffside farms are now abandoned, many small communities still survive and thrive along the water's edge.

Norway's most famous fjords include the Sognefjord, at 204 kilometers (127 miles) the world's second longest, and the UNESCO-listed Geirangerfjord and Nærøyfjord. Hundreds of miles farther north, the mouth of the dramatic Trollfjord is only 100 meters (330 feet) wide, while its mountainsides reach more than 1,000 meters (over 3,500 feet) toward the sky.

Geirangerfjord

Fjord Road Trip

Renting a car opens up a wealth of options to customize a fjord itinerary. Even in high season there will be times when you are all alone on the roads. Turn off the main routes and perhaps you'll end up in a dense forest, or on top of a hill with an unspoiled view of a fjord all to yourself.

Outline a rough itinerary to be sure of good accommodation and restaurant options. Alternatively, tent up and take advantage of Norway's excellent campsites and the freedom to roam laws that permit wild camping.

With two weeks and a rental car, I recommend taking in three of Norway's most dynamic cities and several of the best known fjords, while leaving plenty of time for your own exploration. It's

important to note this itinerary includes a couple of roads that are only accessible May-October, depending on the weather. A winter road trip requires much more advance planning and should only be considered by experienced winter drivers.

Day 1: Oslo Airport to Lillehammer
150 KM (93 MI); 2 HOURS

Maximize your time on the road by renting a car from Oslo Airport Gardermoen and avoiding the high cost of driving in Norwegian cities by heading north, away from Oslo. A stop at Eidsvoll, site of the signing of Norway's constitution, is a must for history buffs. Spend the afternoon in **Lillehammer,** where the **Olympic Museum** and open-air museum at **Maihaugen** offer a terrific introduction to Norwegian society and culture. Spend the night in one of the hotels overlooking the vast Lake Mjøsa.

Day 2: Drive to Åndalsnes
259 KM (161 MI); 4 HOURS

Carve your way through the heart of Norway and along the winding roads of the Rauma valley towards **Åndalsnes.** The visitor center at the **Troll's Wall (Trollveggen),** Europe's tallest vertical rock face, is worthy of a stop. The town itself is unremarkable, so stay in a comfortable cabin at one of the several campsites in the immediate area, and enjoy a relaxing evening walk along the Rauma river in the shadow of the jagged mountains.

Day 3: Geiranger via Trollstigen
95 KM (59 MI); 3 HOURS

Get to the **Trollstigen mountain pass** (May-Oct.) before 10am and you'll beat the tour buses. Driving up the 11 hairpin bends is a memorable experience, as is the incredible view from

the balconies that dangle over the mountain ridge. Continue on the National Tourist Route to **Geiranger,** allowing plenty of time for photo stops. The viewpoint at the 1,500-meter (5,000-foot) summit of **Dalsnibba** mountain (May-Oct., toll road) offers an outstanding bird's-eye view of Geiranger.

Day 4: Geirangerfjord
21 KM (13 MI); 1.5 HOURS

After a quick visit to the modern **Norwegian Fjord Center,** pick up a packet of chocolate from **Geiranger Sjokolade** as a gift or to enjoy on the car ferry to Hellesylt. This one-hour cruise past the famous waterfalls and clifftop farms of the **Geirangerfjord** will leave a lasting impression. Dine and stay overnight in the peaceful village of **Hellesylt,** or a night at the spooky **Hotel Union Øye** is recommended for couples.

Day 5: Royal Fjord Route to Ålesund
120 KM (75 MI); 3.5 HOURS

Cross the underrated **Hjørundfjord** on a car ferry and follow in the footsteps of European

Ålesund

the Flåm Railway

fascinating shapes and colors of the Nigardsbreen glacier

royalty, who have traveled through this valley since the 19th century. Take a lunch in one of the many small villages along the route. **Ørsta** offers the most facilities and the option of an enjoyable waterside walk. Before arriving in **Ålesund,** take a detour through its suburbs up to the summit of **Mount Aksla** for one of Norway's most spectacular urban viewpoints. An evening meal in the restaurant here is worth the cash.

Day 6: Art Nouveau Ålesund
MINIMAL DRIVING IN AND AROUND ÅLESUND

A great choice to break up a Fjord Norway road trip is to spend the day exploring the rich art nouveau architecture of **Ålesund.** Whether you guide yourself or take a walking tour, the charm of the city is intoxicating. During the afternoon, explore the hiking trails and nature reserves of the neighboring **Giske islands** or meet the penguins at the saltwater **Atlantic Sea Park.** The

city's restaurants offer lunch and dinner options to suit all tastes and budgets.

Day 7: Balestrand
313 KM (195 MI); 6.5 HOURS

Make up a packed lunch from your hotel buffet or pick up some snacks from a supermarket for the lengthy drive south. Start your tour of the mighty Sognefjord in the peaceful village of **Balestrand,** perfect for exploring on foot. Treat yourself to dinner and a night in one of the historical rooms of the **Kviknes Hotel** and relax in one of the Sognefjord's most picturesque locations.

Day 8: Blue Ice Hike on a Glacier
173 KM (107 MI); 3.5 HOURS

Drive to Gjerde for a close-up view of the **Nigardsbreen glacier.** Hike in the immediate area, or pre-book a guided blue ice hike for an unforgettable experience. Stay overnight at a nearby campsite, or head to **Sogndal** for more accommodation and dinner choices.

Day 9: Sogndal to Flåm
105 KM (65 MI); 3 HOURS

Visit the magnificently preserved Borgund Stave Church and drive to Flåm via your choice of two of Norway's most intriguing driving experiences. Negotiate the winding Snow Road (May-Sept.) over the Aurlandsfjellet mountains, or experience the unique lighting within the world's longest road tunnel, the 24.5-kilometer (15.2-mile) Lærdal Tunnel. Stay overnight in Flåm and enjoy the range of local food and drink served at the village brewpub.

Day 10: A Day in Flåm
MINIMAL (IF ANY) DRIVING

This remote community may be tiny but it offers plenty of options to keep visitors occupied for a day. Choose between a kayak trip along the Aurlandsfjord, a cruise to the UNESCO-listed Nærøyfjord, or a return trip on the world-famous Flåm Railway. Alternatively, take it easy and stroll along the valley to the 17th-century church in the old village. Spend a second night relaxing in this peaceful location before hitting the roads again.

Day 11: Flåm to Bergen
167 KM (104 MI); 3 HOURS

Drive directly to Bergen and immerse yourself in the Hanseatic history of Norway's second city. The Bryggen wharf and associated museum are a must-see. In the evening, familiarize yourself with the modern side of Bergen. Treat yourself to a feast of New Nordic cooking at one of the city's outstanding restaurants, or take in a concert at one of the many gig venues.

Day 12: A Day in Bergen
MINIMAL (IF ANY) DRIVING

The outstanding Bergen Art Museum deserves at least a couple hours but could easily occupy the day if you have more than a passing interest in art history. The museum's restaurants are great choices for a light lunch or indulgent dinner. If you didn't catch a stave church on your travels, be sure to head out to a leafy suburb on the Bergen Light Rail to see the reconstructed Fantoft Stave Church.

To shorten this trip, leave your rental car at Bergen Airport (with prior agreement, for an additional fee) and return to Oslo by plane or the scenic Bergen Line railway.

Days 13-14: Oslo via Hardanger
463 KM (288 MI); 8 HOURS

Driving back to Oslo in a day is possible, but you'll miss out on even more outstanding natural beauty. It's best to allow two days for the return trip to take in the Hardangerfjord. Cross the fjord on the Hardanger Bridge, one of the world's longest suspension bridges, and drive all the way down the sunny eastern edge of the narrow Sørfjord for an overnight stay in Odda. Alternatively, take in the spectacular Vøringsfossen waterfall as part of a night in Eidfjord.

Skirt the edge of the vast Hardangervidda National Park on Route 7 to return to Oslo. At Hønefoss, continue on the E16 southbound toward the city or eastbound toward the airport.

Best of Oslo

Twenty-first century Oslo is a city transformed. For decades, travelers would head straight for the mountains or the fjords, but today they linger in this cosmopolitan European capital with world-class architecture, art, and museums. Were it not for Norway's stunning natural environment, three days in Oslo would satisfy most travelers. That's because the city is intrinsically linked to nature, surrounded on all sides by forest and fjord. Spend an entire weekend break in Oslo or tag on this three-day itinerary to a longer tour and you will not leave disappointed.

Should the weather be good, consider replacing any of these choices with a day trip to **Drøbak,** a delightful fishing village on the Oslofjord, or to **Fredrikstad** to wander the streets of one of northern Europe's best-preserved fortified districts.

To conserve your budget, make the most of your hotel's breakfast buffet and plan to eat light for lunch. Many hotels offer the opportunity to compose a packed lunch from the breakfast buffet (for an additional charge), or just grab some fruit and snacks from a supermarket.

Day 1: Art and the Waterfront

A visit to the epic **National Gallery** affords the opportunity to see some of Edvard Munch's most famous works with none of the crowds you might expect. Take a leisurely lunch in one of the excellent waterside restaurants on the **Aker Brygge** wharf, or grab a quick bite from a coffee shop and head instead to the **Astrup Fearnley Museum of Modern Art** at the nearby Tjuvholmen development. In the afternoon, explore the buildings that inspired the castle in Disney's *Frozen* at **Akershus Fortress,** before completing your tour of the waterfront with a stroll on the roof of **Oslo Opera House.** The nearby **Oslo Central Station** and **Jernbanetorget** square offer several options for dinner.

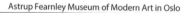
Astrup Fearnley Museum of Modern Art in Oslo

Akershus Fortress in Oslo

Day 2: The Great Outdoors

Oslo's excellent public transit brings forest and fjord within reach of all budgets. Take the metro to the **Frognerseteren** mountain lodge, where you can enjoy a slice of cake and a piping hot cup of cocoa before a walk through the forest to the world-class ski jump at **Holmenkollen.** On your way back to the city, stop off at Majorstuen and walk the short distance to take in the life's work of Gustav Vigeland at the remarkable **Vigeland Sculpture Park.** For an informal dinner head to the busy streets of **Grünerløkka,** where most restaurants turn into lively nightspots as the time ticks by.

Day 3: The Museums of Bygdøy

The Bygdøy peninsula is home to some of the country's best museums, clustered together amid the spacious homes of some of Oslo's wealthiest residents. The **Viking Ship Museum** displays restored ships found in burial mounds along the Oslofjord, together with tools and other objects that reveal much about the daily lives of the Vikings. Continuing the maritime theme, the **Kon-Tiki Museum** tells the fascinating tale of Thor Heyerdahl's Pacific expeditions through the original vessels and documentary films. Finally, watch actors bring an 18th-century farming community to life at the **Norwegian Museum of Cultural History,** a must-do during the summer. Splurge on dinner and drinks in the district of **Frogner,** which offers several high-end options.

Explore the Arctic

The dramatic mountains of Lofoten, the short days of winter and the endless summer nights, the aurora borealis dancing overhead, the vibrant colors and unique sounds of Sami culture, and the vast plains of tundra: Arctic Norway is a land of extremes.

Your best base to explore the Arctic is **Tromsø**, well connected to Oslo with several daily flights. Once you've exhausted options in the party capital of the north, choose to head west to explore the dramatic Lofoten islands or east through the Finnmark plains toward the North Cape.

Tromsø
DAY 1: NORWAY'S ARCTIC CAPITAL

The vibrant town of **Tromsø** is worthy of at least a full day before you set out into the Arctic wilderness. Cross the windswept city bridge for a closer look at the iconic **Arctic Cathedral** before taking the **Tromsø Cable Car** to the Storsteinen mountain summit for an unbeatable panorama of Tromsø's mountainous setting. Once back in the city, a beer at the famous **Rorbua** (ask the locals why it's famous) or **Tromsø Jernbanestasjon**, named after the city's nonexistent railway station, is a must to sample some of the city's well-known nightlife.

Option A: Lofoten
DAY 2: VESTERÅLEN

Start early and cross Senja, Norway's second largest island, to the fishing village of Gryllefjord. Grab a light lunch of fresh shrimp while you wait for the car ferry (summer only) to **Andenes** at the northernmost tip of the Vesterålen archipelago. Follow the National Tourist Route south and overnight among the blue buildings of **Sortland**. Alternatively, extend your trip with an overnight stay in Andenes and join a **whale-watching** boat tour.

cable car on the mountainside overlooking Tromsø

view across the bay in Hammerfest

Family Fun

Children have a prominent place in Norwegian society and will be welcomed anywhere you travel, even on organized trips such as northern lights safaris and shorter glacier hikes.

Spacious campsite cabins provide great value family accommodations for road trips through the fjords, while the most family-friendly attractions are located in Oslo and around the southern coastline to Stavanger.

Some of Norway's top attractions for children include:

- **Norwegian Museum of Cultural History (Oslo):** Children of all ages love exploring the historical farmstead brought to life with actors and animals.

Norwegian Petroleum Museum in Stavanger

- **Tusenfryd (Oslo):** Traditional roller coasters keep adults happy while children are well catered to at this family-friendly theme park just outside Oslo.

- **Kristiansand Dyreparken (Kristiansand):** Norway's biggest theme park includes an exotic zoo, water park, and plenty of unique accommodations within the park itself.

- **Norwegian Petroleum Museum (Stavanger):** Immediately outside the museum is the intriguing **Geopark,** an experimental children's playground that tests new ways of recycling materials and unusual objects from the petroleum industry.

- **Leo's Lekeland:** This chain of indoor play centers has branches in most major towns, including Oslo, Fredrikstad, Kristiansand, Stavanger, Bergen, Trondheim, and Tromsø. See www.leoslekeland.no for more information.

DAY 3: THE CAPITAL OF LOFOTEN

Discover the history of Norway's iconic coastal ferry service at the **Hurtigruten Museum** in **Stokmarknes,** before taking the Melbu to Fiskebøl ferry onto the Lofoten islands. Grab a late lunch and wander the galleries of **Svolvær,** before admiring the ice sculptures over an evening drink in the **Magic Ice** bar.

DAYS 4-5: A DRIVE TO REMEMBER

Stock up on food for a picnic lunch before you leave Svolvær, as you won't want to waste time searching for a restaurant. Head west through the Lofoten islands, allowing plenty of time for stops as the scenery becomes ever more dramatic. Linger around the stunning setting of **Henningsvær,** where you'll find some of the islands' most interesting artworks. The **Lofotr Viking Museum** and the living museum **Nusfjord** in a sheltered bay are other recommended stops. Stay overnight in a waterside timber cabin in **Å** or **Reine,** both stunning examples of traditional Lofoten fishing villages, before starting your return trip.

the World Heritage Rock Art Centre in Alta

Option B: To the North Cape

DAY 2: ALTA

Enjoy the best of **Tromsø** (see Day 1) before making the six-hour drive to **Alta.** A visit to the UNESCO-listed rock carvings at the **World Heritage Rock Art Centre** is the undisputed highlight, but don't miss the opportunity to learn about Sami culture and meet domesticated reindeer at the **Boazo Sami Siida** visitor center. There isn't much to do in Alta itself, so take the opportunity to enjoy the midnight sun or grab an early night, getting ready for a long drive the next morning.

DAY 3: HAMMERFEST

Beware of reindeer on the rural roads leading up to **Hammerfest** and even in the city itself. Put on some walking shoes and explore the historical **trails** around the city, including the steep zigzag path that provides an outstanding view across the bay. The central district with its boardwalk has a modern feel to it, because the town was razed to the ground by retreating Nazi forces at the end of World War II. History buffs should allow a couple hours to fully appreciate the **Museum of Reconstruction,** which depicts the events and subsequent rebuilding of the town and community. Dine at one of the restaurants along Hammerfest's modern boardwalk.

DAY 4: THE EXTREME NORTH

As you travel farther north the roads become narrower, the tunnels more intimidating, and the scenery more desolate. Take your time getting to **Honningsvåg,** a pleasant fishing community that vies with Hammerfest for the title of Europe's northernmost town.

Catch an intimate performance of *Our Northernmost Life* from a local youth group before basing your decision of if and when to drive to the **North Cape** on the weather. Clouds often roll in across the famous plateau, disappointing hundreds of visitors hoping to see the midnight sun. A better-value alternative is to head to any hilltop across the region, where you'll most likely be able to enjoy the midnight sun on your own. Although there are only a handful of restaurants, Honningsvåg will offer a better-value dinner than the overpriced visitor center at the North Cape.

Oslo

Look for ★ to find recommended sights, activities, dining, and lodging.

Highlights

★ **National Gallery:** This impressive collection of artwork from across the ages rivals some of Europe's greatest galleries. The Edvard Munch room is a particular highlight (page 43).

★ **Oslo Opera House:** The award-winning architecture of this striking structure slopes gently into the Oslofjord. Walk up to the roof and take in the views from the top (page 44).

★ **Vigeland Sculpture Park:** Explore the life's work of Gustav Vigeland at the center of Frogner Park. Many of the 200 sculptures take human form (page 54).

★ **Bygdøy Museums:** Oslo's most interesting and unique cultural museums are gathered together on the Bygdøy peninsula. A day here is time well spent (page 55).

★ **Holmenkollen Ski Arena:** The views from the top of the ski jump at this world-class sporting arena are both breathtaking and stomach-churning (page 57).

★ **Nordmarka:** Packed with locals on weekends, the Nordmarka forest is the city's premier destination for hiking and cross-country skiing, less than a 30-minute metro ride from downtown (page 61).

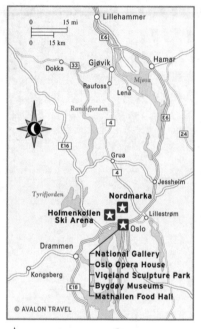

★ **Mathallen Food Hall:** Some of the best restaurants in Oslo are gathered together under one roof (page 72).

Oslo is one of Europe's fastest growing cities and offers a growing list of cultural attractions to tempt the fjord-bound traveler to spend some extra days in the city. The combination of historic buildings, functional commercial districts,

comfortable accommodations, and modern architecture attracts a diverse range of travelers to Norway's dynamic capital.

In recent years, Copenhagen and Stockholm have gotten into a very public battle for the rather meaningless marketing title "Capital of Scandinavia." Approach this subject in Oslo and locals will roll their eyes, safe in the knowledge that their city has become the modern cultural heartbeat of Scandinavia. After years of lying in the doldrums with a frankly deserved reputation of expensive dullness, Oslo's 21st-century renaissance has gathered pace in the blink of an eye.

First came the Aker Brygge fjord-side development of shops, restaurants, offices, and apartments replacing the unsightly Aker shipyard that greeted visitors arriving by sea. The motorway that further blighted the waterfront was ripped up and replaced with a network of tunnels. Oslo's waterfront is now a pleasant car-free environment, and it's set to improve even further.

With Oslo gaining in confidence as an emerging world city, attention turned to redevelopment of the east side. For several years since its opening in 2008, the sparkling white marble and glass Oslo Opera House stood alone as a symbol of the future, but development is finally underway on a new central library and Munch museum to complete the area's revitalization.

Almost all international travelers bound for the fjords will touch down in Oslo, and finally the city has enough to demand attention and insist that all but the most nature-obsessed travelers should spend a day or two exploring the capital.

A city full of surprises to first-time visitors, Oslo is a much more cosmopolitan place than any other Norwegian city. One in three residents were born outside of Norway, so

Previous: Oslo's modern architecture; Oslo City Hall by the waterfront. **Above:** Vigeland Sculpture Park.

Oslo

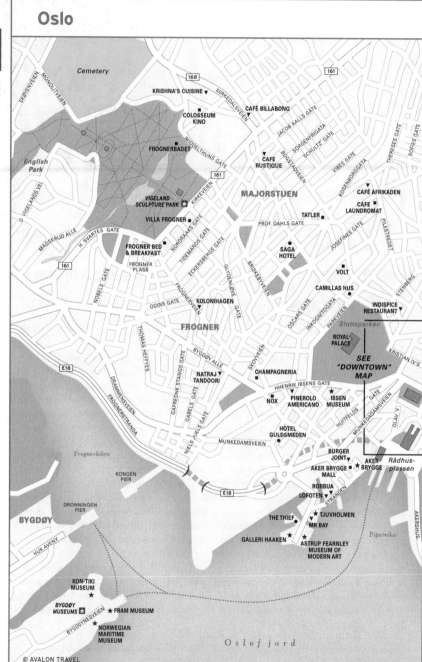

Cemetery

168

KRISHNA'S CUISINE ▼

CAFÉ BILLABONG

161

COLOSSEUM
KINO

FROGNERBADET

CAFÉ
RUSTIQUE ▼

English
Park

161

MAJORSTUEN

CAFÉ AFRIKADEN ▼

VIGELAND
SCULPTURE PARK ✚

CAFÉ
LAUNDROMAT

VILLA FROGNER ●

TATLER ■

PROF. DAHLS GATE

FROGNER BED
& BREAKFAST ●

SAGA
HOTEL ●

FROGNER
PLASS

161

VOLT ▼

KOLONIHAGEN ■

CAMILLAS HUS ●

ODINS GATE

INDISPICE
RESTAURANT ▼

FROGNER

Slottsparken

ROYAL
PALACE

SEE
"DOWNTOWN"
MAP

KRISTIAN IV'S

E18

BYGDØY ALLE

CHAMPAGNERIA ■

NATRAJ ▼
TANDOORI

HHENRIK IBSENS GATE

NOX ▼

PINEROLO
AMERICANO

IBSEN
MUSEUM ▼

HOTEL
GULDSMEDEN ●

MUNKEDAMSVEIEN

BURGER
JOINT ▼

AKER
★ BRYGGE

Rådhus-
plassen

Frognerkilen

KONGEN
PIER

AKER BRYGGE ■
MALL

RORBUA ▼
LOFOTEN ▼ ▼

E18

STRANDEN

Pipervika

DRONNINGEN
PIER

BYGDØY

THE THIEF ●

★ TJUVHOLMEN
MR BAY

GALLERI HAAKEN ★

HUK AVENY

ASTRUP FEARNLEY
MUSEUM OF
MODERN ART

KON-TIKI
MUSEUM
★

BYGDØY
MUSEUMS ✚

★ FRAM MUSEUM

BYGDØYNESVEIEN

★ NORWEGIAN
MARITIME
MUSEUM

Oslofjord

© AVALON TRAVEL

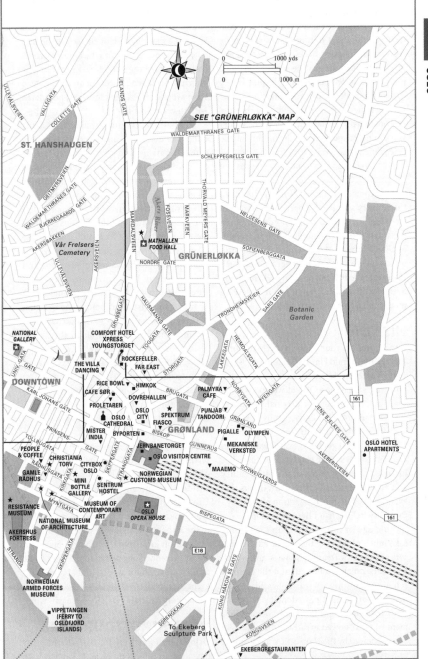

0   1000 yds
0   1000 m

SEE "GRÜNERLØKKA" MAP

WALDEMAR THRANES GATE

SCHLEPPEGRELLS GATE

ST. HANSHAUGEN

VALLEGATA
COLLETTS GATE
ULLEVÅLSVEIEN
UELANDS GATE

GEITMYRSVEIEN
WALDEMAR THRANES GATE
BJERREGAARDS GATE
AKERSBAKKEN
MARIDALSVEIEN
AKERSVEIEN
ULLEVÅLSVEIEN

Vår Frelsers
Cemetery

THORVALD MEYERS GATE
FOSSVEIEN
MARKVEIEN
HELGESENS GATE

★ MATHALLEN
FOOD HALL
GRÜNERLØKKA

SOFIENBERGGATA

NORDRE GATE

Botanic
Garden

TRONDHEIMSVEIEN
SARS GATE
GRUBEGATA
HAUSMANNS GATE
TØYENGATA

NATIONAL
GALLERY ✚

COMFORT HOTEL
XPRESS
YOUNGSTORGET

THE VILLA
DANCING ▼

DOWNTOWN

UNIV.GATA
GATE
KARL JOHANS GATE
PRINSENS.

▼ ROCKEFELLER
FAR EAST

RICE BOWL ▼ ■ HIMKOK
CAFE SØR ■
▼ PROLETAREN
DOVREHALLEN

OSLO
CITY

▲ OSLO
CATHEDRAL

MISTER
INDIA ▼

★ SPEKTRUM
FIASCO ■

■ BYPORTEN

PALMYRA ▼
CAFE

BRUGATA

STORGATA
TOGGATA

PUNJAB ▼
TANDOORI

GRØNLAND

GRØNLAND

PIGALLE ▼
OLYMPEN

NORBYGATA

JENS BJELKES GATE

OSLO HOTEL
APARTMENTS
●

PEOPLE
& COFFEE

CHRISTIANIA
TORV
RÅDHUSGATA
GAMLE
RÅDHUS

★ CITYBOX
● OSLO

MINI
BOTTLE
GALLERY

KIRKGATA
MYNTGATA
TOLLBUGATA
GATE

SKIPPERGATE
STRANDGATA

SENTRUM
HOSTEL

RESISTANCE
MUSEUM ★

AKERSHUS
FORTRESS

MUSEUM OF
CONTEMPORARY
ART

NATIONAL MUSEUM
OF ARCHITECTURE

STRANDA
SKIPPERGATA

NORWEGIAN
ARMED FORCES
MUSEUM

■ VIPPETANGEN
(FERRY TO
OSLOFJORD
ISLANDS)

JERNBANETORGET ■

GUNNERUS

OSLO VISITOR CENTRE

NORWEGIAN
CUSTOMS MUSEUM

MEKANISKE
VERKSTED

MAAEMO ●

SCHWEIGAARDS

AKEBERGVEIEN

161

OSLO
OPERA HOUSE ✚

BISPEGATA

E18

KONG HAKON 5s GATE

161

SØRENGKAIA

KONGSVEIEN

To Ekeberg
Sculpture Park ↓

EKEBERGRESTAURANTEN ▼

mosques, temples, and a vast array of food and shopping options fill the city's streets.

Many visitors are surprised at Oslo's proximity to the great outdoors, offering more recreational opportunities than perhaps any other city of its size in the world. Despite a population of well under a million, the city is surrounded by water and forest, so in the summer there are awesome hiking, biking, and boating opportunities, while in the winter you are never more than a 20-minute metro ride from a cross-country ski trail.

Although it appears to be in the south of the country, Oslo is placed in the center of the region known as Eastern Norway thanks to the country's unusual geography. The region stretches along the Swedish border from the mountains south of Trondheim to the mouth of the Oslofjord. An extended stay in Oslo puts you within easy reach of great cities such as historic Fredrikstad or sporty Lillehammer, both worthy of a day trip if you'll be staying more than a couple days in Oslo.

HISTORY

Depending on your faith in ancient Norse sagas, King Harald Hardråde founded Oslo in 1049. There is evidence of earlier settlement, however, which puts Oslo at well over 1,000 years old. Either way, the original settlement stood at the foot of the Ekeberg hills to the east of today's central district.

The city's first golden age came way back in the Middle Ages. King Haakon V chose to live in Oslo at the beginning of the 14th century and build Akershus Fortress, two things that eventually led to the designation of Norway's capital switching from Bergen to Oslo.

This age of prosperity didn't last long. Like much of Europe, the city faced the horrors of the Black Death in 1349. A union with Denmark quickly followed, and the country remained in union with its Scandinavian neighbors (including Sweden at one point) until 1814. During this period, the development of Oslo slowed greatly and was largely overshadowed by the Hanseatic trading boom in Bergen.

In 1624 Oslo was destroyed by a three-day-long fire. King Christian IV declared that the old wooden city should not be rebuilt. Instead he built a new network of city streets behind Akershus Fortress. As was the king's prerogative, he named the new city Christiana. The old city continued to grow in an unmanaged state around its original location, populated with lower-class citizens.

Shipbuilding eventually pulled Christiana out of the doldrums, and the city's economy slowly began to stand on its own two feet. In the 19th century, Norway finally became an independent nation once again and formed a looser union with Sweden, and the city really took off. New institutions such as the University of Oslo and the National Gallery were opened, the city expanded along the Akerselva river and got its first railway. The Parliament building was constructed and the memory of Danish rule was slowly but surely wiped away. In 1877 the city name was changed to Kristiania, before the original Norwegian name of Oslo was restored in 1925.

Since the discovery of oil in the 1960s, Oslo, along with cities like Stavanger and Haugesund, has entered a boom era, attracting international investment and interest. But it wasn't until the political decisions of the late 20th century to redevelop so much of the waterfront that Oslo started the transition to in-demand tourist destination.

A little bit of Oslo changed forever with the terror attacks of July 2011, when a far-right extremist killed a total of 77 people, mostly children, in the city center and on nearby Utøya island. Then Prime Minister Jens Stoltenberg and the city's people responded to the atrocities with love and hope, a display of emotion and solidarity that gripped the world. An enormous bed of roses lay in front of the cathedral for weeks, and at a rallying event in front of the city hall a few weeks later, Stoltenberg proclaimed that "hope will win."

PLANNING YOUR TIME

Oslo offers something for you whether you have just an afternoon or an entire week. It would be remiss to visit Norway without spending at least a couple of days exploring the capital's unique attractions.

To take in the city's waterside attractions, visit the museums of Bygdøy, and explore at least some of the outdoor possibilities, allow three full days. Oslo is a surprisingly compact city and easy to explore on foot, but the excellent public transit system will speed things along if you're on a tight schedule.

For those spending a longer time in Oslo, it's worth considering some trips to nearby towns like Drøbak or Eidsvoll. A trip to Fredrikstad's beautiful Old Town is a great way to spend a summer's day, while Lillehammer is a must to rekindle memories of the 1994 Winter Olympic Games. Fredrikstad is just over an hour away by train or coach, and while Lillehammer is farther (more than two hours by car or train), it can be a comfortable day trip destination with some advance planning.

If your visit to Oslo is short, try to avoid Sunday and Monday. Almost all shops and some attractions are closed on Sunday, while many museums and galleries close on Monday. Opening hours are also restricted throughout the Norwegian holiday month of July.

Oslo Pass

If you stop by the modern **Oslo Visitor Centre** (Østbanehallen, Jernbanetorget, tel. 81 53 05 55, www.visitoslo.com, 9am-6pm daily), you will be offered the Oslo Pass. Available for 24, 48, or 72 hours, the pass gives you unlimited access on public transit; free parking in municipal car parks; free walking tours; entry to many museums, galleries, and attractions; and discounts in certain restaurants and stores. At 335kr (24 hours), 490kr (48 hours), or 620kr (72 hours), the pass isn't cheap. Note that children under 16 and seniors over 67 pay approximately half the adult rate, while students under 30 can claim a 20 percent discount with identification.

Whether the investment is worthwhile comes down to your traveling style and simple

math. It's difficult to argue for the 24-hour pass unless you plan to rush around the city trying to cram as much as possible into one day. The 72-hour pass, however, is a different story. Consider the alternative: There is no equivalent public transit pass, so you would need to buy a seven-day pass for 240kr. Visiting just four of Oslo's biggest attractions (National Gallery, Viking Ship Museum, the Norwegian Museum of Cultural History, and Holmenkollen Ski Museum) adds 435kr to your bill. At 620kr, the 72-hour pass can be a good value, especially if you visit even more places or take advantage of the discounts. Consider also the convenience factor of avoiding foreign currency transaction fees on your credit card or the accumulation of loose change.

The Oslo Pass can be bought at the Oslo Visitor Centre; Ruter public transit information centers at Jernbanetorget, Aker Brygge, or Oslo Airport; and from most museums and hotels. To obtain the child, senior, or student rate, you'll need to buy your pass at the Oslo Visitor Centre or from a Ruter center. You can also pre-order online and collect your pass at Oslo Visitor Centre. All passes come with a booklet listing the benefits and discounts available at each attraction.

ORIENTATION

The city of Oslo covers an area so large that a lake high up in the hills actually marks its geographic center. The sprawling forest surrounding the city on three sides is fiercely loved by locals and just as much a part of the city as the paved streets below. The forest is split broadly into **Nordmarka** to the north and **Østmarka** to the east, both accessible by public transit.

You'll spend most of your time in the compact **downtown** *(sentrum)* area. The few square miles of interest pivot around the main artery, **Karl Johans gate.** The mostly pedestrianized street slices straight through downtown Oslo, passing Oslo Cathedral, Parliament, and the National Theater on its way from Oslo Central Station to the Royal

Palace. The city's **waterfront** is split into two bays; **Pipervika** to the west is home to the City Hall, Akershus Fortress, and Aker Brygge, while **Bjørvika** to the east is home to the Oslo Opera House, the gleaming office blocks and upscale restaurants of Barcode, and the luxury residential development Sørenga.

A short ferry trip into the **Oslofjord** reaches popular recreational islands. The pick of these is **Hovedøya,** with a nature reserve, important historical monuments, open space, and sheltered beaches.

Oslo's **suburbs** are divided by the Akerselva river. In simplistic terms, west of the river is more upmarket, with parks, expensive boutiques, and clean streets, while east of the river is more working class, with apartment blocks, cheaper shops and restaurants, and majority immigrant communities. Along the river itself is the hybrid **Grünerløkka,** a gentrified district full of boutiques, trendy cafés, and remarkable hairstyles.

Heading west, **Frogner** is an upperclass neighborhood great for shopping and home to most of the world's ambassadors to Norway. The important transit interchange at Majorstuen is a short distance from the sprawling Frogner Park and Vigeland Sculpture Park. Walking from downtown to Majorstuen via the Royal Palace and Frogner is a pleasant experience and great if you like shopping, thanks to the exclusive Bogstadveien shopping precinct.

Further to west is the peninsula of **Bygdøy,** of interest to travelers for the museums, as well as its beaches and hiking trails, which are popular with locals.

Immediately east of downtown, the diverse districts of **Grønland** and **Tøyen** offer the cheapest places to eat and shop in town but are short on sights. Farther east, Oslo's old town **Gamlebyen** doesn't compare to the historical districts of Fredrikstad, Bergen, Trondheim, and Stavanger, so there's no need to make a special journey.

Outside the central area, Oslo stretches for miles to the northeast and southeast with industrial and residential suburbs home to Oslo's rapidly increasing population.

Sights

Much of what you'll need to see in Oslo in located downtown, but don't miss the museums of Bygdøy, and take at least one trip into the hills.

All major museums and galleries have English explanations, either on the exhibits themselves or via a brochure. Where an establishment offers guided tours they are usually in Norwegian, with English available only on Saturday or by prior arrangement, often at a hefty cost. If a guided tour is important to you, inquire in advance.

DOWNTOWN

Oslo's compact center is packed with sights. You could pack in a day's sightseeing and have seen some of the world's most famous paintings and cultural experiences.

National Museum (Nasjonalmuseet)

The **National Museum of Art, Architecture and Design** (tel. 21 98 20 00, www.nasjonalmuseet.no) is spread over a few distinct venues. The National Gallery, Museum of Contemporary Art, and the National Museum of Architecture are all worthy of a visit, especially as a combined ticket for all of the venues is just 100kr. All of the venues are closed on Monday. There is free entry on Thursday with extended opening hours until 7pm.

A new National Museum between the City Hall and Aker Brygge, scheduled to open in 2020, will combine all the museums together for the first time. As that time draws near, some of the exhibitions are likely to be

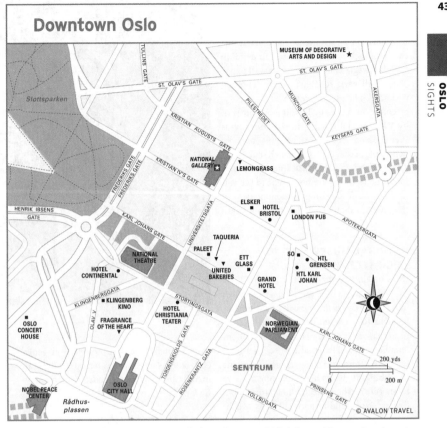

Downtown Oslo

© AVALON TRAVEL

reduced in size as the museums get ready for a logistical nightmare, so do check the latest status in advance if you're planning a special visit. The **Museum of Decorative Arts and Design (Kunstindustrimuseet)** (St. Olavs gate 1) is now closed pending the move.

★ NATIONAL GALLERY
(Nasjonalgalleriet)

The city's star attraction is the vast **National Gallery** (Universitetsgata 13, 11am-6pm Tues.-Fri., 11am-5pm Sat.-Sun., 100kr). You could easily spend an entire day exploring Norway's largest public collection of paintings and sculptures, or just an hour if you want the highlights. Most visitors head straight for the Edvard Munch room, home to his most famous works, including *Madonna* and *The*

Scream, which is located here rather than at the Munch museum itself. If this gallery was in London, Paris, or Rome there would be queues out of the door, but it's quite normal to find yourself all alone in the Munch room with one of the world's most famous artworks. Alone that is, apart from the security guard making sure you don't sneak a photograph.

The gallery is organized into a labyrinth of small rooms, each one representing a specific time period and/or style, so the rest of the highlights are dispersed throughout the building. Although the collection consists of predominantly Norwegian art from the Romantic era and more modern works, there is an impressive collection of works from French impressionists including Paul Cézanne, Édouard Manet, and perhaps the movement's most prolific practioner, Oscar-Claude Monet. Although each painting is captioned only with the title and artist, the theme of each room is described in detail in both Norwegian and English on a wall panel. This is well worth reading when first entering a room as it helps to set context.

Other must-sees include the self-portrait by Vincent van Gogh and the sumptuous French Salon, named for its original purpose of housing plaster copies of French sculptures. The French Salon's marbled stucco walls and fleurs-de-lis decals are now home to the gallery's cozy café. Opening times coincide with the gallery, although food is served only until 4pm.

NATIONAL MUSEUM OF ARCHITECTURE
(Nasjonalmuseet–Arkitektur)

The lesser known of the quartet of museums, yet my personal favorite, is the fabulous **National Museum of Architecture** (Bankplassen 3, 11am-5pm Tues.-Fri., noon-5pm Sat.-Sun.). The building itself is a great example of modern architecture, let alone the exhibits it guards inside. Architect Sverre Fehn refurbished the former Norwegian Central Bank building and achieved the delicate balance of restoring the Regency glory while adding in modern elements such as the glass pavilion to the rear. A film inside shows the story of the refurbishment. The museum is well suited for those who like the technical details of architecture, as plans and models of classical and modernist Norwegian buildings are everywhere.

MUSEUM OF CONTEMPORARY ART
(Museet for samtidskunst)

Immediately adjacent to the National Museum of Architecture, the **Museum of Contemporary Art** (Bankplassen 4, 11am-5pm Tues.-Fri., noon-5pm Sat.-Sun.) is home to thousands of artworks from 1945 to the present day. Photography and drawings are commonplace amid installations and digital media. A permanent exhibition

statue outside the National Gallery

from French-American Louise Bourgeois (1911-2010) showcases her famous sculptural installations known as cells, most notably *Celle VIII.*

★ Oslo Opera House
(Operahuset)

With so much development going on at the waterfront **Bjørvika** neighborhood, you'll need to follow the signs to find the quickest route to the **Oslo Opera House** (Kirsten Flagstads plass 1, tel. 21 42 21 21, www.operaen.no). The striking angular design, somewhere between a glacier, ski slope, and a ship coming in to dock, connects the city to its people in spectacular fashion. The roof rises out of the water, allowing visitors the ability to walk right up to the top. From the top you can clearly see across the city, from the Holmenkollen Ski Jump to the Oslofjord islands, and you also get a front-row view of the striking new vertical development of offices and restaurants named Barcode.

The Italian marble, white granite, and

glass structure shimmers beautifully in the summer sun, imposing yet inviting. With such a memorable design and views across the city and the fjord, you'd be forgiven for forgetting you're standing on top of an opera house. However, with free rooftop concerts held throughout the summer, you're unlikely to make that mistake.

Norwegian architect firm Snøhetta scooped many accolades for the design, including the 2008 culture award at the World Architecture Festival in Barcelona and the 2009 European Union Prize for Contemporary Architecture (Mies van der Rohe award). The interior is covered in oak to bring warmth in contrast to the coolness of the white exterior. A small café and shop are inside. A short distance into the fjord is the floating steel and glass art installation called *She Lies*, constantly moving with the waves and catching the light in a similar way to the giant windows of the Opera House itself.

For further insights, a 50-minute guided tour (1pm Mon.-Fri., noon Sat., 100kr) gives you unique backstage access otherwise off-limits.

You don't get much for free in Oslo, so take advantage of one attraction with free entry close by. The **Norwegian Customs Museum (Norsk Tollmuseum)** (Tollbugata

1a, tel. 22 34 68 76, 11am-3pm Mon.-Fri., free) is appropriately housed in the old Customs headquarters. Original uniforms and items dating back more than 350 years are on display, alongside exhibits documenting the history of imports and exports to and from Norway. You won't need more than 20 minutes here.

Karl Johans gate and the Civic Center

Start your walking tour of Oslo's downtown from the biggest transit interchange in the city. Buses, trams, and people trundle across **Jernbanetorget** square all day while the T-Bane rumbles every few minutes through the tunnel beneath your feet. The statue of the tiger on the city square is one of the city's most photographed. At first glance one may wonder why Oslo is nicknamed the Tiger City (Tigerstaden), given the distinct lack of any orange-and-black striped animals roaming Scandinavia, yet statues of tigers appear all across the city.

The phenomenon actually comes from the 1870 poem *Last Song (Sidste sang)*, in which the Swedish poet Bjørnstjerne Bjørnson described the dangerous city Oslo as a tiger fighting a horse representing the countryside.

Walking up to the roof of the Oslo Opera House is a must-do.

Hardly dangerous by world standings, but for a rural Norwegian the big city was seen as a ruthless place.

The Jernbanetorget square is useful to orient yourself by, with its tall tower marking the Ruter public transit information center, the start of **Karl Johans gate** (downtown's main artery), and just around the corner the sleek modern lines of the Opera House.

OSLO CATHEDRAL
(Oslo Domkirke)

First consecrated in 1697 and previously known as Our Saviour's Church, **Oslo Cathedral** (Karl Johans gate 11, 10am-4pm Mon.-Thurs., 4pm-6am Fri., 10am-4pm Sat.-Sun., free) is an active parish church for downtown Oslo and host of public events for the Royal Family and Government. After the Oslo and Utøya terror attacks of 2011, locals blanketed the streets outside with roses, notes, and candles right up to the tram tracks. Restored to its original baroque style, the interior includes the original pulpit, altar, and carved organ. Don't miss the adjacent Neo-Romanesque bazaar halls, built during the 19th century as butcher shops but today home to cafés and restaurants.

NORWEGIAN PARLIAMENT
(Stortinget)

Past the hustle and bustle of Karl Johans gate is the first of the impressive civic buildings built in the 19th century. The **Norwegian Parliament** (Karl Johans gate 22, tel. 23 31 30 50, www.stortinget.no) is the Oslo Parliament building. The main entrance on Løvebakken was designed to face up to the Royal Palace. Unlike in many parliaments in the world, Norway's Plenary Chamber is located in the semicircular frontage with windows that open out onto the public square below.

Without getting elected to Parliament, the only way to get inside the building is on a tour. Free one-hour guided tours are held in English every Saturday morning at 11:30am on a first-come, first-served basis, with weekday tours added during July.

Oslo Cathedral

The tours look at the history of the building and politics in Norway and take you inside the Plenary Chamber, with plenty of good-natured humor about the Swedes and the Danes, of course. As the building is an active government building, it's advisable to check the website or tourist information to confirm the tours are running on your specific day of interest. Bookings are not possible except for groups, so wait in line outside the rear entrance on Akersgata; as long there are not 30 people (the maximum allowable) in front of you, you'll be fine. It's best to leave bags in your hotel, as you can expect airport-style security.

ROYAL PALACE
(Det kongelige slott)

Spend some time relaxing in front of the Parliament building in Eidsvolls plass, an urban park home to fountains and numerous events throughout the year, including a charming Christmas market in December. This section of Karl Johans gate is often used for processions and other public events, most notably on Norway's Constitution Day, May 17. The crowds fill the street as they approach the **Royal Palace** (Slottsplassen 1, tel. 22 04 87 00, www.kongehuset.no), the official residence of the Norwegian royal family. The palace is open to the public during the summer months but only on an official one-hour guided tour, on which you'll see various state rooms, the banqueting hall, and the palace chapel. They run four times daily in English from mid-June to mid-August starting at noon; book in advance.

A popular free attraction is the changing of the guard that takes place every day at 1:30pm in front of a camera-laden horseshoe of curious tourists. Erected 1845-1849, the Guardhouse is believed to be the oldest building in Norway built in the Swiss style.

A helpful link between downtown and the shopping district of Bogstadveien, the romantic **Palace Gardens (Slottsparken)** are worth a stroll at any time of year. The ponds, statues, and open spaces of the park look especially peaceful covered in snow.

IBSEN MUSEUM
(Ibsenmuseet)

Just behind the palace you'll find the **Ibsen Museum** (Henrik Ibsens gate 26, tel. 22 12 35 50, www.ibsenmuseet.no, 11am-6pm daily June-Aug., 11am-4pm daily Sept.-May, 100kr), dedicated to Norway's most famous playwright. At the turn of the 21st century, the interior of his former home was lovingly restored to the original colors and furniture, allowing visitors a glimpse into his mind as he wrote his dramatic final works. Exhibits from Ibsen's life can be viewed at any time, but the rooms of his home—the library, dining room, parlors, and study—are only available to view by joining a 30-minute guided tour. Available in English and Norwegian, the tours are held every hour on the hour up to one hour before closing. Book in advance to guarantee a spot, as groups are limited to 15.

To mark the importance of Ibsen's work to the Norwegian language, the sidewalks from the Grand Hotel to the museum feature 69 steel quotations inscribed into the ground from some of his most loved characters.

Waterfront

Until the construction work around the Oslo Opera House is complete, **Pipervika** remains Oslo's primary waterfront area, with a mix of old and new architecture.

The Royal Palace stands at the end of Karl Johans gate.

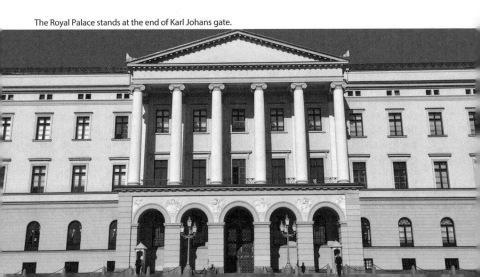

Island Hopping in the Oslofjord

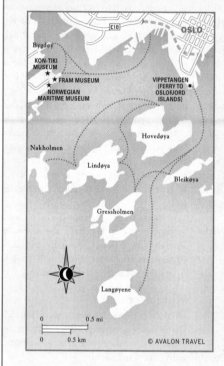

If the weather is kind to you, do as the locals do and head out to the small islands that dot the fjord in front of Oslo. Each island has its own distinctive character, from the beaches and history of Hovedøya to the residential vibe of Lindøya. Each island can be reached by small passenger ferries that run as part of the Ruter public transit system. They all leave from Vippetangen, which is a 20-minute walk or a couple minutes' ride on bus 60 from Jernbanetorget. The ferry runs year-round, although departures are much less frequent outside the summer months, so check www.ruter.no for the latest timetable. Choose to stay on one island for the day, or design your own itinerary and hop between several.

HOVEDØYA

The largest and most popular of the islands, Hovedøya is great for swimming on its western beaches or playing games on the large open grassy area. The east of the island is dominated by a nature reserve and perfect for hiking. Historical monuments abound, including the ruins of a monastery founded by English Cistercian monks in the 12th century and burned down in 1532. You'll also find cannon batteries from the days when

AKERSHUS FORTRESS
(Akershus Festning)

Akershus Fortress might look familiar—it was the inspiration for the castle in the Disney film *Frozen*. A monument to Oslo's history, the fortress has played an important role in the city's fortunes since its construction in medieval times. Turned into a state-of-the-art palace in the 17th century by King Christian IV, the fortress successfully defended all sieges before becoming a prison in the 18th century.

During World War II, the German Wehrmacht occupied the fortress. The Norwegian prisoners were moved and the Germans used the fortress as a prison of their own for those opposed to the Nazi system. Needless to say, conditions were poor, the fortress earning the nickname "Death's waiting room" from locals. After inmates attempted to escape, conditions deteriorated even further, as all furniture and bedding were removed.

The fortress is still an active military area, but the grounds are open to the public until 9pm daily. A small **visitor center** (tel. 23 09 39 17, 11am-4pm Mon.-Fri., noon-5pm Sat.-Sun., free) tells the story of the fortress from medieval castle to war prison. The grounds offer visitors a terrific vantage point of the modern Aker Brygge development and the Oslofjord.

the island was used by the Norwegian army. A few steps from the jetty, the beautiful Lavetthuset is home to a gallery and small kiosk open during the summer.

LINDØYA

Many of the Oslo residents that own one of the 300 summer cottages on Lindøya spend the whole month of July on the island. Peace and tranquility, yet just a 15-minute ferry ride from civilization. That population is served by a small shop and facilities including swimming areas and a football field.

NAKHOLMEN

Similar to Lindøya, Nakholmen is a small island filled with 200 holiday cottages. Not the most interesting of the islands for travelers, but interesting to get an insight into the Norwegian summer house experience.

GRESSHOLMEN

The hilly island of Gressholmen is connected to Heggholmen and Rambergøya with causeways that form an important bay for sea birds. Home to the picturesque Heggholmen lighthouse, the island is notable for holding Oslo's first main airport. Seaplanes landed here from 1927 to 1939, and the former airport is now a boatyard.

BLEIKØYA

One of the less frequented islands is also one of the more intriguing. Bleikøya is home to a former 19th-century sanatorium that housed children suffering with tuberculosis. A nature reserve occupies the northeastern part of the island, which is also home to a small World War II memorial.

LANGØYENE

The only island that permits free overnight camping, Langøyene is a popular place to spend the long summer nights. The large beach, volleyball court, field for ball games, and small kiosk (summer only) attract a younger crowd, especially on weekends.

Akershus Fortress

NORWEGIAN ARMED FORCES MUSEUM
(Forsvarsmuseet)

The **Norwegian Armed Forces Museum** (tel. 23 09 35 82, www.forsvaretsmuseer.no, 10am-5pm daily May-Aug., 10am-4pm Tues.-Sun. Sept.-Apr., free) traces Norwegian military history from the days of the Vikings right through to the present day. The unions with Denmark and Sweden are explored, along with the sea battles of World War II.

RESISTANCE MUSEUM
(Norges Hjemmefrontmuseum)

Located next to a memorial to Norwegians executed during World War II, the **Resistance Museum** (tel. 23 09 31 38, 10am-4pm Mon.-Fri., 11am-4pm Sat.-Sun., longer hours June-Aug., 60kr) chronicles the domestic fight against the Nazi occupation. Most of the original documents, newspapers, posters, and audio recordings that document the struggle are of course in Norwegian, and while written explanations in English are available, it's only worth the entrance fee if you're a real war history buff.

CHRISTIANIA TORV

A few minutes north of Karl Johans gate is the grid-style layout of the Kvadraturen district. Make time to pass through the heart of Kvadraturen, the cobbled square of **Christiania Torv.** Surrounded by a picturesque collection of original buildings from the 17th century, amid the cobbled roadway and centuries-old buildings, you'll find a fountain sculpture of a hand pointing downward. This marks the spot where King Christian IV chose to rebuild Oslo after a fire destroyed the old town in 1624. You won't be the first visitor to repeat his alleged words, "The new town will lie here!" while pointing to the ground!

MINI BOTTLE GALLERY

Hidden away in the Kvadraturen district is the **Mini Bottle Gallery** (Kirkegata 10, tel. 23 35 79 60, noon-4pm Sat.-Sun., www.minibottlegallery.com, 85kr), one of the city's most curious museums. Over 12,500 miniature bottles are on display in various installations, with a further 40,000 kept in a secure vault. Needless to say, it's the world's largest such collection. A popular venue for office parties and product launches, the Mini Bottle Gallery is an intriguing concept, but a visit is only worth the entrance fee if you have a specific interest in bottles beyond their contents.

OSLO CITY HALL
(Rådhus)

Oslo City Hall (Fridtjof Nansens plass, tel. 23 46 12 00, 9am-4pm daily Sept.-June, 9am-6pm daily July-Aug., free) is easy to spot thanks to its distinctive twin brown towers. Despite its brutal post-war brick architecture, the City Hall is a popular building among locals, voted as Oslo's "structure of the 20th century."

The building is known for its bell tower, which rings out on the hour every hour. Featuring such classic composers as Edvard Grieg and Vivaldi, as well as more modern hits such as "Imagine" by John Lennon, the program has in recent years altered based on current events. In 2016, the bells rang out David Bowie's "Changes" to pay tribute to the iconic singer upon his death.

In addition to housing Oslo's city council and administrative offices, City Hall is home to an art gallery featuring predominantly Norwegian artists from the early 20th century. During June and July, free guided tours are held at 10am, noon, and 2pm. Tours are given in Norwegian or English depending on the makeup of the group. Given the number of tourists, it usually ends up being English. Tours in Spanish, German, and French are available upon request.

NOBEL PEACE CENTER
(Nobels Fredssenter)

The City Hall is known internationally for being the home of the Nobel Peace Prize ceremony every November. Next door is a museum chronicling the history of the award. At the heart of the **Nobel Peace Center**

Nobel Peace Prize

Unlike all the other Nobel Prizes, which are awarded in Stockholm, the Nobel Peace Prize is awarded every November in Oslo. The prestigious annual award is intended to recognize those who have "done the most or the best work for fraternity between nations, for the abolition or reduction of standing armies, and for the holding and promotion of peace congresses."

NOTABLE WINNERS

The first winners in 1901 were Switzerland's Henry Dunant, for his role in founding the Red Cross, and France's Frederic Passy, for being one of the main founders of the Inter-Parliamentary Union and also the main organizer of the first Universal Peace Congress.

Other notable winners include Nelson Mandela, Mother Teresa, Aung San Suu Kyi, Theodore Roosevelt, and Desmond Tutu. Organizations are also eligible for the award. Doctors Without Borders took the prize in 1999. In 2012 the European Union took the honor for "over six decades contributed to the advancement of peace and reconciliation, democracy, and human rights in Europe."

CONTROVERSY

Despite the award's prestige, it has not been without its controversy. In 1973 Henry Kissinger and Lê Đức Thọ were awarded the Nobel for their efforts in negotiating the Paris Peace Accords, although fighting continued on to 1975.

Lê Đức Thọ refused to accept the award, and two members of the Norwegian Nobel Committee members resigned in protest. Other controversial winners include Yasser Arafat and Barack Obama, the latter saying he did not feel deserving of the award, which was announced just nine months after he took office.

The prize has also caused controversy for its omissions. "The greatest omission in our 106-year history is undoubtedly Mahatma Gandhi," said Geir Lundestad, secretary of the Norwegian Nobel Committee in 2006. "Gandhi could do without the Nobel Peace Prize. Whether the Nobel committee can do without Gandhi is the question."

(Brynjulf Bulls plass 1, tel. 48 30 10 00, www.nobelpeacecenter.org, 10am-6pm daily, closed Mon. Sept.-May, 100kr) is the Nobel Field, a collection of digital screens surrounded by thousands of LED lights creating a unique ambience. Each screen contains the story of a Nobel laureate.

Other permanent exhibits tell the story of Alfred Nobel, while temporary exhibitions profile the most recent winners. Although by no means required, a guided tour from the ultra-knowledgeable guides is worth the extra planning. Tours in English are included in the ticket price and run at 2pm on weekends throughout the year, daily during the summer.

AKER BRYGGE

The old Aker shipyard dominated the area until its closure in 1982. Four years later, the first part of waterside development **Aker Brygge** opened its doors. Today, over 6,000 people work here and over 1,000 people call it their home. The offices, malls, and residences are linked by several public areas and a pier perfect for an afternoon stroll or people watching from the many restaurants, cafés, and ice-cream kiosks that line the route. A recent extension to Aker Brygge, **Tjuvholmen** (www.tjuvholmen.no) is a modern waterside development with a grim history. Thieves were executed here in the 18th century, and its name directly translates into English as the Thief's Island.

On the walk from Aker Brygge to Tjuvholmen you will pass the always-burning Eternal Peace Flame, dedicated to the city of Oslo by Sri Chinmoy in 2001 and designed to serve as a beacon of light and inspiration.

ASTRUP FEARNLEY MUSEUM OF MODERN ART
(Astrup Fearnley Museet)

Tjuvholmen is the sparkling new location of the **Astrup Fearnley Museum of Modern Art** (Strandpromenaden 2, tel. 22 93 60 60, www.afmuseet.no, noon-5pm Tues.-Wed. and Fri., noon-7pm Thurs., 11am-5pm Sat.-Sun., 120kr), a private collection of works that focuses on meaningful individual pieces rather than time periods or movements. In addition to the range of Norwegian contemporary artists, the collection has a strong American influence. The museum welcomes a regular carousel of touring exhibitions, including the likes of Alex Israel, Matthew Barney, and Cindy Sherman. Damien Hirst's diamond skull *For the Love of God* appeared here during the opening season.

Explore the waterside sculpture park right outside and you'll discover a small hidden beach. If you're in the mood for more artwork, take a few steps behind the Astrup Fearnley Museum to discover **Galleri Haaken** (Tjuvholmen allé 23, tel. 22 55 91 97, www.gallerihaaken.com, noon-5pm Wed.-Fri., noon-4pm Sat.-Sun., free), which showcases a range of Norwegian contemporary artists in a much more intimate setting. The curator is usually on hand to answer questions and will happily discuss all things art and all things Tjuvholmen.

GRÜNERLØKKA & EASTERN OSLO

Most visitors to eastern Oslo go for shopping or nightlife rather than sightseeing, but nevertheless there are some sights of note. A stroll northward along the Akerselva river bypasses Grünerløkka and takes you past former mills and factories, many now converted to arts- and design-related trades. As you head farther, the feel of Oslo becomes more gritty, yet there are some sights to take in.

Munch Museum
(Munchmuseet)

Until its long-awaited move to a new high-profile location next to Oslo Opera House, the **Munch Museum** (Tøyengata 53, tel. 23 49 35 00, www.munchmuseet.no, 10am-4pm daily Oct.-June, 10am-5pm daily July-Sept., 100kr) remains open in Tøyen. Although the most famous works of Edvard Munch (1863-1944) are housed in the National Gallery, the museum still holds over 1,000 paintings, yet it is no ordinary art museum. During Munch's childhood, his mother died of tuberculosis and one of his younger sisters was diagnosed with mental illness. The museum reveals how this challenging childhood led to the dark psychological symbolism that defines much of his work. Munch once wrote, "My father was temperamentally nervous and obsessively religious to the point of psychoneurosis. From him I inherited the seeds of madness. The angels of fear, sorrow, and death stood by my side since the day I was born."

You'll never look at *The Scream* in the same way again.

University Botanical Garden
(Universitetets Botaniske hage)

The green lung of the otherwise urban eastern Oslo, the **University Botanical Garden** (Sars' gate/Monrads gate, tel. 22 85 17 00, 7am-9pm daily, free) offers a pleasant shortcut through to Grünerløkka. The fragrant garden, alpine garden, and old ornamental plants from Eastern Norway line your route. At the southwestern end, the Viking Garden displays the natural resources available during from the Viking Age. A caged hemp plant, herbs, rocks, and other plant life are all showcased within a Viking ship-themed outdoor exhibit.

North of the gardens is the **Natural History Museum (Naturhistorisk museum)** (Sars' gate 1, tel. 22 85 50 50, www.nhm.uio.no, 11am-4pm Tues.-Sun., 50kr), which encompasses a zoological museum popular with children. Known locally as Ida, the world's oldest complete primate skeleton has been on display since 2009, coinciding with the 200th anniversary of Darwin's birth and the 150th anniversary of the publication of *The Origin of Species*. The bone structure

Grünerløkka

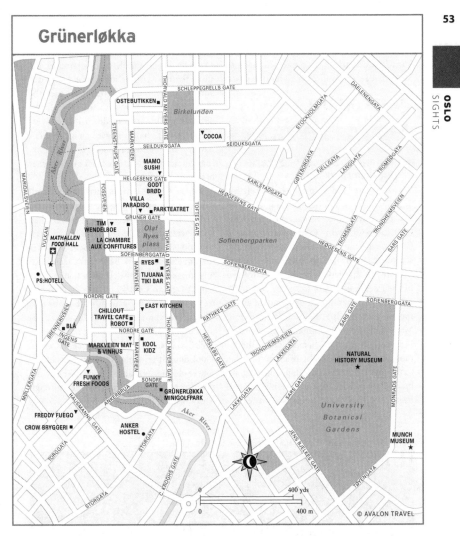

is so well preserved that historians can tell Ida is female and have placed the skeleton's age at an astonishing 47.8 million years. The lemur is likely to be the closest living relative alive today.

Ekeberg Sculpture Park
(Ekebergparken)

Farther out into Oslo's suburbs, **Ekeberg Sculpture Park** (Kongsveien 23, tel. 21 42 19 19, www.ekebergparken.no, free) doesn't have the crowds of Vigeland Park but offers just as much intrigue. The sculpture-laden natural forest and parkland offers outstanding views across the fjord and ever-expanding city. Salvador Dalí's *Venus de Milo aux Tiroirs* and Per Inge Bjørlo's *Inner Space VI—The Life Cycle* are two of the park's most visited spots, along with the very spot that inspired Edvard Munch to paint *The Scream*. It is believed Munch's mentally ill sister Laura Catherine was a patient at the nearby asylum at the time. In 2013, Serbian filmmaker Marina Abramovic filmed 270 citizens of Oslo screaming out their emotions from Ekeberg Park in a disturbing, dramatic homage to Munch. A Scream-selfie here is hard to resist.

WESTERN OSLO

★ Vigeland Sculpture Park (Vigelandsparken)

Wander the truly unique **Vigeland Sculpture Park** (Nobels gate 32, tel. 23 49 37 00, www.vigeland.museum.no, open daily, free) and get drawn in to the bizarre mind of Gustav Vigeland (1869-1943). More than 200 sculptures in bronze, granite, and wrought iron are on display in the park, which Vigeland himself designed. Walk from one end to the other in just 10 minutes, or spend an entire morning examining the human condition. Many sculptures take human form, and there is an eerie realism to them, not least the famous *Angry Boy,* its hand a different color due to the myth that if you touch it, you get good luck. (Park officials discourage this, though, because of deterioration to the sculpture.)

There are plenty of abstract sculptures too, such as the man being attacked by angry babies and the park's famous centerpiece, a 14-meter-high monolith consisting of 121 stone figures writhing around on top of one another in a desperate attempt to reach the sky. Critics of Vigeland say he was a Nazi sympathizer and his art is made up of fascist aesthetics, but it's hard to agree on a summer's day with the fountain flowing and locals mixing happily with tourists from every corner of the world.

The sculpture park is surrounded on all sides by the much larger **Frogner Park.** Oslo's biggest inner city playground is filled with locals walking dogs, barbecuing *pølser* (hot dogs), and playing Frisbee. It makes for a much nicer walk back to the transit interchange at Majorstuen once you're done with Vigeland's work. Often skipped over by visitors, the **City Museum (Bymuseet)** (Frognerveien 67, tel. 23 28 41 70, www.oslomuseum.no, 11am-4pm Tues.-Sun., free) is set back in the park's southern corner and worth a look due to the fabulous 18th-century atmosphere of Frogner Manor. Inside the museum, the history of Oslo and the Frogner borough is examined largely through paintings and

Vigeland Sculpture Park is one of Norway's most visited attractions.

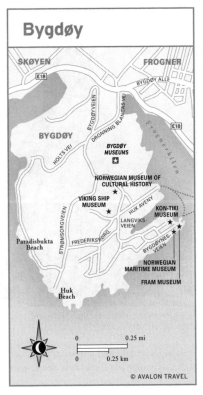

Bygdøy

SKØYEN
FROGNER
BYGDØY ALLE
E18
BYGDØYVEIEN
DRONNING BLANCAS VEI
Frognerkilen
E18
BYGDØY
HOLTS VEI
BYGDØY MUSEUMS ✪
NORWEGIAN MUSEUM OF CULTURAL HISTORY ★
VIKING SHIP MUSEUM ★
HUK AVENY
KON-TIKI MUSEUM
LANGVIKS-VEIEN
STRØMSORGVEIEN
FREDERIKSBORG.
BYGDØYNES-VEIEN
Paradisbukta Beach
NORWEGIAN MARITIME MUSEUM
FRAM MUSEUM
Huk Beach
0   0.25 mi
0   0.25 km
© AVALON TRAVEL

The 10-minute ferry trip is quicker than the 20-minute bus trip, but a standalone ticket (35kr one-way, 55kr round-trip) is required from the booth before you board, as the regular public transit passes are not valid on the Bygdøy service. However, the ferry trip is complimentary for Oslo Pass holders.

NORWEGIAN MUSEUM OF CULTURAL HISTORY
(Norsk Folkemuseum)

If for some reason you're not heading out to the western fjords after your time in Oslo, then the **Norwegian Museum of Cultural History** (Museumsveien 10, tel. 22 12 37 00, www.norskfolkemuseum.no, 125kr) is a must-do for a taste of rural Norwegian life. The highlight of the center is a genuine medieval stave church from the town of Gol, which was relocated to Oslo by King Oscar II in the 19th century. Other farmsteads from all across the valleys of Norway have been acquired and relocated here, including a mustard yellow 19th-century farmhouse from Stiklestad with a refurbished interior to show how a busy farming family would have lived during the 1950s. Other notable highlights include the parsonage (1752) from Sogn and an open-hearth house, barn, and stable comprising the Setsedal farmstead (1739).

The park is open daily year-round, although the experience in the summer season from mid-May to mid-September is far richer. Open 10am-6pm, the open-air museum comes to life with hosts in traditional folk dress ready to show you their farmsteads and explain their lives to you, to the soundtrack of live folk music. Make it clear you're an English speaker and the hosts will happily switch languages.

Outside summer, the opening hours are drastically reduced to 11am-3pm (4pm on weekends), and the museum adopts a more serious demeanor, although there is still plenty to see for those with an interest in Norwegian culture.

photographs, one of the biggest collections in Norway.

★ Bygdøy Museums

Whether by accident or design, Oslo's most distinctive museums of cultural history are bunched together on the otherwise wealthy residential peninsula of Bygdøy.

To reach Bygdøy, you can take bus 30, which runs a regular route from Jernbanetorget (outside Oslo Central Station) year-round, but the more interesting and quicker way is to take the ferry (Mar.-Oct.) from Pier 3 by City Hall. The first stop serves (by way of a short walk) the Norwegian Museum of Cultural History and the Viking Ship Museum, while the second stop drops you right outside the Kon-Tiki, Fram, and Norwegian Maritime Museums. Bus 30 stops outside all the Bygdøy museums.

VIKING SHIP MUSEUM
(Vikingskipshuset)

Neighboring the Museum of Cultural History, the **Viking Ship Museum** (Huk Aveny 35, tel. 22 13 52 80, 9am-6pm daily May-Sept., 10am-4pm daily Oct.-Apr., 100kr) is one of the most popular attractions on Bygdøy and with good reason. Three genuine Viking ship discoveries from Gokstad, Oseberg, and Tune are on display in the purpose-built building. Two of them are in spectacular condition, considering they were built in the 9th century. As much as the ships play a starring role, the exhibits around the periphery take you on an eye-opening journey into Viking life. Discover sledgehammers and household objects such as tools, textiles, and utensils that were used.

The ships provide the foundation for continuing research. The Gokstad grave was excavated in 1880 but until recently was never investigated using modern methods. A recent research project, Gokstad Revitalized, has revealed a marketplace at nearby Heimdalsjordet, providing yet more insight into the daily life of the Vikings.

the stave church from Gol at the Norwegian Museum of Cultural History

KON-TIKI MUSEUM
(Kon-Tiki Museet)

In 1947, Norwegian explorer Thor Heyerdahl set sail from Peru on a hand-built raft called *Kon-Tiki*. He wanted to prove it was possible to sail to Polynesia as ancient myths told. After an 8,000-kilometer (5,000-mile) journey across the Pacific Ocean, his raft reached the Tuamotu Archipelago. His success backed up his theory that, contrary to popular belief that Polynesia was populated from west to east, there had been ancient contact from South America to Polynesia. Largely dismissed by modern anthropologists, Heyerdahl's theories and adventures nevertheless inspired an Academy Award-winning documentary movie. The **Kon-Tiki Museum** (Bygdøynesveien 36, tel. 23 08 67 67, www. kon-tiki.no, 10am-6pm daily June-Aug., 10am-5pm daily Mar.-May and Sept.-Oct., 10am-4pm daily Nov.-Feb., 100kr) tells the tale of Heyerdahl and houses original vessels and equipment from his expeditions.

FRAM MUSEUM
(Frammuseet)

While you're in the mood for expeditions, explore a genuine polar vessel at the **Fram Museum** (Bygdøynesveien 36, tel. 23 28 29 50, www.frammuseum.no, 9am-6pm daily June-Aug., 10am-4pm daily Sept.-May, 100kr), adjacent to the Kon-Tiki Museum. The strongest wooden ship ever built, *Fram* survived journeys to both polar caps. Although principally focused on the vessel, the museum also profiles Norwegian polar explorers Fridtjof Nansen (who helped fund and specify the ship), Otto Sverdrup, and Roald Amundsen and the Scottish-Norwegian ship designer Colin Archer and has exhibits on polar bears and penguins.

NORWEGIAN MARITIME MUSEUM
(Norsk Maritimt Museum)

Next door to the Fram Museum is the **Norwegian Maritime Museum** (Bygdøynesveien 37, tel. 24 11 41 50, www.marmuseum. no, 10am-4pm Tues.-Sun., 100kr), which completes the series of museums of Bygdøy but is only worthwhile to those with a specific interest in maritime culture and history. Exhibits principally focus on the technical details of the shipping industry, although the hall of traditional boats and the maritime art gallery hold some interest.

NORTHERN OSLO

Northern Oslo is defined by its vast Nordmarka forest, where its hiking trails and lakes become the city's playground. But other than the ski arena, sightseeing opportunities are thin on the ground.

★ Holmenkollen Ski Arena
(Holmenkollen nasjonalanlegg)

The main attraction at **Holmenkollen Ski Arena** (Kongeveien 5, tel. 22 92 32 00, www.holmenkollen.com) is the **Holmenkollen Ski Jump (Holmenkollbakken),** visible from all across the city. This world-class sporting arena, which hosted the 1952 Winter Olympics and was rebuilt in 2011, is free to walk around, take in the remarkable views across the city, and feel your stomach churn at the thought of sailing off into the skies.

For the true Holmenkollen experience, take an elevator ride up the **ski jump tower** to see the views the jumpers get just before they set off. It's not for the faint-hearted. At the foot of the tower is the **Ski Museum (Skimuseet),** the world's oldest museum dedicated to skiing, profiles famous Norwegian polar explorers right through to present-day snowboarding. Never tried winter sports? **Simulators** allow you to give it a go in

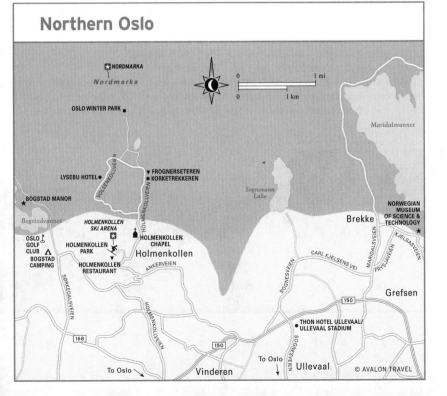

Northern Oslo

relative safety, although there's no guarantee you won't be embarrassed.

The ski jump tower, museum, and simulators are open 10am-4pm daily with extended hours of 9am-8pm from June to August. A 130kr ticket buys you entrance to the ski jump tower and museum, and the simulator costs 75kr, but the ski jump arena and gift shop are free to explore.

A word of warning: The only way to reach Holmenkollen by public transit is the T-Bane. As pleasurable as the Holmenkollen line is, a 10-minute uphill walk is required to reach the Ski Arena from Holmenkollen station. If you're visiting in the winter, check in advance at www.holmenkollen.com for any major events that will impede access for tourists. It's not uncommon to see Olympic-level athletes training in the biathlon arena and on the cross-country trails around Holmenkollen.

KOLLENSVEVET ZIP LINE

From April through October, Oslo's home of ski jumping plays host to another extreme activity. The **Kollensvevet Zip Line** (tel. 22 08 30 00, www.kollensvevet.no, 730kr) is an expensive yet exhilarating opportunity to get the same view as the professional ski jumpers who soar over the city. From mid-June through August, the line is open 11am-6pm Monday-Friday and noon-6pm Saturday-Sunday; outside those few weeks, hours are on weekends only. Arrive early to avoid a long wait, especially on weekends, when advance reservations are possible but only for an additional 500kr.

HOLMENKOLLEN CHAPEL
(Holmenkollen kapell)

Standing proudly overlooking the ski arena is **Holmenkollen Chapel** (Holmenkollveien 142, tel. 23 62 94 70), a traditional-looking church that hides a dark history. In 1993, musicians from Norwegian black metal band Emperor torched the original chapel, one of a series of church arsons in the early 1990s. The church was rebuilt a few years later to strongly resemble the traditional Norwegian stave churches, and is now one of the city's most popular venues for weddings. It's only open for services at 11am on Sunday.

Bogstad Manor
(Bogstad gård)

One of the few Norwegian country estates, **Bogstad Manor** (Sørkedalen 826, tel. 22 06 52 00, www.bogstad.no) is an oasis of calm

cross-country skiers at Holmenkollen Ski Arena

just 10 kilometers (6 miles) northwest of Oslo. The history of the estate dates back to 1649, up until which the land had been cultivated and rented out to farmers. Morten Lauritzen bought the land from the Danish-Norwegian King Fredrik III and used the forested areas to boost the local timber trade.

Peder Anker, who became the first Norwegian prime minister in Stockholm in 1814 during the long union with Sweden, improved the estate during the 18th century. Inspired by the grand architecture of Versailles and Rome, he built a ballroom, collected paintings, and created Norway's first English landscape park, which housed exotic plants from all over the world inside greenhouses.

Guided tours (1pm Tues.-Sun. May-Sept.) of the museum are only available in Norwegian, but an English language booklet is provided. The fully restored 18th-century lakeside park is free to explore year-round. The café, gift shop, and small exhibition about the manor are open noon-4pm Tuesday-Sunday. To reach Bogstad Manor, travel to Røa T-Bane station and then take a 5-minute bus ride on route 41 or a 40-minute walk.

Norwegian Museum of Science & Technology
(Norsk Teknisk Museum)

If you are traveling with kids who love planes, trains, and automobiles, the **Norwegian Museum of Science & Technology** (Kjelsåsveien 143, tel. 22 79 60 00, www.tekniskmuseum.no, 11am-6pm daily mid-June to mid-Aug., 9am-4pm Tues.-Fri., 11am-6pm Sat.-Sun. mid-Aug. to mid-June, 150kr) is a must-visit attraction. The museum tells the story of Norway's development from an agrarian to an industrial society, and it's all done through bright, colorful, and interactive exhibits that are just plain fun. Founded over 100 years ago, the museum stays fresh by updating its exhibits on an annual basis. Because of its rather unusual location away from all other museums, it's best to combine a visit here with a hiking or swimming trip at nearby Sognsvann or a stroll along the Akerselva river.

VICINITY OF OSLO

A number of sights are all within easy reach of downtown Oslo by public transit.

Bærums Verk

In 1610, King Christian IV (of Denmark and Norway) founded an iron ore production facility 16 kilometers (10 miles) west of Oslo. Over 400 years later, **Bærums Verk** (tel. 67 13 00 18, www.baerumsverk.no, free) is now a thriving shopping destination. Verksgata is home to a blacksmith, glassblower, textile shop, carpenter's workshop, and other traditional Norwegian crafts, while supermarkets and other shops service the neighboring village of the same name. The oven museum houses a unique collection of antique cast-iron ovens produced at the ironworks, from the baroque style of the 1700s up to the end of production in 1964.

The complex is open daily but opening hours vary for each shop. Go 10am-5pm (noon-4pm Sun.) to guarantee most places being open. From the end of November, the Christmas Street *(Julegaten)* opens every weekend, offering gift ideas, festive food, and entertainment, including leisurely reindeer-pulled sled rides.

To reach Bærums Verk, take bus 143, which has regular departures from Oslo Bus Terminal and stops right outside the complex. As the destination is outside the city of Oslo, a two-zone bus ticket is required for the 50-minute ride.

Eidsvoll House
(Eidsvollsbygningen)

Continue north past the airport on the E6 highway or the train and you come to **Eidsvoll,** a picturesque small village of wooden houses and churches. The real attraction here is the **Eidsvoll House** (Carsten Ankers veg 19, tel. 63 92 22 10, www.eidsvoll1814.no, 10am-5pm daily May-Aug., 10am-3pm Tues.-Fri., 11am-4pm Sat.-Sun.

Sept.-Apr., 125kr), which marks the place where Norway became an independent country in 1814.

In April 1814, 112 elected representatives arrived at Eidsvoll and immediately divided in two. One group wanted complete independence for Norway, while the unionist half believed a union with Sweden was the best way forward. It took over a month for the battle to be settled and for a constitution to be drawn up and signed, declaring Norway an independent state.

Extensive restorations have turned the former manor house into a national monument to be proud of and where this history can be rightly remembered. In addition to the former manor itself, the visitor center highlights stories of global democracy from past and present, while the charming coffee house and gift shop are worthy stops.

Located 60 kilometers (37 miles) northeast of Oslo, Eidsvoll House can be reached by a 30-minute train journey from Oslo S station to Eidsvoll, followed by a 20-minute walk or a 5-minute bus ride on route 811. A three-zone ticket will be required. By car, the journey from downtown Oslo will take around 40 minutes.

Tusenfryd

While the name literally means *a thousand joys*, the Viking-themed **Tusenfryd** (Vinterbro, tel. 64 97 64 97, www.tusenfryd. no, from 299kr) theme park offers only 35 attractions—but kids will want to stick around for the day. Racing through the water rapids on Ragnarok and experiencing the 4D-motion ride Thor's Hammer are the must-dos, while two traditional roller coasters are worth the queues. The Formula-1 themed Speedmonster takes you from stationary to 90 kph (56 mph) in just two seconds, while speeds on the Thundercoaster top 100 kph (62 mph).

The park is open daily in June and July, plus most weekends in May and August. Opening hours vary and exceptions apply, so check carefully before you travel, especially as advance online booking secures the cheapest rate.

Located 20 kilometers (12.5 miles) south of Oslo, Tusenfryd can be reached in just 30 minutes on express bus 500, which leaves Oslo Bus Terminal half-hourly, or you can book park tickets through **Adventure Oslo** (tel. 41 14 64 74, adventureoslo.no) for inclusive bus travel from the city center.

Sports and Recreation

Oslo might be a cosmopolitan capital packed with art and culture, but that doesn't mean it's lacking in outdoor opportunities. Surrounded on all sides by forest and water, Oslo has plenty to offer those seeking an active outdoorsy break from the city.

TOURS
Walking Tours
If your time in Oslo is limited or you want to get your bearings on the first day of a longer stay, **Free Walking Tours** (www. freetouroslo.com) leave the tiger statue on Jernbanetorget square at 10am daily, with an additional 4pm tour Friday-Sunday. The 90-minute walk takes in the Oslo Opera House, Christiania Torv, Aker Brygge, Oslo City Hall, and all the attractions along Karl Johans gate.

While the tours are advertised as free, tips of around 50kr are expected by the English speaking-guide, who is usually an energetic university student. On weekends, groups can be uncomfortably large, but it's nevertheless a good way to orient yourself and decide what you want to take a closer look at during the afternoon.

Boat Tours
Båtservice Sightseeing (Rådhusbrygge 3, tel. 23 35 68 90, www.boatsightseeing.com) runs a selection of fjord cruises from Pier 3

in front of the City Hall. The most popular is the two-hour **Fjord Sightseeing** (299kr) tour of the Opera House, Akershus Fortress, Aker Brygge wharf, and the inner Oslofjord islands. From mid-June to mid-August, there are six daily departures (starting at 10:30am), reduced to three in the shoulder season (Mar.-Sept.) and just two through the winter.

Their three-hour **Oslofjord Evening Cruise** (7pm most days June-Aug., 420kr) takes you out into the fjord in an old wooden sailboat with the sun low in the sky. Although the chance of taking to the water in a classic vessel is a tempting one, it's an expensive trip, given the only food served is a simple buffet of shrimp with bread and butter.

Inquire and buy tickets for both trips from the ticket booth on the pier or from Oslo Visitor Centre.

Bus Tours

When the weather is not so good, a bus tour from **HMK Sightseeing** (tel. 22 78 94 00, www.sightseeingoslo.com) is a good solution to see a lot of the city in relative comfort. If time is tight, the 2.5-hour **Panorama Tour** (270kr) ticks off the major attractions, including a brief stop for photos at Holmenkollen Ski Jump and a walking tour of the Vigeland Sculpture Park.

The longer **Full Day Sightseeing Tour** (420kr) also includes entrance to the Viking Ship Museum and your choice of the Fram Museum or Kon-Tiki Museum on the Bygdøy peninsula. Lunch is not included, so it's a wise move to bring your own; otherwise, you'll need to visit a museum cafeteria rather than the exhibits.

All tours are given in English, Norwegian, and German and start from behind City Hall.

HIKING

Oslo's city streets can be surprisingly quiet on a Saturday morning. That's because the locals head out to the hills. The forests to the north and east of the city are accessible by public transit, so within 30 minutes you can go from sipping a latte downtown to a 360-degree view of vast untouched forest.

★ Nordmarka

Just as much a symbol of the city as the Opera House or Royal Palace, the **Nordmarka** forest is the city's premier destination for hiking in the summer and fall and skiing in the winter and spring. The far-reaching trails climb hills, piercing a path through dense forest

The Nordmarka forest is a popular recreation spot year-round.

and around large lakes in a seemingly endless maze.

Reaching Oslo's wilderness is easy thanks to metro routes 1 and 6, which whisk you to Frognerseteren and Sognsvann stations, respectively, in under a half hour.

In contrast to the city streets, Nordmarka is bustling on Sunday. Norwegian families spanning multiple generations walk together and even come out of their shells a little. Try saying hello!

One of Nordmarka's most popular routes is the steady three-mile hike from **Frognerseteren** to the popular cabin at **Skjennungstua** (Ullevålseterveien 60, tel. 90 15 59 20, www.skjennungstua.no). The cabin's kiosk is staffed sporadically (most often 11am-4pm on Wednesdays and weekends), but there is also an unstaffed small cabin open year-round should you need to take shelter or grab a bite to eat. Payment for coffee and dried foods is made on an honesty policy, so carrying some cash on a hike is a wise idea. The hike to Skjennungstua is straightforward, albeit hilly, and should take around one hour.

You can reach the same destination from **Sognsvann,** but the distance is a little longer. For those after an easier stroll, a 45-minute loop around **Sognsvann lake** on the 3.7-kilometer (2.3-mile) cycle-free footpath is a great option, while heading east to the much larger **Maridalsvannet lake** is a great option for those on two wheels or who fancy a longer hike. The marked trail from Sognsvann to and around Maridalsvannet lake is 15.3 kilometers (9.5 miles) round-trip, with two mild ascents; the hike can take from three hours to an entire day, depending on your pace.

BIKING

Bicycles from **Oslo City Bike (Oslo Bysykkel)** (www.oslobysykkel.no) are available from over 100 stations across the city center and can be used for up to three hours at a time. Available from 6am to midnight from early April to late November, the bikes are only accessible by way of a season ticket costing 299kr per year.

A better alternative for tourists is the better quality rental bikes from **Viking Biking** (Nedre Slottsgate 4, tel. 41 26 64 96, www.vikingbikingoslo.com), available from 200kr per day. Bikes are available from April to October and the rest of the year weather-permitting. It's best to book online in advance. The company also offers guided sightseeing tours starting at 240kr. The daily Oslo Highlights tour is the most popular, but the River Bike tour opens up the Oslo missed by many and is highly recommended.

WINTER SPORTS
Skiing and Snowboarding

Less than a half-hour from downtown Oslo is the city's biggest winter sports facility, **Oslo Winter Park** (Tryvannsveien 64, tel. 22 14 36 10, www.oslovinterpark.no). Better known by locals by its former name Tryvann, the park can be reached by the free shuttle bus (or a short walk) from the Voksenkollen metro stop.

The season depends on snowfall, but in the majority of years, most of the 18 runs are open by December, thanks to artificial snow production facilities filling the gap. Once the season has started, snow production facilities and floodlights keep the park open 10am-10pm Monday-Friday and 10am-5pm Saturday-Sunday right through to mid-April.

A daily lift pass costs 400kr; access to the beginners' area is 200kr. Equipment rental runs at around 400kr, while lessons with patient English-speaking instructors are also available (695kr for 1hr, 1,570kr for 3hrs).

Snowboarders can use the park with a dedicated area, although for the international standard superpipe it's best to use the second entrance several miles away at Wyller. Take the metro to Røa and connect with the 41 bus. The long Wyllerløypa black run and express chair lift links the two sections of the park.

More serious skiers should consider the international standard slopes of the Hafjell and Kvitfjell resorts, just north of Lillehammer.

Tobogganing

Oslo's best toboggan run, **Korketrekkeren** (Frognerseteren, tel. 22 49 01 21, www. korken.no) sits on the hill that was formerly home to the 1952 Olympic bobsled and luge track. The 2,000-meter (6,562-foot) run starts at Frognesteren metro station and ends at Midstuen, where you can board the metro to start all over again. Daily sled rental from the outlet next to Frognerseteren restaurant costs 100kr, while the run itself is free to use. A day ticket for the metro is a wise investment.

SWIMMING

Swim for free in the Oslofjord or at selected lakes in Oslo's forests. The city's most popular beach is **Huk** on the Bygdøy peninsula, with the nearby **Paradisbukta** better suited for children. Both are within a short bus trip from downtown Oslo. On warm days, locals head for the islands of the inner Oslofjord, reachable by public ferry. **Hovedøya** is the best choice for sunbathing and swimming.

The most accessible lake open for swimming is at **Sognsvann** on the end of the metro line 6. Diving is possible and there is plenty of space for picnics in the surrounding forest and parkland.

For those who prefer more managed facilities, **Frognerbadet** (Middelthuns gate 28, tel. 23 27 54 50), an outdoor pool on the fringes of Frogner Park, is open from June to August, but you'll do well to find space on a hot summer weekend when queues to get in can snake down the street. The best alternative is the **Tøyenbadet** (Helgesens gate 90, tel. 23 46 22 90, 7am-7pm Mon.-Fri., 9am-7pm Sat.-Sun., 100kr) indoor public swimming center, which is open year-round. Tuesday and Thursday mornings are reserved for local schools.

GOLF

The par-71 championship course at **Oslo Golf Club** (Ankerveien 127, tel. 22 51 05 60, www. oslogk.no) is set on the shores of Bogstad lake, with a small waterfall providing the backdrop to the 12th green. Norway's oldest golf club welcomes members of other clubs to use its facilities. A handicap certificate of at least 28 for men and 32 for women is required, and arrangements should be made in advance. Greens fees are 950kr, with a 15 percent discount available in the Norwegian holiday month of July.

For those who don't take their golf quite so seriously, **Grünerløkka Minigolfpark** (Søndre gate 1, tel. 22 38 00 27, www.minigolf-parken.no, noon-8pm daily, 50kr) is a fun alternative for all. Set next to the Aker river, the 18 holes are open every day, weather permitting. Giant street chessboards can also be played (free).

SPECTATOR SPORTS
Soccer

The Oslo region boasts three clubs competing in the Norwegian Premier League, with games taking place March through October. The **Vålerenga Fotball** (www.vif-fotball.no) team currently plays at the national **Ullevaal Stadion** (Sognsveien 75), three kilometers (two miles) north of downtown Oslo, although they are scheduled to move to their own purpose-built 18,000-capacity stadium at their traditional home in the east of the city in time for the 2018 summer season.

Their biggest local rivals are **Lillestrøm SK** (www.lsk.no). Their **Åråsen Stadion** holds 12,250, and with an average attendance of half that, tickets are available for almost all games on the day. It's 16 kilometers (10 miles) northeast of Oslo and an easy train ride from the capital.

Since returning to the top tier of Norwegian football in 2013, family-friendly **Stabæk** (www.stabak.no) enjoyed something of a renaissance under Bob Bradley, former boss of the U.S. men's national team. Their small

Nadderud Stadion (Haukeveien) is not the grandest sporting arena but is within walking distance of Bekkestua metro station, 10.5 kilometers (6.5 miles) west of downtown Oslo.

1952 Winter Olympics. The arena is in the picturesque Kampen neighborhood just 2.5 kilometers (1.5 miles) east of downtown Oslo, and easy to reach on foot, by T-Bane, or by bus.

Ice Hockey

Ice hockey in Norway is a popular winter sport, yet the domestic teams lack international success when compared to their Nordic neighbors. Still, while the crowds are orders of magnitude less than what you can expect at an NHL game, the **Vålerenga Hockey** (www.vif-hockey.no) team attracts anything from a few hundred to a few thousand spectators, who get a great view of the action at the asymmetrical and somewhat dated **Jordal Amfi** (Jordalgata 12) arena, originally built for the

American Football

As evidenced by more and more NFL games taking place in London, American football is growing in popularity across the Atlantic. The trend is mirrored in Norway, where a thriving amateur league is capturing the interest of both American expats and Norwegians. The **Oslo Vikings** (www.oslovikings.com) play their home matches in front of decent crowds at Frogner Stadion in Majorstuen, while the **Vålerenga Trolls** (www.viftrolls.no) play next to the ice hockey stadium at Jordal.

Entertainment and Events

NIGHTLIFE

Due to Norway's high taxes on alcohol, the nightlife scene in Oslo is not as thriving as in many European cities. Norwegian youths will typically host a gathering at home called a *vorspiel* (fun fact—this comes from the German word for foreplay) before heading out to a bar or club for the final few hours.

As almost all clubs and bars must stop serving alcohol at 2am, there will be no dancing the night away in Oslo. Most locals prefer to get up early in the morning and head to the hills for skiing or hiking. This means that nightlife can seem subdued, but if you're looking for an after-dinner drink, you nevertheless have options.

Oslo is known for its brown bars—English-style pubs that focus on beer, often showing sport—while the gastropub phenomenon has spread across Oslo like wildfire.

The city's liveliest nightspots tend to center around Youngstorget and Grünerløkka. Covers are not common except for live concert venues and dedicated nightclubs, where you can expect to pay at least 100kr. Dress code is surprisingly casual in most venues except for

the most exclusive spots. Age limits tend to be high, and it's not uncommon to see those under 23 turned away from clubs unless they happen to know the door staff.

Downtown

Techno-heads need look no further than intimate dance venue **The Villa** (Møllergata 23-25, tel. 93 25 57 45, www.thevilla.no, 11pm-3am most Friday and Saturday nights), one of Oslo's top underground nightspots. Appearances from the likes of Guy Gerber, Debbie Harry, and Bonobo frequently see hour-long queues along Møllergata. Farther up the street, the basement nightclub at **Revolver** (Møllergata 32, tel. 22 20 22 32, www.revolveroslo.no, 10pm-3am Fri.-Sat.) hosts regular local bands that lean toward the heavier side of rock.

The bared-down interior of **Himkok** (Storgata 27, tel. 22 42 22 02, 5pm-3am Sun.-Thurs., 3pm-3am Fri.-Sat.) is home to a microdistillery proving immensely popular with those in the know. In-house spirits, cocktails, and craft ciders from around the world are the reward for those who wait in the weekend queues. The same owners run the nearby Crow Bryggeri (Torggata 32, tel. 21 38 67 57, www.crowbryggeri.com, 3pm-3am daily), a microbrewery with a vast selection of imports also on offer. Its industrial decor attracts a curious mix of hipsters alongside those who are there for the beer. A similar crowd frequents the exposed metalwork, bare-brick walls, and giant wall maps at Grønland's Oslo Mekaniske Verksted (Tøyenbekken 34, tel. 45 23 75 34, www.oslomekaniskeverksted.no, 3pm-2am Mon.-Fri., 1pm-2am Sat.-Sun.), a bar where beers and wines are the staple choices. Because the venue allows patrons to bring their own food, the nearby pizza places do a roaring trade.

Prices are lower at the down-to-earth Cafe Sør (Torggata 11, tel. 41 46 30 47, www.cafesor.no, 10am-midnight Mon.-Thurs., 10am-3am Fri.-Sat., 11am-midnight Sun.), which attracts an eclectic mix of old and young, locals and visitors to its downtown location. Get there early to snag a spot on the street-facing terrace.

The word quirky was invented for Cafe Laundromat (Underhaugsveien 2, tel. 21 38 36 29, www.laundromat.no), a bar, café, and library tagged on to a laundromat in the Bislett neighborhood northwest of downtown (take the tram or bus to Bislett Stadion). Freshen up your traveling clothes while reading from the vast library and sampling one of the various whiskeys, tap beers, or cocktails. You may just need that extra rinse cycle.

Grünerløkka and Eastern Oslo

Start your evening out in Grünerløkka with a beer in the rockabilly-themed bar Ryes (Thorvald Meyers gate 59, noon-1am Sun.-Tues., noon-3am Wed.-Sat.), before heading across the square to the former cinema turned bar and concert venue Parkteatret (Olaf Ryes plass 11, tel. 22 35 63 00, www.parkteatret.no, 11am-late daily). The bar is a lively place for music lovers, regardless of whether you have tickets to whoever is playing in the adjacent concert venue. If live music isn't your thing, perhaps you'll prefer the Mexican atmosphere

and rum- and tequila-packed cocktails of the Tijuana Tiki Bar (Thorvald Meyers gate 61, tel. 90 07 71 91, www.tijuana.no, noon-4am Mon.-Sat., noon-midnight Sun.).

There's usually a band on most nights at intimate riverside club Blå (Brenneriveien 9, www.blaaoslo.no, hours vary). Almost part of the furniture, the funky 18-person Frank Znort Quartet play a free jazz/blues show every Sunday afternoon prior to their main evening gig. These Sunday sessions are an Oslo institution and the laid-back atmosphere draws many people back week after week. Legendary cocktail bar Pigalle (Grønlandsleiret 15, tel. 24 10 19 99, 4pm-1am Tues.-Thurs., 4pm-3am Fri.-Sat.) has enjoyed a long-overdue makeover and now sports a modern interpretation of a 1920s art-deco establishment, complete with plants, custom-designed furniture, and an overhauled drinks menu.

Western Oslo

Head to Frogner if you like your nightlife a little more high-brow, but be prepared to pay for the experience. Enjoy a glass or two of fizz at Champagneria (Frognerveien 2, tel. 21 08 09 09, 4pm-1am Mon.-Wed., 3pm-3am Thurs.-Fri., 1pm-3am Sat., 1pm-midnight Sun.). The rooftop terrace and focus on champagne, cava, and wine attract a more mature crowd. From here, take the short walk to the red carpet of swish nightclub Nox (Henrik Ibsens gate 100, tel. 22 55 40 00, www.clubnox.no, 11pm-3am Fri.-Sat.) to enjoy a glass of wine or classic cocktail in its lavish interior.

LGBT

Norway's cities are generally very accepting of LGBT lifestyle and thus there are only a few specific gay bars. You're likely to find as many LGBT couples in the bars of Grünerløkka as you are in the gay bars. Those bars are clustered together on a couple of streets downtown.

The first stop for many is Oslo's largest gay venue, London Pub (C. J. Hambros plass 5, tel. 22 70 87 00, www.londonpub.no,

3pm-3:30am daily), which offers a frankly bizarre mix of camp music, drag queens, and pool tables in an English pub-style basement bar. The upstairs nightclub (cover is charged) is underwhelming, so most patrons seeking a dance floor head over to the nearby **Elsker** (Kristian IVs gate 9, tel. 45 21 41 33, www.elsker-oslo.no, 6pm-3am Wed.-Sat.), an intimate bar with music so loud there's no point in even trying to strike up a conversation. Norway's only lesbian bar, **So** (Arbeidergata 2, www.so-oslo.no, 7pm-1am Thurs. and Sun., 9pm-3am Fri.-Sat.), is a popular alternative combining a dance floor with a quieter lounge area. Both Elsker and So run regular quiz nights and other events that may make them a dance floor-free zone for an evening.

A chilled-out brasserie by day, **Ett Glass** (Rosenkrantz' gate 13, tel. 91 77 53 90, www.ettglass.no, 11am-1am Mon.-Tues., 11am-3am Wed.-Fri., noon-3am Sat., noon-1am Sun.) becomes a popular nightspot for cocktails once the kitchen closes at 10pm. Frequented by everyone gay, straight, and everything in between, the stylish bar is one of Oslo's most established.

The city's LGBT communities come together every June for **Oslo Pride** (www.oslopride.no), Norway's largest LGBT festival. Usually held in the public square in front of the City Hall, Oslo Pride's highlight is the parade that makes a very visible statement along Oslo's main drag, Karl Johans gate. The festival also has a serious side though, touching on literature, art, and political debates throughout its week-long program.

While not strictly an LGBT event, the Eurovision Song Contest is hugely popular within the LGBT community. Run by state broadcaster NRK, the annual **Melodi Grand Prix** (www.nrk.no/mgp) is held over several weeks in January to choose Norway's entry for the annual showcase of all things kitsch. The February final, usually held in Oslo, attracts as much interest as many major sporting events. Tickets are available to the public but sell out well in advance.

PERFORMING ARTS

Oslo in a music-loving city and there is live music somewhere in the city on any night of the week. The likes of Adele, Justin Bieber, and Rihanna play at the vast but soulless **Telenor Arena** (Widerheveien 1, www.telenorarena.no), while the smaller but much better-located **Spektrum** (Sonja Henies plass 2, www.oslospektrum.no) also welcomes major artists and events.

Smaller bands and shows are held almost every night at one of the three downtown venues part of the **Rockefeller** group (www.rockefeller.no), all located on Torggata. Tickets go fast for any international names, so be sure to check out any concerts you might want to attend in advance of your arrival.

The **National Theater (National Theatret)** (Johanne Dybwads plass 1, tel. 22 00 14 00, www.nationaltheatret.no) is an imposing 19th-century home to playwrights and artists built from private funds to mark the secession from Sweden. The writers of the opening performances, Ludvig Holberg, Henrik Ibsen, and Bjørnstjerne Bjørnson, are immortalized in statues out front, and their names are carved in the stonework on the front facade. Today the theater is Oslo's premier arts venue, hosting everything from Shakespeare to the International Ibsen Festival.

The **Oslo Philharmonic (Oslo Filharmonien)** (www.ofo.no), the city's symphony orchestra, has a proud history that can be traced back to the days of Edvard Grieg. Since 2013, Russian Vasily Petrenko has been chief conductor of the orchestra, which gives over 100 concerts a year, many at its home **Oslo Concert House (Oslo Konserthus)** (Munkedamsveien 14, tel. 23 11 31 11, www.oslokonserthus.no). In addition to the many performances from the city orchestra, the concert house hosts a Jazz Café on most Saturday afternoons in Glasshuset, for which tickets start at a very reasonable 125kr.

Home of the Norwegian National Opera and Ballet (Den Norske Opera & Ballett), **Oslo Opera House (Operahuset)** (Kirsten Flagstads plass 1, tel. 21 42 21 21, www.

operaen.no) hosts regular free performances on its roof and in the café, alongside the scheduled program. The venue holds regular opera and ballet performances throughout the year.

Nordisk Film Kino runs seven cinemas across Oslo with international releases alongside Norwegian films. International films will often have Norwegian subtitles, and only children's films tend to be dubbed. If in doubt, ask in advance. The biggest of the cinemas is **Colosseum kino** (Fridtjof Nansens vei 8, Majorstuen), while **Klingenberg kino** (Olav Vs gate 4) is most convenient for those downtown.

FESTIVALS
AND EVENTS

In recent years Oslo has become the festival capital of Scandinavia, with events coming thick and fast throughout the summer season. Yet the Norwegian capital isn't the place to find traditional Norwegian festivals. As an ambitious growing city, Oslo focuses on bringing the newest trends from around the world to its streets. Oslo rivals cities many times its size for the sheer number and diversity of its internationally focused festivals. From business and innovation to music and

films from around the world, there's a festival in Oslo for it.

Constitution Day

There are parades in even the smallest village on May 17 to mark Constitution Day, celebrating the independence of Norway. Although not unique to Oslo, the capital's parade is certainly the biggest and best. Noted most of all for its absence of military, the parade is formed by children from every school across Oslo. They march along Karls Johans gate up to the Royal Palace, where the king and his family are waiting to greet them. Although a rare display of national pride from the Norwegians (you can't move two feet without encountering a Norwegian flag), foreigners are welcome observers and locals are only too pleased to share their day. Just be wary that almost all tourist attractions will be closed on May 17 and many restaurants are booked up weeks in advance.

Music Festivals

The SXSW of Scandinavia is how **By:larm** (www.bylarm.no) wants to be described, combining a music festival of largely unsigned or breaking acts from across Scandinavia with a conference on the latest industry trends.

Øya Festival is the city's main contemporary music event.

The conference element has grown massively in recent years and now covers many talks about digital trends and cultural talking points. Taking place across multiple venues over four days in early March, the music festival offers passes for the day or the entire event, which go on sale approximately three months beforehand.

The short summer season kicks off in early June with the one-day **Musikkfest Oslo** (www.musikkfest.no), where up to 30 outdoor stages quite literally fill the streets with music, all for free. A couple weeks later, **Norwegian Wood** (www.norwegianwood.no) takes place at Frogner Park with the likes of Bob Dylan, Sting, and Lou Reed having graced its stage. The festival tends to attract an older crowd for its three-day run.

August is the month for music lovers to visit Oslo, as festivals pack the calendar. Held at Tøyen Park, **Øya Festival** (www.oyafestivalen.no) has broadened its rock traditions in recent years with the likes of New Order, Kraftwerk, and Massive Attack joining the lineup, which also features many breakthrough Norwegian acts. Passes for the four-day mid-August event sell out months in advance, but availability of single-day tickets is better.

Also held in mid-August, **Oslo Jazz Festival** (www.oslojazz.no) is a week-long showcase of the best in Nordic jazz, with selected guests from overseas providing some bulk to the lineup. Finally, broaden your cultural horizons at **Mela** (www.mela.no), an annual performing arts festival featuring international rhythms with a strong Asian influence. The festival and its 300,000 attendees takes over Rådhusplassen in front of City Hall for one weekend in mid- to late August every year.

In mid-September, 17 of Oslo's arts institutions get together for the week-long **Ultima** (www.ultima.no), a contemporary music festival with a focus on high artistic quality that also features an international symposium.

Film Fra Sør

Screening over 100 films from Asia, Africa, and Latin America, **Film Fra Sør** (www.filmfrasor.no) brings quality films to the people of Oslo each fall. The organizers aim to reach the multicultural audience in Norway as well as expose Norwegians to new thoughts and debates about the southern hemisphere. To help achieve its artistic goals, the festival runs a fund to support film production in the non-western world. Held over 10 days in early October, screenings are individually ticketed, and tickets should be bought online in advance.

Shopping

DOWNTOWN

Downtown Oslo has malls aplenty, with **Oslo City** (Stenersgaten 1, tel. 81 54 40 33, www.oslocity.no, 10am-10pm Mon.-Fri., 10am-8pm Sat.) and **Byporten** (Jernbanetorget 6, tel. 23 36 21 60, www.byporten.no, 10am-9pm Mon.-Fri., 10am-8pm Sat.) directly opposite one another by Jernbanetorget square.

Fashion dominates the upscale mall that lies behind the restaurant strip at **Aker Brygge** (Bryggegata 9, tel. 22 83 26 80, www.akerbrygge.no, 10am-8pm Mon.-Fri., 10am-6pm Sat.).

You'll find Oslo's biggest bookstore, with a great selection of English language books, including many Moon titles, on the ground floor of the boutique-filled **Paleet** (Karl Johans gate 37-43, tel. 23 08 08 11, www.paleet.no, 10am-8pm Mon.-Fri., 10am-6pm Sat.), between Parliament and the Royal Palace.

GRÜNERLØKKA AND EASTERN OSLO

The vibrant district of Grünerløkka is the number one destination for vintage clothing and trinkets. You'll find boutiques, thrift stores, and everything in between on the grid system of streets. During the summer, Birkelunden square hosts a Sunday thrift market (noon-6pm), while the buildings around the Blå nightclub host a Sunday crafts market (noon-5pm) year-round.

Head to the **Chillout Travel Cafe** (Markveien 55, tel. 22 35 42 00, www.chillout.no, 10am-7pm Mon.-Fri., 10am-6pm Sat., noon-6pm Sun.) for a better range of outdoor clothing and hiking/camping equipment than you'll find in most sports stores, plus traveling advice from the seasoned traveler staff. Before you move on, mull over the extensive travel library in the basement lounge with a chili mocha from the in-store café.

Next door, behind the funky exterior of **Robot** (Korsgata 22, tel. 22 71 99 00, 11am-6pm Mon.-Fri., 11am-5pm Sat., noon-5pm Sun.) you'll find a small selection of vintage clothes and retro bags, with staff that know exactly what will suit you. As the name suggests, **Kool Kidz** (Markveien 56, tel. 90 19 28 25, www.koolkidz.no, noon-6pm Mon.-Fri., 11am-5pm Sat., 1pm-5pm Sun.) is a boutique that specializes in children's clothes. Slogan-filled tees and designer dresses sit alongside pop-up books and other gifts, with many exclusive Scandinavian brands stocked.

The neighborhood is also great for food shopping. In addition to the goodies available at the Mathallen food hall, the French-inspired **La Chambre aux Confitures** (Olaf Ryes plass 6, tel. 92 16 19 17, 11am-6pm Mon.-Sat.) is stacked floor-to-ceiling with specialty jams and preserves, while **Ostebutikken** (Thorvald Meyers gate 27, tel. 22 37 80 65, 4pm-10pm Mon.-Tues., noon-10pm Wed.-Sun.) has a busy cheese counter frequented by locals and is a great choice for helping to compose a picnic to enjoy in one of the nearby parks.

WESTERN OSLO

Trailing off from behind the Royal Palace up toward Majorstuen is Oslo's most exclusive shopping street. Most stores on **Hegdehaugsveien** and **Bogstadveien** (essentially two different stretches of the same street) are open 10am-6pm Monday-Saturday, but almost all are closed on Sunday.

Sport meets fashion at **Tatler** (Bogstadveien 2, tel. 22 60 29 58, www.tatler.no), where shelves are filled with Ralph Lauren, Acne, Canada Goose, Ugg, and Gudrun. Be wearing one of these brands when you enter or you'll get a few dirty looks. A few steps away is the flagship store of Scandinavian menswear

Chillout Travel Cafe has an excellent travel bookshop.

retailer **Volt Magasin** (Hegdehaugsveien 30b, tel. 23 21 85 97), and there are many luxury brand stores, such as **Lacoste** (Hegdehaugsveien 34, tel. 22 56 69 00). A **farmers market** (noon-6pm) takes place on leafy Valkyrie plass most Saturdays.

Food

DOWNTOWN
Cafés and Light Bites

The flagship outlet of **United Bakeries** (Karl Johans gate 37-43, tel. 94 02 41 02, 7:30am-8pm Mon.-Fri., 9am-6pm Sat., 11am-5pm Sun.) is the best downtown choice for an on-the-go breakfast or a quick bite at any time of day. Fresh pastries are always on offer, and although the tables around the service area might seem cramped, there's plenty more seating out back.

Perfectly positioned for a stop before or after a visit to Akershus Fortress, **People & Coffee** (Rådhusgata 21, tel. 40 29 62 22, www.peopleandcoffee.no, 7am-6pm Mon.-Fri., 11am-6pm Sat.-Sun.) is an independently run coffee shop with an international vibe thanks to its mix of regulars from the business district and passing tourists. Sandwiches, salads, and soups are served all day, although most people just grab a quick coffee to go.

Traditional Scandinavian

With new Nordic flavors all the rage, traditional Norwegian cooking is surprisingly hard to find on the streets of Oslo. Get your fill of salted meats and boiled potatoes in the unique atmosphere of **Dovrehallen** (Storgata 22, tel. 22 17 21 01, 10am-midnight Mon.-Thurs., 10am-3am Fri.-Sat., noon-midnight Sun., 135-199kr), a traditional Norwegian dining hall hidden up some stairs from a busy rundown shopping street. On Friday and Saturday evenings, a live folk band entices the clientele—mainly elderly Norwegian couples—onto the dance floor.

New Nordic

See for yourself why Esben Holmboe Bang is the new star of new Nordic at ★ **Maaemo** (Schweigaards gate 15b, tel. 22 17 99 69, www.maaemo.no, 6pm-midnight Tues.-Fri., noon-midnight Sat.), which leads the way in Oslo's fine dining revolution, scooping up Michelin stars like they're going out of fashion. The simple, clean interior is deliberately designed to put the focus on the food, which brings the best Scandinavian seasonal ingredients from biodynamic farms together on a bewildering series of plates. Call several months in advance to stand a chance of booking a table, and expect to cough up around 4,000kr per person (including wine).

Arctic cod dominates the menu at **Gamle Rådhus** (Nedre Slottsgate 1, tel. 22 42 01 07, www.gamle-raadhus.no, noon-4pm and 5pm-10pm Mon.-Fri., 5pm-10pm Sat., 289-435kr), where they try perhaps a little too hard to blend French classic with new Nordic. The restaurant is set inside Oslo's original 17th-century city hall. Snag a table out in the secluded garden from May through August.

Seafood

Down at Aker Brygge, the rustic **Rorbua** (Stranden 71, tel. 22 83 64 84, www.rorbua.as, noon-10pm Tues.-Sat., noon-9pm Sun.-Mon., 179-329kr) is perhaps the only unpretentious spot on the whole promenade, save for the golden arches of course. Taking its design cues from a northern Norwegian fisherman's cottage, the lively pub has a menu to match, with fish soup the best budget option. For an introduction to the flavors of the ocean, the northern Norwegian plate includes marinated trout, stockfish, elk sausage, and smoked whale.

Named after the region from where much of its produce originates, **Lofoten** (Stranden

75, tel. 22 83 08 08, www.lofoten-fiskerestaurant.no, 11am-11pm Mon.-Sat., noon-10pm Sun., 200-425kr) serves a similar selection to Rorbua but in a modern setting where white tablecloths and wine glasses trump long wooden tables and beer glasses.

American

Thanks to its location between the train and bus stations, the rowdy rock-themed **Fiasco** (Schwegaardsgate 4, tel. 47 17 40 00, www.fiasco.no, 11am-midnight Mon.-Thurs., 10am-2am Fri., 11pm-2am Sat., noon-midnight Sun., 130kr) is a popular after-work spot with locals. A decent range of draft and bottled beers is on offer at reasonable (for Oslo) prices. The burgers are delicious but, as the kitchen is tagged on to the bar almost as an afterthought, be prepared for a wait. While the burgers are decent value, it's a bit mean spirited to charge an extra 35kr for sides. For something a little different, try the bacon jam burger.

The light, airy interior of ★ **Pinerolo Americano** (Henrik Ibsens gate 60, tel. 22 55 00 47, www.pinerolosolli.no, 4pm-10pm Mon.-Sat., 199kr) brings a touch of New England elegance to the heart of Oslo, just a stone's throw from the old U.S. Embassy. Compose your own two-course Boston (445kr) or three-course New York (545kr) menu, on which the seafood-based starters are especially appetizing. Order some mac-and-cheese, truffle fries, and chili corn on the cob to share; an after-dinner Hamptons Sour will complete your dose of Americana in this good-value eatery.

The 200-gram (nearly half-pound) handmade patties at gourmet fast-food outlet **Burger Joint** (Holmens gate 3, tel. 21 08 22 75, www.burgerjoint.no, 11am-10pm Mon.-Thurs., 11am-midnight Fri., noon-midnight Sat., noon-10pm Sun., 175kr) are up there with the best in Norway, but it's a bit mean-spirited to charge separately for fries. Double up on your burger for an extra 75kr. The limited seating in this intimate venue means eating in can be a challenge, but there are plenty of places to sit on the nearby Aker Brygge wharf. Alternatively, grab a table at the neighboring Beer Palace, from where you can order and eat from the Burger Joint menu.

Asian

The Thai café **Rice Bowl** (Youngs gate 4, tel. 22 41 20 06, www.ricebowl.no, noon-10pm Mon.-Sat., 2pm-9pm Sun., 150kr) is filled with locals all day due to the rare combination of great prices and decent portion sizes. The informal café atmosphere encourages swift eating despite plenty of seating. No alcohol is served, so if you prefer a beer with your food, head to the nearby family-run Vietnamese **Far East** (Bernt Ankers gate 4, tel. 22 20 56 28, 1pm-midnight daily, 175kr), although be wary of the sometimes slow service and, unusually for Oslo, a lack of spoken English by the (often just one) wait staff. The restaurant bears clear signs of not being an original restaurant and has a somewhat jumbled approach to decor.

Upscale Vietnamese and Thai restaurant **Mr Bay** (Olav Selvaags plass 1, tel. 22 83 22 01, 11am-midnight Mon.-Fri., 1pm-midnight Sat., 1pm-9pm Sun., 279kr) is a fashionable alternative on Tjuvholmen. Hungry diners can tackle the vast 10-course chef's menu (789kr pp), which is served tapas style all at once. From the regular menu, the succulent tenderloin is an especially good platform for the kitchen's authentic eastern spices. The restaurant boasts an impressive wine list, and advance booking is essential.

Caribbean

Lemon, lime, and ginger are used to great effect in this popular Caribbeanesque restaurant that's more themed than authentic. The colorful **Lemongrass** (Kristian Augusts gate 14, tel. 22 20 12 22, www.lemongrass.no, 4pm-10pm Sun.-Thurs., 4pm-11pm Fri.-Sat., 259kr) specializes in chicken (jerk or nut) and lighter fish dishes, such as sea bass, which work well with the citrus accompaniments. The flavor-packed mango and avocado salad is a popular choice for vegetarians. The restaurant is often open 11am-3pm offering a slimmer lunch menu, while after 10pm it transforms into an upscale nightspot.

Indian

Attentive service and authentic Indian food rarely go hand-in-hand in Norway, so ★ **IndiSpice Restaurant** (Welhavens gate 2, tel. 22 20 96 08, www.indispice.no, 4pm-10pm daily, 239kr), just a few streets away from the Royal Palace, is a real find. Servings are generous, so skip starters and go straight for the mains. Ginger slivers and punchy coriander add a freshness to the plates, which the staff will go to great lengths to ensure are served at a heat level you are comfortable with. The upscale interior, mood lighting, and stylish furniture add a touch of class rarely seen in Norway's Indian restaurants. Reservations are recommended for weekends.

The outstanding Persian-inspired ambience of **Mister India** (Dronningens gate 19, tel. 22 41 42 00, www.mister-india.no, 3pm-10pm Mon.-Sat., 3pm-9pm Sun., 249kr), just steps from Karl Johans gate at the heart of downtown Oslo, is a worthy alternative. The menu of lesser-known dishes, such as the lamb-based *achari gosht* curry and vegetarian-friendly *kaikari kuruma,* makes a welcome change from the norm.

Mexican

The Norwegian take on Tex-Mex is popular throughout the capital, but you have to look a little harder for something a little more authentic. The small *lucha libre* (Mexican wrestling) themed **Freddy Fuego** (Hausmanns gate 31a, tel. 40 06 64 28, www.freddyfuego. no, 11am-9pm Tues.-Sun., 120kr) is a burrito bar with fresh salsas made daily. The lines can be out the door during the early Norwegian lunchtime, but head there after 1pm and you should walk straight up.

Tacos and quesadillas fill the menu at **Taqueria** (Karl Johans gate 39, tel. 23 89 86 40, www.taqueria.no, 11am-11pm Mon.-Thurs., 11am-midnight Fri.-Sat., 120kr), and although the servings are on the small side,

the prices are reasonable considering its prime location on Karl Johans gate. Despite the efforts of the decor, the atmosphere bears little resemblance to a bustling Mexican taco stand and feels all too Norwegian, so you may prefer to get takeout.

Vegetarian

Tucked away behind City Hall, the **Fragrance of the Heart** (Fridtjof Nansens plass 2, tel. 22 33 23 10, 7:30am-6pm Mon.-Wed., 7:30am-7pm Thurs.-Fri., 10am-7pm Sat., 11am-5pm Sun.) café serves vegetarian and vegan soups, pies, sandwiches, and wraps. They actively promote the Lemon Diet, a supposedly effective cleansing diet based around a cocktail of water, lemon juice, syrup, and cayenne pepper—but you won't be turned away if you all want is a caffeine hit, as this is an airy coffee shop first, vegetarian café second.

Although billed as a restaurant, the atmosphere at the Norwegian Centre for Design and Architecture's **Funky Fresh Foods** (Hausmannsgate 16, tel. 45 91 57 79, 10am-5pm Mon.-Tues., 10am-10pm Wed.-Fri., noon-10pm Sat., noon-7pm Sun., 99-179kr) is that of a fast food café. The limited menu features freshly made hamburgers and salads alongside milkshakes. The riverside location makes this a great vegan lunch option for those heading to or from Grünerløkka.

A quick pit stop for those downtown, **Proletaren** (Torggata 7, tel. 91 65 18 65, 11am-6pm Mon.-Sat., closed in July, 50kr) offers a largely vegetarian menu of take-away soups. The six soups rotate regularly, but expect the likes of spinach and squash, carrot and lentil, mung bean, and cream of mushroom to feature, all served with bread. Lines are common but service is swift.

GRÜNERLØKKA AND EASTERN OSLO
★ **Mathallen Food Hall**

Inspired by the food halls of continental Europe, **Mathallen** (Vulkan 5, tel. 40 00 12 09, www.mathallenoslo.no, 8am-1am Tues.-Thurs., 8am-3am Fri., 9:30am-3am Sat.,

lunch at Mathallen food hall

from 6pm, with questions given in both Norwegian and English.

Stock up on cheeses, cured meats, and other delicacies for later from the boys at **Gutta på Haugen** (www.gutta.no). They have a bigger store at St. Hanshaugen, but the selection at Mathallen is good enough to avoid an out-of-the-way trip to the 'burbs.

The mezzanine floor offers far more than a chance to take in the atmosphere and aromas from below. The menu of the day at Latin American backpacker-themed **Hitchhiker** (tel. 95 45 14 66, www.hitchhiker.no, 11am-1am Tues.-Sat., noon-10pm Sun.) presents sharing plates crammed with street food with a slight Norwegian twist. Fish tacos anyone? The restaurant slowly transforms into a bar with a late-night DJ getting the party started on Friday nights, although it's drinks only after 10pm.

CULINARY ACADEMY (Kulinariskakademi)

During the daytime, the mezzanine plays host to a series of food classes from Oslo's **Culinary Academy** (tel. 23 23 15 80, www.kulinariskakademi.no), including wine pairing, sushi making, and sausage making. Most courses are held in Norwegian and run around 1,200kr, but classes in English are available at peak times, so check in advance.

Cafés and Light Bites

Norwegian barista ★ **Tim Wendelboe** (Grünersgate 1, tel. 40 00 40 62, 8:30am-6pm Mon.-Fri., 11am-5pm Sat.-Sun.) is the undisputed king of Nordic coffee culture, and his micro-roastery and coffee bar does a roaring trade with locals. This isn't the place to relax over a latte, as the solitary table is likely to be taken. Pop in for a black coffee brewed to order and experience a taste sensation. Not sure what to order? The menu is available in both Norwegian and English, and Tim's staff are knowledgeable bordering on obsessive about the origin of the beans. Just tell them if you prefer your coffee with nutty, chocolaty, or fruity tones, and they'll recommend the

9:30am-1am Sun.) brings the best of Oslo's restaurants and food shopping under one roof. The centerpiece of the emerging riverside Vulkan neighborhood, Oslo's biggest food hall is a destination in itself. At the center of the hall are large benches encouraging social interaction and sharing of dishes, while some self-contained restaurants dot the perimeter of the spacious redbrick former factory. Fresh fruit and vegetables, a fishmonger, and a butcher counter are all available inside. Note that several of the individual shops and restaurants have different opening hours to the center itself, which is entirely closed on Mondays.

Highlights inside include **Vulkanfisk** (www.vulkanfisk.no), which sells arctic cod from Tromsø, shrimp from Kirkenes, crayfish and lobster from Møre, and organic salmon from Aukra. The selection of craft beers at basement bar **Smelteverket** (www.smelteverketoslo.no) is so vast they have built Norway's longest bar to serve them from. Join the fun at the weekly pub quiz on Wednesday best option for you. You're unlikely to meet the man himself, as he spends several months every year working on location with the farmers to improve the production process.

Perfect for a winter visit, the menu at **Cocoa** (Toftes gate 48, tel. 92 80 84 40, 10am-7pm daily) is packed with hot chocolate options, and, of course, they serve coffee too. Most of the light bites are made in-store by the owner, with savory pies such as spinach and feta sitting alongside sweet temptations. The retro interior is charming, but even if it's busy, you can pick up cocoa to go from the serving window.

The Grunerløkka branch of **Godt Brød** (Thorvald Meyers gate 49, tel. 23 22 90 40, 6am-6pm daily) is the best option for breakfast or a light lunch. All sandwiches are made to order, and there's a bigger range of fresh toppings and sauces, and more seating than most other cafés in Oslo. The coffee's good, too!

Traditional Scandinavian

If you need to shake off the hipster attitude of Grünerløkka and desire something more formal, **Markveien Mat & Vinhus** (Torvbakkgt 12, tel. 22 37 22 97, www.markveien.no, 4pm-1am Mon.-Sat., 275kr) is the place for you. This is the kind of warm, cozy restaurant where you make an evening of it. Fish and seafood feature strongly on the menu, with an excellent five-course set menu available for 600kr. The associated wine bar is one of Oslo's oldest, and you will be hard pressed to ignore the tantalizing range of wines on offer to accompany your meal, even if they could double the price.

Amid the thrift stores and takeaways of multicultural Grønland is the surprisingly stylish **Olympen** (Grønlandsleiret 15, tel. 24 10 19 99, www.olympen.no, noon-midnight Sun.-Mon., 11am-1am Tues.-Thurs., 11am-3am Fri., noon-3am Sat., 220kr). Reminiscent of a German *bierkeller* (basement pub), the dark wooden interior is in complete contrast to the bright and spacious rooftop terrace open during the summer months. Popular with groups, Olympen serves traditional Scandinavian fare, although the menu is often limited to one meat and two fish dishes. This is no place for vegans.

With perhaps the best view from any restaurant in Oslo, **Ekebergrestauranten** (Kongsveien 15, tel. 23 24 23 00, www.ekebergrestauranten.com, 11am-midnight Mon.-Sat., noon-10pm Sun.) is in a modernist building within the peaceful surroundings of Ekeberg Park. Prime cuts of meat or fish are served simply yet elegantly with terrific views and a direct tram link to the city. Expect to pay around 180kr for a simple lunch of cured salmon or a hamburger, while a more formal dinner will run around 285kr for your entrée.

Asian

Always a comforting sign for a sushi restaurant, **Mamo Sushi** (Helgesens gate 16, tel. 22 37 10 38, 3pm-10pm Sun.-Thurs., 3pm-11pm Fri.-Sat., 109-195kr) attracts a lot of Japanese guests. Its popularity and relatively small interior mean booking is advisable if you want to enjoy the generous sharing plates. If you're especially hungry, start with the excellent spicy Thai soup.

For a budget option, check out the Chinese, Vietnamese, Thai, and sushi menu at the shabby yet busy **East Kitchen** (Markveien 50, tel. 22 71 96 58, 11am-10pm Mon.-Fri., noon-10pm Sat., 1pm-10pm Sun.). Their midweek lunch deal (11am-3pm) for under 100kr has to be one of the best culinary bargains in the city, and the locals know it. Head here after the lunchtime rush and you might not need much of an evening meal.

Indian

Grønland is home to a concentration of Indian restaurants, the best of which is **Punjab Tandoori** (Gronland 24, tel. 22 17 20 86, www.punjabtandoori.no, 11am-11pm daily, 110kr). The interior feels like a fast-food outlet, and you will need to listen out for your order as it's shouted from the counter. Be especially attentive when it's busy, which is most of the time given that it's one of Oslo's best-value places to eat a decent-sized meal.

Tucked away on a residential street in nearby Tøyen, **Palmyra Cafe** (Norby gata 15, www.palmyra.no, 11am-9pm daily, 110kr) is a no-frills South Indian and Sri Lankan restaurant with a focus on simple, traditional food. Don't let the school cafeteria-style plastic serving trays put you off; this is authentic and great value food from the Indian subcontinent.

Italian
For thin and crispy Italian-style pizza, look no further than **Villa Paradiso** (Olaf Ryes plass 8, tel. 22 35 40 60, www.villaparadiso.no, 8am-11pm Mon.-Fri., 10am-11pm Sat.-Sun., 181kr), even if the crusts are often a little overdone. Located on one of Grunerløkka's busiest squares, the pizzeria is always popular in the evenings, so be sure to book ahead. Walk-ins are usually possible for lunch, and takeout is always available, but orders are not accepted over the phone. The outside terrace fills up fast, but there's plenty more seating inside the warm Italian bar area.

WESTERN OSLO
Cafés and Light Bites
The airy **Cafe Rustique** (Majorstuveien 33b, tel. 22 59 35 00, 8am-6pm Mon.-Fri., 10am-6pm Sat.-Sun.) is known for its international atmosphere, but that's down to the global nature of its staff and clientele rather than the food. The much-lauded empanadas aren't worth the premium price, so save your money and stick to a croissant and coffee instead. Choose between the moody cramped interior or one of the few sidewalk tables on the street corner.

Traditional Scandinavian
It might be a little tricky to find (look for the plants!), but **Kolonihagen** (Frognerveien 33, tel. 99 31 68 10, www.kolonihagen.no, 11am-11pm Mon.-Sat., 11am-5pm Sun., 279kr) is worth the effort. Set back from the street in the upscale residential neighborhood of

Frogner, Kolonihagen brings the freshest Scandinavian ingredients from the farm to your plate in a relaxed rustic environment. Also available as a vegetarian version, the seasonal tasting menu is the best way to sample the taste of Kolonihagen, although taking the accompanying drink pairings will push the check over 1,100kr per head.

International
The Ivorian chef at **Café Afrikaden** (Pilestredet 75c, tel. 21 39 61 06, www.cafeafrikaden.no, 4pm-9pm Mon.-Fri., 2pm-10pm Sat., 130kr) focuses on authenticity with a rotating weekly menu. The café offers a rare chance to sample African food in Oslo. Rice and fried plantains are common accompaniments, but you might need sunglasses to protect your eyes from the vivid mismatched decor.

There are plenty of cheaper Indian restaurants in Oslo, but **Natraj Tandoori** (Bygdøy allé 8, tel. 22 44 75 33, www.natraj.no, 4pm-11pm Mon.-Sat., 3pm-10pm Sun., 199kr) serves generous flavorful portions in a colorful atmosphere that has placed it as a firm favorite among diners in western Oslo.

A great choice for those passing through Majorstuen due to its proximity to the metro station, **Café Billabong** (Bogstadveien 53, tel. 22 60 42 97, www.cafebillabong.no, 11am-1am Mon.-Thurs., 11am-3am Fri.-Sat., noon-midnight Sun., 140kr) offers a daily special on top of its vast range of pizzas, burgers, and pasta dishes. The food is nothing special, but it's filling, good value, and served quickly. As the day progresses, the atmosphere transforms from sleepy to lively as the booths become home to groups for drinking games galore.

Vegetarian
The menu changes daily at **Krishna's Cuisine** (Sørkedalsveien 10, tel. 22 60 62 50, 11am-8pm Mon.-Fri., 11am-7pm Sat., 150kr) but is always limited to one combination of curry, soup, rice, and sides. Drinks are limited to juice, coffee, water, or lassi, a traditional Indian yogurt-based drink. Set inside a mall, this is not

the place to come for a romantic dinner, but it's a great value option for vegetarians on this side of the city.

NORTHERN OSLO
Traditional Scandinavian

Traditional Norwegian food in a rustic cabin environment with sensational views across Oslo—there's not much not to like about **Frognerseteren** (Holmenkollveien 200, tel. 22 92 40 40, www.frognerseteren.no, noon-10pm Mon.-Sat., 1pm-9pm Sun., 365kr). Top quality reindeer, lamb, and local fish are served with simple accompaniments. During the daytime, the adjacent café serves a slimmer sandwich menu alongside an abundance of fresh cakes to keep hungry hikers and skiers satisfied before they continue their journey into the Nordmarka forest.

Farther down the hill, the **Holmenkollen Restaurant** (Holmenkollveien 119, tel. 22 13 92 00, www.holmenkollenrestaurant.no, noon-9pm Tues.-Sat., 1pm-7pm Sun., closed in July, 299kr) serves a Norwegian menu with the odd international twist in a traditional mountain lodge setting. The biggest pull here is not the food, but the outstanding views across the Oslofjord.

Accommodations

Recent years have seen a wave of simple budget hotels arrive in the Norwegian capital, a trend we hope to see spread to the smaller cities in due course. Chain hotels still dominate the city, though, and in some areas of central Oslo you can't walk more than a block without hitting a Thon or Scandic hotel. Thon alone boasts 16 hotels across the city.

Hostel beds are expensive in comparison to other European capitals, but availability is good. However, for not much more money you can now get motel-standard rooms in central locations, without having to share a bathroom with anyone.

DOWNTOWN
Under 500kr

Anker Hostel (Storgata 55, tel. 22 99 72 00, www.ankerhostel.no, dorm beds from 250kr pp) offers beds in a simple six- or eight-bed dormitory just across the bridge from Grünerløkka. The biggest dorms contain kitchenettes, which can prove an invaluable money-saver. Borrow a pan from reception and whip up some noodles from the budget supermarket across the street. The 24-hour reception staffed by locals is handy for late arrivals or questions about transportation.

Buses and trams trundle by the entrance en route to most parts of the city.

An alternative budget option is the **Sentrum Pensjonat** (Tollbugata 8a, tel. 22 33 55 80, www.sentrumpensjonat.no, dorm beds from 290kr pp). The central location means pretty much anywhere in downtown Oslo is within a 10-minute walk. Dorm rooms are dated, the walls are salmon-pink, and noise can be an issue in this area, but that aside it's the best value accommodation in the city center. Private twin/double rooms are also available from 670kr.

500-1,000kr

The best of the recent budget bunch is the ★ **Comfort Hotel Xpress Youngstorget** (Møllergata 26, tel. 22 03 11 00, xpress.young-storget@choice.no, 900kr), aimed squarely at hip young things. From the free coffee and fast Wi-Fi to retro arcade machines in reception, this hotel is on the stylish side of budget. The comfortable minimalist rooms with a splash of color are small, but storage isn't a problem.

The tiny rooms at **Citybox Oslo** (Prinsens gate 6, tel. 21 42 04 80, www.citybox.no, 795kr) will not please those with a lot of

Black, copper, and gold dominate The Thief hotel.

1,000-2,000kr

Despite now being a part of the identikit Thon hotel chain, the **Hotel Bristol** (Kristian IV's gate 7, tel. 22 82 60 00, post@bristol.no, 1,645kr) retains its historic name and independent character. Sophisticated and traditional design combine with a live piano bar to provide a timeless elegance for its guests to enjoy, in both the rooms and common areas. The hotel's Winter Garden and Library Bar has a strong history in the city's cultural circles and offers freshly baked cakes and coffee daily to guests.

A good self-catering option, the popular **Oslo Korttidsutleie** apartments (Rostockgata 7, tel. 92 01 09 70, www.oslo-korttidsutleie.no, from 1,200kr) at the new Barcode development get booked up fast. This will suit those who want a taste of how the other half live, with spotless modern studio and one-bedroom apartments with balcony views of the Oslo Opera House and Oslofjord.

Prices vary seasonally at the **Hotel Christiania Teater** (Stortingsgate 16, tel. 21 04 38 00, stay@christianiateater.com), but rooms with striking design and bold colors can usually be found for under 2,000kr. The original theater building dates back to 1917, and the hotel's common areas are filled with nods to Oslo's cultural history, from early performances of *Peer Gynt* to when Norwegian opera icon Kirsten Flagstad played her first major lead role. Today, the Christiania Teater puts on regular musicals, and the National Theater is merely steps away.

Sustainability is high on the agenda at the **Hotel Guldsmeden** (Parkveien 78, tel. 23 27 40 00, www.guldsmedenhotels.com, 1,495kr), with organic toiletries in all the rooms and local produce for breakfast. It has a sister hotel in Bali and it shows, with a unique combination of Balinese decor crossed with a Norwegian cabin. Most rooms contain four-poster beds and reindeer furs for a warm and welcoming stay.

luggage, but they're fine for an individual or a couple traveling light. The outstanding location just a few minutes' walk from Oslo Central Station is perfect for late-night arrival. The automated reception won't please everyone, but there is usually a member of staff on call. The hostel-style social lounge with library and TVs helps to make up for the small rooms.

The outstanding value **HTL Karl Johan** (Arbeidergata 4, tel. 97 99 56 30, 799kr) has spacious rooms with LED lights and a modern TV system that you stream videos to from your tablet or laptop. A comfortable lounge fills the lobby area with friendly service from the bar at your seat. Included in the room rate is a quality breakfast but with not much variety—fine for one or two nights, but any more and you'll find yourself seeking some variety in the nearby cafés. If the hotel is full, try your luck at the almost identical **HTL Grensen** (Grensen 20, tel. 97 99 56 20, 799kr), literally around the corner.

Over 2,000kr

Five-star luxury doesn't come cheap, although ★ **The Thief** (Landgangen 1, tel. 24 00 40 00, www.thethief.com, 2,940kr) is named after its waterside location where thieves were executed rather than the price of its rooms. The striking black, copper, and gold lobby gives you an inkling of what to expect. The walls of the lobby are adorned with modern art from the neighboring Astrup Fearnley Museum, while tablet computers control the amenities within the contemporary luxury rooms. The buffet breakfast is outstanding, with hot options cooked to order and a fine range of fresh juices sourced from local orchards.

The **Grand Hotel** (Karl Johans gate 31, tel. 23 21 20 00, www.grand.no, 2,336kr) is a landmark hotel dating back to 1874. Dominating the city's primary plaza and overlooking the Parliament, the Grand Hotel plays host to visiting Nobel Peace Prize laureates and was the preferred haunt of Norwegian playwright Henrik Ibsen. Despite the hotel's age the rooms are surprisingly modern, with white and gold decor lending an airy feeling. Despite renovations, the character of the whole building has been preserved, and the stores out front are unable to use glaring billboards.

The crowning glory at **Hotel Continental** (Stortingsgata 24/26, tel. 22 82 40 00, www. hotelcontinental.no, 2,095-3,030kr) is the bar lounge Dagligstuen, home to one of Norway's largest private collections of Edvard Munch's work. The lounge hosts afternoon tea every Saturday. The upscale rooms are decorated in subdued tones, but only the upgraded rooms feature seating areas. If you want to spend even more money, the hotel offers packages combining lavish dinners or spa treatments, or a romantic package that features fruit, wine, room service, early check-in, and a late check-out.

For a boutique luxury experience, look no further than the seven exquisite bedrooms of **Camillas Hus** (Parkveien 31, tel. 94 85 60 15, www.camillashus.no, 1,999kr s, 2,750kr d), located just behind the Royal Palace park and named after one of Norway's most renowned female authors, Camilla Collett. You'll feel like royalty in the individually decorated rooms in which the extravagant bathrooms are the main feature. The personal touches like fresh fruit and flowers in the bedrooms make all the difference, while a cooked-to-order hot breakfast is the icing on the cake.

GRÜNERLØKKA AND EASTERN OSLO

Because it's surprisingly bereft of accommodation options, most people interested in the Grünerløkka neighborhood simply stay downtown. One great option is the riverside ★ **PS:Hotell** (Maridalsveien 13c, tel. 23 15 65 00, www.pshotell.no, 1,250kr pp) at the heart of the emerging Vulkan district with the Mathallen food hall as its neighbor. The hotel is staffed by people who need guidance, knowledge, and experience on their way back to employment. As a result, customer service is a priority here, and any queries or problems are quickly addressed. The 31 rooms are basic (some of the double rooms actually come with bunk beds) yet with an urban style designed to appeal to a younger, socially conscious patron.

For longer stays in Oslo, do as the locals do and stay in a fashionable apartment complex. The cost-effective weekly rate at the **Downtown Apartments** (Nedre gate 8, tel. 22 60 83 00, www.dta.as) ranges from 4,704kr for a studio to 10,605kr for a four-bed option. Head farther east to Tøyen for a cheaper option at the **Oslo Hotel Apartments** (Kjølberggata 29, tel. 24 07 40 03, www.oslohotelapartments.com), which offers dorm beds from 210kr, a room in a shared apartment from 490kr, or standard double rooms from 770kr.

WESTERN OSLO

The leafy western suburbs of Oslo are dominated by apartments and guesthouses rather than hotels. One exception is the popular **Saga Hotel** (Eilert Sundts gate 39, tel. 22 55 44 90, www.sagahoteloslo.no), whose 19th-century exterior hides a cutting-edge design inside. Gold and copper tones add a sense of luxury to the 47 rooms. The hotel also operates apartments in the vicinity, just steps away from the exclusive boutiques and restaurants of Bogstadveien.

The homey feel of **Villa Frogner** (Nordraaks gate 26, tel. 22 56 19 60, 1,195kr), together with its location just steps from Vigeland Sculpture Park, draws many travelers away from downtown. A friendly host, free tea and coffee, and vintage furniture in the communal areas give this bed-and-breakfast an altogether different feel from the soulless chain hotels all too common elsewhere in Oslo, as do the individually decorated spacious rooms. There's a cheaper alternative just a few streets away at the three-room **Frogner Bed & Breakfast** (Kirkeveien 5, tel. 92 42 03 65, post@frognerbb.no, 850kr), where the small rooms are simply furnished. There's a lack of common areas and no permanent reception, so it feels more like a lodging than a commercial B&B.

Plenty of accommodation options are available through **Frogner House** (tel. 93 01 00 09, www.frognerhouse.no), a network of intimate apartments across the neighborhood. Especially good for a short stay are the apartments in the ornate former hotel at Bygdøy allé 53, where all rooms contain a kitchenette and smart TV.

NORTHERN OSLO

Leaping out of the pages of a Norwegian folk tale, the rustic **Lysebu Hotel** (Lysebuveien 12, tel. 21 51 10 00, www.lysebu.no, 1,950kr d) is possibly the finest accommodation choice in Oslo. Surrounded by forest yet just a short stroll from Oslo's T-Bane network, the hotel features a swimming pool and well-stocked wine cellar that make Lysebu a destination in itself. This is an absolutely perfect choice if you want to explore Oslo's forest and the Holmenkollen area any time of year. Designed by architect Magnus Paulsson as a monument to Danish-Norwegian cooperation during World War II, Lysebu showcases a range of art from the two countries. Combine this setting with the light, rustic bedrooms

and you'd be hard-pressed to find a better venue for a romantic getaway, especially in the winter.

Few hotels in the city offer views as good as the **Scandic Holmenkollen Park** (Kongeveien 26, tel. 22 92 20 00, holmenkollenpark@scandichotels.com, 1,390kr), sandwiched between Holmenkollen and the city below. The striking contrast of the fanciful architecture resembling a Norwegian stave church with the modern ski jump is an exciting one, yet many of the hotel's 300-plus rooms are located in a far less interesting modern block. Still, for fresh air and access to Holmenkollen and Oslo's forests, this is a great choice. The hotel is extremely busy in winter, especially during major skiing events.

Primarily a conference hotel, **Thon Hotel Ullevaal** (Sognsveien 77C, tel. 22 02 80 00, ullevaalstadion@thonhotels.no, 1,116kr) is nevertheless a good choice for sports fans. The hotel is immediately adjacent to the national soccer stadium and soccer museum, and the restaurant used for breakfast comes with a view across the soccer pitch. Rooms can be picked up for under 1,000kr a night at weekends, but rates shoot sky-high when the stadium is in use.

Camping might not be your first thought when staying in a destination famed for its winter climate, but Oslo has its own year-round campground at **Bogstad Camping** (Ankerveien 117, tel. 22 51 08 00, www.bogstadcamping.no), which is close to Bogstad Manor, Holmenkollen Ski Arena, and Oslo Winter Park. Nightly camping fees start at 200kr for two people without a car, while hookups for RVs are also available amid the 800 pitches on offer. The 55 comfortable cabins range 550-1,400kr depending on size and season, while a new kitchen block is free to use for all camping guests. Although the campground is one of Norway's biggest, it rarely feels busy due to its proximity to outdoor recreation. Its neighbors include a popular lake, a golf course, and a myriad of hiking and cross-country skiing trails.

AIRPORT HOTELS

For those with an early departure or late arrival at Oslo Airport Gardermoen, a range of hotel options will meet your needs. Be aware that although cheaper than hotels downtown, all airport hotels except the Radisson and Park Inn require an expensive shuttle bus trip or an even more pricey cab. Your best option is probably to stay downtown close to Oslo Central Station.

As you would expect for an airport hotel, the staff at the **Radisson Blu Oslo Airport** (Hotellvegen, tel. 63 93 30 00, info.airport. oslo@radissonblu.com, 1,995kr) are fully knowledgeable about procedures at Oslo Airport and are only too willing to help.

The food and drinks are eye-wateringly expensive but good quality. For a luxury beginning or end to your holiday this is a good pick, but if you're watching your budget try one of the cheaper alternatives outside the airport ring.

The best of the bunch is the **Comfort Hotel Runway** (Hans Gaardersvei 27, tel. 63 94 88 88, co.runway@choice.no, 799kr), where its simplicity is disguised by contemporary design features and a view of the runway, giving the impression that you're staying in a much higher quality hotel. The lobby includes a small convenience store and restaurant that provides a free breakfast or an early-bird "grab bag" from 4am.

Information and Services

VISITOR INFORMATION

For general information about attractions and things to do in Oslo and free Wi-Fi, head to the modern **Oslo Visitor Centre** (Østbanehallen, Jernbanetorget 1, tel. 81 53 05 55, www.visitoslo.com, 9am-6pm daily) near Oslo Central Station. City maps are available from most hotel receptions. If you ever get lost in Oslo, ask a local. Everyone speaks English and most are only too happy to help a tourist, especially with the confusing T-Bane system or bus routes.

POST OFFICES AND COURIER SERVICES

Posten is the national post service and handles all domestic and international mail. Many supermarkets have an in-store postal service (*post i butikk*), but for parcels and detailed questions, you're best to head to the main **Posten** (Klingenberggata 7, 7:30am-6pm Mon.-Fri., 10am-3pm Sat.) at Vika. If it's just a stamp you need, most souvenir shops sell them alongside postcards.

EMBASSIES AND CONSULATES

Most nations have an embassy or consulate in Oslo. Most are located in western Oslo. Be aware that most follow Norwegian holidays as well as the holidays of their own country.

The **Embassy of the United States** (Henrik Ibsens gate 45, tel. 23 96 05 55, http://norway.usembassy.gov) remains at its city center location until the lengthy move to new premises at Huseby is finally completed. The emergency hotline for U.S. citizens (tel. 21 30 85 40) deals with lost/stolen passports, crime, deaths, and contact information for health-care providers. For all other issues, an appointment must be made to visit the embassy in person. They cannot act as your travel agent, bank, interpreter, employment office, lawyer, investigator, or law enforcement agent, or assist with personal legal or medical matters, but they can advise you on where to receive help on such matters.

Similar emergency support and services are available from the **Embassy of Canada** (Wergelandsveien 7, tel. 22 99 53 00, oslo@

international.gc.ca) and the **British Embassy** (Thomas Heftyes gate 8, tel. 23 13 27 00, UKinNorway@fco.gov.uk). Australian citizens should contact the **Australian Embassy in Denmark** (tel. +45/7026 3676, http://denmark.embassy.gov. au); the Oslo Consulate closed in 2013.

INTERNET ACCESS

Wireless Internet connectivity is commonplace in Norwegian hotels, shopping centers, and cafés.

As an alternative or to surf for longer periods of time, try the main branch of the **Oslo Public Library** (Arne Garborgs plass 4, tel. 23 43 29 00, 9am-7pm Mon.-Fri., 10am-4pm Sat.). Head to the top floor for the most seats and quietest environment.

For more comprehensive business services, ask at your hotel or head to **Arctic Internet** (Jernbanetorget 1, tel. 22 17 19 40, 9am-11pm daily) on the mezzanine floor of Oslo Central Station. There you will find printers, webcams, headsets, scanners, and CD burners in addition to regular Internet terminals.

NORWEGIAN LANGUAGE COURSES

Norwegian is a language of many dialects, but the Oslo version (Eastern Norwegian) is the one considered easiest for foreigners to learn. The **University of Oslo** (www.uio. no) runs an International Summer School in Norwegian language and culture but restricts its pure language courses to students and employees. Private language schools have exploded in popularity in recent years but tend to require a commitment of at least five weeks for beginners, costing from 4,000kr.

Alfaskolen (Kongens gate 15, tel. 22 41 01 20, www.alfaskolen.no) runs an intensive summer school at 1,800kr for the first week, with discounts for extra weeks.

Undoubtedly your best financial option is to study beforehand and use your time in Oslo to put into practice what you've learned. Many enterprising Norwegians living abroad offer lessons via video chat. Because of the lower cost of living, they are able to offer lessons at far cheaper rates than can teachers needing to meet Oslo's stratospheric cost of living.

MONEY

Banking in Oslo is largely conducted digitally. Although all shops still accept cash, times are changing fast and credit cards, wireless, and mobile payments are fast replacing bills and coins. Most shops are likely to accept all international cards, although the smallest might only accept credit cards. If in doubt, it's wise to make sure you have at least some cash on you at all times.

Cash and travelers checks can be exchanged at **Forex Bank** (Jernbanetorget 1, tel. 22 17 22 65, 7am-9pm Mon.-Fri., 9am-6pm Sat., 10am-5pm Sun.) inside Oslo Central Station and is usually a better option than hunting out a bank. Many Norwegian bank branches no longer deal with cash transactions, directing you toward the ATMs. Larger branches open later include **DNB** (Karl Johans gate 27, 9am-6pm Mon.-Fri., 10am-4pm Sat.), **Nordea** (Prinsensgate 12, 9am-3pm Mon.-Fri.), and **SpareBank** (Youngstorget 5, 9am-6pm Mon.-Thurs., 9am-3pm Fri.).

Most ATMs *(minibank)* around Oslo accept international debit and credit cards and often offer a decent exchange rate, depending on your own bank's charges.

HEALTH

Many risks typically associated with traveling are minimized in Oslo. Tap water is generally drinkable.

Urgent Care

Oslo has a number of first-aid centers *(legevakt)* that act as emergency rooms. Waits can be long, but for urgent care this should be your first port of call. **Legevakt Storgata** (Storgata 40, tel. 22 11 72 96) is the main downtown center and is open 24 hours. For illnesses including fevers, vomiting, and diarrhea, the nearby **Legevakt Aker** (Trondheimsveien 235, tel. 23 48 72 00) is also an option, but opening hours are restricted (4pm-1:30am Mon.-Fri., 10am-1:30am weekends and holidays).

Pharmacies

Every shopping center will have at least one of the major pharmacy *(apotek)* chains. Boots, Apotek 1, and Vitusapotek are the main names to look out for. There are at least 10 in the vicinity of Oslo Central Station. **Vitusapotek Jernbanetorget** (Jerbanetorget 4B, tel. 23 35 81 00) is open 24 hours, as is the **Apotek1 Legevakten** (Storgata 40, tel. 22 98 87 20) at the Storgata urgent care center.

Dental Services

Dental treatment in Oslo is expensive, so much so that medical tourism to eastern Europe is big business. Nevertheless there are options should you need emergency treatment. Precious few dental centers open on Sunday, and those that do charge a premium.

The City of Oslo runs an emergency room for dental treatment that is only open on evenings and weekends. **Oslo Tannlegevakten** (Schweigaardsgate 6, tel. 22 67 30 00, 7pm-10pm Mon.-Fri., 11am-2pm and 7pm-10pm Sat.-Sun.) is on the third floor of The Gallery above Oslo Bus Terminal. Credit cards are accepted, but with rates starting at 565kr for just 10 minutes, the bill is likely to make your eyes water just as much as the treatment.

Oslo Tannlegesenter (Tordenskiolds gate 6B, tel. 22 42 49 50, www.oslotannlegesenter.no, 8am-9pm Mon.-Fri., 10am-5pm Sat.-Sun.) welcomes emergency calls, although on a Sunday you will need to call 95 36 65 28 to inquire about the availability of a dental practitioner.

Transportation

GETTING THERE
Air
OSLO AIRPORT GARDERMOEN

Although a 49-kilometer (30-mile) drive northeast of the city center, **Oslo Airport Gardermoen** (Edvard Munchs veg, Gardermoen, tel. 64 81 20 00) is the main international hub for Norway, with flights to the United States, Middle East, and Asia alongside domestic and European routes. Both international and domestic terminals have undergone a massive expansion, so congestion issues should now be a thing of the past.

A must-know is the complicated luggage rules. If you are connecting onto a domestic flight from an international arrival at Gardermoen, you must collect your baggage and clear customs and re-check your bags. The extra time required for this and the additional security check mean you should allow at least 90 minutes for a connection at Gardermoen. Trials for an expedited process called *Connecting Norway* are underway for selected flights, although this seems unlikely to be rolled out beyond arrivals from select other northern European nations. If you're transferring with hand-luggage only, you can pass through a separate section of the airport and straight into the domestic terminal.

If you need to transfer on to a domestic flight, check the latest regulations with staff on-site at Oslo Airport. Based on previous experience, airline staff in other countries and even cabin crew are unlikely to know the very latest processes.

To reach Oslo, choose between the nonstop 20-minute journey on the modern **Airport Express Train (Flytoget)** (www.flytoget.no, 180kr) or the 30-40-minute ride on the commuter train from **NSB** (www.nsb.no, 93kr). Both options run from approximately 5am to midnight. The express option has much more room for luggage, but the commuter service is a great budget option for those traveling light.

In contrast, the **Airport Express Coach (Flybussen)** (www.flybussen.no, 150kr) is both expensive and slow. It can take up to an hour to reach the city at busy times.

OTHER AIRPORTS

Previously known as Oslo's second airport, Moss Airport Rygge ceased operations in late 2016 following the withdrawal of low-cost carrier Ryanair. The only alternative airport for Oslo is now **Sandefjord Airport Torp** (tel. 33 42 70 00, www.torp.no), approximately 110 kilometers (68 miles) south of Oslo, on the western side of the Oslofjord. Although Sandefjord Airport is commonly advertised as Oslo Torp by low-cost carriers, the compact regional airport is actually an expensive two-hour bus transfer to and from the capital. Nevertheless, it's worth considering, as bargains can be had from the United Kingdom and continental Europe.

Bus

Located at the eastern edge of downtown, **Oslo Bus Terminal** (Schweigaards gate 6-14) is the arrival point for all international bus routes. **Swebus** (www.swebus.se) runs regular coaches from Stockholm, Gothenburg, and Copenhagen, from where **Eurolines** (tel. +49/6196-2078-501, www.eurolines.de) offers connections to Berlin, Frankfurt, and Hamburg. **Czech Transport** (tel. +420/776-677-890 Mon.-Fri., www.czech-transport.com) runs a weekly service from Prague.

When arriving at Oslo Bus Terminal, be sure to keep hold of your belongings and head straight for the neighboring Oslo Central Station. Although Oslo is generally considered to be a safe city, care should be taken inside and in the area immediately outside the bus station.

Rail

Also on the east of downtown, **Oslo Central Station** (Jernbanetorget 1, tel. 81 50 08 88, www.oslo-s.no) is linked into the European rail network via Swedish cities Gothenburg and Stockholm. Three daily trains make the four-hour journey from Gothenburg, and tickets can be booked via the Norwegian state railway company **NSB** (tel. 81 50 08 88, www.nsb.no), but to make the five-hour journey from Stockholm, you must book in advance with the Swedish state company **SJ** (tel. +46/771 757 575, www.sj.se).

If you are arriving by rail and plan to continue your journey around Norway by rail, it's worth investigating the rail passes on offer. Non-Europeans can use Eurail (www.eurail.com) and European citizens Interrail (www.interrail.eu). Both passes are particularly good value for those under 25 and for families traveling together.

Boat

In addition to the increasing numbers of cruise ships, three international ferry operators service Oslo. **DFDS** (tel. +44/330 333 0245, www.dfdsseaways.co.uk) operates overnight boats from Copenhagen, while **Color Line** (tel. 81 00 08 11, www.colorline.no) runs a daily service to and from Kiel in northern Germany. **Stena Line** (tel. 23 17 91 30, www.stenaline.no) operates a 24-hour round-trip service to and from Fredrikshavn in northern Denmark known locally as a "booze cruise." Oslo locals take advantage of the duty-free regulations on board, often stumbling back into Oslo with crates of beer in tow.

GETTING AROUND
Public Transit

Oslo's public transit system is extensive and collectively managed under the umbrella organization **Ruter** (www.ruter.no). This means that, although the metro, tram, bus, train, and ferries are operated by different companies, there is one ticketing solution for more or less the entire network. The Ruter network extends out of Oslo and into the surrounding Akershus county. Pay attention to the multiple zone ticketing system, although you will only need a ticket for more than one zone if you are traveling outside of Oslo.

The excellent English version of their website helps you plan your travel around the city and gives up-to-date information on fares and passes. Whichever mode of transport you choose, you in most cases need to purchase your tickets in advance and ensure they are validated or you risk a heavy fine. Ignorance is no excuse in the eyes of the Oslo public transit cops. A single fare (valid for 60 minutes including transfers on bus, metro, and tram) for one zone costs 33kr when bought in advance, with a 24-hour ticket at 90kr good value if you are planning a hectic day of sightseeing. Children under 4 travel fee, with a discount (usually 50 percent) applied for children under 16 and seniors above 67.

At almost all public transit stops you will find live information screens detailing how long you will need to wait for any particular service. These tend to be accurate, but there are paper timetables at the majority of stops too, just in case. Smoking is banned on all public transport and also at the stops. The usually shy and reserved Norwegians won't hesitate to interrupt a visitor who violates this law.

Most modes of transport are up and running by 6am through to midnight, with some bus lines running throughout the night. The rush hour in Oslo tends to be early, so you'll find public transport at its busiest before 8am and 3-5pm.

METRO

Oslo's metro network, known as **T-Bane** (look for the T logo), is extensive considering the compact nature of the city. The lines all converge into one tunnel that serves all six stations in the vicinity of downtown Oslo, meaning you can get onto any line from any station in the city center. Many of the lines reach out far into the surrounding suburbs and offer great connectivity into Oslo's *marka,* the forested areas that envelop the city. Line 1 serves Holmenkollen Ski Arena and passes through dense forest on its way to Frognerseteren and Nordmarka, while line 3 serves the hiking and skiing trails around Sognsvann lake. It's not uncommon for both lines to be packed with winter sports enthusiasts in the winter or locals heading into the hills for a weekend hike.

TRAM

There's a certain charm to Oslo's aging tram *(trikk)* network, which is undergoing a major renovation and expansion. New lines run along the waterfront Barcode development, with more planned in due course to fill in the gaps of the T-Bane network.

BUS

The metro and tram are usually sufficient for visitors to Oslo, but there is also an extensive network of buses that fill in the gaps, in particular to residential suburbs. Green buses are regional, whereas the red ones are local and stay within the city limits. Almost all bus routes pass through the downtown area somewhere close to Jernbanetorget square.

FERRY

Oslo's passenger ferry network provides a vital transportation link from nearby islands and peninsulas to the downtown area. But they are great use to travelers, too. A daily service runs year-round from Vippetangen serving the small islands of the inner Oslofjord. All Ruter tickets and passes are valid on these ferries, with the exception of the Bygdøy tourist ferry, which requires a separate ticket.

Taxi

There is almost never a need to take a taxi in Oslo. That's a good thing, because the cost of short trips is astronomical, with prices starting at 109kr. Expect a per-kilometer rate of around 14kr, rising to almost 20kr depending on the time of day. If you really do need a taxi, **Oslo Taxi** (tel. 22 38 80 90, www.oslotaxi.no, 24 hours) is your best bet. All their taxicabs accept major credit cards, including Diners Club and American Express.

Car Rental

All international car rental companies are represented at both Oslo Airport and in the city itself. Expect to pay around 3,000kr for a week's basic rental from the likes of **Avis** (tel. 67 25 55 10, www.avis.no) or **Hertz** (tel. 64 81 05 50, hertz.no) from Oslo Airport.

A good alternative option, **Rent-a-wreck** (www.rent-a-wreck-scandinavia.com) rents out used cars starting at 300kr per day, although they charge additional fees for extensive mileage. They have outlets at Økern (Østre Akervei 21) and Jessheim (Ringveien 31), near Oslo Airport.

Oslofjord

A world away from the dramatic western Norwegian fjords, the Oslofjord is nevertheless a vast expanse of water stretching over 80 kilometers (50 miles) south from the Norwegian capital. Almost half of Norway's population lives within a one-hour drive from the fjord, so there's plenty to see along the shoreline, from idyllic islands, skerries, and lighthouses to major commercial centers of trade and industry.

The quaint fishing village Drøbak marks the entrance to the Inner Oslofjord, where the waterway narrows, the population increases, and the islands become increasingly inhabited. Seagulls, oystercatchers, terns, and geese are commonly sighted along these narrow waters.

The region is one of Norway's warmest, and on summer days Oslo's residents head south and locals dash to their boats to make the most of the sunshine. The agreeable climate has attracted settlers since the days of the Stone Age and Bronze Age, so it's no surprise that some of the world's best preserved Viking ships were discovered on these shores. The fjord was a strategically important waterway in World War II, and as such historical monuments and former military installations are commonplace.

If you can't afford the time or money to visit the fjords of western Norway, then a day trip to one of these Oslofjord destinations is a respectable alternative, and a great way to break up a few days in Oslo.

DRØBAK

Largely unheard of by tourists, this quaint fjordside town at the narrowest point of the Oslofjord is one of the most popular day trips taken by residents of Oslo on a warm summer day. The big draw of Drøbak is its beaches and gentle waterside walks, while the lively harbor is busy with boat traffic, due to the many nearby islands and plentiful stocks of cod, coalfish, pollock, ling, haddock, and mussels. In the 19th century, when the inner Oslofjord used to freeze over, Drøbak acted as the winter harbor for Oslo.

Drøbak is just a one-hour bus ride or 40-minute drive from Oslo, or accessible via a sightseeing boat during the summer, so a last-minute decision to travel here is possible.

Sights
OSCARSBORG FORTRESS
(Oscarsborg festning)
Strategically located on an island in the narrowest part of the Oslofjord, the horseshoe-shaped **Oscarsborg Fortress** (Søndre Kaholmen, tel. 64 90 41 61) is best known for defeating the German cruiser *Blücher,* which still remains at the bottom of the fjord, during World War II. Visitors can enjoy a small museum, traditional smithy, art exhibition, marina, a marked trail, and a café. Opening hours vary throughout the year but are typically 10am-3pm for the museum and 11am-9pm for the café. Outside of high season (June-Aug.), it's best to bring your own food just in case the café is closed, or call in advance to check the hours.

The fortress can only be reached by boat, which runs daily year-round from Sundbrygga pier at the town harbor, at a cost of 100kr round-trip (admission is included).

Outside Oslo

Journeys begin at 7am and run approximately hourly through to 11pm, but do check the schedules in advance, especially outside the summer season.

DRØBAK AQUARIUM
(Drøbak Akvarium)

Built by the local boat society, **Drøbak Aquarium** (Havnegata 4, tel. 91 10 84 20, www.drobakakvarium.no, 10am-4pm daily, 60kr) is intended to recreate the waters of the Oslofjord for enjoyment and education. Local fishers have filled the aquarium with lobsters, codfish, sea porcupines, and flounders, all sustained by a constant stream of salt water pumped in from the fjord.

TOWN CENTER

The protected status of the small town center helps to preserve its traditional 19th-century look and feel. Numerous art galleries and sidewalk cafés help to create an atmosphere that's more continental Europe than Norway.

The gallery at the **Newspaper Cartoonists' House (Avistegnernes Hus)** (Lindtrupbakken 1, tel. 66 93 66 32, www.avistegnerneshus.no, noon-4pm Tues.-Sun., 30kr) is a tribute to the artistry of comedic journalism and the universal freedom of expression. The Cartoonists' House is more than just a gallery. It offers free accommodations and workspace for persecuted newspaper cartoonists from all over the world, once they are accepted as political refugees into Norway. Exhibitions change regularly, and a wide selection of illustrated books are available for purchase.

Experience a Scandinavian Christmas in the middle of the summer at **Tregaarden's Christmas House (Tregaardens Julehus)** (Havnebakken 6, tel. 64 93 41 78, www.julehus.no, 10am-5pm Mon.-Fri., 10am-3pm Sat. Jan.-May; 10am-5pm Mon.-Fri., 10am-3pm Sat., noon-4pm Sun. June-Oct.; 10am-5pm Mon.-Fri., 10am-4pm Sat., noon-4pm Sun. Nov., 10am-8pm Mon.-Fri., 10am-4pm Sat., noon-4pm Sun. Dec.). While the ground floor of the spectacular former chapel building sells traditional Scandinavian Christmas decorations from candles to stockings, the top floor doubles as Santa's Post Office, from where you can arrange for postcards to be sent out during December.

Food and Accommodations

Enjoy lunch amid the bustling harbor atmosphere at **Skipperstuen** (Havnebakken 11, tel. 64 93 07 03, noon-10pm Mon.-Sat., 1pm-8pm Sun.), which is one of Norway's few restaurants with more seating outdoors than in. Unsurprisingly the catch of the day comes highly recommended. Before 4pm, this is served together with bread and aioli for 235kr. The atmosphere turns a touch more formal for the evening service, when more extravagant mains run up to 350kr. If you just want to graze in the afternoon sun, pick up some olives, cured meats, or cheese from the snack menu.

Spanish omelets, topped focaccia breads, and seafood tapas are among the excellent choices at the informal **Galleri Cafe Teskje** (Niels Carlsensgate 7, tel. 64 93 09 91, www. teskje.no, 10am-5pm Tues.-Sat., noon-5pm Sun.), midway along a charming street lined with galleries and boutiques. The neighboring **Kumlegaarden** (Niels Carlsensgate 11, tel. 64 93 89 90, www.kumlegaarden.no, 11:30am-8pm Mon., 11:30am-10pm Tues.-Sat., 1pm-8pm Sun., 245kr) is set inside two of Drøbak's oldest timber buildings. A raw claystone fireplace tops off a remarkable

interior strewn with trinkets and flowers that will keep you occupied until the food arrives. Expect traditional Norwegian fare, generally with a choice of beef, game, or fish. Saturdays aside, lunchtime tends to be much quieter, whereas reservations for dinner are recommended throughout the week.

Accommodation options are limited, but the 28-room **Reenskaug Hotel** (Storgata 32, tel. 64 98 92 00, www.reenskaug.no, 1,590kr d) would not be out of place in the capital. Rooms are individually decorated, so it's pot luck whether you'll end up with traditional elegance or sleek modern, but all come with a pod coffee maker, flatscreen TV, and a private bathroom. The comfortable outdoor terrace helps to make this historical hotel a great choice in which to spend a day away from the capital.

Information and Services

The harborside **Drøbak Tourist Information** (tel. 64 93 50 87, 8:30am-4pm Mon.-Fri., 10am-2pm Sat.-Sun.) will help you orient yourself, suggest hikes, and confirm return transport options to Oslo. Follow signs for Drøbak Aquarium to find the office.

Getting There

Drøbak is 39 kilometers (24 miles) south of central Oslo along the main E6 highway. If making the 40-minute drive, exit the E6 onto Rv23 and follow the signs for Drøbak. Parking is free for four hours at the AMFI shopping mall, a 30-minute walk from the harbor. Street parking costs 33kr per hour (free 5pm-8am).

Public bus route 500 departs Oslo Bus Terminal every half hour throughout the day. The one-hour journey requires a two-zone ticket (52kr advance, 70kr on board), which is not covered by the Oslo Pass or the regular public transit pass, unless you specifically bought a zone extension.

FREDRIKSTAD

An easy day trip from Oslo thanks to fast rail and bus links, the otherwise ordinary

Fredrikstad is worth a look because of its remarkable Old Town. The fortified streets drip character from every corner, and even though many of the old buildings now house boutiques and cafés, it's all been done with a sense of dignity.

Founded in 1567 by Denmark-Norway King Fredrik II as a trading post between the European mainland and western Scandinavia, Fredrikstad was fortified to protect itself from the risk of Swedish invasion. Burned to the ground twice, the fortifications were strengthened with the distinctive jagged moat to a point when Fredrikstad became the best protected city in Norway. Because the modern city grew up on the other side of the Glomma river, the Old Town has been left largely intact and its 17th-century character preserved.

This is Østfold, the smallest and least mountainous of Norway's counties. The flat meadows, forest, and scenic farm buildings mark the transition to the south of Sweden. Traces of habitation dating back 8,000 years can be found across the county. With more time, explore the historical monuments from the Stone, Bronze, and Iron Ages along the Rv110 between Fredrikstad and Skjeberg, also known as the **Ancient Road (Oldtidsveien)**. Burial mounds, fortified hamlets, and rock carvings are some of the highlights. Pick up an information leaflet from the tourist information center in Fredrikstad to explore this further.

Sights
OLD TOWN

There's precious little to see in the modern downtown district, so visitors should waste no time in heading straight for the **Old Town (Gamle Fredrikstad)**, which requires a pleasant ferry ride across the river. From the train station, turn left and continue on down to the river bank. Pick up the compact free-of-charge **City Ferry (Byferga)**, a passenger service that runs between here and the Old Town plus a couple of suburbs throughout the day. The crossing to the Old Town takes just a couple of minutes, or you can stay on the ferry for a 30-minute tour of the river and Fredrikstad's suburbs.

Simply soaking up the atmosphere is a good use of time here, as is a ramble along the grassy embankments of the perimeter. But there are plenty of sights on this easy-to-navigate grid system of cobbled streets, if you know where to look. Head to the southern end of the district (turn right from the ferry) to see the skeletons found buried under the city

Fredrikstad's Old Town is one of Norway's best.

hospital and now on display at **Fredrikstad Museum** (Tøihusgaten 41, tel. 69 11 56 50, noon-4pm daily, 75kr). The small museum won't take up too much of your time, but make sure to ask about some of the area's best preserved buildings, such as the convict prison and stone storehouse.

Continue your tour of Fredrikstad's history at the well-preserved embankments, turrets, and stone walls of **Kongsten Fort** (tel. 81 57 04 00, grounds always open), standing guard on a gentle hill behind the Old Town. Pick up a map to follow a self-guided tour, or just explore the pleasant grounds by yourself and let your mind wander to a time long forgotten. Alternatively, do as the locals do—bring a picnic and just relax.

A curious addition to the Old Town's attractions, the **Model Railway Center (Gamlebyen Modelljernbanesenter)** (Voldgaten 8, tel. 90 50 98 74, www.gbmj.no, 11am-4pm Mon.-Sat., noon-4pm Sun. mid-June to mid-Aug., noon-4pm Sat.-Sun. mid-Aug. to mid-June, 40kr) is a must for kids, as well as adults with even a passing interest in the railroad. Model trains run between different rooms, each with its own landscape. The attention to detail in the scenes is stunning, from people arguing in the streets to an almost-hidden couple sunbathing in the forest. Kids can control a small track themselves, while adults may feel inspired to dig out their dusty old train sets when they hear the entire center was the vision of just one man.

Food and Accommodations
OLD TOWN

A little bit of everything is on offer at the often-busy **MorMors** (Rådhusgaten 18a, tel. 69 32 16 60, 11am-5pm Mon.-Fri., 11am-6pm Sat., noon-5pm Sun.) at the heart of Fredrikstad's Old Town. Make the most of finding a table and order a heavy slice of homemade cake just like the ones your grandmother used to bake. Alternatively, grab a focaccia or light sandwich to go, then find a space on the curb outside.

The most distinctive hotel in the entire city, ★ **Gamlebyen Hotell** (Voldportgaten 72, tel. 40 05 39 09, www.gamlebyenhotell. no, 1,190kr s, 1,490kr d) is the only accommodation located within the atmospheric Old Town. Unlike the streets outside, the interior has been thoroughly modernized, with a touch of sophistication and more than a nod to the past. White wood dominates the interior, and the 15 bright rooms are individually decorated. No breakfast is included, but a discounted deal is available with the adjacent café.

The cheapest accommodation in town is hidden away behind the Old Town. **Fredrikstad Motel & Camping** (Torsnesveien 16/18, tel. 99 22 19 99, www. fredrikstadmotel.no) offers basic double motel rooms from 550kr, but the higher-quality cabins feel more like hotel rooms. They range from 850kr for a two-bed option up to 1,250kr for a cabin that sleeps up to six. Pitches for tents (150kr) and campervans (250kr) are available, with power hookups a further 50kr. Wi-Fi is available throughout, and access to the basic kitchen and bathroom facilities is included in camping rates.

CENTRAL FREDRIKSTAD

While there are few sights in the modern district, central Fredrikstad is awash with quality food and accommodation choices. Head west toward the river for the best-quality eateries or into the pedestrianized shopping streets for quick bites.

There's little argument between locals about the best restaurant in Fredrikstad. Advance booking is a must to secure a table at **Slippen** (Verkstedveien 12, tel. 99 46 99 88, www.restaurantslippen.no, 11am-10pm Tues.-Fri., noon-10pm Sat., 2pm-8pm Sun., 295kr). Outstanding presentation adds a modern twist to the classic Norwegian dishes of stockfish, fried sea trout, and oven-baked cod. Head there before 4pm to enjoy the lighter lunch menu for under 200kr.

There's no doubt **Hotel Victoria** (Turngata 3, tel. 69 38 58 00, www.hotel-victoria.no, 895kr) has seen better days, but nevertheless it offers the most budget-friendly hotel accommodations in central Fredrikstad. The decor shoots for English country elegance but ends up more like your grandmother's garish living room. Breakfast is included in all room rates.

The pick of the chain hotels is **Quality Hotel Fredrikstad** (Nygata 2-6, tel. 69 39 30 00, q.fredrikstad@choice.no, 1,195kr), the most modern hotel in the city by quite a distance. Just half a mile from the train station, the hotel's 172 modern but boxy rooms are brightened up by large windows and a fjord-inspired color scheme. A filling breakfast buffet is served until 10am, 11am on weekends.

Information and Services

It might seem sensible to house the **Fredrikstad Tourist Office** (Kirkegaten 31B, tel. 69 30 46 00, 9am-4pm Mon.-Fri.) in the Old Town, but by the time you've reached it most of your questions (where is the Old Town and how do I get there?) will have been answered. It's also strange to find a tourist information center closed on Saturday.

Getting There

Fredrikstad is located on the eastern side of the Oslofjord close to the Swedish border. By car, the 93-kilometer (58-mile) drive along the E6 should take just over one hour.

NSB (www.nsb.no) trains run hourly from Oslo Central Station to Fredrikstad throughout the day. Look for trains marked Halden or Göteborg, all of which should stop at Fredrikstad. The scenic one-hour journey costs 215kr. Alternatively, a **TIMEkspressen** (www.nettbuss.no) express bus service leaves Oslo Bus Terminal on the hour. A ticket for the 80-minute journey costs around 200kr.

Getting Around

Other than the small passenger ferry linking the Old Town to the rest of Fredrikstad, day visitors should be able to get around comfortably on foot. Otherwise, local company **Østfold Kollektivtrafikk** (tel. 69 12 54 70, www.ostfold-kollektiv.no) runs bus routes around the city and to nearby towns around the region. Single tickets cost 40kr.

TØNSBERG

Founded by the Vikings and one of Norway's most important cities in the Middle Ages, Tønsberg lays claim to be the country's oldest city. Although Tønsberg is overlooked by many international travelers, Viking burial mounds and church ruins draw in large

Tønsberg Wharf

numbers of domestic visitors, especially during the summer months when the Oslofjord is blessed with Norway's warmest climate.

For international visitors, Tønsberg makes a curious day trip of history and culture or an excellent overnight stop on a journey farther south. It is the starting point of the **Vestfold Viking Trail,** a series of ancient settlements and burial mounds from the Viking Age dotted along the coastline.

Sights

Start your exploration at **Tønsberg Wharf (Tønsberg Brygge),** the focal point of the city for more than 1,000 years. Several wooden trading warehouses from the early 19th century still stand, reminiscent of Bergen's more famous wharf. It was here that the economy of Tønsberg developed, while today the pier is noted for its restaurants and nightlife just as much as its guest marina. The pedestrian bridge across the canal is opened five times daily to allow taller ships to enter the city's main harbor.

SAGA OSEBERG

One of the most famous Viking finds in Norway took place near Tønsberg, when in 1904 the small *Oseberg* ship was discovered in a burial mound. Although the original 9th-century vessel is on display in Oslo's Viking Ship Museum, the *Saga Oseberg* (Ollebukta 3, osebergvikingskip.no) is a full-scale copy of the ship built to the original specifications and moored in the harbor just a short stroll south of Tønsberg wharf. Previous attempts to reconstruct the ship failed, including one that capsized just 20 seconds into its maiden voyage. The vessel is only taken out of its mooring for special events and research.

SLOTTSFJELL MUSEUM

Although parts of the city and its surroundings are one big museum, the **Slottsfjell Museum** (Farmannsveien 30, tel. 33 31 29 19, www.slottsfjellsmuseet.no, 11am-4pm Tues.-Sun., 70kr) adds some context to what you are seeing. The museum is constantly growing,

with an ambition to become a medieval museum of international interest. The biggest draw is the *Klåstad* Viking ship, the only ship from the nearby finds on display outside Oslo. Following the success of the *Oseberg* replica, plans are now underway to build a new version of the *Klåstad* ship.

Immediately above the museum is the strongest pointer to Tønsberg's importance in the Middle Ages. Ruins of a 12th-century church and fortress, part of the former Royal Residence, are spread across the top of the small mountain **Slottsfjellet.** The **Slottsfjelltårnet** stone tower was erected in 1888 to celebrate the city's 1,000-year anniversary. Climb to the viewpoint for a 360-degree view of the city and fjord.

HAUGAR VESTFOLD ART MUSEUM

The star attraction at the **Haugar Vestfold Art Museum (Haugar Vestfold Kunstmuseum)** (Gråbrødregaten 17, tel. 33 30 76 70, www.haugar.com, 11am-5pm Mon.-Fri., noon-5pm Sat.-Sun. June-Aug.; 11am-4pm Tues.-Fri., noon-5pm Sat.-Sun. Sept.-May, 70kr) is the Andy Warhol paintings that were inspired by Edvard Munch's *The Scream.* Warhol's portrait of Queen Sonja is also on loan from Oslo's National Museum, so that all of Warhol's Norway-inspired work can be viewed in one location. Every Tuesday from September to May, entrance is free.

Sports and Recreation
TOURS

Explore the sun-drenched archipelago to the east of Tønsberg with a summer boat trip to **Østre Bolærne** island.

From mid-June to mid-August, the **MS Viksfjord** (tel. 95 03 57 51, www.msviksfjord.no) leaves the Fiskebrygga quayside (a 15-minute walk from Tønsberg Wharf) at 10am daily. Stay on the boat's sun-trap rooftop terrace for a relaxing 2.5-hour cruise around the archipelago, or choose to stay on Østre Bolærne and pick up the return trip at 3:30pm or 5:40pm. The round-trip costs 250kr, or 200kr if you stay on the boat for the immediate return. Family tickets (two adults and up to three children under 16) are great value at 490kr/440kr. In the shoulder seasons (mid-May to mid-June and mid-Aug. to mid-Sept.), round-trips (no stay on the island) run at 10am and 2pm Saturday-Sunday, and 5pm Friday.

Around 3.2 kilometers (two miles) southeast of the island is the famous **Fulehuk Lighthouse (Fulehuk fyr)** (www.fulehuk. no), originally built as a stone tower in 1821. Residential buildings, a boathouse, and a steel fog bell were added some years later to help warn incoming ships of the archipelago. Today the lighthouse is used for company banquets and private celebrations, and can be seen from the cruise.

HIKING

Salty sea air, all manner of birdlife, and a glittering watery horizon are just some of the reasons for seeking out the coastal paths in and around Tønsberg. For an easy introduction to the region's hiking possibilities, explore the **Ilene Nature Reserve (Ilene Naturreservat)** northwest of the city. The 7.4-kilometer (4.6-mile) round-trip family-friendly trail signed from the wharf is lined with bird-watching stations and quiet spots for a picnic. Ask at Tønsberg Tourist Information for maps and suggested trails on the pretty coastal paths of Nøtterøy island, across the water from Tønsberg.

Entertainment and Events

Every year in early June, thousands of people flock to the top of Slottsfjellet to enjoy the pageantry of the **Tønsberg Medieval Festival (Tønsberg Middelalderfestival)** (www. tonsbergmiddelalderfestival.no, 400kr). The family-friendly daytime activities include juggling, theater, live music, and jousting tournaments, before the attention turns to an adults-only medieval banquet in the evening. Cheaper day-only tickets are available alongside a pass for the entire weekend.

At the height of summer in mid-July, **Slottsfjellfestivalen** (www.slottsfjell.no,

2,500kr) music festival welcomes a primarily Norwegian lineup of contemporary artists to the hilltop over the course of four days. The event is best known for Kastellnatt, its subterranean warehouse after-party. Despite the central location, camping is available, as the thousands of visitors far outstrip the number of hotel beds available in the city. Day tickets and after-party-only tickets are available alongside festival passes.

Food

The city's best restaurants are clustered together on Tønsberg Wharf. One of the longest-running is **Esmeralda** (Nedre Langgate 26c, tel. 33 31 91 91, 11am-2am Mon.-Sat., noon-11pm Sun., 199-329kr), where you can expect to enjoy excellent thin-crust pizza or fresh fish with colorful crispy vegetables while you watch the world go by from the outdoor terrace.

Stop by **The Sense** (Nedre Langgate 18, tel. 45 96 40 00, 3pm-10pm Mon.-Thurs., 3pm-2am Fri., noon-2am Sat., noon-11pm Sun., 199-297kr) for an Asian-inspired meal that still utilizes the freshest local ingredients. Light dishes of chicken satay and salmon salad are packed with flavor but won't fill you up. Grab a generous bowl of mussels for the table to ensure you leave satisfied. The modern restaurant's terrace tends to have more availability than the more traditional restaurants farther along the wharf.

For a morning pick-me-up, call in to **Bare Barista** (Øvre langgate 44, tel. 48 89 98 36, 8am-6pm Mon.-Fri., 9am-5pm Sat., 10am-5pm Sun.), a few streets back from the wharf. Although the focus is on the quality of the espresso, light sandwiches and sweet snacks are available to enjoy in the spacious backyard.

Accommodations

Modern chain hotels dominate the compact central area near the wharf, so for something with a bit more character or less expensive you'll need to look farther afield.

One exception lies at the foot of the

city's hilltop near the railway station. The friendly hostess at **Tønsberg Vandrerhjem** (Dronning Blancas gate 22, tel. 33 31 21 75, 895kr d) runs a charming B&B standard hostel that books up fast with repeat visitors during the summer months. The 24 hotel-standard rooms are tight but tastefully decorated in a traditional Scandinavian style. The more spacious family rooms with bunk beds that sleep six are great value at 2,300kr, while pancakes for breakfast are a nice unexpected touch.

A five-minute walk east of the rail station is the grand **Wilhelmsen House** (Halfdan Wilhelmsens Allé 22, tel. 97 13 50 00, www. wh.no, 1,495kr d), named after the wealthy Wilhelmsen family whose international shipping empire began in the city. Light brown and beige dominate the 49 modern rooms, the biggest of which come with a well-equipped kitchenette. The luxury Jensen beds, down duvets, and oversize flatscreen TVs are some of the reasons this independent hotel has made such an impact since opening in 2015. Substantial discounts are available outside of high season.

Across the bridge on Nøtterøy island, the maritime-themed **Active Hotel** (Stalsbergveien 5, tel. 33 34 59 10, www.activehotel.no, 795kr s, 895kr d) includes free entry to the neighboring fitness center and Badeland water park for all its guests. Rooms are simply furnished and compact, but all come with private bath. A basic breakfast buffet is available for 100kr, while baguettes and salads can be bought from reception throughout the day.

Information and Services

Located inside City Hall (Rådhuset), **Tønsberg Tourist Information** (Tollbodgaten 22, tel. 33 34 80 00, 8am-3pm Mon.-Fri. year-round, 8am-3pm Sat.-Sun. mid-June to mid-Aug.) offers hiking maps, boat tour timetables, and information on small local events and markets.

Getting There

Tønsberg is a 103-kilometer (64-mile) drive south of Oslo down the E18 on the western side of the Oslofjord. **NSB** (tel. 81 50 08 88, www.nsb.no) runs an hourly regional train service from Oslo Central Station to Larvik that calls at Tønsberg. A single ticket for the 80-minute journey costs 244kr.

The city is close to **Sandefjord Airport Torp** (Torpveien 130, Sandefjord, tel. 33 42 70 00, www.torp.no), a small regional airport with Widerøe routes to Bergen and Trondheim, alongside many routes to the United Kingdom, Spain, and Poland on European budget carriers. Take the free shuttle bus between the airport and Torp railway station, which is just a 15-minute train ride (50kr) away from Tønsberg with an hourly service for much of the day.

Lillehammer

Decades before the 1994 Winter Olympics put Lillehammer on the map, this small Norwegian city and its surrounding valleys had long been a destination for winter sports fanatics. Northern Europe's highest mountain, biggest lake, and a plethora of national parks are all within range of Lillehammer.

When the city was declared host of the Olympic Games, the world checked a map. Never before had a Winter Olympics been held somewhere so small—its population is a shade over 25,000—so the city's infrastructure received substantial investment. The successful event and subsequent boost in visitors has benefited the city and the region's ski resorts ever since, and so it is much better equipped to welcome visitors than almost all other Norwegian cities of its size.

As the journey by train or car takes more than two hours, a day trip while not impossible is not advised. Better to plan an overnight stop or make the city your first port of call in a road trip toward Trondheim or the western fjords.

CLIMATE

Most major Norwegian cities hug the coastline for a milder climate and access to plentiful fishing grounds. Although built on the shores of the 365-square-kilometer (141-square-mile) Lake Mjøsa, Lillehammer is far inland, which has a major impact on the town's climate.

From mid-November to mid-March temperatures will likely be at or below freezing, and snow is expected. While summer days can reach a pleasant 15-20°C (59-68°F) or even higher, May to September is the wettest time of year.

ORIENTATION

Despite its status as a sporting capital, central Lillehammer is ultra-compact. The majority of shops and central attractions are located on or just off **Storgata,** which is just minutes from the railway station and bus terminal. The Maihaugen open-air museum, the Olympic Museum, and the Olympic Park are all a 15- to 20-minute walk east of the central area, but the steep hill on the way surprises many who've only glanced at a map. Buses and taxis are available.

SIGHTS
Maihaugen

Open-air museums are commonplace throughout Norway, but Lillehammer's **Maihaugen** (Maihaugvegen 1, tel. 61 28 89 00, www.maihaugen.no, 10am-5pm daily June-Aug., 11am-4pm Tues.-Sun. Sept.-May, 170kr summer, 130kr rest of year) is one of the best. Set on the hillside overlooking the city, the museum is split into three sections.

Follow the paved trail around the log cabins to find the first section, a village of three rural farms presented as they would have been in the 18th and 19th centuries. During the summer, the village is brought to life with actors playing the parts of farmers, maidens, and even the local schoolteacher.

The second section, the show town, is modeled on Lillehammer at the turn of the 20th century, so much so that many of the houses were actually moved piece by piece from the town itself. The best of those, Olsengården, housed three generations of craftsmen with hens and rabbits in the backyard.

Check out the original steam locomotive before wandering through the third section, a residential area that shows how quickly the standard of living developed during the 20th century. Typical Norwegian houses of all shapes and sizes can be found here, including a prefabricated single-story "future house" developed by Norwegian corporate giant Telenor.

Make time to visit the indoor exhibitions, including the dental office of Anders Sandvig (featuring an 1850s dentist chair and drill) and a unique range of carved folk art collected from across the Gudbrandsdalen valley. Finally, the gift shop at Maihaugen is one of Norway's best. Colorful memorabilia from the Olympic Museum sits alongside ceramics, glass, knitwear, and local crafts.

Norwegian Olympic Museum
(Norges Olympiske Museum)

The highlight of any visit to Lillehammer, at least for non-skiers, is the **Norwegian Olympic Museum** (Maihaugveien 1, tel. 61 28 89 00, http://ol.museum.no, 10am-5pm daily June-Aug., 11am-4pm Tues.-Sun. Sept.-May, 130kr). Beware of old brochures that direct you to Håkons Hall at the Olympic Park. In 2016, the museum relocated to the basement of the main building at the Maihaugen open-air museum.

Rather than focus on the 1994 Games, the underground exhibits document the history of the global Olympic movement, both summer and winter, from ancient times through to the present day. Video installations will help you recall unforgettable moments, record-breaking performances, and inspiring opening ceremonies from around the world. Half of the museum is dedicated to Norway's Olympic history. Media coverage from Lillehammer 1994 and Oslo 1952 and a biathlon simulator are some of the highlights for non-Norwegians.

Olympic Park
(Olympiaparken)

Since the Olympic Museum relocated to Maihaugen, visitor numbers to the **Olympic Park** (Sigrid Undsets vei, www.olympiaparken.no) have dropped, but it's still worth a visit for sports fans. This compact site hosted the majority of events during the 1994 Games, including ice hockey, ski jumping, and the memorable opening ceremony.

On a clear day, climb the steps at **Lillehammer Ski Jumping Arena (Lysgårdsbakkene)** (9am-7pm daily mid-June to mid-Aug., 9am-4pm daily mid-May to mid-June and mid-Aug. to early Sept., 25kr) or take the chair lift (additional 35kr) for a clear view across the city and Lake Mjøsa. Even in the snow-free months of summer, serious jumpers still practice on the hill thanks to the artificial surface laid a few years ago.

Lillehammer Art Gallery
(Lillehammer Kunstmuseum)

Art meets architecture on the glistening silver-blue facade of the Weidemann Gallery at the **Lillehammer Art Museum** (Stortorget 2, tel. 61 05 44 60, www.lillehammerartmuseum.com, 11am-5pm daily late June to mid-Aug., 11am-4pm Tues.-Sun. mid-Aug. to late June, 100kr). The new addition was a collaboration between leading architecture firm Snøhetta and legendary Bergen-born artist Bård Breivik, who sadly passed away weeks before the project's opening in 2016. He was also responsible for the tranquil sculpture garden with stone and running water that links the museum's buildings.

Three private collectors donated the core of the gallery's permanent collection of 19th-century Norwegian art, which has been supplemented in recent years by the purchase of more contemporary artworks. New temporary exhibitions and retrospectives are introduced quarterly.

Family Attractions
HUNDERFOSSEN FAMILY PARK

Discover Norwegian fairy tales at the **Hunderfossen Family Park** (tel. 61 27 55 30, www.hunderfossen.no, 385kr), which is one of Norway's best family destinations despite its short summer season (mid-June to mid-Aug.). In the land guarded by a 46-foot-high troll, your family will meet Norwegian princes

ski jump in Lillehammer's Olympic Park

and princesses as you create your very own fairy-tale experience based around Norwegian folk tales.

Younger children are catered to with an indoor play center, boat pool, and splash pool, while rollercoasters will keep bigger kids amused. The five-minute ride on the simulated rapids is a must-do, but be prepared to get wet! The park is a 16-kilometer (10-mile) drive north of Lillehammer but is accessible by train or a free bus from central Lillehammer.

LILLEPUTTHAMMER

On the opposite side of the Gudbrandsdalslågen river from the Hunderfossen Family Park lies an attraction suited for younger children. At the center of **Lilleputthammer** (Hundervegen 41, tel. 61 28 55 00, www.lilleputthammer.no) is a miniaturized version of Lillehammer's main street, Storgata. The surrounding adventure park with electric-powered cars, a mini-rollercoaster, playgrounds, and colorful characters is best suited for children under 8, while the new climbing frames and zip lines of Olas klatrepark will keep children up to 12 occupied. Opening hours and prices vary wildly during the short opening season. Expect the longest hours (9am-8pm daily) but the longest queues and highest prices (314kr) throughout July. Late June and early August (10am-6pm daily, 249kr) are more reasonable, and the park is open weekends in early June and Saturdays from mid-August through September (10am-5pm Sat.-Sun., 199kr). Children under 6 receive discounted entry, while children under 3 go free. A free shuttle bus runs from Lillehammer throughout high season.

SPORTS AND RECREATION
Olympic Bob and Luge Track

Complete the Lillehammer Olympic experience at the **Olympic Bob and Luge Track** (Hunderfossvegen 680, tel. 61 05 42 00, www. olympiaparken.no), next to Hunderfossen Family Park, 16 kilometers (10 miles) north

of Lillehammer. The center offers varying experiences depending on season, using Scandinavia's only artificially frozen bobsled and luge track. Try the four-man bobsled to reach speeds of up to 120 kph (75 mph) and 5G force, or the skeleton sled, where your nose hovers barely an inch above the ice. Check the calendar in advance and book ahead to avoid disappointment, as only a limited number of runs are possible each day.

During the summer, a wheelbob (wheeled bobsled) run costs 250kr per person and is available 10am-5pm daily throughout July. The track also opens most weekends in May, June, and August. Winter opening depends on events but is typically 3pm-8pm Wednesday and noon-5pm Saturday. Bobrafting (on a rubber bobsled) costs 250kr per person, while taxibob (on an actual bobsled) or skeleton (2 runs) costs around 1,000kr per person. All bobsleds are piloted by experienced pros. A short movie of your ride can be purchased for 150kr.

Hafjell Ski & Bike Resort

One of Norway's major ski centers, **Hafjell** (Hundervegen 122-124, Hafjell, tel. 61 28 55 50, info@hafjell.no, Dec. to mid-Apr.) is just 16 kilometers (10 miles) north of Lillehammer close to the Bob and Luge Track and Hunderfossen Family Park, and linked by regular shuttle buses throughout the season. The resort is known for its Olympic-standard slopes, but it has a vast range of gentler slopes (11 blue, 10 green), seven slopes dedicated to children, plus four different terrain parks. Hafjell is also the starting point for an incredible 300 kilometers (186 miles) of prepared cross-country trails. A day's lift pass costs 405kr, with big discounts for longer stays or evening skiing. Rental gear varies 325-445kr depending on standard, with a complete cross-country package available for 200kr.

Winter sports lovers are spoiled for choice in the Lillehammer region. Hafjell lift passes are also valid at nearby **Kvitfjell** (Fåvang, www.kvitfjell.no), 30 kilometers (18.5 miles) north of Hafjell, built specifically for the Olympics. The resort tends to attract the more serious skier.

During the summer, Hafjell is transformed into one of Norway's most challenging mountain bike parks. Open from late June, **Hafjell Bike Park** (10am-5pm Thurs.-Sun. late June to Aug., 10am-5pm Sat.-Sun. Sept.) consists of three expert-level forest trails with large stepdowns and gap jumps galore, plus 11 other trails of varying difficulty. The easiest is suitable for families. A day's lift pass costs 305kr, and pro bikes can be rented for 275-795kr.

Spectator Sports

Major national and international winter sports events take place in and around Lillehammer from December to April. Check in advance because attractions, hotels, and restaurants will be overrun when the world's skiers come to town. Grabbing a ticket for a live ski jumping or biathlon event adds a truly different sporting experience to your trip. The best place to discover upcoming international events is the **International Ski Federation** (www.fis-ski.com), while **Lillehammer Tourist Information** (Jernbanetorget 2, tel. 61 28 98 00) will be up to speed on the domestic calendar.

ENTERTAINMENT AND EVENTS
Festivals
PEER GYNT FESTIVAL
(Peer Gynt ved Gålåvatnet)

The annual **Peer Gynt Festival** (www.peergynt.no) is a real highlight on the Norwegian cultural calendar. Taking place on the banks of the Gålåvatnet lake an hour north of Lillehammer, the play brings Henrik Ibsen's dramatic poem to life through song and dance. Although performed in Norwegian, it's subtitled in English through a booklet and audio headset.

In addition to these daily lakeside performances, concerts are held high up in the mountains and in local churches, while art exhibitions and guided hikes around the Gudbrandsdalen valley complete the program. Tickets should be booked well in advance for the 10-day festival, which takes place in early August.

BIRKEBEINERRENNET

The city is the finish line for the world's largest ski race, **Birkebeinerrennet** (www.birkebeiner.no). On a crisp March weekend, more than 12,000 professional and keen amateur skiers complete the epic 54-kilometer

Hafjell ski resort is within easy reach of Lillehammer.

(33.5-mile) trail through the mountains east of Lillehammer. Thousands more take part in smaller events over the course of the weekend, including many children.

All participants in the main race carry a backpack weighting 3.5 kilograms (7.7 pounds) to commemorate the original Birkebeinerne that rescued the infant Norwegian prince, Haakon Haakonsson, from a rival faction in 1205-1206. The prince eventually became the king who united Norway after hundreds of years of civil war. The story was immortalized in the 2016 movie *Birkebeinerne*, released internationally as *The Last King*.

FOOD
Cafés and Light Bites
The Italian Renaissance-inspired building of the Kulturhuset Banken theater is the grand setting for **Cafe Stift** (Kirkegata 41, tel. 94 05 31 79, www.cafestift.no, noon-1am Tues.-Fri., noon-3am Sat., 179kr). Despite the imposing exterior, the café itself is light and informal, at least until 9pm, when the food service abruptly stops and the DJs arrive. Up until then, enjoy great-value sandwiches, fish soup, burgers, and even a Norwegian take on a burrito—we won't spoil the surprise—all for well under 200kr.

A heaped plate of miniature Dutch-style pancakes served sweet or salted is the simple yet delicious concept of cottage-like **Det Lille Pannekakehuset** (Storgata 46, tel. 91 99 30 52, 10am-6pm Mon.-Fri., 10am-4pm Sat.), located at the heart of Lillehammer's shopping district. Although savory options and soups are available, one sight of the pancakes covered in berries, ice cream, or chocolate sauce heading out of the kitchen will make up your mind. The sidewalk seating is popular even in the winter, thanks to the blankets and warming cocoa.

New Nordic
The impressive almost-but-not-quite art nouveau exterior of **Hvelvet** (Stortorget 1, tel. 90 72 91 00, www.hvelvet.no, 4pm-11pm Mon.-Sat., 305kr) is hard to miss, and the name (The Vault in Norwegian) hints at the building's history. The former Norges Bank building once held all of Norway's gold reserves, secretly moved from Oslo shortly before the Nazi invasion at the beginning of World War II. The renovated interior is now a fine dining restaurant serving Norwegian ingredients with a touch of Mediterranean flair. The immaculately presented portions are on the small side, so consider the three-course (475kr) or four-course (525kr) set menus, which change monthly.

Chinese
Although less busy than the cluster of restaurants along the main drag of Storgata, **Ming Restaurant** (Storgata 130, tel. 61 26 04 71, 3pm-10pm Tues.-Thurs., 3pm-11pm Fri.-Sat., 2pm-10pm Sun., 189kr) scores highly on all counts. Fragrant dishes from Canton, Beijing, and Sichuan, friendly service, and excellent set menus make this well-kept restaurant the most authentic in the area, despite the simplistic decor.

Pub Food
Riverside sports bar **Nikkers** (Elvegata 18, tel. 61 24 74 30, www.nikkers.no, 11am-11pm Mon.-Thurs., 11am-3am Fri.-Sat., 1pm-10pm Sun.) serves up a British-style pub menu in its separate restaurant. Pick up a lunchtime sandwich or omelet for under 150kr. Most mains run under 200kr, but the house specialty, a fragrant wild game stew and mash, is a great choice for couples at 239kr per person.

Free popcorn sides mean you won't need more than a single course at the stylish **Heim Gastropub** (Storgata 84, tel. 61 10 00 82, www.heimlillehammer.no, 3pm-noon Mon.-Thurs., 3pm-3pm Fri., noon-3am Sat., 169-229kr). Use that money to instead sample some of the Norwegian brews both bottled and on tap, a staggering range from fresh fruity saison ales through to heavy stouts. The beef bourguignon, battered fish-and-chips, and house burger are better value than the meat and cheese platters, which may still leave you hungry. Despite the late opening hours, the kitchen closes at 10pm.

Although beer is the star of the show at the local brewery's pub, **Lillehammer Bryggeri** (Elvegata 19, tel. 95 01 91 08, www.lillehammerbryggeri.no, 5pm-11pm Wed.-Thurs., 5pm-1am Sat.-Sun., 200kr), you can order plates of filling stew, chicken wings, and cured meats to enjoy alongside the ales in this underground watering hole, tucked away on a back street beside the Mesna river. The small-batch brewery produces an outstanding IPA among its constantly revolving selection. Ask the enthusiastic staff about the best beer pairing for your food and you're likely to make a friend for life.

ACCOMMODATIONS

A former chain hotel now happily independent, ★ **Lillehammer Hotel** (Turisthotellvegen 6, tel. 61 28 60 00, www.lillehammerhotel.no, 1,000kr d) stands above the city, conveniently located between Maihaugen and the Olympic Park. The exterior and hallways of this historic building retain a strong sense of dignified tradition, yet many of its 300 rooms are decked out in a contemporary style with images of winter sports adorning the walls. Two restaurants, two bars, and various lounges mean there are plenty of places to relax after a day on the slopes.

After 130 years as a working millhouse, the tall mustard-colored **Mølla Hotel** (Elvegata 12, tel. 61 05 70 80, www.mollahotell.no, 990kr s, 1,290kr d) is one of Norway's most unique accommodations. Original machinery and thick stone walls leave you in no doubt of the building's history, while Olympic memorabilia on the walls does the same for the city. The cramped rooms are comfortable, but there's little room for spreading out to relax, so most guests head for the hotel's rooftop **Toppen Bar** (8pm-2am Mon.-Sat.) to enjoy an iced cocktail with a view.

The city's best budget option is also one of its best located. Simple, hotel-standard rooms with no-frills hostel-style service are the thing at **Lillehammer Stasjonen Hotel & Hostel** (Jernbanetorget 2, tel. 61 26 00 24, www.stasjonen.no, 850kr s, 950kr d), located inside the railway station. Spacious family rooms (1,400kr) and dorm beds (300kr) are also available. Guests have access to a breakfast buffet (99kr) or lighter options (35kr) in the station café every morning, and a 15 percent discount on lunch and dinner. Check-in after 10pm requires prior arrangement.

Those skiing, visiting Hunderfossen, or just driving through the region should consider the diverse range of hotels, apartments, chalets, and mountain cabins managed by **Hafjell Resort** (tel. 61 28 55 50, www.hafjellresort.no), 16 kilometers (10 miles) north of Lillehammer. A comfortable double room with private bath and buffet breakfast can be booked for 1,090kr.

INFORMATION AND SERVICES

Handily located inside the train station is **Lillehammer Tourist Information** (Jernbanetorget 2, tel. 61 28 98 00, 8am-4pm Mon.-Fri., 10am-2pm Sat.). The staff can help you with accommodation bookings and directions to attractions. Several brochures and city maps are free, although you'll have to pay for the more detailed hiking and skiing maps, which are on sale alongside a small selection of Norwegian souvenirs, postcards, and postage stamps. When the office is closed, brochures about Lillehammer and the surrounding area plus detailed maps are available on the walls outside.

GETTING THERE

The 184-kilometer (114-mile) drive from Oslo to Lillehammer along the E6 highway takes just over two hours, a quicker option than the shorter route using Rv4. Add on an extra 10-15 minutes to reach Hafjell, Hunderfossen Family Park, and the Bob and Luge Track.

NSB (tel. 81 50 08 88, www.nsb.no) runs trains once per hour from Oslo Central Station to Lillehammer, with almost all calling at Oslo Airport on the way. A single ticket bought on the day of the 2.25-hour journey costs 414kr. Four trains per day travel from Trondheim at a cost of 754kr for the 4.5-hour journey. Book your tickets at least 24 hours in advance for a discount of at least 40 percent. **Lillehammer Station** (Jernbanetorget 2) is also home to the city's bus station, a modern waiting room, and a café.

GETTING AROUND

While Lillehammer's compact center is easy to navigate on foot, the steep hills of the surrounding area and harsh winter weather will soon have you looking for other options. The local bus service in and around Lillehammer is managed by **Opplandstrafikk** (Kirkegata 76, tel. 61 28 90 00, www.opplandstrafikk.no). Single tickets within the city cost 37kr, with most travel to/from Hunderfossen/Hafjell covered by a 50kr two-zone ticket. Expect buses to run approximately 7am-10pm, but check timetables for specifics, especially on weekends and late in the evening.

For taxi service, call **06565 Drosjene** (tel. 06565, booking@06565.no), which has cars based in Lillehammer and the Hunderfossen/ Hafjell area. Expect to pay 207-279kr for an eight-kilometer (five-mile) journey, depending on the time of day. Minimum prices run 102-138kr regardless of distance.

Southern Norway

Look for ★ to find recommended
sights, activities, dining, and lodging.

Highlights

★ **Norwegian Petroleum Museum:** The discovery of oil changed the face of Stavanger. This modern and highly enjoyable museum tells the tale (page 107).

★ **Stavanger Old Town:** Dating back to the 18th and 19th centuries, this collection of whitewashed timber cottages is no museum. It's a lively and fiercely proud neighborhood (page 107).

★ **Museum of Archaeology:** See real Viking runes from more than 1,000 years ago and learn about early medieval life at the Iron Age farm (page 109).

★ **Preikestolen:** A cruise down the beautiful Lysefjord can be combined with a hike to this dramatic cliff. Will you dangle your feet over the edge (page 120)?

★ **Kjeragbolten:** This world-famous boulder is wedged above a one-kilometer drop at the end of the Lysefjord. For experienced hikers only (page 122)!

Although dominated by the modern cities Stavanger and Kristiansand and vast inland forests, southern Norway is best known by locals for its string of pristine fishing villages and yacht-based summer getaways.

Largely ignored by tourists, the North Sea coast is a perfect choice for those looking for a quintessentially Norwegian summer experience.

Stavanger itself is considered part of the vast Fjord Norway region by the national tourist board because of the outstanding Lysefjord, but it's also the perfect point to start or end your exploration of this vast region of Norway. With some outstanding museums, a picturesque Old Town, and a world-famous fjord within easy reach, Stavanger can be considered a worthy rival to Bergen, despite its reputation as Norway's oil capital.

With its central beaches and vast amusement park, Norway's southernmost city, Kristiansand, is a child-friendly place to visit. The small coastal village Flekkefjord makes for a pleasant stop-off between the two.

CLIMATE

The word to sum up the climate of southern Norway is variable. The climate in Stavanger and the western coastline has similar weather to the fjord region, so plan for rain and sudden changes in weather whatever the time of year.

The southern coastline around Kristiansand is known as the Norwegian Riviera because of the warm sunny summers. The area can be particularly pleasant in the winter because temperatures often stay above freezing and snow is less common than almost anywhere else in Norway. That said, it's a different story inland, where snow can cover the higher ground October through April.

PLANNING YOUR TIME

Because of its proximity to the Lysefjord, a few days in Stavanger is a great alternative to the fjords farther north, or a good third

Previous: Vågen harbor in Stavanger; Preikestolen. **Above:** house in Stavanger's Old Town.

Southern Norway

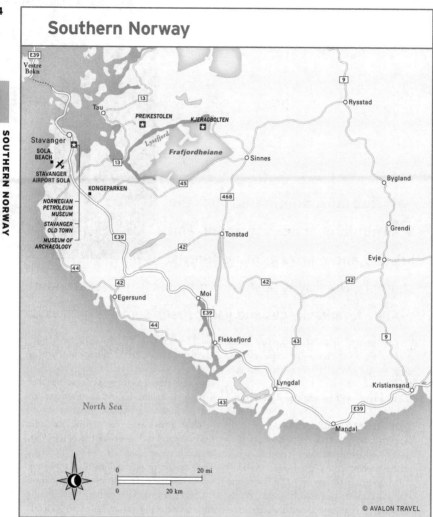

© AVALON TRAVEL

point for an Oslo-Bergen triangle. Families may find the international vibe of Stavanger an easier adjustment than other destinations.

One full day is enough in Stavanger unless you have a specific interest in cultural history or the oil industry. For a longer stay, spend a day touring the Lysefjord or the beaches of the Jæren region, south of the city, as you travel toward Flekkefjord and Kristiansand.

Stavanger

Like all other Norwegian cities along the vast west coast, Stavanger owes its success to the sea. Although not formally established until 1125, evidence exists of settlements in and around modern-day Stavanger stretching back to the days following the last Ice Age.

For centuries a traditional fishing settlement driven by herring, Stavanger's fortunes began to wane midway through the last century when the population of herring dropped. After a couple of tough decades, Stavanger's fortunes were transformed when oil was discovered in the North Sea in the 1960s. But more important for the city than the discovery itself was the decision of the Norwegian government to base Statoil, the state oil company, in Stavanger.

In the decades since, Stavanger has been transformed into one of Europe's most important oil industry hubs, attracting thousands of talented engineers from around the world. This in turn has led to a diverse cultural scene and a staggering variety of international restaurants. More languages are spoken here than in any other city barring Oslo, and English is an official language in all but name.

Yet despite this economic development, Stavanger has retained its traditional feel, with hundreds of white timber houses preserved not only in the Old Town, but right across the central district. That tradition is layered with a gritty modern edge thanks to the many giant murals created as part of the city's thriving street art scene. Take a casual stroll around the streets of Stavanger and you are essentially taking in a free cultural history and contemporary art tour.

ORIENTATION

Stavanger's compact city center pivots around the **Vågen harbor,** lined on both sides by traditional streets. To the west are the cobbled streets of the **Old Town** while the eastern side is home to a thriving commercial district centered around the colorful **Øvre Holmegate.** To the southeast of the harbor is the city's main transport hub, centered on the **Breiavatnet lake.** Bus stops for all city lines dot the perimeter, while the bus and

Stavanger's Breiavatnet city lake is a helpful navigation point.

Stavanger

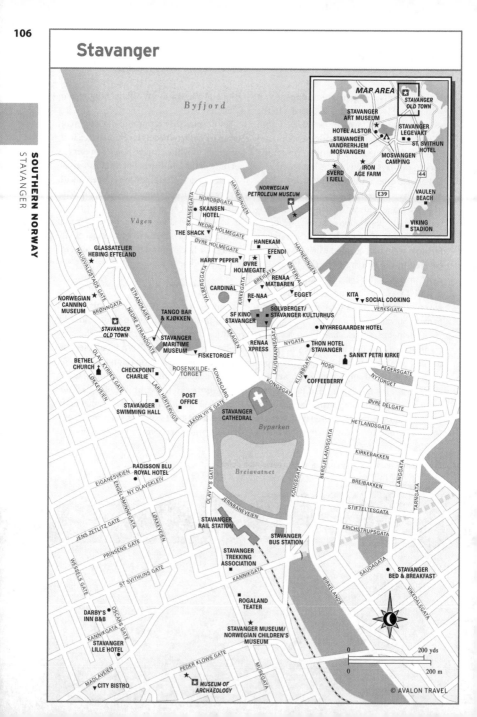

MAP AREA

STAVANGER OLD TOWN

STAVANGER ART MUSEUM

HOTEL ALSTOR

STAVANGER LEGEVAKT

STAVANGER VANDRERHJEM MOSVANGEN

ST. SVITHUN HOTEL

MOSVANGEN CAMPING

SVERD I FJELL

IRON AGE FARM

44

E39

VAULEN BEACH

VIKING STADION

Byfjord

Vågen

Vågen

NORWEGIAN PETROLEUM MUSEUM

HAVNERINGEN

NORDBØGATA

SKANSEGATA

SKANSEN HOTEL

NEDRE HOLMEGATE

THE SHACK

ØVRE HOLMEGATE

HANEKAM

EFENDI

HARRY PEPPER

ØVRE HOLMEGATE

HAVNERINGEN

GLASSATELIER HEBING EFTELAND

HAUGVALDSTADS GATE

VALBERGGATA

KIRKEGATA

CARDINAL

BREIGATA

RENAA MATBAREN

ØSTERVIG

RE-NAA

EGGET

KITA

SOCIAL COOKING

NORWEGIAN CANNING MUSEUM

BRØNNGATA

STRANDKAIEN

NEDRE STRANDGATE

TANGO BAR & KJØKKEN

SF KINO STAVANGER

SOLVBERGET/ STAVANGER KULTURHUS

VERKSGATA

MYHREGAARDEN HOTEL

STAVANGER OLD TOWN

SKAGEN

RENAA XPRESS

NYGATA

LAUGMANNSGATA

THON HOTEL STAVANGER

SANKT PETRI KIRKE

STAVANGER MARITIME MUSEUM

FISKETORGET

BETHEL CHURCH

OLAV KYRRES GATE

CHECKPOINT CHARLIE

LARS HERTERVIGS

ROSENKILDE-TORGET

KONGSGÅRD

HOSP

KLUBBGATA

COFFEEBERRY

PEDERSGATE

NYTORGET

LØKKEVEIEN

STAVANGER SWIMMING HALL

POST OFFICE

HÅKON VII'S GATE

KONGSGATA

KONGSGATA

ØVRE DELGATE

STAVANGER CATHEDRAL

Byparken

HETLANDSGATA

RADISSON BLU ROYAL HOTEL

EIGANESVEIEN

ENGELSMINNEGATA

NY OLAVSKLEIV

Breiavatnet

OLAV V'S GATE

BERGJELANDSGATA

KIRKEBAKKEN

BREIBAKKEN

LANGGATA

TARNGATA

JENS ZETLITZ GATE

LØKKEVEIEN

JERNBANEVEIEN

STIFTELTESGATA

PRINSENS GATE

STAVANGER RAIL STATION

STAVANGER BUS STATION

ERICHSTRUPSGATA

STAVANGER TREKKING ASSOCIATION

WESSELS GATE

ST SVITHUNS GATE

KANNIKGATA

SAUDAGATA

STAVANGER BED & BREAKFAST

BIRKELANDS

VIKEDALSGATA

DARBY'S INN B&B

OSCARS GATE

ROGALAND TEATER

KANNIKGATA GATE

STAVANGER LILLE HOTEL

STAVANGER MUSEUM/ NORWEGIAN CHILDREN'S MUSEUM

MADLAVEIEN

CITY BISTRO

PEDER KLOWS GATE

MUSEGATA

MUSEUM OF ARCHAEOLOGY

0   200 yds

0   200 m

© AVALON TRAVEL

train stations lie to the south. Many of the city's museums are also clustered together south of the lake.

SIGHTS
★ Norwegian Petroleum Museum
(Norsk Oljemuseum)

Known by most as simply the Oil Museum, the **Norwegian Petroleum Museum** (Kjeringholmen 1a, tel. 51 93 93 00, www.norskolje.museum.no, 10am-7pm daily June-Aug., 10am-4pm Mon.-Sat., 10am-6pm Sun. Sept.-May, 120kr) is a lot more interesting than it sounds. Find out not just how oil is made and extracted from the ground, but also how it feels to be a worker waiting for the helicopter ride out to the North Sea rigs. A short film reveals the daily life of a dive crew, while the control room of a rig just begs to be explored.

The main hall contains many models of real rigs currently at work in the ocean, while a large portion of the museum is devoted to the human side of the industry, most notably when more than 100 workers were killed by the 1980 capsizing of the Alexander L Kielland platform in the Ekofisk oil field. Allow at least a couple of hours here, more if you intend on grabbing an indulgent lunch at the excellent in-house café/restaurant with an excellent harbor view.

The museum's port location north of the central district has opened up a new waterfront area with space to stretch out. Immediately outside the museum is the intriguing **Geopark,** an unconventional urban space that at first glance looks like something out of a dystopian blockbuster. In fact, the graffiti-laden experimental children's playground tests new ways of recycling materials and unusual objects from the petroleum industry.

★ Stavanger Old Town
(Gamle Stavanger)

Although much of central Stavanger consists of delightful old timber houses, the oldest and best preserved are clustered together west of the harbor in **Stavanger Old Town.** Most of the 200 or so houses dating back to the 18th and 19th centuries are privately owned, and residents take immense pride in their property, keeping the white paint bright and the windowboxes colorful year-round.

But it was so nearly not to be. In the years following World War II, city planners wanted to rebuild the area with modern concrete

the Geopark outside of the Norwegian Petroleum Museum

structures. The plan was not as outrageous as it may seem. In the post-war years the area's buildings were run down and seen as an undesirable place to live. Thanks to the campaign led by city architect Einar Hedén, the city council voted to conserve the area in 1956. Since then, many of the buildings have been fully restored and the area has a vibrant community feel.

Wandering the cobbled streets to admire the immaculate white buildings is a must and won't take longer than half an hour. Make time to combine your walk with a visit to the **Norwegian Canning Museum,** or a peek around the showroom of stained-glass producer **Glassatelier Hebing Efteland** (Mellomstraen 4, tel. 41 38 77 64, www.glassatelier.no, 11am-4pm Tues.-Fri., 11am-3pm Sat.), where you can learn about the HotPot method of glass fusing.

Museum Stavanger

A series of museums under the banner of **Museum Stavanger** (www.museumstavanger.no), styled MUST, dominates the cultural history scene in Stavanger. Each museum has an entrance charge of 90kr, but the ticket is valid for all other venues under the Museum Stavanger banner on the same day. Note that not all the museums are located in the same place, so it's best to plan in advance where you want to visit, especially in the event of poor weather. For specific historical interest, the Maritime Museum and Canning Museum are top picks, while the Stavanger Museum is best for general interest.

STAVANGER MUSEUM

Located just outside the central district but only a 10-minute walk south of Stavanger Cathedral, **Stavanger Museum** (Muségata 16, tel. 51 84 27 00, 10am-4pm daily June-Aug., 11am-3pm Tues.-Fri., 11am-4pm Sat.-Sun. Sept.-May) is really two separate museums of cultural history and natural history sharing the same premises and making up the main collection of MUST. The cultural history half profiles Stavanger's development from ancient landscape through fishing and farming to today's modern oil capital. Artifacts from Asia, America, and Africa show that Stavanger's history as an international city go back far beyond the discovery of oil.

Curious disfigured animals and smiling skeletons fill the natural history museum. As the museum opened, gifts came pouring in from the local community. Game caught by local hunters and exotic stuffed animals

Stavanger Old Town

brought back to Stavanger by returning sailors and missionaries make up the intriguing collection.

NORWEGIAN CHILDREN'S MUSEUM (Norsk Barnemuseum)

In the same building as Stavanger Museum is the **Norwegian Children's Museum** (Muségata 16, tel. 51 84 27 00, 10am-4pm daily June-Aug., 11am-3pm Tues.-Fri., 11am-4pm Sat.-Sun. Sept.-May), designed to showcase children's culture and the history of childhood both in Norway and around the world. While the interactive exhibits entertain the kids, adults are kept amused with various old toys that will transport you back to your own childhood.

STAVANGER MARITIME MUSEUM

Popular with day visitors due to its proximity to the cruise ship terminal, **Stavanger Maritime Museum** (Strandkaien 22, tel. 40 76 96 79, 10am-4pm Fri.-Wed., 10am-7pm Thurs. June-Aug.; 11am-3pm Mon.-Fri., 11am-4pm Sat.-Sun. Sept.-May) displays some of its vast archive of model ships, photographs, artifacts, and documentation from the city's coastal history. Ask for one of the free multilingual audio guides, which add some much needed context to the exhibitions, otherwise your stay will be a brief one. Of most interest to the casual visitor is the building itself, a 19th-century boathouse restored to its former glory.

NORWEGIAN CANNING MUSEUM (Norsk Hermetikkmuseum)

Set in the middle of the charming Old Town, the **Norwegian Canning Museum** (Øvre Strandgate 88, tel. 40 72 84 70, 10am-4pm daily mid-May to mid-Sept., 11am-3pm Tues.-Fri., 11am-4pm Sat.-Sun. mid-Sept. to mid-May) is an exceptionally well-preserved herring canning factory. Original machinery and English language audio give an insight into what life as a herring worker was like during the pre-oil days. Thankfully for those with an aversion to the rather pungent aroma, the only thing missing is the herring itself, although a more palatable chocolate version can be bought in the gift shop. The upstairs, where employees used to change, is now home to an activity area for kids and a gallery of the unique herring can artwork.

STAVANGER ART MUSEUM (Stavanger Kunstmuseum)

Originally founded as an art association by a group of private citizens, **Stavanger Art Museum** (Henrik Ibsens gate 55, tel. 51 84 27 00, 10am-4pm Tues.-Wed. and Fri.-Sun., 10am-7pm Thurs. June-Aug., 11am-4pm Tues.-Wed. and Fri.-Sun., 11am-7pm Thurs. Sept.-May) showcases a vast collection of mainly Norwegian art from the 19th century through to more contemporary styles. The collection of personally influenced landscapes of local artist Lars Hertervig (1830-1902) is a highlight. The museum is located at Lake Mosvatnet, 2.6 kilometers (1.6 miles) southwest of central Stavanger, and can be easily reached by a 35-minute walk or a 12-minute bus ride on bus route 2 or 3. The museum is especially busy on Saturday, when the entrance charge is waived.

★ Museum of Archaeology (Arkeologisk Museum)

One of the few museums not in the Museum Stavanger family happens to be one of the city's best. The highlight of the **Museum of Archaeology** (Peder Klows gate 30a, tel. 51 83 26 00, http://am.uis.no, 10am-5pm Mon.-Fri., 10am-4pm Sat.-Sun. June-Aug.; 11am-8pm Tues., 11am-3pm Wed.-Sat., 11am-4pm Sun. Sept.-May, 50kr) is the Viking exhibition featuring large rune stones and information on how the Vikings constructed ships and navigated around the waters of the north. The rest of the museum is devoted to life in Norway during the Stone Age, including a 7.5-foot-long polar bear skeleton found at Finnøy in the 1970s. The museum is south of the central area close to Stavanger Museum. Bus routes 2, 3, 6, and 7 pass close to the museum (look for the Kannik stop), but the easiest option is to take a 12-minute walk from Stavanger Cathedral.

The museum also runs the **Iron Age Farm (Jernaldergarden)** (Ullandhaugveien 165, tel. 51 83 26 00, 11am-4pm daily July, 11am-4pm Sun. mid-May-June and Aug. to mid-Sept.), located at Ullandhaug near the university campus and a 20-minute walk east of the Sverd i fjell monument. From the central area, take bus X60 directly to the farm or route 6 or 7 to the university campus, from where the farm is just a few minutes' walk. The bus ride should take no more than 15 minutes.

The reconstructed farmstead is based on an archaeological dig in the 1960s that uncovered the foundations of the original buildings dating back to AD 350-550. During July, actresses demonstrate daily life on the farm, and children can try their hand at spinning thread or even making fire with steel and flint.

Øvre Holmegate

Known locally as Fargegaten ("the colorful street"), **Øvre Holmegate** changed forever in 2005 when local hairdresser Tom Kjørsvik wanted to create a vibrant environment to draw more visitors to his salon and the neighboring businesses. The houses on either side of the street were painted in different colors, based on a *Miami Vice*-inspired color scheme suggested by the Scottish artist Craig Flannagan. It's not the individual colors that make the street work, but the color combinations. Each house was given a series of colors for its facade, doors, and window frames, designed to harmonize with its neighbors.

Problems with the project came not from the local council, who eventually approved the final design, but from the individual building owners and especially because of the color pink. Stereotype it may be, but some men refused to paint their buildings pink, while some women specifically requested it. After each change was agreed on, the entire street had to be redesigned to ensure harmony. Eventually, all except one building owner agreed, and the street is now one of Stavanger's most visited and most photographed landmarks, lined with cafés, boutiques, and restaurants and enjoying a lively atmosphere throughout the day and well into the night.

Churches

Stavanger Cathedral (Stavanger domkirke) (Haakon VIIs gate 2, tel. 51 84 04 00, www.stavangerdomkirke.no, 9am-4pm Mon.-Thurs., 9am-6pm Fri., 11am-4pm Sat.,

Øvre Holmegate is known as "the colorful street" by locals.

11am mass Sun., 30kr) has been in continuous use for 900 years. The original Norman architecture has seen substantial Gothic additions and varying decor from across the centuries. The interior is richly decorated thanks to the city's post-Reformation growth of the 17th century, but it also features the beautiful St. Olav Tapestry from the 1920s and the much older stone baptismal font from the 14th century.

The most notable feature is the stunning colorful pulpit that details the complete story of the Bible from Adam and Eve through to a triumphant Christ crowning the canopy. The pulpit was the master work of 17th-century Scottish Cartilage baroque craftsman Andrew Smith, who also carved and painted the five grand epitaphs dotted around the cathedral.

Tucked away behind the Arkaden Torgterrasen shopping mall, the distinctive bright red walls of **Sankt Petri kirke** (Nykirkebakken, tel. 51 84 04 20, www.stpetri.no) are hard to miss. Concerts are held sporadically throughout the year. For a service held in English, the Anglican **Bethel Church** (Løkkeveien 59, tel. 48 60 40 61, www.stavangeranglicans.net) hosts a Holy Communion in English every Sunday at 10:30am to which tourists are welcomed. The church is a 10-minute walk west from Stavanger Cathedral. Alternatively, the nearby **Stavanger International Church** (Misjonsmarka 12, tel. 51 11 22 15, www.sic.no) draws a congregation from a range of Christian faiths to its Sunday services. Previous sermons can be listened to online.

Outside Central Stavanger
SVERD I FJELL

Literally translating as "swords in rock," the **Sverd i fjell** (Madlaveien) monument stands beside the Møllebukta bay overlooking the Hafrsfjord. Consisting of three 33-feet tall bronze swords planted in the rocky ground, the monument commemorates the Battle of Hafrsfjord in the year 872, more than 250 years before the city of Stavanger was founded. The three unique crowns topping each sword represent the three districts of Norway that were united under the crown of Harald Hårfagre, known as Harald Fair Hair and remembered as the first king of Norway.

The Møllebukta bay is a popular recreational area, with a small beach, grassy area for picnics and games, and a safe bathing area. The monument is 5.5 kilometers (3.4 miles) southwest of central Stavanger, but it's easy to reach on public transit. Bus route 16 stops at Madlaleiren bus stop, just a couple minutes' walk from the monument, every half hour during the daytime. The bus journey takes 10-15 minutes.

FLOR & FJÆRE

A collection of tropical gardens on the small island Sør-Hidle, **Flor & Fjære** (tel. 51 11 00 00, www.florogfjare.no, mid-May to mid-Sept.) is open for visitors but only as part of a lunch or dinner package. A former family retreat, the gardens are now run by the Bryn family as a tourist attraction and an experiment to see which international plants and flowers will adapt to a Nordic climate. The exotic gardens are surrounded by tall trees along the shoreline to help protect the vulnerable plants from the often harsh winds of the Norwegian Sea.

A boat trip on the MS *Rygerfjord* (noon Mon.-Sat.) from Skagenkaien (the eastern side of Vågen harbor) to Hidle island, including a tour of the tranquil gardens and a lunchtime buffet, costs 1,090kr (1,150kr Saturdays). A similar evening tour (5pm) with a more substantial buffet is also available on selected days at a slightly higher cost. Both tours take a total of 4.5 hours and must be booked online in advance.

SPORTS AND RECREATION
Hiking

Most hikers in Stavanger will look to the opportunities available around the nearby Lysefjord, but many pleasant walks are available throughout the city and its surroundings. The 1.6-kilometer (one-mile) circumference of the **Mostvatnet lake,** just 2.5 kilometers (1.5 miles) southwest of the city center, is a popular family-friendly walk, and further urban trails fan out to the west and south. An 11-kilometer (6.8-mile) circuit known as the **Museum Tour (museumsturen)** circles Mostvatnet lake and takes you past many of the city's museums before returning to central Stavanger through the cobbled streets of the Old Town. Allow around two hours to complete the circuit.

Maps for this and other suggested hikes can be obtained from the Stavanger Tourist Information office and the **Stavanger Trekking Association (Stavanger Turistforeningen)** (Olav Vs gate 18, tel. 51 84 02 00, 10am-4pm Mon.-Fri., 10am-3pm Sat.)., which also sells quality hiking gear.

Biking

The **Stavanger Tourist Information office** (Strandkaien 61, tel. 51 85 92 00, 9am-4pm daily May-Sept., shorter hours rest of year) has a handful of bicycles available for rental to explore the city, pedal the coastal paths, and take the popular ride to the Sverd i fjell sculpture. Expect to pay 60kr per hour or 200kr for a day.

Beaches

The small sandy and rocky **Vaulen Beach** (Stasjonsveien) is on the shores of the Gandsfjord five kilometers (3.1 miles) south of central Stavanger. Bus routes 2 and 3 stop at Sørhallet, a 10-minute walk from the beach, or you can take the train to Mariero station and follow the coastal path for 15 minutes to the beach. Basic facilities including toilets are available, and the beach is also the starting point for several excellent fjordside walks.

A 20-minute drive south of Stavanger and close to the runway of the city's airport is the region's best beach. Backed by wooden holiday cabins and grassy dunes, the soft, sandy **Sola Beach (Solastranden),** with plenty of room to stretch out, is the best place to spend a sunny day, although winds can often be

---

Stavanger's Street Art

In stark contrast to the pretty white timber houses that dominate downtown, the colorful modern artworks show the city is more modern than first meets the eye. Among the first cities to accept the practice as a valid art form, Stavanger is now one big public street art gallery.

The best known Norwegian artist, Dot Dot Dot, uses a combination of spraycan, stencils, and freehand painting in his work. His iconic Johnny Rotten work can be seen at Vinkelgata (close to Pedersgata, east of the central district), with more pieces at Bakkegata and Muségata at the Rogaland Teater.

The Nuart festival's smartphone app (available all year) provides a handy overview of Stavanger's street art, sorted by location, artist, and date.

---

frustratingly strong. This makes the beach a haven for wind- and watersport enthusiasts. Public restrooms and a sheltered area for changing are located at the southern end of the beach, while parking and further facilities are available at the Sola Strand Hotel.

Swimming

Public opening hours at the municipal **Stavanger Swimming Hall (Stavanger svømmehall)** (Lars Hertervigs gate 4, tel. 51 50 74 51, 65kr) vary wildly throughout the week due to its use by schools and community groups, but it's generally open to the public 7am-11am daily and on Wednesday afternoons. A more hectic experience can be enjoyed on weekends during the family swimming hours (10am-4pm Sat., 11am-4pm Sun.).

Golf

On the shoreline of the Store Stokkavsatnet lake five kilometers (3.1 miles) west of the city center, **Stavanger golfklubb** (Longebakke 45, tel. 51 93 91 00, www.sgk.no) is known for its tight greens and undulating tree-lined fairways. Guests are welcome to play the par-71 18-hole course (500-600kr), but tee times should be booked in advance.

Soccer

The local Premier League soccer club **Viking FK** (www.viking-fk.no) plays their home matches at the smart 16,000-capacity **Viking Stadion** (Gamle Jåttåvågen, tel. 51 32 97 00). Tickets (from 200kr) rarely sell out, so they are usually available on the day for games every other weekend during the April to October season.

Theme Parks
KONGEPARKEN

The region's only theme park, 25 kilometers (15.5 miles) south of central Stavanger, is **Kongeparken** (Kongsgata 20, Ålgård, tel. 51 61 26 66, www.kongeparken.no, 299-399kr). Its main attraction is The Eagle (Ørnen), a gut-wrenching 260-foot high tower with two gondolas that rotate at more than 40mph. The Waterfall (Fossen) log flume sends passengers both forward and backward, while the park's rural setting is reflected in the many tractor-themed attractions especially for children. Opening hours vary wildly but are typically 10am-6pm daily during high season (mid-June to mid-Aug.) and 10am-5pm weekends May and September. Check online in advance for specific opening hours.

ENTERTAINMENT AND EVENTS
Nightlife

Start your evening in the cafés of Øvre Holmegate, many of which serve beer long into the night. The eclectic decor of **Hanekam** (Øvre Holmegate 26, tel. 78 01 02 99, 10am-2am Mon.-Sat., noon-2am Sun.)—surfboard tables, artwork made from blue and pink cassette tapes, and a mural-strewn backyard—is matched by its mix of patrons, everything from regulars to cruise ship day trippers intrigued by the mismatched funky furniture out front. Avoid the basic food menu and stick

to the great espressos by day and the range of craft beers by night.

An older clientele frequents the beer specialist **Cardinal** (Skagen 21, tel. 98 20 42 00, www.cardinal.no, 3pm-1am Sun.-Thurs., noon-1am Fri.-Sat.), which sells around 20 on tap plus hundreds of bottles, including many from Britain and the United States. Prices are not cheap, but the range cannot be bettered. Avoid Thursday nights, which tend to feature a Norwegian language quiz night.

The best known nightspot in Stavanger, **Checkpoint Charlie** (Nedre Strandgate 5, tel. 51 53 22 45, www.checkpoint.no, 8pm-2am Mon.-Sat., 8pm-midnight Sun.) has been around since the 1980s. Expect a casual atmosphere with pool tables to a soundtrack of heavy rock music. It gets rowdy on Saturday nights.

Performing Arts
THEATER

Norwegian actress Liv Ullmann made her name at the **Rogaland Teater** (Teaterveien 1, tel. 51 91 90 00, www.rogaland-teater.no), playing the lead role in a Norwegian version of *Anne Frank's Diary*. Since then the theater became known internationally for its adaption of *Peer Gynt* and today hosts performances year-round, mostly in Norwegian.

CINEMA

As the city's only cinema, **SF Kino Stavanger** (Sølvberggata 2, tel. 51 51 07 00, www.sfkino.no) is frequently booked out at weekends. All international releases with the exception of children's movies are subtitled rather than dubbed, making a visit here possible for non-Norwegian speakers. Select screenings of major Norwegian movies will be subtitled in English. Check in advance for details.

SØLVBERGET, STAVANGER KULTURHUS

Home to the city's main library, **Sølvberget, Stavanger Kulturhus** (Sølvberggata 2, tel. 51 50 74 65, www.stavanger-kulturhus.no) is also a meeting place for a wide variety of cultural events. For visitors, free Internet access, the cinema, and the selection of English language books are the reasons to visit.

Festivals and Events

NUART FESTIVAL

The international contemporary street and urban art **Nuart Festival** (www.nuartfestival.no) was founded by Brit Martyn Reed in 2001 as a small art project with a budget of just US$900. Since then, Nuart has grown phenomenally to become a global expo on the art form. Exhibitions during the early September festival vary yearly but always include the live creation of new art and weekend walking tours. Artists, academics, media, and industry experts participate in the Nuart Plus debates. Even the local bus company gets in on the act, operating a series of designer electric buses on several popular routes. Although the festival proper only lasts a couple of days, exhibitions run on for weeks and much of the art created during the event stays permanently.

MUSIC FESTIVALS

One of the city's most popular events, **MaiJazz** (www.maijazz.no) celebrates the arrival of better weather with concerts across all sub-genres of jazz. Tickets are sold separately for each concert during the six-day event, held at various venues across central Stavanger in early May.

Held in early August every year, the **International Chamber Music Festival (Kammermusikkfestivalen)** (tel. 51 84 66 70, www.icmf.no) aims to bring classical music to a wider audience. Participants live, work, eat, and play together during the six-day festival, where new ensembles are created just for the event. Late evening concerts in the city's cathedral are a highlight.

FOOD FESTIVALS

Firmly established in the minds and stomachs of the local population, the **Gladmat** (www.gladmat.no) food festival is one of the biggest of its kind in Scandinavia. Held over four days in mid-July, Gladmat transforms the city's waterfront into a showcase for the best farms and restaurants from the city and wider Rogaland region. Most street stalls offer free samples and are free to explore, although most other events, from live music to cooking courses, carry a charge.

Norway is not known as a nation of wine drinkers, but the annual **Stavanger Wine Festival** (www.stavangervinfest.no), held in late March, has been aiming to change that since its inception in 1999. The four-day festival's main attraction, known as The Lunch, brings 14 restaurants together under one roof to offer perhaps the country's most indulgent banquet, while the Wine Train visits eight of Stavanger's restaurants to sample wines in the company of producers and importers.

FOOD

A new take on the cookery class that has taken Stavanger by storm, **Social Cooking** (Verksgata 2, tel. 96 82 89 27, www.socialcooking.no) hosts international culinary classes where the focus is on having fun and getting to know people from all around the world over a shared interest of food. Classes ranging from vegan falafel to the Russian spicy sour soup *solyanka* are held every couple of days at their central premises. The 400kr course fee covers the ingredients and expenses, but the volunteer teachers are only paid through tips at the end of the session. All bookings should be made online in advance.

Cafés and Light Bites

Choose the family-run ★ **Coffeeberry** (Klubbgata 3, www.coffeeberry.no, 7am-7pm Mon.-Fri., 9am-6pm Sat., 11am-6pm Sun.) over the chain coffee stores on the same street. Bright red walls, soft copper lighting, and former school stools add to the retro atmosphere. Head there early in the morning to snag the corner sofa and enjoy the fragrant cinnamon buns fresh out of the oven, or simply grab a latte to go.

Colorful Øvre Holmegate is lined with cafés spilling out onto the sidewalk. The best of the bunch for an evening coffee is **Efendi**

(Øvre Holmegate 25, tel. 40 10 80 54), which also has a great range of Turkish teas and indulgent homemade desserts. The only downside is the erratic opening hours, largely due to the friendliest host in all Stavanger only opening up when he's finished making a fresh batch of lentil soup and desserts for the day ahead.

Traditional Scandinavian

Although it's a little way out of central Stavanger, the one-mile walk to **City Bistro** (Madlaveien 18, tel. 51 53 95 70, www.city-bistro.no, 5pm-midnight Tues.-Sat., 335kr) is worth it to build up an appetite for an intimate experience of classic seasonal Norwegian dishes. Don't expect a fine dining atmosphere in the two floors of a former residential timber house, but the service is good and the raw ingredients outstanding. The meat is sourced from a local hunter and the fish from the Lofoten islands, while the manager's deep knowledge of the wine list is impressive. In the run-up to Christmas, locals flock here to enjoy the Norwegian delicacy lutefisk, said to be the best in the city.

New Nordic

Firmly established as the city's most popular dining brand long before the award of the first Michelin star outside of Oslo, ★ **Re-naa** (Steinkargata 10, tel. 51 55 11 11, www.restaurantrenaa.no) offers everything from coffee and croissant through to fine dining. Enjoy an intimate culinary evening at owner and head chef Sven Erik Renaa's 21-seat experimental **Re-naa** studio (6pm-10pm Tues.-Sat., 1,200kr), where you will sample up to 20 courses of seasonal produce gently cooked and beautifully presented. Expect to hear details on specific farms each plate was sourced from. The more informal **Matbaren** (11am-11pm Mon.-Sat., 1pm-11pm Sun., 249kr) retains the same focus on quality raw ingredients but presented in a more typical bistro menu of steaks, seafood, and lighter bites. The gourmet open-faced sandwiches on dark rye bread are a popular lunchtime choice. Booking months in advance is essential for the fine dining experience, while a reservation the day before is a wise idea for the bistro.

For a speedier option, **Renaa Xpress** (Sølvberggata 2, tel. 94 00 93 48, 10am-10pm Mon.-Thurs., 10am-midnight Fri.-Sat., noon-10pm Sun.) sells light sandwiches, salads, and soups alongside great coffee in a fast-food-like environment. Despite this concept, it is often

Warm colors and comfy furniture help to make Coffeeberry Stavanger's coziest café.

packed at lunchtime with people in no rush to leave their tables, so takeout is popular.

There is no fixed menu inside the cramped **Egget** (Steinkargata 23, tel. 98 40 77 00, 6pm-11pm Tues.-Sat.). Instead, the chalkboard above the bar reveals the most likely dishes of the day based on the chef's recommendations, which can be adapted based on your preferences. This is a place where seasonality is at the heart of the menu, so much so that if the right berries aren't available, then dessert is off the table. A couple should expect to pay around 2,000kr for the full dining experience including a selection of outstanding paired wines. Booking is essential.

Seafood

More than just a fresh fish market, the bustling harborside **Fisketorget** (Strandkaien 37, tel. 51 52 73 50, 11am-10pm Mon.-Sat., 249kr) is especially popular with the after-work crowd, so head here early in the day for a quieter lunch. The fish stew rarely disappoints, while the catch of the day is often competitively priced. A light three-course meal can be enjoyed for around 369kr.

American

Burgers, ribs, and Asian-style fried chicken make up the simple yet mouthwatering menu at the central branch of **The Shack** (Breidablikkveien 6, www.theshack.no, 11am-10pm Mon.-Fri., noon-10pm Sat., 1pm-10pm Sun.). Most burgers run 149kr, while a full rack of ribs will set you back 239kr. This informal restaurant halfway between a diner and a pub is a place to come and eat when time is tight, as you'll be done in a half hour. Takeout is popular with Stavanger's youth thanks to the smartphone ordering app.

Asian

For the best sushi in town you need to head east along Pedersgata to the no-frills **Sabi Sushi** (Pedersgata 38, tel. 90 40 60 70, www.sabi.no, 11am-10pm Mon.-Sat., 1pm-10pm Sun.). Takeout is the most popular option; the excellent website details the full menu

with photographs and allows online ordering. Sharing plates for two start from 250kr, although couples should expect to pay around 400kr for a full meal.

The Déjà Vu delicatessen transforms itself into smart Japanese eatery **Kita** (Verksgata 2, tel. 51 89 65 55, www.dejavu.no/kita, 7pm-1am Tues.-Sat.) in the evening. The modern *izakaya* menu is a tapas-style serving of Nordic ingredients cooked in a modern Japanese style. At 640kr, the signature menu of best sellers is broadly equivalent to a three-course meal, while snacks including crispy king crab taco and virgin herring tempura can top up your order.

Italian

A short walk east of central Stavanger, the noisy intimate atmosphere of **Casa Gio** (Pedersgata 48, tel. 92 43 82 27, 5pm-11pm Wed.-Fri., 1pm-11pm Sat., 5pm-10pm Sun.) is a neighborhood favorite, and reservations are recommended. Baked beets and chopped nuts make a thoughtful addition to the classic Caprese salad appetizer, while you watch the chef grind out the pasta for your main dish in the open kitchen. Experimental dishes are often on the menu, such as herb-infused pasta and purple gnocchi.

Mediterranean

Reservations are required for the trendy **Tango Bar & Kjøkken** (Nedre Strandgate 23-25, www.tango-bk.no, 6pm-1am Mon.-Fri., noon-1am Sat., kitchen closes 10pm), where a three-course set menu will set you back 695kr although it comes with a few additional snacks. Dessert often takes the form of a cheese board. The chalk-white walls and tablecloths create a somewhat bland environment, but the view across the colorful harbor from the window tables more than makes up for that. A lighter bistro menu including pizza, oysters, halibut, and baked potatoes runs around 165kr and can be enjoyed from 5pm in a more informal environment. Food is salted to Norwegian tastes, so be sure to specify if you'd like less salt, especially on fish dishes.

Mexican

One of Norway's first Mexican restaurants, **Harry Pepper** (Øvre Holmegate 15, tel. 51 89 39 59, 4am-10pm Sun.-Thurs., 4pm-1am Fri., 1pm-1am Sat.) is easy to miss on the more sedate stretch of Øvre Holmegate. The menu is made up of Mexican-style steaks and sauces with a strong influence from north of the border. End your three-course meal (495kr, any combination from the menu) with a cocktail utilizing their vast range of tequilas, said to be the best in Norway.

ACCOMMODATIONS

As a compact city yet a hub for the international energy business, Stavanger suffers from a lack of midweek hotel capacity, especially during the busy conference seasons of spring and fall. This lack of availability will force you to pay top dollar for central accommodations or stay miles outside the city. On the plus side, availability is much better on weekends, when prices for some of the top business class hotels can halve. Bear this in mind and book accommodations as early as possible.

500-1,000kr

Tucked away in a quiet residential area yet just minutes from the railway station, ★ **Stavanger Bed & Breakfast** (Vikedalsgaten 1, tel. 51 56 25 00, www. stavangerbedandbreakfast.no, 790kr s, 890kr d) is central Stavanger's best value accommodation. Rooms are bright and modern, and although toilet facilities are shared, some rooms contain a private shower and basin. A basic breakfast buffet (homemade bread and cold cuts) and evening waffles and coffee are included in all room rates.

The already good rates at the centrally located **Skansen Hotel** (Skansegata 7, tel. 51 93 85 00, www.skansenhotel.no, 995kr) can drop on weekends if you book far enough in advance. However, the 28 rooms are small and tatty around the edges, and it can be difficult to sleep on weekends because of the rowdy cocktail bar below. On the upside, an

excellent breakfast buffet at the neighboring Best Western hotel is included in the low rate.

The handful of no-frills rooms at the homely **Stavanger Lille Hotel** (Madlaveien 7, tel. 51 53 43 27, www.slh.no, 990kr d) provide a good standard of private accommodations just a 10-minute walk from downtown. Free car parking is a rare benefit for a hotel so close to the central area. The hotel also runs a couple guesthouses with rooms from 670kr s, 840kr d, although these are farther away from central Stavanger.

If you don't mind sharing the breakfast canteen with hospital patients and mothers of newborn babies, the **St. Svithun Hotel** (Gerd-Ragna Bloch Thorsens gate 8, tel. 51 51 26 00, www.st-svithun-hotell.no, 840kr s, 940kr d) is a good value option albeit a 10-minute bus ride from central Stavanger. The 137 rooms in this hospital hotel are unsurprisingly clean and allergy-free, with many adapted for accessibility. The hospital kiosk co-located in the reception area sells drinks, snacks, salads, and sandwiches around the clock, while the canteen also serves great-value evening meals well under 200kr. This is often the first go-to choice for business travelers when downtown hotels fill up.

Both private rooms and dorm beds are available at **Stavanger Vandrerhjem Mosvangen** (Henrik Ibsens gate 19, tel. 51 54 36 36, http://stavangerhostel.com/rooms, June-Aug.) on the shores of Mosvatnet lake, a 35-minute walk or short bus ride south of the city center. Guests have access to a common dining room, laundry room, and TV lounge, and while the breakfast buffet costs an additional 60kr, a fully equipped modern kitchen is available. Dorm beds start from 250kr, private rooms from 600kr.

Adjacent to the hostel, **Mosvangen Camping** (Henrik Ibsens gate 21, tel. 51 53 29 71, info@mosvangencamping.no, May to mid-Sept.) owns 19 simple cabins (550-750kr) and plenty of space for motorhomes and tents, with rates starting from 200kr per night. Although kitchen and bathroom facilities are basic, an on-site kiosk and bicycle rental help to elevate this campsite into a place worth considering.

Another of the cluster of accommodations along the Mosvatnet lake, **Hotel Alstor** (Tjensvollveien 31, tel. 52 04 40 00, www.hotellalstor.no, 995kr d) has a surprising range of facilities for the price, most notably an indoor swimming pool and sauna. This is an excellent option if you have your own transport, as there is free on-site parking, although central Stavanger is only a three-kilometer (1.8-mile) walk away, the first third of which is a lovely lakeside path. The room quality varies considerably, although most are now refurbished in a contemporary style with lots of black and gray.

1,000-1,500kr

The distinctive brick exterior of the ★ **Myhregaarden Hotel** (Nygata 24, tel. 51 86 80 00, www.myhregaardenhotel. no, 1,095kr s, 1,395kr d) continues inside. Although the feather and down duvets and modern artwork on the exposed-brick walls give the feel of a boutique hotel, the hotel actually has 53 rooms, most naturally lit with tall windows. Although a little rough around the edges in places, the rooms are spacious and surprisingly quiet given the central location.

While the **Darby's Inn** (Oscarsgate 18, tel. 47 62 52 48, 1,180) offers just a handful of rooms, do check availability because this intimate bed-and-breakfast is a class above most of the city's hotels, set in a quiet residential area just a few minutes' walk from the central train and bus stations. Guests can expect traditionally decorated rooms with an atmosphere more akin to a personal bedroom than a hotel room, in-room TVs with British and American news networks, bathrooms with heated floors, and access to a modern kitchen.

1,500-2,000kr

Bold colors and contemporary design touches fill the 147 rooms of the **Thon Hotel Stavanger** (Klubbgata 6, tel. 51 59 95 00, stavanger.booking@thonhotels.no, 1,995kr d), a full-service hotel with prices to match.

Well-equipped for millennials, the rooms feature fast Wi-Fi and a smart TV and Bose sound system that will stream video from your smartphone or tablet. A free light meal is served from Monday to Tuesday in the jazzy second-floor lounge.

As the biggest of the central business-class hotels, the **Radisson Blu Royal Hotel** (Løkkeveien 26, tel. 51 76 60 00, reservations. royal.stavanger@radissonblu.com, 1,595kr d) often has last-minute availability, especially during the quiet July period and at weekends. Contemporary artwork adorns the walls of the 215 rooms, while the airy atrium restaurant rarely feels busy. A small indoor swimming pool is available for guest use.

INFORMATION AND SERVICES
Visitor Information

In 2016 **Stavanger Tourist Information** (Strandkaien 61, tel. 51 85 92 00, 9am-4pm daily May-Sept., shorter hours rest of year) moved from its central location to new premises by the cruise ship terminal. Though useful for cruise arrivals, the new location is frustrating for independent travelers arriving by train or bus, so combine a visit there with a walk around the cobbled streets of the Old Town. City maps, tour information, and bicycle rental are among the services available.

Urgent Medical Care

For urgent medical care, **Stavanger Legevakt** (Armauer Hansens vei 30, tel. 51 51 02 02) is always open, but appointments must be made by telephone so priority can be assessed. In life-threatening situations, call for an ambulance on 113. The center is on the site of the University Hospital, two kilometers south of central Stavanger. Bus routes 4 and X31 pass by the hospital campus.

Post Offices and Courier Services

For postage services, **Stavanger sentrum postkontor** (Haakon VIIs gate 9, 9am-6pm Mon.-Fri., 10am-3pm Sat.) is handily placed between the harbor and the Breiavatnet city lake. Any shop selling postcards will likely also sell postage stamps, especially those along Strandkaien between the cruise ship terminal and the city center.

GETTING THERE
Car

From Oslo, take the E18 highway around the southern coastline via Kristiansand and Flekkefjord, either of which would make a great overnight stop. You should allow around 7.5 hours for the 552-kilometer (343-mile) drive. Alternatively, explore some of Norway's forest and mountains by taking the E134 highway through the heart of the Telemark forest. From Dalen, continue on to the Rv45 before picking up Fv337 through the Sirdal valley and on to Stavanger. This more picturesque option shaves 100 kilometers off the distance but takes a similar amount of time. Be wary of snow-related road closures from fall through late spring.

From Bergen, allow at least five hours for the 210-kilometer (130-mile) journey along the E39 coastal highway that includes two ferries. Although tiresome for locals, these ferries provide natural breaks in the journey (and restrooms!), with departures every half hour during the daytime. Check timetables in advance with **Fjord1** (www.fjord1.no) if you are planning to drive late in the evening or overnight. The compact coastal town of Haugesund, 80 kilometers (50 miles) north of Stavanger, is a sensible place to break up the drive. The town had important status in the Viking Age and grew up on the herring industry but today is devoted to the oil industry, much like Stavanger. Its pink neoclassical town hall is a striking centerpiece.

Air

Stavanger Airport Sola (Flyplassvegen 230, tel. 67 03 10 00), 13 kilometers (eight miles) southwest of the city center, is busy throughout the day with oil industry commuters to Oslo, Bergen, the northeast United Kingdom, and also by helicopter to the oil rigs along the

Norwegian coastline. Although it's an international airport, most travelers will arrive on a domestic connection from Oslo. Both SAS and Norwegian run many daily services to and from the capital.

The **Airport Express Coach (Flybussen)** (tel. 51 59 90 60, www.flybussen.no) leaves every 20 minutes. There are two routes, one via the Forus business park and one via the hospital, but both services call at the Breiavatnet lake (outside the Radisson Blu hotel) and the bus station in the city center. The fare for the 20- to 30-minute journey is 120kr one-way, 180kr round-trip.

If time is of the essence or you are traveling with a group, take a taxi from right outside the terminal building. Because it's a business airport, the wait at the taxi rank is minimal. The fare for the 15-minute journey will run at least 290kr.

For rental cars, Avis, Budget, Europcar, Hertz, Sixt, and Enterprise all have desks close to the arrivals terminal. Avis and Budget have the best opening hours for evenings and weekends, but all reservations should be made in advance.

Rail

Budget travelers should consider taking the train from Oslo to **Stavanger Station** (Jernbaneveien 3) at the southern end of the city center. The 600-kilometer (373-mile) journey from operated by **NSB** (tel. 81 50 08 88, www.nsb.no) takes between 7.5 and 8.5 hours, but unlike the Bergen, Trondheim, and Bodø lines there's not a great deal to see as this line generally runs inland away from the coast. Spend the extra 90kr for a premium seat and buy a good book. The walk-up fare is 997kr, but discounts of at least 50 percent can be gained by booking just 24 hours in advance.

Bus

Lavprisekspressen (tel. 67 98 04 80, www.lavprisekspressen.no) runs bus services once or twice daily from Oslo to Stavanger. The double-decker coaches are comfortable, with reclining seats, bathroom facilities, and free Wi-Fi, and the service stops for 30 minutes in Kristiansand midway through the nine-hour journey. Substantial discounts on the 580kr full fare can be obtained with advance booking online.

Boat

The most economical way to reach Stavanger from Bergen is on the daily ferry service from **Fjordline** (tel. 81 53 35 00, www.fjordline. com). Tickets should be booked online in advance and start from just 200kr for a foot passenger. To take a car on the six-hour journey, calculate an extra 500kr. The service continues on to the Danish port of Hirtshals, providing an interesting option for continuing on a Scandinavian tour.

GETTING AROUND
Bus

The public transit system of buses in Stavanger is run by **Kolumbus** (tel. 177, www.kolumbus.no). All city buses stop either at the **Bus Station (Byterminalen)** (Jernbaneveien 3) or close by at one of the stops that line the perimeter of the Breiavatnet city lake. Check on the numerous information charts and maps found on most bus stops for the specific stop you need. Most buses leave on a half-hourly schedule between 6am and midnight, although service frequency will be less in the evenings and on weekends. A single ticket bought in advance from the station or an automatic ticket machine costs 35kr, with a 24-hour ticket costing 90kr. Cash can be paid on the bus, but the tickets cost an extra 20kr.

Rail

A local commuter rail service from **Stavanger Station** (Jernbaneveien 3) to Sandnes runs every 15 minutes throughout the day (5am-8pm) and every 30 minutes during the evening (8pm-11pm), with every other train continuing on to Egersund. Contact national rail operator **NSB** (tel. 81 50 08 88, www.nsb.no) for specific timetables and fares.

Taxi

Taxis are largely unnecessary to get around the city due to the compact nature of the central area and the high cost of the service. Should you require a taxicab, **Stavanger Taxi** (tel. 51 90 90 90, www.stavanger-taxi. no) will have the most cars available across the city. The absolute minimum fare regardless of distance is 143-178kr, with costs escalating after 6pm and at weekends.

Car Rental

The only car rental outlet in central Stavanger is **Hertz** (Olav Vs gate 13, tel. 51 53 82 02, 8am-4pm Mon.-Fri., 9am-1pm Sat.), but opening hours are limited.

LYSEFJORD

Despite the fame enjoyed by the fjords between Bergen and Ålesund farther north, the Lysefjord has long been called the most beautiful of Norway's fjords by poets, writers, and painters. Life seems to slow down on a visit here, although that's because it's impossible to rush such a visit. Those sailing from Stavanger have few distractions on board, enabling them to concentrate on taking in the narrow 42-kilometer (26-mile) fjord snaking inland east of the city and pick out its waterfalls and hidden caves. Those exploring the mountains on foot, including the major tourist draws Preikestolen and Kjeragbolten, must navigate several hours of hiking, which shouldn't be attempted without a reasonable level of fitness.

Despite the famous photographs from Preikestolen of the glittering granite cliffs and deep blue water, layers of mist are a common sighting along the Lysefjord. Although for many this adds to the atmosphere, it can be disappointing for the unprepared. It's all part of the fjord experience.

TOP EXPERIENCE

★ Preikestolen

Also known as Pulpit Rock, **Preikestolen** is the region's biggest tourist attraction. A cubed cliff 604 meters (1,982 feet) above the

Lysefjord, Preikestolen is known around the world for the photographs of tourists dangling their feet over the ledge. Whether you choose to engage in that daring activity or not, the hike to Preikestolen is a worthwhile activity in itself. The 625-square-meter (6,724-square-foot) top of Preikestolen is almost entirely flat, a remarkable natural feature that just so happens to present its visitors with spectacular views along the sparkling Lysefjord.

Allow around two hours each way for the hike, which starts from Preikestolen Mountain Lodge and should only be attempted by those with a reasonable level of fitness. Some clambering up rocks is necessary, along with a couple of steep inclines, which can be tricky when the weather is poor, so consider the weather forecast before you book a trip. Needless to say, if you don't cope well with heights, this probably isn't the trip for you. Norwegians will tell you the hike is straightforward, but what's easy for a Norwegian can be challenging for those who didn't grow up with the Nordic terrain on their doorstep. If you choose the hike, take a packed lunch and plenty of water, and allow more time than you expect. Alternatively, there's no shame in picking a relaxing fjord cruise over the hike!

GETTING THERE BY PUBLIC TRANSIT

From central Stavanger, take the car ferry (as a walk-on passenger) to Tau, from where you can pick up a connecting bus to **Preikestolen Mountain Lodge (Preikestolen Fjellstue).** The timetable varies by day and by season, but generally there are at least three ferry departures before 11am. The ferry-bus round-trip combination ticket offered by **Tide Reiser** (tel. 55 23 87 00, www.tidereiser. no, Apr.-Sept.) can be bought for 300kr from the tourist information office in Stavanger or on the ferry itself. Note that the ferry to Tau leaves from the Fiskepiren pier, east of central Stavanger, and not the main Vågen harbor. Be sure to allow plenty of time to catch the last return bus from the lodge at 5pm (Apr. and Oct.) or 9pm (May-Aug.).

GETTING THERE BY CAR

With your own transport, take the car ferry to Tau and make your own way to the mountain lodge. Expect to pay 150kr one-way for the car ferry plus 52kr per additional passenger, and a further 100kr for the lodge's parking lot. Following the 35-minute ferry journey, it should take a further 30 minutes to reach Preikestolen Mountain Lodge, clearly signed

view of the Lysefjord from the hike to Preikestolen

off route Rv13, 20 kilometers (12.5 miles) southeast of Tau.

GETTING THERE BY CRUISE

Rødne Fjord Cruise (www.rodne.no, 480kr) offers a three-hour cruise, available year-round but with limited departures October through April. From May to September, daily departures leave Vågen harbor at 10am, with an extra noon departure during July and August. While this cruise gets you up close and personal with the waterfalls and caves of the Lysefjord, the view of Preikestolen from below is nothing to write home about. That said, this is still a relaxing and enjoyable way to see one of Norway's most naturally beautiful fjords.

From mid-May to August, you can choose to depart the cruise at **Oanes,** at the narrow mouth of the Lysefjord, and be transported by bus up to the mountain lodge to start the hike, and by bus back to Tau for the public ferry afterward. This eight-hour option costs 780kr, but you have to factor in an additional 52kr per person for the ferry back from Tau. Although expensive, this is a great option to combine the Preikestolen hike with a longer boat trip, but the ferry-bus combination ticket from Tide Reiser is much better value for those who are most keen on the hike.

★ Kjeragbolten

The five-cubic-meter (180-cubic-foot) stone boulder wedged between two cliffs of the Kjerag mountain above the Lysefjord provides one of Norway's most famous vistas. Daredevils step out on to the **Kjeragbolten** boulder, which hovers above a 984-meter (3,228-foot) drop, and typically do a star jump for one of the most iconic travel photographs in the world. But many casual visitors don't realize that the only way to get to the boulder is via a demanding five- to six-hour round-trip hike, which even Norwegians won't attempt without some preparation. Experienced hikers are rewarded with a classic hike involving prepared trails, gravel paths, and some clambering across rocks, although no specific

Kjeragbolten boulder

climbing equipment is required. In addition to hikes, the Kjerag mountain is a popular BASE jumping destination. More than 50,000 jumps have been attempted since 1994, with several fatal accidents.

If you are physically fit and have sturdy hiking boots, the hike to Kjeragbolten should be high on your bucket list. Accessible from June to early September depending on snow conditions, the easiest trail starts from the **Øygardstøl** restaurant and visitor center (tel. 97 51 16 51, www.visitkjerag.no, 10am-6pm daily), accessible from the fjordside village **Lysebotn** via the 27 hairpin bends of steep mountain road Fv500.

GETTING THERE

From Stavanger, **Tide Reiser** (tel. 55 23 87 00, www.tidereiser.no, 550kr) runs daily bus trips to Kjeragbolten, leaving Stavanger Bus Station at 7:30am and returning by 7pm. The hike itself is not guided, so you should come prepared with enough food and water to last the day. Although the trails are marked, a map from tourist information or the visitor center is a wise purchase, and it's worth repeating that sturdy hiking boots and suitable clothing are essential.

By car, Lysebotn is accessible via the Sirdal valley mountain road (Fv986/Fv500), but only during the summer months. When the road opens around late May, it is surrounded by 20-foot high banks of snow, which makes for a spectacular start to your Kjeragbolten experience. The alternative, quicker route from Stavanger is the 42-kilometer (26-mile) drive via the E39 south and Rv13 east to **Lauvvik,** where you can pick up the tourist car ferry to Lysebotn run by **Kolumbus** (www.kolumbus.no). The one-hour ferry runs several times daily (varies by season) and will cost from 366kr. Not only is the ferry quicker than the three-hour 150-kilometer (93-mile) drive via Fv45 and the Sirdal valley mountain road, it also doubles as a Lysefjord sightseeing cruise.

Southern Coastline

Known locally as the Norwegian Riviera, the southern coastline from Stavanger right around to Oslo is a summer paradise for Norwegians but largely ignored by international tourists. Choose to spend a day or two exploring the towns, fishing villages, and islands along the coastline and you will be rewarded with a truly Norwegian atmosphere.

KRISTIANSAND

The fifth largest and southernmost major city in Norway, Kristiansand is known for its pleasant summer weather. A beautifully modern boardwalk surrounding the historic fortress, some of the country's best beaches, and great opportunities for recreation are some of the reasons to plan a day in Kristiansand into your schedule.

Head for the grid-based central district known as Kvadraturen, where the majority of commercial activity takes place. At the very least, grab an ice cream from one of the family-owned Hennig-Olsen ice cream kiosks and take a walk along the waterfront.

Kristiansand is Norway's summer city.

Sights

KRISTIANSAND DYREPARKEN

A must for families, **Kristiansand Dyreparken** (tel. 97 05 97 00, www.dyreparken.no) is a 150-acre amusement park and zoo 12 kilometers (7.5 miles) northeast of the central district along the E18 highway. Much loved by Norwegian schoolchildren, **Cardamom Town (Kardemomme by)** is an exact re-creation of the town featured in the book *When the Robbers Came to Cardamom Town (Folk og røvere i Kardemomme by)*, by Thorbjørn Egner. During the summer, actors play the parts of the commissioner, tram conductor, and three robbers.

Another major attraction is the **theme park** focused on Norwegian children's character Kaptein Sabeltann (Captain Sabertooth), featuring pirate ship rides and a haunted house. The **zoological gardens** are home to Norway's biggest collection of exotic animals, including tigers, lions, cheetahs, zebras, and orangutans. Finally, **Badelandet** (Apr.-Sept.) is a self-contained water park with rides suitable for all ages.

With such a vast choice of activities on offer, opening hours and entrance fees vary considerably, from 189kr in the off-season to 299kr or even higher at peak times. Booking online in advance is recommended, not least to check the exact opening hours and entrance fees on the day you are planning to visit.

If you plan on spending a full day at Dyreparken, consider staying at the pirate-themed accommodations within the park. The 171 rooms and apartments at **Abra Havn** feel like a movie set and are a very special treat for children. The accommodations and prices vary hugely and start from 300kr per person, but you can expect to pay at least 1,500kr for a good-standard family apartment. If you are staying overnight, a second day at Dyreparken can be booked for just 100kr.

CENTRAL KRISTIANSAND

Similar to Stavanger, the houses of Kristiansand's **Old Town (Posebyen)** are all occupied, and it is very much a residential area. Nevertheless, it's a great place for a leisurely walk to see what Kristiansand was like before a fire in 1892 destroyed much of the rest of the city. The 19th-century **Bentsens Hus** (Kronprinsens gate 59) is the best preserved house in the city, while the former **Post Office** (Kronprinsens gate 45) dates back to the late 17th century.

The rest of the central district is best explored along the modern waterfront. The pedestrian-friendly **Kristiansand Boardwalk (Strandpromenaden)** runs from the Fiskebrygga wharf to the city beach, past parkland, a marina, and the grounds of the 17th-century **Christiansholm Fortress (Christiansholm festning)**. Originally built by King Christian IV on an islet to defend the city, the fortress has since been linked to the mainland and is now a popular recreational area, although the fortress itself is usually only open for specific cultural events.

Sports and Recreation

You don't have to travel far to enjoy a lazy afternoon on the beach, because the best one is at the very heart of the city. The child-friendly **City Beach (Bystranda)** is one of just five blue flag beaches in Norway. Facilities include a swimming pier, sun deck, skatepark, and restrooms.

For short hikes, cross the footbridge by the Fish Market onto **Odderøya** island. The former naval base is now a popular recreational area with two miles of marked footpaths, old cannons, and great views back across to the city. When the City Beach is busy, the rocky beaches on the eastern side of Odderøya provide a great alternative for swimming.

Food and Accommodations

Grab a craft beer and play some shuffleboard at **Håndverkeren** (Rådhusgata 15, tel. 38 04 02 00, 3pm-2am Mon.-Fri., 1pm-2am Sat.-Sun.) for a true local experience. Although it's undoubtedly a pub atmosphere with sports on the TV, the menu is vast and there are plenty of choices to suit all tastes, from hamburgers to *moules frites*. Evenings can be lively with live concerts and quiz and improv nights commonplace.

For fish and seafood, head to the **Fish Wharf (Fiskebrygga)**, where five restaurants are clustered together. Many people simply buy some fishcakes or shrimp to eat on the harbor steps. During the long summer evenings, the atmosphere is buzzing with boats coming and going and locals gathering to share the latest gossip.

The 55 basic, modern rooms at the **Yess! Hotel** (Tordenskjoldsgate 12, tel. 45 90 90 88, www.yess.no, 779kr d) are substantially cheaper than the city's chain hotels. Expect comfortable beds, bright en suite bathrooms, and a basic breakfast buffet included in the price.

The city's best value chain hotel is the child-friendly ★ **Scandic Kristiansand Bystranda** (Østre Strandgate 74, tel. 21 61 50 00, 1,399kr d), set back from the City Beach from which it takes its name. The 229 stylish rooms with striking contemporary design all feature writing desks, flatscreen TVs, and en suite bathrooms with powerful showers. A children's playroom, a 24-hour kiosk selling snacks, and a generous breakfast buffet meeting many dietary needs make this a top choice for families visiting Kristiansand. Ask for a room on the upper floors for an excellent sea view.

Information

For city maps and general information, **Kristiansand Tourist Information** (Rådhusgata 18, tel. 38 07 50 00, 8am-3pm Mon.-Fri.) is located in the City Hall.

Getting There

Easy to reach by car, Kristiansand is a 234-kilometer (145-mile) drive southeast along the E39 from Stavanger and a 319-kilometer (198-mile) drive southwest along the E18 from Oslo. Driving directly, allow 3.5 hours from Stavanger and at least four hours from Oslo. From Stavanger, Flekkefjord makes a pleasant stop, while Arendal and Lillesand are picturesque options on the road from Oslo.

Several flights a day link Oslo with **Kristiansand Airport Kjevik** (Kjevikveien, tel. 67 03 03 30), 15 kilometers (9.3 miles) northeast of the city, close to Kristiansand Dyreparken. Alternatively, the city is midway on the Oslo to Stavanger railroad. **Kristiansand Station** (Gyldenløves gate) is centrally located, and several daily departures leave for Oslo (4.5 hours, 726kr) and Stavanger (3 hours, 512kr). Price savings of around 50

This beautiful beach is at the very heart of Kristiansand.

percent can be obtained by booking a specific departure at least 24 hours in advance through national rail operator **NSB** (tel. 81 50 08 88, www.nsb.no).

The **Sør-Vest Ekspressen** bus service runs three times daily between Stavanger and Kristiansand's bus terminal next to the railway station. The service operated by **Boreal** (tel. 38 18 30 35) takes just under four hours and costs 410kr. A small discount can be obtained by booking a specific departure in advance on www.nor-way.no.

The city is often referred to as Kristiansand S in public transit schedules to distinguish it from the similar-sounding Kristiansund.

FLEKKEFJORD

Midway between Stavanger and Kristiansand, Flekkefjord is a charming small town surrounded by calm water and luscious green hills perfect for hiking, biking, and just exploring.

During the 1800s, herring drove the expansion of the sleepy village into a thriving commercial town and attracted many fishermen and traders from the Netherlands. Several large posters with funny notes about Dutch history are placed around town, most notably in **Holland Town (Hollenderbyen),** a picturesque old district of narrow lanes and white timber houses. Stavanger's love of street art has rubbed off here, as several of the district's houses are brightened up by murals from international artists.

If time is tight, make **Flekkefjord Tourist Information** (Kirkegaten 33, tel. 38 32 80 81, 10am-4pm Mon.-Sat.) your first port of call to ensure you make the most of your visit.

Sports and Recreation
The most well-known attraction is the **Flekkefjord Railroad (Flekkefjordbanen)** (tel. 97 65 79 33, www.flekkefjordbanen.no), a 17-kilometer (10.5-mile) stretch of railroad closed to train traffic since 1990. The line is now a popular **biking** route. Special tandem rail bikes, some with additional seating for children, can be rented for 350kr at noon and 4pm each day from the former train station on Jernbaneveien. The full route takes you through 17 tunnels, one over one kilometer long, and takes approximately three hours.

Food and Accommodations
You can't miss the octagonal towers of the impressive Swiss-style **Grand Hotell Flekkefjord** (Anders Beersgate 9, tel. 38 32 53 00, www.grand-hotell.no, 1,095kr s, 1,295kr d) on the edge of Hollanderbyen. In contrast to the grand exterior, the 29 rooms are modern albeit small, and the facilities are more akin to a friendly B&B than a hotel. Rooms of such standard in Flekkefjord are few and far between, so book well in advance if you want to overnight here during the summer.

The hotel's restaurant **Grand Gastro** (4pm-10pm Mon.-Sat., 2pm-6pm Sun.) is also the pick of the town's eateries. The small menu changes frequently depending on what's in season, although locally caught fish is always available. The wine list is limited, but otherwise the bar is well stocked for a small hotel restaurant.

Getting There
From Stavanger, Flekkefjord is a 128-kilometer (79.5-mile) drive southwest along the E39, although a diversion through the agricultural lowlands of Jæren along Rv44 is a more scenic alternative and adds just 30 kilometers (19 miles) and about 30 minutes to the two-hour journey.

Public transit is limited to the three daily departures of the **Sør-Vest Ekspressen** bus service from Stavanger or Kristiansand. The service operated by **Boreal** (tel. 38 18 30 35) takes two hours from either Stavanger or Kristiansand, with the same 260kr fare applying from either direction. A small discount can be obtained by booking a specific departure in advance on www.nor-way.no.

Bergen and the Fjords

Look for ★ to find recommended
sights, activities, dining, and lodging.

Highlights

★ **Bryggen:** Learn about medieval Bergen as you explore the narrow alleyways between the Hanseatic trading buildings at this UNESCO World Heritage Site (page 133).

★ **Fløibanen Funicular:** A quick gravity-defying railway journey whisks you to the top of Mount Fløyen for fantastic views and the start of many hiking trails (page 137).

★ **Bergen Art Museum:** Must-sees at this superb collection include Edvard Munch's darkest works and a vast collection of Chinese handicrafts (page 138).

★ **Art Nouveau Ålesund:** This truly unique Norwegian city was rebuilt in the iconic art nouveau style after a devastating fire (page 168).

★ **Geirangerfjord:** Norway's most photographed fjord is Mother Nature at her very best, dotted with slender waterfalls and ancient farmhouse buildings perched high on the sheer cliffs (page 179).

★ **Flåm Railway:** This marvel of engineering is a worthy contender for the world's most beautiful railroad. The one-hour journey descends 865 meters (2,838 feet) down to the very heart of Fjord Norway (page 187).

★ **Nærøyfjord:** This narrow fjord is hemmed in by mountains up to 1,660 meters (5,446 feet) high. Mountain goats, seals, and gulls call it home (page 189).

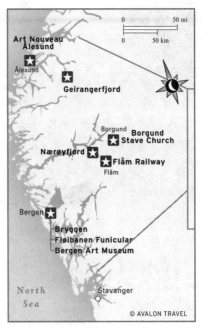

★ **Borgund Stave Church:** The most authentic of Norway's stunning stave churches has been lovingly preserved since its construction in the late 12th century (page 191).

Aside from the northern lights, the first images that come to mind when thinking of Norway are undoubtedly the western fjords. Puncturing the coastline, the fjords penetrate many miles inland to the glaciers and mountains at the heart of the country. Choose between visiting the epic Sognefjord, the longest and deepest; one of the UNESCO-listed fjords, Geirangerfjord or Nærøyfjord; or countless smaller arms and tributaries throughout the region.

The Norwegian tourist board defines Fjord Norway—or *vestlandet*—as stretching from Stavanger at the south all the way to Kristiansund, but in this chapter we focus on the two main cities, Bergen and Ålesund, and the fjords within easy reach of them.

For many travelers, the combination of an urban break in a dynamic city like Bergen with easy access to the fjords, rivers, mountains, and hiking trails of the great Norwegian outdoors is a dream combination—so much so that many people don't look beyond this region when planning a trip to Norway.

Bergen makes for a good base, especially if you lack your own transit, as options to reach the fjords via railroad or fast ferry are great value for the money. The fact that the city is rich with culture and history is just the icing on the cake. The spirit of 19th-century composer Edvard Grieg is everywhere, yet the city remains forward-looking with a busy calendar of contemporary festivals.

Consider a visit to Ålesund, a city quite unlike any other in Norway. Rebuilt in a dashing art nouveau style at the turn of the 20th century, this compact city charms all visitors with its architecture, color, and waterside walks. It makes a great alternative base for exploring the fjord region, as the Geirangerfjord and Hjørundfjord are within easy reach.

Be aware when practicing your Norwegian in Bergen and the surrounding fjords. Most locals speak in the unique Bergensk dialect, which is very difficult to understand for those with a basic grasp of the language. On top of that, many people write in Nynorsk (an alternative form of written Norwegian), especially in rural areas and the inner Sognefjord. As

---

Previous: Hjørundfjord; Bergen. **Above:** Kviknes Hotel on the waterfront of Balestrand.

Bergen and the Fjords

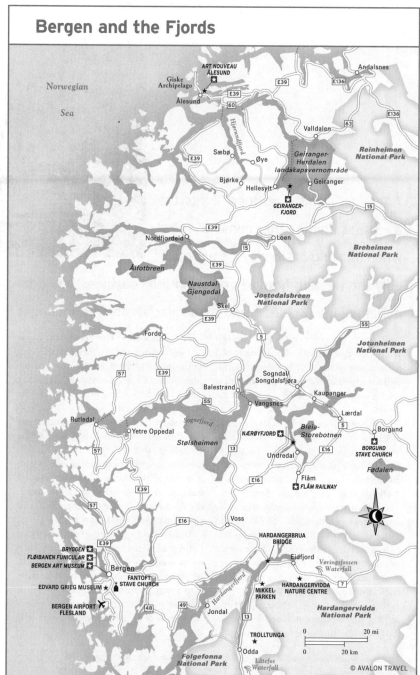

Norwegian
Sea

ART NOUVEAU
ÅLESUND
Giske
Archipelago
Ålesund
E39
E39
E136
Andalsnes
60
Hjørundfjord
Valldalen
63
E136
Reinheimen
National Park
Sæbø
Øye
Geiranger-
Herdalen
landskapsvernområde
Bjørke
Hellesylt
Geiranger
GEIRANGER-
FJORD
15
E39
Nordfjordeid
Loen
Breheimen
National Park
15
Ålfotbreen
E39
Naustdal-
Gjengedal
Jostedalsbreen
National Park
Skei
E39
Jotunheimen
National Park
Forde
5
55
57
E39
Sogndal/
Songdalsfjøra
Balestrand
Kaupanger
55
Vangsnes
Lærdal
Rutledal
Sognefjord
NÆRØYFJORD
Bleia-
Storebotnen
5
Borgund
Yetre Oppedal
BORGUND
STAVE CHURCH
57
Stølsheimen
13
Undredal
E16
E39
Flåm
FLÅM RAILWAY
Fødalen
E16
57
Voss
E16
HARDANGERBRUA
BRIDGE
BRYGGEN
FLØIBANEN FUNICULAR
BERGEN ART MUSEUM
E39
Eidfjord
Vøringsfossen
Waterfall
Bergen
FANTOFT
STAVE CHURCH
EDVARD GRIEG MUSEUM
MIKKEL-
PARKEN
HARDANGERVIDDA
NATURE CENTRE
7
BERGEN AIRPORT
FLESLAND
48
49
Jondal
Hardangerfjord
13
Hardangervidda
National Park
TROLLTUNGA
0   20 mi
Folgefonna
National Park
Odda
Låtefos
Waterfall
0   20 km
© AVALON TRAVEL

such, spellings of place-names and attractions may vary slightly from those listed in this guide.

CLIMATE

Here's what the travel magazines and TV shows don't tell you: It rains a lot in Bergen and the fjords. In fact, Bergen is one of the wettest cities in Europe. Its residents have to put up with an astonishing 220-230 days with rainfall every year, compared with 160 days in Oslo and just 150 days in America's Pacific Northwest. There is no dry season in Bergen, although May tends to have less rainfall than the rest of the year.

The fjords have a similar climate to Bergen, with regular rainfall to be expected at any time of year, although as a rule of thumb, the farther inland you travel the less rainfall you will encounter. The fjords reach as far inland as the glacial mountains that dominate Norway's topography. Here, the temperatures are much lower than on the coast.

PLANNING YOUR TIME

To get the most out of your visit to the Norwegian fjords, some advance planning is essential. Even if you rent a car, you will be reliant on public transportation in the form of public ferries to cross fjords. Schedules can be frustratingly infrequent, especially in the evening and on Sundays, when waits of up to two hours can occur. The majority of car ferries are run by **Fjord1** (tel. 57 75 70 00, www.fjord1.no). Timetables and prices can be downloaded from their website in advance or copies obtained from all tourist information offices. Locals will likely have committed the ferry schedules to memory, so just pull over and ask if you are unsure of timings or how things work.

This slow approach to travel should encourage you to slow down and enjoy the natural surroundings. Never plan too much into a road trip itinerary, because the outstanding scenery around every corner will have you pulling over and reaching for your camera far more often than you expect. If you're planning a three-day drive, add an extra day and you'll be glad you did.

If you are reliant on public transport, make Bergen your base and take advantage of the train connection to Myrdal for the Flåm Railway down to the Aurlandsfjord and Nærøyfjord, or the fast ferry from Bergen to Sogndal.

With a car, consider driving from Bergen to Ålesund via the enormous Sognefjord, or skip Bergen altogether and spend your time exploring the breathtaking scenery between Ålesund and the Geirangerfjord. Tag on nearby Åndalsnes and the Rauma valley and you will have experienced some of Norway's most outstanding natural features in under a week.

If time is tight, the popular **Norway in a Nutshell** tours from **Fjord Tours** (www. fjordtours.com) are worth considering. The classic tour starts from Oslo or Bergen and includes trips on Norway's most famous railroads (the Bergen Line and the Flåm Railway), a sightseeing ferry trip along the UNESCO-listed Nærøyfjord, and a coach trip through the lush valley between Gudvangen and Voss. The tour is self-guided, and what you are essentially getting is a discount on a set of pre-booked tickets. Because of this, the booking process is flexible, and although the tour can be completed in one day, overnight stops are easy to include in your itinerary. Rates start from 1,440kr per person, and the tour is available year-round.

Bergen

Norway's second city vies with Oslo to be the country's cultural capital. Bergen has long been a magnet for Norway's artists, musicians, and creatives. As such, a fierce rivalry exists between residents of Oslo and Bergen, something you'll quickly discover when striking up a conversation with a local.

Central Bergen gets uncomfortably crowded during the summer when multiple cruise ships bring thousands of American, British, and German tourists to the Bryggen Hanseatic wharf every day. As such, daytimes are best spent exploring the city's rich cultural attractions beyond the wharf, such as the outstanding Bergen Art Museum or the fairy-tale Fantoft Stave Church, one of the few easily accessible stave churches in the country. As the biggest city along the vast west Norwegian coast, Bergen is the perfect start or end point for exploring the Hardangerfjord or mighty Sognefjord, with or without a car. Fast ferries leave for the fjords daily, while a rail trip on the famed Bergen Line connects with the magnificent Flåm Railway and a boat tour of the UNESCO-listed Nærøyfjord.

Although tourism is a major income source for the city, Bergen is known as a leading destination for maritime research and the base of the Royal Norwegian Navy. Much of Norway's media business is based here, while a large student population studies on a campus within walking distance of the central district.

HISTORY

Originally just a small coastal village, Bergen's success is thanks to geography. The Vågan bay—where the Bryggen wharf is today—was sheltered from Atlantic storms by the islands of Askøy, Holsnøy, and Sotra, while the seven mountains surrounding what is today the city provided some protection from southeasterly winds. The arable land surrounding the village was ideal for farming.

With its excellent location and deep harbor, Bergen quickly became one of the most important trading centers in northern Europe in the post-Viking era. Traders traveled from Orkney, Shetland, Iceland, England, and even as far south as Germany, Holland, and Belgium. The primary export was fish,

The colorful Bryggen wharf is Bergen's most famous sight.

in particular dried fish, from the Lofoten and Vesterålen islands. The foreign traders brought corn and other foods not available in Norway, along with luxury decorative items for the home. Such international influence also led to the importing of culture, including architecture, arts, and literature.

With the growing trade in fish and other commodities, royalty started to show an interest in Bergen. King Olav Kyrre and successive kings built several large churches around the town in the 12th century. Once Bergen became a cathedral town and the capital of Norway, the town's expansion grew at pace. Toward the end of the Middle Ages, Bergen could boast two hospitals, five monasteries, and more than 20 places of worship, more than any other Nordic town.

In the 13th century, trading restrictions were introduced and German merchants began to stay in the town for longer periods, leading to civil disturbances and prostitution. However, this was just the beginning of Bergen's troubles. In 1349, a ship from England unwittingly unleashed the Black Death on Bergen. The plague decimated the population of not only Bergen, but the entire country, with an estimated two-thirds killed. Trade and industry were hit hard. Although the royal interest in Bergen would cease, the city recovered as a trading center and was back on its feet within 50 years, although the population took longer to fully recover.

As foreign traders began to flood back to the town, the German Hanseatic League emerged as a key player in the years following the Black Death. A census shows that during the 15th century, Bergen's population of 7,000 was made up of more than 2,000 Germans, a number that increased during the summer. Although not permitted to marry, many German residents began to form relationships with Norwegian women, and some fathered children. Some became craftsmen, including a large portion who manufactured shoes. The influence of the Hanseatic League began to

wane in the 17th century as more local people began to take over trading routes, especially to the north.

As fishing and trade continued to drive Bergen's economy, shipbuilding emerged to service the growing need for transport. Bergen remained the largest city in Norway until the rapid development of Oslo, then Christiania, in the early 19th century. As Oslo became a more important city in Norway, the Bergen Line railroad was opened in 1909 to link Norway's two biggest cities and replace a long journey by ship or a dangerous trek over the mountains.

During the 20th century, Bergen's city limits expanded significantly, and many residential developments were built on new land, leading to a rapid increase in population. In the years following World War II, city planners considered demolishing historical neighborhoods including Bryggen and Nordnes, but the plans were largely scrapped because of significant local opposition.

ORIENTATION

Bergen's central area is small and fairly easy to find your way around with two key navigation points: the **Fish Market** at Vågan harbor and the **city lake** known as Lille Lungegårdsvannet. The **Bryggen** wharf is to the north of the Fish Market, while the modern **central area** lies between the Fish Market and the lake. To the southwest of central Bergen, the **university campus** is within walking distance.

SIGHTS
★ Bryggen

The brightly colored wooden facades are one of the most iconic images of Bergen, but there's a lot more to the Bryggen wharf than first meets the eye. This UNESCO World Heritage Site is perfect for a quick photo opportunity or an entire day spent puttering about the narrow alleyways and museums to learn the fascinating history of this famous district.

Bergen

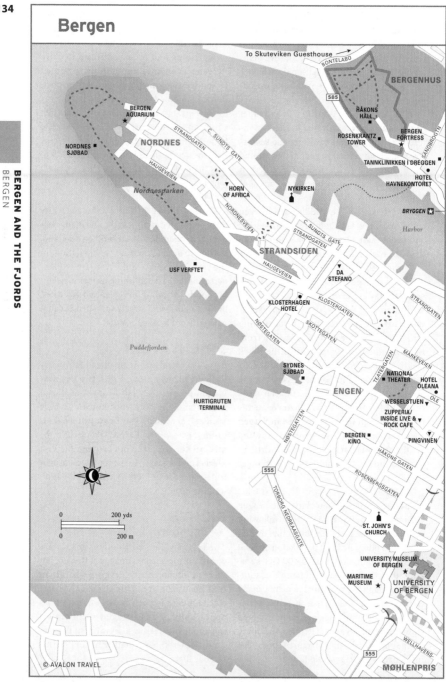

To Skuteviken Guesthouse

BONTELABO

BERGENHUS

585

HÅKONS HALL

BERGEN AQUARIUM

ROSENKRANTZ TOWER

BERGEN FORTRESS

SANDBROGTN.

NORDNES SJØBAD

NORDNES

STRANDGATEN

C. SUNDTS GATE

TANNKLINIKKEN I DREGGEN

HOTEL HAVNEKONTORET

HAUGEVEIEN

Nordnesparken

HORN OF AFRICA

NYKIRKEN

BRYGGEN ★

Harbor

NORDNESVEIEN

C. SUNDTS GATE

STRANDGATEN

STRANDSIDEN

USF VERFTET

HAUGEVEIEN

DA STEFANO

KLOSTERGATEN

STRANOGATEN

KLOSTERHAGEN HOTEL

SKOTTEGATEN

Puddefjorden

NØSTEGATEN

MARKEVEIEN

SYDNES SJØBAD

TEATERGATEN

NATIONAL THEATER

HOTEL OLEANA

OLE

ENGEN

WESSELSTUEN

HURTIGRUTEN TERMINAL

ZUPPERIA/ INSIDE LIVE & ROCK CAFE

BERGEN KINO

PINGVINEN

NØSTEGATEN

HÅKONS GATEN

555

ROSENBERGSGATEN

0   200 yds

0   200 m

TORBORG NEDREAASSGATE

ST. JOHN'S CHURCH

UNIVERSITY MUSEUM OF BERGEN

MARITIME MUSEUM

UNIVERSITY OF BERGEN

WELLHAVENS.

555

MØHLENPRIS

© AVALON TRAVEL

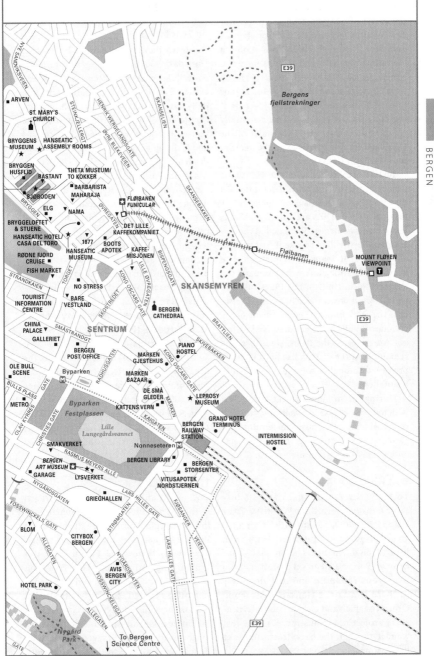

Today home to shops, restaurants, and cafés, these former trading houses were the driver of Bergen's economy for centuries. Wealthy German traders from Lübeck met here with fishermen from Lofoten to trade grain, salt, and textiles for dried Norwegian cod in the 14th century. The oil from Norwegian cod lit lamps across Europe until well into the 19th century. As trading increased, Bryggen became essentially a German enclave, and a reminder of the Hanseatic era remains today in the name of the local lager, Hansa.

Just as the influence of the Hanseatic League began to wane, the district suffered a disastrous fire, so these houses, rebuilt in their original style in 1702, are almost all that is left of medieval Bergen. Remarkably, the district very nearly didn't make it past the end of World War II. Many locals wanted it gone because of its strong links with Germany, but archaeological finds in the 1950s inspired an interest in preservation and helped to secure the area's future. However, many of the communal buildings were destroyed by fire and torn down in the 1950s. Since then, the remainder of the district has been lovingly preserved through a continual program of restoration.

During the summer, Bryggen is packed with tourists because the wharf links the city center with the busy cruise ship terminal. On clear days, arrive early to grab one of the outdoor tables to enjoy a leisurely lunch.

WALKING TOUR

To really dig into Bryggen and its history, consider joining a **Walking Tour** (tel. 55 30 80 30, 150kr) with an English language guide, held daily at 11am from June through August. The one-hour tour through Bergen's medieval past starts from **Bryggens Museum** and includes entry to there and to the Hanseatic Museum. Otherwise, pick and choose your own itinerary from the various museums or just wander through the backstreets and take in the atmosphere.

HANSEATIC MUSEUM & ASSEMBLY ROOMS (Det Hanseatiske Museum og Schøtstuene)

Step inside the former merchant's house of the **Hanseatic Museum** (Finnegården 1a, tel. 55 54 46 90, http://hanseatiskemuseum.museumvest.no, 9am-6pm daily June-Aug., 11am-3pm daily rest of year, 150kr) for more insight into the people who originally occupied these houses. The building itself dates back to 1704 and is the only house on Bryggen to have its original interior intact.

Original layouts and furnishings will shed light on the tough lifestyle of its occupants, despite the wealth generated by the traders. Although you will be surprised at the basic conditions, especially the tight sleeping quarters for merchants' apprentices, the accommodation retained heat well and so was more pleasant than you might think at a time when heating was not allowed for fear of fire.

The same ticket also entitles you to enter the **Hanseatic Assembly Rooms (Schøtstuene)** (Øvregaten 50, tel. 55 31 60 20, 10am-6pm daily June-Aug., 11am-3pm Sun. only rest of year) at the other end of the Bryggen district, a five-minute walk away. The communal space was a popular place to socialize, especially during the cold, dark winters. Hot evening meals were served in the spacious yet dark wooden halls, while during the daytime teaching and legal matters took place.

THETA MUSEUM

One of the hidden delights of Bryggen is the secret one-room headquarters of the Norwegian resistance from World War II. It took years for the Nazis to discover what is now the **Theta Museum** (Enhjørningsgården, 2pm-4pm Tues. and Sat.-Sun. June-Aug., 20kr), and even today you're likely to need a helping hand to find it.

Pass through the tight alleyway behind the Enhjørningen restaurant (look for the unicorn carving!) on Bryggen and head up the narrow staircase to the top-floor loft,

The Fløibanen funicular gives a great view of central Bergen.

mid-May to mid-Sept., noon-3pm Sun. only mid-Sept. to mid-May, 80kr), one of Scandinavia's best Renaissance-era monuments, where you can climb the narrow staircase all the way to the roof for a great view across Bergen. Over the years the tower acted as a residence to a diverse range of guests, from the king of Norway to somewhat less illustrious guests in the dungeon. The unusual floor plan reveals many curious rooms filled with a selection of memorabilia from the building's former uses.

Much of interest about both the hall and tower can only really be learned on a guided tour (20kr), held hourly in Norwegian or English on request. For example, during World War II, an ammunition ship packed with dynamite exploded in the harbor, destroying local neighborhoods and sending the ship's anchor miles into the hillside. The hall and tower were damaged but survived.

where you'll find original radio equipment, clothing, and a knowledgeable English-speaking guide who will tell a few more personal tales.

BERGENHUS FORTRESS
(Bergenhus Festning)
At the far end of Bryggen are the grounds of **Bergenhus Fortress**, a stirring reminder of the city's former status as capital of Norway. Originally a garrison with a tower acting as the royal residence and a large banqueting hall, the fortress grounds are better known today as an outdoor concert and festival venue. Nevertheless, both the tower and hall remain as a reminder of Bergen's importance during the early medieval times.

The largest secular medieval building in Norway, **Håkons Hall** (tel. 47 97 95 77, 10am-4pm daily mid-May to mid-Sept., 80kr) is still used today for grand banquets but is not so interesting beyond its jagged stone exterior. Better save your kroner for **Rosenkrantz Tower** (tel. 47 97 95 78, 10am-4pm daily

BRYGGENS MUSEUM
To complete your tour of this historic district, visit the modern **Bryggens Museum** (Dreggsalmening 3, tel. 55 30 80 30, www.bymuseet.no/en, 10am-4pm daily mid-May to Aug., 11am-3pm Mon.-Fri., noon-3pm Sat., and noon-4pm Sun. rest of year, 80kr) showcases the archaeological findings from Bryggen through the ages.

The permanent exhibition reveals the discoveries from the 1950s dig that saved the district, along with some World War II memorabilia and stories from Bergen's time as Norway's most important city during the Middle Ages. Museum highlights include original tenement building foundations dating back to the 12th century (the museum was built over the top) and the remains of a 100-foot-long ship found nearby.

★ Fløibanen Funicular
Start your visit to Bergen with the short trip on the **Fløibanen Funicular** (Vetrlidsallmenningen 21, tel. 55 33 68 00, 8am-11pm daily, 90kr). This will not only help you get your bearings but also give you an

unforgettable view of central Bergen in context with the surrounding peaks and ocean.

More than 1.3 million visitors take the six-minute journey up the steep side of Mount Fløyen every year. The train makes several stops on its way up to the top, and as popular as it is with tourists, locals who live on Mount Fløyen use it as a commuter service and to reach the starting point of the endless hiking points at the summit. As a round-trip ticket is valid through the end of the day, take some time to explore the area. A playground will keep kids occupied, while a small kiosk, gift shop, and café serving the usual Norwegian fare of black coffee and waffles is open daily 10am-6pm (9am-10pm May-Aug.). For those with more time, do as the locals do and explore the sprawling forest along the network of trails that radiate out from the funicular station.

An easy hike for families and a great choice for bird-watchers is the 1.5-hour round-trip to the **Fløyvarden cairn.** From the top of the funicular, follow the signs for Blåmansveien and follow the path to the Blåmansveien-Skomakerdiket junction. Follow the signs for Fløyvarden and atop some steps you will see the cairn, along with an outstanding view across Bergen, with none of the crowds from the funicular station. From here, continue north to a further viewpoint before returning along the marked trail. For more demanding hikes, see the *Hiking* section.

Although the railway is scheduled to run half-hourly in both directions, there is no need to book in advance. The operators run the service continuously to meet demand at busy times, so you should never be waiting too long for a place.

★ Bergen Art Museum
(KODE Kunstmuseene i Bergen)

Lining the edge of Lille Lingegårdsvannet lake, the four buildings (labeled KODE 1-4) of **Bergen Art Museum** (Rasmus Meyers allé 9, tel. 53 00 97 04, www.kodebergen.no, 11am-5pm daily mid-May to Aug., 11am-5pm Tues.-Fri., 11am-5pm Sat.-Sun. rest of year, 100kr) together make up one of Scandinavia's largest museums for art, craft, design, and music.

KODE 4 hosts a vast permanent exhibition of art history from around the world, including works by such greats as Picasso, Miró, and Klee. It also features KunstLab, which encourages younger art lovers to explore the paintings of said greats through play and interaction.

The four buildings of Bergen Art Museum surround the city lake.

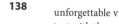

The Oslo to Bergen Railway

Consistently voted as one of the world's most remarkable railway journeys, the **Bergen Line (Bergensbanen)** soars over the Hardangervidda mountain plateau at 1,200 meters (4,000 feet) above sea level. A true engineering wonder, the 371-kilometer (230-mile) track was completed in 1909 to connect Norway's two biggest cities. In each direction, once the train clears suburbia, the ride offers magnificent views across some of Norway's most beautiful yet inhospitable landscape. Passengers are a curious mix of budget-conscious Norwegians, locals traveling to their cabins, and mesmerized travelers.

Several stops along the route, including Finse and Myrdal, can only be reached by the train. Finse is a popular stop with *Star Wars* fans as it was the setting for the ice planet Hoth, and you'll see snow here on almost every day of the year.

Tickets for the 6.5-hour ride can be booked via the Norwegian state railway company **NSB** (tel. 81 50 08 88, www.nsb.no). The best bit? Advance tickets known as *minipris* can be grabbed for as little as 249kr with a couple weeks' notice. If you're taking the full journey, pay an extra 90kr to upgrade to comfort class to enjoy comfier seats, more legroom, and complimentary hot drinks.

Next door in KODE 3, the undisputed highlight of the Rasmus Meyer Collection is the rooms featuring some of Edvard Munch's darkest works, including *Melancholy, Jealousy,* and *By the Death Bed.* Norwegian romantics feature heavily throughout the museum, including the abstract fjord landscapes of Nikolai Astrup, which in 2016 were finally given an international platform. This collection focuses on the colorful naïvism of his early works and includes many childhood drawings. Appropriately, the museum has produced an excellent children's book about Astrup's life and work.

As much as paintings dominate the collections, there are also thousands of drawings, sculptures, installations, and videos throughout. The most notable is the 2,500-item China Collection, one of Europe's largest collections of Chinese artwork and artisanal handicrafts, some dating back as far as the Stone Age. Amid the hundreds of paintings you'll see bronze and clay sculptures and objects made of white marble, sandstone, and limestone.

True art lovers will need more than a day to fully appreciate the museum's collections, but thankfully the ticket is valid for two consecutive days. Each building has a small gift shop, but the store inside KODE 2 is open to those without a ticket and doubles as one of Norway's largest art bookstores, with children's books and drawing supplies.

Central Bergen
LEPROSY MUSEUM
(Lepramuseet)

It doesn't seem right to recommend a **Leprosy Museum** (Kong Oscarsgate 59, tel. 48 16 26 78, 11am-3pm daily mid-May to Aug., 80kr) as a highlight of any trip, but the former hospital is a genuine site of historical interest. Although leprosy, also known as Hansen's disease, has affected humanity for centuries, the causative agent wasn't discovered until 1873 by Gerhard Armauer Hansen, a Norwegian physician working in Bergen. Following this discovery, the city quickly became the European center for research into the disease.

At the time, leprosy was still thought to be highly contagious, so three hospitals were founded to cope with Europe's largest concentration of patients. The oldest of the three, St. George's (St. Jørgen's in Norwegian), remained open up until 1948, when the last two patients died. The hospital is now a monument to the thousands of personal tragedies and an important center for the dissemination of Norwegian medical research.

Tiny bedrooms line both sides of the dimly lit hall of the main building. Inside some of the rooms, which are presented as they would have been at the time, the harrowing personal stories of former residents are told. The hospital's kitchen and other facilities are also open to explore, while information boards reveal a detailed account of the disease and the hospital itself. Much of the description is in Norwegian, but an information booklet in English is available to borrow from reception.

Conditions at the hospital were never fantastic. Indeed, one hospital chaplain described it as "a graveyard for the living." It's a moving place to visit but at times disturbing, so this is no place for children. For the complete story, be sure to visit the small church adjacent to the hospital, where both patients and the general public attended services together, although it is thought the patients sat in a separate area with a dedicated entrance. The church can only be visited on request, so ask at reception when you arrive. A visit to the museum and church will take no more than one hour, but be aware of the short opening season and hours.

BERGEN AQUARIUM
(Akvariet i Bergen)

Despite the warm welcome from the adorable penguin population that once called the Falkland Islands home, **Bergen Aquarium** (Nordnesbakken 4, tel. 55 55 71 71, 9am-6pm daily May-Aug., 10am-4pm Mon.-Fri., 10am-6pm Sat.-Sun. Sept.-Apr.) appears small at first glance. But step inside the doors and you soon find three floors of exhibits, the most exciting of which is the tropical underground floor that is home to snakes, lizards, and other creepy-crawlies.

Children are well catered to with crab pools and a tunnel under the giant aquarium that surrounds you with sharks and tropical fish of all shapes, sizes, and colors. Hourly feedings or exercise sessions are held throughout the day in the outdoor pools with either the penguins or sea lions. Check the day's schedule on arrival.

Admission prices vary by season. Tickets range 220-270kr for adults, 160-185kr for children. Family tickets (two adults, two children) are available for 650-750kr.

The aquarium is at the far end of the Nordnes peninsula, which is the piece of land directly opposite the Bryggen wharf. Choose from a pleasant 20-minute stroll through a largely residential area, local bus 11 (10 min., hourly departures from Stadsporten or Nygaten), or the colorful ferry that leaves from the Bradbenken pier near Bryggen every 10 minutes (7:30am-4pm weekdays year-round, plus 11am-4pm Sat. May-Aug.). A one-way ticket for the ferry's five-minute journey costs 25kr. Even if you don't plan on visiting the aquarium, the boat trip is worthwhile for the unique perspective of Bryggen from the water.

CHURCHES

The steps of **Bergen Cathedral (Bergen domkirke)** (Domkirkeplassen 1, tel. 55 59 32 70, hours vary, typically 9am-4pm Mon.-Fri.) act as a meeting point for Bergen locals. The 12th-century stone structure has been damaged by fire multiple times but remains standing, albeit with plenty of restoration and modernization. Inside is a spacious but ordinary place of worship, in part because of the Franciscan friars who called the church home in the 13th century, with more recent additions including 19th-century stained-glass windows and an organ from 1997. Much of interest is outside the church itself, including the splendid stonemasonry of the entrance hall, carved by the same artisans who worked on Westminster Abbey's chapter house. Don't miss the cannonball still wedged in the outer wall, a constant reminder of the 1665 battle between the British and Dutch navies. Entrance is free but donations (20-50kr) are appreciated.

Bergen's oldest building and the finest example of Romanesque architecture in the region, **St. Mary's Church (Mariakirken)** (Dreggsallmenningen 15, tel. 55 59 32 70, hours vary, 50kr) is a wonderful old church hidden away behind the end of the Bryggen wharf. Recently reopened after an extensive five-year restoration, this church is worth a look for its unique rococo-style pulpit and paintings, somewhat at odds with the otherwise simple interior. Ask for an information leaflet to learn the fascinating history of some of the scenes depicted in the artwork, or take the short English language guided tour (3:30pm weekdays June-Aug., 75kr).

University Area

Despite being home to some of Bergen's more interesting museums and delightful small colorful wooden houses, the university area is surprisingly tourist-free.

ST JOHN'S CHURCH
(Johanneskirken)

The 19th-century neo-Gothic St John's Church (Johanneskirken) (Nygårdshøyden, tel. 55 59 32 70, 10am-1pm Tues.-Fri. mid-May to mid-Aug., sporadic opening rest of year) is easy to spot from the pedestrianized commercial street Torggaten, thanks to its position atop Sydneshaugen hill. Its tall steeple adds to the vertical appearance, so you can get quite a shock inside when you are greeted with more than 1,200 seats. The modern surroundings of the historical church act as the gateway between the bustling downtown district and the academic quarter.

UNIVERSITY MUSEUM OF BERGEN
(Universitetsmuseet i Bergen)

The University Museum of Bergen (Haakon Sheteligs plass 10, tel. 55 58 31 40, 10am-4pm Tues.-Fri., 11am-4pm Sat.-Sun. June-Aug., 10am-3pm Tues.-Fri., 11am-4pm Sat.-Sun. Sept.-May, 60kr) holds a detailed record of natural and cultural history from this part of the world, although the natural history department is closed for refurbishment through 2019. Although certain exhibitions and the greenhouse are closed, the city's former botanical gardens remain open (7am-6pm daily, until 8pm June-Aug.), as do the museum's exhibitions on cultural

history, which include a large collection of archaeological materials and artifacts from indigenous communities from around the world.

MARITIME MUSEUM
(Sjøfartsmuseum)

While the Hanseatic Museum on Bryggen focuses on the trading aspect of Bergen's maritime history, the Maritime Museum (Haakon Sheteligs plass 15, tel. 55 54 96 00, www.bsj.uib.no, 10am-4pm Mon.-Fri., 11am-4pm Sat.-Sun. June-Aug.; 11am-3pm daily Sept.-May, 70kr) presents a detailed look at the ships themselves. Original Viking finds dating back to the 5th century sit alongside models of the more well-known findings from the Oslofjord area. Methods of wooden shipbuilding and the transition to modern techniques are also in focus, along with an exhibition looking at some of the 1,000 Norwegian vessels involved in World War II.

BERGEN SCIENCE CENTRE
(VilVite)

From the city center, cross Nygårdsparken park to unleash your inner child at Bergen Science Centre (Thormøhlens gate 51, tel. 55 59 45 00, www.vilvite.no, 9am-3pm Tues.-Fri., 10am-5pm Sat.-Sun., 175kr). Although designed for children, it still has plenty to interest adults. The interactive energy zone, where you can cycle in a 360-degree loop and discover how hydrogen rockets work, is the highlight, while kids will enjoy making their own weather report and learning about the ocean through wave machines and ship simulators.

Given the high price (a family ticket for two adults and two children is 530kr), this isn't somewhere to pop into for an hour. If you are traveling as a family, plan to spend a full day, whereas individuals or an adult couple might want to pass. As an alternative to walking via the university campus, take the short six-minute trip on Bergen Light Rail line from downtown Bergen to Florida station, a five-minute walk away from Bergen Science Centre.

South of Bergen
MOUNT ULRIKEN CABLE CAR
(Ulriksbanen)

Soaring to 643 meters (2,109 feet) above sea level in just seven minutes, the **Mount Ulriken Cable Car** (Haukelandsbakken 40, tel. 53 64 36 43, www.ulriken643.no, 9am-9pm daily Easter to mid-Oct., 10am-5pm Tues.-Sun. rest of year, 160kr round-trip) takes you twice as high as the Fløibanen Funicular. Whereas Fløibanen is great for a lofty view of downtown, the views from Mount Ulriken set the city in context with its stunning natural surroundings.

Ignore the pushy sales tactics from the downtown street vendors and don't book in advance. Instead, wait until the day you plan to visit and make a visual check of the weather. If it's cloudy on the mountains to the southeast of the city or if there are high winds, don't make the journey.

For an extra 100kr you can take the brightly colored antique double-decker bus (you can't miss it!) from downtown to the bottom of the cable car. The bus departs from the Fish Market on the hour 9am-6pm May-September. Otherwise, public bus routes 2 and 3 both call at Haukeland Hospital N, which is a 10-minute walk along Haukelandsbakken to the bottom cable car station. Both routes leave from Småstrandgaten in central Bergen, and the journey will take approximately 10 minutes.

Mount Ulriken Cable Car

FANTOFT STAVE CHURCH

Hidden away in a leafy suburb seven kilometers (4.3 miles) south of central Bergen, the remarkable **Fantoft Stave Church** (Fantoftvegen 38, tel. 55 28 07 10, 10:30am-6pm daily mid-May to mid-Sept., 55kr) has an equally remarkable history. Moved piece-by-piece from its original location outside the tiny village of Fortun in the Sogn region in 1883 to prevent demolition, the church was burned to the ground in 1992 as part of a series of church arsons by members of the early Norwegian black metal music scene.

Five years later, the church was rebuilt as close as possible to its original specifications, with planks, columns, and supports dovetailed or pegged together rather than joined with glue or nails.

The notable stylized dragon heads on the exterior are a result of the conflict between the original pagan beliefs of Norse mythology and the emerging Christianization of Norway when the church was originally built around the year 1150. The belief that dragons could keep evil spirits away was one Norse belief it was decided would be best not to risk ignoring.

The interior, which can seat just a handful of people, is kept dimly lit and features a small altar and some interesting Norse-inspired carvings. Outside the church stands an original stone cross from Tjora, near Stavanger.

Fantoft Stave Church is open from mid-May to mid-September and can be viewed free of charge from a viewing platform outside the perimeter fence. To get a closer look

Outside Bergen

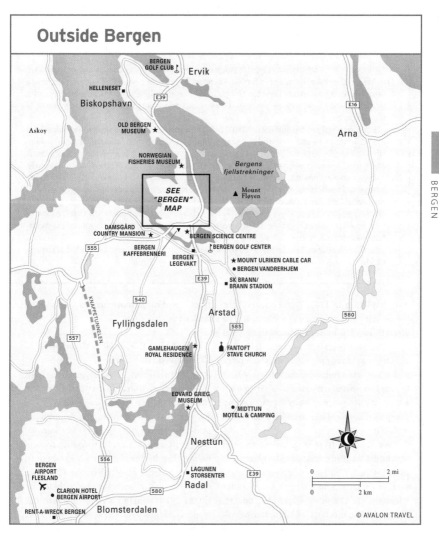

inside the perimeter fence and to look inside the church itself, you'll need to pay and, unusually for Norway, you'll need cash. The church is atop a hill and can only be accessed by a short yet very steep walk from either the Fantoft or Paradis stop on the Bergen Light Rail line. Although well worth a visit, it's unfortunately not an appropriate destination for those who find walking difficult, even if you drive to the car park.

EDVARD GRIEG MUSEUM

At the Troldhaugen country estate eight kilometers (five miles) south of Bergen, the **Edvard Grieg Museum** (Troldhaugvegen 65, tel. 55 92 29 92, www.griegmuseum.no, 9am-6pm daily May-Sept., 10am-4pm daily Oct.-Apr., 100kr) is a popular stop for music lovers the world over. The charming pastel-yellow villa was built in 1885, and Grieg lived here with his wife during the summers

Edvard Grieg, Master Composer

Although most Norwegians celebrate Norway's most famous composer as one of their own, in Bergen they take things a step further. Founded in 1765, the Bergen Philharmonic Orchestra once had Grieg as Artistic Director. Grieg's residence at Troldhaugen has become a popular tourist attraction and concert venue, and it also hosts an annual piano competition in honor of the composer.

Born in the city in the summer of 1843, Grieg struggled in school at any subject aside from music, although he still preferred to discover things for himself than follow any set curriculum. His musical education continued in Leipzig, Germany, where Grieg studied the work of Mozart and Beethoven while being exposed to the more contemporary styles of Schumann and Wagner.

After a stint in Copenhagen, where he became reacquainted with his first cousin, Nina Hagerup, who would soon become his wife, Grieg returned to Norway to help develop the music scene in the capital Oslo. After a tough period, Grieg moved to Troldhaugen and began working with the Norwegian author Bjørnstjerne Bjørnson and with playwright Henrik Ibsen. The latter collaboration would produce Grieg's most noted work, the score for *Peer Gynt*, which includes the world-famous *In the Hall of the Mountain King*.

Sadly, it was Grieg's success that led to his death from chronic exhaustion in 1907, at the age of 64.

until his death in 1907. Twenty years later, the building was reopened as a museum. The ground floor has been left almost untouched as a tribute to the master composer. His original Steinway piano from 1892 stands in place and is still used today for recordings. Along the rugged path down to the lake, Grieg built a modest hut to escape from distraction and composed some of his most famous works within it.

Every Sunday from mid-June to the end of August, evening recitals take place, featuring some of Norway's best-known classical musicians. The 250kr ticket includes admission to the villa before the concert. Daily piano concerts (160kr including admission) are held throughout the summer season at 1pm.

Inquire about concert tickets at the **Bergen Tourist Information Centre** (Strandkaien 3, tel. 55 55 20 00, 9am-8pm daily May-Sept., 9am-4pm Mon.-Sat. Oct.-Apr.), which also offers bus transportation to/from the concerts and a guided tour of Grieg's villa for an additional 100kr. Otherwise, Grieg's rural hideaway is awkward to reach without your own transport. The easiest way is to take the Bergen Light Rail to Hop station (22 minutes from downtown), from where it is a 20-minute walk to the museum.

DAMSGÅRD COUNTRY MANSION (Damsgård Hovegård)

A less-trafficked alternative to Grieg's Troldhaugen estate, **Damsgård Country Mansion** (Alleén 29, Laksevåg, tel. 47 97 95 84, www.bymuseet.no/en, noon-4pm daily mid-June through Aug., 80kr) is an exquisite example of 18th-century wooden rococo, believed to be the finest such example in Europe. Minster of War Joachim Christian Geelmuyden Gyldenkrantz built the estate in the 1770s, during a time in which the trend among Bergen's elite was to build or obtain luxurious countryside retreats, and as such is a shining example of how the wealthy used to live.

The fully restored ballroom, blue lounge, red cabinet, and the bedrooms gleam with color but can only be visited on a one-hour guided tour run at noon and 2pm. Visit on a sunny day to make the most of the rose gardens, with ponds, sculptures, and flora as they would have been two centuries ago, when the mansion played host to the noble Danish-Norwegian Gyldenkrantz.

To reach Damsgård, take bus route 16 or 17 from Olav Kyrres gate in downtown Bergen. Buses run every 15-30 minutes throughout the day and take less than 10 minutes to reach the estate. Alternatively, the estate can be reached in about 35 minutes on foot via the bridge that crosses the Damsgårdssundet sound, south of downtown.

GAMLEHAUGEN ROYAL RESIDENCE

Fans of such stately homes are spoiled in and around Bergen. The art nouveau exterior of the **Gamlehaugen Royal Residence** (Gamlehaugveien 10, tel. 53 00 51 15, www.gamlehaugen.no, 80kr) hides a medieval-style Norwegian interior that can only be visited on a one-hour guided tour. English-language tours run at noon on Tuesday, Thursday, Saturday, and Sunday June-August and should be booked in advance.

Still the king's official residence in Bergen, Gamlehaugen's appearance evokes the 16th-century rural castles of France's Loire Valley and is one of the city's most recognizable buildings. The contrast between the exterior and interior is highlighted by the rococo and neo-renaissance furniture of the entrance hall, music room, library, and winter garden. Built in 1899, the estate was originally home to shipowner and statesman Christian Michelsen, before being purchased by the state upon his death in 1925.

Five kilometers (3.1 miles) south of Bergen along Rv556 toward Fjøsanger, Gamlehaugen can be reached by public transit. Bus routes 51 and 67 both leave from Nordahl Bruns gate I in downtown Bergen and take around 10 minutes to reach Fjøsangerkrysset, from where it is a 10-minute walk to the estate.

North of Bergen
NORWEGIAN FISHERIES MUSEUM
(Norges Fiskerimuseum)

Just 1.5 kilometers (one mile) north of Bryggen is the **Norwegian Fisheries Museum** (Sandviksboder 23, tel. 53 00 61 80, http://fiskerimuseum.museumvest.no, 10am-5pm daily May-Sept., 11am-3pm Sat.-Sun.

Oct.-Apr., 90kr), set in beautifully preserved wharfside warehouses that are as good as anything at Bryggen. The setting alone is worth the price of admission, as the buildings, built on wooden foundations and surrounded by canals and a busy harbor, give a feel for what Bergen was like during medieval times.

The history of the Norwegian fishing industry is explored inside the timber walls, but the real fun is to be had outdoors. From mid-June to mid-August, two rowboats are available to rent for 100kr per hour, while children can fish for crabs and search for sea creatures using a free species map.

To reach the museum from downtown Bergen, take a pleasant 25-minute walk past Bryggen and through Bergenhus Fortress or combine your visit with a ride on Beffen, a delightful old wooden ferry. The 20-minute trip (daily mid-May to mid-Sept., 60kr) doubles as a sightseeing tour of historic Bergen, as you sail past Bryggen and the fortress on your way to the museum. The ferry leaves its Bryggen pier every 40 minutes from 10am and includes admission to the museum with a round-trip ticket (150kr). Alternatively, the museum is a five-minute bus ride from Torget in central Bergen on bus route 3, 4, or 5.

OLD BERGEN MUSEUM
(Gamle Bergen Museum)

A further 1.5 kilometers north of the city along the coastal road, the 40-or-so 18th- and 19th-century buildings making up the **Old Bergen Museum** (Nyhavnsveien 4, tel. 55 39 43 00, www.bymuseet.no/en, 9am-4pm daily mid-May to mid-Sept., 100kr) are only worth a visit if you haven't already visited one of the other outdoor museums elsewhere in Norway. Parts of Bergen are historic enough that the cobbled streets and wooden nostalgia don't have quite the same impact here as in more modern cities like Oslo.

The museum tells the story of Bergen in the 19th century, when it was Europe's biggest wooden city. Stroll the park and enjoy the historical atmosphere, or peek inside the windows and doors to meet actors playing the roles of masters and servants. Wealthy ship-builder Rasmus Rolfsen built the Elsesro summer house and English-style gardens next to the shipyard for his wife in the 18th century, while the other wooden buildings were moved from central Bergen in the 1950s and 1960s, once the site had become a museum.

SPORTS AND RECREATION

Tours

With the nickname Gateway to the Fjords, Bergen is the perfect starting point to explore the outstanding natural beauty of western Norway. Although a car opens up many options, those without their own transport can choose from many options from Bergen, from excursions of a couple of hours through to day trips or longer.

SIGHTSEEING BOAT TOURS

To experience Bergen from the water, **Rødne Fjord Cruise** (tel. 51 89 52 70, www. rodne.no) runs a **Bergen Sightseeing** tour (160kr) from the Zachariasbryggen pier next to the Fish Market. The vintage MS *White Lady* is your host as you take in the sights in and around Bergen's harbor, including the Bryggen wharf, Bergenhus Fortress, and the Old Bergen Museum, before exploring the Puddefjord on the other side of the city center. While this won't give you the spectacular fjord experience of the more expensive tours, it is nevertheless a good-value way to see the best of Bergen from a different perspective.

The same company offers one of the quickest ways to see a fjord with the three-hour **Osterfjord/Mostraumen Cruise.** While it lacks the dramatic cliffs of the Geirangerfjord or Nærøyfjord, the Osterfjord does get narrow around the waterfalls of Mostraumen and is a great way to see a natural fjord landscape if you are short on both time and money.

Tours leave year-round from the Zachariasbryggen pier twice daily at 10am and 2pm, with an extra 6pm evening departure added on select days during July and August.

Call ahead for winter departures (Nov.-Feb.), as tours are weather dependent. The trip costs 550kr (350kr under 16). A family ticket (two adults, two children) costs 1,500kr.

NUTSHELL TOURS

Although the **Norway in a Nutshell** (www. fjordtours.com) tour from Oslo can be horrifyingly busy in high season, taking the tour in the opposite direction and as a round-trip from Bergen can result in a much more pleasant experience. The tour can be customized, but typically you leave Bergen by train before 9am to Voss, take a bus through the lush valley to Gudvangen, from where you take a two-hour ferry trip along the Nærøyfjord and Aurlandsfjord. You have time for a quick lunch before making your way up the Flåm Railway and returning to Bergen by rail from Myrdal station (where the Flåm Railway connects with the Bergen Line) in time for dinner.

This self-guided tour is available daily year-round and starts at 1,620kr for a round-trip, or from 2,070kr for a one-way trip ending in Oslo. Because it's an entirely self-guided tour, you get tickets and an itinerary, but you are responsible for making all connections. There is no tour guide. **Hardangerfjord in a Nutshell** and **Sognefjord in a Nutshell** are also on offer at similar prices.

Hiking

There are many more mountains that surround Bergen, but the famous collection of seven peaks—Lyderhorn, Damsgårdsfjellet, Løvstakken, Ulriken, Fløyen, Rundemannen, and Sandviksfjellet—draws hikers from across the country to test themselves in an environment only usually available in more remote areas.

Serious hikers should contact **Bergen and Hordaland Trekking Association (Bergen og Hordaland Turlag)** (Tverrgaten 4-6, tel. 55 33 58 10, www.bergenoghorda-landturlag.no) in advance for detailed maps, itinerary advice, and information on cabins. Every year, the association runs a **7-Mountain Hike,** a 35-kilometer (21.7

Many of the Bergen area's best hiking routes start from Mount Fløyen.

miles) test of endurance for committed hikers, who receive a commemorative T-shirt for completing the route.

MOUNT FLØYEN

Mount Fløyen (425 meters/1,394 feet) is the starting point of so many hikes that it's not uncommon for the first Fløibanen Funicular journeys of weekend mornings to be packed with locals planning to spend the entire day up in the mountains.

The **best-known hike** is to/from **Mount Ulriken** (643 meters/2,110feet), popular because of the easy access at both ends. Most locals start the hike by taking the Mount Ulriken cable car and finish in the heart of downtown, thanks to the Fløibanen Funicular at the end of the walk, but it's possible to do the reverse journey, too. The 15-kilometer (9.3-mile) hike is moderate in difficulty, but loose rocks, mud, inclement weather, and its approximately five-hour duration make it more challenging for inexperienced hikers. Much of the trek covers high, open mountain

terrain, so dress appropriately and take plenty of food and water.

Many other **shorter hiking trails** are possible from Mount Fløyen and are described in detail on www.floyen.no and the information boards at the top of the funicular railway. An easy seven-kilometer (4.3 mile) round-trip hike to the **Aasebu and Brushytten cabins** is perfect for a quiet early morning or summer evening walk of approximately three hours. Cyclists are banned from this trail, which has been upgraded with woodchip to make it one of the more comfortable hikes in the area.

GUIDED HIKE

If navigation isn't your strongest point, you can still experience the forests of Mount Fløyen on a two-hour **guided hike** (11am Mon.-Fri. mid-June to mid-Aug., 350kr) bookable in advance at the **Bergen Tourist Information Centre** (Strandkaien 3, tel. 55 55 20 00, 9am-8pm daily May-Sept., 9am-4pm Mon.-Sat. Oct.-Apr.). The hike starts promptly from the Fløistuen Varmestue building at the top of the funicular, so be sure to arrive in plenty of time. An experienced mountain guide will take you on a moderate hike and discuss not just the forest, flora, and fauna, but also local culture and the Norwegian love of the outdoors.

Mountain Biking

The Fløistuen Varmestue building at the top of the Fløibanen Funicular is the destination for **mountain bike rental** (tel. 55 33 68 03, floyen.no, 10am-6pm May-Aug., 300kr for 3hrs, 400kr per day). These are good-quality hard-tailed mountain bikes suitable for the trails on and around Mount Fløyen. Check maps and signs carefully before you pick up a trail, as some are designated for use by pedestrians only. Mountain bikes can also be rented out of season with advance booking and subject to conditions.

Beaches

Helleneset is a popular ocean swimming spot 5 kilometers (3.1 miles) north of Bergen, accessible by local bus routes 5 and 6. Despite being promoted by the local tourist office as a beach, Helleneset's sandy area is actually very small, but the large rocky outcrop, diving boards, grassy areas, and a separate children's pool make this an enjoyable place to enjoy a summer's day.

Behind the Royal Residence 5 kilometers (3.1 miles) south of Bergen, the **Gamlehaugen** (Gamlehaugvegen) bathing area offers a small beach and large lawn for sunbathing. Swimming in the shallow waters is also possible here.

Skiing and Snowboarding

Although Bergen has a good network of cross-country ski trails, snowfall is unpredictable and renting cross-country gear not so easy. Instead head east to Voss, the winter sports capital of Norway. It's an easy 1.5-hour journey by road or railroad, so it makes an easy day or evening trip.

Swimming

The heated saltwater swimming pools of **Nordnes Sjøbad** (Nordnesparken 30, tel. 53 03 91 90, 7am-7pm Mon.-Fri., 7am-2pm Sat., 10am-2pm Sun., mid-May to mid-Sept. only, 75kr) throng with people on weekends but tend to be pleasantly quiet on weekdays. The outdoor complex is next to Bergen Aquarium and is easy to reach on foot (25 minutes from the Fish Market) or local bus route 11. On weekends with particularly good weather it will stay open until 7pm.

A free alternative within walking distance of central Bergen is the **Sydnes Sjøbad** (Nøstegaten), a bathing facility next to the Hurtigruten ferry terminal. This small enclosed space is the perfect solution for a quick dip, but it's not big enough to hold your interest for long.

Golf

Par-68 course **Bergen Golf Club (Bergen Golfklubb)** (Ervikveien 120, tel. 55 19 91 80, www.bgk.no), 9.3 kilometers (5.8 miles) north of the city, is the premier links for miles around. The club permits guests to play at certain times, but contact the club well in advance to check seasonal opening and reserve a spot. Greens fees for guests range 250-400kr.

Much closer to central Bergen and better suited to casual players, **Bergen Golf Center (Bergen Golfsenter)** (Klaus Hanssensvei 22, tel. 55 20 49 00, www.bgs.no, 10am-5pm Mon.-Fri., 10am-3pm Sat.) has an indoor driving range and HD simulator, allowing you to sharpen your skills year-round.

Spectator Sports

SOCCER

Very much the pride of Bergen despite their limited success in recent years, **SK Brann** (tel. 55 59 85 00, www.brann.no) plays its home games at the 17,500-capacity **Brann Stadion** (Kniksens Plass 1) at the foot of Mount Ulriken. With just one league title in 55 years, Brann is considered the sleeping giant of Norwegian football. Home games typically take place every other Sunday from April through October. Check the league standings in addition to the schedule, because if Brann is battling for a top three place, you'll need to book tickets well in advance. To fully appreciate the match-day atmosphere, ride the Bergen Light Rail from the city center to the stadium along with thousands of Brann fans.

AMERICAN FOOTBALL

One of the oldest American football teams in Norway, **Bergen Storm** (www.bergenstorm. no) has its home field at **Varden Kunstgress** (Allestadveien 12) in the Fyllingsdalen suburb, eight kilometers (five miles) southwest of central Bergen. Local bus route 31 brings you to the neighboring Varden Amfi shopping mall.

ENTERTAINMENT AND EVENTS

Nightlife

LIVE MUSIC

Much of the best of Bergen's nightlife centers on the live music scene. From the constant references to famed composer Edvard Grieg to a plethora of live music venues, you'll soon discover how loud and proud the Bergenese are about their fine musical heritage. Some international acts even pick Bergen over Oslo on European tours—such is the reputation the city has in music circles.

One of the liveliest venues is **USF Verftet** (Georgernes Verft 12, tel. 55 30 74 10, www. usf-verftet.no), a striking brick sardine cannery turned arts, film, and music center. Artists across all genres perform most Friday and Saturday nights and selected weekdays, while films and art shows run throughout midweek.

Another venue to catch a touring band or a show is the centrally located **Ole Bull Scene** (Øvre Ole Bulls plass 3, tel. 55 32 11 45, www.olebullhuset.no), with lesser-known and unsigned artists likely to feature in the smaller room, named **Lille Ole Bull**. Bergen's best pub for lovers of rock music is **Garage** (Christiesgate 14, tel. 55 32 19 80, www.garage. no, 3pm-3am daily), where you can enjoy a local beer to a heavy rock soundtrack, or venture downstairs to check out one of Bergen's hottest unsigned bands.

For a more informal experience, one of Bryggen's old wharf buildings is the home of **Sjøboden** (Bryggen 29, tel. 55 31 67 77, www.sjoboden-bergen.no, 7pm-2:30am daily), which presents local live music every night of the week. Free entry and one of the city's largest range of beers create a lively atmosphere most nights, especially for the Monday night jam sessions.

BARS AND CLUBS

The Bergenese tend to stay late in bars and restaurants rather than move on to dedicated nightclubs. That said, the cozy **No Stress** (Hollendergaten 11, tel. 93 83 31 12, 5pm-2am Sun.-Thurs., 5pm-3am Fri.-Sat.) is a cocktail bar of mismatched furniture and colorful murals where you'll be lucky to snag a table even early in the evening. The bar replaced a streetwear store, and this is reflected in the design and hip-hop soundtrack.

The multicolored retro charm of **BarBarista** (Oevregaten 12, tel. 46 94 07 34, noon-midnight Sun.-Thurs., noon-1am Fri.-Sat.) is well worth seeking out. Tucked away behind the Bryggen wharf, the cramped bar is a walk down memory lane with chairs, lamps, tables, parasols, and posters from across the decades and across the world. It's perfect for an afternoon coffee and waffle or a pre-dinner drink.

Performing Arts
THEATERS

The history of the grand **National Theater (Den Nationale Scene)** (Engen 1, tel. 55 54 97 00, www.dns.no) stretches back to the time of playwright Henrik Ibsen, who was one of the first writers-in-residence and art directors of the theater. Alongside minor productions, jazz concerts, and comedy shows, the resident company presents around 20 major performances every year of both Norwegian and international classics.

It's impossible to miss the sharp angular lines of **Grieghallen** (Edvard Griegs plass 1, tel. 55 21 61 00, www.grieghallen.no), best known for hosting the 1986 Eurovision Song Contest. The venue hosts concerts, theater productions, and international ballet throughout the year.

CINEMA

Consisting of 13 screens across two buildings, **Bergen kino** (Neumanns gate 3, tel. 55 56 90 50, www.bergenkino.no) is downtown Bergen's only cinema, so advance bookings are essential for weekend screenings and recommended throughout the week. All films are shown in their native language with Norwegian subtitles, so you needn't miss out on the latest releases during your visit.

Festivals and Events
BERGEN INTERNATIONAL FESTIVAL
Festspillene i Bergen

Although classical music and theater are the main themes of the two-week-long **Bergen International Festival** (www.fib.no), visitors can enjoy art in all its guises, including live music, dance, opera, and visual art. The whole region comes out to play for the 250 events held across 20 venues in late May and early June. Tickets are sold for individual events and should be booked in advance to avoid disappointment.

MUSIC FESTIVALS

Hot on the heels of the Bergen International Festival comes **Bergenfest** (www.bergenfest. no), a more contemporary music festival that aims to showcase local Norwegian acts alongside international stars. Held over four days at the Bergenhus Fortress in mid-June, major acts such as Patti Smith and Robert Plant are spread out across the lineup, making single day tickets a popular purchase. Expect to pay 2,000-2,500kr for a full festival pass depending on how far in advance you order.

The longest-running jazz event in northern Europe, **Natt Jazz** (www.nattjazz.no) is a collection of concerts spread over two weekends and the week in between that blur the lines between traditional jazz, electronica, folk, and rock. The lineup is announced on a rolling basis, and tickets are purchased for individual concerts rather than the festival itself. The festival is usually held around the end of May.

Veering from contemporary into experimental territory, **Borealis** (www.borealisfestival.no) is one of Bergen's most interesting and varied festivals. Claiming to celebrate music that "falls between the gaps," Borealis takes the live music experience to different venues, from art galleries to warehouse spaces. Run by a board of 16 music societies, galleries, and venues, the five-day festival is held in early March and puts out a 24/7 live stream called *Radio Space* throughout the month. Festival passes and tickets for individual events are available and should be purchased online in advance.

OTHER FESTIVALS

Second in size to Oslo, **Bergen Gay Pride (Regnbuedagene)** (www.bergenpride. no) has nevertheless grown substantially in recent years. Held over a week in early June, the festival covers political debates, art shows, concerts, films, and nightclub events before culminating in a colorful parade through the city's streets on the final weekend.

Held annually in late September, the weeklong **Bergen International Film Festival (Bergen Internasjonale Filmfestival)** (www.biff.no) brings some of the world's most cutting-edge documentary films to cinemas across the city. Tickets can be purchased for individual shows, although the lineup tends to be announced only a few weeks beforehand.

Local farmers from across Hordaland county and along the Sognefjord bring their wares to the city for a weekend in early September for the annual **Bergen Food Festival (Bergen Matfestival)** (www.matfest.no), where you can sample the region's best honey, cheese, meat, and seafood. In recent years, some of Bergen's finest restaurants have also set up stalls to give you a sample of what's on offer from their kitchens. Children have their own section of the festival arena, while adults can enjoy the accompanying Beer Festival (Ølfestival), all held within the grounds of Bergenhus Fortress.

If you happen to be visiting Bergen in the run-up to Christmas, don't miss the **Gingerbread Town (Pepperkakebyen)** (www.pepperkakebyen.org), the world's largest such event. Kindergartens, schools, businesses, and thousands of individuals have contributed to the annual festival at the heart of Bergen since its creation in 1991. Expect Bergen in miniature: houses, trains, cars, and ships made from real gingerbread, and of course, plenty of opportunities to buy gingerbread, too. The town is created inside Sentralbadet (Teatergaten 37) and runs daily from mid-November through the end of the year. An entrance fee of around 90kr applies for adults, but children under 12 go free.

CONSTITUTION DAY

As with the rest of Norway, one of the biggest events of the year in Bergen is **Constitution Day (Nasjonaldagen)** on May 17, which most Norwegians refer to simply by the date, *syttende mai*. Being in Bergen on this day is a double-edged sword. On the one hand, the colorful parades, marching bands, and celebratory atmosphere are infectious, but almost all shops are closed, and those few restaurants that aren't booked up will be even more expensive than usual.

The day begins early (around 7am) with a 21-gun salute and a parade of local community groups at around 10am, which merges with a parade of school bands from across the city before ending at the main festival site at the Lille Lungegårdsvannet lake. Various activities take place throughout the afternoon before a torchlight procession and fireworks in the evening. Exact times can vary each year, so check with any hotel reception for the latest information.

SHOPPING
Bryggen

Amid the usual tourist trap stores selling anything and everything that can have Norway stamped on it, Bryggen does actually offer some unique souvenirs inside its crooked houses and narrow alleyways. In particular, clothes from Dale of Norway and Oleana, along with Norwegian silver, are popular gift choices.

The festive **Julehuset** (Holmedalsgården 1, tel. 55 21 51 00, 10am-5pm Mon.-Fri., 10am-4pm Sat.) draws crowds year-round with its collection of brightly painted wooden toys and decorations. Pick up a soft *julenisse*, a traditional Scandinavian Christmas pixie, for a truly Nordic addition to your own Christmas decor. **Bryggen Husflid** (Bryggen 19, tel. 55 32 88 03, www.sweaterspecialist.com, 9am-9pm daily) carries hand-knitted Norwegian sweaters, woolen jackets, Røros tweed blankets, wooden carvings, and reindeer skins among its range of more typical souvenirs, while the intimate **Elg** (Bryggen 11, tel. 55 21 54 88, 11am-6pm Mon.-Sat., noon-6pm Sun., mid-June to mid-Aug. only) stocks colorful moose-themed clothes and souvenirs.

Just behind Bryggen next to St. Mary's Church is the working outlet store of **Arven** (Sandbrogaten 11, tel. 55 55 14 00, www.arven. no, 10am-4pm Mon.-Thurs., 10am-7pm Fri., 10am-4pm Sat., June-Sept. only), a local manufacturer of gold and silver stretching back to 1868. As a member of the global Économusée network of traditional artisans, its quality is assured. Its silver cutlery is especially popular with Norwegian families, with the beautiful *Stork* brand of children's cutlery and trinkets making an excellent gift.

Marken

Together with Bryggen, the cobbled street Marken that links Bergen railway station with the central area is the city's best shopping destination. The boutiques here skew more toward fashion and interiors.

The delightful **De små gleder** (Marken 23, tel. 95 87 87 10, www.desmagleder.no, 10am-5pm Mon.-Fri., 10:30am-5:30pm Sat.) translates as The Small Pleasures, an appropriate name for a retro store filled to the brim with modern clothing and pastel trinkets. Immediately next door, **Kattens vern** (Marken 25, tel. 55 36 58 65, www.kattens-vern.org, noon-4pm Mon.-Sat.) is a charity store perfect for bargain-hunting pet lovers. All monies spent support the care and rehoming of homeless cats in Bergen. Cat ornaments, dolls, and T-shirts are among the goods on offer. Farther up the street, the factory outlet store **Marken Bazaar** (Marken 7, 10am-5pm Mon.-Sat.) stocks women's fashions with a particular focus on South Asian saris and accessories.

Shopping Malls

Bergen's indoor malls are mostly clustered around the wide Torgallmenningen pedestrian boulevard and the Lille Lungegårdsvann lake. The most central is **Galleriet** (Torgallmenningen 8, tel. 55 30 05 00, 9am-9pm Mon.-Fri., 9am-6pm Sat.), with an abundance of main-street stores, while there is more of a fashion focus in the stores within **Bergen Storsenter** (Strømgaten 8, tel. 55 21 24 60, www.bergenstorsenter.no, 9am-9pm

Mon.-Fri., 9am-6pm Sat.), handily located between the city's train and bus stations.

The biggest shopping mall in the region, **Lagunen Storsenter** (Laguneveien 1, Rådal, tel. 55 11 74 00, www.lagunen.no, 10am-9pm Mon.-Fri., 10am-6pm Sat.) is 12.5 kilometers (7.8 miles) south of the city and not worth a special visit from Bergen. It is, however, a useful stopping point for those driving in or out of the city on the E39 to/from Stavanger and Haugesund because of the large number of shops, restaurants, and services.

FOOD

Bryggen

CAFÉS AND LIGHT BITES

For those who value dedication to coffee over fancy interiors, the award-winning baristas of **Kaffemisjonen** (Øvre Korskirkealmenning 5, tel. 98 81 96 11, 7:30am-6pm Mon.-Fri., 10am-6pm Sat.-Sun.) attract a crowd of people who know their Kenyan Karinga from their Ethiopian Konga. Homemade pastries and cakes make this sleek modern coffeehouse a top choice for a leisurely late breakfast or afternoon treat, although you must do battle with the laptop brigade for a table. Run by the same people, **Blom** (John Lunds plass 1, 8am-5pm Mon.-Fri., 10am-5pm Sat.) is an equally fine choice if you are visiting the museums near the university campus southwest of downtown.

Tucked away in the narrow lanes of Bryggen, **Bastant** (Jacobsfjorden 4, tel. 40 07 22 47, 11am-5pm daily) is a welcome alternative to the pricier options in the more trafficked parts of the wharf. Grab a hearty bowl of soup for around 125kr or one of the excellent nut-packed brownies to enjoy alongside a fragrant espresso. There are always good vegetarian and vegan options on the soup and sandwich menu, too.

Escape completely from the crowds of Bryggen by seeking out **Det Lille Kaffekompaniet** (Nedre Fjeldsmau 2, tel. 55 31 67 20, 10am-8pm Mon.-Fri., 10am-6pm Sat.-Sun.), nestled in a delightful cobbled residential street just above the lower stop of the

Fløibanen Funicular. The hyper-knowledgeable staff focus on drip-brewed coffee for a superior taste, with Aeropress or French press methods also available on request. It's one of Norway's smallest coffee shops, you're unlikely to snag a table, but a stroll around the surrounding neighborhood is just as enticing.

TRADITIONAL SCANDINAVIAN

If you're prepared to pay for the experience, **To Kokker** (Enhjørningsgården 29, tel. 55 30 69 55, 5pm-11pm Mon.-Sat., 340kr) serves dishes of red deer, catfish, and steamed halibut in an atmosphere that simply oozes history from its red wooden beams and landscape paintings. The sister to fish-focused Enhjørningen, this restaurant has more choice and more seating and just as authentic an atmosphere.

Serving the most authentic dishes in town, **Bryggeloftet & Stuene** (Bryggen 11, tel. 55 30 20 70, www.bryggeloftet.no, 11am-11pm Mon.-Sat., 1pm-11pm Sun.) offers bland and heavily salted dishes, with mounds of bread and potatoes on the side. Most house specials are acquired tastes, in particular the lutefisk (cod treated with lye then boiled) and salted meat with dumplings. Its elderly clientele has been coming for decades, and they do lend the place a certain charm. Perfect if you value tradition over taste.

NEW NORDIC

Bookings are essential for the formal dining experience of **1877** (Vetrlidsallmenningen 2, tel. 92 87 18 77, www.restaurant1877.no, 6pm-9pm Mon.-Sat., also noon-4pm Sat.), set amid the brick, wood, and brass of the old market hall next to the Hanseatic Museum. The popular five-course set menu (725kr) featuring shellfish, fish, meat, cheese, and desserts changes every six weeks but always includes local flavors such as rhubarb, strawberries, and cherries.

SEAFOOD

Locally caught fish dominates the menu at **Enhjørningen** (Enhjørningsgården 29, tel. 55 30 69 50, www.enhjorningen.no, 4pm-11pm

Mon.-Sat., 340kr), easily identifiable thanks to the unicorn sculpture leaping out of the wooden facade. The interior has been carefully restored to its 18th-century splendor, complete with garish walls and creaky floorboards. The salads are equally colorful, with generous helpings of fresh vegetables, but the real star of the show is the fish. The steamed halibut and baked salmon are the tastiest choices, but if you can't decide, order the Fish Duo for a taste of both.

ASIAN

Japanese fusion, sushi, and fresh citrus cocktails all feature on the vast inventive menu from **Nama** (Lodin Lepps gate 2b, tel. 55 32 20 10, www.namasushi.no, 1pm-11pm daily). As tempting as the familiar sushi or noodle dishes are, order from the fusion menu to sample outstanding Norwegian-Japanese creations, including king crab with coconut and lemon jelly, or clams cooked on the *robata* grill and served up with *shiso* pesto and ginger foam.

The lightly spiced curries at **Maharaja** (Rosenkrantzgaten 5, tel. 55 31 25 55, www.maharajas.no, 3pm-11pm Mon.-Fri., 3pm-midnight Sat., 2pm-10pm Sun., 220kr) are authentic despite the heat levels being adjusted for the Norwegian palate. The service, much like the bland interior, is far from perfect, but it makes the cut because of its excellent range of vegetarian options, a rarity in this part of Norway.

MEXICAN

In the ground floor of the Hanseatic Hotel, **Casa del Toro** (Rosenkrantzgate 6, tel. 55 55 03 10, casa@finnegaarden.no, 4pm-10pm Mon.-Fri., 3pm-10pm Sat.-Sun., 219kr) serves American-style Mexican food, from homemade nacho chips through to juicy steaks. Most patrons opt for the filling burritos or enchiladas, served with generous sides of rice, corn, and vegetables. The service is somewhat informal considering the price.

Central Bergen
CAFÉS AND LIGHT BITES

The filling sandwiches at **Smakverket** (Rasmus Meyers allé 3, tel. 92 24 91 04, 11am-5pm daily) make a perfect quick lunch for those spending the day at Bergen Art Museum. Alternatively, make an afternoon of it by sampling the bustling art café's wine list, most of which is served by the glass.

If your destination is the museums on the university campus, take an extra few minutes to walk to the vast **Bergen Kaffebrenneri** (Thormøhlens gate 45, tel. 92 01 34 69, www.bergenkaffebrenneri.no, 8am-6pm Mon.-Fri., noon-6pm Sat.-Sun.), an independent roastery and coffee bar set in a former shipyard. You'll soon forget the run-down industrial setting as the strong aroma of freshly roasted beans hits you the moment you open the door. Hungry? Their famed dumpster pizza is topped with leftover vegetables from local restaurants that would otherwise go to waste.

TRADITIONAL SCANDINAVIAN

Pingvinen (Vaskerelven 14, tel. 55 60 46 46, www.pingvinen.no, noon-3am daily, 250kr) is known for its beer and rowdy late-night bar, but earlier in the day it's a popular place to chew on generous helpings of traditional Norwegian dishes such as meatballs or lamb stew. This is the food your grandmother made, if she were Norwegian. The food doesn't touch the quality of some other Bergen establishments, but for a taste of a hearty traditional meal you can do a lot worse.

The dark wood-paneled interior of **Wesselstuen** (Øvre Ole Bulls plass 6, tel. 55 55 49 49, 11am-midnight Mon.-Sat., 2pm-11pm Sat., 309kr) evokes memories of a Bergen long since gone. Traditional dishes of reindeer steaks and stockfish stew served by polite well-dressed staff who may have actually come from that era complete the illusion. It's an expensive option, but few places will give a more authentic experience of a traditional Norwegian dining hall.

NEW NORDIC

Although located in Bergen Art Museum, ★ **Lysverket** (Rasmus Meyers allé 9, tel. 55 60 31 00, www.lysverket.no, 11am-1am Tues.-Sat., 11am-5pm Mon.) is no mere after-thought, and booking is required to secure a table. Founders include Fredrik Saroea from local band Datarock and gold-toothed chef Christopher Haatuft, who spent years honing his craft in New York City and brought some of that attitude back to what has become one of the city's places to be seen. The sleek cock-tail bar is separated from the dining room by a wall covered in sheep's wool, but your focus will soon switch to the modern Nordic menu, likely featuring scallops and stockfish. Choose from the four-course (695kr) or mon-ster eight-course tasting menu (895kr).

Combining a single-minded focus on in-gredients from around the west Norwegian fjords with a tapas serving style, **Bare Vestland** (Vaagsallmenningen 2, tel. 91 90 04 56, www.barevestland.no, 4pm-10pm Mon.-Wed., noon-10pm Thurs., noon-11pm Fri.-Sat., 3pm-9pm Sun.) is a great choice to appreciate a range of local flavors all within one meal. Expect crispy flatbreads, smoked mackerel, local fish, beer-braised stew, and a cheese selection. Four plates run 400kr.

SEAFOOD

Munch on everything from shrimp baguettes to fish cakes at the aromatic **Bergen Fish Market** (Torget, 7am-7pm daily June-Aug., 7am-4pm Mon.-Sat. Sept.-May), which focuses more on fast-food style meals to eat at covered picnic tables over a traditional fish market. The selection varies by season, and most stall-holders will compose a plate of your own de-sign, although a simple dish of shrimp served with bread and butter is a timeless favorite. Expect to pay 150-200kr for a pre-composed plate, less for individual items. Expensive, but you won't find fresher seafood in all of Bergen.

AMERICAN

Inside Live & Rock Cafe (Vaskerelvsmauet 7, tel. 55 90 19 00, inside@insiderock.no,

Bergen Fish Market serves fast food alongside the day's fresh catch.

2pm-10:30pm Mon.-Tues., 2pm-1am Wed.-Thurs., noon-3am Fri.-Sat., noon-10:30pm Sun., 159-199kr) serves a tantalizing range of burgers in a lively rock-and-roll setting. The Orgasmatron with pineapple and honey mus-tard and the Antarctica with local blue cheese are popular choices. The 1.6-kilogram Suicide Solution, complete with wedges, costs 666kr—or nothing if you can finish it within an hour. Book in advance to take the challenge.

ASIAN

The popularity of great-value soup specialist ★ **Zupperia** (Vaskerelven 12, tel. 55 55 81 14, www.zupperia.no, noon-midnight Mon.-Sat., 2pm-10pm Sun., 109-169kr) has seen the Bergen institution expand to four venues across the city. The Vaskerelven branch is your best chance of snagging a table to enjoy the Asian-inspired menu, although the reindeer soup is a perennial—and worthy—traveler fa-vorite. Allow plenty of time because the ser-vice is notoriously slow.

The excellent lunchtime deals at **China**

Palace (Torgallmenningen 3a, enter on Strandgaten, tel. 55 21 28 38, noon-11pm Mon.-Sat., 1pm-11pm Sun.) are filling thanks to the mound of steamed rice served with all plates. The stars of the expanded evening menu include the hot-pots and crispy duck. But what you'll remember most about China Palace is the lavish red and gold interior complete with paper lanterns and fish pond. Ask for a window seat for a bird's-eye view of the busy Torgallmenningen pedestrian street below.

ITALIAN
For authentic pizza, look no further than the Italian-run Da Stefano (Strandgaten 96, tel. 55 24 24 44, 10am-10pm Mon.-Sat., noon-9pm Sun., 149-189kr), which transforms from a busy delicatessen by day to an outstanding restaurant by night that wouldn't look out of place on the streets of Naples. Don't overindulge on dough, though, as it would be a terrible shame to miss out on the excellent tiramisu or authentic gelato desserts that Da Stefano is known for.

VEGETARIAN
Surprisingly in a city of this size, vegetarians and vegans will struggle to find a restaurant with more than one suitable option anywhere in Bergen. Indian, Chinese, and Thai restaurants tend to offer the greatest variety of vegetarian dishes on their menus.

Although far from exclusively vegetarian, Horn of Africa (Strandgaten 212, tel. 95 42 52 50, 5pm-10pm Tues.-Sun., 179kr) is widely known as a good vegetarian hangout. The liberally spiced vegetarian platters (419-499kr, can include beef cubes and chicken stew on request) showcase the best of authentic Ethiopian cuisine just a 15-minute walk from Bergen Fish Market. Meat-eaters have many options, and the location on the Nordnes peninsula makes it an ideal stop for those heading back from the Bergen Aquarium.

ACCOMMODATIONS
Finding good value accommodations in central Bergen can be a challenge because hotels are often block-booked by tour companies. Prices on weekends outside July can be much lower than stated here. Advance booking is essential for all price ranges.

Bryggen
500-1,000KR
Located in the residential Skuteviken neighborhood just above Bryggen, the Skuteviken Guesthouse (Skutevikens smalgang 11, tel. 93 46 71 63, www.skutevikenguesthouse.com, 900kr d, 1,050kr t) is actually a collection of five high-standard apartments in a traditional wooden home. Ideal for independent couples or those valuing flexibility, each apartment is tastefully decorated and equipped with a kitchenette and basic utensils.

1,000-2,000KR
The stunning Hanseatic Hotel (Finnegaarden 2a, tel. 55 30 48 00, www.dethanseatiskehotell.no, 1,295kr) is the best choice to continue your Bryggen experience through the night. Each one of the cozy 37 rooms is completely unique, with decor ranging from elegant light shades through to a contemporary take on a traditional country cabin. Unfortunately, its 300-year-old wooden walls don't prevent the sound of a lively Friday or Saturday night seeping in from the streets below, so light sleepers may prefer to look elsewhere. The hotel's stylish FG Bar (6pm-1am Tues.-Fri., 4pm-1am Sat.) evokes the atmosphere of a gentlemen's club and is a popular spot for an after-dinner cocktail.

The best of the chain hotels along Bryggen is the Hotel Havnekontoret (Slottsgaten 1, tel. 55 60 11 00, 1,695kr d) from Clarion Collection. A substantial breakfast buffet, a light evening meal (usually a soup or stew), and free hot drinks and fruit available around the clock mean the hotel is better value than many of its competition. The neoclassical stone building at the end of the wharf hides a fashionable interior, with warm tones and large windows creating an inviting atmosphere throughout the hotel, while a quiet library lounge and a sauna will help you relax after a day's fjording.

Central Bergen

UNDER 500KR

If you just need a place to rest your head with the absolute minimum of services, the self-service **Piano Hostel** (Kong Oscars gate 48, tel. 92 88 12 46, www.pianohostel.no, 200kr) has converted a former two-bedroom apartment into basic accommodations for 12. Conditions are cramped but you won't find cheaper. Popular with eastern European backpackers, the hostel must be booked in advance and is a good place to mix with a diverse range of travelers. Basic kitchen and bathroom facilities are available, but be prepared to wait for a power socket and a shower.

Mere seconds from the railway station, the **Intermission Hostel** (Kalfarveien 8, tel. 55 30 04 00, www.intermissionhostel.no, mid-June to mid-Aug., 200kr) is geared toward the young and the social. The 39 beds are crammed into one giant dormitory of triple bunks. Despite this lack of privacy, the hostel has attracted regulars from around the world who return every summer. A positive attitude and a smile are essential if you book a bed here, with new friends from across the world guaranteed.

The city's most stylish hostel, **Marken Gjestehus** (Kong Oscars gate 45, tel. 55 31 44 04, www.marken-gjestehus.com, 260kr), is also the best equipped, with workspaces, reading lights, and lockable storage units in every dorm room. The largest 10-bed dorm even has its own private bathroom. A large TV lounge, kitchen, and laundry are available for all guests. Near-hotel standard private rooms run 575-960kr. The hostel is open year-round, although reception hours are limited to 9am-4pm from October to April.

500-1,000KR

Much improved after a rushed launch, **CityBox Bergen** (Nygårdsgaten 31, tel. 55 31 25 00, www.citybox.no, 450kr s, 600kr d, 800kr t) has finally completed its renovations and is now a good choice for centrally located economy accommodations. Rooms are larger than you'd expect for the price range but with very basic furnishings. All rooms have a private bathroom or one shared with just one other room. The only drawback is the lack of a reception if anything goes wrong overnight. Check-in is done by machine.

1,000-2,000KR

The unique ambience of the **Hotel Oleana** (Øvre Ole Bulls plass 5, tel. 55 21 58 70, 1,320kr s, 1,420kr d) hits you as soon as you step inside the lobby. Bright funky furniture and liberal use of plants give a modern elegance to the public areas, while the decor turns sensual in the larger bedrooms as the dim lighting, deep purple shades, and semi-exposed shower seem designed to encourage romance. Some of the rooms on higher floors are much smaller and more basic in design.

Despite the historical nature of Bergen, many of the city's hotels are located inside unremarkable modern buildings. Not so the 19th-century **Hotel Park** (Harald Hårfagresgate 35, tel. 55 54 44 00, www.hotelpark.no, 1,190kr d), whose 33 rooms spread over two buildings are all individually designed with simple elegance dominating. The hotel is a short walk from central Bergen but up a hill, so bear this in mind if you have luggage. Don't miss the delicious homemade brownies served during the afternoon. The smell will alert you when they're ready!

An alternative choice for a historical stay is the ★ **Grand Hotel Terminus** (Zander Kaaes gate 6, tel. 55 21 25 00, www.grandterminus.no, 1,250kr d), located slightly outside central Bergen beside the railway station. It's known across Norway for its well-stocked oak-walled whiskey bar, and the hotel's elegant architecture and photography on the walls recall memories of the Arctic explorers and Norwegian royalty who have stayed here throughout its proud history. Perfectly complementing the atmosphere of the public areas, the 131 elegant rooms are lifted by bright cushions and bedding. If your time in Bergen in short, take advantage of the free cycle rental to zip down to Bryggen in a matter of minutes.

On the grounds of the former monastery on the Nordnes peninsula, the **Klosterhagen Hotel** (Strangehagen 2, tel. 53 00 22 00, 1,495kr) is a good choice for those arriving or leaving on the Hurtigruten ferry. The contemporary en suite rooms and bright breakfast room are in stark contrast to the traditional exterior and historical neighborhood outside. Continuing the tradition of the monastery, items for the hotel's breakfast buffet are sourced from local farms. The only downside is that the 15 rooms tend to book out well in advance, but if you do secure a room you can expect personal attention from the staff.

Outside Bergen

When the central hostels are fully booked, look to **Bergen Vandrerhjem** (Johan Blytts vei 30, tel. 55 20 80 70, bergen.montana@hihostels.com), also known as the Montana Youth Hostel, on the hillside of Mount Ulriken (bus 12 from downtown Bergen). Accommodation options vary from en suite private rooms for one to four (715-1,345kr), family rooms (945kr), and, from May to August only, a bed in a small or large dormitory (220-310kr). The diverse range of accommodations attracts a diverse clientele, from backpackers and job seekers right through to families traveling on a budget, especially during the off-season, when prices are around 25 percent lower. An unlimited breakfast buffet is included with all accommodations, although an extra charge is applied if you want to make up a packed lunch.

An industrial suburb is a strange setting for a campground, but **Midttun Motell & Camping** (Midtunheia 3, tel. 55 10 39 00, www.mmcamp.no) offers a great value option for longer stays. Having your own car is preferable, although the Bergen Light Rail is a 20-minute walk away in Nesttun. Open year-round, the 32 basic motel rooms are all equipped with a basic kitchenette and a private bathroom. Camping is permitted from 190kr per night.

By the Airport

The contemporary **Clarion Hotel Bergen Airport** (Flyplassvegen 551, tel. 56 10 00 00, cl.bergen.airport@choice.no, 1,795kr s, 1,995kr d) is packed with modern art and offers outstanding runway views from most of its 200 rooms. It's often booked solid during the week with conferences and business travelers, but occupancy and prices plummet by up to 50 percent on weekends. With early morning "grab-and-go" breakfasts available and a staff with thorough knowledge of airport procedures, this hotel is a great option for those with an early flight out of Bergen.

INFORMATION AND SERVICES
Visitor Information

Despite its prominent location behind the Fish Market, finding **Bergen Tourist Information Centre** (Strandkaien 3, tel. 55 55 20 00, 9am-8pm daily May-Sept., 9am-4pm Mon.-Sat. Oct.-Apr.) is something that trips up many visitors, who end up in a seafood restaurant. To reach the office, you need to take the staircase or elevator to the left of the building entrance.

Most travelers use this office to book tours, including local fjord tours and the popular Norway in a Nutshell itineraries. Tickets for rail journeys throughout Norway and local concerts can also be bought here, along with a selection of postcards and simple souvenirs. The office gets very busy at peak times, so plan to visit as early as possible in the day.

Post Offices and Courier Services

The main **Bergen Post Office (Postkontor)** (Småstrandgaten 3, 9am-6pm Mon.-Fri., 10am-3pm Sat.) is centrally located between the Fish Market and the Lille Lungegårdsvannet city lake. For basic needs, all souvenir shops on the Bryggen wharf that stock postcards will sell international postage stamps from the counter. Ask for the nearest postbox, as they can be hard to find.

Internet Access

All hotels, most hostels, and the majority of coffee shops and cafés offer free high-speed Internet to their patrons. For a more dedicated workspace and access to PC terminals with print/copy/scan/fax facilities, the central **Bergen Library (Bergen Offentlige Bibliotek)** (Strømgaten 6, tel. 55 56 85 00, 8:30am-8pm Mon.-Thurs., 8:30am-5pm Fri., 10am-4pm Sat., noon-4pm Sun.) is cheaper and more secure than an Internet café.

Money

Almost all banks in Bergen follow similar opening hours. Typically, they will close by 4pm weekdays, and most do not open at all on weekends.

ATMs inside bank branches are usually accessible when the branch is closed. Alternatively, most branches of 7-Eleven and Narvesen will have an ATM (minibank), but these charge at least 20kr on top of your own bank's charges.

Urgent Health Care

The city's main **emergency room (Bergen legevakt)** (Solheimsgaten 9, tel. 55 56 87 00) is always open but with a reduced overnight service 10pm-8am. Take the Bergen Light Rail to Danmarksplass and cross the main E39 highway. Wait times can be long, so call ahead for an appointment and/or advice. In a medical emergency, always call for an ambulance on 113.

Pharmacies

The closest pharmacy to the Bryggen wharf is **Boots apotek** (Vetrlidsalmenningen 11, tel. 56 12 54 00, 9am-5pm Mon.-Sat., 10am-4pm Sun.). Branches of Apotek1 are located throughout central Bergen, but for evening or Sunday service, head to **Vitusapotek Nordstjernen** (Strømgaten 8, tel. 55 21 83 84, 8am-11pm Mon.-Sat., 1pm-11pm Sun.) in the Bergen Storsenter shopping mall, next to Bergen railway station.

Dental Services

For urgent dental care, **Sentrum Dental** (Markeveien 4c, tel. 55 60 66 77, www.sentrumdental.no, 8am-4pm Mon.-Fri.) and **Tannklinikken i Dreggen** (Dreggsallmenningen 10, tel. 55 31 72 10, www.tannklinikken-as.no) both offer online booking and emergency care options on weekends.

GETTING THERE

Car

With the vast majority of Norway's international visitors arriving at Oslo Airport Gardermoen, renting a car and driving directly to Bergen is a popular option. It would be a terrible mistake to plan the 476-kilometer (296 miles) drive along the E16 and Route 7 in one go, as you would miss out on spectacular mountain scenery and some of Norway's best fjords within easy reach. Sensible places to plan an overnight stop include ski resort **Voss** and one of the small villages on the inner reaches of the Hardangerfjord, such as **Eidfjord.**

If you are driving to Bergen along the E39, the highway that links Bergen with the major coastal towns to the north and south, plan additional time to take into account the time you will spend waiting for ferries. For example, the Sandvikvåg to Halhjem crossing between Stavanger and Bergen takes 40 minutes, but you could be waiting up to 45 minutes for a departure.

Air

Having recently undergone a desperately needed overhaul, **Bergen Airport Flesland** (Flyplassvegen 555, tel. 67 03 15 55) is now an airport worthy of Norway's second biggest city. The brand-new terminal 18 kilometers (11 miles) southwest of central Bergen welcomes a handful of international flights, but you are more likely to arrive on a domestic connection from Oslo. Bear in mind when transferring onto a domestic flight to Bergen from an international arrival at Oslo, you are required to collect your bags to clear customs in Oslo unless you are specifically told otherwise.

To reach Bergen without a rental car, the regular **Airport Express Coach (Flybussen)** (tel. 05505, www.flybussen. no, 100kr one-way, 170kr round-trip) takes around 30 minutes. Buy your ticket onboard with cash or credit card. For destinations outside of central Bergen or if you are traveling in a group, taxis are normally available directly outside the terminal entrance or can be booked through **Bergen Taxi** (tel. 55 99 70 50), which is advisable for late-night arrivals. The 25-minute trip will cost at least 400kr, with prices rising considerably in the evening and on weekends.

A planned extension to the Bergen Light Rail to link the airport with central Bergen is due to launch by early 2018. Although the new link will likely be the cheapest public transit option, it will also be the slowest.

Bus

The main **Bergen Bus Station (Bergen busstasjon)** (Lungegårdskaien) is one kilometer southeast of the Fish Market, co-located with the Bergen Storsenter shopping mall just a few steps south of the central railway station.

At the time of writing there is no direct bus connection linking Bergen with Oslo, so the train is the preferable option. It's quicker, more comfortable, and often cheaper than other modes of transport, especially when booked in advance. If you are prepared to book in advance and hunker down for a 10-hour trip, then bargains can be found from the long-distance bus operator **Nettbuss** (tel. 05070 within Norway, www.nettbuss. no), with regular fares running 700-1,000kr.

Kystbussen (tel. 52 70 35 26, www. kystbussen.no) runs hourly services from Stavanger to Bergen. Tickets for the 4.5- to 5.5-hour journey run 600kr, with savings of around 25 percent available with online advance purchase.

Rail

Bergen Railway Station (Strømgaten 4) is the western terminus of the world-famous Bergen Line from Oslo. The 371-kilometer (230-mile) journey is much more direct than any road connection and soars 1,237 meters (4,058 feet) above sea level to cross the Hardangervidda mountain plateau, making it Europe's highest railroad. Tickets for the 6.5-hour ride can be booked via the Norwegian state railway company **NSB** (tel. 81 50 08 88, www.nsb.no). Booking in advance is highly advisable, as the walk-on fare is around 1,000kr. Booking even just 24 hours in advance can save around 33 percent, with bargains of less than 400kr obtained a month or more before travel.

It's also possible to reach Bergen by rail from Stavanger, Kristiansand, and Trondheim, but only by changing trains at Oslo. This can be a bargain, but it takes up more than a day, so it should only be considered by those on the tightest of budgets.

Upon arrival the railway station appears to be in the middle of nowhere, but it's actually less than a one-kilometer (0.6-mile) walk from the Bryggen wharf. The beginning of the Marken shopping street is directly in front of the station entrance. Follow the cobbled street and you'll eventually hit the water.

Boat

Bergen is the southern terminus of the famous **Hurtigruten** (tel. 77 59 70 20, www. hurtigruten.com) coastal ferry. While many passengers will be embarking on an epic coastal cruise, the service is also a great option to travel up the coast to Ålesund, Kristiansund, or Trondheim. Cabin bookings are mandatory for overnight transit, so book well in advance if you intend to travel in high season. Prices vary wildly depending on season and ship.

The most economical way to reach Bergen from Stavanger is on the daily ferry service from **Fjordline** (tel. 81 53 35 00, www.fjord-line.com). Tickets should be booked online in advance and start from just 200kr for a foot passenger. To take a car on the six-hour journey, calculate an extra 500kr. The service actually starts at the Danish port of Hirtshals, making a budget crossing possible from Denmark to Bergen. Tickets for the 16-hour crossing via Stavanger start at a bargain 300kr without a car.

GETTING AROUND
On Foot

Most of Bergen's attractions are located in the very compact central area, and cobbled streets aside, the city is easy to experience on foot. However, much of the greater Bergen area is built on mountainous terrain, and even some of the hotels and restaurants close to the central districts are up steep hills.

Public Transit

All local buses and the light-rail system are operated by **Skyss** (www.skyss.no). One-way tickets for the central zone (which covers far beyond the city center) cost 37kr in advance and are valid on buses and light rail. Buy tickets from the customer service desk at Bergen bus station (9am-6pm Mon., 9am-5pm Tues.-Fri., 10am-3pm Sat.) or from one of the ticket machines at most transit stops. Paying on board the bus costs 60kr with no change given; 24-hour cards cost 95kr, while a seven-day pass is good value at 245kr.

Bus lines crisscross the city, and although the operating hours of each individual line vary, most run regularly 7am-11pm, although service is less regular in the evenings and on Sunday. The Skyss website is fully translated into English and is an excellent resource to plan your local bus travel. Large maps are available at most central transit stops.

BERGEN LIGHT RAIL

There is just one line of the **Bergen Light Rail (Bybanen)** (www.bybanen.no) system, but it's very useful to reach Brann Stadion and Fantoft Stave Church from the downtown terminus on Starvhusgaten near the Lille Lungegårdsvannet lake. Prices are the same as for the bus, but boarding the light rail without a ticket is not permitted. By 2018 the line will be extended to reach the renovated Bergen Airport Flesland.

Bergen Light Rail is a useful service for travelers.

Taxi

Because of the high cost, taxis should only be considered where there is no public transit alternative or for large groups. Taxi ranks are available at Bryggen and the railway station, or you can pre-book a car with **Bergen Taxi** (tel. 55 99 70 50). Expect an eight-kilometer (five-mile) ride to cost 220-330kr, depending on the time of day.

Car Rental

Bergen's branch of budget car rental firm **Rent-a-Wreck** (Lønningshaugen 15, tel. 98 83 45 75, www.rentawreck.no, 9am-5pm Mon.-Fri.) is handily placed just outside the airport. With advance booking, your car can be delivered and collected at the airport, even on weekends when the office is closed. **Avis** (tel. 55 11 64 30), **Budget** (tel. 67 25 56 20), **Hertz** (tel. 55 22 60 75), **Europcar** (tel. 55 22 73 20), and **Sixt** (tel. 55 22 81 66) are all represented in the airport terminal, but pre-booking is essential during the high season.

To rent a car in central Bergen, **Avis**

Bergen City (Nygårdsgaten 43, tel. 55 55 39 55, 7am-6pm Mon.-Fri., 8am-2pm Sat., 9am-3pm Sun.) has the widest selection of cars and the best opening hours.

VOSS

Located 100 kilometers (62 miles) east of Bergen along the E16 highway or the Bergen Line railroad, Voss has long been a destination for travelers looking for an outdoors vacation. Today, Voss is known across Europe as a ski resort and a center for extreme sports.

Sights

At the heart of the otherwise modern central area, the medieval stone **Voss Church (Vangskyrkja)** (Vangsgata 3, tel. 56 52 38 80, 10am-4pm Tues.-Sat. May-Aug., 15kr) is believed to have been built in the 13th century on the site of a former Germanic pagan temple.

A beautifully preserved farmstead in the hills overlooking the town, **Voss Folk Museum (Voss Folkemuseum)** (Mølstervegen 143, tel. 47 47 97 94, www.vossfolkemuseum.no, 10am-5pm daily June-Aug., 10am-3pm Mon.-Fri., noon-3pm Sun. Sept.-May, 90kr) provides a genuine window into the past. The wooden buildings of the Mølstertunet farmstead are unchanged from as far back as the 16th century and reveal how tough daily life was in this part of the world before transport links, electricity, and computers.

Sports and Recreation

Spring is the best time for kayaking or white-water rafting on the rivers. Hikers should wait until the snow clears in mid-June, but the trails are at their best in September and October.

SKIING

Norwegians flock to Voss because, not only is it the largest ski destination in western Norway, it's also one of the most reliable areas for snow throughout Europe. In addition to the two major alpine resorts, cross-country ski touring and freeskiing are popular in the surrounding mountains.

The best known resort is **Myrkdalen** (tel. 47 47 16 00, www.myrkdalen.no, open daily Dec.-Apr.), known for excellent off-piste skiing and floodlit cross-country trails. Many of the 22 slopes are suitable for beginners and families. A day pass costs 399kr, with cheaper half-day and evening options available. All ski and snowboard equipment is available to rent at 200-300kr per day.

First-timers or lapsed skiers can hone their skills at the Myrkdalen Ski School, which offers private and group lessons in alpine, telemark, cross-country, and snowboarding. A two-hour private lesson will set you back 1,195kr per person or 1,550kr for a couple. A free bus connects with the arrival from Bergen at Voss railway station daily at 10am, returning from Myrkdalen at 3:40pm. There are extra departures on weekends.

Keen skiers may prefer to stay at the resort itself in the **Myrkdalen Hotel** (tel. 56 52 30 40, www.myrkdalen.no). Rooms are modern with a light color scheme and high-standard bathrooms. Prices vary wildly, but a special midweek offer of one-night accommodation plus a two-day lift pass from 995kr is outstanding value. The hotel offers three restaurant choices, while the Pudder Afterski bar gets rowdy at weekends.

A further 22 slopes are available closer to the town at **Voss Resort** (Bavallsvegen 227, tel. 47 00 47 00, www.vossresort.no), which can be reached by the free resort bus departing Voss train station at 9am, 10am, and 11:20am daily. A full day's skiing costs 395kr, while a special Friday night plus weekend pass costs 805kr. Ski rentals and lessons are available.

WHITE-WATER KAYAKING

Throw yourself into the spirit of Voss by taking to the crystal-clear waters, even with no prior kayaking experience. A one-day course from **Voss Elvesport** (Vangsgata 45, tel. 91 37 49 95) begins by learning basic paddling techniques on calm water, before testing out your newfound skills on a more exciting river. The course costs from 1,500kr per person. More extensive guided tours can be booked for experienced kayakers.

INDOOR SKYDIVING

If you've ever considered skydiving, three minutes in the wind tunnel at **Voss Vind** (Tvildemoen, tel. 40 10 59 99, www.vossvind. no, noon-8pm Wed.-Sun. mid-Aug. through Dec.) is an ideal introduction to the sport. The first such attraction in northern Europe simulates the experience of freefall skydiving in a safe environment. It's the biggest adrenaline rush in Voss, save for the real thing, and has been enjoyed by ages 5 through 93! The first-timer package (765kr) including instruction must be booked in advance, and an HD video of your entire flight can be purchased for an additional 150kr.

HIKING

The mountains surrounding Voss are prime hiking territory, with miles of marked trails that weave their way through valleys, along lakes, and past former farmsteads for a taste of rural Norwegian life as it used to be. Keen hikers can challenge themselves with the demanding hike from Voss Folk Museum to the summit of **Lønahorgi** (trail open June-Oct.), a 1,200-meter (3,937-foot) climb that can take up to eight hours for the round-trip.

For the less experienced, **Voss Active** (Nedkvitnesvegen 25, tel. 56 51 05 25, www. vossactive.no) runs a selection of guided hikes, including a popular easy-to-medium half-day hike (530kr) along a riverside path to the Kronæ farmstead. Transport to/from Voss, hot drinks, and snacks are included. On longer hikes, soup and bread are served.

Food and Accommodations

Join the after ski crowd at **Inside Voss** (Uttrågata 42, tel. 90 22 28 60, www.inside-voss.no, 3pm-1am Tues.-Thurs., 3pm-3am Fri., 2pm-3am Sat., 2pm-1am Sun.), a rock café with loud music, pinball machines, and great burgers (193kr). Visit earlier in the day

to enjoy a late lunch or early dinner in a laid-back family-friendly atmosphere, or at night to rock out with a great selection of beers in the basement nightclub.

The friendly atmosphere, spacious terrace, and cozy interior mean **Tre Brør** (Vangsgata 28, tel. 95 10 38 32, 10am-10pm Sun.-Wed., 10am-11pm Thurs.-Sat.) is often busy with diners, but the real highlight is the drink service. Choose your favored brewing method (Chemex is a local favorite) to enjoy the best coffee in Voss, or come from 8pm onward when the bar presents 20 different varieties of beer from Norwegian microbreweries in 200-milliliter tasting glasses.

The grand old lady of Voss hotels, ★ **Fleischer's Hotel** (Evangervegen 13, tel. 56 52 05 00, www.fleischers.no) has been run by the Flesicher family since its opening in 1864. The main building gives off the feel of a Swiss mountain lodge with its 19th-century decor and elegant restaurants. A dip in the indoor swimming pool is the perfect way to relax those aching muscles after a day on the slopes. Despite the low prices advertised on the hotel website, expect double rooms to run at least 1,850kr. Alternatively, the hotel also owns a self-catered motel block 100 meters away with prices half what you will pay in the main hotel.

Budget options include the dated **Vinje Turisthotel** (Vinjadalen 58, tel. 56 52 24 09, www.vinjeturisthotel.no, 450kr d), 19 kilometers (11.8 miles) north of Voss and very convenient for skiing at Myrkdalen, and the simple cabins at the lakeside **Voss Camping** (Idrottsvegen 5, tel. 56 51 15 97, www.voss-camping.no, 700kr d), which also offers space for tents on a first-come, first-served basis. Most Norwegians will choose a cozy cabin over a hotel. Contact the Voss Tourist Information office to understand the options available, as facilities, prices, and locations vary wildly.

Information and Services

Pick up hiking maps or get more information on available tours and activities from the

Voss Tourist Information office (Skulegata 14, tel. 40 61 77 00, 9am-6pm Mon.-Fri., 9am-6pm Sat., 10am-5pm Sun. mid-June through Aug., 9am-4pm Mon.-Fri. rest of year), just a few minutes' walk from the train station.

Getting There

Voss is easy to reach by road or rail and, as such, is a good choice to break up the journey from Oslo to Bergen. Located on the E16 highway, Voss is a mere two-hour drive from Bergen or a five- to six-hour drive from Oslo. By rail, the Bergen Commuter Line connects Bergen to the centrally located **Voss Station (Voss Jernbanestasjon)** (Stasjonsvegen 5) in under two hours. Expect approximately one hourly departure from 6am to midnight and a fare of 204kr. Four daily departures are available from Oslo to Voss at a cost of 826kr, although discounts are available for booking at least 24 hours in advance.

HARDANGERFJORD

While not as long or deep as the mighty Sognefjord, the Hardangerfjord nevertheless carves its way 179 kilometers (111 miles) inland to the southeast of Bergen. The fjord is at its narrowest and most impressive far inland, where the imposing Folgefonna, the southernmost glacier in Norway, helps to shape understanding of how fjords are formed.

The fjord is a popular option for road-trippers traveling from Oslo to Bergen, and is a popular domestic tourism destination in its own right. Hiking opportunities are almost limitless among the orchards and waterfalls of the rich valleys, and summer skiing and guided glacier hikes are available in Folgefonna National Park. The region's fruit farms provide rich pickings for the roadside farm shops.

Without private transport, the **Hardangerfjord in a Nutshell** tour from **Fjord Tours** (tel. 81 56 82 22, www.norway-nutshell.com, May-Sept.) is a great solution to see the best of the inner Hardangerfjord in as little as one day. The round-trip from Bergen or Oslo (one-way also available) takes in the villages of Ulvik and Eidfjord, the Vøringsfossen and Steinsdalsfossen waterfalls, the Hardangervidda Nature Centre, and a couple of ferry trips on the iconic fjord. The round-trip, which is generally less busy than the better-known Norway in a Nutshell tour, starts from 1,430kr and can be customized to include overnight stops or extra activities.

Folgefonna National Park

Folgefonna National Park

Made up of three separate glacial plateaus, the **Folgefonna National Park** (tel. 53 48 42 80) is a remarkable wilderness at the heart of south-central Norway. The largest outflow glaciers, Blomstølskardbreen, Bondhusbreen, and Buarbreen, the latter two retreating over the past 20 years, provide several entry points and opportunities for hiking and summer skiing. The high mountains and harsh temperatures of the park are not conducive to much wildlife, although grouse, golden eagles, and red deer call the park their home.

Although appearing solid and safe, any glacier is a dangerous place to be, and an adventure here should only be attempted with a qualified guide and full safety equipment.

JONDAL

Beyond the 19th-century **timber framed church** (10am-8pm daily mid-June to mid-Aug., free) that has an appearance of one much older, **Jondal** is an otherwise unremarkable village, but it's the best place to base your exploration of the park. The Akjerhaugen village green features a mound of stones from the Bronze Age, while the **Jondal School Museum** (open by appointment) reveals what remote school life was like in 1903. Contact **Jondal Tourist Information** (tel. 53 66 85 31, www.visitjondal.no) to arrange a guided tour of the museum or for more information on the village.

At the heart of Jondal overlooking the harbor, the newly refurbished **Jondal Hotel** (tel. 53 66 85 63, www.jondalhotel. no, 950kr s, 1,090kr d, 1,330kr t) is impossible to miss. The white-paneled bedrooms are compact, with beds built into cozy cubbyholes to help keep the summer sun at bay while you sleep. A few self-catering apartments are also available, where two persons can pay around 5,500kr for a full week's accommodations. The hotel's café is a popular place to wait for the ferry with a slice of apple cake, while the restaurant serves traditional Norwegian and German dishes in a fine-dining setting.

FONNA GLACIER SKI RESORT

Not many of the world's ski resorts are only open during the summer, so people of all nationalities take advantage of the unique season at the **Fonna Glacier Ski Resort** (tel. 46 17 20 11, www.visitfonna.no, 9am-4pm daily May-Sept.), 19 kilometers (11.8 miles) southeast of Jondal along a signed track that has an 80kr toll payment. A daily ski pass costs 380kr, with rental of ski or snowboard equipment a further 300kr. Perfect for non-skiers who want to experience the resort, snowshoes are also available to rent (250kr), but you'll need decent hiking boots to use them. For 250kr (plus a further 320kr for equipment rental if necessary), the five-kilometer cross-country trail offers some of the greatest views in all of Norway, yet it's flat enough for the inexperienced to enjoy.

From mid-June to mid-August, **Norled** (Strandkaien 15, Bergen, tel. 51 86 87 00, www. norled.no, office open 8am-3:30pm Mon.-Fri., 2pm-4pm Sun.) runs a daily ski bus package, leaving Bergen bus station at 7:25am and returning to the city around 7pm. The 990kr price includes bus and ferry travel direct to the ski resort, a day pass, and approximately five hours on the slopes.

HIKING

From an office at the Fonna Glacier ski resort, **Wilderness Norway** (tel. 95 17 77 92, www. wilderness-norway.no) runs daily guided glacier hikes from mid-June through August. For the bargain price of 720kr, you'll be taken to the Juklavass section of the glacier, known for its blue ice. Depending on the wishes of the group, the hike can stick to flat ice or venture into more challenging crevasses. Although crampons, an ice ace, harness, rope, and mountain boots are all provided, you must remember to bring sunscreen and sunglasses, and be prepared for a five- to six-hour hike covering up to six kilometers (3.7 miles). Even on cloudy days, the reflection of light off the glacial ice can be dazzling. Outside the summer season, contact the company for rental of cross-country skis or guided snowshoe hikes.

For ice-free hiking, pick up a hiking map from any of the local supermarkets in Jondal. The 4.2-kilometer (2.6-mile) **Vassenden-Vatnasete hike** is a relatively easy way to explore the region's scenery, including the Vatnasetevatn lake. The four-hour round-trip is possible May through October, but be sure to take plenty of food and water because cell phone coverage is poor. The hike can be made more demanding by following signs to Dåren or Vatnasete, or combined with a fishing trip. Ask at the Jondal Tourist Information office for permit information.

GLACIER KAYAK TOURS

For a unique perspective of the Folgefonna glacier's blue ice, **Wilderness Norway** (tel. 95 17 77 92, www.wilderness-norway.no) also runs a full-day guided adventure tour of the glacier by kayak (1,990kr) from its Jondal office. Shorter three- to four-hour kayak tours of the fjord are also available from 790kr.

Eidfjord

At the innermost point of the Hardangerfjord lies the dramatic fjord spur and village of **Eidfjord**. A small community surrounded by mountains and water, Eidfjord is a picturesque place for lunch or an overnight stop on your journey.

HARDANGERVIDDA NATURE CENTRE
(Hardangervidda Natursenter)

Geology meets botany at the **Hardangervidda Nature Centre** (Øvre Eidfjord, tel. 53 67 40 00, www.hardangerviddanatursenter.no, 9am-7pm daily mid-June to mid-Aug., 10am-6pm daily rest of year, 130kr), with a dose of animal and birdlife thrown in for good measure. The center profiles the environment of the vast **Hardangervidda National Park** that lies southeast of Eidfjord.

Northern Europe's most extensive highland plateau and Norway's largest national park, Hardangervidda is home to Europe's largest wild reindeer herd and is the southernmost

habitat of the arctic fox. The 20-minute widescreen movie *Fjords, Mountains and Waterfalls* sums up the area's outstanding natural beauty for those stopping by the center on their way to Oslo or Bergen.

VØRINGSFOSSEN WATERFALL

A national symbol that has drawn tourists to the area since the late 19th century, the 182-meter (597-foot) waterfall **Vøringsfossen** (Fossatromma, signed off Route 7) is 17 kilometers east of Eidfjord. Plentiful parking and a café and souvenir shop make this a handy picnic spot. Park your car on the side road by Storegjel, between the second and third tunnels in the Måbødalen valley. Follow the footpath and pick up the signed trail. Although the trail is less than two kilometers (1.25 miles) from the parking spot, part of it runs over unstable rocks that can be slippery and crosses the river on a rickety suspension bridge.

HARDANGERBRUA BRIDGE

Driving west along Route 7, most travelers will cross the Eidfjord on Norway's longest suspension bridge, the impressive **Hardangerbrua.** Opened in 2013 to replace a ferry crossing and shorten the driving distance between Oslo and Bergen, the 1.4-kilometer-long toll bridge crosses the Eidfjord at a height of 200 meters.

MIKKELPARKEN

Young kids will love **Mikkelparken** (Kinsarvik, tel. 53 67 13 13, www.mikkelparken.no, 10:30am-6pm daily mid-June to mid-Aug., 10:30am-6pm Sat.-Sun. mid-May to mid-June and mid-Aug. to mid-Sept., 229-299kr), an outdoor water park a few miles south of the Hardangerbrua Bridge along Route 13. The park includes a swimming pool, paddling boats, miniature golf, a climbing net, and slides.

SIGHTSEEING TOUR

May-September, **Tide** (www.tide.no) runs a sightseeing tour of Eidfjord that includes entry to the Hardangervidda Nature Centre and a bus trip along the Måbødalen valley to the Vøringsfossen waterfall. The 2.5-hour lunchtime tour costs 350kr, but if you have your own transport, save the money and make the trip yourself.

Taking the tour only makes sense if you are arriving in Eidfjord on the Hardangerfjord sightseeing tour from Bergen operated by **Norled** (tel. 51 86 87 00, www.norled.no, 770kr). The daily tour leaves Bergen Bus Station at 7:25am and includes a three-hour ferry ride to Eidfjord, from where you can either explore the village or pick up the Tide tour. You then return to Bergen on the same ferry and bus combination, arriving back in the city at around 7pm.

FOOD AND ACCOMMODATIONS

Stay in one of the 28 bright modern rooms at the **Eidfjord Fjell & Fjord Hotel** (Lægreidsvegen 7, tel. 53 66 52 64, www.effh. no, 1,395kr), where the conservatory restaurant (noon-9pm daily May-Aug., contact in advance during low season) serves a set menu of local delicacies with outstanding views across the water.

Odda

A dagger-like spur of the Hardangerfjord cutting 38 kilometers (24 miles) into lush countryside, the **Sørfjord,** often called Sørfjorden i Hardanger to distinguish it from similarly named fjords, is one of the few narrow fjords you can actually drive along. County Road 550 runs down the western side while Route 13 skirts the eastern side. Both roads are fairly narrow, but the plentiful parking spots are great places to pull over and enjoy a picnic or simply admire the fjord.

At the end of the Sørfjord is the small town of **Odda,** the main commercial center of the inner Hardangerfjord region. Known among Norwegians for its unique dialect and among travelers as the best place to recharge your batteries on a long road trip, Odda has the perfect combination of stunning location and useful services. The town is set in a deep valley with snowcapped mountains towering overhead

on both sides, the Sørfjord ahead and the Sandvinvatnet lake behind.

LÅTEFOSS WATERFALL

About 14 kilometers (8.7 miles) south of Odda on Route 13, the spectacular 165-meter (541-foot) **Låtefoss Waterfall** is a breathtaking example of nature's power. The stone bridge and twin cascade are known around the world and have doubtless inspired many fairy tales over the years. Be prepared to get wet as the water smacks into the rocks below, creating a near-deafening roar and sprays of mist that can change direction and soak you in seconds. A parking lot is available after you drive past the waterfall, so there is no need to stop on the road itself.

TROLLTUNGA

Despite the appearance of the famous photographs, the hike to Norway's most spectacular rock formation is not for the inexperienced. Hikers ascend 900 meters (2,952 feet) over the hike from Skjeggedal to **Trolltunga,** which rolls out like a tongue (the name literally translates as Troll's Tongue) and dangles 700 meters (2,296 feet) over the Ringedal lake. The hike can only be attempted once the snow has melted around mid-June, with the season generally lasting to mid-September. Allow 10-12 hours for the full 23-kilometer (14.3-mile) round-trip.

All but the most experienced hikers should obtain detailed maps and information on conditions from the Odda Tourist Information office before attempting the hike. Consider joining a guided hike from **Trolltunga Active** (tel. 90 82 45 72, www.trolltunga-active.com), which offers a range of tours including the classic hike (850kr), a hike plus cycle tour (1,100kr), and an overnight hike (2,500kr) to see the sunset from this iconic location. An above-average level of physical fitness is required for all tours.

The trailhead at Skjeggedal is a 12.7-kilometer (7.9-mile) drive from Odda. Head north along Route 13 to Tyssedal and follow the signed road to Skjeggedal.

FOOD AND ACCOMMODATIONS

The town and its surroundings host the best range of accommodation and food options in the Hardangerfjord region. Despite first appearances, the ugly **Hardangerfjord Hotel** (Eitrheimsveien 13, tel. 53 64 64 64, 1,395kr d) is the place to be. Book early to grab one of the 50 dated rooms that are nevertheless comfortable and well equipped. The hotel also runs the nearby **Smeltehuset** restaurant and bar (Røldalsvegen 4, tel. 45 90 88 33, noon-10pm Mon.-Thurs., noon-10pm Sun.), where pizza (179-205kr) is the house specialty.

A budget accommodation alternative can be found on the lake side of the town at **Odda Camping** (Jordalsvegen 25, tel. 94 14 12 79, www.oddacamping.no), which offers four cabins (1,190-1,690kr), a handful of motel rooms (590kr), and camping facilities including a kiosk and 24-hour sanitary building. In the low season (Sept.-May), camping is still permitted, although the facilities are only open on demand.

INFORMATION AND SERVICES

Call in to the centrally located **Odda Tourist Information** (Torget 2, tel. 48 07 07 77, www.hardangerfjord.com, 9am-7pm daily May-Sept., 9am-3pm Mon.-Fri. Oct.-Apr.) for hiking maps and tour bookings.

Ålesund

TOP EXPERIENCE

In stark contrast to other fishing towns that are filled with white, dark red, and mustard yellow wooden houses, central Ålesund's fairy-tale art nouveau architecture has more in common with Paris, Prague, and Brussels.

After a 1904 fire devastated the former wooden city, German money and young Norwegian designers came together to rebuild the city in the fashion of the time. More than 100 years later, the turrets and towers of Ålesund stand head and shoulders above any other northern European city as a shining example of the style.

The city and its surroundings are delicately balanced on a collection of islands of all shapes and sizes, helping to create beautiful vistas from almost anywhere in town. Sunsets at the end of summer can be truly spectacular, and there is no better place to watch them than the summit of Mount Aksla, the vertical rock that towers over central Ålesund.

HISTORY

The islands of the Sunnmøre region have been dedicated to fishing and trade since records began. If you believe the local legend (and the family tree in Giske Church), Rollo the Viking, who went on to become the first ruler of Normandy, was born here on the islands.

As trade became more important to Norwegian coastal life, Ålesund itself emerged as the key trading center for the region. The town grew quickly through the 19th century from a population of just hundreds to more than 10,000. The construction of so many wooden houses in confined spaces contributed to disaster on a stormy winter night in 1904, as almost all the houses burned to the ground, leaving thousands of people homeless. Remarkably, only one recorded death was caused by the fire.

Kaiser Wilhelm of Germany often vacationed in Ålesund and was so shocked to hear of the news that he sent four ships with people and materials to help the rebuilding efforts. Local Norwegian designers and architects were inspired by the art nouveau style popular in Germany and across Europe at the time, so they set about building a city in that image.

Despite emerging unscathed from World War II, Ålesund had been a key base for the Norwegian resistance, especially for launching secret flights to England.

SIGHTS
★ Art Nouveau Ålesund

The best way to experience Ålesund's fairytale architecture is to allow at least an hour for a stroll around this very walkable city. Start your walk from **Lorkenstorget,** the square by the canal bridge that links the two halves of the city center.

Head up **Notenesgata** before turning left onto the beautiful waterside path **Skansegata.** The Ålesund Tourist Information office at **Skateflukaia** is a sensible place to turn around and retrace your steps back to the bridge. Cross the bridge and turn right on to **Apotekergata** for a view back across the water. Continue along **Molovegen** to a once-seedy waterside district now dominated by academic institutes and galleries. Walk along the pier to the 150-year old **Molja Lighthouse (Molja fyr)** for an interesting perspective on the town center, harbor, and Mount Aksla. The lighthouse doubles as room 47 for the nearby **Hotel Brosundet** (Apotekergata 5, tel. 70 11 45 00, www.brosundet.no) and offers a truly unique accommodation option with breakfast delivered to the door. Contact the hotel for prices and availability.

The Art Nouveau Centre itself is one of Ålesund's best examples of the architecture.

WALKING TOUR

For the stories behind the town's resurrection, join a 1.5-hour **Walking Tour** (noon daily mid-June to mid-Aug., 100kr) run by an English-speaking guide from the Ålesund Tourist Information office. This is especially useful if you don't have time to discover the history for yourself at the Art Nouveau Centre or Aalesunds Museum.

ART NOUVEAU CENTRE
(Jugendstilsenteret)

Although the city's streets are an art nouveau museum in themselves, the **Art Nouveau Centre** (Apotekergata 16, tel. 70 10 49 70, 10am-5pm daily June-Aug., 11am-4pm Tues.-Sun. Sept.-May, 80kr) tells the story behind the city's renaissance from the devastating fire through a 15-minute multimedia experience

that's well worth the admission fee. Also on display are textiles and furniture from the era.

The center is housed inside one of the city's finest examples of the architecture, with a pristine exterior overlooking a cobbled street and the city's canal. The reception area retains the original fittings from the building's former use as a pharmacy.

Your ticket also covers entrance to the Kube Art Museum, next door. Entry is free for under 18s.

Art Galleries

The **Kube Art Museum (Kunstmuseet Kube)** (Apotekergata 16, tel. 70 10 49 70, www.kunstmuseetkube.no, 10am-5pm daily June-Aug., 11am-4pm Tues.-Sun. Sept.-May, 80kr) is the city's home of contemporary art and design. The entire collection changes on an annual basis, although Norwegian artists are very much the focus. If you've already been to the Art Nouveau Centre next door, then your ticket also covers entrance here. Entry is free for under 18s.

The cobbled streets north of here are awash with art galleries, many run by the artists themselves. Opening hours tend to be daily through the summer but will be much less frequent in low season. Contact the artists in advance to know for sure. Particularly worth a look are the vivid paintings of maritime artist **Bjarte Ytterland** (Brunholmgata 16, tel. 91 86 36 30, www.bjarteytterland.com, noon-5pm daily, free), which demonstrate the outstanding natural light enjoyed along this part of the Norwegian coast. Step inside the open workshop of **Ingrids Glassverksted** (Molovegen 15, tel. 80 12 53 77, www.ingridsglassverksted.no, noon-5pm Mon.-Fri., noon-3pm Sat., free) during the afternoon for a chance to see the glassblowers at work, still using traditional methods.

Aksla Viewpoint

Dominating the downtown area, the 130-meter (426-foot) **Aksla** mountain is impossible to miss from just about anywhere in the city. At its foot, the **City Park (Byparken)** is a pleasant albeit hilly place to wait while you decide if you will climb the 418 recently improved steps to the summit.

If you decide to go for it, reward yourself with an overpriced ice cream and coffee from the **Fjellstua** café (tel. 70 10 74 00, www.fjellstua.no, 11am-5:30pm daily) or a more substantial dinner in the restaurant (6pm-9pm Wed.-Sat.) while you admire one of the most famous panoramic views in all of Norway, placing the colorful downtown in context with its stunning natural setting. An alternative way to reach the summit is by car along the winding Fjelltunvegen road through a residential suburb. Prepare yourself to meet large tour buses on the narrow approach to Fjellstua. Parking can also be a struggle when cruise ships are in dock.

Ålesund Church
(Ålesund kirke)

The original church could lay claim to be the unluckiest victim of the 1904 fire. Despite its brick construction, the building was heavily damaged despite neighboring wooden buildings surviving. At a time when young architects flocked to the city, the design competition for the new stone **Ålesund Church** (Kirkegata 22, tel. 70 16 53 00, www.kirken-aalesund.no, hours vary, 30kr) attracted great interest. Winning architect Sverre Knudsen took inspiration from medieval churches rather than the art nouveau trend that swept across the city at the time, which is why the

The view from Mount Aksla is stunning at any time of day.

rectangular shape and gable roof suggest a much older construction date than 1909.

The church is generally open for tourists 10am-2pm Monday-Friday, but hours vary depending on season and events. The chances that the church is open are much higher if a cruise ship is in dock. Must-sees inside include the glass gable windows (a gift from Kaiser Wilhelm II), the Italian marble font, and one of the country's largest church organs.

Museums

There's more to the town's history than the 1904 fire and subsequent rebuilding. **Aalesunds Museum** (Rasmus Rønnebergs gate 18, tel. 70 16 48 42, 9am-3pm Mon.-Fri. year-round, also noon-4pm Sat. mid-June to mid-Aug., noon-4pm Sun. May-Sept., 50kr) does a fine job of filling in the gaps, including the rapid expansion of 19th-century Ålesund through to the town's critical role in helping the Allied forces win World War II.

The fire is discussed by way of a 15-minute film with English subtitles, but it's the replica lifeboat named *Uræd (Fearless)* that steals the show. Visitors can explore the interior of the egg-shaped 18-foot long craft to feel what it was like to stay for weeks in the cramped conditions, as four Norwegians did more than 100 years ago when they sailed to Pavilion Beach in Gloucester, Massachusetts. Excellent photography is featured throughout the museum, and although many of the captions are only in Norwegian, staff are happy to help with English translations. A ticket here is valid at the Fisheries Museum and vice versa.

While in the area, take a walk east along Parkgata. Here you'll come to a museum that conjures up memories of visiting distant relatives whom you can't quite remember. The three older ladies who run the **Waldehuset Museum** (Fjellgata 2, tel. 98 08 39 00, noon-4pm Wed.-Thurs. and Sat.-Sun., free) treat you like one of their own family, making fresh coffee and offering a delicious homemade cake while they explain the fascinating story of the house. One

of the few to escape the city fire, the wooden house originally built in 1870 has been kept as it was with no refurbishment. The post-fire photographs show just how remarkable its survival was, but it's the storytelling that makes this small museum so memorable. Such is the power of their conviction; the ladies may even convince you of their tale that an angel told the owner to stay in the house and it would be saved!

Only venture inside the **Fisheries Museum** (Molovegen 10, tel. 70 16 48 42, 9am-3pm Mon.-Fri., noon-4pm Sat.-Sun. mid-June to mid-Aug., 50kr) if you don't mind the smell of cod liver oil. It's worth passing by the exterior regardless, as it's one of the few wooden buildings that survived the city fire and gives you an inkling as to what the city might have looked like if disaster never struck. The museum documents the town's main economic driver of the last centuries: the production of dried cod. A ticket here is valid at Aalesunds Museum and vice versa.

Nearby Ålesund
ATLANTIC SEA PARK (Atlanterhavsparken)

The pricey **Atlantic Sea Park** (Tueneset, tel. 70 10 70 60, www.atlanterhavsparken.no, 10am-6pm Sun.-Fri., 10am-4pm Sat. June-Aug., 11am-4pm Mon.-Sat., 11am-6pm Sun. Sept.-May., 180kr) will keep children occupied for hours, but adults may get bored quickly. The highlight is the feeding of the penguins and seals, so contact the aquarium in advance to find out the times to make the most of your visit. The staggered seating to view the giant aquarium is helpful, although the detailed descriptions of North Atlantic wildlife throughout the aquarium skew too much toward scientific explanation to hold mild interest for long.

The 45-minute walk west of central Ålesund is very pleasant on a sunny day. If you're pushed for time, a 10-minute shuttle bus (May-Aug. only) runs from Apotekertorget at 11am and noon, returning from the aquarium at 1:15pm and 2:15pm.

SUNNMØRE MUSEUM

Log cabins and farm buildings dating back to the Middle Ages line the lakeside of the former trading post at **Sunnmøre Museum** (Museumsvegen 1, tel. 70 16 48 70, 10am-4pm Mon.-Fri., noon-4pm Sun., also Sat. noon-4pm during July, 80kr), which is equally interesting from an architectural and cultural perspective. The best time to visit is on Wednesday during the summer season, when costumed actors bring the medieval atmosphere to life.

By the dock you will find a large collection of boats including the *Kvalsund* ship, the oldest complete boat ever found in Norway, dating back to 690 AD. It is believed the 18-meter-long oak and pine warship had been buried in sacrifice to the gods, before it was discovered in 1920.

Although there is an indoor exhibition, most of your time here will be spent outside, so a visit is best made in clear weather.

Also on-site and included in the ticket price is the archaeological exhibition at the **Medieval Museum (Middelaldermuseet)** (noon-3pm Mon.-Fri., noon-3pm Sun. June-Aug., also open noon-4pm Sat. during July only), built across an excavation site and showing finds from the old medieval trading community who once lived here. Take a stroll outside to discover traces of old religious buildings and the trading port.

If time isn't tight, visit **Borgund Church (Borgund kyrkje)** (Borgundgavlen 30, tel. 70 16 53 41) on the southern border of the museums. Although it was rebuilt in the early 20th century, the architects chose to stick with the original Romanesque style. Part of the transept dates back to the former basilica that stood on the site in the 12th century. The interior of the parish church is usually only open for Sunday services and by prior appointment.

The museums are 5.5 kilometers (3.4 miles) east of Ålesund, just off the main E139 road, so they make a great stop when arriving or leaving this charming town. To reach the museums without a car, take bus 618 (every 15 mins, less frequent on weekends) from the bus station. The bus stops outside the museum and the journey takes less than 10 minutes.

Giske Archipelago

Home to many interesting ancient monuments from the Vikings and the Middle Ages, the islands of the Giske archipelago are linked to Ålesund by a series of modern bridges and tunnels.

From Godøya, which resembles one giant piece of rock, to the nature walk of Valderøya to the grassy residential paradise of Giske itself, each island has its distinctive character and appeal. Each island also has its own burial grounds revealing the cultural and historical importance of the area. There are Roman and Iron Age remains on Valderøya and Vigra, while the Mjelthaugen burial ground on Giske dates back to the Bronze Age.

Access to the islands, which lie immediately north and west of Ålesund, really requires a car, because you are likely to want to make multiple stops on a tour rather than spend several hours in one place. However, local bus routes are available from Ålesund bus station (Ålesund rutebilstasjon); they take approximately 20 minutes depending on your destination. Bus 662 links Ålesund with Valderøya and Vigra, while bus 664 serves Giske and Godøya. Services run approximately hourly during the day with a limited service on evenings and weekends. Due to the tunnels linking the islands, walking to the archipelago is not possible.

GODØYA

Tucked away on the island of Godøya is **Alnes Lighthouse and Cultural Center (Alnes fyr og opplevelsessenter)** (Alnesgard, tel. 70 18 50 90, www.alnesfyr. no, noon-5pm daily), one of Norway's most famous lighthouses because of its proximity to Ålesund, just a 20-minute drive using the excellent tunnels and bridges to hop across the islands of Giske.

There have been lighthouse operations at Alnes since 1852. There were constant complaints that the height of the lighthouse's beam was too low, and in 1937 funds were granted for a new 18-meter-tall angle iron tower with exterior plating. The lighthouse is still in operation (automated since 1982), and since 1993 the facility has also functioned as a local and regional cultural center in a unique countryside setting. Dug into the ground so as not to distract the visual focus from the lighthouse, the local cultural center is open during the summer months as an art gallery. The lighthouse café is renowned for its homemade cake, the ingredients for which are kept a closely guarded secret.

GISKE

On the grassy residential island of Giske, the 12th-century **Giske Church (Giske kyrkje)** (Gjerdevegen, tel. 70 18 09 90, www.giske. kyrkja.no, 10am-5pm Mon.-Sat., 1pm-5pm Sun. July to mid-Aug., 35kr) is a pleasant five-minute detour from the tunnel to Godøya along the narrow roads that circle the island. What's not immediately obvious because of the chalk covering is that the church is built of white marble. A stroll around the small graveyard reveals many graves with the surname Giske, hinting at the importance of the family to the island of the same name. Restored in the 18th century, the basic interior of the church was given a new pulpit and altarpiece. Also inside is a family tree showing the ancestry of the islanders stretching back to Rollo. The **Mjelthaugen burial ground** on Giske dates to the Bronze Age.

VALDERØYA

As a nice stop-off to or from the Ålesund airport, the three-kilometer (1.9-mile) **Culture Road (Kulturvegen)** is a marked nature trail on the west coast of Valderøya island. Park at the Valdervoll sports ground, which is found by taking the first right after you emerge from the undersea tunnel onto Valderøya. Bathroom facilities are available at the car park.

White-tailed eagles are commonly sighted soaring overhead, while along the path you can find rock formations, caves, and monuments to the area's cultural history. The most popular spot to explore is the ancient **Skjonghellaren** cave, which, despite being created by seawater, lies 187 feet above sea level. Traces of human life during the Neolithic age and wildlife stretching back more than 30,000 years have been found here. The cave stretches more than 300 feet into the steep cliff and is found toward the end of the trail.

SPORTS AND RECREATION
Central Ålesund
HIKING

Aside from climbing the steps to the top of Mount Aksla, the most popular hike around Ålesund is to the 314-meter (1,030-foot) summit of **Sugar Loaf Top (Sukkertoppen)**, a mountain on Hessa island at the western end of Ålesund. The beginner-friendly trail up the eastern ridge is the most popular and starts from the parking lot at Hessa School (Hessa skole), which you can reach by following the signs for Aspøya/Hessa from central Ålesund. Follow the residential Sukkertoppvegen road until you pick up the signed trail between houses. The trail does split off into smaller paths, but they all converge farther up the mountain.

Allow about two hours for the 3.6-kilometer (2.2-mile) round-trip hike, including a good amount of time at the summit to enjoy the 360-degree views. The trail can be slippery and muddy, especially after overnight rain, so proper walking boots are recommended. Experienced hikers should contact the Ålesund Tourist Information office for information on more challenging routes to the summit.

KAYAKING

As the town is surrounded by water, the best way to see it and the surrounding islands is by sea kayak. After launching the first-ever commercial sea-kayaking trips in Norway's Lofoten islands in 1998, **Kayak More Tomorrow** (Notenesgata 3, tel. 95 11 80 62, www.kayakmoretomorrow.com) has switched its attention to the calm waters of Sunnmøre.

Launching from a dock in the center of town, the four-hour sea-kayak tours of the archipelago (1,300kr) are the most popular excursion. The physically fit should consider the eight-hour sea-kayak tour combined with guided hike (1,775kr) to the summit of Sula mountain. All trips are suitable for children (around 20 percent cheaper) and include a packed lunch.

SOCCER

If you see a lot of families walking around the town in distinctive bright orange shirts, chances are there's an **Aalesunds FK** (tel. 70 10 77 80, www.aafk.no) match later that day. Despite relatively small numbers, their fans are the most visible in Norwegian soccer, thanks to the lurid orange team color. Games take place March-October at the smart 10,778-capacity **Color Line Stadion** (Sjømannsveien 14), and tickets (180-290kr) generally only need to be bought far in advance for the year's big games against Rosenborg and fierce local rivals Molde.

Giske Archipelago

The entire Giske archipelago is perfect for hiking, but be aware that walking through the tunnels is prohibited. For a leisurely walk, take the **Culture Road (Kulturvegen)** on Valderøya island.

For a more demanding hike, head to Godøya island's **Godøyfjellet** peaks, from where you can enjoy terrific views across Ålesund to the Sunnmøre Alps. Several routes are available. At 497 meters (1,630 feet) the tallest peak on the islands, Storhornet appears as an imposing wall when seen from the town, but the peak has a perfect cone shape when viewed from the west and is not as difficult as it first appears.

You can take on the hike from Alnes village (park at the supermarket and pick up the trail through the neighboring farm) or from the school at Gjuv village on the south side of the island. The ascent takes 1.5-2.5 hours

depending on your route (up to three kilometers one-way), but great views are available throughout the trails, so tackling the trail's steepest inclines is not necessary to appreciate the views.

Sandvika Beach straddles both sides of the road as you arrive on Giske and is a popular spot for sunbathing, swimming, ball games, or simply relaxing. Turn right into the small parking lot immediately after leaving the bridge.

ENTERTAINMENT AND EVENTS
Nightlife

A former cod liver oil factory is today one of the town's most cutting-edge performance venues. Expect comedy nights, theater, and the occasional concert at **Teaterfabrikken** (Moloveien 22, tel. 70 10 04 10, www.teaterfabrikken.no).

The floor-to-ceiling glass windows of **Milk Bar & Lounge** (Skaregata 1a, tel. 70 12 42 53, 6pm-1am Tues.-Thurs., 6pm-2am Fri.-Sat.) attract a fashionable young clientele who dress to be seen amid the deep blue and purple lighting. The waterside club skirts the line between hip and pretentious and just about ends up on the right side. Enjoy a cocktail from the large menu, along with a view across the water.

Beer-loving locals will surely direct you to **Hoffmann** (Kongensgate 11, www.chb.no, 9am-11pm Mon.-Wed., 9am-3am Thurs., 10am-3am Fri.-Sat.), which transforms from sleepy daytime café serving average food into a lively, late-night watering hole for Thursday, Friday, and Saturday nights. Most of the beer selection is bottled, which is a downside for those who prefer tap beers. The café tables mean it's a good gathering spot for groups, especially on Friday and Saturday nights when live music tends to be scheduled.

Music Festivals

The largest music festival between Bergen and Trondheim, the well-organized **Jugendfest** (www.jugendfest.no) fills the soccer stadium, **Color Line Stadion** (Sjømannsveien 14), with more than 20,000 people over two days in mid-August. Scandinavian artists dominate the bill, with the odd international name thrown in to help shift tickets. The soccer stadium also hosts big-name international artists for occasional one-off gigs. Elton John and A-ha are two of the artists to have played in the shadow of the Sunnmøre Alps.

Throughout June, smaller festivals fill the city's streets to mark the lightest month of the year. Ålesund's midsummer bonfire is Norway's largest, while the best of Norway's contemporary musicians take over St. Olavs plass for two consecutive evenings for **Ålesund Live** (www.alesundlive.no), usually held a week or so before the midsummer celebrations.

On Giske island in early July, the free one-day **Sommerfesten** (www.momentium.no/sommerfesten) showcases mainly Norwegian artists, with a smattering of talent from the United Kingdom and occasionally farther afield. The family-friendly event is Ålesund's most established and eagerly anticipated summer festival.

Throughout the year, one-off concerts from touring Norwegian acts are held most weekends at **Terminalen** (Sjøvegen 77, tel. 90 20 46 20, www.momentium.no/terminalen), next to the city's bus station.

SHOPPING

Ålesund's Art Nouveau Centre is a haven for independent boutiques and galleries. The largest of these is **Artifex Kunst & Antikk** (Apotekergata 10, tel. 91 35 09 94, 11am-4pm Tues.-Sat., noon-4pm Sun.), a curious mix of antiques, trinkets, and modern paintings from local artists.

Music lovers must make time to peek inside **Jukebox Recordstore** (Kipervikgata 1b, tel. 70 12 68 85, 11am-6pm Mon.-Sat.) for free transportation to a bygone era when vinyl ruled the music business. A Wurlitzer takes pride of place in the heart of this intimate store.

Shopping Malls

They are easy to miss, but the small entrances of **Ålesund Storsenter** (Grimmergata 1, tel. 90 70 04 00, www.alesundstorsenter.no, 10am-8pm Mon.-Fri., 10am-6pm Sat.) lead to the town's largest shopping mall. More than 70 outlets include a mass of clothing and homeware stores, a travel agency, two cafés, and a bookshop with a small English language selection.

If you're driving into town, it's impossible to miss Norway's third largest shopping complex, **Amfi Moa** (Langelandsvegen 25, tel. 70 17 75 60, www.amfi.no/moa, 10am-8pm Mon.-Fri., 10am-6pm Sat.), 11.4 kilometers (7 miles) east along the E136 highway. More than 150 big brand stores are gathered here, including sports and hiking specialists XXL and electronics giant Elkjøp.

For one of Norway's most distinctive shopping experiences, take the fast ferry to the **Devold Factory (Devold Fabrikken)** (Geilneset, Langevåg, tel. 70 30 11 11, www.devoldfabrikken.no, 10am-6pm Mon.-Wed. and Fri.-Sat., 10am-8pm Thurs.) for a mix of big brands and studio workshops in a former industrial setting. This is where the likes of Moods of Norway, Norrøna, and Helly Hansen run their clearance sales. The glass-blowing studio of Swede Cornelia Skuggen (closed Mon.), an old smithy and forge, an art gallery, and a homey café mean it's easy to spend an entire day here. The scheduled Ålesund-Langevåg ferry service from **Norled** (www.norled.no, half-hourly Mon.-Fri., hourly Sat., 65kr) takes less than 10 minutes and is much quicker than driving.

FOOD

While in and around Ålesund, try a *svele*, the traditional light and fluffy buttermilk pancake that locals enjoy in the place of waffles or cinnamon buns with their coffee. Homemade cakes are also popular throughout the region. As Ålesund is a fishing town, restaurant menus are unsurprisingly dominated by fish and seafood. The local specialty

Søstrene Fryd is a popular, mostly organic restaurant.

(Kipervikgata 1, tel. 70 12 53 00, www.lyspunktet.as, noon-5pm Mon., 10am-10pm Tues.-Fri., noon-9pm Sat.-Sun.), but the roaring brick fireplace, relaxed seating arrangements, and a vast café menu provide a welcome environment for a casual meal any time of day. Mexican-inspired dishes made with Norwegian *lefse* in place of corn tortillas and the warming bowls of soup served with chunky bread are popular choices. Free refills on filter coffee and sodas are a nice touch, but note that the kitchen closes at least an hour before the advertised times.

There are no strictly vegetarian or vegan restaurants in Ålesund, so most people head to the organic restaurant **Søstrene Fryd** (Kongens gate 28, tel. 70 10 05 12, 11am-11pm Mon.-Sat., 1pm-9pm Sun.) for a quick lunch or casual dinner. It's known for its gluten-free bakery, and the vegetarian options, such as the quinoa bowl, outstrip the tired hamburgers and pizzas on the menu. The casual atmosphere of this shabby chic diner seems to extend to the staff, so be sure to chase after them if you want glasses refilled or a quick turnaround.

bacalao can refer either to a tomato-flavored stew made with clipfish (salted dried cod) or the fish itself.

Many restaurants are situated in or around Kongens gate, so a daytime walk along the commercial street may help you decide where to spend your evening. More than half the city's restaurants are closed on Sunday, so reservations are a good idea.

Cafés and Light Bites

For a morning espresso-based pick-me-up, the modern **Invit** (Apotekergata 9b, tel. 70 15 66 44, www.invit.no, 8:15am-4:30pm Mon.-Sat.) has firmly established itself in the hearts and minds of Ålesund commuters. Don't pigeonhole this as an espresso bar though. The cozy basement lounge and outside deck with yachts sailing by are perfect places to enjoy their fantastic café menu. The zesty shrimp salad with cucumber and fruit followed by a slice of nutty chocolate cake makes a perfect indulgent lunch.

A quiet lunch is unlikely at **Lyspunktet**

Traditional Scandinavian

Although the café atop Mount Aksla is known as an overpriced tourist trap, the evening transformation into a modern minimalist restaurant is surprising. **Fjellstua** (Aksla, tel. 70 10 74 00, 6pm-9pm Wed.-Sat., 265kr) serves a slim-line ocean-themed menu, with the traditional potato and light salad sides putting the focus squarely on the freshness and flavor of the fish. Wines, local beers, and juices are available to accompany your meal, which you can enjoy to the backdrop of a stunning sunset across the islands. Book in advance to guarantee a window table.

For a true western Norway experience, **XL Diner** (Skaregata 1b, tel. 70 12 42 53, www.xldiner.no, 5pm-11pm Mon.-Sat., 320kr) has you covered with seven options inspired by how the Italians and Portuguese eat their clipfish. For those who can't stomach the saltiness, a fresh fish platter and reindeer are also available, but it's the *bacalao* that people flock here for, so much so it's difficult to get a table here even on weekdays, and reservations won't guarantee you a prime waterside seat.

New Nordic

The four- or six-course tasting menus (580kr/750kr) at the Hotel Brosundet's **Maki** (Apotekergata 5, tel. 70 11 45 00, 6pm-10pm Mon.-Sat.) are the ideal way to experience a range of coastal flavors in one satisfying meal. Expect beautiful presentation both on the plates and in the restaurant, where timber beams contrast with the contemporary furnishings. Heavily salted dishes are common, so notify your waiter if you would prefer yours adjusted. Reservations recommended.

Asian

The staff at **Zuuma** (Kongens gate 13, tel. 70 12 70 70, www.zuuma.no, 3pm-9pm Mon.-Tues., 11am-10pm Wed.-Sat., 2pm-9pm Sun., 159-189kr) do their best to find a table even at busy times. Service can be slow, so it's best to order as much sushi as you think you'll need from the start. Well-known dishes sit alongside the house special mackerel sushi on the vast menu. Chicken in peanut sauce is a tasty alternative choice, while the simple 49kr desserts are a great value way to end your meal. Takeout is a great option at busy times when the sun is shining, as there's plenty of waterside space to enjoy your food just a block away.

Good Indian options in Norway are few and far between, but **Taj Mahal** (Kongens gate 18, tel. 70 12 03 00, www.tajmahaltandoori.no, 2pm-10pm Sun.-Thurs., 3pm-10pm Fri., 265kr) takes a deserved place on the list despite the high prices. Skip over the average starters and instead order one of the excellent naan breads to eat alongside your main dish. Spice levels are adjusted down to the Norwegian palate, so expect creamy and lightly spiced dishes rather than heat.

International

It's easy to get bored with fish and boiled potatoes if you're staying in Ålesund for more than a couple days. The rich flavors on the nine-course tapas menu (325kr) at trendy bistro cum wine bar **Kabb** (Kongens gate 19, tel. 70 12 80 08, 5pm-10pm Tues.-Fri., 3pm-10pm Sat.-Sun., 289kr) are the perfect antidote. Asian lamb hot pot and roasted pork leg hocks are popular. Although the modern restaurant seems spacious, much of the space near the bar is reserved for wine drinkers, so table reservations are wise.

Italian

Tempting as it is to order pizza, the light menu at swish eatery **Anno** (Apotekergata 9, tel. 71 70 70 77, www.anno.no, 6pm-10pm Mon.-Sat.) is where the best value and taste lie. Tagliatelle in creamy or white wine sauce, shellfish salad, and filling creamy fish soup can all be enjoyed for well under 200kr each, while regular mains run over 300kr. For a less formal experience earlier in the day, pizza with a liberal helping of arugula and lighter pasta or focaccia dishes can be enjoyed on the outside terrace (11am-5pm Mon.-Fri., 2pm-5pm Sat.). After hours Anno transforms into a trendy nightspot with DJs and regular live music.

ACCOMMODATIONS
Central Ålesund
UNDER 1,000KR

The cheapest central accommodation by some distance, dorm beds at **Ålesund Vandrerhjem** (Parkgata 14, tel. 70 11 58 30, alesund@hihostels.no, 285kr) book up fast during the summer season. The quiet location at the foot of Mount Aksla, generous buffet breakfast of cold cuts, and spacious rooms will leave you questioning its status as a hostel. In fact, their one- to four-bed private rooms (690-1,140kr) are of a hotel standard if a bit dated in terms of decor. A spacious kitchen with two full-size ovens makes self-catering a breeze.

It's cramped, and maintenance schedules can sometimes slip in the busy summer season, but **Volsdalen Camping** (tel. 70 12 58 90, www.volsdalencamping.no) is the only campground within walking distance of central Ålesund, and its relatively low price reflects the facilities. Basic cabins without running water sleep two (550kr) and four (950kr), while tents can be pitched for 150kr. Expect to wait for a shower in high season. Open year-round, the prices drop further outside of the May to mid-September high season.

The best of the city's cheaper hotels is the dark and moody **First Hotel Atlantica** (Rasmus Rønnebergs gate 4, tel. 70 12 91 00, 995kr). The pricing is dynamic based on capacity across the city, so prices can dip as low as 750kr or rise considerably higher in the summer. Plus points include the central location, modern rooms, and an in-house bar and restaurant that offers a daily set menu at prices less than many of the city's restaurants. The lobby aside, the hotel lacks a certain character, but its value can't be questioned.

1,000-1,500KR

The distinctive green waterfront building of the ★ **Hotel Brosundet** (Apotekergata 5, tel. 70 11 45 00, www.brosundet.no, 1,252kr d) offers the standout accommodation in Ålesund. Perfect for couples, half of the 46 rooms come with a view across the canal. Space is at a premium, but the exposed wooden beams and hardwood floors add a sense of occasion well beyond most of the other chain hotels who fill the buildings of central Ålesund with identikit interiors. The Hotel Brosundet also administers the bedroom built into the Molja Fyr lighthouse a short walk away. Known as room 47, the lighthouse is typically used by honeymooners and can only be booked directly with the hotel.

Rivaling the Brosundet in the romance stakes is the **Hotel Bryggen** (Apotekergata 1-3, tel. 70 10 33 00, bryggen@choice.no, 1,399kr) from Clarion Collection, just a few steps farther down the cobbled street. Room rates tend to run slightly higher, but all guests are entitled to a light supper, typically a soup or stew, served in the early evenings. The old salt cod warehouse limits the room sizes, and even some superior rooms have slanted walls,

but there is plenty of space to relax in the warm-toned lounge and contemporary bar.

Outside Ålesund

The elegant **Storfjord Hotel** (Øvre Glomset, Skodje, tel. 70 27 49 22, www.storfjordhotel.com, 2,500kr) is one of Norway's most luxurious country retreats. Overlooking the fjord with the Sunnmøre Alps mountain range as the backdrop, the natural setting is hard to beat. That same beauty has been brought inside the hotel's timber walls with curated antiques and artwork filling the bright lounge and library. Each room resembles a cozy log cabin, lit only by small lamps and the daylight, creating a romantic evening ambience. Well-appointed bathrooms provide a further dash of luxury. Pricey, but a special experience and one that would make a great surprise for a loved one as you travel between Ålesund and the Geirangerfjord or Hjørundfjord.

Giske Archipelago

To stay close to the airport for an early morning flight, look no further than the five rooms offered by **Flyplasservice** (Ålesund Airport, Vigra, tel. 48 27 17 98, www.flyplasservice. as, 650kr s, 750kr d). Despite the somewhat strange setting in a shared office facility, the rooms are hotel standard, and although no breakfast is offered, a fridge is available to store food and hot drinks are complimentary.

Despite the suggestive name, **Aalesund Airport Hotel** (Ytterland 1, Valderøya, tel. 70 18 26 11, www.aaah.no, 875kr d) is six miles south of Ålesund Airport on a different island. Motel standard rooms include a buffet breakfast with a selection of English-style hot options. The strange setting above a supermarket is actually a good base to explore the nature trail on Valderøya island, but there's very little else to do out here aside from watching the sunset on the terrace of the hotel's bar (8pm-11pm Wed.-Sat.).

An alternative for those with their own transport is the delightful **Glede på Reisen** guesthouse (Postvegen 46, Vigra, tel. 70 18 50 99, gledereisen@hotmail.com) in a quiet residential part of Vigra island. Rooms are tight, but the quiet suntrap terrace more than makes up for that. For a relaxing stay for a group of up to six sharing two bedrooms, the two cabins at **Alnes Rorbuer** (Alnes, tel. 70 18 51 96, www.alnesrorbuferie.no, 1,100kr) include a rowboat, fishing gear, and a private floating dock in the price.

INFORMATION AND SERVICES
City Spelling
A minor but important note. The town's name starts with the letter Å, the last letter of the Norwegian alphabet. In a curious attempt to prevent confusion, the town is sometimes referred to as Aalesund, so the city's name could come at the beginning or end of any alphabetized list you come across. To confuse things further, Ålesund is almost always spelled Alesund in website URLs.

Tourist Information
The **Ålesund Tourist Information** office (Skateflukaia, tel. 70 16 34 30, 8:30am-6pm daily June-Aug., 9am-4pm Mon.-Fri. Sept.-May) covers the entire region, so any questions you have about traveling to the fjords or even farther afield can be answered here. Several languages are spoken, and a wide variety of free publications, including maps, are available to browse and take with you.

GETTING THERE AND AROUND
Car
In this part of the world, getting there is half the fun of a road trip. Driving distances to Ålesund tend to be longer than they first appear due to the terrain being littered with mountains, glaciers, and fjords. Although Ålesund and Bergen are linked by the E39 highway, you should allow at least 7-8 hours for the 423-kilometer (263-mile) journey—and that's if you avoid stopping in any of the delightful fjordside villages you pass through.

You will also cross two fjords on car ferries. **Norled** (www.norled.no) operates the 25-minute journey from Oppedal to Lavik across the mighty Sognefjord, which costs 102kr per car plus an additional 38kr for every passenger besides the driver. Departures typically run 2-3 times hourly with an hourly service throughout the night, although consult the online timetable for weekend driving. On the approach to Ålesund, the E39 is also interrupted by the Festøya to Solavågen ferry operated by **Fjord1** (www.fjord1.no), which costs 94kr (car plus driver) plus 37kr for each additional passenger for the 20-minute crossing. Departures run every 30 minutes and approximately once per hour throughout the night.

It takes a similar amount of time to reach Ålesund from Oslo. The 545-kilometer (338-mile) drive via the E6 to Lillehammer and Dombås and then E136 through the fertile Romsdal valley is a memorable one, with plenty of options to stop along the way. Norway's winter sports capital Lillehammer and the hiking opportunities in and around Åndalsnes are two of the best.

From the Atlantic Road near Kristiansund, the drive is a more tolerable 126 kilometers (78 miles) along the E39 via Molde, and should take less than three hours. The 299-kilometer (186-mile) Trondheim-Ålesund drive takes around 5.5 hours but should be extended with a coastal drive to Kristiansund and the Atlantic Road, which will tack on an additional 60 kilometers (37 miles) and at least two hours, including stopping time at the Atlantic Road. If time is of the essence, do as most locals do and take the E6 via Dombås instead. Although much longer in distance at 408 kilometers (254 miles), it takes less time as the drive is ferry-free.

Air
The compact **Ålesund Airport Vigra** (AES) (tel. 67 03 21 21, www.avinor.no) is mainly served by SAS and Norwegian shuttles to the capital. A useful SAS service links the airport to Trondheim and to Stavanger via Bergen. Tickets are rarely cheap on the latter service but can still work out better value than a car rental. Dutch carrier KLM runs up to two

daily hopper services to their international hub in Amsterdam, which is a fantastic yet largely unknown option for reaching Ålesund from the United States.

Local public transit provider Fram runs an **airport shuttle** *(flybussen)* connecting with all arrivals. The return shuttle picks up and drops off at Skateflukaia (by the Ålesund Tourist Information office) and the bus station. The 20- to 25-minute journey costs 95kr one-way, 140kr round-trip. Taxis wait outside the airport terminal, but the 15-minute ride will cost at least 300kr. If arriving late at night, pre-order from **Ålesund Taxi** (tel. 70 10 30 00). For car rental, Avis, Budget, Hertz, Europcar (closed weekends), and Sixt operate desks inside the terminal, but opening hours are limited and pre-booking is essential.

Rail

There is no railroad station in Ålesund. However, it is possible to reach the town by bus connection from Åndalsnes, which is linked to Oslo and Trondheim via Dombås station. The Dombås to Åndalsnes line is a scenic 80-minute meander through the lush Romsdal valley that connects with arrivals from Oslo and Trondheim at Dombås station. Through-tickets should be bought from Oslo or Trondheim, but if you're traveling from Dombås to Åndalsnes you can expect to pay 257kr for a one-way ticket. From Åndalsnes, **Fram** (www.frammr.no) operates bus route 681 to Ålesund. Although the two-hour journey only runs 4-5 times daily, twice on weekends, departure times are set to meet the train. A one-way adult ticket costs 212kr, payable on the bus.

Boat

Cruise ships arrive into Ålesund's large harbor on the southern side of the city center, with all central attractions within comfortable walking distance. The terminal for the **Hurtigruten** (tel. 77 59 70 48, www.hurtigruten.no) coastal service is on the northern side of the city, close to the Ålesund Tourist Information office, and is also within easy walking distance of the city's main attractions. Hurtigruten offers two daily departures. The northbound service arrives at midday and leaves toward Trondheim at 3pm, while the southbound service arrives shortly after midnight before continuing on toward Bergen at around 1am.

Bus

Local buses in and around Ålesund are run by **Fram** (www.frammr.no), with a single ticket valid within the city costing 34kr when bought in advance. All local and regional buses leave from **Ålesund Bus Station (Ålesund rutebilstasjon)** (Keiser Wilhelms gate), close to the cruise ship terminal.

TOP EXPERIENCE

★ GEIRANGERFJORD

Its calm waters, slimline waterfalls, ancient mountain farms, and the greenest greens you'll ever see are just some of the reasons why the **Geirangerfjord** tops the list of Norway's must-see fjords. The 15-kilometer (9.3-mile) UNESCO-listed arm of the Storfjord carves through the mountains, leaving almost vertical drops on both sides. At its widest point the fjord is just 1.5 kilometers (0.93 miles) across, so any boat trip along arguably the country's most famous waterway will provide outstanding 360-degree views.

The **Hellesylt-Geiranger car ferry** (May-Oct. only) doubles as a one-hour sightseeing cruise. The modern boat skirts close to the most famous of the waterfalls and 17th-century mountain farms with commentary given in multiple languages. Although expensive at 505-990kr depending on how many passengers you have (260kr pp without a car), the ferry trip leaves few patrons disappointed. The ferry has 4-8 daily departures between 8am and 6pm.

The most famous of the fjord's many waterfalls, the **Seven Sisters (De syv søstrene)** is a collection of seven narrow streams of water tumbling down the rocky cliff into the fjord from a height of 410 meters (1,350 feet), including a freefall of up to 250 meters (820 feet). Just to the north of the waterfall, the timber farm buildings at **Knivsflå** were abandoned in 1898 due to the increasing risk of avalanche and falling rocks.

Opposite the waterfall and perched on a mountain ledge 270 meters (886 feet) above the fjord, the former mountain farm **Skageflå** achieved fame in 1993 when Norway's King Harald and Queen Sonja celebrated their silver wedding anniversary at its secluded setting. Only accessible via demanding hikes from Geiranger village or a steep climb from the fjord itself, the farm is kept relatively tourist-free but can be seen atop the ledge from the fjord below.

Geiranger

Every day of the summer, Geiranger is transformed from sleepy rural hideaway to thriving commercial hub as cruise ships and tour buses descend on the tiny hamlet. Although there is little to see in the village itself, Geiranger is the gateway to the fjord, with most tours and activities starting from its small port. Stay here overnight to see the village and fjord in an entirely different light, free of the crowds and with room to breathe.

A quick visit to the **Norwegian Fjord Center (Norsk fjordsenter)** (Geiranger, tel. 70 26 38 10, www.fjordsenter.com, 10am-6pm daily May-Sept., 10am-3pm daily Oct.-Apr., 115kr) is recommended if you won't be spending long around the fjords. Visitors will learn how fjords were created, how humans have adapted to the challenges of living in such a unique environment, and the story of the UNESCO World Heritage award and ongoing preservation work. The center is a short five-minute walk from the port.

For a view of the Geirangerfjord from above, you have three choices in and around Geiranger. If traveling from the north along Route 63, you will drop down to the village by way of several hairpin bends, each one bringing an even more impressive view of the fjord's final stretch toward Geiranger. Pull over at the **Ørnesvingen** bend, where recent improvements to the parking facilities and lookout point have made this spot the best place to view the Geirangerfjord.

A few miles above Geiranger along Route 63 toward Stryn is the car park for the **Flydalsjuvet** lookout. The view down to the village and the fjord from here is wonderful, but for the most iconic view and clearest photograph you'll need to hike 100 meters (328

Geiranger village is nestled at the end of the Geirangerfjord.

The Wave

Norway's first disaster movie, *Bølgen* (released with subtitles as *The Wave* in English markets) depicts a tsunami caused by a rockslide that surges down the Geirangerfjord and destroys the village of Geiranger. Unlike many Hollywood disaster movies, *The Wave* is based on a proven risk. As the intro to the movie states: It has happened before. It will happen again. In 1934, over 40 people died as a rockslide created a tsunami that washed over the villages of Fjørå and Tafjord in Møre og Romsdal county, while similar incidents have occurred in mountain lakes.

The risk today is very real. Standing high above the entrance to the Geirangerfjord, the Åkerneset mountain is pulling itself apart. Geology experts agree that it's not a matter of if, but when. Should a large enough section of Åkerneset collapse into the water, residents of Geiranger would have approximately 10 minutes to climb to safety.

The movie is an entertaining and at times gripping watch, and as the disaster it depicts is very much a worst-case scenario, it shouldn't put you off visiting this magnificent fjord.

feet) down a slippery trail, and be prepared to queue at busy times.

For the most stunning vista—and the only way to truly appreciate the Geirangerfjord in context with the mountains that created it— head to the **Dalsnibba** (tel. 45 48 13 01, www. dalsnibba.no) lookout. Drivers need to pay an 85kr toll to access the five-kilometer (3.1-mile) road to the lookout, which starts from the Djupvatnet lake, approximately 16 kilometers (10.1 miles) above Geiranger along Route 63 toward Stryn. Be prepared for much colder weather as you ascend 1,500 meters (4,921 feet) for the on-top-of-the-world feeling. Clouds and mist often add to the atmosphere but also frequently obscure the view down to the fjord. Those without a car can take a bus (mid-June to mid-Aug., 180kr round-trip) that runs three times daily from the Geiranger Tourist Information office, briefly stopping at Flydalsjuvet on the way up. Allow around two hours for a return trip from Geiranger by car, three hours by bus.

SIGHTSEEING BOAT TOURS

If you are basing yourself in the village of Geiranger, **Geiranger Fjordservice** (Geiranger, tel. 70 26 30 07, www.geiranger-fjord.no) presents a range of exciting ways to get out on to the water and enjoy the Geirangerfjord without the expense of the Geiranger-Hellesylt car ferry. The 90-minute

Fjord Sightseeing ferry trip (several departures daily May-Sept., 230kr) takes you up close to the sheer cliffs and waterfalls at the water's edge, or choose the speedy one-hour **RIB Tour** (several departures daily June-Aug., 695kr) for a more exhilarating experience.

SIGHTSEEING KAYAK TOURS

For a more intimate relationship with the fjord, **Active Geiranger** (tel. 70 26 30 68, www.activegeiranger.no) rents single and double sea kayaks. The fjord's inland location and dog-leg entrance mean it's rarely windy here, and the waters tend to be calm, making for ideal kayaking conditions even for children. Sample prices are 250kr for one hour, 400kr for three hours, and 1,300kr for two days. Although they no longer offer scheduled guided kayak tours to the waterfall and mountain farm, it's worth getting in touch with them to inquire if this is something that interests you.

HELICOPTER TOURS

Experience the sculpted landscape of Fjord Norway from the air with **Fjord Helikopter** (tel. 97 48 40 40, www.fjordhelikopter.no, 1,500kr). Rides include at least 20 minutes in the air and require a minimum of four passengers to go ahead. If you don't have a party of four, contact the company in advance to see if you can share a ride.

FOOD

Located inside a former boathouse, the cozy ★ **Geiranger Sjokolade** café (Holenaustet, tel. 96 72 52 05, hours vary) serves rich hot chocolate made in the factory downstairs. The store sells nicely packaged sets of individual chocolates that make great gifts and transport well. For a unique flavor, try the famed blue cheese chocolates, or a bar flavored with sweet berries from the region's valleys. To arrange a visit of the boutique factory, contact the owner and chief chocolatier, Bengt, in advance.

Dining options are limited in fjord villages, and despite its fame, Geiranger is no exception. Immediately opposite Geiranger Sjokolade, **Café Olé** (Holenaustet, tel. 70 26 32 30, www.olebuda.no, 9am-5pm daily May-Sept.) is the best of the bunch for a quick lunch in the village. Coffee, snacks, homemade cakes, and light meals such as sandwiches and soups are served throughout the day in the traditional yet informal atmosphere of a whitewashed timber house.

handmade chocolate from a Geiranger factory

You might expect a restaurant next to a major port to be something of an overpriced tourist trap, but nothing could be further from the truth at **Brasserie Posten** (Stranda, tel. 70 26 13 06, www.brasserieposten.no, noon-10pm daily May-Sept., noon-4pm daily during Oct., 250kr), where the popular creamy fish soup is given extra flavor with halibut bones and locally brewed wheat beer. Excellent value raw salads and beautifully presented lamb shank are also popular.

ACCOMMODATIONS

Several of Geiranger's hotels are in dire need of modernization, and coupled with the hectic daytime atmosphere of the tiny village, staying central is not recommended. Instead, look to the historical splendor of the ★ **Grande Fjord Hotel** (Ørnevegen, tel. 70 26 94 90, www.grandefjordhotel.com, 1,350kr d), just one kilometer north of the village on Route 63. Once the cruise ships have moved on, the spacious outdoor terrace is the perfect place to soak up the serene atmosphere with a glass of wine from the bar (4pm-11pm daily). The hospitality is something many traditional Norwegian hotels can learn from. Complimentary coffee, snacks, and homemade lemonade are available around the clock, while the included buffet breakfast meets many dietary needs with its wide range of tasty options.

In front of the hotel, **Geirangerfjorden Feriesenter** (Ørnevegen, tel. 95 10 75 27, www.geirangerfjorden.net, May-Sept.) rents self-catered cabins for groups of 4-6 (850-1,090kr) and fjordside pitches for motorhomes and tents (160-190kr). Cabins must be booked, but the campsite doesn't take reservations, so it's first-come, first-served. Several other campsites operate in or just above the village itself. **Geiranger Camping** (tel. 70 26 31 20, www.geirangercamping.no, mid-May to mid-Sept.) is the most centrally located and offers pitches from 85kr (on foot or bike) up to 175kr (with car or motorhome).

INFORMATION AND SERVICES

Housed in a new building right by the port, the **Geiranger Tourist Centre** (Geirangervegen 2, tel. 70 26 30 99) is the best place to inquire about the availability of fjord tours and maps for hiking trails. They will also have the latest weather reports and information on road closures to hand.

GETTING THERE

Driving to Geiranger outside the summer season requires some additional planning. Due to snowfall, many of the mountain roads around the region are closed, especially the National Tourist Route (Route 63) from Geiranger to Åndalsnes via Trollstigen. The stretch between Langevatnet to Geiranger is typically closed from November to May, while the Trollstigen mountain pass closes up to a month earlier. Route 15 heading east toward Otta is also closed over the winter. Check with the **Norwegian Public Roads Administration (Statens Vegvesen)** (tel. 91 50 20 30, www.vegvesen.no) for detailed

the powerful waterfall at the heart of Hellesylt village

information if planning a road trip outside of the summer months.

Hellesylt

This small village is at the western end of the Geirangerfjord, and although it also welcomes cruise ships, Hellesylt tends to enjoy a more sedate atmosphere than its famous brother, Geiranger. For that reason, walking in the hills above the village can be a more enjoyable experience than in Geiranger, and many savvy travelers base themselves here instead.

Many marked trails of varying degrees of difficulty start from the hills above the village, so consult one of the information boards near the ferry dock or pick up a map from the tourist information office to make the most of your stay. Start your walk with a stroll up the steep paths through the village's residential core to take a closer look at the 19th-century **Sunnylven Church (Sunnylven kirke),** from where you can also enjoy a picturesque view across the rooftops to the fjord. The church is open sporadically, but visitors are usually welcome whenever a cruise ship is in port. Donations are appreciated.

Even if you're just passing through via the Geiranger-Hellesylt car ferry, make time to see the **Hellesyltfossen** waterfall, which literally splits the village in two. In contrast to the slender beauty of the fjordside waterfalls, Hellesylt's version showcases the raw power of nature, as a flood of water thunders over the granite rocks despite its height of only 20 meters (66 feet). The cascade is at its most impressive from April to early June, when melting snow from the surrounding mountains swells the flow. A steep path on the northern side of the water leads you up to a stone bridge for the best vantage point.

A curious addition to the region's culture is the **Peer Gynt Gallery (Peer Gynt Galleriet)** (Hellesylt, tel. 95 01 31 70, www.peergyntgalleriet.no, 10am-6pm daily June-Aug., shorter hours rest of year, 120kr), home to a series of extravagant wooden carvings from a local artist depicting the famous *Peer Gynt* story, which was set over 300 kilometers

(186 miles) away in the Gudbrandsdalen valley. While an interesting cultural aside to your fjord road trip, even the addition of a half-hour movie about the carvings fails to deliver value for money for all but the most ardent fans of the Ibsen play.

FOOD AND ACCOMMODATIONS

If you're waiting for the Geiranger ferry, ignore the rip-off pizza restaurant by the car park and seek out the **Hellesylt Boutique & Bar** (Gata 29, tel. 40 51 65 35, 10am-6pm daily June-Aug., weekends only May and Sept.) tucked away on the quiet residential street that leads to the church. Expect excellent coffee, snacks that lean toward sweet over savory, books to read, and friendly, attentive service in this cozy café.

The basic private rooms at the **Hellsylt Vandrerhjem** (tel. 70 26 51 28, hellesylt@hihostels.no, May-Sept., 750kr d) offer the best value accommodations around the Geirangerfjord. There are no bells and whistles whatsoever other than the simple breakfast buffet, just about served in time to catch the first ferry to Geiranger, but you'll need to eat fast. Dorm beds can be had for 260kr, but without your own bedding and towels the price goes up to 330kr. The other downside is the 15-minute trek up a very steep hill from the port to reach the hostel.

HJØRUNDFJORD

A less well-known alternative to the busy Geirangerfjord, the 35-kilometer (22-mile) **Hjørundfjord** is nevertheless the locals' fjord of choice. Easy to visit as a day-trip from Ålesund or to combine with the Geirangerfjord on a longer loop, the Hjørundfjord is entirely encircled by the Sunnmøre Alps, clearly visible from Ålesund. Its forested sides and mountainous backdrop create a distinct, wilder, yet just as beautiful experience as its more famous sister to the east.

European royalty has visited the magnificent fjord and nearby Norangsdalen valley since the 19th century, leading to its nickname embraced by the local tourist offices, the **Royal Fjord Route.** To follow in their footsteps, follow the E136 out of Ålesund and turn south onto the E39 (signed Stavanger). Cross the Storfjord on the Solavågen-Festøya car ferry (94kr car plus driver, plus 37kr for each additional passenger for the 20-minute crossing; departures run every 30 minutes and approximately once per hour throughout the night) run by **Fjord1** (tel. 57 75 70 00, www.fjord1.no) and continue to **Ørsta,** where you should make time for a quick stroll around the scenic harbor path.

Leave Ørsta on the eastbound Fv655 and you will reach the shore of the Hjørundfjord at Sæbø. A number of ferries depart here, but by far the most popular is the Sæbø-Lekneset crossing run by **Fjord1** (tel. 57 75 70 00, www.fjord1.no). Departures run every 30-60 minutes between 6:30am and 10:30pm and you will pay 87kr for a car plus driver, plus 35kr for each additional passenger for the 15-minute crossing. From Lekneset, continue on through the lush Norangsdalen valley to Hellesylt and the Geirangerfjord. The 85-kilometer (53-mile) drive from Ålesund to Sæbø should take 2-2.5 hours, including time for the ferry crossings.

Without a car, visiting the Hjørundfjord is easy thanks to the four- to five-hour **Sightseeing Cruise** (mid-June to mid-Aug., 890kr) that includes a light two-course lunch at the historic Hotel Union Øye. The tour departs daily at noon from Dronning Sonjas plass in Ålesund and can be booked via the tourist information office in Ålesund (Skateflukaia, tel. 70 16 34 30, 8:30am-6pm daily June-Aug., 9am-4pm Mon.-Fri. Sept.-May).

Sæbø

Just a couple minutes' walk from the ferry terminal, **Hjørundfjord Camping** (Skuleplassen 13, tel. 70 04 00 16, www.hjorundfjord-camping.no, June-Aug.) must be a contender for the most picturesque campsite in Norway's fjord region. Staying right on the shoreline of the Hjørundfjord in the peaceful village of Sæbø, you can go from the comfort of your cabin to kayaking in one of Norway's best fjords in mere seconds. Basic cabins all sleep four and start from 350kr, double that for ones with a kitchenette and bathroom. Pitches are available for camper vans, caravans, and cars with tents from 170kr, or 80kr for just a tent pitch. Electrical hookup costs an additional 30kr.

Services are basic although newly refurbished and the campground is kept clean. Shared toilet, shower, and kitchen facilities are available, along with a room for preparing fish. Although the campsite is only open during high season, the biggest cabins can be rented year-round.

Bjørke

The tiny village of Bjørke at the extreme southern end of the Hjørundfjord is the idyllic location for the **Indiefjord** (www.indiefjord. com) music festival. Inspired by the Britpop movement of the 1990s, Indiefjord brings together fans of the genre for two days in mid-July to dance, bounce, and sleep right on the shoreline. The festival is kept small to keep the intimate vibe and not overload the delicate local environment.

Øye

The historic ★ **Hotel Union Øye** (Norangsfjorden, tel. 70 06 21 00, www. unionoye.no) is the standout hotel around the Hjørundfjord. All 25 rooms are individually decorated with modern touches despite the predominantly 19th-century aesthetic. Doubles start from 1,640kr. Upgraded rooms with a four-poster bed or a balcony run at least an extra 500kr. A stay at the Union is an all-inclusive experience that includes a lavish three-course dinner followed by coffee served in the grand lounge, where European royals and the wealthy have relaxed for decades.

Those of a nervous disposition may wish to give the hotel a wide berth, as the hotel's resident female ghost regularly tips over lamps in the dark hallways and blows out candles over dinner. Even if you don't set foot in the hotel, you won't be able to resist pulling over for a photograph as you approach the magnificent cream and maroon exterior set against the lush green backdrop of the foothills of the Sunnmøre Alps.

the day lounge at the historic Hotel Union Øye

Inner Sognefjord

Impossible to miss on even the largest-scale map, Norway's most awesome fjord splits apart the northwest and southwest fjord region with a 205-kilometer-long (127-mile-long) body of water. The picturesque villages, idyllic farmsteads, fruit orchards, and hiking trails of the fjord would take months to explore in-depth, so it's the most outstanding section—east of Balestrand, almost two-thirds of the way along the fjord—where we focus our attention.

It's here that things get interesting, as the Sognefjord's narrow fingers reach deep inland to the foot of glaciers and some of Norway's tallest mountains. The whole region feels like a vast living museum, so prepare yourself for dramatic landscapes, narrow fjordside lanes, and hidden cultural gems.

AURLAND

The Sognefjord's two southernmost arms (Aurlandsfjord and Nærøyfjord) reach into the heart of Aurland municipality, one of the most popular tourist destinations in the entire country. Known as Norway's Grand Canyon,

the 40-kilometer-long (25-mile-long) Aurland valley is a paradise for hikers and cyclists, who flock here in the summer from right across the country. Filled with ancient forest trails and long-abandoned farmsteads, the valley's cultural significance is just as appealing as its natural beauty.

The most popular way to experience Aurland's highlights is through the classic one-day **Norway in a Nutshell** (www.norwaynutshell.com, year-round, 1,320kr) train-bus-ferry combination tour from Oslo or Bergen. The tour's popularity is its downside, as from June to August the buses, ferries, and small villages along the route are overrun with people.

Although utilizing public transit, the self-guided Nutshell tours are nevertheless recommended for those who don't want to plan out an otherwise complicated itinerary. Add in an optional overnight stay in Flåm or book the various legs of the trip independently to escape the worst of the crowds. A newer alternative, the **Sognefjord in a Nutshell** tour (May-Sept., 1,540kr) includes a fast ferry

The Sognefjord is Norway's longest and deepest fjord.

Inner Sognefjord

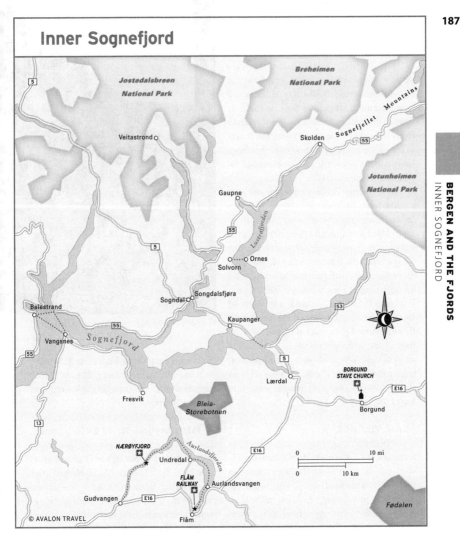

service to/from Bergen with an optional hike on the Nigardsbreen glacier. This tour can also be done in one day, or extended with optional overnight stays.

★ Flåm Railway
(Flåmsbana)

The reason Aurland is so accessible from the country's two major cities is the remarkable **Flåm Railway** (tel. 57 63 21 00, www.visit-flam.com), which regularly tops the charts of world's most beautiful railroads. How on earth this railroad was ever built in the days before computer-aided engineering (it opened in 1940) will top your list of questions as you trundle from Myrdal station (on the Bergen Line) down through the lush Flåm valley. The one-hour journey circles around bridges and through tunnels as you descend more than 800 meters at a 5 percent gradient to the quaint community of Flåm, which is the starting point for tours of the Aurlandsfjord and Nærøyfjord.

As primarily a tourist route, the train stops midway to allow photographs at the **Kjosfossen** waterfall, which includes a small power station that powers the line itself. Be wary of the Huldra, a seductive forest creature from Norse mythology who uses the power of song to tempt men to their fate. She's been known to make more than the occasional appearance at the waterfall!

The renowned **Rallarvegen hiking and cycle path** runs down the valley, so an option for the more energetic is to take the railway up to Myrdal station and meander down the valley in your own time. Allow several hours for the hike, which takes you up close to even more waterfalls with many secluded spots for an outstanding view while you rest. As enjoyable as the hike is, the path is uneven and steep in places, and is not recommended for those without a good level of fitness. **Myrdal** itself offers nothing of interest bar the station and a couple of holiday cabins, so while waiting for the train you should consider taking a short walk along the trail to explore the very top of the valley.

FLÅM VILLAGE

If you're not on a tight intinerary, Flåm itself is worthy of an overnight stop. Even if time is tight, call in to the **Flåm Railway Museum (Flåmsbanamuseet)** (tel. 57 63 23 10, 9am-8pm daily June-Sept., 9am-7pm daily May, 1pm-4pm daily Oct.-Apr., free) by the train station to answer those questions about how the railway was built. Exhibitions include an authentic EL-9 locomotive and many black-and-white photographs.

If you are staying more than a few minutes in Flåm, pick up a hiking guide from the **Flåm Tourist Information** office (Flåm station, tel. 95 43 04 14, 9am-6pm daily Apr.-Sept., 9am-3pm Thurs.-Sat. Oct.-Mar.) to enjoy the village and its surroundings once the crowds have left. The riverside **Flåm Church (Flåm kyrkje)** is a postcard-worthy 17th-century

The Flåm Railway stops by Kjosfossen waterfall.

church an easy three-kilometer (1.9-mile) walk back along the railway. The tourist information office rents out **bicycles** at 150kr for three hours.

The only nightspot of note is the lively ★ **Flåmsbrygga** (tel. 57 63 20 50, www. flamsbrygga.no, noon-4pm and 5pm-10pm daily May-Aug., evenings only rest of year) from local craft brewery Ægir. Named after the seafaring Norse creature of the Jotunn race, the Ægir brewery has created a Viking-themed brewpub centered around a roaring open fireplace. Sample their range of ales around the fireplace or at a cozy private table, or head upstairs to enjoy the fabulous menu in which any dish that could contain beer, does contain beer. Take your time to peruse the menu, as snippets of Viking history sit alongside each dish. Best value is the five-course Viking plank, featuring reindeer, shellfish, soup, pork, and chocolate cake with matching samplers from across the Ægir range for 475kr (vegetarian option available). Ordinary mains run 245-295kr.

Just make sure to save room for the flamboyant desserts.

For overnight stays, the **Fretheim Hotel** (tel. 57 63 63 00, www.fretheimhotel.no, from 1,890kr d) offers a range of accommodations, from the 19th-century farmhouse through to a more modern block that offers a mountain view. Figure at least an extra 500kr to stay in the oldest, highest standard rooms, which are individually decorated and feature clawfoot bathtubs. The **Heimly Pensjonat** (tel. 57 63 23 00, post@heimly.no, 895kr d), a 1930s home converted into a quiet guesthouse 500 meters (1,640 feet) away from the busy village port, is a great budget alternative. The 22 rooms are very small but well-equipped, each with a private bathroom. The attentive staff know the village's hiking trails and ferry schedules inside out, and also offer bicycles to rent. The cute waterside garden is the perfect location to watch a sunset.

Despite its small size, Flåm is accessible by car via the E16 from Bergen and Oslo. Allow around 2.5 hours to cover the 168-kilometer (104-mile) route from Bergen, with Voss the most sensible place to stop and stock up on fuel or groceries. From Oslo, allow at least five hours to cover the 351-kilometer (218-mile) journey, which passes by Borgund Stave Church and through the impressive 24.5-kilometer (15.2-mile) Lærdal Tunnel, the world's longest road tunnel.

★ Nærøyfjord

Together with the Geirangerfjord, the Nærøyfjord makes up the west Norwegian fjords listing on the UNESCO World Heritage list. More intimate than its big brother, the fjord narrows to just 250 meters (820 feet) at its narrowest point, with towering mountains creating a somewhat enclosed feeling. On photogenic clear days or atmospheric cloudy days, a trip on the Nærøyfjord, an arm of the mighty Sognefjord, has been known to bring tears to grown adults' eyes.

From May through September, a popular two-hour **Sightseeing Cruise** (from 310kr one-way, 490kr round-trip) transports passengers from Flåm to Gudvangen via the Aurlandsfjord and Nærøyfjord. In 2016, the futuristic *Vision of the Fjords* hybrid eco-ferry was launched on the route, quickly bagging global awards for its design and improving Norway's eco-rankings. In the most vulnerable areas, the vessel switches to battery power and all you can hear is the screeches of the birds circling overhead.

If planning your own itinerary and/or

the narrow Nærøyfjord

staying overnight in Flåm, taking one of the earlier or later ferries can help to miss the Nutshell rush. As a round-trip by ferry can take up to five hours, a 20-minute shuttle bus (pre-book via Flåm Tourist Information, 55kr) travels through the road tunnel between Flåm and Gudvangen to bring the return journey down to around three hours.

For an even more intimate experience with the Nærøyfjord, book a two-hour **Fjord Heritage Safari** (690kr), which mirrors the sightseeing cruise (Flåm-Gudvangen-Flåm) but with one advantage: The RIB boat can get closer to what you want to see. On the route, the driver will stop near the ancient Stigen farmstead perched precariously on the mountainside and talk about the history of each small hamlet by the fjordside. Seals, porpoises, and eagles are frequently spotted.

Book all Nærøyfjord tours with **Flåm Tourist Information** (Flåm station, tel. 57 63 33 13, 9am-6pm daily Apr.-Sept., 9am-3pm Thurs.-Sat. Oct.-Mar.), or in advance at www. visitflam.com.

Undredal

The tiny population of **Undredal,** the most beautiful of Aurland's small fjordside villages, is outnumbered by its population of goats. Based on that fact, you won't be surprised to learn of Undredal's claim to fame. The village runs the **Geitostfestivalen (Goat's Cheese Festival)** (late July, www. geitostfestivalen.no, 700kr), marking the village's proud history of cheese production. Held most years, the three days of festivities include cheese tossing and betting on which square a goat will poop in first. Group hikes and concerts on the pier round off one of Norway's most unique events.

Outside of the festival period, **Eldhuset** museum is the place to learn about the village's cultural history, from its cheese making to other farming traditions of the Undredal valley. The museum is open by appointment and must be visited as part of a one-hour package that includes a lecture and tasting buffet of local cheeses, cloudberry jam,

crisp breads, and local fruit juices. Contact **Undredal Tourist Information** (tel. 57 63 31 00, www.visitundredal.no) for booking and price information.

Undredal is home to Scandinavia's smallest stave church still in regular use. Guided tours of the tiny timber **Undredal Stave Church (Undredal stavkirke)** (Kyrkjevegen, tel. 95 29 76 68, 10am, 2:30pm most days mid-June to mid-Aug.) take place twice a day, lasting for approximately 30 minutes. Built in 1147 but completely restored in 1722, the tiny church nevertheless retained some of its older features, including a medieval bell, baptismal font, and a deer-head chandelier.

From June to August, a **Guided Tour of Undredal** leaves Flåm by coach. Participants receive a guided tour of the Eidfjord museum and the church before returning to Flåm by boat along the Aurlandsfjord. This tour does not sail down the Nærøyfjord, but is good value at 490kr. Book with **Flåm Tourist Information** (Flåm station, tel. 95 43 04 14, 9am-6pm daily Apr.-Sept., 9am-3pm Thurs.-Sat. Oct.-Mar.).

Undredal is a 13.5-kilometer (8.4-mile) drive north of Flåm via the E16 tunnel and Route 601. The drive takes just 15 minutes. Local bus 144 links the villages but runs just twice per weekday, and not at all on weekends. Check with **Kringom** (www.kringom.no) for the latest timetable and fare information.

Gudvangen

With just one restaurant and campsite, Gudvangen isn't set up for long stays and so most tourists pass straight through, whether on a Nutshell tour or not. Before you check out, browse the homemade knitwear and trinket-filled shelves of **Nærøydesign** (tel. 57 63 39 58), a short walk from the dock.

The village marks the start of the picturesque road trip back to Voss and Bergen. As the hairpin bends of the E16 climb the ever more green valley, be sure to stop at the **Stalheimskleiva viewpoint** for a memorable photograph back down toward Gudvangen. Allow around 2.5 hours to

Borgund Stave Church

complete the 147-kilometer (91.3-mile) drive from Gudvangen to Bergen, with Voss as the most obvious point for a break.

LÆRDAL

Lærdal village is the historical center of the ripe valley, but sadly, in 2014 many of its well-preserved timber homes from the 18th century were destroyed by fire, spread by the high winds of a winter storm. Even so, the historical center remains a charming walk as the long process of restoration continues. Traveling between Aurland and Lærdal is half the fun, with two of Norway's most breathtaking driving experiences to enjoy.

Throughout large parts of the summer, dramatic cliffs of snow line both sides of the 45-kilometer (28-mile) National Tourist Route between the villages of Aurlandsvangen and Lærdalsøyri (known by most people as Aurland and Lærdal), leading to its nickname, the **Snow Road (Snøvegen)**. Although the Snow Road is closed from October through April, the portion of Route 243 from Aurland

to the **Stegastein Viewpoint** is open year-round. The elegant viewing platform hovers above the pine tree forest, while its glass front gives a view right down to the fjord below. At the highest point of the mountain pass, the modern **Flotane** rest stop is powered by solar panels at its rear.

The alternative way to reach Lærdal using the E16 highway is much more direct but no less intriguing. At 24.5 kilometers (15.2 miles), the **Lærdal Tunnel (Lærdalstunnelen)** is the longest road tunnel in the world. Because of the mental strain on drivers for the dark 20-minute journey, the tunnel is separated into four sections by blue mood lighting and yellow-lit large turnaround points. Security stations count the number of cars entering and exiting to enable a quick response to any accidents. A dedicated air treatment plant removes dust and nitrogen dioxide, leading to surprisingly high air quality.

The small **Lærdal Tourist Information** office (Øyraplassen 14, tel. 48 27 75 26, 10am-5pm daily June-Aug.) is open during the summer. During the summer months, take the Snow Road to Lærdal and come back via the tunnel (or the reverse) to get the complete driving experience.

★ Borgund Stave Church
(Borgund Stavkyrkje)

Norway's best preserved stave church, built in 1180, also happens to be its most aesthetically stunning. The major pull of Lærdal is the magnificent **Borgund Stave Church** (Borgund, tel. 57 66 81 09, www.stavechurch.com/borgund, 10am-5pm daily June and Aug.-Sept., 8am-8pm daily July, 90kr), located 27 kilometers (16.8 miles) east of Lærdal along the E16, yet another picturesque mountain road.

The designers made the critical decision to build the church on a raised stone foundation to keep the timber frame from coming into contact with the damp ground during a Norwegian winter. The very fact the church is still standing proudly over eight centuries later is testament to their incredible foresight.

The basilica-plan layout is distinguished by a raised central nave and a shingle-covered roof. As with many other stave churches of the era, Norse mythology is reflected in the interior and exterior carvings, as Norway's transition to Christianity took many hundreds of years to fully bed down. In the same vein, several runic inscriptions are visible on the western walls.

The construction and conservation techniques at Borgund serve as a model for other stave church restoration projects, and as inspiration for replicas all around the world. The entry fee also gives admission to an exhibition on other stave churches and archaeological finds from the Viking era in a modern building by the parking lot.

SOGNDAL

Leaving Lærdal on Route 5, cross the Sognefjord on the Fodnes-Mannheller car ferry operated by **Fjord1** (tel. 57 75 70 00, www.fjord1.no) to arrive in Sogndal municipality. The ferry runs every 20 minutes (7am-10pm, hourly overnight) and costs from 114kr for the 15-minute crossing.

Kaupanger

The first village you come to from the ferry offers plenty of interest for those passing through. You'll find **Kaupanger Stave Church (Kaupanger stavkyrkje)** (tel. 57 67 88 40, 10am-5pm daily June-Aug., 70kr), still in regular use today as a parish church. While not as exquisite as Borgund, Kaupanger's effort is still a great example of the architecture. Although the building dates back to the mid-12th century, the pulpit, altarpiece, and font are all 17th-century additions. You can judge for yourself whether the 19th-century modernizations were brutal or beautiful, a debate that rages on. The entrance fee is only required if you want to go inside the church, where you'll find local student guides who tell you as much about living along the Sognefjord as they do the history of the church.

Five kilometers (3.1 miles) farther along

Route 5 is the **Sogn Museum (Sogn Folkemuseum)** (Vestreim, tel. 57 67 82 06, 10am-5pm daily June-Aug., 10am-3pm daily May and Sept., 10am-3pm Mon.-Fri. Oct.-Apr., 80kr May-Sept., free Oct.-Apr.). The **Heiberg Collections (De Heibergske Samlinger)** reveal how people from the valley have lived and worked for generations, and why so many chose to emigrate to the new world in the late 19th century. Thirty buildings make up an open-air museum (May-Sept.), including an open-hearth cottage dating back to medieval times and various crofters homes. Hunting, fishing, and agricultural exhibits dominate the indoor museum (year-round).

Back in the center of Kaupanger village, the arguably more interesting **Sogn Fjord Museum** (tel. 57 67 82 06, 10am-5pm daily June-Aug., free) exhibits traditional boats that were once the primary mode of transport for the fjord region. You can see original equipment and the workshop of a boat builder. A 30-minute video presentation with English subtitles documents a modern boat builder trying to use traditional construction techniques.

If you need to stay overnight in the area, some of the 107 cozy cabins with comfy lounge areas and separate bedrooms at **Vesterland Feriepark** (next to Sogn Museum, tel. 57 62 71 00, www.vesterland.no) are usually available, with rates from 1,200kr (2-3 people) to 1,525kr (4-5 people); prices are lower outside the mid-June to August high season. At an extra 140kr per person the buffet breakfast is on the expensive side, so call into one of one the nearby supermarkets and take a DIY approach.

Sogndalsfjøra (Sogndal)

A friendly community has grown up around the intersection of Route 5 and Fv55, kind to travelers in part due to the local airport, **Sogndal lufthamn, Haukåsen** (SOG), which receives daily visitors from Oslo and Bergen on Widerøe prop planes. An airport bus service (75kr) is timed to meet all arrivals.

Car rental is possible only through advance booking with **Europcar** (tel. 57 67 66 70).

Despite its small population of just a few thousand, Sogndal (officially known as Sogndalsfjøra but known simply as Sogndal by locals) is the inner Sognefjord's commercial capital. With its varied (for the fjords) choice of restaurants and accommodations, Sogndal itself is best used as a base for getting out to explore the surrounding areas.

FOOD AND ACCOMMODATIONS

The **Quality Hotel Sogndal** (Gravensteinsgata 5, tel. 57 62 77 00, q.sogndal@ choice.no, 1,500kr s, 1,800kr d) primarily caters to business guests and hosts conferences that want a fjord location. This means the lounge and catering facilities are excellent, with a generous buffet breakfast provided for all guests. The 115 contemporary rooms are mostly high-standard with vivid colorful decor, although a few still await refurbishment. Room rates drop on weekends when the business crowd is long gone. The name gives away the house specials of in-house restaurant **Vågal Burger & Gin** (3pm-10pm Mon.-Sat., 1pm-10pm Sun.), where artisan burgers can be enjoyed for around 155kr, but while the range of 13 gins is impressive for Norway, they come at a premium.

At the other end of the price scale but in a more impressive location closer to the fjord, **Sogndal Vandrerhjem** (Helgeheimsvegen 9, tel. 57 62 75 75, June to mid-Aug., 410kr s, 620kr d) hires out simple private rooms all with shared bathroom facilities. Tag on an additional 110kr for towels and bed linens unless you bring your own. On-site facilities include an outdoor grill house and beach volleyball court, while staff will be pleased to help you book day trips into the mountains or fjords.

While not outstanding quality, it's the sheer range of dining options available at downtown **Den Gamle Nabo** (Almengingen 4, tel. 57 67 15 53, noon-10pm Mon.-Thurs., noon-2am Fri.-Sat., 1pm-10pm Sun.) that we like. After a long day driving, the ability to order pizza, salad, burgers, quesadillas, pasta, or beef all

from one restaurant will help to prevent arguments. After 10pm on weekends, the cozy yet lively downstairs pub opens.

INFORMATION AND SERVICES

Located inside a kiosk, **Sogndal Tourist Information** (Parkvegen 5, tel. 99 23 15 00, 10am-10pm daily) is best for picking up leaflets and maps rather than getting questions answered in any great detail.

Sognefjellet

The National Tourist Route 55 through the **Sognefjellet** mountains is one of the country's greatest driving experiences and well worth planning a full day for.

Originally the mountain pass from Sogndal to Lom was riddled with highwaymen looking to take advantage of the vital trade link between the coastal and inland communities. Today the road is a great choice for those visiting Sognefjord who want a taste of the raw mountain landscape that dominates the majority of Norway.

The best time to drive through Sognefjellet is straight after its springtime opening, when enormous banks of snow line both sides of the narrow road on what must be one of the world's most dramatic drives. Notable rest points along the road include the **Vegaskjelet viewing point,** which faces the 2,000-meter (6,561-foot) peaks of the Skarsnebb and Steinetind mountains, and **Sognefjellshytta,** a mountain lodge where some of Norway's top international skiers choose to train. The two traditional timber buildings are linked by a modern glass-fronted lounge. From the outside this contrast looks ludicrous, yet from the inside the warm bright environment for a coffee break will leave you praising the vision of the architects.

To take into account the number of stops you are certain to take, allow 3-4 hours for the 137-kilometer (85-mile) drive from Sogndal to Lom. Return the same way for a different perspective on the scenery, or to have a road all to yourself take the narrow Tindevegen from the remote Turtagrø hotel to stay above the tree line and truly appreciate the wilderness, before a steep descent through birch forest to **Øvre Årdal,** a fjordside village whose charm is sadly ruined by a large aluminum smelting plant. Then take Route 53 toward Lærdal and the car ferry to either Kaupanger or Sogndal.

Urnes Stave Church
(Urnes stavkirke)

If stave churches are of interest, take a detour to visit the UNESCO World Heritage listed **Urnes Stave Church** (10:30am-5:30pm daily May-Sept., 90kr) in the tiny village of Ornes on the banks of the Lustrafjord. Although not quite as spectacular as Borgund, this church is still a charming example of the rare architectural style. It makes the UNESCO list as the oldest of Norway's 28 remaining stave churches, believed to have been completed sometime in the 1130s. The church contains more modern elements such as a 17th-century extension to the nave and windows from the 18th century.

To reach the church, take Route 55 north of Sogndal and follow signs for Urnes stavkirke. It should take less than an hour to make the 22.5-kilometer (14-mile) journey, which includes a five-minute ferry crossing. Be aware that the timetable for this particular ferry is extremely limited although hourly services run 10am-5pm May-September. Check in advance with operator **Lustrabaatane** (tel. 91 72 17 19, www.lustrabaatane.no) to avoid disappointment. The ferry crossing costs 110kr for a car plus driver, with a 40kr charge for each additional passenger.

JOSTEDALSBREEN NATIONAL PARK

Come face to face with the remnants of the last Ice Age at the epic **Jostedal Glacier (Jostedalsbreen)** on the northern side of the Sognefjord. Mainland northern Europe's largest ice cap had for years continued to grow rather than retreat, but in recent years this has started to change. Nevertheless, the glacier still covers an area of 474 square kilometers (183 square miles) and is up to 600 meters (1,968 feet) thick in parts. In 1991, the Norwegian government declared the glacier and surrounding areas a protected area, creating **Jostedalsbreen National Park.**

The national park is a nature lover's dream, with the landscape ranging from lush valleys and waterfalls right through to harsh Arctic conditions. Much of the park can only be reached on foot, so the opportunities for **hikers, cyclists, and skiers** are immense. While several hiking paths provide easy access to the glacier, hiking on the glacier itself is fraught with risk and not allowed without a qualified guide.

Of the 28 frosty arms of the glacier, **Nigardsbreen** is the easiest to access from Sogndal, a 60-kilometer (37.3-mile) drive via Route 55 and Route 604 that should take around one hour. The spellbinding blue ice is the backdrop for a challenging yet enjoyable walk for adults and children as young as six. Book a leisurely rope-assisted one-hour **Glacier Walking Tour** from **Jostedalen Breførarlag** (tel. 57 68 31 11, www.bfl.no, mid-May to mid-Sept., 270kr) for an unforgettable experience. The more daring can learn to use crampons and ice axes while they listen to the incredible crackling sounds of the glacier on a five-hour **Blue Ice Hike** (990kr) inside spectacular ice tunnels and crevices.

All tours leave from the foot of the Nigardsbreen glacier arm. Head to **Jostedal Tourist Information** (Breheimsenteret, tel. 57 68 32 50, www.jostedalsignatur.no, 10am-5pm daily May-Sept.), a few miles north of Gjerde on Route 334, to begin your trip. The modern building doubles as a **visitor center** (70kr) for the national park with interactive exhibits and a short subtitled film that takes you on and under the glaciers to explain their fascinating history. The car park for the glacier itself is a couple of miles behind the visitor center. From the car park, it's a 45-minute walk around the edge of the lake to the glacier, so allow plenty of time to reach your guide. During the summer a boat runs the length of the lake, but organized groups take priority, so walking is the best option.

The small village of **Gjerde** is the perfect place to base yourself for a day (or more) of glacier exploration. The simple rooms at the **Jostedal Hotel** (tel. 57 68 31 19, www.jostedalhotel.no, 920kr s, 1,190kr d) are just a few miles from the glacier. Accommodation is basic although the hotel is better known for its restaurant, sourcing its ingredients from the surrounding mountain and the Sognefjord. For a better-value option, a handful of cabins at **Jostedal Camping** (tel. 97 75 67 89, www.jostedalcamping.no) are available for 450-620kr, but you must bring your own bed linen. Although they don't have running water, each cabin has a refrigerator and electric stovetop, making self-catering easy.

From mid-June through August, a daily **Glacier Bus** (tel. 57 67 66 00, 158kr) leaves Sogndal at 8:30am and 1:45pm, returning from Jostedal Tourist Information at 5pm. The journey takes about 80 minutes.

BALESTRAND

The most relaxing of the inner Sognefjord's villages, Balestrand, with its lush vegetation and colorful timber houses, just begs to be explored at a leisurely pace. Marked hiking trails spread out into the surrounding hills, but an enjoyable walk is available within the village itself.

Pick up a free map at **Balestrand Tourist Information** (Holmen 9, tel. 94 87 75 01, 9am-4pm daily June-Aug., 10am-4pm Mon.-Fri. May and Sept., closed rest of year) to follow the **Culture Trail,** a two-mile self-guided walk around the village. Most of the information boards along the route are printed in English, while handy benches with the best fjord views are a great spot for a picnic.

The walk takes you on the old road along the shoreline from the harbor, past 19th-century villas built in the popular Swiss style of the period by locals attempting to introduce a dose of Romanticism into Norwegian architecture. The dragons' heads from the gables are influenced by the decor of the region's many stave churches. Two burial mounds from the Viking Age and a statue of King Bele, a gift from German emperor Wilhelm II in 1913, are other highlights on the trail.

The **Kreklingen nature trail,** with a mild ascent through the forest to the south of the city, is a popular family-friendly alternative. Allow around two hours for a lazy wander along the three-kilometer trail. With such lovely views of the fjord and mountains, you won't want to rush.

For a dose of local history, stay at the sprawling ★ **Kviknes Hotel** (Kviknevegen 8, tel. 57 69 42 00, www.kviknes.com, 1,310kr). Run by the Kviknes family since 1877, the Swiss-style waterside hotel has been expanded over the years but still retains its special character, thanks in part to the vast private collection of paintings and antiques lining the corridors. Don't miss the Høyvik Room, filled by the life's work of craftsman Ivar Høyvik. The standard across the 190 rooms varies, and although all are comfortable, you'll pay more for one in the oldest part of the hotel or for a fjord view. At under 2,000kr per night, the demi-suites with balcony are a surprisingly affordable option to add a treat to your travels.

With Norwegian craft breweries now as common as troll souvenirs, a meal at **Ciderhuset** (Sjøtunsvegen 32, tel. 90 83 56 73, www.ciderhuset.no, 4pm-10pm Sun.-Fri. mid-June to mid-Aug.) will make a refreshing change. The Mediterranean-inspired menu is accompanied by crisp apple cider and fruit wines, made on the premises using produce from their own orchard. A cider-tasting experience with light lunch is also available in the early afternoon. Book in advance.

GETTING AROUND
By Fast Ferry

Although driving is the best way to truly connect with the lush valleys and small communities around the Sognefjord, it is possible to enjoy this region of Norway without joining a Nutshell tour and just using public transit, thanks to the system of high-speed ferries run by Bergen-based **Norled**

(Strandkaien, Bergen, tel. 51 86 87 00, www. norled.no, office open 8am-3:30pm Mon.-Fri., 2pm-4pm Sun.).

The fast passenger ferries are a great option for those who don't want to or can't drive as they also double as a sightseeing cruise of the Sognefjord. The five-hour service from Bergen to Sogndal runs once per day in the early evening year-round. From May to September, an additional service links Bergen with Flåm, via Vik, Balestrand, and Leikanger. This service can also be used for traveling between the small towns of the Sognefjord, but as departures are limited it's wise to keep a copy of the timetable on you to avoid an unplanned overnight stop. Although individual journeys can be expensive, the Norled **Fjord Card** (May-Sept.) is one of Norway's best travel bargains, enabling unlimited travel on the network for five days for 1,250kr.

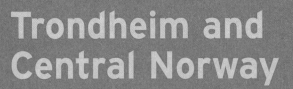

Trondheim and Central Norway

Look for ★ to find recommended
sights, activities, dining, and lodging.

Highlights

★ **Nidaros Cathedral:** The northernmost cathedral in the world is covered with hundreds of sculptures and ornate carvings (page 204).

★ **Bakklandet:** Trondheim's photogenic old town is a bustling mix of sidewalk cafés, boutiques, and cyclists passing by (page 207).

★ **Røros Museum:** The former copper-mining town in the mountains is a beautifully preserved living museum (page 226).

★ **Snøhetta Pavilion:** With award-winning architecture, views of the mountains, and the chance to see wild reindeer, this viewpoint makes a perfect stop on a road trip through the mountains (page 231).

★ **Musk Ox Safari:** A few hours spent with a local guide searching for herds of musk oxen is time well spent! These immense creatures can't be found anywhere else in Europe (page 231).

★ **Trollstigen Mountain Pass:** This pass is only open in the summer months. Head there early to navigate the hairpin bends in relative peace, and don't miss the walkways to the exceptional viewpoints at the summit (page 236).

★ **Atlantic Road:** Norway's most famous road trip dances across skerries and islets—and the journey through Averøy island to get there is as captivating as the road itself (page 245).

Often overlooked by international visitors, Trondheim and Norway's central mountains receive a huge influx of domestic tourism each year. So what exactly do Norwegians know that foreign visitors don't?

Firstly, the scenery of this largely rural region is varied and offers landscapes just as spectacular as the rest of the country, only far less well known. From the towering Snøhetta mountain (one of Norway's tallest) to the hiking trails, cabins, rivers, and waterfalls of the many national parks, central Norway draws hikers, cyclists, and cross-country skiers in the thousands. Rare animals, including wild mountain reindeer and Europe's only herds of musk oxen, complete the region's compelling natural attractions. Farther west, the green Romsdal valley marks the border with Fjord Norway and culminates with the island-based city of Kristiansund and its world-famous neighbor, the island-hopping Atlantic Road.

Secondly, Trondheim is Norway's oldest major city and is packed full of history. The cobbled streets and wooden buildings of the beautiful city center whisper their secrets as you pass through. Nidaros Cathedral is a spectacular monument of national importance as the burial site of Saint Olav (Olav Haraldsson), the patron saint of Norway. Yet modern Trondheim is far from a sleepy place full of memories. It's a vibrant international city with a massive student population and a packed calendar of cultural events throughout the year.

Outside of Trondheim you'll find rock carvings, battlefields, fortresses, and stave churches that live to tell the tale of those who came long before. So many key events took place in central Norway that history buffs will leave here fully satisfied. The death of Olav Haraldsson at the battle of Stiklestad in 1030 represented the introduction of Christianity to Norway, while the discovery of copper in the mountains toward the Swedish border created a new town (Røros) and an industry that lasted for hundreds of years.

Less than 10 percent of the country's population live in this vast region, so in spite of the

---

Previous: Trondheim's Nidaros Cathedral and the Nidelva river in the winter; camping in the mountains.
Above: trolls, a cultural icon of rural Norway.

Trondheim and Central Norway

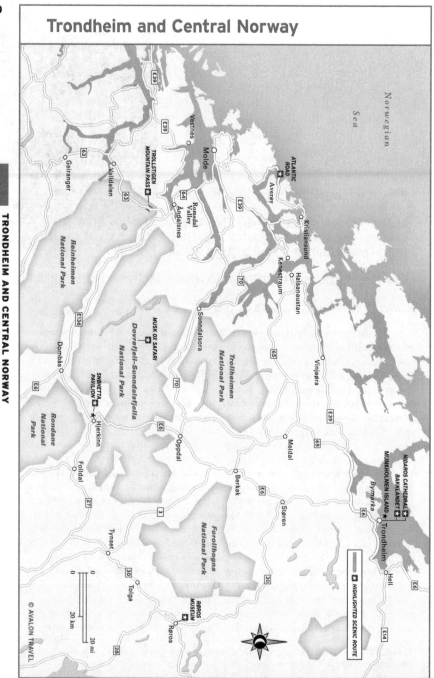

© AVALON TRAVEL

huge number of things to do, you'll never feel rushed or outnumbered.

PLANNING YOUR TIME

The majority of visitors to Norway's midriff will spend a day or so in Trondheim as part of a cruise or passing through on their way to or from the Arctic. If you are arriving by ship, you should have enough time for a two-hour sightseeing walk around the compact central area to take in the city's main sights.

If you have more time, Trondheim can serve as a base for exploring central Norway. The city has enough going on to keep you entertained for a few days, although you should certainly consider taking a day trip to the remarkable mountain town of Røros, accessible by car, bus, railroad, or plane. For longer stays, a day or two around Kristiansund and the Atlantic Road is time well-spent, as are the mountains of Dovrefjell-Sunndalsfjella National Park. You don't need to plan a multi-day hiking trip to experience the mountains, as many of the park's highlights and shorter hikes are accessible from the E6 highway and numerous railway stations.

Drivers plan a road trip through this area for one reason: the Atlantic Road. Suitable as an add-on to a trip to Trondheim or around the western fjords, the Atlantic Road is a must-do for drivers, although since it's at least 215 kilometers from Trondheim, you'll want to plan an overnight stop in Kristiansund, Åndalsnes, or one of the region's many campsites.

Trondheim

With strong Viking roots and a long history in trade, mining, and fishing, Trondheim has a long, proud, and visible history. From the old town of Bakklandet to the fortress watching over the city, from the wooden riverside wharves to the narrow cobbled alleyways, a stroll around Trondheim will leave you in little doubt of the city's importance over the years.

Many kings are buried here, and Nidaros Cathedral hosts coronation ceremonies. Such is the historical importance of the cathedral that people still make the pilgrimage across the central mountains to this day.

Modern Trondheim bills itself as Norway's technology capital due to its high concentration of high-tech firms. Perhaps a better title would be knowledge capital, for academia is where the city truly shines. The Norwegian University of Science and Technology (NTNU), its University Hospital, and the independent SINTEF research institute (the largest such organization in Scandinavia) dominate the city's economy.

The 25,000 students in a population of around 180,000 give the town a youthful, vibrant feel, so much so that the town is noticeably more peaceful in the summer months.

Trondheim has a strong musical heritage, particularly in heavy metal and classical music. Live music can be heard somewhere in the city most nights of the week, while the number of music festivals held throughout the year would be enough for a city three times its size. Award-winning violinist Arve Tellefsen, Diesel Dahl from metal band TNT, and Bent Sæther from psychedelic rock band Motorpsycho are just some of the professional musicians who have called Trondheim home. You can explore some of this heritage at two of Norway's best music museums, Rockheim and Ringve Music Museum.

HISTORY

People have lived in the region for thousands of years, evidenced by the large number of rock carvings dotted around central Norway. During his short reign as Viking king, Olav Tryggvason founded Trondheim in 997, although the city was known as Nidaros

Trondheim

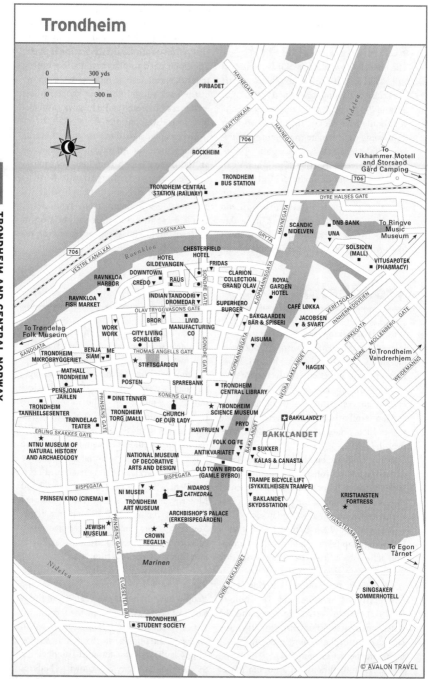

0   300 yds
0   300 m

PIRBADET

706

ROCKHEIM

To
Vikhammer Motell
and Storsand
Gård Camping

TRONDHEIM
BUS STATION

706

TRONDHEIM CENTRAL
STATION (RAILWAY)

DYRE HALSES GATE

FOSENKAIA

Nidelva

706

VESTRE KANALKAI

Ravnkloa

SCANDIC
NIDELVEN

DNB BANK

To Ringve
Music
Museum

UNA

CHESTERFIELD
HOTEL

SOLSIDEN
(MALL)

HOTEL
GILDEVANGEN

FRIDAS

VITUSAPOTEK
(PHARMACY)

RAVNKLOA
HARBOR

DOWNTOWN

CLARION
COLLECTION
GRAND OLAV

CREDO

RAUS

ROYAL
GARDEN
HOTEL

RAVNKLOA
FISH MARKET

INDIAN TANDOORI
DROMEDAR

CAFÉ LØKKA

OLAV TRYGGVASONS GATE

SUPERHERO
BURGER

To Trøndelag
Folk Museum

WORK
WORK

BROR

LIVID
MANUFACTURING
CO

BAKGAARDEN
BAR & SPISERI

JACOBSEN
& SVART

CITY LIVING
SCHØLLER

SANDGATA

BENJA
SIAM

ME

AISUMA

THOMAS ANGELLS GATE

TRONDHEIM
MIKROBRYGGERIET

HAGEN

STIFTSGÅRDEN

MATHALL
TRONDHEIM

To Trondheim
Vandrerhjem

WEIDEMANNS

POSTEN

SPAREBANK

PENSJONAT
JARLEN

KØNENS GATE

TRONDHEIM
CENTRAL LIBRARY

TRONDHEIM
TANNHELSESENTER

DINE TENNER

BAKKLANDET

TRØNDELAG
TEATER

TRONDHEIM
TORG (MALL)

CHURCH
OF OUR LADY

TRONDHEIM
SCIENCE MUSEUM

ERLING SKAKKES GATE

PRYD

NTNU MUSEUM OF
NATURAL HISTORY
AND ARCHAEOLOGY

HAVFRUEN

BAKKLANDET

FOLK OG FE

NATIONAL MUSEUM
OF DECORATIVE
ARTS AND DESIGN

ANTIKVARIATET

SUKKER

KALAS & CANASTA

BISPEGATA

OLD TOWN BRIDGE
(GAMLE BYBRO)

TRAMPE BICYCLE LIFT
(SYKKELHEISEN TRAMPE)

PRINSEN KINO (CINEMA)

NI MUSER

NIDAROS
CATHEDRAL

BAKLANDET
SKYDSSTATION

KRISTIANSTEN
FORTRESS

TRONDHEIM
ART MUSEUM

JEWISH
MUSEUM

ARCHBISHOP'S PALACE
(ERKEBISPEGÅRDEN)

CROWN
REGALIA

To Egon
Tårnet

Marinen

SINGSAKER
SOMMERHOTELL

Nidelva

ELGESETER BRU

TRONDHEIM
STUDENT SOCIETY

BRATTØRKAIA

HAVNEGATA

HAVNEGATA

GRYTA

KJØPMANNSGATA

SØNDRE GATE

PRINSENS GATE

PRINSENS GATE

ØVRE BAKKLANDET

NEDRE BAKKLANDET

KIRKEGATA

NEDRE MØLLENBERG GATE

VERFTSGATA

INNHERREDSVEIEN

KRISTIANSTENSBAKKEN

© AVALON TRAVEL

throughout the Viking Age. It is believed he chose the area as his base due to the curvature of the Nidelva river giving natural protection from land attacks.

From 1015, Olav Haraldsson ruled Norway, and following his death at the Battle of Stiklestad in 1030, his body was enshrined in Nidaros Cathedral, built over his burial site. It is believed that both Olav Tryggvason and Olav Haraldsson played important roles in Norway's conversion to Christianity. Olav Haraldsson was canonized 134 years after his death by Pope Alexander III, forever confirming Nidaros as a place of historical importance.

Nidaros was the capital of Norway until 1217, when a period of civil unrest began over a succession struggle. Haakon IV eventually triumphed and chose to sit in Bergen. The city of Nidaros continued to grow as a trading post, and during the Middle Ages the name Trondhjem first began to appear. This spelling is still used today by those of a certain generation, while the name Nidaros lives on in the title of many local companies and sports clubs. The university's American football team is known as the Nidaros Domers.

Many great fires destroyed the city during the 16th and 17th centuries, when the population was still under 10,000 with almost all people living within the bounds of the current downtown area. In 1681, the city was reconstructed with wide avenues such as Munkegata created to try to prevent any future fires from spreading so quickly. This period also saw the construction of Kristiansten Fortress, to help prevent attacks from Swedish forces from the east.

In 1760 the Trondheim Society was created, an organization that would eventually become the Norwegian University of Science and Technology (NTNU) after a series of mergers.

Trondheim was occupied by Nazi Germany from the very first day of the invasion of Norway during World War II. The Germans used the city as a naval operations base and had planned to significantly expand the urban area southward.

In 1964, the current city of Trondheim was created by merging the neighboring municipalities of Strinda, Tiller, Leinstrand, and Byneset with the former city. This move doubled the city's population, and it has grown steadily ever since.

CLIMATE

Despite its watery surroundings, Trondheim is actually quite a long way from the open ocean and therefore doesn't get anywhere near as much rain as the likes of Bergen and Stavanger. The rain that does fall tends to be concentrated between September and November. Snow can be expected from December to March, but that can stretch weeks on either side, sometimes falling as early as September and as late as May.

Summer temperatures reach the 70s fairly often. You'll notice a transformation in the mood of locals any day over 15°C (60°F), especially in the late spring as the city emerges from its winter hibernation.

ORIENTATION

Known as **Midtbyen** (literally "middle city"), Trondheim's city center is still on the same small piece of land on which Olav Tryggvason founded the city over 1,000 years ago. Almost an island, the land is characterized by a grid layout of streets and is easy to navigate on foot.

Most of the city's attractions are located in or very close to Midtbyen, and it takes no more than 20 minutes to walk across it in any direction. **Nidaros Cathedral** and its grounds take up the southern portion. Across the river to the east you will find the **Bakklandet** old town neighborhood, while farther north is the **Solsiden** development of restaurants, bars, and a shopping mall on the site of a former shipyard.

Between Midtbyen and the Trondheimsfjord to the north is **Brattøra,** an artificial island that is home to the city's railway station, bus station, port, and ferry terminal. This keeps Midtbyen a relatively pleasant place, free from industry.

In contrast to the compact nature of

downtown, the residential areas of Trondheim spread for miles into the hills on the west and east of the city, and following the route of the river to the south. The sprawling **Bymarka** forest visible from across the city is the city's main recreational area, along with the fjord and river.

SIGHTS

Thanks to a natural boundary formed by the fjord and the Nidelva river that almost entirely encircles it, Trondheim's downtown is small, compact, and easy to navigate on foot. A walking tour taking in the main sights can be completed in a couple of hours at a leisurely pace.

Downtown
★ NIDAROS CATHEDRAL
(Nidarosdomen)

The world's northernmost medieval cathedral, **Nidaros Cathedral** (Bispegata 11, tel. 99 43 60 00, www.nidarosdomen.no, 9am-3pm Mon.-Fri., 9am-2pm Sat., 9am-4pm Sun., 90kr) is the most important, historic, and impressive ecclesiastical building in Scandinavia and the undisputed highlight of Trondheim. To this day, pilgrims walk great distances across Scandinavia to visit Nidaros and pay their respects to Saint Olav, who is buried inside. The tower can be seen from across the city, and its imposing western front, reminiscent of those at Salisbury and Wells in England, delights curious visitors from around the world.

Although construction began as a memorial to Saint Olav in 1070, the cathedral wasn't finished until around 1300, although it had been in use for more than a century. Since then, the structure was damaged by fire several times and it has been repaired, restored, and expanded over the years.

Major reconstruction has taken place on the entire structure but most notably on the western front. It isn't known how many sculptures there were on the original design, but today over 50 sculptured figures line three rows around the rose window. Those immortalized in stone include kings and prophets

the sculpture-rich west front of Nidaros Cathedral

of the Old Testament, Norwegian saints, the three theological virtues, and the four cardinal virtues. The sculpture of Saint Olav stands atop a dragon-like creature said to represent paganism. His figure is often decorated with a garland at times of celebration, such as during the St. Olav's Festival held every summer.

The rose window was restored at the beginning of the 20th century from a design by local architect Gabriel Kielland. The window, which is faced to the sunset and symbolizes doomsday, is made up of 10,000 individual pieces of glass and regarded as Kielland's masterpiece. Around the same time, the famous Norwegian sculptor Gustav Vigeland carved some of the gargoyles for the northern transept.

It's a common sight to see locals on their lunch breaks sitting on the benches across the atrium, taking in the view. Take a stroll around the cathedral's exterior and you'll notice other Gothic-style carvings. Paying to enter the cathedral isn't a must, as you can gain a lot just from studying the western front and strolling around the exterior. If you only have time for a quick stop on a walking tour of Trondheim, there's no need to pay the entrance fee.

Having said that, those with an interest in Norwegian history or Christianity will get a lot of value from a look inside. Features to look out for include the octagonal shrine to Saint Olav, two principal altars, and a medieval chapter house. June-August, 30-minute guided tours are offered throughout the day and can be requested in advance during the rest of the year. Guides tend to be local students and are full of stories from centuries past.

For an additional 40kr you can go up the tower and take a look at the breathtaking views across Trondheim. Included in the regular entrance fee is an unaccompanied journey down to the crypt. This stuffy, warm area is not the most comfortable area to stay in for a long period, but it's worthwhile to study the collection of tombstones, many made from marble.

Formerly the residence of some of Norway's most powerful people, the **Archbishop's Palace (Erkebispegården)** (10am-3pm Mon.-Sat., noon-4pm Sun., 90kr) is immediately adjacent to the cathedral. Today it functions as a museum, home to some original relics from the cathedral and a fascinating tale of its construction and restoration through a series of exhibits and a subtitled movie. The **Crown Regalia** (10am-3pm Mon.-Sat., noon-4pm Sun., 90kr) in the neighboring building contains coronation memorabilia, including the crowns of the king and queen of Norway. Made in Stockholm in 1818, the king's crown is made of gold with amethysts, pearls, and tourmaline, lined with a red velvet cap.

A combined ticket can be bought for all three attractions for 180kr, saving 90kr on individual entries. The café and gift shop mean you could easily spend an entire day in and around the cathedral grounds, which are a pleasant place to enjoy a sunny day. The area in front of the western front and the green bank alongside the river are the prime spots.

TRONDHEIM ART MUSEUM
(Trondheim kunstmuseum)

Although merely steps from Nidaros Cathedral, **Trondheim Art Museum** (Bispegata 7b, tel. 73 53 81 80, www.trondheimkunstmuseum.no, 10am-4pm daily June-Aug., noon-8pm Wed., noon-4pm Thurs.-Sun. Sept.-May, 100kr) is frequently missed by tourists. A small selection from the gallery's vast permanent collection is always on display, including works by Norwegian landscape painters Johan Dahl and Thomas Fearnley. Many carvings, sketches, and lithographs from Edvard Munch are also part of the collection, but if you are really keen to see them, call ahead to check that they are currently on display. The museum's biggest draw is the regular rotation of temporary exhibitions focusing on contemporary art, sometimes controversial, from Norway and beyond. Check the website for the latest lineup.

NATIONAL MUSEUM OF DECORATIVE ARTS AND DESIGN
(Nordenfjeldske Kunstindustrimuseum)

The **National Museum of Decorative Arts and Design** (Munkegata 3-7, tel. 73 80 89 50, www.nkim.no, 10am-4pm Mon.-Sat., noon-4pm Sun. June-Aug., 10am-3pm Tues.-Wed. Fri.-Sat., noon-8pm Thurs., noon-4pm Sun. Sept.-May, 100kr) has a diverse collection of material collections spanning textiles, furniture, and metalwork. The rooms on the lower floors showcase the bourgeois lifestyle of Trondheim over the years.

Don't miss the room dedicated to Belgian architect Henry van de Velde. The art nouveau pioneer designed several iconic furniture pieces that were groundbreaking in their day. The 14 tapestries from Swedish-Norwegian textile artist Hannah Ryggen (1894-1970) were so influential that they are frequently out on temporary loan, although their home is here in Trondheim. She was known for using a standing loom and dying the fabric with local plants. Since the museum's opening over 100 years ago, a Japanese collection of ceramic arts, Samurai armor, and pots dating back to the Jomon period (14,000-300 BC) has been amassed.

NTNU MUSEUM OF NATURAL HISTORY AND ARCHAEOLOGY (Vitenskapsmuseet)

Explore prehistoric central Norway at the **NTNU Museum of Natural History and Archaeology** (Erling Skakkes gate 47a, tel. 73 59 21 45, www.ntnu.no/vitenskapsmuseet, 10am-4pm Tues.-Fri., 11am-4pm Sat.-Sun., 60kr), just a short walk from the central shopping district. Exhibits include a pair of shoes from the Iron Age, rock carvings from the Stone Age, and the original Kuli stone, a monument from the Viking Age featuring a cross with clear runic inscription. It marks the first ever known reference to Christianity in Norway. The museum also contains an exhibition known as The Ark that helps children study animals and in particular how certain species have evolved.

TRONDHEIM SCIENCE MUSEUM (Vitensenteret)

Located in a grand building formerly home to the Bank of Norway, **Trondheim Science Museum** (Kongens gate 1, tel. 72 90 90 07, www.vitensenteret.com, 10am-4pm Mon.-Fri., 11am-5pm Sat.-Sun., 85kr) describes itself as a place for "aha!" moments. It creates these by allowing visitors to get hands-on with experiments in kitchen chemistry and interact with robots. It's primarily aimed at children.

JEWISH MUSEUM (Jødisk museum)

The former building of Trondheim's first railway station is now home to the **Jewish Museum** (Arkitekt Christies gate 1b, tel. 40 16 98 01, 50kr), which explores Jewish history, culture, and identity in the Trondheim area. Although the Jewish population of the city is small, they were greatly affected by the occupation of Trondheim by Nazi Germany in World War II, and these stories form

the basis of the exhibits at the museum. Of all the World War II-focused museums in Norway—and there are a lot—this one tells some of the most harrowing personal tales. This small museum is only open from mid-June to mid-August (10am-4pm Mon.-Fri., noon-3pm Sun.) and on the first Sunday of every month (noon-3pm) outside of the summer season.

STIFTSGÅRDEN

Only open to visitors during the summer, the royal residence at **Stiftsgården** (Munkegata 23, tel. 73 84 28 80, www.nkim.no/en/stiftsgarden, 90kr) runs tours on the hour 10am-3pm Monday-Saturday, noon-3pm Sunday. The 30-minute tours in Norwegian and English guide you around the wooden palace that was built in the late 18th century, during the transitional period between rococo and classicism. The somewhat basic furnishings are in stark contrast to the delightfully extravagant wall paintings. The 140-room home was originally built for an affluent widow and today serves as the official royal residence in Trondheim. Although the smart yellow building is prominently located in the center of town, it is only possible to visit Stiftsgården on a guided tour. You can, however, stroll through the small but pleasant gardens at the building's rear in daylight hours.

CHURCH OF OUR LADY (Vår Frue kirke)

The medieval **Church of Our Lady** (Kongens gate 5, tel. 73 80 55 20, 9am-6pm daily, free) would be much better known were it not for Nidaros Cathedral stealing the show. The church is known locally for opening its doors to the city's less fortunate citizens and giving them a place to rest their heads at night and providing a warming cup of coffee during the day. Hundreds of volunteers have kept this open church policy going in the very heart of Trondheim since 2007. The Romanesque and Gothic stone exterior, including the 18th-century tower, are worth seeking out, although the interior is fairly plain with the exception of the impressive tall altar adorned with sculptures and paintings.

★ BAKKLANDET

Just a few minutes' walk from Nidaros Cathedral is the charming old town of Bakklandet, known for its cobbled streets and wonky wooden houses. Originally built in the 17th century to house traders, factory workers, and fishermen, the district's wooden houses are today home to cafés, restaurants, boutiques, and some of the city's most desirable apartments. Pull up a chair and watch the world go by.

To reach Bakklandet from Nidaros Cathedral, head east across the **Old Town Bridge (Gamle Bybro),** where I challenge you not to whip out your camera and take a photo. Without doubt Trondheim's most photographed spot, the bridge crosses the Nidelva river, lined on both sides by colorful wooden buildings on stilts.

Shocking as it may seem, the area was nearly demolished in the 1970s to make way for a new four-lane highway to bypass the city center. Thankfully common sense prevailed, but only after a decade of grassroots lobbying from groups of concerned residents.

If you can resist the aroma of the freshly brewed coffee and cinnamon buns from the cluster of cafés, immediately in front of the bridge is the **Trampe Bicycle Lift (Sykkelheisen Trampe),** the only one of its kind in the world. That it's become a tourist attraction is a source of great amusement to Trondheim's cyclists, who use the lift (which is essentially little more than a moving foot plate) as part of their daily commute.

ROCKHEIM

The contemporary music museum **Rockheim** (Brattørkaia 14, tel. 73 60 50 70, www.rockheim.no, 11am-7pm Tues.-Fri., 11am-6pm Sat.-Sun., 130kr) is more of an interactive experience than a museum. Housed in a former grain warehouse in a largely industrial area north of downtown, Rockheim leads you through a musical journey from the 1950s to the present day, profiling both Norwegian and international artists through a series of interactive exhibits.

Try your hand at electric guitar with on-screen guidance from Ronni Le Tekrø, guitarist for the Trondheim-based heavy metal band TNT, while in the neighboring room your whole family can jam together on stage, if you have the talent! Staff are on hand to help

view of the Nidelva river warehouses from Bakklandet

with all the interactive exhibits and help make sure you don't miss any of the fun.

Although Rockheim is classed as the city center, it is a short walk from what most people consider downtown. The most direct route is to head to the Trondheim railway station and take the large pedestrian stairway over the tracks (lift available). Once over the tracks, follow the path to the right. It will take around 20 minutes from Nidaros Cathedral.

Outside the Center
RINGVE MUSIC MUSEUM
(Ringve Musikkmuseum)

For a look back at how musical instruments have shaped culture over time, take the short trip to the beautiful country estate that is now home to **Ringve Music Museum** (Lade allé 60, tel. 73 87 02 80, www.ringve.no, 11am-4pm daily May, 10am-5pm daily June-Aug., 11am-4pm Tues.-Sun. Sept.-Apr., 120kr) on the Lade peninsula, northeast of central Trondheim. Pick up bus route 3 or 4 from Munkegata (toward Lade) to reach the museum in less than 15 minutes.

Over 2,000 musical instruments are split across two collections. The barn presents classical musical instruments from around the world and demonstrates how they were used by the upper classes in the form of musical societies and private concerts. You can try your hand at a number of the instruments, including one of the first electronic instruments, the theremin.

The 19th-century wooden manor house is home to the second collection, including a house organ, disc music box, and a self-playing piano, and is in process of being restored following a damaging fire in 2015. This part of the museum requires a short guided tour (included in the price), which can be arranged upon your arrival.

The museum is surrounded by the beautiful **Ringve Botanical Garden** (Lade allé 58, tel. 73 59 22 69, always open, free), which is a pleasant place to extend your stay on the peninsula when the weather is nice. Highlights of the garden include the Renaissance herb garden from the 17th century, a northern hemisphere arboretum, and a historical park planted in an English landscape style.

TRØNDELAG FOLK MUSEUM
(Trøndelag Folkemuseum)

Trøndelag Folk Museum (Sverresborg allé 13, tel. 73 89 01 00, www.sverresborg.no, 10am-4pm daily June-Aug., 10am-3pm Tues.-Fri., noon-4pm Sat.-Sun. Sept.-May, 150kr

Ringve Music Museum is set inside a country estate.

summer, 115kr otherwise) is arguably the best of all Norway's outdoor folk museums, with more than 60 timber buildings from the 18th and 19th centuries combined with a photographic exhibition and a small ski museum, showcasing the importance of the sport to this region of Norway. A terrific family attraction, the museum is best visited during the summer months when the outdoor exhibits come alive with actors and live music fills the air.

Located in the suburb of Sverresborg high in the hills to the west of the city, the museum can be reached by taking bus route 18 from Kongens gate (toward Havstad). The journey to the museum takes just 10 minutes.

KRISTIANSTEN FORTRESS
(Kristiansten festning)

Overlooking downtown Trondheim from a perch high above the east of the city, **Kristiansten Fortress** (Kristianstensbakken, tel. 81 57 04 00, 10am-4pm Mon.-Sat., noon-4pm Sun. mid-May to mid-Sept., grounds always open, free) has a fascinating history. The fortress was built in the late 17th century when the city was reconstructed after a great fire. In 1718, Swedish forces attacked in the latter stages of the Great Northern War. The fortress did its job, and the city was held.

Inside the meter-thick white walls of the former cannon tower is a small museum. It's worth a quick look for the charming wooden interior, and to see if you dare to climb the steep creaky staircases. If you don't, follow the signed Fortress Trail to discover all the points of interest, although the written descriptions are only in Norwegian.

The fortress can be reached on foot from Bakklandet via the steep Brubakken, home to the Trampe bicycle lift, in about 10 minutes or alternatively by taking the gentler (though still uphill) Lillegårdsbakken in about 15-20 minutes. Alternatively, take bus 63 from Kongens gate (toward Strindheim), alight at Festningsgata after around eight minutes, and cross the park (five-minute walk) to the fortress.

MUNKHOLMEN ISLAND

Out in the bay is **Munkholmen Island,** a small island with a big history. It was originally an execution ground used by Olav Trygvasson in the Viking era. Benedictine monks built a monastery on the island very early in the 11th century. In 1658 it was converted into a prison and fort, later becoming a custom house. Today the island is a popular recreational area for the people of Trondheim thanks to its green spaces and good bathing possibilities. Inside the numerous preserved buildings on the island you'll find a restaurant/café and the **Husflid Galleri** (open when the boats run) gallery and gift shop, selling a surprisingly wide variety of arts, crafts, and textiles.

You can reach Munkholmen from mid-May to September on a scheduled boat tour from **Tripps** (tel. 95 08 21 44, www.trippsbatservice.no). Ferries depart from the Ravnkloa fish market hourly 10am-4pm (times can vary, so be sure to check in advance), and one hour is enough for most people to wander around the island. The five-minute ride costs 90kr (tickets valid for both journeys) and, unusually for Norway, only cash is accepted on board. The nearest ATM is a five-minute walk away on the market square opposite the Trondheim Torg shopping mall.

SPORTS AND RECREATION

Sports and outdoor activities are second nature to anyone from central Norway. Trøndelag, the county that covers much of central Norway, produces more Olympic gold medalists than any other region of Norway. International observers continue to be baffled at Norway's Olympic success (although their performance at the Sochi Games of 2014 was underwhelming), yet locals point toward government investment in regional sports centers as the key to success. As such, facilities in and around Trondheim are world-class.

Bymarka

Covering miles of western Trondheim, the

city forest known as **Bymarka** is the city's playground. Trails for **hiking** and **cross-country skiing** work their way through the forest, at some points dense and lonesome, at others open and with unbeatable views across the city below.

On weekends Bymarka is filled with families spanning multiple generations enjoying the outdoors and picking berries. Many of the trails closest to the city are even suitable for baby carriages.

Due to its accessibility by public transport, one of the most popular weekend routes is from the Skistua lodge to the Lian restaurant at the Lianvatnet lake. One of the largest lodges across Bymarka, **Skistua** (Fjellseterveien, tel. 94 88 94 50, www.skistua.no, 11am-3pm Mon.-Fri., 11am-5pm Sat.-Sun.) is served by bus 10, which departs from Kongens gate at 10am and 2pm on Monday and Friday. A more extensive service operates on weekends, with departures starting from 9:50am on Saturday and from 10:15am on Sunday. The journey into the woods takes around 25 minutes.

Skistua is the starting point of many classic trails. Your first port of call should be the short two-kilometer (1.2-mile) round-trip hike to the summit of **Gråkallen** for the best possible view across Trondheim. Although the walk is short, you do ascend 100 meters, so a reasonable level of fitness is required. It's then a 4.8-kilometer (three-mile) walk to **Lian,** from where you can take the tramway back to the city center, but many other possibilities exist for side-trips or taking a longer route to Lian. The **Lian Restaurant** (Lianvegen 36, tel. 72 56 51 10) is a good place to stop for coffee and waffles before taking the tram back into the city. Opening hours during the week verge on random, but the restaurant is always open on Sunday (the popular hiking day among Norwegians) from midday to around 5pm.

Bymarka trails are clearly signed, but buy a specialized hiking map from a sports store downtown to help decipher the signposts if you plan on exploring trails other than those listed here.

Biking

Although the exact dates depend upon the weather conditions, **Trondheim Bysykkel** (www.bysykler.no) offers city bike rental from around April to October. Primarily intended for residents, the 150 bikes can also be used by tourists through the rental of an access card at **Trondheim Tourist Information office** (Nordre gate 11, tel. 73 80 76 60, 9am-6pm Mon.-Sat., also Sun. during July). Rental costs 75kr for one day, 120kr for two days, and 300kr for one week, with a 200kr deposit also required. Bikes can be picked up and returned at one of 20 automated rental stations around the city, including Nidaros Cathedral, St. Olav's Hospital, Bakklandet, Solsiden, and Fjordgata.

Skiing

Cross-country skiing dominates to the point of obsession in Central Norway. In summer months you will almost certainly see roller-skiers zipping around the cycle paths of Trondheim. These are likely professionals or keen amateurs keeping in shape until the snowfall returns. Once the snow does fall, the hikers of Bymarka become skiers, and it's not uncommon for the city center to be eerily quiet on a Saturday morning as locals head for the hills. **Trondheim Ski Club (Trondhjems Skiklub)** (tel. 72 56 03 31, www.skiklubben.no, 9am-3pm Mon.-Fri.) rents out cross-country skis, boots, and poles at 120kr per day or 450kr per week from their base at Skistua. Contact the club in advance as preference will be given to members.

For those who prefer the downhill variety, **Vassfjellet** (Vassfjellveien, tel. 72 83 02 00, www.vassfjellet.com) is the main ski resort for Trondheim, 24 kilometers (15 miles) south of the city center. Equipment rental and a ski school are provided through the on-site **Vassfjellet Skishop** (tel. 45 23 61 11, www.vassfjellet.no). Without your own transport, the only option to reach the resort is by taking the **Skibuss** (www.skibussen.no), which leaves Trondheim at 10am on weekends and during school holidays, returning from Vassfjellet at 4:30pm. A round-trip costs 450kr including a day's ski pass, or 150kr for the transport only. Stops in central Trondheim include the railroad station, Munkegata, the Student Society building, and the Lerkendal Stadium.

Because Vassfjellet and the hills around Trondheim sometimes suffer from a lack of snowfall, serious alpine skiers head farther south to the bigger resort at **Oppdal** or make the 166-kilometer (103-mile) journey east across the Swedish border to **Åre,** arguably the best ski resort in Scandinavia. Two daily trains run from Trondheim S to Åre at a cost of around 300kr for the 2.5-hour journey. Contact **NSB** (tel. 81 50 08 88, www.nsb. no) for details.

Swimming

One of the best aquatic centers in Norway, **Pirbadet** (Havnegata 12, tel. 73 83 18 00, www.pirbadet.no, 7am-9pm Mon., Wed., and Fri., noon-9pm Tues. and Thurs., 10am-7pm Sat.-Sun., 155-175kr) is on the expensive side, but you get your money's worth with two fast water slides, a wave pool, diving boards, several children's pools, and a sauna. An in-house café and the ability to take your own food into

the pool area mean a trip here could easily last the day.

Although the temperatures are low, fjord swimming is a free and enjoyable activity. The excellent beach at **Korsvika** is a prime swimming spot and great for barbecues and summer picnics. Follow the Ladestein trail from the end of Ormen Langes vei to the Lade barnehage kindergarten, a total walk of around three kilometers (1.9 miles) from downtown Trondheim, or ride 10 minutes on bus route 3 from Munkegata to Krutthusbakken (every 30 minutes), which stands above the beach.

Alternatively, a small charge gains you admission to changing facilities and diving platforms at the outdoor **Sjøbadet** swimming facility (St. Olavs Pir, www.sjobadet. no, noon-6pm daily June-Aug., 60kr) in the Trondheimsfjord, which is just a 15-minute walk from Pirbadet along the waterfront path.

Kayaking

Trondheim Kajakk (Bostadvegen 11, tel. 48 33 83 18, www.trondheimkajakk.no, 8am-midnight daily Mar.-Oct.) is a well-established company that offers kayak tours along the Nidelva river or just the rental of the equipment. A tour takes approximately two

Kayaking along the Nidelva river is popular throughout the summer.

hours and costs 400kr, which includes kayak rental and all necessary safety equipment. Alternatively, you can rent the equipment all day for the same price, or over a weekend (Fri.-Mon.) for 800kr.

Golf

Two golf courses offer terrific views across the city. A reciprocal golf club membership is required to play at **Trondheim Golfklubb** (Gamle Bynesvei, tel. 73 53 18 85, www. golfklubben.no, 450-600kr). A less formal alternative is the pay-and-play concept at the nearby **Trondheim Par 3** (Statsråd Kroghs veg 15a, tel. 91 17 24 05, www.trondheimpar-3golf.no), where you can play the nine short holes with rented clubs for 110kr.

Spectator Sports

SOCCER

The most decorated soccer club in Norway, **Rosenborg BK** play their home matches at the **Lerkendal Stadion** (Klæbuveien 125). The season runs April through October, and although the Lerkendal is one of Norway's biggest soccer stadiums, games do sell out frequently. Check the schedules and order online in advance at www.rbk.no.

If Rosenborg isn't playing at home, you can try your luck with the much smaller club **Ranheim IL** (Ranheimsvegen 166, tel. 73 57 45 85, www.ranheimfotball.no), where buying tickets on game day is usually fine.

HANDBALL

Pride of the city in handball circles are the ladies of **Byåsen Håndball Elite** (www. byaasen.no), who have competed in the country's top division since 1982 and frequently represent Norway in the European Champions League. Home games are played at the 3,000-capacity **Trondheim Spektrum arena** (Klostergata 90, www.trondheimspektrum.no) at Øya, a pleasant 15-minute walk west of downtown.

During late April, the **Trondheim Handball Cup** (www.trondheimhandballcup.no) attracts over 3,000 players, who compete in over 500 games across the four-day event.

ENTERTAINMENT AND EVENTS

Nightlife

As a student city, Trondheim's nightlife is inevitably skewed toward the younger generation. The distinctive red circular building of the **Trondheim Student Society (Studentersamfundet)** (Elgesetergate 1, tel. 99 21 59 10, www.samfundet.no) is the heartbeat of the city's student scene, playing host to a mix of local bands and high-profile touring acts. As any local will inevitably tell you, the Sex Pistols once played here. Opening hours of the building's various bars depend on events, and nonmembers are usually welcome for live shows.

In the central area, most nightclubs are centered around Fjordgata and Nordre gate. The over-20 policy of **Downtown** (Nordre gate 28, tel. 73 50 40 00, www.downtown. no, 10pm-2:30am Mon.-Sat.) seems to be in name only, as the dance floor is often filled with students on Friday and Saturday nights. Across the street, the more sophisticated **Raus** (Nordre gate 21, tel. 48 32 72 00, www.enrausbar.no, 7pm-2am Tues.-Sat.) is one of the few nightspots in the city focused on wine and cocktails rather than filling a dance floor or selling food. The elegant interior creates an ideal atmosphere for an after-dinner drink, although as with most places in Trondheim, it can get very busy on weekends.

LGBT

As a youthful and international city, Trondheim is very gay-friendly and the LGBT community is well integrated into the nightlife scene in general. The one gay bar opens on Friday and Saturday nights, but the small cavernous **Me** (Dronningens gate 15, 10pm-2am Fri.-Sat.) is a place to dance rather than meet and talk. Occasional midweek salsa nights add some variety.

Trondheim Pride (www.trondheimpride. no) is a low-key event held every year, usually

medieval marketplace at St. Olav's Festival

Festivals and Events
ST. OLAV'S FESTIVAL
(Olavsfestdagene)

The main festival of the year, **St. Olav's Festival** (www.olavsfestdagene.no) is one of the biggest and most important multi-day festivals in the whole country. Named after the former Viking king Olav Haraldsson, the festival runs over 10 days in late July and early August. Over 150,000 visitors attend the festival, which includes concerts, live entertainment, and a medieval craft market. Although it has a religious history, the festival has a rich and varied cultural program that is suitable for everyone.

Held over the main weekend of St. Olav's Festival in the city's market square (Torvet) is the **Trøndersk Food Festival (Trøndersk Matfestival)** (www.oimat.no). The main draw for visitors is the food market, with a range of farmers from across the region offering plenty of samples to taste. Expect dried meats, cheeses, breads, and berries. Cookery courses and activities for children are also available.

MUSIC FESTIVALS

Trondheim's leading music-only festival, **Pstereo** (www.pstereo.no) is held on the third weekend in August in the beautiful riverside grounds of Nidaros Cathedral. International headliners complement up-and-coming acts from across the Nordics, before a series of after-parties are held across the city. Previous headliners have included Franz Ferdinand, Sigur Ros, and Band of Horses.

One of the few Norwegian festivals outside the summer season, **Trondheim Calling** (www.trondheimcalling.no) showcases unsigned bands from central Norway and further afield. Usually held the first weekend in February, the festival has a symposium bringing together the Norwegian music business to debate issues and hear from international speakers, but the evenings are devoted to live music. A festival pass gains you access to the participating venues, many of which are

in early September. Lectures, debates, art shows, and concerts are held before the week-long event culminates with a parade through the city streets.

Performing Arts

Built in 1816, **Trøndelag Teater** (Prinsens Gate 18-20, tel. 73 80 51 00, www.trondelag-teater.no) is one of Scandinavia's oldest running theaters. Major Norwegian performances feature strongly on the schedule. The occasional international play features, albeit likely translated into Norwegian.

Prinsen kino (Prinsens Gate 2b, tel. 73 80 88 00, www.trondheimkino.no) is the bigger of the city's two cinemas, and it features major Hollywood blockbusters alongside Norwegian films. English-language movies are almost always subtitled rather than dubbed, except for movies aimed at children. Occasionally, major Norwegian releases are shown with English subtitles, but you should check with the cinema in advance for this.

grouped around the Solsiden district, north of Bakklandet.

SHOPPING

Head to **Bakklandet** for boutique shopping opportunities, although many of the shops are only open on weekends and when large cruise ships are in port. The stock at design collective **Sukker** (Nedre Bakklandet 9a, tel. 93 09 38 44, www.sukkerdesign.no, 2pm-5pm Fri., 11am-4pm Sat.-Sun.) is constantly changing, but it usually includes a selection of jewelry, bags, pottery, paintings, and other interior design pieces. Designers are often present, and conversations about their craft are actively encouraged.

The opening hours are a little more visitor friendly at another design collective right across the street. **Pryd** (Nedre Bakklandet 22, tel. 95 02 95 15, www.pryd.no, 11am-5pm Wed.-Fri., 11am-4pm Sat., noon-4pm Sun.) is home to the work of five local designers, including Indian-influenced textiles and unique, colorful ornaments.

Downtown is pretty much the exclusive realm of main-street stores, but one place worth checking out is **Livid Manufacturing Co** (Olav Tryggvasons gate 19, tel. 40 67 54 42, www.lividjeans.com, 10am-6pm Mon.-Sat.).

The small business manufactures jeans right here in their workshop and headquarters. Denim products sit alongside shirts and handmade leather goods, available for both men and women.

Trondheim Torg (Kongens gate 9, tel. 73 53 69 94, www.trondheimtorg.no, 9am-8pm Mon.-Fri., 9am-6pm Sat.) is the main shopping mall in the city center, but the modern mall at **Solsiden** (Beddingen 10, tel. 73 60 10 00, www.solsidensenter.no, 9am-9pm Mon.-Fri., 9am-6pm Sat.) is a nicer experience and surrounded by good restaurants. The out-of-town malls Sirkus and City Syd are not worth a special journey, as almost every store can be found downtown.

FOOD
Cafés and Light Bites

★ **Jacobsen & Svart** (Ferjemannsveien 8, tel. 90 24 42 26, www.jacobsensvart.no, 7am-6pm Mon.-Fri., 9am-6pm Sat., 11am-6pm Sun.) is the current reigning champion of the Trondheim coffee scene. Roasted in-house and brewed by hand, a cup of coffee here is as much a work of art as a pick-me-up. Light open sandwiches and locally made ice cream are also available. Locals know to ask

The Pstereo music festival takes place every August on the banks of the Nidelva river.

The shops and restaurants of Solsiden sit among remnants of the former shipyard.

coffee and craft beers while you pass the time playing shuffleboard or a retro video game.

For a more substantial lunch to break up a sightseeing tour, the excellent **Ni Muser** (Bispegata 9, tel. 73 53 63 11, www.nimuser.no, 11am-11pm daily) art café is just a few steps from Nidaros Cathedral. Enjoy filter coffee with free refills, filling sandwiches, and supersized salads served with fresh bread. The outdoor terrace is popular even when it's chilly thanks to the heaters, blankets, and colored lights creating a cozy atmosphere.

A lazy café by day, **Antikvariatet** (Nedre Bakklandet 4, tel. 73 18 50 14, 2pm-1am Mon.-Fri., noon-1am Sat.-Sun.) transforms into a bustling venue by night, often squeezing live performances into any corner they can spare. A small menu is usually on offer, but most people stop by for a cup of coffee, glass of beer, or slice of cake as they go about their day. Ask if the backroom is open, as the atmospheric library with riverside views is the perfect place to spend an hour playing board games and mixing with locals.

Traditional Scandinavian

The ever-popular ★ **Credo** (Ørjaveita 4, tel. 73 53 03 88, www.restaurantcredo.no, 6pm-10pm Tues.-Sat.) retains its position as Trondheim's best restaurant by consistently serving up a great quality experience of central Norwegian cuisine. The team works closely with two farms in Orkdal, southwest of Trondheim in the region's agricultural heartland, to use only the finest seasonal ingredients. Their multi-course menus ranging 700-950kr may be on the expensive side, but they're worth every krone. Book well in advance to secure a table.

The Danish influenced café-cum-restaurant ★ **Baklandet Skydsstation** (Øvre Bakklandet 33, tel. 73 92 10 44, 11am-1am Mon.-Fri., noon-1am Sat.-Sun.) is popular with travelers thanks to its photogenic bright yellow rustic exterior and charming, intimate interior. The Danish herring table draws in the city's elders, but most visitors plump for the less acquired taste of fish soup, *bacalao,*

especially for a scoop of ice cream with an espresso shot. Magic!

Drop into one of the several branches of **Dromedar** (Olav Tryggvasons gate 14, tel. 73 50 22 00, www.dromedar.no, 7am-7pm Mon.-Fri., 9am-7pm Sat., 10am-6pm Sun.) for an excellent cinnamon bun. Each barista has their own signature drink alongside a seasonal menu of caffeine-infused creations, so ask their advice if you want to try something different. Another well-located branch for tourists is the intimate location a few steps from the Old Town Bridge (Nedre Bakklandet 77, 7:30am-6pm Mon.-Fri., 10am-6pm Sat., 11am-6pm Sun.).

Work Work (Munkegata 58, tel. 92 65 12 68, www.work-work.no, noon-midnight Mon.-Thurs., noon-2am Fri.-Sat., 3pm-midnight Sun.) is a video game themed bar on the ground floor of a gaming-focused coworking space. Expect to find young entrepreneurial minds chewing the fat over a latte and laptops. The food menu is basic (think sandwiches and nachos), but you can enjoy a good range of or warm liver pâté. This isn't the place for calorie counters, as homemade cakes dominate the menu, with the filling warm apple cake the best of the bunch. It's also one of the best places in town to try the Norwegian national spirit, Aquavit.

For a modern twist on Scandinavian food, book one of the handful of tables at **Folk og Fe** (Nedre Bakklandet 6, tel. 97 51 81 80, www.folkogfe-bistro.no, 5pm-11pm Tues.-Sun.) well in advance. This intimate bistro is known for its limited seasonal menu yet attentive, knowledgeable service. Three courses are available at 495kr and five courses at 625kr. In addition to wine pairings, the staff are only too pleased to recommended beer pairings from their selection of local craft ales.

In addition to stocking a wide range of fresh produce from across the mid-Norway region, **Mathall Trondheim** (Kongens gate 30, tel. 45 90 65 55, www.mathalltrondheim.no, 11am-9pm Mon.-Thurs., 11am-9pm Sat.) also functions as a restaurant on the mezzanine level. The atmosphere can be noisy, but it is a good option for getting a taste of traditional Norwegian dishes with a contemporary twist. The three-course menu with limited choice runs 485kr. A lighter menu is available at lunchtime, but much better value is available elsewhere.

Seafood

The prestigious **Havfruen** (Kjøpmannsgata 7, tel. 73 87 40 70, www.havfruen.no, 4pm-10pm Mon.-Sat., 295kr) is not cheap but is the undisputed king of fish and seafood in Trondheim. During the summer months, you can even borrow a rod from the restaurant to catch your own fish from the river. You can expect fresh arctic cod, clams, and whale on the menu, along with a creamy fish soup to start. The atmospheric setting inside an old wharf building overlooking the river is well suited for romantic meals or a celebration. A set five-course tasting menu is available at 649kr.

Ravnkloa (Munkegata 70, tel. 73 52 55 21, www.ravnkloa.no, 10am-5pm Mon.-Fri., 10am-4pm Sat.) is the city's fish market; it

doubles as a seafood café. Due to the opening hours it's only really suitable for lunch, but it's ideally located for a quick bite before or after the ferry to Munkholmen. The homemade fishcakes are an especially popular takeout option. Don't contemplate a meal here unless you really enjoy the aroma of all things aquatic, as the café's seats are merely feet away from the fresh fish counter! Ravnkloa is also one of the few places in Trondheim from where you can buy whale meat.

American

For tasty burgers and outstanding craft beers, few places top the lively pub atmosphere of ★ **Trondheim Mikrobryggeriet** (Prinsensgate 39, tel. 73 51 75 15, 3pm-midnight Mon., 3pm-2am Tues.-Fri., noon-2am Sat., 189kr). Booking is advisable for Friday and Saturday evenings, although there is usually room at the bar if you just want to sample the local brews. On that note, the sampling tray of whichever 5-8 beers are currently on offer is a great choice, if a little expensive (price depends on the beers). If you don't get the chance to stop by in person, a selection of their bottled beers is now available for purchase in the state-run alcohol store (Vinmonopolet) and selected Rema 1000 supermarkets. Although open for drinks into the night, the kitchen stops taking food orders at 10pm.

For a cheaper burger while still enjoying some excellent beers, try out the nearby **Bror** (Olav Tryggvasons gate 29, tel. 45 83 15 26, www.brorbar.no, 11am-12:30am Mon.-Thurs., 11am-2:30am Fri.-Sat., 1pm-2:30am Sun., 119kr). Their excellent sides include mac-and-cheese, homemade slaw, and sweet potato fries, while the wide range of imported beers both on tap and bottled often includes several American craft brews.

Superhero Burger (Olav Tryggvasons gate 1, tel. 73 51 33 40, 11am-10pm Mon.-Wed., 11am-3am Thurs.-Sat., noon-11pm Sun., 129kr) is known by locals as a late-night refueling stop, but it's also a good value choice for a quick lunch. Although it's dressed up as a superhero-themed fast food joint, board games and beer are available to encourage you to linger.

If you're in the vicinity of Solsiden, **Café Løkka** (Dokkgata 8, tel. 40 00 09 74, www. cafelokka.no, 11am-1am Mon.-Sat., noon-midnight Sun., 185kr) is a popular after-work choice for Trondheimers. Good value food along with board games means those people are often still propping up the bar when the sun goes down. Expect a typical bar menu of burgers and salads, with lighter bites (from 110kr) available until 2pm.

Asian

The best of Trondheim's collection of Asian restaurants is **Benja Siam** (Ravelsveita 6, tel. 73 53 38 88, www.benja-siam.no, 2pm-10pm Mon.-Thurs., 2pm-11pm Fri., 1pm-11pm Sat., 2pm-10pm Sun., 185kr), a charming Thai restaurant inside an old wooden building. The charm extends to the presentation of the food, which is often served with an orchid flower. The menu is vast, but those in the know go for the soups or Thai salads, both of which are filling and good value.

Indian cuisine isn't so popular in Trondheim, but try the straightforwardly named **Indian Tandoori** (Søndre gate 22a, tel. 73 52 70 00, www.tandooritrondheim.no, 2pm-11pm Sun.-Thurs., 2pm-midnight Fri.-Sat., 229kr), where the tandoori is cooked in an authentic clay oven. The Taste of India starter platter is great for sharing, while the lamb and shrimp mains make good use of high-quality local ingredients. There are several options for vegetarians and vegans. Although prices are a touch high, you will leave satisfied.

International

The contemporary yet formal setting of **Bakgaarden Bar & Spiseri** (Kjøpmannsgata 40, tel. 45 22 24 88, www.bakgaarden.com, 11am-11pm Mon.-Sat., 3pm-10pm Sun.) suggests a fine dining restaurant, but this kitchen actually serves a tapas concept. Select a menu (160-215kr at lunch, 305-395kr at dinner) or

compose your own by ordering the individual dishes at 35-120kr. The salted baked potatoes with mojo sauce are a good accompaniment to any of the meat dishes.

The food philosophy at **Kalas & Canasta** (Nedre Bakklandet 5, tel. 92 85 25 27, www. kalasogcanasta.no, 11am-midnight Mon.-Thurs., 11am-1am Fri., noon-1am Sat., 1pm-9pm Sun., 189kr) is to showcase the very best in natural ingredients without altering flavor. Set on busy Bakklandet, the restaurant is a place to stop, graze, and people-watch rather than rush. The cheese and cured meat platter is a popular choice, served with their homemade fruit and nut bread. A tasting menu is available from 485kr.

I'm going to include ★ **Egon Tårnet** (Otto Nielsens veg 4, tel. 73 87 35 00, taarnet@ egon.no, 10am-11pm Mon.-Sat., 11am-10pm Sun., 159-299kr) on the list, not for the food but for the experience. Egon is a chain restaurant, and you can expect exactly the same food and service in each of the identikit branches across Trondheim. Having said that, the menu is vast, with a wide selection of pizza, pasta, meat, fish, steaks, burgers, and salads, so you are sure to find something to suit everyone's taste. The main draw to this particular branch is the revolving restaurant set 250 feet above ground atop a TV tower. The restaurant takes approximately one hour to revolve once, and you can expect at least one 360-degree view of Trondheim while you eat. It's a popular venue for children's parties, so booking is essential Friday-Sunday and advisable at other times. Bear in mind that at busy times it can take up to 15 minutes to queue for the elevator, so plan to arrive with plenty of time to spare.

Italian

Pizza is a popular evening option across Trondheim, with many restaurants offering a selection, although the quality varies considerably. Italian themed **Una** (Beddingen 14, tel. 40 00 70 03, www.unapizzeria.no, 11am-11pm Mon.-Thurs., 11am-midnight Fri.-Sat., 1pm-11pm Sun., 170kr) serves the best pizza in town, along with an excellent choice of authentic antipasti and salads. Located at the Solsiden development, the restaurant can fill up quickly, so head there for a leisurely lunch or book ahead for dinner.

Inside an atmospheric old wharf building beside the river, **AiSuma** (Kjøpmannsgata 57, tel. 73 54 92 71, www.aisuma.no, 4pm-10pm daily, 265kr) serves Italian cuisine with a contemporary twist. Shunning the oh-so-typical pizza and spaghetti dishes, the chefs instead favor seafood, Mediterranean-style meat dishes, and fresh gnocchi. The outstanding homemade vanilla panna cotta is an excellent way to round off your evening.

Mexican

The exceptional ★ **Fridas** (Fjordgata 15, tel. 73 53 50 07, www.restaurantfrida.no, 4pm-10:30pm Sun.-Thurs., 4pm-11:30pm Fri.-Sat., 259kr) acts as a hub for Trondheim's Latin American community, who in turn introduce the locals to authentic Mexican food, a real rarity in Norway. The colorful interior inspired by the Mexican revolution helps to add to the authentic atmosphere. The vast sharing platters are the best value, and although you won't need starters, be sure to ask for extra tortillas. Most wait staff speak Spanish alongside English and Norwegian. Booking is essential on any day of the week.

Vegetarian

Hagen (Nedre Bakklandet 75, tel. 40 54 43 09, www.matfrahagen.no, 10am-7pm Mon.-Fri., 11am-6pm Sat., noon-6pm Sun., 95-140kr) is one of Trondheim's most popular choices for lunch, whether you're a vegetarian or not. To understand the menu concept, the name Hagen translates into English as The Garden. Sandwiches including avocado and tomato, or eggplant and sweet potato, come in at under 100kr, while the popular Hot Box menu at 140kr includes a carrot burger, grilled falafel, or grilled tofu, all served with a fresh salad side.

ACCOMMODATIONS
Under 500kr

Set in a quiet residential area around a 10-minute walk from Solsiden, **Trondheim Vandrerhjem** (Weidemanns vei 41, tel. 73 87 44 50, www.trondheimvandrerhjem.no) has a choice of single beds in basic four-person dorm rooms from 330kr, or tiny studios with shared kitchen and bathroom facilities from 475kr. The hostel was totally rebuilt in 2013, so you shouldn't find peeling wallpaper or scuffed furniture here, and there is a TV lounge to relax in and meet other guests. While a long way from hotel standard, it's a solid choice if you are on a tight budget.

In the summer months, **Singsaker Sommerhotell** (Rogerts gate 1, tel. 73 89 31 00, http://sommerhotell.singsaker.no) is another peaceful option in a beautiful old building just steps from Bakklandet. Beds in dorm rooms including linen can be had from as little as 300kr a night. Private rooms start at 559kr with shared facilities and 779kr with bathrooms, but at these prices you're better off looking at a dedicated budget hotel.

500-1,000kr

The best value budget option within easy walking distance of central attractions is the ★ **Pensjonat Jarlen** (Kongens gate 40, tel. 73 51 32 18, www.jarlen.no, 549kr s, 690kr d). The light, bright rooms feature wooden floors, kitchenettes, flatscreen TV, and free Wi-Fi, at prices somewhere between a hostel and a budget hotel. Larger groups should consider the six-bed room available at a nightly rate of just 1,920kr.

Book directly with **City Living Schøller** (Dronningens gate 26, tel. 73 87 08 00, www. cityliving.no, 699kr) for their best rates. Overlooking a shopping street, the 50 spacious rooms are comfortable with a modern design but do not have a private bathroom. For an additional 100-150kr, the superior rooms have a private bathroom, kitchenette, and room for extra beds if required. The 19th-century building is at the very heart of downtown with a sushi restaurant on the ground floor and supermarkets and chain stores all within a few minutes' walk.

Following the closure of the Hotel

Britannia for an extensive refurbishment, the pick of the Thon hotels in Trondheim is the **Hotel Gildevangen** (Søndre gate 22b, tel. 73 87 01 30, gildevangen@thonhotels.no, 950kr), notable for its beautiful stone architecture dating back to 1908. In contrast to the striking exterior, the rooms are light and modern although they do have the feel of a business hotel. A light evening buffet is included in the room rate and served 5pm-8pm Monday-Thursday, although this is sadly not available during the summer season from mid-June to mid-August.

1,000-1,500kr

The excellent ★ **Radisson Blu Royal Garden Hotel** (Kjøpmannsgata 73, tel. 73 80 30 00, info.trondheim@radissonblu.com, 1,200kr) doesn't have the history of the city's other full-service hotels, but it is nevertheless a top pick. Built in the 1980s, the hotel's unusual architecture resembles the row of wooden buildings it replaced. The striking glass exterior and airy atrium are indicative of what to expect from the almost 300 tasteful modern rooms, all complete with a generous splash of color. A vast breakfast buffet is included with both hot and cold options, while the restaurant is a popular choice for dinner not just with hotel guests.

It's worth checking the website of the **Chesterfield Hotel** (Søndre gate 26, tel. 73 50 37 50, www.cht.no, 1,099kr) before booking, as they run regular special offers and weekend packages that take the nightly rate well under 1,000kr even for larger family-sized rooms. It's a short walk from Trondheim Central Station. The public areas of the hotel have seen better days, but the refurbished bedrooms nevertheless offer a comfortable stay for those on a budget. A breakfast buffet is included for all guests.

One of the most expensive standard hotel rooms in the city is at the **Clarion Collection Grand Olav** (Kjøpmannsgata 48, tel. 73 80 80 80, cc.grand.olav@choice.no, 1,250kr), but there is good reason. The fact that each guest receives a complimentary evening meal consisting of soup, a light main course, and salad bar makes this a perfect choice if you want to spend your day sightseeing without worrying about finding a place to eat. Featuring a bold splash of color around every corner, this trendy hotel also serves as a temporary home for artists and musicians playing at the Olavshallen concert hall under the same roof. Secure underground parking is available at 168kr per day.

Over 1,500kr

The main reason to stay at the ★ **Scandic Nidelven** (Havnegata 1-4, tel. 73 56 80 00, nidelven@scandichotels.com, 1,600kr) isn't the view across the adjacent marina or its proximity to the railway station, as good as these things are. The award-winning breakfast is known across Norway for taking the Scandinavian breakfast buffet concept to new standards. Expect fresh smoothies, eggs cooked to order, and even a barista on hand to brew your coffee. Sadly, it's rarely possible to enjoy your breakfast in peace as its popularity ensures the room is often packed. Locals can—and often do—pay an eye-watering 295kr to join the feast on weekends. Allergy-free and pet-friendly options are among the 343 modern rooms on offer, most of which come with a marina view, yet you'll be thankful for the blackout curtains during the long summer nights.

Near Trondheim

Overlooking the Trondheimsfjord, **Storsand Gård** (Storsandveien 1, Malvik, tel. 73 97 63 60, www.storsandcamping.no) is a large modern campsite with 72 cabins available to rent. A pleasant sandy beach, good spots for fishing and swimming, and an on-site kiosk make the area a viable alternative to staying in the city. Cabin rental starts from 570kr for a simple four-berth with access to shared toilets and showers. Bus route 38 (every 30 minutes) links Storsand with both downtown Trondheim and Trondheim Airport Værnes, and despite its location 18 kilometers (11.2 miles) east of the city, it is covered on a regular bus ticket.

From central Trondheim, pick up the bus at Dronningens gate (toward Stjørdal) for the 30-35 minute ride.

Also close to Trondheim Airport Værnes, the basic modern rooms at the **Vikhammer Motell** (Vikhammerløkka 2, tel. 73 97 61 64, www.vikhammer.no, 575kr s, 675kr d) are a good budget choice for longer stays or for those passing through the region on a road trip. The adjacent campsite offers cabins (500-1,350kr) and lots of space for tents (180kr) and motorhomes (230kr) year-round. Take bus 38 to Vikhammerløkka, right outside the campsite, or the hourly train service from Trondheim S or the airport to Vikhammer station, which is less than a 10-minute walk from the motel and campsite. From Trondheim, allow 25 minutes for the bus ride and 15 minutes for the train.

Because the airport is a relatively long way from Trondheim, the **Radisson Blu Trondheim Airport** hotel (Lufthavnsveien 30, Stjørdal, tel. 74 84 36 00, www.radissonblu.com, 1,225kr) is a good choice for a stress-free start or end to your trip. Just steps from the airport terminal and train station, half of the 180 contemporary rooms come with runway views. Ask for a room on a high floor for the best view of the planes, and of the surrounding mountains and fjord. Unlike at central hotels, the generous breakfast buffet is quietest later in the morning. The restaurant remains open all day and serves an extensive menu with a particular focus on grilled meats.

INFORMATION AND SERVICES
Visitor Information
For general information about attractions and things to do in Trondheim, free Wi-Fi access, and one of the less tacky gift shops out there, head for the **Trondheim Tourist Information** office (Nordre gate 11, tel. 73 80 76 60, 9am-6pm Mon.-Sat., also Sun. mid-June to mid-Aug.). Browse the selection of locally made gifts and food products while you try in vain to get the wall of digital information

monitors to work. If the touchscreens don't play ball, there are plenty of paper leaflets and maps in the rack.

If you're staying in the city for a couple days and want to know what's on in the evenings, pick up a copy of Trondheim's English-language listings magazine. Produced every two months, *The List* (thelist.is) is available from Trondheim Tourist Information office, the information desk at Trondheim Torg mall, and many of the city's independent shops and cafés. The magazine contains articles about local people and culture alongside thorough listings for festivals, concerts, arts, and sporting events.

Post Offices and Courier Services
Although many supermarkets offer postage services, the best service will be from the main branch of the **Post Office (Posten)** (Munkegata 30, 9am-5pm Mon.-Fri., 10am-3pm Sat.). Take a ticket as you walk in and wait until your number is called. Their English is not the best, so be patient. Most kiosks and some supermarkets (look for Post i Butikken signs) sell stamps to international destinations.

Internet Access
In Trondheim, there is a city-wide wireless network called **Wireless Trondheim** (www.tradlosetrondheim.no). The service isn't free, but at just 10kr for 3 hours and 30kr for 24 hours, it's one of the rare things in Norway that come with a token price tag. Coverage is far from extensive but is reasonably reliable around the downtown shopping district. It's also worth knowing that the majority of city buses operated by AtB offer free Wi-Fi.

As an alternative, try **Trondheim Central Library (Hovedbiblioteket)** (Peter Egges plass 1, tel. 72 54 75 00, 9am-6pm Mon.-Thurs., 9am-4pm Fri., 11am-4pm Sat.), or ask at your hotel for the nearest Internet café. Having said that, even the most budget hotels should offer free Wi-Fi, and many have a computer for guest use.

Norwegian Language Courses

Folkeuniversitet (Dronningens gate 10, tel. 70 17 26 60, www.folkeuniversitetet.no) offers the widest selection of courses from complete beginner through to advanced. The standard course length is 48 hours, structured as twice a week for a couple of months, but intensive courses are available, particularly during the summer. Expect to pay at least 4,750kr for a 48-hour course.

Money

Cash and travelers checks can be exchanged at **Forex Bank** (Munkegata 34, tel. 73 50 15 40, 9am-7pm Mon.-Fri., 9am-4pm Sat.), which is usually a better option than hunting out a bank. If you require banking services, the biggest branches include **DNB** (Beddingen 16, 9am-6pm Mon.-Thurs., 9am-3pm Fri., 10am-3pm Sat.) and **SpareBank** (Søndre gate 4, 9am-3:30pm Mon.-Sat.).

Most ATMs *(minibank)* around Trondheim accept international debit and credit cards and often offer a decent exchange rate, depending on your own bank's charges.

Health
URGENT CARE

St. Olav Hospital (Prinsesse Kristinas gate 3, tel. 06800) is the main hospital for central Norway and has a large campus just south of the city center. For genuine emergencies, call 113 for an ambulance. For other urgent matters, there is an **emergency room** *(legevakt)* (Prinsesse Kristinas gate 3), but it requires calling ahead (tel. 73 96 95 80 or 116 117) to allow a nurse to screen your case and give you a time to visit.

PHARMACIES

Every shopping center has at least one of the major pharmacy *(apotek)* chains. Boots, Apotek 1, and Vitusapotek are the main names to look out for. **Vitusapotek Solsiden** (Beddingen 4, tel. 73 88 37 37, 8:30am-midnight Mon.-Sat., 10am-midnight Sun.) has the longest opening hours in the city, and is one of the few to open on Sunday.

DENTAL SERVICES

Dental treatment in Norway is expensive, so a visit to a clinic should be for nothing less than an absolute emergency.

Dine Tenner (Kongens gate 11, tel. 73 99 19 99, www.tannlegetrondheim.net) has good availability on weekdays. It's on the fourth floor of a nondescript office building next to the Trondheim Torg shopping mall. Look for the tooth-shaped door handle at street level and you're on the right track.

For weekend care, try **Trondheim Tannhelsesenter** (Kongensgate 49, tel. 73 53 45 45), which is open 10am-2pm on weekends, but only for emergency treatment. Call ahead and be prepared to pay for the convenience.

GETTING THERE
Car

Trondheim is on the E6 highway that runs almost the entire length of the country. From Oslo, the 534-kilometer (332-mile) drive should take around 6-7 hours nonstop. Lillehammer, Dombås, and Oppdal are the most useful rest stops.

Air

Trondheim Airport Værnes (Luft-havnsveien, Stjørdal, tel. 67 03 25 00) is the main air hub of central Norway but is actually 30 kilometers (18.6 miles) east of the city next to the town of **Stjørdal**. Most travelers arrive on one of the many daily flights from Oslo or Bergen. There are connections designed to connect with long-haul flights most days to London Gatwick, Copenhagen, and Amsterdam, along with weekly departures to many other European destinations. Direct flights are also available to Kristiansand, Stavanger, Ålesund, Bodø, Tromsø, and small regional airports. Due to the airport's location sandwiched between a fjord and mountains, landing at Værnes can be a bumpy ride.

The international terminal is in a separate building accessed via the domestic terminal. International arrivals will collect their luggage and proceed through customs to the domestic arrivals terminal. The airport is compact but offers good facilities, including a coffee shop in the arrivals hall.

To reach Trondheim, take the **Airport Express Coach (Flybussen)** (www.flybussen.no, 180kr). Be wary of the rival Værneseksspressen bus, which claims to be faster but is more expensive, irregular, and unreliable. A trip into Trondheim by bus takes around 40 minutes, and the bus serves all major hotels. Listen to the driver's announcements for your hotel.

There is a railway station at the airport, but services to Trondheim are limited to once per hour. However, the price is just 82kr, so it's worth checking the timetable when you arrive (there's an information screen in the arrivals hall) if you are without significant luggage and time is not a problem. The train journey takes 35 minutes, and you will be rewarded with fjord views if you snag a seat on the right-hand side of the carriage.

Rail

Commonly referred to as Trondheim S, **Trondheim Central Station (Sentralstasjon)** (Fosenkaia) is the terminus of some of Norway's longest rail lines. The 9.5-hour **Nordland Line (Nordlandsbanen)** service to Bodø and the seven-hour **Dovre Line (Dovrebanen)** service to Oslo start their journeys here, while twice a day a train runs east to the Swedish city Östersund, via a brief stop at the border town Storlien. Contact the Norwegian state railway company **NSB** (tel. 81 50 08 88, www.nsb.no) for timetable and ticket information.

Located on the artificial island of Brattøra, the station is no more than a 15-minute walk from all downtown hotels. Cross the harbor on Søndre gate toward the colorful wharf buildings to reach the main downtown district, or head east past the bus station to reach the shops, bars, and restaurants of the modern Solsiden development in the former shipyard.

Bus

Adjacent to the train station is **Trondheim**

Bus Station (Fosenkaia), home to the city's regional and long-distance bus routes. **Nor-Way Bussekspress** (tel. 81 54 44 44, www.nor-way.no) links Trondheim with Oslo and Bergen, although journey times are long, taking up to 14 hours to reach Bergen. **Lavprisekspressen** (tel. 67 98 04 80, www.lavprisekspressen.no) offers a cheaper alternative route to Oslo with fares dropping as low as 99kr with advance booking, although you'll more likely pay around 300kr. The 8.5-hour route sells out quickly though, so book well in advance to secure one of the bargain fares. The Lavprisekspressen network also offers connections to Kristiansand and Stavanger from Oslo.

Boat

The **Coastal Express (Kystekspressen)** (tel. 73 89 07 00, www.kystekspressen.no) links Trondheim to Kristiansund and the coastal communities between. Three daily services run all the way and a one-way trip costs 632kr.

The Hurtigruten ferry calls at Trondheim in late morning on both its northbound and southbound journeys. For those without a car it's a good choice to reach Ålesund, which will cost less than 1,000kr without a cabin for the 14-hour daytime journey.

GETTING AROUND

Trondheim's compact downtown area is flat and straightforward to navigate on foot, but to reach some of the city's sights you'll need to take a bus.

Public Transit

AtB (yes, it means A to B) is the company that oversees public transit in Trondheim and much of the central Norway region. The English version of their website (www.atb.no) helps you plan your travel around the city and gives up-to-date information on fares and passes.

At almost all public transit stops you will find live information screens detailing how long you will need to wait for any particular service. These tend to be accurate, but there are paper timetables at the majority of stops too, just in case. Smoking is banned on all public transport and also at the stops. The usually shy and reserved Norwegians won't hesitate to interrupt a foreigner who is blissfully unaware of the law.

BUS

The primary form of public transit in Trondheim is the green city bus. The buses are green in more ways than just their color, as many of them are now electric or hybrid powered. This does mean they can be quieter than you'd expect, so be extra careful when crossing roads. Most bus lines run every 30 minutes throughout the day from around 6am to midnight. Frequency is often higher 7am-9am and 3pm-5pm but can be less in the evenings and on Sunday.

All bus drivers accept cash but cannot give change. It's far more economical to buy your tickets in advance from one of the many downtown convenience stores (Narvesen, Deli de Luca, 7/11), the AtB office (Kongens gate 34), or from an automatic ticket machine available at the bigger bus stops. If you're in Trondheim for more than a day, consider investing in a pass or downloading the AtB smartphone app, which lets you buy passes or single tickets at a discount.

Single tickets bought in advance from an automatic machine cost 41kr or 33kr on the AtB smartphone app, compared to 50kr for the walk-on fare. A 10-ride card can be purchased in advance for 328kr, with 24-hour (105kr), 72-hour (165kr), and 7-day (235kr) passes also available. Single tickets are actually valid for 90 minutes on unlimited buses, which is useful if you need to change lines downtown.

AtB has announced sweeping changes to the bus network that will affect every route in Trondheim from summer 2019. Be sure to plan your routes online or pick up an information leaflet and route map if you are visiting the city after this time.

TRONDHEIM TRAMWAY

The city still operates one tram line from the downtown area all the way up to Lian in the Bymarka forest. It's primarily intended as a commuter line but is used by hikers and skiers year-round. Taking the tram up to Lian for a walk around the lake before returning on the tram makes for a very pleasant afternoon. There are 20 stops en route and the journey takes 20-25 minutes, with departures every 15-30 minutes from 6:30am to midnight. On Sunday, the service is still half-hourly but doesn't start until midmorning. Tickets for the tramway are the same as for the buses, with transfers to and from the buses permitted.

Taxi

Expect a per-kilometer rate of around 11kr, rising to almost 20kr depending on the time of day. If you absolutely do need a taxi, **Trønder Taxi** (tel. 93 00 73 73, www.07373.no, always open) is your best bet, as they have the most availability. All their taxicabs accept major credit cards, including Diners Club and American Express. To help with your planning the website offers a price calculator to help estimate charges, although it is in Norwegian only. The firm also offers a sightseeing tariff of 750kr per hour (1,000kr on weekends).

Car Rental

The best place to hire a car is from Trondheim Airport, where most major brands have an office. Expect to pay around 3,000kr for a week's basic rental from the likes of **Avis** (tel. 67 25 56 10, www.avis.no) or **Hertz** (tel. 73 50 35 00, www.hertz.no).

A good alternative option in the city itself is **Allways Leiebiler** (Kjøpmannsgata 73, www.allways.no, tel. 90 81 40 00), based inside the Radisson Royal Garden Hotel. Their range of cars rivals the big-name brands and the prices tend to be up to 25 percent cheaper. Weekend deals can be especially good, but be wary that their return times are not quite so flexible.

HELL

Less than one mile (1.5 kilometers) south of Trondheim Airport Værnes, the village of Hell is a popular tourist draw for those wanting a photograph next to the railway station sign. Yet the village hides a more interesting secret up in the forest. Follow the signs up a quiet residential street to Helleristninger to see a couple of **rock carvings** dating back to the Stone Age. It's less than a 10-minute walk from the main road through Hell, but you do have to negotiate a hill and some forested terrain.

Along the E14 road to Sweden, 12 kilometers (7.5 miles) east of Hell, further rock carvings can be seen just past the village of Leirfall at a site managed by **Bergkunstmuseet** (tel. 74 82 70 21, www.bergkunstmuseet.no). Again, look for the signs to Helleristninger to see the carvings depicting a hunter-gatherer society that were discovered between 1910 and 1960. Free guiding is available 11am-5pm Tues.-Sat., noon-5pm Sun. from mid-June to mid-August.

THE ROAD NORTH

The journey north to Bodø and onward to Lofoten takes a full day to drive along the direct but largely uninteresting E6 highway. Many people take the Hurtigruten or fly instead, but another option is the Nordland line (Nordlandsbanen) railway. While it takes a similar time as driving—more than nine hours from Trondheim to Bodø—you can opt for an overnight sleeper or relax on the day train rather than stress out behind the wheel.

If you do choose to drive, the historical Stiklestad makes a sensible first stop, around 100 kilometers (62 miles) north of Trondheim. This is where one of the most famous battles in Norway's history took place back in 1030. The Battle of Stiklestad saw the fall of Olav Haraldsson, later canonized and now entombed in Trondheim's Nidaros Cathedral. A visit to **Stiklestad National Cultural Center (Stiklestad Nasjonale Kultursenter)** (Leksdalsvegen 1, Verdal, tel. 74 04 42 00, www.stiklestad. no, 180kr) lets you discover more about medieval Norway, from the 30 well-preserved buildings to various exhibitions about cultural life. Visit in July and August (exhibitions 9am-8pm daily, folk museum 11am-4pm daily) for the best experience when all attractions are open. For the rest of the year, only the exhibitions in the cultural house are open (9am-6pm daily).

Consider taking route 17, otherwise known as the **Coastal Route (Kystriksveien),** to complete the 620-kilometer (385-mile) trip from Stiklestad to Bodø. Allow several days to explore the landmarks along the route, such as the Seven Sisters mountains (De Syv Søstre), the Svartisen glacier, and countless islands. The route is dotted with unique accommodations, biking and hiking opportunities, and excellent local food.

However, if you are on a tight schedule, I highly recommend skipping this region and heading straight for Lofoten. The choice is yours.

Central Mountains

South of Trondheim, the Norwegian landscape is characterized by lush green valleys and some of Europe's tallest mountains. National parks are ten a penny in this part of the world and as such are hugely popular areas for domestic tourism. Biking, hiking, and skiing between cabins is a pastime loved by Norwegians of all ages. Although it can be tough to befriend the locals, bump into one on a hiking trail and they will be only too pleased to help, point you in the right direction, and share their coffee.

The mountains of central Norway are some of Europe's last sanctuaries for wild reindeer, mountain foxes, golden eagle, ravens, and rodents, who all share this phenomenal natural environment. For this reason, the national parks are extremely vulnerable to human activity, so take care to walk only on marked trails, keep your distance from herds of wild animals, and leave no litter behind.

To properly explore the mountains a car is advisable, but many stunning locations are accessible by public transit. The main rail line and the E6 highway from Oslo to Trondheim pass over the mountains.

CLIMATE

You should be prepared for all types of weather at any time of year in the Norwegian mountains. Weather conditions can change suddenly and so windproof and waterproof clothing is essential. Røros is one of the coldest inhabited parts of Norway, and temperatures in winter can regularly drop below 23°C (-10°F). Although rare in June and July, snowfall is possible at any time of year throughout the region.

Crisp winter and spring days can present a surprising danger: the sun. Even when temperatures are close to freezing, a clear sky can result in sunburn quicker than you would imagine. Snow blindness is also a risk, most notably during the brighter days of March and April when snow coverage is still high.

If you are planning a trip anywhere in the central mountains, check the weather forecast regularly and ask at a tourist information office or hotel for advice about current conditions.

TOP EXPERIENCE

RØROS

For more than 300 years, Røros was a remote mining community. Today it's a surprisingly vibrant community focused on sustainable tourism and local food production. The town is incredibly well preserved, and as you stroll through the center you could be forgiven for thinking you've traveled back in time. There's nowhere quite like Røros anywhere in Scandinavia, perhaps even anywhere in the world.

Two years after the first copper deposits were found in 1644, the mining town of Røros was established. At this time, knowledge of mining was scant in Norway, and therefore experts were sent for, mainly from Germany and Denmark.

The copper works received several privileges, including the exclusive right to all minerals, forests, waterways, and people within a 40-kilometer radius. In the early 18th century, the company had to look outside the area to continue the supply of wood to the burning furnaces in the smelting hut. This excessive industry has left its mark on the landscape for miles around.

The whole town of Røros is a living museum. At the very least, take a walk along Kjerkgata or Bergmannsgata up to the church and copper-mining works before returning along the other side of the river. This short 20-minute walk will both orient you and help you decide where to spend the rest of your time.

DNT: The Norwegian Trekking Association

The network of marked trails and mountain lodges maintained and operated by the **Norwegian Trekking Association (Den Norske Turistforening)** is a vital part of planning any hiking, skiing, or camping holiday in Norway.

So much more than a simple volunteer organization, DNT is a Norwegian cultural icon and the very definition of the Norwegian word *friluftsliv*, which roughly translates as a love of the outdoors lifestyle. DNT has grown from an initial 223 members in 1868 to more than 260,000 today. More than 5 percent of the entire Norwegian population are members, giving more than 175,000 volunteer hours every year.

The result of this incredible effort is a world-leading national network of marked hiking trails totaling more than 19,000 kilometers (more than 12,000 miles) in length, plus over 6,000 kilometers (4,000 miles) of ski tracks marked each winter. Of the 500 cabins in the DNT network, a small number in southern Norway (primarily near Oslo) are staffed lodges that serve food and have electricity and warm showers. Most other cabins in central and southern Norway are equipped with firewood, gas, utensils, bedding, and a basic selection of dried and canned food. The cabins in northern Norway are primarily for shelter, and although they will have some equipment, you'll need your own food and sleeping bag. Most staffed lodges are open from late June until early September, but opening hours outside the summer vary from cabin to cabin.

To access unstaffed DNT lodges you will need a membership key. Nonmembers can borrow a key against a deposit of 100kr from staffed cabins and DNT offices around the country. Nonmembers can expect to pay 180-395kr depending on the standard of accommodation.

For more information about DNT and its network of cabins and trails, see the detailed English-language website at www.dnt.no.

Sights

★ RØROS MUSEUM
(Rørosmuseet)

The actual Røros Museum is made up of several sites in and around the town. The **Smelting House (Smelthytta)** (Lorentz Lossius gata, tel. 72 40 61 70, www.rorosmuseet.no, 11am-3pm daily Sept.-May, 10am-4pm daily June-Aug., until 6pm during July, 100kr) shows a 20-minute film (alternating between English and Norwegian) about the history of the town and mining operations, before you take a trip underground to see scale models and original equipment. Genuine copper ingots produced in Røros make a great gift idea.

Behind the smelting house are slag heaps that you can climb for an even better view across the town and surrounding mountain plateau. You'll get a deeper understanding of the deforestation that took place during the mining boom. Below the slag heaps is the **Sleggveien** road, where you'll find original workers' houses preserved and open to the public 11am-4pm daily from mid-June to mid-August. On Thursday evenings during July, special events take place in the street from 6pm. The street's dark timber houses are a great photo opportunity at any time of year, and are particularly atmospheric when covered in snow.

Signed off Route 31 approximately 11 kilometers (7 miles) northeast of the town is one of Røros Copper Works' most important sites. **Olavs Mine (Olavsgruva)** ran continuously from 1645 to 1972. Today the mine can only be visited on a one-hour guided tour costing 120kr. During the summer season these run four times a day, but from September to May the only opportunity to visit the mine is at 3pm every Saturday. Bookings must be made in advance by telephone (tel. 72 40 61 70), at the smelting house museum, or at the tourist office in Røros. A combined ticket for the smelting house and the mine can be purchased for 180kr.

RØROS CHURCH
(Røros Kirke)

Røros Church (Kjerkgata 39, tel. 72 41 95 31, www.roroskirke.no) is so much more than just a place of worship—it's a focal point for a community. Built in 1784 for the miners and their families, the church hosted prayers every morning, midday, and evening. The black and white paneled exterior is so unique that it has become a symbol of the town, instantly recognizable across Norway, while the distinctive turquoise and cream interior is surprisingly lacking in religious iconography. The pulpit stands high above the altar, which likely indicates the authority of the clergy at the time. Despite the small population of Røros, the church has space for hundreds of people. For an alternative view of the church and its setting, walk behind it and up into the vast graveyard.

Getting inside the church can be a challenge as opening hours are limited, but various open days throughout the year provide extra opportunities, and they are only too willing to open the church on request for the keen traveler. At a minimum, the church is open 11am-1pm Monday-Saturday throughout the year, with extended hours from mid-June to mid-August.

Short 20-minute guided tours are available at noon every Saturday throughout the year, and at 11:30am, 1:30pm, and 3:30pm Monday-Saturday in the summer season at a small charge of 50kr. Most tours are given in Norwegian, but if the group is small guides will happily answer questions in English.

DOKTORTJØNNA OUTDOOR RECREATION PARK
(Doktortjønna friluftspark)

If you are traveling with children, then a visit to **Doktortjønna Outdoor Recreation Park** (Johan Falkbergets vei 16, tel. 72 40 61 70, 11am-4pm daily mid-June to mid-Aug.) is recommended. Located on the main road (Route 30) out of Røros, the center offers canoeing, a log cabin playhouse, nature trails, and the opportunity to meet livestock and try out fishing. Meanwhile, a basic exhibition about the remote Femundsmarka National Park, southeast of Røros on the Swedish border, and a simple café will keep adults entertained. Entrance is free, but some activities carry a small charge.

RØROS REIN

A local Sami family runs **Røros Rein** (Hagaveien 17, tel. 97 97 49 66, www.rorosrein.

TRONDHEIM AND CENTRAL NORWAY
CENTRAL MOUNTAINS

the mining town Røros

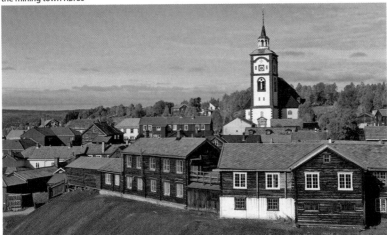

no), a working reindeer farm and activity center within walking distance southeast of the central streets that showcases these wonderful animals and the unique lifestyle of reindeer herders. Weather permitting, the center offers reindeer-pulled sled rides during the winter season (approximately Nov.-Apr.) together with opportunities to feed the animals. All activities must be arranged in advance by contacting the center directly or via the tourist office. For a rather macabre souvenir of your trip, reindeer meat products are available from the farm shop and in stores across Røros.

Recreation

Hiking and jogging are possible along **marked trails** that radiate out from the town center. Ask at your hotel for directions to Fjellkirka, an old mountain church, or Småsetran, a cozy mountain hamlet.

If you will stay in Røros for a day or more, consider renting a **bicycle** to explore the surrounding areas. **Røros Sport** (Bergmannsgata 13, tel. 72 41 12 18, 9am-5pm Mon.-Fri., 10am-3pm Sat.) offers cycle rental of both regular cycles and electric bikes, but it may be more convenient to book a cycle rental with **Destination Røros,** which offers packages with pickup from Røros Hotel, Bergstadens Hotel, and Idrettsparken Hotel. Expect to pay 200-400kr depending on the length of hire, from a few hours to a full day.

Each rental comes complete with maps of three recommended routes around the region that vary from a few hours to a full day. In the Footsteps of the Miner takes you to the former mine at Storwartz (great to combine with a visit to the Olavs mine); Biking in Falkbergets Realm guides you around Nordgruvfeltet, the inspiration for many of Norwegian author Johan Falkberget's famous works; and Remains of the Ice Age introduces you to the scenery of Mølmannsdalen valley. The last is the easiest tour. QR codes are dotted around the sites, so make sure you have a QR code reader on your smartphone if you want to learn more on your travels.

Events

Twice a year this tiny town is swamped with visitors. If you plan on attending either of these events, book your accommodations well in advance or consider making a day trip from Trondheim. Dress appropriately—although temperatures are likely to be -15 to -1°C (5-30°F), they can drop as low as -32°C (-25°F) in the winter. The markets will go ahead regardless!

If they can cope with the cold, kids will adore the **Røros Christmas Market (Julemarked)** (www.julemarkedroros.no), usually held around the first weekend of December. They will think they are in the North Pole, with guaranteed snow, reindeer-pulled sled rides, Arctic huskies, and more. The final of the annual gingerbread house competition is a sight to behold. Enjoy the festivities over a warming cup of cocoa for the kids and mulled wine for the adults. Market stalls showcase local products and offer an opportunity to buy some truly unique Christmas gifts.

The bigger sister of the Christmas market, the mid-February **Røros Winter Fair (Rørosmartnan)** (www.rorosmartnan.no) begins with a horse-pulled sled procession from the neighboring municipalities, valleys from throughout central Norway, and even from the mountains of Sweden. Held by way of a royal decree since 1854, the fair attracts around 75,000 people to the tiny town (remember, the year-round population is just a few thousand!), transforming the sleepy former mining town into a bustling market-led metropolis for a week. By day cultural events, fun activities, and a thriving marketplace dominate, while a fun fair, dance hall, and concerts keep the crowds entertained long into the evening.

Food

The attractive yet anonymous frontage of ★ **Frøyas Hus** (Mørkstugata 4, tel. 92 88 35 30, www.froyashus.no) hides a delightful little café in the shadow of Røros Church. Open daily 10am-7pm during the summer season (mid-June to mid-Aug.), the exotic backyard is dotted with antiques, plants, blankets, and pillows for you to relax in whatever the temperature. The menu varies but usually features snacks such as waffles and pancakes through to more substantial soups, cured meats, and sharp cheeses. Friendly owner Ellen also opens the café during the town's winter events when there are seats in the equally charming barn to keep you warm. Antiques, blankets, and oil lamps are for sale.

The historic **Kaffestuggu** (Bergmannsgata 18, tel. 72 41 10 33, www. kaffestuggu.no, 11am-5pm Sun.-Wed., 11am-11pm Thurs.-Fri., 10am-11pm Sat., 179-290kr) is popular with locals and the elderly, which should tell you a lot about the traditional style of food here. There's a local element to every dish no matter where its origin. The burger comes with a blue cheese sauce from Selbu, while Norwegian staples *bacalao* (dried cod in a tomato sauce) and elk are popular choices. Find a table first, especially on busy days, before ordering from the bar.

Former servants' quarters have been transformed into one of central Norway's finest dining establishments at **Vertshuset** (Kjerkgata 34, tel. 72 41 93 50, www.vertshusetroros.no, 6pm-10pm Tues.-Sat.), the restaurant of the equally fine hotel. Choose between a three-course (525kr) and five-course (798kr) menu, which will most likely feature the nationally known Røros lamb, salmon caught from the region's rivers, and blue cheese from Selbu. Despite the formal setting, service is friendly and the focus is very much on the food, which is presented beautifully.

If you prefer things a little more casual, the same building offers a more accessible gastropub menu at **Berkel** (Kjerkgata 34, tel. 72 41 93 50, www.vertshusetroros.no, noon-10pm daily, 165-225kr). The products from the basement microbrewery are especially popular with locals. If you don't have time to sample the beers in the pub, bottles are available to buy from most stores in the town, including Røros Delikatesser and Coop Mega.

Located inside the Bergmann's wing of the Bergstadens Hotel, **Peder Hiort Mathus** (Osloveien 2, tel. 72 40 60 20, 2pm-10pm daily, 149-249kr) gives guests the feeling of being down the mine with low ceilings, timber beams, and intimate tables surrounded by artifacts and photographs from the old mining days. The food is more up-to-date, however, with international favorites such as pizza, pasta dishes, and hamburgers getting top billing. An outdoor terrace is available in warmer weather. If you're in a rush or you just want to grab a lighter meal, try the associated **Hiort** sports pub immediately next door.

Accommodations

Few lodgings are better located than the historical ★ **Vertshuset Hotel** (Kjerkgata 34, tel. 72 41 93 50, www.vertshusetroros.no, from 1,050kr d) at the very heart of the town. Traditional timber dominates the interior of the 19th-century building Rammgården, which houses the reception, restaurant, lounge, and some of the superior rooms and apartments. Next door, the former wool factory Uldvarefabrikken houses smaller, more contemporary loft-style rooms. You'll be staying in a part of Røros history at the very heart of the town whichever option you choose.

One of the bigger and most well-known hotels in this part of the country, **Bergstadens Hotel** (Osloveien 2, tel. 72 40 60 80, www.bergstadenshotel.no, 1,250kr d) presents 90 well-equipped rooms, many newly refurbished and some with a balcony. Nonallergenic rooms and rooms suitable for pets are also available. The hotel is a popular choice during the winter due to its proximity to the train and bus stations and its choice of several restaurants under the same roof.

A 10-minute walk from the main shopping streets, **Røros Hotel** (An-Magrittveien 48, tel. 72 40 80 00, www.roroshotell.no, 1,000kr d) often has rooms available when other hotels are full. Rooms are on the cramped side and only half can be described as modern, but the reception, lounge, and bar areas have all been upgraded in a mountain lodge style and are a pleasant place to spend the evening.

The selection at breakfast is limited but of a good quality.

Because of extensive media coverage it can be difficult to secure one of the seven rooms at the budget-friendly **Solheim Pensjonat** (tel. 95 52 37 06, www.solheimpensjonat.no, 800kr d), so get in touch well in advance of your trip. Step back in time as you enter one of Norway's most distinctive guesthouses, lovingly restored to its original post-war condition and decor. Sofas complete with cross-stitch pillows and bold patterned wallpaper provide a familiar homey feel of days long gone.

Information and Services

Given the short time most day trippers have in Røros, it's sensible to make a quick stop at **Destination Røros** (Peder Hiortgata 2, tel. 72 41 00 00, 9am-6pm Mon.-Sat. and 10am-4pm Sun. mid-June to mid-Aug., 9am-3:30pm weekdays and 10am-4pm Sat. rest of year) upon arrival to make sure that you're not going to miss out on any events happening that day. Information is posted outside when the office is closed. Things tend to change quickly in small communities, so head here, just a few minutes' walk from the railway station, for the latest lowdown.

Getting There and Around

Despite its small size Røros does have an airport, which is served by flights to and from Oslo from Norway's domestic airline Widerøe. Typically, there are two daily departures on weekdays and one on Sunday afternoon. The airport is a 20-minute walk south of the town center. Taxis will be on hand to meet flights, or you can book one in advance from **Røros taxi** (Johan Falkbergets vei 2, tel. 72 41 12 58).

Railway is perhaps the most common way to arrive at Røros. Direct trains make the 2.5-hour journey from Trondheim three times a day, and Oslo can be reached in around five hours by changing trains at Hamar. A one-way ticket from Trondheim costs around 304kr, with a small saving usually available for buying at least 24 hours in advance. From Oslo to Røros, expect to pay 810kr on-the-day, with prices of under 400kr usually available when booking in advance. Contact national rail operator **NSB** (tel. 81 50 08 88, www.nsb. no) for timetable information and advance bookings.

Bus 340 is a useful alternative from Trondheim and opens up more possibilities for day trips. Four daily departures make the three-hour journey from Trondheim, and a one-way ticket costs 220kr. The bus is operated by Boreal on behalf of the regional bus company **AtB** (tel. 02820, www.atb.no).

Driving is a pleasant albeit time-consuming way to reach Røros. From Oslo, the five-hour northbound drive along Routes 3 and 30 takes you through the valleys and mountain plains of eastern Norway that few tourists ever see. From Trondheim, head south on the E6 to Støren and pick up the eastbound Route 30 to Røros to arrive in approximately 2.5-3 hours. An interesting alternative for scenery and wildlife spotting is the mountain Route 705 through Selbu, although this route adds an hour to your journey time and is not recommended (and is in fact often closed) outside of the summer season. Parking in Røros is straightforward and mostly free of charge.

The downtown area is so small that walking is the only sensible option, even if you are stopping off for a few hours. In the winter, kick-sleds known as sparks are popular ways to move around the city. Ask to borrow one at your hotel.

DOVREFJELL-SUNNDALSFJELLA NATIONAL PARK

The most easily accessible of the national parks is set around the mighty Dovre mountain range, which separates Trondheim from the southern half of Norway. A drive along Norway's arterial E6 highway will introduce you to the range, and simply selecting any one of the many turnouts and campsites along the route for a brief hike is a sensible idea.

If you are traveling south from Trondheim, a good starting point is the town of **Oppdal,** an easy 119-kilometer (74-mile) drive south along the E6. Previously known as one of Norway's best ski resorts, the slopes have seen better days although the town itself has been spruced up with recent improvements to its central area. The drive from Oppdal to the town of Dombås is steep and slow but takes you through some of Norway's most scenic mountain areas. Allow around one hour to drive the 75 kilometers (46 miles) south along the E6. If you only have time to stop once, choose the tiny village of **Hjerkinn**, more than 1,000 meters above sea level, between Oppdal and Dombås.

The town of **Dombås** is the crossroads of central Norway. Road, rail, and rivers meet here, along with the borders of several national parks. There's nothing especially of note but it's worth planning Dombås into your journey as a refueling point, for both yourself and your vehicle. The town center is essentially a shopping arcade with a couple of supermarkets, souvenir shops, gas stations, and fast food outlets.

★ Snøhetta Pavilion

The **Norwegian Wild Reindeer Centre (Besøkssenter villrein)** (Hjerkinnhusvegen 33, tel. 95 05 47 55, www.villrein.no) is

responsible for promoting the preservation and sustainable management of Norway's wild reindeer population and their natural habitats. The office is in process of establishing an educational center, but for now its chief attraction for visitors is the **Snøhetta Pavilion,** a contemporary wooden shelter and a great place for spotting herds of wild reindeer. The short one-kilometer hike from the nearby (signposted) car park is worth it for the scenery and to see the striking architecture of the pavilion, even if you don't see any wild animals. The pavilion, which picked up a World Architecture Award in 2011, is open year-round from late May to September, weather dependent.

★ Musk Ox Safari

Dovrefjell-Sunndalsfjella National Park is the only place in Europe to see a herd of musk oxen roaming in the wild. Imported from eastern Greenland in the mid-1900s, these enormous creatures are vegetarian, but are still a threat to humans given their immense 400-kilogram (880-pound) weight. Your tour guide will almost certainly tell you the cautionary tale of a tourist who had to be airlifted to hospital in Trondheim after trying to feed one of the animals.

the Snøhetta Pavilion in Dovrefjell-Sunndalsfjella National Park

Guided tours operate across the national park by **Moskus Safari Dovrefjell** (tel. 46 42 01 02, www.moskus-safari.no), with pickup from either Hjerkinn or Dombås. Because herds of musk oxen roam the mountains, the tours can take up to five hours, and warm clothing and hiking boots are strongly recommended. Tours cost 350kr per person and run daily from 9am (Dombås) or 10am (Hjerkinn). Pre-booking is not required from mid-June to mid-August. Outside of these times, call in advance.

The real benefit of this safari is the chance to tour Dovrefjell-Sunndalsfjella National Park with a knowledgeable local guide, who will tell you all about the natural environment of the mountains, and the animals that call it home.

Recreation

HIKING

Hiking is free and numerous trails start from Hjerkinn. Hikes can last anything from a couple hours to a couple days. Lengthier hikes higher in the mountains are only recommended during the period of May-September due to the risk of sudden snowfall. For advice, the **Dombås National Park Center (Dombås Nasjonalparksenter)** (Dombås Senter, tel. 61 24 14 44, 9am-8pm Mon.-Sat., 9am-4pm Sun. mid-June to mid-Aug., 9am-4pm Mon.-Fri. rest of year) is your best bet.

One of the most popular starting points is **Kongsvold,** which also happens to be one of the best places to see musk oxen in the wild. The 16-kilometer (10-mile) hike to the Reinheim cabin is relatively demanding but can be completed in around five hours. Expect to see musk oxen, wild reindeer, and mountainous landscape along the way. Serious hikers will consider going on to climb **Snøhetta,** the highest mountain in Norway outside of the Jotunheimen range. It's an approximately five-hour round-trip from the Reinheim cabin. Expect snow on the ground even in summer, and crampons and waterproof clothing are recommended.

SKIING

Dovrefjell-Sunndalsfjella National Park is a mecca for cross-country skiers, with marked trails crisscrossing the park in all directions. For downhill skiing and snowboarders, **Oppdal Skisenter** (Kjerkvegen 112, tel. 72 40 44 80, www.oppdalskisenter. no) offers the region's best slopes. A day's ski pass costs 410kr, with equipment rental costing 350kr for basic gear and 450kr for better quality gear. Cross-country rental (skis and boots) costs 195kr for a day with discounts available for multiple days. A week's rental is 500kr.

HORSE RIDING

The mountain lodge **Hjerkinn Fjellstue & Fjellridning** (tel. 61 21 51 00, www.hjerkinn. no) offers horseback riding through the plains, rivers, and forests of the area. Riding starts at 9:30am Tuesday-Sunday from mid-June to mid-August and costs 950kr per person for up to seven hours of guided riding.

RAFTING

Take to the river Driva, one of Norway's best known rafting rivers. The company **Opplev Oppdal** (tel. 72 40 41 80, www.opplevoppdal.no) runs three different tours, varying in difficulty, from Granmo Camping (Dovreveien 638).

One tour is suitable for families and children, a second requires previous rafting experience, while the third is well suited to both beginners and thrill-seekers. Wetsuits and safety equipment are provided, but you should take a swimsuit, woolen socks, and running shoes. Swimming and even cliff jumping are optional extras on the more demanding tours.

The family tour lasts two hours and costs 440kr per person, while the standard 14-kilometer (8.7-mile) tour costs 840-890kr and lasts around three hours. Tours are usually run twice daily, but because availability depends on season and water levels, booking in advance is highly recommended.

GOLF

Open daily May through October, **Oppdal Golfklubb** (Industrivegen, tel. 72 42 25 10, www.oppdalgolfklubb.no, 3pm-8pm Mon.-Fri., 10am-8pm Sat.-Sun.) runs a nine-hole course just two kilometers from Oppdal center. The fairways cross the River Alma four times and are lined by birch and pine forest, providing both enjoyable views and a challenging game. Greens fees start at 250kr with a day pass available from 400kr.

Food

Self-catering is very much the order of the day in the Norwegian mountains. Popular Norwegian hiking food includes the Kvikk Lunsj chocolate bar, hot dogs (*pølser*) kept warm in a flask of hot water, and sweet flatbreads (*lefser*). Most hotels and hostels in the region will allow you to make up a packed lunch (*matpakke*) from the breakfast buffet. Many don't advertise this option, so do ask if there are no supermarkets nearby. You can expect to pay 50-100kr for this. If you plan on hiking all day, there will be few other options.

Every town dotted along the E6 will have at least one restaurant although the quality rarely peaks above fast-food standards, and they are likely to close well before 10pm. There are exceptions, most notably in the upscale restaurant of **Kongsvold Fjellstue** (Dovrevegen 3663, tel. 90 08 48 02, www.kongsvold.no, Feb.-Nov., 200-350kr). Reservations must be made in advance, even for lunch, which is served noon-3pm daily. A three-course menu is served at 7pm. The restaurant focuses on extremely local food, with cured, smoked, and marinated cooking techniques. Reindeer, mountain trout, mushrooms, and pâté feature regularly. From mid-June to mid-August, a smaller café menu is available 1pm-5pm with coffee, porridge, and homemade cakes.

Farther north in the center of Oppdal, an inconspicuous basement pub hides surprisingly good food. A gourmet burger at **Spisbar** (Aunevegen 1, tel. 45 25 21 11, noon-5pm

Mon.-Tues., noon-10pm Wed.-Thurs., noon-3am Fri.-Sat.) will set you back around 182kr, while main courses such as fillet of trout or breast of pheasant will come in at around 289kr. The venue is a popular late-night destination for Oppdal locals and visiting skiers, so the later it gets the livelier and more pub-like it becomes.

Accommodations

Five kilometers (three miles) south of Oppdal, **Granmo Camping** (Dovreveien 638, tel. 99 64 29 47, www.granmocamping.no) offers pitches (from 150kr per night) and cabins ranging in quality and price (400-1,200kr). The campsite is well located along the E6 and is the base for recreational activities including rafting and fishing. Toilets, showers, kitchen, and full laundry facilities are available. A small kiosk is open alongside the reception during the summer months. Prices are high but it saves you a shopping trip into Oppdal.

Hjerkinn Vandrerhjem (tel. 46 42 01 02, www.hjerkinnhus.no) is a hostel located in a former military barracks, a distinctive traditional black and red timber building. The accommodations are basic, with bunk beds and a wash basin in each dormitory and shared bathroom facilities in the corridor, although amenities include a sauna, TV lounge, kitchen, and fitness room. Prices vary depending on the number in your party and time of year, but expect to pay around 500kr for a single bed up to 1,000kr for a group of four. A simple breakfast is available for an additional 100kr per person.

The charming whitewashed **Hjerkinn Fjellstue & Fjellridning** (tel. 61 21 51 00, www.hjerkinn.no 1,395kr d) is a mountain lodge and perfect starting point for a hike. The owners claim it to be the oldest family business in Norway. Whether that's true or not is debatable, but this is one family that knows these mountains inside out, so do ask questions. Campers are welcome to stay at a nightly rate of 280kr with a vehicle or 95kr without. Twelve homey apartments are also available for bigger groups, starting from 1,395kr with additional charges made for bedding and cleaning. **Kongsvold Fjellstue** (Dovrevegen 3663, tel. 90 08 48 02, www.kongsvold.no, 725-995kr pp) has a history stretching back almost 1,000 years. The hostel has offered accommodations to all sorts of people traveling across the mountains, from Scandinavian royalty to pilgrims making the journey north to Nidaros, the original name for Trondheim. Easily accessible via the E6 or Kongsvoll station on the Oslo to Trondheim railway line, the hostel offers 75 beds in a variety of configurations. This is far from the cheapest way to stay in the Dovrefjell mountains, but it's a perfect choice for a comfortable way to start or end a hiking trip, or to break up a journey from south to north.

At the southern edge of the national park, the **Dombås Motell** (Romsdalsveien 6, Dombås, tel. 45 67 19 95, www.dombasmotel. com, 440kr s, 660kr d) is one of the cheapest non-cabin options in and around the Dovrefjell mountains. The mismatched furniture and mattresses have seen better days, and there are no TVs or computer terminals available, but this simplistic approach to accommodation keeps the prices low. The motel is 1.6 kilometers (one mile) from Dombås rail station, which should take just 15-20 minutes to walk.

Information and Services

For detailed information about hiking routes and conditions, call into the **Dombås National Park Center (Dombås Nasjonalparksenter)** (Dombås Senter, tel. 61 24 14 44, 9am-8pm Mon.-Sat., 9am-4pm Sun. mid-June to mid-Aug., 9am-4pm Mon.-Fri. rest of year). They can also supply maps for driving or hiking, and help with booking tours or recreational experiences. The center is easy to find in the commercial center of Dombås, just off the E6.

Getting There

The most convenient access point to

Dovrefjell-Sunndalsfjella National Park is the eastern border. Here you'll find the E6, Norway's main north-south highway, although the road resembles a rural lane at times. Be wary of high winds, especially when overtaking trucks. When driving in the Dovrefjell mountains, and indeed anywhere in central Norway, always have a backup plan because the roads can be closed suddenly due to high winds or sudden snowfall. It's wise to keep a printed map and a list of backup accommodations should bad weather strike.

It takes around four hours to drive the 306 kilometers (190 miles) from Oslo Airport to the southern edge of the park at Dombås along the E6 via Lillehammer. From Trondheim, follow the southbound E6 for 119 kilometers (74 miles) to reach the northern edge of the park at Oppdal in under two hours.

The eastern edge of the park is also easily accessible by train from Oslo and Trondheim on the Dovrebanen line. There are stops at Oppdal, Kongsvoll, Hjerkinn, and Dombås. Prices can drop as low as 249kr when booking in advance with the state railway company **NSB** (tel. 81 50 08 88, www.nsb.no). The journey from Oslo to Dombås takes 4-4.5 hours, while the Trondheim to Oppdal journey takes under two hours.

RONDANE NATIONAL PARK

Similar to the neighboring Dovrefjell-Sunndalsfjella National Park, the Rondane National Park is mountainous, with 10 peaks higher than 2,000 meters (6,000 feet). The highest, Rondeslottet, clocks in at 2,178 meters (7,146 feet). The peaks may not appear as dramatic as you expect because even at the lowest point in the park, you are at least 1,000 meters (3,300 feet) above sea level.

The park is as an important natural habitat for wild reindeer and is characterized by the large number of kettle holes caused by the remains of Ice Age glaciers. The soil is poor above the tree line and so vegetation is limited to reindeer moss and the occasional shrub. The birch forests and lakes of the area give a different feel than the region's other national parks.

Sights

South of the Dovrefjell mountains, you will skirt the western side of Rondane on the E6 highway or on the Oslo to Trondheim railway line. There's plenty to see from the roadside, but to get a closer look in the car, take a detour on your trip away from the E6 at Ringebu (traveling north) or Hjerkinn (traveling south) onto Route 27 to enjoy the 64-kilometer (40-mile) National Tourist Route that skirts the eastern perimeter of the park.

Just a few miles off Route 27 along Route 219 is the quaint **Sollia Church (Sollia kirke)** (Sollia, tel. 95 97 10 97, www.storelvdal.kirken.no), built by local people in 1738 without any funding in order to stop the need to make the arduous trek along the mountains to the closest church at Ringebu. The timber church with its painting-filled interior has been wonderfully preserved. It's usually only open for services, but you can call ahead to arrange a viewing.

North along Route 27, 20 kilometers (12.5 miles) away from the church, is the **Atnabrufossen Waterworks Museum (Atnbrufossen Vannbruksmuseum)** (Nordre Braend, tel. 62 46 37 75), which is a worthy stop regardless of your interest in the subject matter. Located in a birch grove beside a gushing river, the area makes a fine place for a picnic or to simply stretch your legs on a road trip. The former sawmill and hydropower station now hosts art exhibitions and concerts, so opening hours vary.

Just a couple of miles farther north along Route 27, the architecture of the modern lakeside viewing point **Sohlbergplassen** is typical of the modern constructions along the National Tourist Routes. Built to curve around the pine trees rather than interfere with them, the platform beautifully frames the view across the Atnsjøen lake, which straddles the border of Hedmark and Oppland counties. The snow-capped peaks of Rondane make a spectacular backdrop to this ideal picnic spot.

Recreation

During the summer months, most hikers head for DNT's **Rondvassbu mountain lodge** (tel. 61 23 18 66) at the southern tip of Rondvatnet lake. Open to DNT members only, the cabin has 128 beds and is accessible with a straightforward but lengthy 1.5-hour hike from the Sprangen parking lot. During the winter season, there is a marked **cross-country ski trail.** Be aware that the lodge and many of the hiking routes across Rondane are closed from May to early June because of the reindeer calving season. The lodge is staffed during Easter and after the calving season has finished through to late September.

To reach the Sprangen parking lot, travel to **Otta,** which is 46 kilometers (29 miles) south of Dombås along the E6 or a 30-minute train ride. From Otta, take Route 444 to Mysusæter and follow the signs. If you are without your own transport, public bus 538 runs from the transport interchange in Otta (Otta skysstasjon) to the Spranget lot twice a day during July and August. The journey takes 35-50 minutes, and a one-way ticket costs 37kr. Check www.opplandstrafikk.no for schedule information.

From Rondvassbu, many **hiking** opportunities are available, including a relatively straightforward hike to the summit of Storronden. Allow around five hours to negotiate the challenging round-trip on the clearly signed trail.

During July and August, a **boat trip** runs 2-3 times a day from the lodge along the length of Rondvatnet lake. The one-way journey takes just 20 minutes and costs 120kr. The walk back along the lake's western shoreline takes around 2.5 hours, or you can return immediately on the boat.

For specific information on accommodations and hiking options, the **Dombås National Park Center (Dombås Nasjonalparksenter)** (Dombås Senter, tel. 61 24 14 44, 9am-8pm Mon.-Sat., 9am-4pm Sun. mid-June to mid-Aug., 9am-4pm Mon.-Fri. rest of year) also dispenses information about Rondane.

Åndalsnes and the Romsdal Valley

The traditional district of Romsdal straddles the border of central Norway and the vast western fjord region. At this meeting point you find the best of both worlds: imposing mountains and hiking opportunities combined with photogenic fjords and popular tourist attractions. The area is easily explored by car from Trondheim or as an add-on from a tour of the western fjords.

The Romsdal valley is Norway in miniature, with everything from winding rivers and gushing waterfalls to ragged mountain peaks and lush green forest within a relatively small area. Most travelers choose **Åndalsnes** as their base to explore the area. The town is ideally located at the western terminus of the Romsdal railway line from Dombås, where it connects with the Oslo to Trondheim train. By car, Åndalsnes is just an hour and a half from Ålesund and two and a half hours from the Atlantic Road and Geiranger.

The latter route involves a journey along one of Norway's best National Tourist Routes, one that incorporates the Ørnesvingen hairpin bends, the magnificent Gudbrandsjuvet gorge, the one-of-a-kind Trollstigen mountain pass, and different mountain landscapes around every bend.

However, although the setting of Åndalsnes is magnificent, the town itself is rather drab with very few sights of note. The nearby campsites are of a very high standard, so staying there and using the town as a mere refueling stop is your best option.

★ Trollstigen Mountain Pass

As you drive southeast from Åndalsnes toward the **Trollstigen mountain pass,** you get closer and closer to a sheer rock face rising high up into the sky. You won't be the first person to think, "surely this is the end of the road?"

But then you spot a car crawling up the mountain face. "Wait a moment, there's a road

there?" Indeed, there is. Trollstigen loosely translates into English as "The Troll's Path" and replaced a challenging ancient hiking trail to link Åndalsnes with the Valldal valley and on to Geiranger.

Part of Fv63, the Trollstigen mountain road has an incline of 10 percent and 11 hairpin bends on its way up to the 700-meter-high (2,300-foot-high) mountain plateau. The road is largely single track with many passing points, although these are often clogged with cars pulled over for photographs. Halfway up, an old stone bridge crosses the Stigfossen waterfall, which tumbles over 300 meters. Time your drive early in the morning or late in the evening to avoid tourist buses. They struggle with the hairpin bends and can turn an otherwise incredible driving experience into a frustrating one.

Primarily known as an attraction for

The remarkable Trollstigen mountain pass is only open during the summer.

Myth of the Trolls

Norway's folklore is extensive, and much of it dates back to the pagan era but was only written down from the 19th century onward. A major part of folklore across Scandinavia is the supernatural creature known as a troll. Portrayed as spirits of the underground, trolls are able to help or hinder humans, but often choose to do neither. Trolls may be described as small, human-like beings or as tall as men depending on the region of origin of the story. Many tales describe the creatures as being extremely old, very strong, but slow and dim-witted.

As creatures of the countryside they favor peaceful environments and so won't be found in cities. So strong was the belief in the troll folklore that as recently as 300 years ago, villagers would ring church bells for hours in an attempt to keep the trolls away.

Funnily enough, it always worked.

drivers, Trollstigen surprises many by its offering at the summit. The wooden paths around the summit connect you with the rugged mountain landscape, and three viewing platforms allow you to peer down onto the road and valley below. The largest platform dangles 650 feet above a sheer drop, but the glass and steel construction keeps you safe as you take in the spectacular view of the racetrack-like road below. The **visitor center** (10am-5pm daily during season) designed by Reiulf Ramstad Architects bears a striking resemblance to Oslo's Opera House. Within its walls you'll find a café and gift shop packed with troll-related merchandise.

Note that parts of Route 63, including the Trollstigen pass, are closed during winter. The road is usually open from mid-May to early October, but the exact dates are dictated by the weather conditions and so can vary considerably year to year. Check with **National Tourist Routes (Nasjonal turistveger)** (www.nasjonaleturistveger.no) or ask at any tourist office or hotel in the region.

Other Sights

Continuing the troll theme, the **Troll's Wall (Trollveggen)** is a dramatic section of the mountain massif known as the Troll Peaks in **Reinheimen National Park,** approximately 11.4 kilometers (7 miles) southeast of Åndalsnes along the E136 toward Dombås.

The cliff rises 1,700 meters (almost 5,600 feet) and is Europe's tallest vertical rock face. At some points the overhang is as much as 45 meters (150 feet), which has in the past attracted base jumpers from across the world. In 1984 renowned BASE jumper Carl Boenish fell to his death, and soon after the emerging sport was made illegal at Trollveggen. However, this tragedy only served to heighten the area's allure, and the practice has continued over the years, with a total of nine known fatalities, only one of them a Norwegian national.

Safely out of harm's way, the award-winning **visitor center** (near Horgheim, tel. 71 22 06 60, www.visit-trollveggen.com) on the E136 houses a café with terraced seating to enjoy an uninterrupted view of the mountain face. The visitor center is open 10am-5pm daily June-August, but you can stop in the car park and walk around the area to take in the imposing sight at any time of year.

A further 27 kilometers (16.7 miles) southeast along the E136 toward Dombås is the **Vermafossen waterfall.** The powerful waterfall plunges 380 meters (1,250 feet) and provides a terrific photo opportunity. Care should be taken in the vicinity, as the rocks can become slippery from the waterfall's spray. The adjacent stone arch **Kylling Bridge** carries the Rauma line railway across the valley, 60 meters (200 feet) above the river.

The only attraction of note in Åndalsnes itself is the relatively new **Norwegian Alpine Center (Norsk Tindesenter)** (Havnegata 2, tel. 73 60 45 57, www.tindesenteret.no,

10am-6pm daily June-Sept., 140kr), a celebration of Norwegian mountaineering from the 1800s to the present day and a meeting place for all those who love the sport. The exhibition tells true stories from the mountains through an equipment museum and a short movie in a purpose-built rock face auditorium. All exhibits and the movie are titled in both English and Norwegian. The addition of an indoor climbing wall makes the steep entrance fee bearable, although you do have to fork out another 150kr for equipment rental.

Recreation

HIKING

Walkers of all abilities flock to the Åndalsnes area for the spectacular hiking opportunities. Beginners can follow the course of the Rauma river and enjoy the sight of the soaring mountains, while experienced hikers will want to tick the **Romsdalseggen Ridge** off their bucket list.

One of Norway's most famous hiking routes, the Romsdalseggen Ridge is a challenging all-day commitment with a substantial reward. Breathtaking is an overused word in travel guides, but the 360-degree views from the ridge fully deserve the description. On clear days, you can see all the way to Molde and the open ocean beyond, plus you get a unique perspective of the Romsdal mountains that few other tourists get to see.

The 10-kilometer (6.2-mile) hiking route is accessible from July to September and begins with a 9:30am bus (daily) from Åndalsnes to the hike's starting point at **Vengedalen.** You can expect the hike to take 7-8 hours at normal speed. Although the challenging hike doesn't require any specialized equipment, sturdy hiking boots and wind- and waterproof clothing (no matter what the weather is like when you leave) are essential items. The 140kr bus fare includes an information brochure and map. Be sure to take enough provisions to last the day, because hiking the ridge to Åndalsnes is the only way back. Consider your plans carefully if the weather forecast is poor.

FISHING

One of the cleanest fjords in Norway, the Romsdalsfjord contains 68 species, including coalfish, pollock, cod, haddock, and mackerel. Fishing is free along its 80-kilometer (50-mile) shoreline, but it could be more convenient and more fun to join a tour offered by **Rauma Jakt og Fiskesafari** (Tegltun 4, Åndalsnes, tel. 71 22 63 54, www.rauma-jakt-fiskesafari. no, 380kr) in one of their traditional 30-foot fishing boats. Running daily throughout the year subject to suitable weather conditions, the short three-hour trips leave Åndalsnes at 7:30am and 6pm. All fishing and safety equipment is included.

PADDLEBOARDING

The gentler stretches of the Rauma river provide the perfect conditions for stand up paddling, which is great for your balance and a full-body workout. Try it for yourself with an introductory course from **Friluftsek** (Vollan 3, Åndalsnes, tel. 71 22 25 00, www.friluftslek. no, 600kr including wetsuit rental). Call in advance to check times and book. The same company also offers board rental for experienced paddleboarders at 500kr for three hours.

SKIING

Directly across the Romsdalsfjord from Åndalsnes is the **Skorgedalen Ski Center** (tel. 47 26 97 42, www.raumaskisenter.com, 10:30am-4pm Sat.-Sun. in season, daily throughout Easter, 300kr), which opens from the first snowfall of the year through March. Popular with alpine skiers from across the region, the center also offers marked cross-country ski trails.

Food and Accommodations

Staying outside Åndalsnes is recommended, although it is handy to be close to supermarkets. Several campsites offer high-quality cabins with electricity, running water, and full bathroom facilities at rates that are still lower than a hotel. The riverside ★ **Åndalsnes Camping & Motel** (Gryttenveien 1, tel. 71 22 16 29, www.andalsnes-camping.net) is a short one mile walk from the town, yet it feels like you are in the middle of nowhere. Surrounded by the steep ragged peaks of the Romsdal mountains, the campsite offers a wide range of cabins and motel rooms sleeping 2-7 people for 400-975kr. The reception building doubles as a restaurant selling beer and wine along with a menu of hot meals. Alternatively, riverside benches provide the perfect setting for a self-catered meal.

Located at the foot of the Isterdalen valley, **Trollstigen Camping** (tel. 71 22 11 12, www.trollstigen.no, Apr.-Sept.) is the ideal choice if you want to reach Trollstigen before the road is flooded with cars. They have a range of cabins, and prices range 460-910kr depending on standard and season. Tents can be pitched for the night at 110kr with an extra 30kr if you bring a car. Open from mid-May to mid-September, the **Trollstigen Gjestegård** restaurant is behind the camping reception area and serves hot albeit basic food all day. The same company operates the café at the top of Trollstigen, so staff are well-placed to answer any questions you might have about your onward journey.

Open from mid-May to the end of August, **Åndalsnes Vandrerhjem** (Setnes, tel. 71 22 13 82) is a highly regarded HI hostel that is closer in standard to a budget hotel. Set in former farm buildings just one mile from downtown Åndalsnes, the hostel offers dorm beds from 290kr with private rooms ranging 500-1,160kr. A guest kitchen is available, although the hostel offers some good value food options: breakfast (75kr), basic dinner (150kr), and a packed lunch (40kr). The latter is a particularly good deal if you are planning a hike or long road trip.

For a filling evening meal, head into Åndalsnes and visit **China House** (Romsdalsvegen 6, tel. 71 22 82 01, 11am-9pm Mon.-Sat., 180kr). Although the menu also features sushi and a small Norwegian menu, the quality of the Chinese food is far superior and is in stark contrast to the somewhat dated interior. While far from outstanding, it's a lot better than many small-town Asian restaurants elsewhere in Norway. Simpler, slightly cheaper deals are available at lunchtime, and takeaway is available all day.

Information and Services

One reason to call into Åndalsnes is to visit the knowledgeable staff at the office of **Visit Åndalsnes** (Jernbanegata 1, tel. 71 22 16 22, www.visitandalsnes.com, 9:30am-5pm Mon.-Wed. and Fri., 9:30am-7pm Thurs., 10am-3pm Sat.) for maps, tour questions, and activity bookings.

Timber cabins are the most popular accommodations in Romsdal.

Kristiansund and the Atlantic Road

The windswept town of Kristiansund and the nearby Atlantic Road are found in the historical district of Nordmøre, which marks the border of Fjord Norway and the country's central region. Largely open to the elements, the coastal region is famous among international travelers for the Atlantic Road, the 8.3-kilometer-long (5.2-mile-long) stretch of Route 64 that jumps between islands and has been the setting for countless car commercials.

KRISTIANSUND

Kristiansund is a town with a strong maritime tradition. It makes for a pleasant lunchtime or afternoon stop for those traveling from Trondheim to the Atlantic Road, or an overnight stop for those traveling at a slower pace. Split into four sections by the water—Kirkelandet, Innlandet, Nordlandet, and Gomalandet—and linked by bridges and a frequent ferry, Kristiansund is a perfect location for fans of waterside walks.

Some scientists and historians believe that some of Norway's first inhabitants lived near what is now known as Kristiansund, as the

region was one of the first to be ice-free toward the end of the last Ice Age and the sea provided rich pickings for food and trade. Although many battles took place here during the Viking era, it was during the 17th century that something resembling the modern-day town began to develop around the natural harbor.

The town grew as an important trading post, in particular for clipfish. At one point during the 18th century, Kristiansund exported more clipfish products to the Mediterranean than any other Norwegian town.

Sights

The city itself is the main sight, and the best way to explore that is on the iconic **Sundbåten** ferry (Kongens plass 1, tel. 92 85 17 44, www.sundbaten.no, 7am-5pm Mon.-Fri., 9:30am-5pm Sat., noon-4pm Sun.), which claims to be the oldest continuously running public transportation system anywhere in the world. The compact passenger ferry links together the various suburbs and islands

Sundbåten ferries passengers between the islands of Kristiansund.

Kristiansund and the Atlantic Road

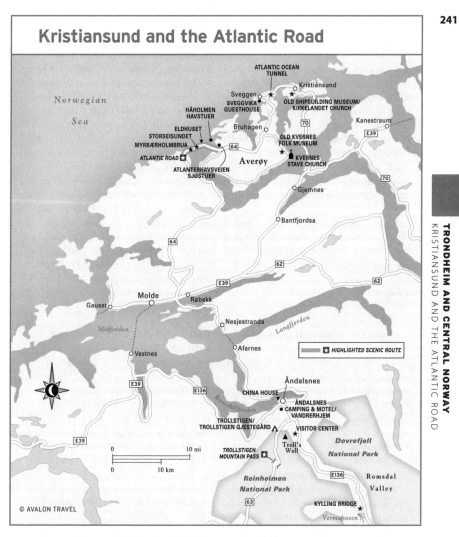

making up the city: Kirkelandet, Innlandet, Nordlandet, and Gomalandet.

KIRKELANDET

Kirkelandet is the main part of Kristiansund, home to the modern town center, most hotels, bars, and restaurants, and modern shopping malls. If you are just passing through the town, this is your best option to grab a light lunch and take a quick stroll along the waterfront.

Unveiled by Queen Sonja in 1992, the waterfront *Klippfiskkjerringa* statue is an icon of the town and a tribute to the town's fishing industry. The bronze statue depicts a woman working with clipfish, the dried and salted cod used to make *bacalao*.

Along the waterfront is the **Old Shipbuilding Museum (Mellemvaerftet)** (Krana vei 22, tel. 71 67 71 95, noon-5pm daily mid-June to mid-Aug., 70kr), the most interesting part of the regional **Nordmøre**

museum. The shipyard's primary function was as a maintenance yard for the large fleet of local fishing boats and sailing ships. An original workshop building with machine shop and forge can be explored. Today the shipyard still functions preserving old ships, so there is a rare opportunity to see a traditional working shipyard in action.

Opened in 1964, **Kirkelandet Church (Kirkelandet kirke)** (Langveien, tel. 71 57 52 80) is a building for those who appreciate brutalist architecture rather than traditional churches. The daring angled design resembling an apartment block splits opinion across the city but has won plaudits for its interpretation of what a modern church should be. The interior is notable for featuring a block-patterned stained-glass window on its entire rear wall.

INNLANDET

The unique coastal architecture of the 18th-century trading center is the main reason to hop off the boat at Innlandet. As Kristiansund's smallest island, it's known locally as Tahiti and even hosts a small music festival, the Tahiti Festival, every year. Hotels and restaurants now populate the waterfront buildings, but other than a popular swimming area, the island is mostly residential.

GOMALANDET

The **Norwegian Clipfish Museum (Klippfiskmuseet)** (Dikselveien 20, tel. 71 58 70 00, noon-5pm daily mid-June to mid-Aug., 70kr) tells the tale of how the town depended on the fishing industry for so many years. The museum's setting, in a former clipfish factory dating back to the 18th century and overlooking the water, only adds to the authenticity of the experience.

GRIP

Although technically part of Kristiansund, the tiny island of **Grip** is actually one of Norway's most isolated communities. At 14 kilometers (8.7 miles) northwest of the mainland, the island can only be reached by scheduled ferry. Once a thriving community thanks to the abundance of fish in its waters, Grip suffered from years of damaging storms and poor fishing yields between 1780 and 1820. Modern-day Grip is largely deserted for most of the year, but the island's fishing village atmosphere is preserved thanks to the hundred or so summer residences. A notable sight is the small red **stave church.** Although an inscription one of the beams indicates it was built in 1621, investigations have concluded the church was built as early as the 15th century.

Gripruta (tel. 92 60 80 45, www.gripruta. no, 350kr) operates scheduled tours from Kristiansund harbor daily (10:30am Mon.-Fri. and 2pm Sat.-Sun. from mid-June to mid-Aug., with an extra daily departure during July). The round-trip takes around three hours, which gives you around 90 minutes to wander around the island with a local guide. Coffee and snacks are available for purchase on the boat.

Food and Accommodations
INNLANDET

The only option for those wanting to stay in Kristiansund's old town is the **Thon Hotel Kristiansund** (Fiskergata 12, tel. 71 57 30 00, 795kr). Although the charming wooden exterior is inviting, step inside and you could be in any chain hotel in any Norwegian town. On the flip side, most of the 98 rooms have a sea view, and the refurbished dock with outdoor seating for the restaurant is a nice touch.

A former boathouse on the waterfront of Kristiansund's old town, **Dødeladen Café** (4pm-11pm Wed.-Thurs., 4pm-2am Fri.-Sat.) is an after-work meeting point for multiple generations. The simple menu includes the likes of a chicken Caesar salad, an open-faced shrimp sandwich, *bacalao,* and a creamy fish soup. Enjoy your meal on the outdoor terrace or grab a takeout coffee if you're just stopping by on a tour of the town.

KIRKELANDET

Seafood also dominates the menus on Kirkelandet. The best of the bunch is inside another former boathouse, a common theme among the better restaurants of Kristiansund. **Smia** (Fosnagata 30b, tel. 71 67 11 70, www. smia.no, 11am-10pm Mon.-Sat., 2pm-9pm Sun., 295kr) specializes in *bacalao* and clipfish, and makes an excellent raspberry dessert. If you are just passing through, the lunch menu is worth a look. For 195kr you can try a tasting plate consisting of pickled herring, whale meat, fishcake, and a salted fish dumpling. Open sandwiches are also available.

The best value accommodations in the downtown area are at the **Astoria Hotel** (Hauggata 13, tel. 71 57 10 20, www.astoriahotell.no, 1,090kr s, 1,290kr d), which offers 73 newly renovated en suite rooms in a great location. Expect bold colors and simple furnishings with free Wi-Fi and a TV but few other frills. A breakfast buffet is included with all room rates. Guests staying a week or longer should inquire about long-stay packages with rooms that include a kitchenette.

GOMALANDET

Those with their own transport might consider the motel at **Atlanten Turistsenter** (Dalaveien 22, tel. 71 67 11 04, www.atlanten. no, 595kr s, 795kr d), located away from the central district but close to the entrance of the Atlantic Ocean Tunnel. Accommodations are basic, rooms are small, and breakfast is simple, but parking is free and it's easily the cheapest motel standard accommodation in the city. Cabins ideal for four people and space for tents, caravans, and motorhomes are available year-round.

Information and Services

Despite the cities being over 645 kilometers (400 miles) apart, foreign travelers often mistake Kristiansund for the bigger Kristiansand at the southern tip of the country. For this reason, the travel industry often refers to the cities as Kristiansund N (for north) and Kristiansand S (for south).

For maps, timetables, and other travel questions, visit the information center of **Destinasjon Kristiansund & Nordmøre** (Kongens Plass 1, tel. 71 58 54 54, www.

visitkristiansund.com, 9am-6pm Mon.-Sat., 9am-3pm Sun. mid-June to mid-Aug., 9am-3pm Mon.-Fri. rest of year) in the shopping district on Kirkelandet.

Getting There

AIR

Scandinavian Airlines operates four daily services from Oslo to **Kristiansund Airport,** located in Kvernberget seven kilometers (4.3 miles) east of the city. The airport is equipped to handle international arrivals, although there are currently just a few charter services over the summer season. Norway's domestic airline Widerøe provides services to Bergen, Florø, Molde, Stavanger, and Trondheim.

There is no express bus service to the city center, although local buses pass by the airport terminal main entrance approximately every half hour with the journey taking around 25 minutes. Taxis and a Hertz car rental desk are also available. **Kristiansund Taxi** (tel. 71 67 22 22, www.kristiansundtaxi. no) will take you into the city center in 10-15 minutes for around 160kr.

BOAT

Hurtigruten ships stop twice a day in Kristiansund and are the best option if you are traveling from Bergen. The journey from Bergen takes around 24 hours, so advance booking is essential to secure an overnight cabin. Prices vary. One daily departure leaves Trondheim mid-morning and takes around six hours to reach Kristiansund. Tickets can usually be booked for around 500kr.

A faster option from Trondheim is the **Coastal Express (Kystekspressen)** catamaran (tel. 73 89 07 00, www.kystekspressen.no), running three times a day at a cost of 648kr. Buy tickets on board for the 3.5-hour trip. It takes a similar time to drive the 198 kilometers from Trondheim to Kristiansund via the E39 highway.

BUS

Because of the relatively fast direct ferry service, bus route 905, which links Kristiansund with Trondheim and is known as the Fram Ekspress, is designed to serve the rural communities on the route rather than through passengers. As such, the journey takes around five hours and only runs once per day at 1:20pm from Trondheim bus station, at a cost of 433kr. The bus is operated by **Fram** (www.frammr.no), but you can search timetables and book seats on www.nettbuss.no. Seniors, children, and youth under 25 receive a 50 percent discount on advance tickets.

Getting Around

The **Sundbåten** passenger ferry (Kongens plass 1, tel. 92 85 17 44, www.sundbaten. no, 7am-5pm Mon.-Fri., 9:30am-5pm Sat., noon-4pm Sun.) links together Kirkelandet, Innlandet, Nordlandet, and Gomalandet. Note that the Sunday service is only operational from mid-May through August. A single ticket costs 35kr and is valid for travel between two points or an uninterrupted round-trip. To hop between the islands, a day pass at 90kr is the most convenient and best-value option. Expect a departure every 15-30 minutes, although as distances are short, it's usually possible to see where the ferry is from any of the four departure piers. In the main part of the town, Kirkelandet, the pier is opposite the **Kristiansund Town Hall (Kristiansund Rådhuset)** (Kaibakken), a few minutes' stroll down the promenade from the bus terminal.

AVERØY

Most tourists passing through Kristiansund head straight for the Atlantic Road. Yet this road trip is just as much about the journey as the destination, and an important part of the journey is the island of Averøy that links the two destinations.

Sights

Upon leaving Kristiansund on the westbound Route 64, you travel through the 5.7-kilometer-long (3.5-mile-long) **Atlantic Ocean Tunnel (Atlanterhavstunnelen)**, which at a depth of 820 feet below sea level is one of the deepest undersea tunnels in the world. The toll is 98kr for a car plus driver, with 40kr due for additional passengers. The tunnel emerges on Averøy, a scenic island with several distractions that can delay your arrival at the Atlantic Road.

Immediately after emerging from the tunnel and toll booths, take the first right to **Sveggen,** where small fishing boats putter around the small sound that separates the two halves of the working fishing village. There's nothing specific to see, but a short break wandering around this picturesque village is a chance to add some relaxation to your itinerary.

The village of **Bruhagen** lies seven kilometers south along Route 64 from the tunnel and is a useful place to stock up on supplies at its two small supermarkets. From Bruhagen, take a 10-kilometer detour along Route 247 to see the impressive **Kvernes Stave Church** (Prestegardsveien, tel. 92 29 94 38, 11am-5pm daily mid-June to mid-Aug., 50kr). Originally built around 1300 and rebuilt in 1633, the church is characterized by long walls with multiple beams, and is one of the smallest stave churches still in existence in Norway. Between the stave church and its modern twin church is the sculpture *Solur* by Rold Øidvin, designed to commemorate recent discoveries of burial mounds dating back to the Iron Age that demonstrate the cultural importance of Kvernes.

The route passing south of Averøy island has long been used by seafarers to avoid the often-rough waters of the exposed northern side of the island. During the Viking Age, various leaders took an interest in this area and made alliances with local chiefs because controlling the sea route, and therefore trade and transport, was of high strategic importance. To discover more about the area's traditions and history, the nearby **Old Kvernes Folk Museum (Gamle Kvernes bygdemuseum)** (tel. 98 06 32 58, www.nordmore.museum.no, 11am-5pm Tues.-Sun. mid-June to mid-Aug., 50kr) showcases a traditional rural farming community with original buildings from the 1700s and 1800s. An archaeological exhibition of artifacts from local excavations and several boathouses revealing the daily life of fishermen are also on display.

From Kvernes, you can continue along the narrow but scenic Route 247 that circles the island to reach the Atlantic Road turnoff in 26.5 kilometers (22.7 miles), or return to Bruhagen, from where the turnoff is 23 kilometers (14.3 miles) along the better standard Route 64.

Food and Accommodations

If the charms of Sveggen work their magic on you, book a room at the **Sveggvika Guesthouse** (Seivågnesveien 107, tel. 400 18 192, www.sveggvika.no, 1,200kr), located in a former waterfront fish warehouse. Rooms are minimally decorated with original features preserved, including the large windows, which all face the ocean. Spend an evening relaxing on the shared deck or take a stroll to the nearby village, where you may be lucky enough to spot a wild deer or a sea eagle soaring overhead. A light breakfast and bar facilities are available, but you'll need to look elsewhere in the area for your evening meal. Light meals are sometimes available during high season, so it's best to inquire in advance.

The village of **Bruhagen** has supermarkets and takeout restaurants, but otherwise look to Kristiansund or the hotels around the Atlantic Road for your meals.

★ ATLANTIC ROAD
(Atlanterhavsveien)

Famous the world over thanks to multiple car television ads, the **Atlantic Road** (also called the Atlantic Ocean Road) is one of Norway's most popular attractions. Linking the western coast of Averøy island with the mainland, the 8.3-kilometer (5.1-mile) stretch of Route 64 dances across skerries and islets interspersed with lookouts, fishing spots, and even the odd hotel. The most famous of the eight bridges is the sweeping **Storseisundet,** which seems to defy engineering logic from certain angles. In fact, the road was voted as Norway's greatest engineering feat in 2005. If you never believed a road could look beautiful, think again.

As it is exposed to open ocean, the road can be struck by sudden changes in weather conditions. In fact, 12 European windstorms interrupted construction from 1983 to 1989.

Driving the famous Atlantic Road is an ambition for many.

Be wary of driving during storms, as high waves can result in water sweeping across the bridges. On calm days, take advantage of the many parking areas to follow the trails around the islets and take in the road and its natural surroundings from all angles.

The road is a popular location for anglers and bird-watchers given its exposure to the ocean, the latter hoping to glimpse the mighty sea eagle. One of the bridges, Myrbærholmbrua, has been specially designed with a pedestrian walkway to better facilitate fishing. A great catch of cod is all but guaranteed even for just hobby fishers, so Myrbærholmbrua is usually bustling with anglers of all nationalities and experience levels.

It's not just anglers who are attracted by the area's unique characteristics. Divers too flock to the Atlantic Road to explore the region's shipwrecks and remarkable life on the ocean floor. Certified divers can join a guided trip run by the experienced Strømsholmen Sjøsportsenter (Strømsholmen, tel. 71 29 81 74, www.stromsholmen.no, daily). Prices vary from 250kr to explore the local reef up to 680kr for a long boat trip to canyons and a seal colony. The same company also offers kiting, kayaking, fishing, and biking experiences. A three-hour fishing trip (noon daily, but call in advance to check) costs 750kr plus equipment rental, but you are guaranteed to come back with a catch.

Food and Accommodations

There are few more atmospheric places to stay anywhere in Norway than the original fishing and trading islet now occupied by Håholmen Havstuer (tel. 71 51 72 50, www.haholmen.no, mid-June to mid-Aug., 1,090kr s, 1,690kr d). Transfer from Håholmen Marina (Håholmen Gjestehavn), halfway along the Atlantic Road, is by boat with departures on the hour 11am-9pm. The 49 spacious double rooms are spread across 25 buildings that also include a pub, restaurant, and museum. Rooms can lack natural light, but the views

out of the small windows and from the island itself are unbeatable.

Located on Averøy island, the wooden cabins of Atlanterhavsveien Sjøstuer (tel. 71 51 23 91, www.atlanterhavsveien.org) overlook the Atlantic Road and the open ocean. Two small cabins sleep two (990kr), while six cabins have enough room for up to six guests (1,400kr). A one-off cleaning charge of 500kr applies to both options. Three of the larger cabins come complete with a sauna. Despite their traditional appearance, the cabins are relatively new and are equipped with Wi-Fi, TV, stovetop, fridge, microwave, and dishwasher.

Food options in the area are largely restricted to expensive hotel restaurants with sporadic opening hours. Your best bet is to do some shopping in Kristiansund and bring a packed lunch or snacks to last the day. One recent addition to the Atlantic Road itself is Eldhuset (Lyngholmen, tel. 970 69 071), a simple café serving sandwiches, waffles, and coffee; it also doubles as a tourist information center. The modern structure is smartly built into a natural cliff so as not to disturb the aesthetics of the area, with a walkway circling Lyngholmen island. Opening times vary, but the typical schedule is daily June-August, weekends only during spring and fall.

Information and Services

Along with a café, the Eldhuset center contains public restrooms and maps that show the area's hiking trails and best spots for fishing. Although the staff are connected with the café only, they are a mine of information and will happily help you out with advice if the café isn't too busy. For more detailed travel planning help, contact the office of Destinasjon Kristiansund & Nordmøre (Kongens Plass 1, tel. 71 58 54 54, www.visitkristiansund.com, 9am-6pm Mon.-Sat., 9am-3pm Sun. mid-June to mid-Aug., 9am-3pm Mon.-Fri. rest of year) in Kristiansund.

Getting There

CAR

From Kristiansund, drive on westbound Route 64 through the Atlantic Ocean Tunnel (98kr car plus driver, plus 40kr for each additional passenger) to Averøy island. Spend time on the scenic island, which has some worthy distractions, or head straight through on Route 64 to the Atlantic Road. The 31-kilometer (19.3-mile) drive from Kristiansund to the Atlantic Road takes 35 minutes.

After the Atlantic Road, Route 64 continues south for 50 kilometers to the town of Molde, from where you can continue a further 58 kilometers (36 miles) along Route 64 to Åndalsnes, or 80 kilometers (50 miles) along the E39 to Ålesund. Both routes include a short trip on a car ferry from Fjord1 (tel. 57 75 70 00, www.fjord1.no). From the Atlantic Road, allow around 2-2.5 hours to reach Åndalsnes and about 3 hours to reach Ålesund.

PUBLIC TRANSIT

Options to reach the Atlantic Road without your own transport are limited, but Fram (tel. 71 28 01 00, www.frammr.no) runs several daily services from Kristiansund to Molde via the Atlantic Road. The buses are regular scheduled services and not sightseeing tours, so you will need to plan in advance how much time you want to spend at the road and plan your return accordingly. Alternatively, you can stay on the bus through to Molde to continue your journey south, although this will seriously limit the experience and likely leave you frustrated. The journey from Kristiansund takes around 50 minutes to arrive at the Atlantic Road and costs 150kr. The service does run on weekends but the frequency is much more limited.

Lofoten

Rugged, dramatic, and intimidating are the words of the north. High above the Arctic Circle, the Lofoten archipelago and its surrounding region is like nowhere else on earth. Nature rules in the north. If you love outdoor activities, this is the destination of your dreams.

The dramatic mountains hide many surprises, from idyllic fishing villages to remarkable beaches that seem more suited to the Caribbean than to Arctic Norway. The waters of Lofoten are crystal clear with shimmers of green. Combine this with stretches of pristine sandy beaches and you honestly have to pinch yourself to remember you are in the Norwegian Arctic, at the same latitude as Nunavut in Canada and Murmansk in Russia.

Many of the best beaches can only be reached on foot, rewarding those willing to make the hike with some of the country's beaches all to themselves. Yet some fabulous finds are right by the side of the road.

The region's biggest urban area by quite some way, Bodø is a functional city yet still surrounded by spectacular mountains and the famous Saltstraumen natural tidal phenomenon.

The few roads in and around Lofoten can get clogged during the short summer season, so for a quieter alternative look a little north to the Vesterålen archipelago. While the scenery is less dramatic than Lofoten, Vesterålen is still impressive and provides similar excellent opportunities for hiking, camping, and whale watching.

CLIMATE

Despite the region's high latitude, temperatures are surprisingly mild. In fact, the Lofoten islands contain one of the biggest temperature anomalies in the world relative to latitude, thanks mainly to the Gulf Stream. Winter temperatures rarely dip below freezing, while in summer anything above 16°C (60°F) is considered warm. Although snow is seen on the mountains of Lofoten well into the summer, actual snowfall on the low-lying

---

Previous: racks of drying cod, a common sight on Lofoten; an Arctic beach. **Above:** a wooden church in a remote part of the Vesterålen archipelago.

Look for ★ to find recommended
sights, activities, dining, and lodging.

Highlights

★ **Norwegian Aviation Museum:** View the history of aviation in Norway through the lens of World War II (page 253).

★ **Saltstraumen Maelstrom:** This intriguing tidal phenomenon forces huge volumes of water through a narrow strait, making a boat ride here an unforgettable experience (page 260).

★ **Trollfjord:** Step into a fairy tale on a trip to Norway's most dramatic fjord, accessible only by boat (page 265).

★ **Henningsvær:** This thriving fishing village, built at the foot of an imposing mountain over several islands that appear like droplets in the ocean, has inspired artists for generations (page 271).

★ **Lofotr Viking Museum:** Experience the daily life of a Viking family at this museum constructed on the site of a former Viking stronghold. Viking banquets are held every evening (page 275).

★ **Reine:** Famously photogenic, the panoramic scenery surrounding this village will take your breath away (page 280).

★ **Å:** This traditional fishing village turned living museum is quite literally the end of the road (page 282).

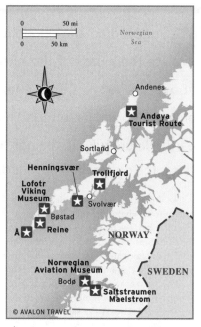

★ **Andøya Tourist Route:** Sandwiched between steep cliffs and open ocean, Norway's newest tourist route helps you explore one of its most remote island communities (page 288).

Lofoten

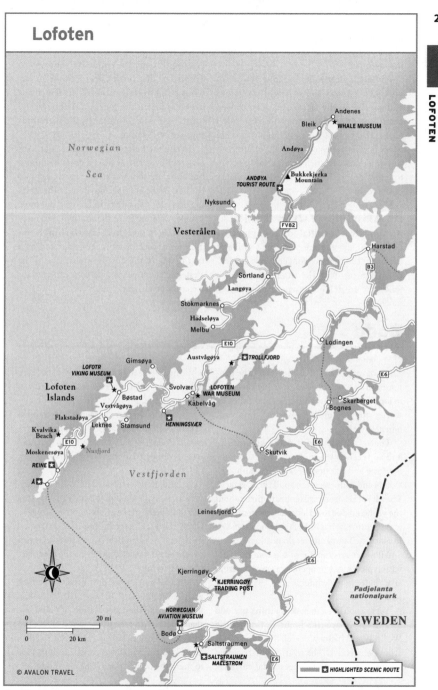

Andenes
Bleik ★ WHALE MUSEUM
Andøya
Andøya

Norwegian

Sea

ANDØYA
TOURIST ROUTE ▲ Bukkekjerka
Mountain

Nyksund

FV82

Vesterålen

Harstad

B3

Sortland
Langøya
Stokmarknes
Hadseløya
Melbu

E10

Lodingen

E6

LOFOTR
VIKING MUSEUM
Gimsøya
Austvågøya ★ TROLLFJORD

Lofoten
Islands
Bøstad
Vestvågøya
Svolvær
Kåbelvåg
LOFOTEN
WAR MUSEUM

Skarberget
Bognes

Flakstadøya
Leknes Stamsund
HENNINGSVÆR

Kvalvika
Beach ★
E10
Moskenesøya   Nusfjord

E6

REINE

Skutvik

Å

Vestfjorden

Leinesfjord

E6

Padjelanta
nationalpark

Kjerringøy
KJERRINGØY
TRADING POST

SWEDEN

0   20 mi
0   20 km

NORWEGIAN
AVIATION MUSEUM
Bodø

Saltstraumen
SALTSTRAUMEN
MAELSTROM

E6

HIGHLIGHTED SCENIC ROUTE

© AVALON TRAVEL

ground tends to be light and limited to just a few months of the year. The wettest months of the year across the region are September to November.

Although all the photography you see of northern Norway shows bright blue skies and calm seas, the fact is that the exposed nature of Bodø, Lofoten, and Vesterålen means that rain, storms, and high winds are never far away, even at the height of summer. But don't despair, such weather only serves to enhance, not inhibit, the natural beauty of the region.

PLANNING YOUR TIME

A car really is essential to fully appreciate Lofoten unless you are planning to hike or cycle, but then a much longer trip is needed. Even in a car, take the time you expect it will take to drive anywhere on Lofoten and double it. Around every corner there is something to see, a new dramatic landscape, just begging to be adored. If you are passing through the region on your way to Tromsø or the North Cape, Bodø is an obvious point to stop as one of the few major urban areas on the journey. Although the town itself is fairly ordinary, the surroundings are captivating.

To add the Lofoten islands into your itinerary will require at least a couple of days, but allow up to a week to properly explore the best of the archipelago. Bodø is the starting point for two ferries to Lofoten, but most people traveling from the south of the country will fly to save time. If you are in the region for a week or more, consider adding a trip to one of the northernmost tips of the Vesterålen archipelago into your itinerary for a change of scenery.

Bodø

The compact city of Bodø (roughly pronounced BOO-duh) is an unremarkable city to look at, yet the surroundings make the city worth stopping off for a day or so on your journey north.

The town lies just north of the Arctic Circle and so receives the midnight sun throughout June and the first week of July, although clouds and rain can often spoil the spectacle. The city receives consistent rain throughout the year, and due to its location on an unsheltered peninsula, it is one of the windiest places in Norway. Temperatures do not vary greatly and it never gets too hot or too cold in Bodø, with typical mean temperatures ranging from -1°C (30°F) in the winter to 13°C (55°F) in the summer.

Yet it would be a mistake to think of Bodø as a dreary place. It's home to fascinating World War II history, especially from an aviation perspective. The nearby Saltstraumen is one of the world's strongest tidal currents, while nearby islands are a natural habitat for broad white-tailed eagles, which can grow to a 2.4-meter (eight-foot) wingspan. The city is surrounded by terrific scenery, from open ocean to mountain ranges. Its compact size means Bodø is easy to get around on foot, and is well connected to the rest of Norway by air, rail, and ferry.

In 2016, Bodø celebrated its 200th anniversary as a city. Although founded in 1816, the city didn't really take off for another 50 years, when the local herring industry attracted merchants, traders, fishers, and a whole bunch of associated services, including the manufacture of herring oil.

Much of the city was destroyed in an attack early in World War II, in May 1940. More than half of Bodø's then-population of 6,000 lost their homes. After the war a period of rebuilding took place, including help from Sweden, and a new town hall was constructed in 1959 to mark the completion of the new Bodø.

SIGHTS
★ Norwegian Aviation Museum
(Norsk Luftfartsmuseum)

Ten percent of the city's population is engaged in the aviation industry, and so the **Norwegian Aviation Museum** (Olav V gate, tel. 75 50 78 50, www.luftfartsmuseum. no, 10am-4pm Mon.-Fri., 11am-5pm Sat.-Sun., 160kr) takes pride of place in Bodø. The largest aviation museum in the Nordic countries tells the story of wartime Bodø through a military exhibition along with a recently revived civil exhibition. From June 15 to August 15, the museum is open daily 10am-6pm and guided tours are available. The tours, which are included in the standard admission price, are given hourly 11am-3pm in both Norwegian and English and take around 40 minutes.

The military exhibition is housed in a large hangar-like building with real planes, stripped-down engines, and models depicting scenes from World War II. Several De Havilland fighter bombers, a Bell UH-1B helicopter, and a tiger striped Northrop F-5 A Freedom Fighter are among the planes on display. The highlight is one of the few Focke-Wulf 190 aircraft left in existence. This model was Nazi Germany's most important fighter plane and is now on display after thousands of hours of restoration work by the Bodø Aviation Historical Society, among others.

Perhaps slightly less interesting for international visitors is the civil exhibition, which tells the story of the development of air travel as a form of transportation within Norway. However, don't miss the opportunity to ascend the tight spiral staircase and visit the old control tower, which overlooks the runway of the city's airport and contains live traffic information about planes arriving and departing.

Nyholmen

Originally built in 1810 to protect the city's grain stocks from British warships, **Nyholmen Fort (Nyholmen skandse)** (Burøyveien) is today a popular recreational area. The remains of the fort are well preserved and a number of cannons have been reconstructed.

Located on a narrow peninsula directly north of the city center, Nyholmen is a pleasant place to walk, have a picnic, or just enjoy the military atmosphere with a view of Bodø and the nearby Litle Hjartøya island. But despite its proximity to the city center,

Bodø harbor

Nyholmen is a 45-minute walk from the downtown hotels through a largely industrial area. You must pass a couple of herring oil factories on the way, and this is not something you want to do on foot. If you want to spend some time on Nyholmen, take a car for the 3.5-kilometer (2.1-mile) drive along Jernbaneveien and Burøyveien, and make sure the windows are closed on the way!

Central Bodø
BODØ CATHEDRAL
(Bodø domkirke)

In keeping with the architecture of the city, **Bodø Cathedral** (Torvgata 12, tel. 75 50 03 00, www.kirken.no/bododomkirke, 9am-3pm daily, closed Sat. Sept.-May., free) is an unremarkable concrete building, completed in 1956 to replace the former church destroyed during the war.

Despite its dour exterior the cathedral is still worth a look. The 40-foot-high stained-glass window behind the altar is an impressive sight, as is the beautiful new 5,000-pipe German-style organ that frames the rose window at the opposite end. On the cathedral's western side (Professor Schyttes gate) stands an independent bell tower; although built from the same concrete as the church, it is of a far more attractive airy design. At the base of the tower is a memorial dedicated to the locals who lost their lives during World War II.

NORDLAND MUSEUM
(Nordlandsmuseet)

The **Nordland Museum** (Prinsensgate 116, tel. 75 50 35 00, www.nordlandsmuseet.no, 11am-4pm daily June-Aug., 9am-3pm Mon.-Fri. Sept.-May, 60kr) is one of the few pre-war buildings still standing in the city center. The distinctive grand yellow building houses exhibitions covering the Viking Age, Sami life, the fishing industry in Bodø and Lofoten, and the turbulent history of the town itself. The collection includes Viking silver found in the rocks just outside Bodø, as well as a reconstructed Sami turf hut and magic drum.

Most, but not all, of the exhibits are

Bodø Cathedral is known for its distinctive bell tower.

described in English, but staff are on hand to help with any questions you may have about some of the more interesting exhibits that are described in Norwegian only. They are especially knowledgeable about the city's war history.

The museum's network includes 17 other sites under the Nordland Museum banner, including a folk museum, mining museum, open-air museum, and a crofter's cottage. The sites are spread across the vast Nordland region and full details can be obtained from the main site in Bodø.

STORMEN LIBRARY
(Stormen Bibliotek)

A welcome modern addition to the city's post-war architecture, **Stormen Library** (Storgata 1a, tel. 75 55 61 00, www.stormen.no, 8am-9pm Mon.-Thurs., 8am-6pm Fri., 10am-4pm Sat., noon-4pm Sun.) is a breath of fresh air for the city. The airy interior is filled with natural light, thanks to enormous vertical windows overlooking the small boat harbor.

The first-floor reading room is a great place to relax and take in the view. English-language books are available for browsing, but the primary interest is the design and architecture. At the very least check out the exterior view of the vertical windows from the harbor side, and know there is a small café in which to take shelter should the rains come.

SPORTS AND RECREATION
Fishing
Giant halibut are frequently caught in the waters off the coast of this part of northern Norway. Try your luck every Wednesday at noon and 6pm when the good folk at **Gone Fishing** (tel. 99 27 83 03, www.gone-fishing. no, 750kr) take a group out into the waters of Bodø on the MY *Petra*, a 54-foot Dutch fishing vessel from the 1960s that was fully restored as a recreational boat in 2006. All clothing and equipment are provided and you can pay on board. On busy days, additional trips are taken by rigid-hulled inflatable boat (RIB).

Hiking
Known locally as **Bodømarka,** the forested mountainous terrain surrounding Bodø offers wonderful opportunities for both serious and recreational hiking. More than 120 peaks rise above 685 meters (2,250 feet) in height, all within easy reach of the city center.

Like many Norwegian cities, Bodø can appear quiet during the weekends because the local population is most likely out exploring the forests. Many will be climbing the **Keiservarden** mountain along an easy marked trail from the Maskinisten parking area (Junkerveien), a three-kilometer (two-mile) drive or a 40-minute walk east of central Bodø. The view from the top of the four-kilometer (2.5-mile) hike is spectacular, ranging from the Bodø peninsula and Vestfjord right across to (on a clear day) the mountains bordering Sweden to the east.

Although you'll be accompanied by locals along the route, it's a wise idea to pick up a map from the Bodø Tourist Information office, or from **Bodø Trekking Association (Bodø og Omegns Turistforening)** (Sandgata 3, tel. 75 52 14 13, www.bot.no, noon-3pm Tues.-Wed., noon-5pm Thurs., noon-3pm Fri.), who can also give you tips for longer and/or more difficult routes.

Swimming
Hidden inside an anonymous building next to the Norwegian Aviation Museum, **Nordlandsbadet** (Plassmyrveien 11, tel. 75 59 15 00, www.bodospektrum.no) is one of Norway's largest and most modern indoor water parks. On the rare occasions the weather is warm enough, you can enjoy the large outdoor area with sunbeds, volleyball areas, and an outdoor pool. For every other day, the complex includes a diving pool, exercise pool, therapy pool, wave pool, children's pool, and three water chutes complete with music and lights. Hot tubs and saunas are available for those who prefer a relaxing time, while a café serves drinks and snacks in both the wet and dry areas of the complex.

Opening hours vary considerably but typically are 3pm-9pm on weekdays, with early morning opening from 7am on Tuesday and Friday. The center is open 10am-6pm on Saturday and Sunday. An adult ticket varies 150-170kr, with family tickets ranging 380-620kr depending on the number in the party.

Golf
Norway's largest golf course above the Arctic Circle, **Bodø Golf Park** (Myklebostad, tel. 75 53 22 20, www.bodogolfpark.no) is arguably one of the most spectacular courses in Europe. Overlooked by mountains, the 18 holes hug the coastline with natural hazards such as forests, rocky shorelines, and the ocean providing a challenge to even the most experienced golfer.

Guests are welcome to play the course for 300kr (9 holes) or 450kr (18 holes), with clubs available to rent from 150kr. Booking in advance is strongly recommended to avoid problems in case of tournaments. The course is typically open daily from mid-April and for as long as the weather allows.

Soccer

The local family-friendly soccer club **Bodø/ Glimt** (www.glimt.no) plays its home games at the **Aspmyra Stadion** (Fridtjof Nansens vei 5), which is within walking distance of the city center. Tickets can be bought online at www.glimt.no or at the stadium for the vast majority of the games, which usually take place on Sunday evening. Expect to pay 170-300kr depending on your choice of seating. Tickets for games against rivals Tromsø and Rosenborg are more expensive and should be ordered in advance. Wear something yellow if wish to endear yourself to the locals!

SHOPPING

Bodø is not a shopping destination, so many of the outlets are the same names you'll see in any Norwegian town. But to satisfy a sweet tooth, make some time to stop by **Craig Alibone** (Storgata 6, tel. 90 25 47 10, www.craigalibone.com, 10am-5pm Mon.-Fri., 10am-3pm Sat.), the store of the independent British chocolatier of the same name. His hand-crafted creations are more art than chocolate, and can be bought to enjoy straight

away or boxed up as gifts. Some of the exciting flavors include passion fruit toffee caramel, tarragon caramel, and gingerbread truffles.

FOOD
Contemporary

Food is not a focus in Bodø, so many restaurants cram as much variety onto the menu as possible in order to bring people through the doors. Nowhere does this more than **Bjørk** (Storgata 8, tel. 75 52 40 40, www.restaurantbjork.no, 10am-10pm Mon.-Sat., 3pm-10pm Sun.), which is likely to be the first name you get when asking a local for a restaurant recommendation. Its vast menu is the reason for its popularity yet also its downfall. Trying to be all things to all people means quality can vary, and waiting times, especially on weekends, can often frustrate. However, if you can't decide on a restaurant and you're not in a rush, it's a good all-around option. The Norwegian tapas and pizzas are popular with locals, while the catch of the day is often outstanding, albeit expensive.

By night, the quayside **Sydøst Restaurant & Bar** (Jakhellngården, tel. 75 54 00 30, www.utibodo.no, 11am-3pm Mon.-Tues., 11am-midnight Wed.-Thurs., 11am-3am Fri.-Sat.)

Arctic tapas, including local cheese and whale meat

is a thriving nightclub, but by day they serve up Norwegian classics in a modern tapas style. A little on the expensive side, Sydøst is a place to sample some unique Norwegian dishes like cured reindeer, grilled stockfish, and red cheese from Kjerringøy, rather than to fill up. Best to come for a lazy lunch rather than an evening meal, when the party is already underway.

A good option for those looking for a more substantial meal yet still with a local focus is **Restaurant Nyt** (Dronningens Gate 26, tel. 92 24 76 38, www.restaurant-nyt.no), where the concept is very much fine dining using the best quality Norwegian ingredients. Short-traveled food and community farms are used wherever possible. King crab, halibut, and ox are frequently on the menu, supported by garnishes such as radish, mountain berries, and local herbs. The full seven-course experience will set you back 795kr, while 545kr buys you the four-course menu.

Another upscale option is the 17th-floor **Roast Restaurant and Bar** (Tollbugata 5, tel. 75 50 38 35, www.scandichotels.com, 11am-1am Mon.-Sat., 11am-5pm Sun.) atop the Scandic Havet hotel. While expensive, the food is top quality and beautifully presented, so it's your decision whether to pay a premium for the outstanding views across the city and surrounding mountains. The kitchen's large charcoal grill produces excellent steaks and grilled fish, while the presented wines match well with the smoky tones of the food.

American

Despite its awkward location above a shopping mall, **Smith's Sportsbar & Grill** (Storgata 15, tel. 48 40 10 01, www.smithsbar.no, 3pm-11pm Mon.-Thurs., 3pm-3am Fri., noon-3am Sat., noon-11pm Sun.) gets especially busy whenever English Premier League soccer is on the screens or the local team Bodø/Glimt is playing at home, both typically on Sunday. This British-owned American-style sports bar serves the best burgers in Bodø by a distance. It's worth shelling out a little extra for the excellent sweet potato fries. On Friday and Saturday nights a DJ transforms Smith's into one of Bodø's busiest nightspots.

Asian

For Asian flavors, try the contemporary surroundings of **Ohma** (Storgata 2, tel. 75 56 46 50, www.ohma-asian.no, 11am-10pm Mon.-Fri., noon-10pm Sat., 3pm-10pm Sun.), in the foyer of the Radisson Blu hotel. Sharing is actively encouraged, and the menu facilitates this with large main courses alongside a pick-and-mix sushi menu. Only tackle the heavily promoted Taste of Ohma sharing menu if you are very hungry. It combines sushi, scampi tempura, crispy duck, and a chocolate dessert for 495kr per person. If you're looking to get the best bang for your buck, an all-you-can-eat buffet is usually available at lunchtime, costing 199kr.

Vegetarian

One of the few places in Bodø with good choice for vegetarians and vegans, the vintage interior of **Kafe Kafka** (Sangata 5b, tel. 93 40 60 03, 11am-11pm Mon.-Thurs., 11am-midnight Fri.-Sat., 3pm-10pm Sun.) is a popular meeting place for a lunchtime coffee and fresh cinnamon bun, or a more substantial evening meal. Not strictly a vegetarian restaurant, Kafka also offers hamburgers and grilled meat dishes, but the vegan soup of the day and vegan cake selection ensure its popularity among non-meat eaters.

ACCOMMODATIONS

Despite the construction of a couple of modern hotels in recent years, the city still suffers from a shortage of hotel rooms. Accommodations should be booked well in advance wherever possible.

500-1,000kr

The 10 rooms at the elegant **Opsahl Gjestegaard** (Prinsens gate 131, tel. 75 52 07 04, www.opsahl-gjestegaard.no, 800kr) vary considerably in size and price, so call ahead to get the best deal. Several of the rooms are dedicated to stars of the silver screen, such as

French cabaret singer and actress Édith Piaf and Norwegian Olympic champion figure skater and film star Sonja Henie. Books from the small library can be enjoyed in the pleasant garden area or on the rooftop terrace, both quiet options despite the city center location. Dinner can be ordered upon request, although no alcohol is available.

Located in a rather anonymous part of town just outside the city center, **Skagen Hotel** (Nyholmsgata 11, tel. 75 51 91 00, www.skagen-hotel.no, 950kr) is the best choice for a quality breakfast. During weekdays a chef is on hand to prepare omelets, eggs, and pancakes to order, a rarity in Norwegian hotels, especially at the budget end of the scale. Sadly this option isn't available during July, when the hotel is most likely to be used by international travelers. Rooms are basic but include a desk, TV, and armchair.

Despite its aged exterior, the ★ **Bodø Hotell** (Professor Schyttes gate 5, tel. 75 54 77 00, www.bodohotell.no, 995kr) is the most contemporary choice in its price bracket. The light, airy rooms with flat-screen TVs and wooden floors are just a few steps from the main Glasshuset shopping mall. For the budget conscious, a bowl of soup is included in the price each evening, along with a generous breakfast buffet and free tea and coffee throughout the day.

1,000-1,500kr

At 191 rooms, the **Radisson Blu Bodø** (Storgata 2, tel. 75 51 90 00, info.bodo@radissonblu.com, 1,195kr) is one of the city's biggest hotels. The interior is modern, although the dark colors that dominate may not be to everyone's taste. Tall windows in the rooms make the most of the views of the fjord to one side and the city with mountains behind on the other. The hotel's best feature is its sky bar, which gets intensely busy late at night as locals mingle with guests to enjoy the spectacular views across the region. The building is also home to the hotel restaurant, a popular Asian restaurant, and a Narvesen kiosk, all useful to have on hand when it's raining or on Sunday when much of the city is closed.

The main high-end competition to the Radisson Blu is the ★ **Scandic Havet** (Tollbugata 5, tel. 75 50 38 00, www.scandichotels.com, 1,299kr), which at 16 floors high is the tallest hotel in northern Norway. The hotel makes the most of its size, with the Roast Restaurant and Bar offering the best views in town, while the bright white exterior has made a striking addition to the seafront. A superior room with sea view costs an extra 300kr, but they are the same size as the regular rooms. Frequent conferences can make the hotel seem cramped despite its 200 rooms, but this is a minor quibble in an otherwise outstanding hotel.

INFORMATION AND SERVICES
Visitor Information

Collect city maps, public transport timetables and book tours at **Bodø Tourist Information** (Tollbugata 13, tel. 75 54 80 00), open weekdays 9am-3:30pm year-round. During the summer months, the office is open 9am-8pm weekdays and 10am-6pm Saturday and Sunday. The office is small but always staffed with knowledgeable locals who will help you plan your stay in Bodø and also your onward travel to Lofoten. It's a good idea to run through your travel plans with a local, in case of any problems with roads, ferries, and so on.

Post Offices and Courier Services

Postage stamps can be bought at most branches of Narvesen and 7-Eleven, but for anything else post-related you'll need to call by **Bodø Post Office (Bodø Postkontor)** (Havnegata 9, 9am-6pm Mon.-Fri., 10am-2pm Sat.).

GETTING THERE
Car

Bodø is a long drive from almost anywhere else in Norway, which is why almost all Norwegians choose to fly here, as it's so much quicker and often works out better value. From Trondheim, the 705-kilometer (438-mile) drive north along the E6 highway will take at least 9.5 hours, but allow at least a few hours more for suitable breaks. The preference for flying also applies when traveling from the High North, because from Tromsø, the 550-kilometer (342-mile) journey along the E6 highway to Bodø will take around nine hours, plus stops.

Air

Bodø Airport (Olav V gate 56-60, tel. 67 03 35 00) is on the same small peninsula as the city center and is just a 15- to 20-minute walk down Hernesveien to most downtown hotels. By taxi, the short five-minute journey will cost up to 150kr. SAS and Norwegian both run multiple daily services to and from Oslo, with direct services from Trondheim and Tromsø also available. Domestic airline Widerøe links Bodø with all regional airports, including those on Lofoten, plus a handy direct route to Bergen.

Rail

Although you can reach Narvik via a train from Sweden, Bodø is as far north as you can go on the Norwegian railway network. The centrally located **Bodø Railway Station** (Jernbaneveien 99) is the terminus of the **Nordland Line (Nordlandsbanen)**, a 729-kilometer (452-mile) track from Trondheim that was completed in the 1960s. Two trains per day travel the whole nine-hour route, one through the daytime and one overnight. Although advance booking with state railway operator **NSB** (tel. 81 50 08 88, www.nsb.no) is not always necessary, prices will drop by at least half when you book at least 48 hours in advance. The on-the-day fare is around 1,100kr.

Bus

Long-distance bus travel is not common in northern Norway simply due to the distances involved between major urban areas. From Bodø, service 23-720 runs twice daily to and from Narvik and Sortland with a fare of at least 400kr. Check with the regional council's bus information service (www.177nordland.no) or ask at the Bodø Tourist Information office for timetables.

Boat

Hurtigruten (tel. 81 03 00 00, www.hurtigruten.com) serves Bodø in the early afternoon on its northbound journey and in the middle of the night on its southbound route. Many travelers choose to take the Hurtigruten from Bodø to Tromsø, to explore the Lofoten islands and Trollfjord from the sea. The journey takes around 27 hours, and cabins must be booked in advance with cost varying by season.

From Bodø, there are direct boat links to the Lofoten islands. Two regular ferries link Bodø with different ends of Lofoten, both run by **Torghatten Nord** (www.torghattennord.no) although leaving from different parts of the city. The quickest route is the daily passenger-only service from **Bodø to Svolvær**, which leaves from the terminal by the Bodø Tourist Information office every evening (times vary). The **Bodø to Moskenes** car ferry leaves from the Hurtigruten terminal four times a day through the summer months and 1-2 times daily otherwise.

GETTING AROUND
Bus

Although Bodø is compact and walkable, several local bus routes can prove useful for travelers in the event of poor weather. Routes 1 and 4 link Bodø Airport with downtown, while Route 3 serves the Norwegian Aviation Museum. Tickets cost 41kr and can be bought on the bus or in advance from the **Central Bus Terminal (Sentrumsterminalen)** (Sjøgata 3, tel. 99 47 39 99, 9am-5pm Mon.-Fri.). In general the major routes run every 10-15 minutes during weekdays but are much less frequent during evenings and weekends, especially Sundays.

Taxi

As in any Norwegian city, taxis are an expensive way to get around and should only be used as a last resort. **Nordland Taxi** (tel. 22 38 83 09, www.nordlandtaxi.no) tends to have the most available cars.

Car Rental

Avis, Budget, Enterprise, Europcar, Hertz, and Sixt all have desks at the airport. Opening hours vary and so booking in advance is highly recommended. Most convenient for those arriving by rail is **Budget Bodø** (Storgata 23b, tel. 75 54 10 00, 7:30am-4pm Mon.-Fri.), which is directly opposite the railway station, although they do not open on weekends.

★ SALTSTRAUMEN MAELSTROM

Unlike the northern lights, the **Saltstraumen** maelstrom is a natural phenomenon that runs to a timetable, thanks to the predictable movement of the moon in relation to earth. Approximately every six hours, up to 400 million cubic meters (523 million cubic yards) of seawater is forced though a 150-meter-wide (500-foot-wide) strait between the open ocean of the Saltfjord and the Skjerstadfjord, which reaches 40 kilometers (25 miles) inland, halfway to the Swedish border.

As gravity pushes water through the narrow strait, water speeds reach up to 40kph (25mph), forming whirlpools. When the current is at its strongest, the difference in water levels between the two sides of the strait can be up to a meter (3.3 feet) and easily visible with the naked eye. While not as powerful to watch as a waterfall or white-water rapids, Saltstraumen is nevertheless a fascinating demonstration of the power of nature. The impressive backdrop of the Børvasstindene mountain range adds to that feeling.

You can experience Saltstraumen from the shoreline or via a boat tour. To travel by road, take a 25-minute drive east of Bodø (along Route 80, then turn south onto Route 17) to the parking areas found either side of the Saltstraum Bridge, which crosses the sound at the water's strongest point. The best vantage point for photos or film is from the highest point of the bridge itself, but it's a 15-minute walk to get there from the parking areas and winds can be high. Either parking area allows close-up access to the water, but take care when the currents are at their strongest. Saltstraumen can also be reached on public bus routes 4, 200,

Saltstraumen is the world's strongest natural maelstrom.

and 300 from Bodø Airport and central Bodø, although there are only a couple of daily departures on each service that run all the way to Saltstraumen. Expect to pay at least 50kr for the 45-minute journey, and check timetables carefully for the return journey.

Tours

The fun option is to take one of the fast inflatable RIB boat tours from Bodø harbor and ride on the water yourself. This option also gives you the potential to see some of the region's excellent birdlife on the route, potentially even some of the world's largest sea eagles swooping overhead.

Operating during the high season (mid-June to mid-Aug.), the two-hour round-trip RIB boat tours from **Stella Polaris** (tel. 75 52 85 08, www.stella-polaris.no, 675kr) leave daily from the Hurtigruten pier at 4pm, although you should be there at least half an hour in advance to get kitted out with the appropriate safety gear. The tours leave at the same time regardless of the current's timetable, so it's worth checking in advance whether a trip will coincide with a high current on any particular day. Tours are available at other times of year for Hurtigruten passengers or large groups.

Fishing

The turbulent waters combined with the sheltered coastline make Saltstraumen a hugely popular fishing location. The season begins in late February with plentiful skrei and cod. Halibut, pollock, and coalfish are available later in the season, which runs until around October. Boats and rods can be rented from the Saltstraumen Brygge hotel with prices varying by season. Call in advance to avoid disappointment.

Food and Accommodations

If you are just passing through the area to see the Saltstraumen maelstrom and don't plan on visiting Bodø itself, consider one of these options. The family-friendly **Saltstraumen Camping** (Knaplund, tel. 75 58 75 60, www. saltstraumen-camping.no) is just a few

minutes' walk from the famous attraction. It's an especially suitable site for fishing as guests get free use of the on-site gutting room and freezing room. Pitch prices range 200-250kr with cabins and apartments of varying standard available from 500kr up to 1,400kr.

At the other end of the scale is **Saltstraumen Brygge** (Tuv Ytre, tel. 92 45 51 00, www.sfc. no), a holiday park best suited for those wanting to spend some time at Saltstraumen, rather than just passing through. Located on the Skjerstadfjord side of the area, Saltstraumen Brygge offers comfortable hotel rooms from 975kr and light, airy apartments sleeping 4-8 guests. The center has 25 boats ranging 60-80 horsepower, although those under 30 will need a boat license. Rods can also be rented.

KJERRINGØY

Under an hour's drive north of Bodø is the charming coastal community of Kjerringøy. With settlement dating back to the Iron Age and still home to around 300 people today, this beautifully preserved slice of northern Norwegian heritage is a must-see if you are driving through the region.

Kjerringøy Trading Post
(Kjerringøy Handelsted)

Part of the Nordland Museum (Nordlandsmuseet), the **Kjerringøy Trading Post** (Kjerringøy, tel. 75 50 35 05, www.nordlandsmuseet.no, 100kr) is open daily 11am-5pm from mid-May through August. Outside these times, the center is usually open 11am-3pm on Saturday. Many Norwegian films have been set here due to the authentic 19th-century atmosphere and spectacular setting of the former trading post. Once as important as Bodø, Kjerringøy was home to the powerful Zahl family, who traded goods and supplies to fishermen in exchange for a fresh catch.

Discover for yourself the lives of this powerful merchant family during the halcyon days as actors play their parts. You are free to explore the 15 buildings, most featuring their original interiors and furnishings. Although the main building feels like something out of

Downton Abbey, the workers' accommodations and boathouses retain a simple rustic feel. A showing of the 20-minute subtitled film *Anna Elisabeth of Kjerringøy* is included in the ticket price, while cultural events and craft demonstrations are held sporadically throughout the summer. Check the website for the calendar. A traditional gift shop sells a surprisingly good range of local food products and handicrafts.

In the vicinity of the village you'll find white sandy beaches, mountain trails, and a white wooden church dating back to the 19th century. Open from mid-June to mid-August, **Zahlfjøsen** (tel. 91 54 29 33, www.zahlfjosen. no, 11am-5pm daily summer only, 50kr) is a restored barn containing a cultural center, library, boatyard, and gallery. The small exhibitions feature local artists and a collection of short Norwegian and foreign films based on the nature journals of writer Knut Hamsun (1859-1952), who won the Nobel Prize in Literature in 1920. His later works portrayed everyday life in rural Norway with elements of irony and humor.

Food and Accommodations

Fitting its typically Norwegian setting, **Kjerringøy Kafe** (Kjerringøy Trading Post, 11am-5pm daily mid-May through Aug., 11am-3pm Sat. rest of year) serves a typically Norwegian selection of small open-faced sandwiches (80-120kr), cakes, waffles, and coffee. Go for the fish soup if it's available and you won't need to eat again for the rest of the day. The café is on the grounds of the museum and keeps the same opening hours, so you can be sure of a place to eat during your visit.

Open from mid-June to mid-August, the restaurant of the **Kjerringøy Havn Bryggehotell** (tel. 76 30 38 22, www.kjerringoybrygge.no, 11am-1am Mon.-Sat., 2pm-11pm Sun., 220-320kr) is the place to go for a special seafood treat, although be prepared to pay for it. The large windows of the quayside restaurant allow you to overlook the same water from which your meal came from. A sumptuous Sunday buffet (2pm-6pm) is popular with locals, while a lighter pub menu is available alongside drinks. In the summer, a spot on the sunny terrace is highly sought-after, with a stroll on the white sandy beach a popular after-meal activity.

The same building also houses a few rooms (1,550kr d) for those wanting to spend a longer time in the relaxing environment. The rooms are simple, yet all have a balcony overlooking the water.

A budget alternative just a mile from the trading post, **Kjerringøy Camping** (tel. 99 01 39 68, kjerringoycamping@hotmail.com) offers seven cabins ranging from 330kr for a basic two-person hut up to 880kr for a fully equipped six-person cabin. Pitches for caravans, motorhomes, and tents start from 165kr per night. The campsite has nothing more than a basic service building, and although it is open year-round, advance booking is required outside the summer season, when you may well be the only guests.

Getting There

Kjerringøy is a short 45-minute drive north of Bodø along Route 834. However, do be aware of the Festvåg to Misten ferry crossing over the Mistfjord, which costs 79kr (car plus driver) plus 33kr for each additional passenger. Although the journey takes just 10 minutes, the ferry operates every 30-60 minutes (6am-11:30pm), so you could be waiting up to an hour for a departure depending on the time of day. Check **Torghatten Nord** (tel. 90 62 07 00, www.torghattennord.no) for the latest timetables before you travel.

Local bus 400 does link Bodø with Kjerringøy, but with just one daily departure most of the year, it's not exactly convenient for travelers. A better alternative is **Polar Tours** (tel. 75 56 30 00, www.polartours.no), which runs guided trips from Bodø every Saturday late June to mid-August departing at 10am. Advance booking is essential at the Bodø Tourist Information office, which is also where the bus departs from. The trip costs 550kr per person and gives you a couple of hours in Kjerringøy, which is plenty of time to explore the museum and surroundings of this charming rural village.

The Lofoten Road Trip

When you stop by the side of the road to take yet another photo of a mountain, glorious beach, or coastal village, you will be struck by one thing—silence. That, and the faint aroma of drying fish floating along on the wind.

The Lofoten road trip is a photographer's dream, but as tempting as it may be, don't make the mistake of focusing too much on your gadgets. Few photographs can ever truly capture the Lofoten islands in all their glory, so be sure you are giving your eyes plenty of opportunities to record the memories too.

A road trip through Lofoten is surprisingly easy to navigate. There's just one main road linking all the islands together, the E10, with minor roads running to coastal villages and beaches. This section of the chapter describes a 128-kilometer (79-mile) road trip beginning at Svolvær, the largest city on the islands, and ending at Å, literally the end of the road. It's equally possible to do the journey in reverse depending on how you arrive on the islands. Although the driving distance from Svolvær to Å seems short, your actual mileage count is likely to be far in excess of this due to the various side trips described along the route. You can easily do the round-trip in a day, but this would be a colossal mistake. To even come close to getting the most out of a Lofoten road trip, plan at least a couple of overnight stops, and give your itinerary plenty of padding. You'll need it.

Treat this section as a rough itinerary of highlights, but I encourage you to get off the beaten track and let your curiosity guide the

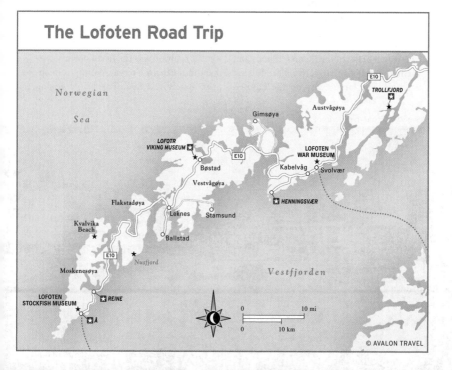

The Lofoten Road Trip

way. Some of Lofoten's most charming villages, hidden beaches, and coastal vistas remain firmly off the tourist trail, and locals aren't likely to give away their secrets! The only way to discover them is by stumbling upon them yourself.

Having said that, planning your day around when you are likely to be passing the urban centers of Svolvær and Leknes is a wise move. Both towns contain all the services you will need (gas stations, supermarkets, restaurants, public toilets), availability of which can be sporadic elsewhere on the islands.

AUSTVÅGØYA

The largest of the Lofoten islands, Austvågøya is where you'll start your journey if driving from the mainland or arriving in Svolvær by ferry. Like much of the archipelago, the island is well-loved among mountain climbers as the area's tallest peak—the 1,146-meter (3,760-foot) Higravstinden—is on the eastern part of the island. To the southeast, the narrow Trollfjord is well worth experiencing.

Svolvær

The region between the Lofoten islands and the mainland is an attractive place to base yourself. The largest city on the Lofoten islands, **Svolvær** remains tiny by international standards, with a population of less than 5,000. However, the town feels a lot more dynamic. It's a regional center, the biggest town for hundreds of miles around. It has everything you would expect from a regional capital, including a shopping mall, clothing stores, supermarkets, a cinema, and a range of recreational opportunities. As a popular stop for the Hurtigruten ferry and other cruise ships visiting Lofoten, it has a number of hotels, high-class restaurants, and art galleries open for business throughout the year.

The rugged backdrop of Svolvær is dramatic. It might be a city but the people are not typical urban dwellers. Ask a local what to do and they will point you with glee to the nearby 569-meter (1,867-foot) Fløyfjellet mountain. Some will suggest biking to the next town and others still a boat trip. One thing's for sure, you won't be left in any doubt that the people of Svolvær are fans of the outdoors life more than anything else.

HISTORY

The nearby village of Vågar, just a few miles west of Svolvær, was the first known settlement in northern Norway, dating from approximately AD 800. The whole region

Svolvær's modern waterfront

thrived thanks to the plentiful supply of cod in the deep waters around Lofoten, and fishing villages spread along the coastline. Svolvær itself was first mentioned in historical records in the late 16th century. The name is likely derived from the Old Norse word *svair,* which means chill.

★ TROLLFJORD

Svolvær is the launch spot for tours to the **Trollfjord,** one of Norway's lesser known yet most dramatic fjords. While the western fjords are known for their size, the Trollfjord is just two kilometers (1.2 miles) long and extremely narrow, as if a thin sliver of rock was deliberately removed from the mountainside.

To add to the drama of a visit, you enter the Trollfjord at its narrowest point, just 100 meters (328 feet) wide, while the surrounding mountains reach more than 1,000 meters (3,280 feet) high. Large cruise ships almost touch the sides as they enter the fjord, and sometimes struggle to turn back around at the other end. On smaller craft, you can drink from the waterfalls if you sail close enough to the sheer mountainsides.

The fjord received national notoriety in 1890 when it was the site of a standoff between the industrial steam ships and traditional open-boat fishermen about access and fishing rights to the fjord. Today the area is known just as much for its local population of sea eagles as for the plentiful stocks of fish. Captains often use fish to lure the breathtaking birds close to the ship for a close-up view.

From June to August, **Trollfjord Cruise** (tel. 45 15 75 87, www.trollfjordcruise. com) operates various sightseeing tours to Trollfjord. The three-hour trips on comfortable boats give you ample opportunity to take in the scenery of Lofoten from a unique angle, spot sea eagles soaring overhead, and experience the tight Trollfjord. Thermal suits, coffee, tea, and snacks are included in the 700kr price, while selected departures also include a short period of fishing. The afternoon departures tend to run a bit longer, up to four hours.

The exact timetable varies depending on weather and group bookings, so check in advance with the operator or at the Destination Lofoten tourist information office.

The same operator also runs a faster tour using high-speed inflatable RIB boats. The twice-daily two-hour tour is slightly more expensive at 750kr but adds more than a little exhilaration to the bird-watching experience, and is the best choice if your time is limited.

LOFOTEN WAR MUSEUM (Lofoten Krigsminnemuseum)

The **Lofoten War Museum** (Fiskergata, tel. 91 73 03 28, www.lofotenkrigmus.no, 10am-10pm Mon.-Sat., noon-3pm and 6pm-10pm Sun. June-Aug., shorter hours rest of year, free) presents a seemingly random collection of items, including a lamp from the battleship *Tirpitz* and the handbag of Adolf Hitler's companion Eva Braun, but it all adds up to a fascinating window into wartime life. With stories told from the Norwegian perspective, the museum is home to Norway's largest collection of World War II uniforms and artifacts despite being a fairly compact place. Not every artifact is well described in English, but any question you have will be answered in astounding detail by the curator.

The strange opening hours are to coincide with the evening arrival of Hurtigruten ships. Outside of the summer period, the museum is usually open, but you should contact them in advance if you are planning a special trip.

OTHER SIGHTS

For such a small town, Svolvær has much to see related to art. The **North Norwegian Art Centre (Nordnorsk Kunstnersenter)** (Torget 20, tel. 40 08 95 95, www.nnks.no, 10am-4pm Tues.-Sun., free) is an artist-run institution that presents contemporary visual art to a wider audience. Frequent artists-in-residence, temporary exhibitions, and even exhibits that tour Lofoten ensure a visit to the Svolvær gallery is always going to result in something new. An important part of the center is the shop, which sells fine art supplies to the artists who flock to Lofoten. It also stocks gifts and artwork designed for the home, and the shop is happy to post purchases to your home address.

Of the numerous galleries, the best is **Galleri Dagfinn Bakke** (Rich Withs gate 4, tel. 76 07 19 98, www.dagfinnbakke.no, 11am-3pm Mon.-Fri., 11am-2pm Sat.), which presents locally inspired watercolors and paintings. Although named after Bakke, the gallery exhibits work from more than 30 local artists, ensuring some nice variety. Artwork can be browsed online beforehand and picked up in person, or bought on-site and shipped to your home.

Although at first glance **Magic Ice** (Fiskergata 36, tel. 76 07 40 11, www.magicice. no, 11am-11pm Sun.-Thurs., 11am-midnight Fri.-Sat., 165kr) might seem like a tacky novelty, the ice bar is actually one of the most impressive in all of Scandinavia. Rather than just a very cold place to enjoy a drink, the bar doubles as an ice sculpture gallery. The natural blue color is enhanced by colorful LEDs to draw the eye to the delicate details on this fairy-tale world of animals, musicians, and buildings. The technical expertise on show is impressive, and so it's no surprise to learn that there is an associated training school in Lithuania that teaches the specialized skills required.

ROCK CLIMBING

Climbers will want to tackle the 150-meter (490-foot) granite **Svolvær Goat (Svolværgeita)**, one of Norway's most popular climbing routes, which stands proudly above the city. First climbed in 1910, the summit offers the unique opportunity to jump the 1.5-meter (five-foot) gap between Storhorn (big horn) and Lillehorn (little horn), the famous duo of vertical rocks at the summit. Many climbers have noted that when taking the jump, one can see the graveyard of Svolvær Church far below.

The route is not technically difficult, but it is very steep and a good level of physical fitness is required, along with ropes and standard climbing equipment. Therefore, your best bet is to join up with **Northern Alpine Guides** (tel. 94 24 91 10, www.alpineguides. no, June-Oct.), who offer half-day round-trip tours from 1,800kr per person. All safety equipment is supplied, but you will need suitable clothing, your own backpack, snacks, and plenty of water.

Galleri Dagfinn Bakke displays landscapes from across northern Norway.

Svolvær's ice bar, Magic Ice, is known for its superb sculptures.

HIKING

Recreational hikers will enjoy the nearby **Tjeldbergtinden** mountain. Although at 365 meters (1,200 feet) the summit is relatively low for Lofoten, Tjeldbergtinden should nevertheless be attempted only by those in good physical condition. The trail begins at Kongsvatveien, near the shipbuilding yard between Svolvær and the village of Kabelvåg. Park at the gas station. Inexperienced hikers can satisfy themselves with the panorama from the radio mast, which can be reached in around 45 minutes.

For keener hikers, though, this is where the real Tjeldbergtinden trail starts. A further 45 minutes along a more demanding trail brings you to the top, from where you can return the way you came or continue on to other nearby summits. The views of the turquoise waters around Svolvær and Kabelvåg are breathtaking and a just reward. The upper parts of the trail can be slippery even in great weather, so good quality hiking shoes or boots are essential.

SUMMER TOURS

In addition to their sightseeing tours of the Trollfjord, **Trollfjord Cruise** (tel. 45 15 75 87, www.trollfjordcruise.com) runs three-hour fishing trips during summer afternoons, and although the scenery is magnificent, these tours do not call at the Trollfjord. The trip will only go ahead if sufficient numbers have booked, so advance contact by email or telephone is essential. The 800kr price includes all safety and fishing equipment.

WINTER TOURS

Trollfjord Cruise (tel. 45 15 75 87, www.trollfjordcruise.com) runs bird-watching tours every Wednesday and Saturday from September to March. The tour, which departs Svolvær Square at 9am, includes a brief lecture about the nature of the area before the group heads out into the icy air of Lofoten in wintertime. White-tailed sea eagles and orcas are frequently seen on this five-hour trip, which includes a lunch (typically a creamy fish soup) and hot drinks in the cost of 1,150kr. Advance booking is essential.

Although the weather can sometimes be a barrier to experiencing the northern lights in Lofoten, your chances increase by taking a tour. Local guides know the weather, the aurora forecast, and the best places to see the natural phenomenon. **Lofoten Lights** (tel. 95 00 59 77, www.lofotenlights.com) runs a northern lights safari from September to March. An English-speaking guide leads you on a 3.5-hour (950kr) or six-hour (1,550kr) journey all through the archipelago seeking the perfect spot to experience the aurora borealis dancing overhead. Warm clothes are essential, and hot drinks are provided throughout the trip. Bookings should be made at least a week in advance.

ENTERTAINMENT AND EVENTS

Run by the North Norwegian Art Centre in September every year, the month-long **Lofoten International Art Festival** (www.liaf.no) brings artists from across the world to place their art in the context of Lofoten's dramatic surroundings. It also functions as a forum and meeting place for local budding artists. What sets this art festival apart from the rest is the constant urge to seek out new venues. In previous years, everything from a war bunker to a fish-drying rack has been used to host exhibitions. The festival's board appoints new curators each year along with a new theme, so no two festivals are ever the same.

In late July or early August, the lineup of contemporary Norwegian artists at the **Lamholmen Festival** (tel. 76 06 64 80, www.lamholmenfestival.no) persuades a small local crowd to cross the bridge onto Lamholmen island for two evenings of live music and street food. Although expensive at 795kr per day (1,350kr for both), there can be few more spectacular music festival sites in all of Scandinavia.

FOOD

Be aware that opening hours for restaurants in this part of the country will be typical for the summer season, but may be cut short at other times of year. These changes are not always advertised, so check in advance if you're making a special journey.

Part seafood bar, part swanky bar, **Bacalao** (Havnepromenaden 2, tel. 76 07 94 00, www.bacalaobar.no, 10:30am-1am Mon.-Thurs., 10:30am-2:30am Fri.-Sat., noon-midnight Sun., 175-205kr) has one of the best locations in town. The large front terrace is a total suntrap and a very pleasant place to stop for coffee, fresh shrimp, or a light lunch. Burgers, nachos, salads, and pasta are also on the menu, although most locals will be ordering the creamy fish soup or *bacalao* balls. Reservations are recommended for evenings as the restaurant slowly transitions into a nightspot.

Consistently voted the best restaurant in Svolvær, the setting of ★ **Børsen Spiseri** (Gunnar Bergs vei 2, tel. 76 06 99 30, www.svinoya.no, 6pm-10pm daily, 300kr) on Svinøya island is simply delightful. The former quayside warehouse seems to float above the water, while inside you can expect an informal approach to fine dining. Almost all the dishes make use of fresh ingredients from the islands, so naturally fish and seafood dominate the menu. In fact, the stockfish comes from the factory just a two-minute walk from the restaurant. The best-value way to get a true taste of Lofoten is with the sharing plate of local delicacies, which includes Lofoten lamb, cured whale, and organic goat cheese, while the cloudberry cheesecake is an indulgent yet light way to round off your meal.

Hidden inside the Thon Hotel, **Paleo Arctic** (Torget, tel. 76 04 90 01, 11am-3pm and 4pm-11pm Mon.-Fri., noon-4pm and 5pm-11pm Sat., 250-295kr) is as the name suggests continuing the long Lofoten tradition of living off the seas and the mountain pastures. The dark interior is brightened by the full-length windows that let the Arctic light flood in from the harbor. The menu varies seasonally, but there will always be a catch-of-the-day available, along with a stockfish-based dish. A lighter lunch menu is available with soups, large sandwiches, and omelets priced around 149kr.

Perfect for a quick bite in the center of town, **Fellini** (Vestfjordgata 8, tel. 76 07 77 60, www.fellinisvolvar.no, 1pm-10:30pm daily, 100-250kr) is known for its vast pizza menu with 25 different varieties. Pasta, salads, hamburgers, fish, and kebabs are also available. Portions are large, so come here to refuel if you are just passing through, or for a great value dinner if you are spending the evening. The small pizzas from 111kr will be more than enough for most people.

For Chinese food, look no further than the simple yet warming ambience of **Ni Hao** (Sjøgata 6, tel. 76 07 79 00, 2pm-10pm Tues.-Sun., 170-250kr), which focuses on Canton- and Sichuan-style cooking. It's a little on the expensive side, but all meals are served with rice and will fill you up. A slimmer takeout menu is available if you prefer to enjoy your meal in the comfort of your own accommodations.

Often missed by tourists, the bright pastel shades of **Hjerterommet** (Vestfjord gata 5, tel. 90 61 19 68, 10am-4pm Mon.-Fri., 11am-4pm Sat.) provide a striking welcome into the best café in town. Enjoy a slice of homemade apple cake with a wide selection of specialty leaf teas and coffees as you enjoy the atmosphere generated by the vintage decor, which includes sewing machines and unique studio-style furniture. Lighter meals such as salads and omelets are available throughout the day.

ACCOMMODATIONS

Even within the beautiful setting of Svolvær, few accommodation choices offer such spectacular views as the former fishing lodges of ★ **Anker Brygge** (Lamholmen 1, tel. 76 06 64 80, www.anker-brygge.no), set on a small island overlooking the harbor and mountain backdrop of the city. The 27 cottages and suites are furnished to a high standard with wooden floors and exposed wooden beams adding to the rustic atmosphere. Each cottage has a quayside terrace, a cozy lounge area, and separate bedrooms, each with its own bathroom. Individual rooms can be booked from 1,595kr, while an entire cottage starts from 2,800kr.

An alternative choice for groups is the very modern harbor-facing apartment building operated by **Lofoten Suitehotel** (Torget 21, tel. 47 67 01 00, www.lofoten-suitehotel.com), which offers one-, two-, and three-bedroom apartments ranging 2,750-5,000kr. Contemporary luxury dominates the décor, and the views from the floor-to-ceiling windows are outstanding, so this accommodation is well suited for a celebration or for those who enjoy the finer things in life. Those just after a bed for the night should most definitely look elsewhere.

A good budget option is the **Vestfjord Hotel** (Fiskergata 46, tel. 76 07 08 70, www.vestfjordhl.no, 1,195kr s, 1,595kr d), hidden away behind the Hurtigruten quay. Ask for a room on the upper floor to make the most of the views of ships entering the harbor or the city's mountainous backdrop. The modern reception and lounge bar area is in stark contrast to the bedrooms, which are spacious but basic with a few tatty corners here and there. A simple breakfast buffet in the adjacent restaurant is included in the price.

The cheapest hotel-standard accommodations in the city center are the small rooms of the ★ **Fast Hotel** (Austnesfjord gate 12, tel. 45 19 86 54, 1,095kr), where the priority is providing simple accommodations at a relatively low cost. All rooms do have a private bathroom with shower, work desk, and electric kettle, but the only food and drink available on the premises is from vending machines. Nevertheless, the 24 rooms book up fast during the summer months, so book ahead to be sure of staying in the lowest cost hotel in Svolvær.

Connected by a bridge to the main city, the island of Svinøya is home to some intriguing options. **Svinøya Rorbuer** (Gunnar Bergs vei 2, tel. 76 06 99 30, www.svinoya.no) offers comfortable wooden fisherman's cabins adapted to modern standards ranging from 1,375kr for a one-bed to 3,000kr for a three-bed, and bigger suites that sleep up to six people for 4,500kr. Discounts are available for longer stays, and prices tend to drop by around 10 percent outside the summer season. Svinøya itself is easy to explore, with rocky coastal paths, fish-drying racks, and great views of Svolvær and the Svolværgeita mountain.

Also on Svinøya, **Kunstnerhuset i Lofoten** (Bernt Salvesens vei 14, tel. 99 55 26 86, www.kunstnerhuset-lofoten.no, 900kr d) is designed as a residence for artists, but rooms are also let to budget-conscious travelers. The eight guest rooms are tight, although they do come with a work desk and chair, but all bathroom and kitchen facilities are shared. Several art studios are available, along with a large lounge where guests mix with the Norwegian artists drawn to Lofoten by the unique light and spectacular scenery.

Around six miles north of Svolvær, **Hammerstad Camping** (Austnesfjordveien 720, tel. 76 07 03 05, www.hammerstadcamping.no) is a good option for those arriving from the mainland. Cabins vary in quality and price, from 550kr for the most basic with a kitchenette but no bathroom, to 1,650kr to a fully equipped cabin that sleeps up to nine. Pitches for motorhomes (185kr) and tents (145kr) are also available. Two four-person boats are available for rent from 450kr for three hours, perfect for a quick sightseeing or fishing trip.

INFORMATION AND SERVICES

Underneath the Thon Hotel is the tourist information office of **Destination Lofoten** (Torget, tel. 76 06 98 00, info@lofoten.info), from where you can book tours and obtain maps of the city and hiking areas. The center is open 9am-7pm daily June-July, 9am-7pm Monday-Saturday March-May and August-mid-October, and only open 9am-3:30pm Monday-Friday mid-October-February. It's best to clear up any queries while you are in Svolvær; although other information centers are available across Lofoten, their opening hours are short.

For basic postal services, head to the Post Office (Posten) desk inside the **Kiwi** supermarket (Sivert Nilsens gate 31, 7am-11pm Mon.-Sat.).

Kabelvåg

As your road trip west of Svolvær begins, your first stop should be at the village of **Kabelvåg,** just 5.7 kilometers (3.5 miles) west along the E10.

Despite being the largest wooden building in northern Norway, **Lofoten Cathedral (Lofotkatedralen)** (Våganveien, tel. 76 06 71 90) is officially just Vågan Church. Built in 1898 to accommodate the hundreds of visiting fishermen, the Gothic revival-style church seats 1,200 and is one of the most aesthetically pleasing churches you'll pass on your journey. Interior features include Swiss-style carvings, pointed arches, and an altar that was relocated from the former parish church that was demolished in 1900. The church is open to visitors (3pm-6pm Mon.-Fri., 9am-6pm Sat., noon-6pm Sun. for the first two weeks in June, 9am-6pm Mon.-Sat., noon-6pm Sun.

mid-June through mid-August), and although not required, a small donation is expected (50kr is recommended).

Based around a former fishing village, the **Skrei Experience Center** (Storvåganveien, www.museumnord.no) is now home to a museum, aquarium, and art gallery. The beautifully preserved main building from 1815 and authentic fishing cabins and boathouses make up the **Lofoten Museum (Lofotmuseet)** (tel. 76 06 97 90, 80kr), which also houses former sailboats and exhibitions about the coastal life. The museum is open 10am-6pm daily June-July and 11am-3pm daily May and August. For the rest of the year, the museum opens 11am-3pm on weekdays only.

Skrei is the Norwegian term for the cod caught around Lofoten. You can learn more about the fish that has driven the Lofoten economy for centuries at the neighboring **Lofoten Aquarium** (tel. 76 07 86 65, 120kr; 10am-6pm daily June-July, 11am-3pm daily May and Aug., 11am-3pm Mon.-Fri. Sept.-Nov. and Mar.-Apr.). The aquarium is completely closed during December and January. A combined ticket can be bought for 200kr, which also gains you access to the **Galleri Espolin** (tel. 76 15 40 00, 80kr), which showcases the expressive art of Norwegian Kaare Espolin Johnson. It may seem strange to couple a gallery with a fishing museum and aquarium, but the constant theme running through the artwork is of coastal lifestyle, so it's an appropriate match, if not an essential visit. It's certainly not worth the steep 80kr entrance fee on its own.

ACCOMMODATIONS

Set in a quiet part of Kabelvåg, four miles from Svolvær, **Lofoten Vandrerhjem** (Finnesveien 24, tel. 76 06 98 80, kabelvag@hihostels.no) is a bright, modern HI hostel perfect for those taking their time journeying through Lofoten. The main attractions of Kabelvåg, the aquarium and museum, are a 25-minute walk away. Private rooms are available from 850kr, along with beds in dormitories starting at 335kr, with all bathroom facilities shared. All guests have access to a shared kitchen, laundry facilities, basic breakfast buffet, and a garden featuring a barbecue area and sea views, while many activities and excursions can be booked here. The only downside is the short summer season, which runs from June to early August.

★ Henningsvær

Set on a group of tiny islands dropped into the Vestfjord at the foot of the mighty Vågakallen mountain, **Henningsvær** is one of Lofoten's best known fishing villages. A beautiful setting in summer or winter, the village is a must-do on any Lofoten trip, especially if you can't make it out to Reine and Å at the extreme west of the islands.

The village is 25 kilometers (15 miles) west of Svolvær along the E10 highway. As you turn out toward Henningsvær on Route 816, you will discover a great example of Lofoten's excellent beaches. **Rørvikstranda beach** is accessed via a short rocky path from the parking area. While not the most spectacular of Lofoten's beaches, its shallow slopes are sandwiched in by imposing mountainsides and make for a nice spot for a beach walk or a light lunch. The beach is suitable for children, although facilities are nonexistent.

As the only way to reach Henningsvær by road, the narrow, winding Route 816 is shared by cyclists, delivery trucks, cars, and even carefree pedestrians. Take special care here; with open water on one side and sheer mountain cliffs on the other, there's lots to distract even the most focused drivers, especially if this is your first taste of Lofoten.

The easiest way to navigate the small village is on foot, so park in the large village square just after the bridge and don't forget your camera.

GALLERIES

Next to the large village square is the bright red wooden building home to **Galleri Lofotens Hus** (Hjelskjæret, tel. 91 59 50 83, www.galleri-lofoten.no, 10am-7pm daily mid-Apr.-May, 9am-7pm daily June-Aug., 10am-4pm daily Sept., 90kr). Although the entrance fee appears high, this is just as much a museum as a gallery. Entrance includes a showing of the short photographic movie *The Magical Archipelago (Det Magiske Øyriket),* which profiles the diverse wildlife of the region and gives you a glimpse of Lofoten's special environment through all four seasons. If you wonder what Lofoten is like during the winter, this will help you find out.

The fishing village of Henningsvær is home to several art galleries.

On the upper floors the beautifully restored wooden structure hosts a mixture of locally inspired artworks and memorabilia from the proud history of the fishing village. There is also an excellent gift shop, which is free to browse.

Ceramic artist Cecilie Haaland, photographer John Stenersen, and glassblowers Mette Paalgard and Heidi B. Kristiansen have formed **Engelskmannsbrygga** (Dreyersgate 1, tel. 48 12 98 70, www.engelskmannsbrygga. no, free), a presentation of traditional arts and crafts in a delightful old waterside wharf (10am-9pm daily mid-June to mid-Aug., 11am-4pm Wed.-Sun. mid-Mar. to mid-June and mid-Aug. through Dec., 11am-4pm Sat.-Sun Jan. to mid-Mar.). Displays of glassblowing and pottery making are held throughout the day in the open studio, while the gallery showcases the finished products.

Last but not least, the whitewashed brick **Kaviar Factory** (Hennningsværveien 13, tel. 90 73 47 43, www.kaviarfactory.com, free) produced fish paste for 40 years but, when facing closure, was bought by Venke and Rolf Hoff. They have transformed the industrial building into a fitting gallery for their vast private collection of contemporary art. In contrast to many local galleries that display traditional landscape paintings, the focus here is on giving the people of Lofoten the opportunity to experience contemporary art from all corners of the world. From mid-June to mid-August, the gallery is open 10am-7pm daily, with 11am-6pm daily opening during early June. In May and late August, expect the gallery to be open for just a few hours in the afternoon, typically Wednesday-Sunday. Viewings outside these months can only be made by appointment.

ROCK CLIMBING

For expert insight into the peaks all around Henningsvær (including the famous Svolværgeita in Svolvær), **Nord Norsk Klatreskole** (Misværveien 10, tel. 90 57 42 08, www.nordnorskklatreskole.no) offers day-long guided climbing tours every day from mid-June to the end of August. Tours must be booked in advance, and the price depends on the size of the group, but you can expect to pay 2,500-3,000kr per person. The same company offers family-friendly packages for beginners at the highly regarded Kalle mountains between Henningsvær and Kabelvåg. This challenging yet fun half-day activity costs around 2,500kr for up to four people, including all equipment.

SNORKELING

The gentle, shallow waters around the Henningsvær archipelago are perfect territory for snorkeling. Henningsvær-based **Lofoten Opplevelser** (tel. 90 58 14 75, www.lofoten-opplevelser.no, 800kr per adult, 700kr per child) provides dry suits and basic training to individuals, groups, and families before heading out in an inflatable RIB boat to the tiny islands surrounding Henningsvær. You will snorkel in several different spots on the two-hour trip, on which you're likely to encounter cod, mackerel, starfish, and jellyfish. Bringing woolen underwear is highly recommended because the sea temperatures are low and the dry suit will keep it from getting wet.

TOURS

From mid-June to mid-August, **Lofoten Opplevelser** (tel. 90 58 14 75, www.lofoten-opplevelser.no) also runs a **Midnight Sun Safari** by inflatable RIB boat. Warm clothes are essential for this trip; although it's only held in summer, the boats head out into the open ocean. Sea eagles, puffins, and grey eagles are often spotted on these trips, and even the occasional whale.

The trips depart Henningsvær at 10pm daily and take up to three hours, costing 850kr for adults and 750kr for children. On cloudless nights the midnight sun adds to the atmosphere, but this trip is a memorable one regardless of the weather.

FOOD AND ACCOMMODATIONS

If you are just passing through Henningsvær and need a quick bite, seek out the candle-laden café **Lysstøperi** (Gammelveien 2, tel. 90 55 18 77, 10am-4pm Mon.-Thurs., 10am-5pm Fri.-Sun.) for an indulgent cinnamon bun, slice of cake, or cup of coffee. During the high season this is a very popular spot, so be prepared for a wait around 1pm-2pm, or do as the Norwegians do and take a light lunch around 11am.

A few steps from the main village square is the waterfront **Fiskekrogen** (Dreyers gate 29, tel. 99 41 79 00, www.fiskekrogen.no, 1pm-10pm daily), arguably Henningsvær's most consistent independent restaurant. Fish and seafood unsurprisingly dominate the menu, although the quality, inventiveness of the dishes, and selection beat anywhere else in Henningsvær. The only criticism from a traveler's perspective is the saltiness of the fish, which is high to suit local tastes.

A good budget option and of special interest to climbers is the main office of Nord Norsk Klatreskole, which in addition to running climbing tours also offers basic accommodations and food. Modern art and music are the themes inside the cozy cabin-style ★ **Climber's Café (Klatrecafeen)** (Misværveien 10, tel. 90 57 42 08, www.nordnorskklatreskole.no), heated by a wood-burning stove at its center, while live music adds to the atmosphere on summer weekends. The house specials are filling dishes such as *bacalao* and creamy fish soup. Available accommodations (tel. 90 95 46 19, post@nordnorskklatreskole.no) include basic single (500kr), double (630kr), and dorm beds (300kr), all with shared bathroom facilities. Although you don't need to be the active type to stay here, you may feel slightly out of place among the young backpackers and keen climbers if you are not the sporty type.

Another venue offering both accommodations and food is the family-run **Finnholmen Brygge** (Hellandsgata 85, tel. 40 05 09 99, www.finnholmen.no, 950-1,295kr d). While very small, the economy rooms are the best value because they still come with a sea view and en suite bathroom. If you hope to stay longer than three or four nights, call ahead to negotiate a discount. The advertised fully licensed restaurant is actually more of a café serving lighter meals, coffee, and waffles throughout the day, and is popular with nonguests.

Accommodations in Henningsvær are limited, and advance booking is required to secure summer lodgings, especially during the Norwegian holiday month of July. The 30 double rooms of the **Henningsvær Bryggehotell** (Misværveien 18, tel. 76 07 47 50, www.henningsvaer.no, 1,195kr) offer the most modern accommodations in town in one of the most historic buildings. Dining is a delightful experience at any time of day thanks to the harbor-view restaurant, where you can enjoy a hearty breakfast or a lovingly crafted gourmet meal of Arctic specialties. Most tours and activities on offer in the local area can be booked at reception.

Thanks to its waterfront location on the tiny Sauøya island on route to Henningsvær, every room at the **Lofoten Arctic Hotel Skata** (Sauøya 2, tel. 76 07 07 77, www.lofotenarctichotel.no, 950kr s, 1,295kr d) enjoys a sea view. The former fishing warehouse has been restored into accommodations ranging from more than 25 standard hotel rooms decorated in white wood and ocean blue to fully restored fishing cabins for bigger groups. Ask to see the film about the site's former use as a landing spot for fishermen.

The same company runs another hotel in the center of Henningsvær. The eight rooms within the 19th-century **Lofoten Arctic Hotel Knusarn** (Dreyers gate 8, tel. 41 56 52 61, www.lofotenarctichotel.no, 950kr s, 1,250kr d) were recently upgraded to modern standards, and all are en suite with LCD TVs. Knusarn is best known as a bar and restaurant, which offers a seasonal fish-dominated à la carte menu throughout the year. The outdoor terrace is one of the best places in town to enjoy a cool Lofoten pilsner on a warm summer's evening.

GIMSØYA

A few days in Svolvær and/or Henningsvær makes a memorable trip in itself, but continuing west along the E10 is when your road trip really gets going. Pass through the village of **Kleppstad** and you will come to the first of Lofoten's impressive bridges linking the islands together. The 839-meter (2,752-foot) **Gimsøystraumen bru** bridge that crosses the 17-kilometer (11-mile) sound separating the islands of Austvågøya and Gimsøya is best viewed from the **Gimsøystraumen rasteplass** parking area immediately prior to the bridge. A modern community center with public restrooms is available.

Once you've crossed the bridge, continue along the E10 to the main attractions on the much bigger Vestvågøya island if you're pushed for time. If you have time to spare, take an immediate left turn to loop around the edge of Gimsøya island on the narrow coastal road for a scenic drive and short stop at the white wooden **Gimsøy Church (Gimsøy kirke)** (Gimsøysand, tel. 76 06 71 90) hidden just off the road (signed) and overlooking the water. The history of churches on the island stretches back to the 15th century, although this one was built around 1800.

Most of the island's recreational options are at its northern tip, including the small residential community of **Hov,** which offers a small beach and some rocky paths along the coastline to explore.

Sports and Recreation
GOLF

Most visitors to Gimsøya are here to play the spectacular 18-hole championship course at **Lofoten Links** (Tore Hjortsvei 389, tel. 76 07 20 02, www.lofotenlinks.no), on which the ocean, rocks, and sandy beaches act as hazards. The course is built around ancient Viking tombs, while sea eagles, black-tailed curlews, grouse, and oystercatchers are commonly sighted overhead.

Play is possible 24 hours a day under the midnight sun, which lasts from late May to mid-July, with daylight opening hours for the full season, which runs May to October, depending on weather. Members are given priority, so it's worth contacting the club well in advance if you are keen on including a round in your itinerary. The course is part of the Troon membership program, which means Troon members can reserve tee times and make all arrangements online. Clubs can be rented from the pro shop in the clubhouse, which also offers accommodations in package deals for visitors keen to play over multiple days. A great time to play the course is late in the season, from late August to October, when the northern lights could appear overhead. Guests can expect to pay around 850kr in fees to play the full 18 holes, with a discount given for those staying at the club.

HIKING

Behind the golf course is the unmissable **Hoven** mountain. Despite standing just 365 meters (1,200 feet) tall, it dominates the otherwise flat marshlands of northern Gimsøya. Although there are far taller summits on Lofoten, the relatively easy hike to the top of Hoven rewards you with 360-degree views of the island, ocean, and even the distant Vesterålen islands on clear days.

No special equipment is needed beyond comfortable shoes that are suitable for sodden ground. Park at the Lofoten Links golf course and walk south to pick up the marked trail to the summit, which should take no more than one hour.

HORSE RIDING

The descendants of the Icelandic horses of the **Hov Riding Centre (Hov Hestegård)** (Hov, tel. 97 55 95 01, www.hovhestegard.no) stretch back to the Viking Age. It feels only natural then to explore the ancient landscape surrounding Hov on one of these magnificent animals. Suitable for more experienced riders, the flagship 2.5-hour Viking tour (offered year-round) takes in the beach and the Viking Age trail through Gimsøya Nature Reserve and costs 950kr per person. Expect to hear stories of the Vikings who lived and worked in these lands. Other tours are offered to suit all skill levels, including midnight sun tours on the long summer evenings and northern lights tours from late September to early April.

Recommended for beginners and families, the short 1.5-hour Lofoten by Horse tour is a walking pace ride along the beach and a ridge with excellent views. Weather permitting, the tour runs daily year-round at 11am with an additional 5pm tour in the summer, and costs 650kr per person. All tours must be booked in advance.

Food and Accommodations

Although primarily intended for golfers, the **Lofoten Links Lodge** (Hov, tel. 76 07 20 02, www.lofotenlinks.no) is open to all. Each lodge sleeps up to six and can be booked in its entirety from 3,600kr or by individuals (950kr) or two people sharing a room (1,400kr). Each lodge is furnished to modern standards and includes a shared living space with fireplace, small kitchen, and a terrace with an uninterrupted ocean view.

A few apartments overlooking the golf course are available from 990kr, based on two people sharing. Breakfast can be pre-booked at the clubhouse for 125kr or delivered to the lodge for 175kr, while meals

throughout the day are available to purchase at the clubhouse.

VESTVÅGØYA

Marshes and agricultural land dominate this island, with mountains and remote fishing villages to the north and south. Although you may be tempted to drive straight through toward the more famous sights to the west, Vestvågøya is home to some picturesque fishing villages, good accommodations, and services in the town of Leknes.

★ Lofotr Viking Museum

The major family attraction is the **Lofotr Viking Museum** (Prestegårdsveien 59, Bøstad, tel. 76 15 40 00, www.lofotr.no), where you can meet "real" Vikings and experience their lifestyle down to the food they ate. The museum is built on what is believed to have been a site of great importance during the Viking era, on high ground at the center of the island. The reconstructed chieftain's long-house is built over a site where artifacts indicate a real chieftain's home once stood.

During the summer, activities led by crafters take place. Sunday is a great day for families to visit, with outdoor Viking games and both entertaining and educational activities

The scenery becomes ever more spectacular as you head west to Vestvågøya.

geared toward children. There's plenty to see for adults, too, such as exploring the living quarters and learning about the weaving and leather-making skills of the time. Don't miss the 15-minute subtitled movie *Dreaming of Borg*, which tells a love story through the eyes of a Viking family, revealing much about their way of life.

Opening hours vary considerably during the year. From May to mid-September the museum is open 10am-5pm daily, staying open until 7pm during June and July. From February to April and mid-September to October, the hours are noon-3pm Wed.-Sat., while for the rest of the year the hours are limited to just noon-3pm on Wednesday and Saturday. Entrance is 140-200kr for adults and 100-150kr for children under 16, with family tickets (two adults with up to three children) available for 430-600kr. Children under six get in free.

To fully immerse yourself in the Viking experience, join the local chieftain and his wife for an authentic Viking feast, held every evening the museum is open. Enter the chieftain's house for an evening of food, mead (a Viking-era honey wine), storytelling around the open fire, and maybe some traditional song and dance. The simple meal typically consists of Lofoten lamb, although dietary needs can be accommodated if noted when booking. Advance booking is required (780kr adults, 535kr children under 16).

From June to August the museum café serves a range of Viking-themed sandwiches, cakes, and hot dishes. Outside of these times, snacks are available from the museum shop.

A short five-minute detour brings you to **Borge Church (Borge menighet)** (Prestegårdsveien 75, Bøstad, tel. 76 05 67 30). Built in 1986 to replace the previous church, which was destroyed by fire, the modern design of the church isn't that attractive, yet its location is. Perched atop a hill, the view across the local area is worth the short drive.

Stamsund

A traditional trawl fishing village on the southern side of the island, **Stamsund** has a population of just 1,000 but enjoys a vibrant cultural life thanks to local theater groups and artists who have set up here. The village enjoys daily visits from the Hurtigruten coastal express, so amenities are greater than one would expect for a village of its size. It's worth the short 15-minute drive from the E10 at Leknes to experience a working Lofoten trawl fishing village.

SKIING

Located in Stamsund, **Lofoten Alpine Center (Lofoten Alpinsenter)** (tel. 76 08 94 11, 6pm-9pm Wed. and Fri., noon-5pm Sat.-Sun.) has limited opening during the winter season (weather dependent) but is the best choice on the islands for those who must get in some skiing or snowboarding. A day card costs 300kr. Call ahead to check availability if you wish to rent equipment.

ENTERTAINMENT AND EVENTS

Every year in late May, the five-day **Stamsund Theatre Festival** (www.stamsund-internasjonale.no) presents a platform for new and exploratory performing arts. The local art school usually opens the festival with a mainstream performance before local and international artists take to the various stages. The action centers around the Skjærbrygga pub, and there is also a varied program aimed at children and young adults. Tickets for individual performances can be purchased for around 200kr, with a festival pass available for 1,000kr.

FOOD AND ACCOMMODATIONS

As every building in Stamsund seems to be, **Skjærbrygga** (Skjæret, tel. 76 05 46 00, noon-10pm daily) is delicately balanced on wooden stilts above the water. A former shipping and fish production warehouse, the building previously used to dry out freshly caught fish is today home to a thriving restaurant and pub. Main dishes such as whale steak, baked cod, and shellfish soup run 195-255kr, while pizzas and lighter meals are also available, from around 150kr.

Few hostels in all of Norway can have a better location than **Stamsund Vandrerhjem** (Hartvågen 13, tel. 76 08 93 34, Mar.-Oct.), teetering above the water with a backdrop of mountains. Ask anyone who's stayed here their opinion and you're almost certain to hear about the eccentric host, Roar. While not to everyone's tastes, Roar tells it like it is and is full of stories and advice about the local area. Rare in this day and age, the hostel can only be booked by telephone. Dorm rooms from 175kr, private rooms from 500kr.

Leknes

Whether you are spending a lot of time exploring Vestvågøya or driving straight on to Flakstadøya and Moskenesøya, include time in your itinerary for a brief recharging stop at **Leknes.** The E10 cuts through the small city on the western side of the island and has a shopping mall, gas station, and several options for food.

Known as Lofoten's second city after Svolvær, Leknes is 68 kilometers (42 miles) west of Svolvær. The drive would take just over an hour in the unlikely event you don't stop at any of the attractions along the route.

BEACHES

One of the best known Lofoten beaches that's reachable by car, **Haukland Beach** is a strip of white sand and crystal blue waters reminiscent of somewhere thousands of miles farther south. To reach the beach, take the signposted Leiteveien from the E10 approximately five kilometers (three miles) north of Leknes. Turn right when you reach the coastline and the parking area is just a couple of minutes farther along to the left. Camping is not permitted, but it's a pleasant place to enjoy a packed lunch or relax for an hour, even in wintertime.

If you're in the mood for beaches, this is the right part of Lofoten to visit, as another three kilometers (two miles) north from Haukland Beach is possibly the most famous of all Lofoten beaches, in part due to the sheer number of photographers who flock here. The north-facing **Uttakleiv Beach** brings

northern lights hunters here in great numbers during the winter, while wild camping under the midnight sun on the beach itself or the grassy dunes beyond is popular during the summer.

HIKING

For a short, straightforward one-hour hike near Leknes with fantastic views of Haukland Beach, consider the round-topped summit of **Holandemelen** mountain, with an elevation of 434 meters (1,424 feet). The partly forested trail is unmarked but easy to follow from the parking area by the side of the road on Voieveien, approximately three kilometers (two miles) south from Haukland Beach. If you reach the turn off for Voie, you've driven too far.

ENTERTAINMENT AND EVENTS

Country music events are not so common in Norway, so the **Lofoten Country Festival** (www.lofoten-countryfestival.no) attracts country fans from all across northern Norway to Leknes each September. Norwegian acts are joined by headline guests from as far afield as the United States for this four-day festival held across three venues. Camping is permitted at the main festival venue Lofothallen, just outside Leknes.

FOOD AND ACCOMMODATIONS

For those who aren't keen on fish or seafood, Leknes offers a rare opportunity on Lofoten to dine on something different. Although neither option is exactly gournmet, the pizzas at **Lille Milano** (Storgata 57, tel. 76 08 20 55, 1pm-11pm Mon.-Sat., 1pm-10pm Sun., 150kr) and the simple yet filling meals at **Kan Thai** (Storgata 51, tel. 76 08 00 10, 2pm-10pm Tues.-Thurs., 2pm-11pm Fri.-Sat., 2pm-9pm Sun., 169kr) are good value ways to add some variety into your vacation diet. The latter's Sunday buffet for 199kr is extremely popular and will fill you up for the day.

The only full-service hotel for miles around, the **Best Western Leknes** (Lillevollveien 15, tel. 76 05 44 30, www. lofotenhotell.no, 1,140kr) provides comfortable modern accommodations with free parking at the halfway point of your Lofoten road trip. The 60 rooms are bright and clean albeit with slightly dated decor. The casual setting of the associated **Restaurant Bevares** (245-295kr) is a good pick to sample a seasonal menu, although Lofoten lamb and fresh fish will likely feature at any time of year.

INFORMATION AND SERVICES
Midway along the main street of Leknes is one of the two main offices of **Destination Lofoten** (Storgata, tel. 76 08 75 53), from where you can book tours, get public transport information, and obtain hiking maps. (The other main office is in Svolvær.) From mid-June to mid-August, the office is open daily (9:30am-7pm Mon.-Fri., 10am-4pm Sat., noon-4pm Sun.). Outside these months, it is closed on Sunday (9:30am-4:30pm Mon.-Fri., 9:30am-3pm Sat.). It's best to clear up any queries here, because although there are other smaller offices on Flakstadøya and Moskenesøya, the opening hours can be sporadic, and nonexistent outside the summer months.

For basic postal services, **Leknes Post Office (Leknes postkontor)** (Storgata 8, 7am-11pm Mon.-Sat.) is located within the Coop Extra supermarket, just off the northern end of the main shopping street.

FLAKSTADØYA
An undersea tunnel brings you to Flakstadøya, the penultimate island that you can reach by car. The scenery gets notably more dramatic and photo opportunities can be found around every corner. Although most of the island's population lives on the flatter northern shore, it's the mountainous scenery to the south that captivates. A side trip to the Nusfjord resort and one of the island's many excellent beaches are recommended stops here.

Nusfjord
Of the many possible side trips off the E10, the 10-minute drive to **Nusfjord** (tel. 76 09 30 20, www.nusfjord.no) along Route 807 is perhaps the most worthwhile. On arrival, your senses will be overloaded by the sheer mountain faces that rise from the water, the red and ochre wooden buildings, the bright white fishing boats, the smell of a fishing village, and the overall sense of history. In 2005 the fishing industry abruptly ended and the entire village has since been converted into a holiday resort, with the vast majority of fishing cabins restored and available for rent. Day visitors are required to pay a 50kr fee to enter the village.

Nusfjord has two options for food. Best suited for overnight visitors, the crisp white tablecloths and ocean views of the **Karoline Restaurant** encourage you to savor the moment and enjoy the specialties caught outside the window. It's one of the most popular restaurants in Lofoten, so advance booking is recommended. Next door you'll find **Oriana Kro,** a café bar serving simple yet filling pub-style food in a more casual atmosphere.

To stay in such a beautiful location is for many what visiting Lofoten is all about. By day Nusfjord can be overrun by tourists, but by night it's the perfect secluded spot to write, paint, walk, fish, or simply reflect on the beauty Mother Nature has bestowed on this part of the world. The high-standard cozy cabins available for rent from **Nusfjord Rorbuer** vary from 1,495kr to 2,695kr, but even the smallest contain a private bathroom, running water, and a coffeemaker. On selected days, the resort offers sea fishing and tours of the Lofoten fishery.

Sports and Recreation
BEACHES
Immediately after arriving on Flakstadøya, take the sharp left turn marked Myrland for the short drive to **Storsandnes Beach,** 13 kilometers west of Leknes. Just two kilometers (1.2 miles) farther along the road, the boulder-strewn sandy **Myrland Beach** comes into view. Both are good alternatives to the busier beaches of Vestvågøya.

The ultimate aim for most Lofoten road trippers is to make it to Moskenesøya, the 182-square-kilometer (72-square-mile) island that marks, quite literally, the end of the road.

It is characterized by an uneven shoreline and the spikiest peaks in the entire archipelago. At 1,029 meters (3,376 feet), the Hermannsdalstinden mountain stands tallest among the jagged range that covers the northern half of the island, interrupted only by the occasional fjord or lake. The entire island is a target for experienced hikers, but there are hiking options for the curious, too.

The island was occupied by the German army during the early days of World War II, and was the venue of a British, Norwegian, and Polish raid that destroyed radio transmitters and sank ships. An operational Enigma coding machine was recovered from one of the sunken ships, providing a tactical advantage to the Allied forces in the years to come.

Lofoten is a prime spot for northern lights hunters.

Kvalvika Beach

On the northern side of Moskenesøya is the isolated **Kvalvika Beach.** Despite its golden sands, shallow turquoise waters, and steep cliffs of Ryten mountain making this one of the most picturesque beaches on the islands, it is often quieter than you might expect because it's only accessible by foot. The two-kilometer (1.2-mile) hike is straightforward but is rocky and can be slippery after rainfall. It takes just over one hour to reach the beach.

The start of the trail is near **Fredvang** village, which is easier to reach from Flakstadøya than Moskenesøya itself. From the E10 take the turn marked Fredvang a couple of kilometers past Ramberg. Turn south in Fredvang village and follow the road just three kilometers (two miles) along the coastline to the small parking spot just past a fairly anonymous boathouse. Although not in place at the time of writing, a parking charge is expected to be introduced, so keep some change on hand.

Although facilities are nonexistent, camping at the grassy dunes and beach is permitted

Beaches dot the coastal stretch of the E10 around the small communities **Flakstad** and **Ramberg** on the northern shore. The best of the bunch is the flat, sandy **Skagsanden Beach,** a haven for photographers and northern lights hunters year-round thanks to its north-facing aspect and the impressive backdrop of the Hustinden mountain.

Shopping

Facing open ocean and backed by an imposing mountain face is the small community of **Vikten.** This is the unlikely location for **Glasshytta** (tel. 97 71 60 23, www.glasshyttavikten.no, 10am-7pm daily June-Aug.), a glassblowing studio started by local fisherman Åsvar Tangrand in the 1970s after being inspired on a trip to Finland. Small glass candle holders, dishes, and bowls, all with ocean-themed decoration, are popular purchases. The workshop is on Route 804 and is signed from the E10 around five kilometers (three miles) west of the undersea tunnel from Vestvågøya.

and indeed recommended in the summer for an outstanding view of the midnight sun with very few others around.

★ Reine

The island village of **Reine** is one of the most famous sights in Lofoten simply because of the sheer number of photos in circulation. If you're visiting Lofoten because of a magazine article, it's highly likely at least one photograph of Reine accompanied it.

Words cannot do justice to the breathtaking scenery on the approach to Reine, which rivals the Atlantic Road for the honor of best driving experience in Norway. The E10 winds its way across islands and skerries for a couple of miles, with open ocean, mirror-like lakes, and ragged snowtopped mountains visible in every direction. It's wise to take your time on this stretch to pause at one of the many parking areas and stroll around what is a truly remarkable location.

Your first glimpse of Reine will be as you take the bridge from the seafood restaurant and cabins of tiny **Sakrisøya** island. You approach the village from the east before spiraling around the edge of the bay, almost circling the village in its entirety before turning to enter the village from the south. As you

turn off the E10, a parking area to the left offers an uninterrupted panorama of the island with its famous mountainous backdrop. On a clear calm day, the view is surely the most spectacular in the country that doesn't require mountain climbing.

The village itself is well equipped for visitors, especially during the summer season, when cafés and restaurants compete for your attention. The narrow roads and limited space mean it's prudent to find a parking spot quickly, and at just 72 acres, the village is easy to navigate on foot.

One of the first points of interest is **Reine Culture Centre (Reine Kultursenter)** (www.reinekultursenter.no, 11am-6pm daily May-Sept.), a former school now functioning as an art gallery and community center. The works of northern Norwegian artist Eva Harr, featuring strong use of light and color, are presented in a permanent exhibition, along with exhibitions of photography and a nature exhibition of local bird and animal life. There's also a small café.

To enjoy Moskenesøya from a unique perspective, take a round-trip on the **MS Fjordkyss** (tel. 76 09 20 90, www.reinefjorden.no). This is a regular scheduled ferry rather than a tour, but it takes in highlights

Biking is a great way to see the Lofoten islands away from the highway.

of the Reinefjord, including the imposing Hermanndalstinden mountain, waterfalls, and tiny farming hamlets. The timetable varies by day and season, but there is normally at least one morning and one afternoon departure. The one-hour round-trip costs 130kr.

HIKING

Budding photographers looking to mimic the most iconic shots of Lofoten and keen hikers alike flock to Reine to tackle the 1,470-foot high **Reinebringen** mountain. While not recommended for beginners, the hike is relatively short (no more than two hours to the summit) and rewards you with an outstanding view of Reine and the nearby islands at the so-called "Lofoten wall" of mountains that dominate Moskenesøya. Begin the trail by taking the paved pedestrian alternative to the Ramsvik Tunnel on the E10, just past the entrance to Reine. Beware of slippery rocks throughout the hike.

FISHING

The waters around Moskenes are ideal deep-sea fishing territory, and it's almost unheard of for a boat to come back empty-handed. Hundreds of cod weighing more than 30 kilograms (66 pounds) are caught every year. **Aqua Lofoten** (Reine, tel. 99 01 90 42, www.aqualofoten.no) runs daily fishing trips ideal for beginners into the plentiful waters surrounding Reine. A professional fisherman will teach you everything you need to know to catch a fish using the traditional jigger wheel method, although it is up to you to catch the fish yourself! The four-hour trip costs 800kr (600kr children under 14) and needs a minimum of four people to go ahead.

KAYAK AND BIKE RENTAL

For a truly relaxing way to experience western Lofoten's unique environment, rent a kayak from **Reine Adventure** (tel. 93 21 45 96, www.reineadventure.com), starting from 450kr per person per day. Choose between a self-guided adventure or book a three-hour guided tour for an additional 500kr.

The same company also offers cycle rental for those wanting a break from the car. Mountain bikes (200kr) and road bikes (300kr) are available for daily rental depending on your planned itinerary, along with children's bikes (150kr).

TOURS

For those staying overnight in or near Reine, a boat trip and hike to the isolated **Bunes** beach is available from **Aqua Lofoten** (Reine, tel. 99 01 90 42, www.aqualofoten.no) on summer evenings to coincide with the midnight sun. The three-hour trip costs 500kr (300kr children under 14) and is available daily in June and early July, subject to demand.

FOOD AND ACCOMMODATIONS

Just 1.6 kilometers (one mile) outside of Reine on Sakrisøya island is the family-run **Anita's Sjømat** (tel. 90 06 15 66, 10am-8pm Mon.-Sat., noon-6pm Sun.), which serves freshly caught fish and seafood (you can see the fishing boats right outside!). The seafood bar concept offers shrimp and a hugely popular homemade fish burger to eat on the waterside terrace out back. Other snacks are also available.

In Reine itself, the 32 cabins of **Reine Rorbuer** (tel. 76 09 22 22, www.reinerorbuer. no, 1,395-3,045kr) are the best option beyond individual lets. All cabins have been upgraded to modern standards while retaining their traditional atmosphere. All come with a kitchenette so you can prepare and cook a fish you caught that day, but in case you weren't so lucky, the cozy **Gammelbua** bar and restaurant serves fresh fish and other local produce. Indulgent desserts include the sweet *søtgrøt* porridge, cloudberry cream with wafer cones, or the meringue and vanilla cream *kvæfjordkake*. Opening hours vary throughout the year, and it's advisable to call ahead to book during the summer.

A holiday resort consisting of former fishermen's cabins on the tiny island of Hamnøy, **Eliasen Rorbuer** (Hamnøy, tel. 45 81 48 45, www.rorbuer.no, 790-1,990kr) is a truly unique place to stay in the wilds of western Lofoten, and within easy reach of Reine. Most of the 35 cabins stand on stilts above the rocky coastline and have unbeatable views of the jagged mountains just across the water. In contrast to the daytime rush of cars, an evening in one of the high-spec cabins with kitchenette and private bathroom or out on the patio watching the midnight sun or northern lights is true relaxation, Lofoten style. A shuttle service is available from Moskenes ferry terminal for 100kr per person.

★ Å

Just nine kilometers (5.6 miles) south of Reine is the literal end of the road. The E10 ends abruptly as a car park in the ancient fishing village of Å (often referred to as Å i Lofoten on road signs and buses to distinguish it from other places named Å), which today functions mainly as a living museum.

Despite the fact that most of the village is an exhibit, there are a lot of accommodations in Å, from hotels and cabins to private rentals, which makes it a popular choice with travelers, especially those who are starting or ending their trip with the nearby ferry to the mainland from the port at Moskenes.

NORWEGIAN FISHING VILLAGE MUSEUM
(Norsk Fiskeværsmuseum)

Founded by the Moskenes History and Museum Society, the main function of the Norwegian Fishing Village Museum (Å i Lofoten, tel. 76 09 14 88, www.museumnord.no, 9am-7pm daily June-Aug., 10am-5pm Mon.-Fri. rest of year, 80kr) has been to preserve the fishing village rather than to build anything new. The old boathouse has been converted to hold most of the museum's exhibitions, but the whole village is the real exhibition.

Having said that, if you're planning on anything more than a quick stroll around the village, then it's worth paying the museum's entrance fee to explore some of the fascinating buildings, including the 19th-century stone oven bakery that still produces bread and aromatic cinnamon buns to sell in the village café. Other buildings worth a look include the former cod liver oil factory, the forge, and the boathouse, most of which contain exhibitions detailing what life was like in each particular building. The original 19th-century grocery shop still functions as a shop today, selling local food, literature, and groceries to the small number of local residents and holidaymakers.

LOFOTEN STOCKFISH MUSEUM
(Lofoten Tørrfiskmuseum)

Lofoten stockfish (dried cod) is a protected brand in the EU alongside the likes of Roquefort and Chablis. If this and the drying racks of fish throughout the islands have piqued your curiosity, find the answers at Lofoten Stockfish Museum (Å i Lofoten, tel. 76 09 12 11, 11am-5pm daily mid-June to mid-Aug., 80kr), which demonstrates how the work at a conventional fish landing station is undertaken.

A 30-minute film with English subtitles explains the process from catch to delivery, and you can then dive into detail by looking around the landing station, gutting shed, and production hall. You also get an opportunity to try the stockfish snacks beloved by locals that are eaten like a packet of potato chips.

The owners speak fluent Italian, which highlights the importance of stockfish exports to Italy to this corner of Norway. It should go without saying that anyone who has a dislike of the taste or smell of fish should steer well clear.

FOOD AND ACCOMMODATIONS

A sister hostel of the one in Kabelvåg outside Svolvær, Lofoten Vandrerhjem Å (tel. 76 09 12 11) is split between the upper floors of the Lofoten Stockfish Museum and the 19th-century Hennumgården house within the wider grounds of the Fishing Village Museum. Both buildings contain a guest kitchen and shared bathroom facilities. Unfortunately, given its unique location and somewhat captive market, the hostel is priced rather steeply at 260kr for a dorm bed, although the private rooms starting at 590kr offer reasonable value.

If you have a bit more cash to spend, the small yet comfortable double rooms on the upper floors of the wharf (815kr) or the fishing cabins (starting at 1,290kr for two persons) of **Smaken av Lofoten** (tel. 76 09 21 00, www.smakenavlofoten.no) are well worth considering. The entire complex has undergone substantial restoration, and the cabins in particular are furnished to a very high standard. The ground floor of the wharf is devoted to a restaurant offering snacks such as whale burgers, fish soup, and vegetarian salads (noon-10pm daily mid-May to Aug.). A more formal à la carte menu is on offer from 6pm.

Information and Services
The **Moskenes Tourist Information Centre** (Sørvågen, tel. 98 01 75 64, 10am-7pm daily mid-June to mid-Aug., 10am-2:30pm Mon.-Fri. May to mid-June and mid-Aug. to mid-Sept.) on Moskenesøya is frustratingly located in Sørvågen—between Reine and Å—rather than in one of the tourist hot spots. Tourist information boards are located in Reine and Å, and staff across the island's hotels and restaurants are more than used to giving directions and advice. Pay particular attention to parking regulations, which have become more strictly enforced in recent years.

GETTING THERE
The best method of transport to Lofoten depends on how the islands fit into your overall itinerary, the time you have available, and your budget. As a broad rule of thumb, the less time you want to spend getting here, the more money you will pay.

Air
If money is less of a concern, fly to **Svolvær Airport Helle** (SVJ, tel. 67 03 39 50), just 5.5 kilometers (3.4 miles) east of the city. Domestic airline Widerøe serves the airport with flights to Bodø, which is connected by several daily flights to Oslo from both SAS

and Norwegian. In 2017, Widerøe began to experiment with direct flights between Oslo and Svolvær. It's worth checking for availability on this route as it will slash your travel time from the capital. Car rental desks available include **Avis** (tel. 76 07 11 40), **Europcar** (tel. 95 45 06 20), **Hertz** (tel. 95 13 85 00), and **Rentacar Lofoten** (tel. 47 64 35 60). Given the short distance to Svolvær there is no special airport bus service, but a taxi for the five-minute journey costs around 150kr.

An alternative airport for Lofoten is **Evenes Airport** (EVE, tel. 67 03 41 00) also named Harstad/Narvik as it is sited midway between those two cities. Although the airport is 164 kilometers (102 miles) driving distance east of Svolvær, SAS and Norwegian both run direct services from Oslo, which generally run much cheaper than Widerøe flights. Public bus 23-760 (www.177nordland. no) connects Evenes Airport to Svolvær. The three-hour journey runs just twice daily and costs around 280kr. Numerous car rental desks are available, including **Avis** (tel. 76 98 21 33), **Budget** (tel. 76 98 21 73), **Europcar** (tel. 76 98 21 20), **Hertz** (tel. 41 58 22 28), and **Sixt** (tel. 76 98 23 00).

Boat
Two regular ferries link Bodø with different ends of Lofoten, both run by **Torghatten Nord** (www.torghattennord.no) although leaving from different parts of the city.

The quickest route is the daily passenger-only service from **Bodø to Svolvær,** which leaves from the terminal by the tourist information office every evening (times vary). A one-way ticket for the 3.5-hour crossing costs 443kr.

The **Bodø to Moskenes** car ferry leaves from the Hurtigruten terminal and is a good option if you want to do the road trip in reverse or just see the highlights of Moskenesøya island. In summer season there are at least four crossings a day, but this drops to just one or two during the winter. A one-way passenger ticket for the 3.5-hour journey costs just 196kr, but expect to pay at least an additional

700kr to take a car. Be wary that this open sea crossing can often be rough, even in apparent good weather, so those not used to travel by ferry should be prepared or consider another option. In high season, it's wise to make a reservation online in advance.

Finally, the **Hurtigruten** (www.hurtigruten.com) coastal express links Bergen, Ålesund, Trondheim, Bodø, and Tromsø (and many other smaller coastal towns) with Stamsund and Svolvær on Lofoten. Although prices tend to be higher and times slower than the regular ferries, it is an option to consider to add a certain level of comfort to your trip.

Car

If you are driving north on Norway's E6 highway, you have two choices to reach Lofoten once you reach the small town of **Fauske.** You can take the **car ferry** from **Bodø to Moskenes** and then return to the mainland by following our suggested road trip in reverse, which allows for an overnight stop in Bodø.

Alternatively, you can reach **Svolvær,** the starting point for our suggested road trip, from the mainland by continuing north on the E6 until you connect with the E10. This 290-kilometer (180-mile) route will take 5-6 hours depending on how long you need to wait for the Bognes-Lødingen ferry.

GETTING AROUND

Although a car is highly recommended to get the best out of a visit to Lofoten, don't despair if renting a car is not an option for you. Many choose to extend their trip on Lofoten and use public transport, bicycles, or car sharing. Hitchhiking is much more common here than anywhere else in Norway, although due care should of course be taken.

Car Rental

In addition to the usual suspects available at the region's airports, **Rentacar Lofoten** (tel. 47 64 35 60, www.rentacar-lofoten.com) has an office in Svolvær and a particularly convenient location at the ferry terminal in Moskenes. Advance booking is highly recommended.

Pay attention to car parking rules and regulations, especially in the tourist hot spots, as local councils have clamped down in recent years. Notices are displayed on noticeboards in town centers and should at least have a summary translated into English, but ask a local if you are unsure.

Bike Rental

Bicycles can be rented from locations across Lofoten, including most hotels and cabin rental companies. Rates from **Reine Adventure** (tel. 93 21 45 96, www.reineadventure.com) vary 200-300kr, with road bikes, mountain bikes, and children's models all available. Call ahead to reserve in high season.

Bus

If you are taking at least a week to explore Lofoten, then the public bus network could be a very effective option for you. The most useful services for tourists include the 18-741 linking Svolvær to Leknes and the onward 18-742 from Leknes to Reine and Å, both running 5-7 times daily. The service is generally reliable but can be slow going as the buses tend to call at most small villages and hamlets near the E10. Allow a minimum of 1.5 hours to travel between Svolvær and Leknes, and a further 1.5 hours to reach Å. Check www.177nordland.no or ask at a tourist information office for timetable and fare information.

Vesterålen

Frequently ignored by travelers in lieu of the more famous Lofoten islands, the vast Vesterålen archipelago is worthy of so much more attention than it gets. While the landscape is just as mountainous, its rounded peaks are not as dramatic as Lofoten and the fishing villages more functional than picturesque. However, such landscape is a haven for outdoor enthusiasts, with hiking, biking, and camping opportunities around every corner.

The exact border of Vesterålen is complex, but its main islands are **Hadseløya**, the vast **Langøya**, parts of **Hinnøya**, and the northernmost **Andøya**. Although **Harstad** (on Hinnøya) is the largest settlement, Vesterålen's central city and therefore public transit hub is **Sortland** (on Hadseløya). Although the town offers little to the traveler, it's a convenient place to stay.

HADSELØYA

Many tourists arrive in Vesterålen on the Fiskebøl-Melbu ferry crossing, and some never venture farther than Hadseløya. That's because the island, although small, contains some of the biggest attractions in the entire archipelago, and a day trip from Svolvær is easily manageable.

Melbu

It seems by design that but minutes after driving off the ferry you come to the **Vesterålen Museum (Vesterålsmuseet)** (Maren Frederiksens allé 1, Melbu, tel. 76 15 40 00, vesteraalsmuseet@museumnord.no, 11am-5pm Tues.-Sun. mid-June-mid-Aug., 50kr), as if to scream at visitors, "You are no longer in Lofoten!"

Set inside the former stately home of enterprising industrialist local Christian Fredriksen, the manor house and farmlands preserve the Vesterålen way of life from the turn of the 20th century. Unlike the fishing-dominated economy of Lofoten, the Vesterålen economy was more diverse thanks to Fredriksen's investment in the port at Melbu, and in production of herring oil, soap, margarine, and textiles. The furniture, artwork, and decor of his home make up the principal exhibits of the museum.

Stokmarknes

A pleasant 15-kilometer (nine-mile) drive around the eastern perimeter of Hadseløya brings you to **Stokmarknes**, the original home of the Hurtigruten company, one of Norway's most recognizable icons. Thanks to the 1956 ship MS *Finnmark* standing proudly ashore, you cannot miss the entrance to the **Hurtigruten Museum (Hurtigrutemuseet)** (Havnegata, tel. 76 11 81 90, www.hurtigrutemuseet.no, 90kr).

In July 1893, the original *Vesteraalen* ship sailed from Trondheim, under the command of Captain Richard With, a cofounder of the company. He sailed through the night to Bodø, where he was greeted by brass bands and thousands of people in their Sunday best. A visit here returns to those days when the Hurtigruten was the only viable method of traveling along the Norwegian coast. Various multimedia exhibits reveal how the company dealt with the disruption of World War II and grew from an important logistical service to the major tourism attraction it is today. The museum's big draw is the chance to explore the stately interiors of the MS *Finnmark*, including the restored captain's cabin.

The only frustration is the limited opening hours. Although the museum is open daily 10am-6pm from mid-June to mid-August, the hours are limited to noon-4pm daily a month on either side of that (mid-May to mid-June and mid-Aug. to mid-Sept.), and just 2pm-4pm daily the rest of the year. Southbound Hurtigruten passengers receive a 40kr discount on admission.

Directly opposite the imposing MS

Finnmark is the fairy-tale-like red wooden building of **Rødbrygga** (Markedsgata 6, tel. 76 15 26 66, www.rødbrygga.no, 9am-1am Mon.-Thurs., 9am-3am Fri., 11am-3am Sat., 4pm-1am Sun.), a popular pub and restaurant. By day the sun-facing terrace is the perfect place to grab a light lunch plate featuring hot dogs, beef, or meat cakes (112kr), while by night the place transforms into a lively sports bar with live music, when pizzas, nachos, hamburgers, and salads are served through the evening.

To break up your journey, consider a night in a room or cabin at the **Vesterålen Kysthotell** (Børøya, tel. 76 15 29 99, http://vesteralenkysthotell.no), just over the bridge on the small island of Børøya. Options vary from modern double rooms (1,160kr) with private bathrooms in the main building to a family-size waterside cabin (3,280kr) that sleeps up to eight. Camping is also available, with electric hookups and free Wi-Fi. A basic service building is home to a kitchen, showers, and restrooms, while hot tubs and a sauna are available for rent.

LANGØYA

Norway's third biggest island, **Langøya** makes up much of western Vesterålen. Despite its large size of 850 square kilometers (328 square miles), you are never far from water, because of the jagged coastline and the 25-kilometer-long (16-mile-long) Eidsfjord, which slices into the island.

Sortland

An ordinary town with little to interest the casual traveler, **Sortland**'s central location means anyone touring Vesterålen will pass through the town multiple times. Its accommodations, restaurants, shopping, and services mean it's the obvious choice to base yourself, despite the lack of attractions in the town itself.

FOOD

Although the prices are a little on the high side, the upscale bistro **Sortland Mat &**

Vinhus (Torggata 27, tel. 76 20 12 10, www.matogvinhus.no, 10am-10pm Mon.-Sat., 330kr) serves the best-quality dishes for miles around, with an excellent choice of wines and beers to match. However, the service can be slow even at quiet times despite the lack of variety on the menu. Seasonal fish dominates the à la carte evening menu, while the lighter lunch menu is better value with items such as pizza, omelets, and fish soup available for around 125kr.

For a livelier, less pretentious atmosphere, join the crowd of locals for lunch at the bright blue ★ **Expedisjonen** (Rådhusgata 26, tel. 76 20 10 40, 10am-6pm Mon.-Tues., 10am-10pm Wed.-Thurs., 10am-11pm Fri., 11am-11pm Sat.), where almost nothing on the menu is more than 200kr despite the generous portion sizes. The informal atmosphere welcomes all whether you're planning an indulgent meal or just popping in for coffee and cake. The homemade sourdough bread served with sandwiches, soups, and salads is a top pick.

ACCOMMODATIONS

The anonymous-looking **Sortland Hotel** (Vesterålsgata 59, tel. 76 10 84 00, www.sortlandhotell.no, 1,395kr) has a fascinating past. For more than 100 years the hotel has welcomed the great and the good through its doors, but there's precious little to celebrate that fact in the rather basic accommodations with beds that can best be described as average. An investment in art helps to justify the high price of the hotel, along with an impressive library that doubles as a restaurant and bar. The grandest room in the hotel hints at what used to be.

A mile or so out of town, **Sortland Camping & Motel** (Vesterveien 51, tel. 76 11 03 00, www.sortland-camping.no) is a quiet, large complex of 15 basic cabins, 24 bungalows, a small motel, and plenty of space for motorhomes and tent camping. Open year-round, there's almost always space here, but rates vary enormously by season. Expect to pay 200kr for a tent pitch (280kr with a car) and 500-1,200kr for basic cabins. A clean

Why Sortland Painted Itself Blue

In Sortland, even the banks are painted blue.

Much like many towns on Lofoten and Vesterålen, Sortland is an ordinary small city that provides services in an area of outstanding natural beauty. There's not a great deal else on offer. Except the people of Sortland (and one man in particular) tried to put their city on the map for something unique.

Local artist Bjørn Elvenes came up with the idea of turning his hometown into a three-dimensional artwork using a blue color palette. Elvenes studied Fine Art in Krakow, Poland, which at the time was a gray city with little optimism, yet it provided the inspiration for the idea.

In the summer of 1998, the mayor of Sortland presented the idea of painting the town blue to a pessimistic pool of local journalists. Questions were asked about cost and practicalities, but the idea captured the imagination of the townspeople. Love it or hate it, everyone had an opinion, and the local newspaper played the role of mediator.

The blue city project was adopted as a millennium project by the city. However, this was the beginning of the problems! While the artist wanted the freedom to create his vision of a three-dimensional painting that you could enter and interact with, the architects preferred using color to emphasize the features of individual buildings, while the local bureaucrats insisted on a managed process.

The artist fell out with the council and started to cooperate with selected building owners directly, while others implemented the council's plans. The result is a mishmash of styles and colors that keeps a stroll around Sortland's city center an interesting one.

The city is by no means completely blue, but enough buildings are blue to raise a curious eyebrow from visitors.

service building, small café, and TV lounge are all on-site.

INFORMATION AND SERVICES

The tourist information center of **Vesterålen Reiseliv** (Kjøpmannsgata 2, tel. 76 11 14 80) is open year-round and can provide detailed advice about activities, hiking maps, and tour suggestions for your specific circumstances. A few souvenirs are available. Although opening hours vary by season, the office is always open 10am-3pm weekdays, with extended opening hours including weekends from June through August.

Nyksund

While in Sortland, it's well worth taking the one-hour drive north via the small town of Myre to this tiny fishing village with a big history. Many Norwegian fishing villages have been through turbulent cycles of activity, but none more stark than **Nyksund**. A once thriving destination that was home to hundreds of cod fishermen, Nyksund was abandoned in the 1970s due to advances in fishing technology that left the shallow waters and isolated village without a purpose.

After decades of decay, an enterprising German brought young Berliners to the village to help restore the weather-weary buildings, and soon enough the village had life again, including hostels, cafés, and galleries. While the village remains eerily quiet in the wintertime, the summer sees a population of around 30 serve curious backpackers and day trippers. Even at the height of summer, Nyksund still feels like the end of the world.

Because of the exposed nature of the village and lack of light pollution, it's one of the best places in the region to see the northern lights, although accommodation options are limited outside the summer.

Even Queen Sonja has paid Nyksund a visit, and given her name to the hiking trail over the mountain to the neighboring village of **Stø**, a livelier but less interesting fishing village. The **Dronningruta** trail (which means Queen's Route in Norwegian) is actually two routes that run between Nyksund and Stø, forming a circle; both routes are well marked. A straightforward five-kilometer (three-mile) walk tours the sandy beaches of the coastline, while a tougher 14.5-kilometer (nine-mile) hike over the mountain is only recommended for experienced hikers. A loop of both routes should take around nine hours, or around four hours using the coastal route both ways.

The homey **Holmvik Brygge** guesthouse (Nyksund, tel. 76 13 47 96, 800kr s, 950kr d) is filled with trinkets, art, and fishing equipment chronicling the history of Nyksund. Rooms are basic, some with bunk beds, but the facilities elsewhere in the house make up for the tight nature of the accommodations. Guests are encouraged to make themselves at home in front of the cozy fireplace in the lounge and prepare their own meals in the kitchen. Open June-August, the fully licensed restaurant **Holmvik Stua** (11am-late daily) serves arctic char and wild reindeer, both smoked on-site.

ANDØYA

The northernmost Vesterålen island is arguably the most beautiful of them all. Following the coastal road that loops right around the island, you are never more than a stone's throw from the water, close to some of the country's best beaches and with great opportunity to see wildlife, including sea eagles swooping overhead and even whales out at sea. The center of the island is characterized by peat bogs and the proliferation of golden cloudberries, while the rocks found on the island are a geologist's dream, including stone coal and fossils from the Jurassic limestone period.

★ Andøya Tourist Route

The western half of the island is the latest addition to Norway's network of National Tourist Routes. The road clings to the coastline, sandwiched in between sheer cliff faces and the open North Atlantic Ocean. The narrow road demands due care, especially in poor weather, but many passing points and parking areas are provided along the route. Highlights include Bleik Beach (the longest in northern Europe), the rock formation Bukkekjerka, and outstanding conditions for bird-watching, hiking, and camping.

Following the brown tourist route signs, it should take about one hour to drive the 58-kilometer (36-mile) western route from Risøyhamn to Andenes, but allow an extra hour or so for the several stops you are likely to make. For a speedier return in around 45 minutes, take the eastern coastal road.

BUKKEKJERKA

Approximately eight kilometers (five miles) north of the small settlement of **Bø** on the western side of Andøya is the impressive **Bukkekjerka** mountain formation, once used by the indigenous Sami people as a place of sacrifice. A new parking area and viewpoint adjacent to the road provides an unobstructed view of the giant rock said to resemble a pulpit.

BLEIK

Despite its remote location 28 kilometers (17 miles) north of Bukkekjerka, settlement at **Bleik** dates back to the Iron Age. Today the village is best known for its 2.4-kilometer (1.5-mile) golden sandy **beach** and rocky breakwater, both perfect for a stroll to break up the drive.

One of the best campsites in the region, **Midnattsol Camping** (Gårdsveien, Bleik, tel. 47 84 32 19, www.midnattsolcamping. com) is right by the beach, perfect for ocean swimming or camping under the midnight sun, yet within easy walking distance of a grocery store, café, and bar in the village. Tents can be pitched for 100kr (one person) or 150kr (two or more people), while double rooms are available in a large cabin for 750kr. All rooms share bathroom, kitchen, and lounge facilities, but substantial discounts are available for stays of one week or more.

In Bleik village, **Nærbutikken** (Skoleveien 45, tel. 76 14 22 00, 9am-8pm Mon.-Fri., 10am-6pm Sat., noon-6pm Sun.) stocks groceries but also doubles as a simple café serving soup, sandwiches, coffee, and ice cream.

Take a last look at the open ocean from the **Kleivodden** rest area, north of Bleik, at the foot of steep mountainsides before the road cuts inland. From this sheltered spot you can admire the **bird cliffs** on **Bleiksøya** island. The cliffs are home to thousands of white-tailed eagles, gannets, and puffins. To get a close-up view, consider a bird-watching tour from Andenes.

The Andøya Rocket Range at Oksebåsen, halfway between Bleik and Andenes, sends up rockets as part of a space research program and for commercial purposes. Here the **Andøya Space Center** (tel. 76 14 46 00, www.spaceshipaurora.no, 10:30am-5:30pm daily mid-June to mid-Aug.) presents the science behind rockets and the northern lights in an exhibition suitable for all ages. A widescreen film with English subtitles about the northern lights is worth a watch if you are here outside of northern lights season, but the real highlight is a ride in Spaceship Aurora, an interactive experience taking

the ragged, lonely coastline of Andøya island

guests on a virtual trip into outer space. As entertaining as the experience is, education is the focus, with scientific experiments to complete as part of your mission, which leaves every hour on the hour. Adults pay 350kr for the full mission experience or 125kr to see the film and exhibitions, with children under 15 paying half.

Andenes

The northern tip of the Vesterålen archipelago is 10 kilometers north of Bleik. With around 2,000 inhabitants, the fishing port of **Andenes** is one of the larger coastal fishing communities on the islands. With direct access to the rich waters off the continental shelf, Andenes has been a thriving fishing village since the Middle Ages, although tourism drives the local economy today. The port is dominated by the 40-meter (131-foot) bright red **Andenes Lighthouse,** dating to 1859.

the distinctive Andenes Lighthouse

WHALE MUSEUM
(Andenes Hvalsenter)

The **Whale Museum** (Hamnegata 1c, tel. 76 11 56 00, www.whalesafari.no, 8:30am-4pm daily June to mid-Sept., longer July hours), operated by Whale Safari, is usually visited in combination with a whale-watching tour but can be visited without a tour for 110kr. Entry includes a 45-minute tour with an English-speaking guide educated in marine biology. In addition to research about the different species of whale and the ocean conditions around Andenes, the museum also displays a real skeleton of a sperm whale.

WHALE WATCHING

Other than sheer curiosity, the reason to travel all this way is for the chance to see a mighty whale out in the open ocean. Sperm whales (summer) and humpback whales (winter) love the waters around the Vesterålen islands, so much so that many of the local tour companies offer guaranteed sightings or a free second trip.

Whale Safari (Hvalsafari) (Hamnegata 1c, tel. 76 11 56 00, www.whalesafari.no) runs a daily **Summer Safari** (945kr) from June to mid-September, which includes a guided tour in the Whale Museum before the trip, with a guide, snacks, and hot drinks aboard the boat. Tour duration varies 2-4 hours depending on the conditions, with up to four departures daily. A **Winter Safari** (9am Tues. and Fri., 990kr) can be taken December-March.

For a more intimate alternative, **Sea Safari Andenes** (Hamnegata 9, tel. 91 67 49 60, www.seasafariandenes.no, Nov.-Mar., 1,000kr) fills its high-speed inflatable RIB boats with no more than 12 people. The three-hour tours reduce the risk of seasickness and allow you to spend more time out at sea, potentially getting closer to the magnificent ocean creatures.

BIRD WATCHING

From May to August, **Sea Safari Andenes** (Hamnegata 9, tel. 91 67 49 60, www.seasafariandenes.no) runs daily 1.5-hour **Birdwatching Tours,** on which you can expect to see white-tailed eagles, gannets, and puffins at the Bleiksøya bird colony off the coast of Andøya island.

FOOD AND ACCOMMODATIONS

It's rare to find quality independent coffee shops outside the main cities, let alone in such an isolated location. But the passionate family behind **Kaffehuset Strøm Eriksen** (Storgata 9b, tel. 94 17 56 12) subsidizes their small but thriving local café with a smart online coffee subscription operation. Coffee aficionados will feel right at home chatting about the latest blends, while those just after a caffeine hit can grab a latte and go.

The 29 en suite rooms at **Hotel Marena** (Storgata 15, tel. 91 58 35 17, www.hotellmarena.no, 1,040kr s, 1,340 d) have provided some much needed hotel-standard accommodations in Andenes, which has led to increased tourism to the town. Rooms are small but thoughtfully decorated with input from local designers and photographers. Breakfast is included.

INFORMATION AND SERVICES

A satellite office of the **Vesterålen Reiseliv** (Kong Hans gate 8, tel. 76 14 12 03) tourist information office is open year-round, and staff can answer specific questions on any aspect of traveling around Andøya or the wider Vesterålen area. Given the exposed nature of the island, it's a good idea to check the latest weather forecast here if you are planning any hiking or camping trips. Although opening hours vary by season, the office is always open 10am-3pm weekdays, with extended opening hours including weekends from June through August.

GETTING THERE AND AROUND

Car

Assuming you are traveling from Lofoten, the easiest way to reach Vesterålen is via the **Fiskebøl-Melbu car ferry** crossing. The journey takes approximately 30 minutes and departures run approximately every 75 minutes throughout the day, although you should check timetables with **Torghatten Nord** (tel. 90 62 07 00, www.torghattennord.no) if you plan to travel in early morning, evening, or on Sunday. Fares start from 123kr for a small car plus 44kr for each passenger, and there are restrooms on board. A well-stocked café serves coffee, waffles, and snacks.

If traveling from the mainland, **Sortland** is a 161-kilometer (100-mile) drive west from the main E6 highway at **Bjerkvik,** which is 33 kilometers (21 miles) north of Narvik.

From mid-May to the end of August, Andenes can be reached by **car ferry** from the island of **Senja,** which is a 220-kilometer (137-mile) drive from Tromsø. **Torghatten Nord** (www.torghattennord.no) operates 2-3 daily departures between Andenes and the village of **Gryllefjord** on Senja. The fare is 615kr for car plus driver, with additional passengers charged 240kr adults, 120kr children/seniors.

Air

At the northernmost tip of Vesterålen, **Andøya Airport, Andenes** (ANX, tel. 67 03 40 50) is within walking distance of the town, although taxis are available, especially in bad weather, for a fee of approximately 85kr. Daily Widerøe flights serve Bodø and nearby local airports, but during the summer Norwegian Air operates direct services to and from Oslo, often at low prices.

Alternatively, **Evenes Airport** (EVE, tel. 67 03 41 00), also named Harstad/Narvik as it is sited midway between those two cities, is 120 kilometers (75 miles) southeast of Sortland. SAS and Norwegian both operate direct services from Oslo. Numerous car rental desks are available, including **Avis** (tel. 76 98 21 33), **Budget** (tel. 76 98 21 73), **Europcar** (tel. 76 98 21 20), **Hertz** (tel. 41 58 22 28), and **Sixt** (tel. 76 98 23 00). A scheduled airport coach service (www.flybussen.no) operates several times per day between Sortland and Evenes at a one-way cost of 310kr.

Bus

The local authority runs bus routes across the region that may prove useful for travelers without a car, but departures are usually limited to just a couple per day. Various routes link Sortland with the E6 at Narvik, and Svolvær and Leknes on Lofoten. Check www.177nordland.no or ask at a tourist information office for timetable and fare information.

Tromsø and the High North

Look for ★ to find recommended
sights, activities, dining, and lodging.

Highlights

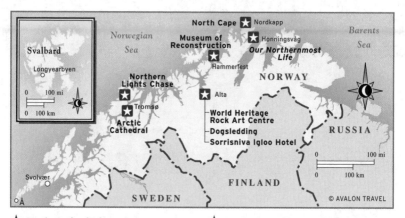

★ **Arctic Cathedral:** This church has become a modern icon of Tromsø (page 298).

★ **Northern Lights Chase:** Maximize your chances of seeing the magical aurora borealis dancing overhead by following an experienced guide (page 302).

★ **World Heritage Rock Art Centre:** Explore this remarkable collection of carvings of all shapes and sizes in their natural setting (page 312).

★ **Dogsledding:** Alaskan huskies pull you across the vast, white Arctic landscape—a trip you will remember forever (page 315).

★ **Sorrisniva Igloo Hotel:** These overnight accommodations are truly unique. A night on a bed made from ice is warmer than you think (page 318)!

★ **Museum of Reconstruction:** Get eye-opening insight into the destruction of the town of Hammerfest—and its recovery over the following decades (page 323).

★ **North Cape:** Journey through barren yet beautiful landscapes to catch a glimpse of the midnight sun at one of Europe's northernmost points (page 328).

★ *Our Northernmost Life:* A fun-filled amateur play depicts life in the harsh conditions of 71 degrees north (page 331).

Vast, frozen, forbidding—just some of the words used to describe Finnmark, mainland Norway's northern-most and biggest county at 48,618 square kilometers (18,772 square miles). The strong indigenous Sami community and

influence from neighboring Sweden, Finland, and Russia create a truly unique culture, different from anywhere else in Norway.

To the west of Finnmark is Tromsø, northern Norway's biggest city and undisputed cultural capital, with a glittering annual program of festivals and events. Norwegians from Tromsø and Finnmark are notably friendlier and more welcoming than their southern counterparts, even if their English isn't always as strong. In fact, you're just as likely to hear the local Sami language, Finnish, or Russian across the region as you are Norwegian or English.

The literally endless days of summer last from May 20 to July 22 in Tromsø, when the midnight sun produces a brilliant deep red-orange light in place of a sunset. The farther north you go the longer this period lasts, up to a week longer on both sides of the summer solstice at the North Cape.

Conversely, in the winter, the sun doesn't rise for 6-8 weeks. Even though the sun remains below the horizon for most of December and January, the days aren't pitch black. Tromsø in particular is bathed in a deep midnight blue in the early afternoon as the residual light reflects off the blue sea and the white snow. These long winter nights are one of the reasons Tromsø and Finnmark county are some of the best places in the world to see the northern lights.

CLIMATE

Despite their location at the extreme north of Norway, Tromsø and Finnmark county are not as cold as one might expect, thanks to the warming waters of the Gulf Stream. However, there are significant climate variations between Tromsø, coastal areas, and the inner mountains.

In Tromsø and many coastal locations, summers are cool but winters are moderate. Farther inland, especially in the Sami

---

Previous: northern lights; crowds gathering to watch the midnight sun at the North Cape. **Above:** World War II history at the Tirpitz Museum in Kåfjord.

territories around Kautokeino and Karasjok, summer temperatures can top 27°C (80°F), but winters get extremely cold. Karasjok holds the unwelcome record of the coldest temperature ever measured in Norway: -52.4°C (-62.3F) on New Year's Day in 1886. The climate is affected by the behavior of the sun at these high latitudes. From the end of November to the end of January, the sun never rises, whereas from mid-May to late July, the sun never dips below the horizon.

Finnmark county is the driest part of the country. Coastal areas receive most rainfall from September to December, while areas inland tend to experience more rainfall during the summer. Snow can fall at any time of year, although summer flurries are rare. If you are visiting the High North at any time outside of the summer, pay attention to weather forecasts because severe snowstorms can arrive suddenly and close roads at a moment's notice.

PLANNING YOUR TIME

With both Tromsø and Alta linked to Oslo with daily direct flights, visiting this remote part of Norway has never been easier.

As the urban center and cultural capital of northern Norway, Tromsø is a worthy inclusion on any itinerary. To fully explore the more isolated Finnmark county, renting a car from Tromsø or Alta is strongly recommended. However, this region trips up many casual travelers who just glance at a map when planning their trip. Roads are narrow, facilities are rare, and distances are long. Outside of the summer months, snowdrifts can close roads at a moment's notice, so a road trip across Finnmark needs careful planning.

Almost all travelers visit northern Norway in the summer (typically mid-June to mid-August) for the midnight sun, or in early fall (September-October) or late winter (February-March) for the northern lights. Early fall and late winter are especially good times to visit because the weather tends to be more agreeable, with lighter skies and less chance of rain.

The Hurtigruten ferry is a vital transport link in this part of the country, calling at most major towns and even some tiny villages. The Svolvær (Lofoten) to Tromsø stretch shows off some of Norway's most impressive coastline, and is a handy alternative to a long monotonous drive or expensive set of flights.

Tromsø

The capital of Arctic Norway, Tromsø is the biggest city for hundreds of miles around. In fact, after the Russian cities of Murmansk and Norilsk, it is the biggest city above the Arctic Circle anywhere in the world. As such, it punches way above its weight in cultural events and things to do considering its small population of just 72,000.

Although the city is the perfect spot to base yourself during an Arctic adventure or for northern lights hunting, there's so much more to see and do within the city itself. The numerous museums and galleries mean a day trip probably isn't long enough to get the most out of Tromsø.

Don't miss the city's famed nightlife. Live music is commonplace, and the bars and pubs are busy all through the week. Locals will be only too pleased to tell you about their lives in the Arctic and, after a few glasses of the local Mack brew, how much better their city is than Oslo or Bergen.

HISTORY

Archaeological excavations show the area around Tromsø has been inhabited since the Stone Age, with evidence of buildings up to 10,000 years old found. Throughout the Middle Ages, Tromsø functioned as a Norwegian outpost in a mainly Sami region,

Tromsø

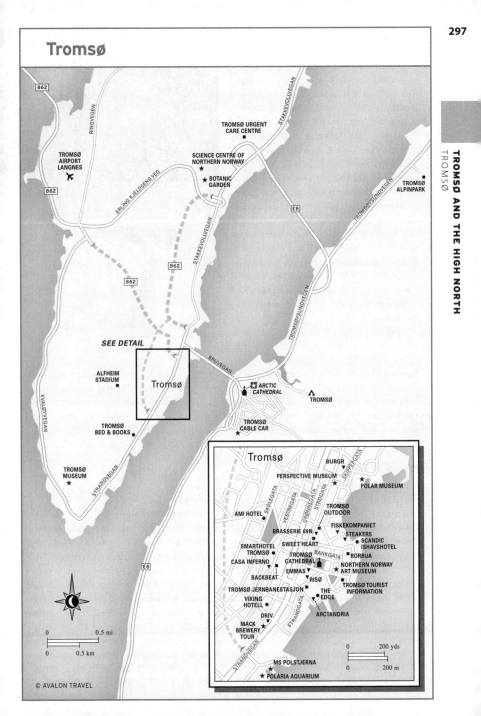

862

RINGVEGEN

TROMSØ AIRPORT LANGNES ✈

862

ERLING KJELDSENS VEG

STAKKEVOLLVEGEN

TROMSØ URGENT CARE CENTRE ■

SCIENCE CENTRE OF NORTHERN NORWAY ■

★ **BOTANIC GARDEN**

STAKKEVOLLVEGEN

E8

TROMSØYSUNDVEGEN

TROMSØ ALPINPARK ■

862

862

SEE DETAIL

BRUVEGAN

Tromsø

ALFHEIM STADIUM ■

KVALØYVEGAN

TROMSØ BED & BOOKS ●

STRANDVEGAN

ARCTIC CATHEDRAL ✚ ✦

△ **TROMSØ**

TROMSØ CABLE CAR ★

E8

TROMSØ MUSEUM ★

0   0.5 mi

0   0.5 km

☾

© AVALON TRAVEL

Tromsø (detail)

SKOLEGATA

VESTREGATA

GRØNNEGATA

STORGATA

SKIPPERGATA

BURGR ★

PERSPECTIVE MUSEUM ■

★ **POLAR MUSEUM**

AMI HOTEL ●

TROMSØ OUTDOOR

BRASSERIE 69N ▼

FISKEKOMPANIET ▼

STEAKERS ▼

● **SCANDIC ISHAVSHOTEL**

SMARTHOTEL TROMSØ ●

SWEET HEART ▼

BANKGATA

TROMSØ CATHEDRAL ⛪

■ **RORBUA**

CASA INFERNO ■

EMMAS ▼

■ **NORTHERN NORWAY ART MUSEUM**

BACKBEAT ■

RISØ ▼

TROMSØ JERNBANESTASJON ■

THE EDGE ●

TROMSØ TOURIST INFORMATION

VIKING HOTELL ●

STRANDGATA

DRIV ★

ARCTANDRIA

MACK BREWERY TOUR ★

STRANDVEGAN

MS POLSTJERNA ★

★ **POLARIA AQUARIUM**

0   200 yds

0   200 m

but also as a frontier city toward Russia in the days when the Norway-Russia border was placed much farther west.

During the 18th and 19th centuries, Tromsø quickly grew to become an important trading post in cod, with a shipping industry soon developing. Many Arctic explorers used Tromsø as a base to launch their expeditions because of the locals' knowledge of the ice cap, which was much closer in those days. Roald Amundsen and Fridtjof Nansen were among the famous Norwegian explorers who passed through Tromsø and even recruited some of their crew from the population.

Unlike the rest of northern Norway, especially Finnmark, which was almost completely razed to the ground, Tromsø escaped World War II relatively unscathed. Many of the fleeing population from Finnmark moved to Tromsø in the months and years following the war's end.

Modern Tromsø is an important center for academic research, with over 18,000 students and staff calling Tromsø their home. Formerly the University of Tromsø, the Arctic University of Norway is the northernmost university in the world and as such takes a special interest in climate change, the exploitation of Arctic resources, and environmental threats.

ORIENTATION

Half of the city's people live on **Tromsøya** island, linked to the mainland by bridges and tunnels. Many others live on the mainland and on neighboring **Kvaløya** island. Surrounded by mountains, the 22.8-square-kilometer (8.8-square-mile) Tromsøya island is home to downtown Tromsø, the Arctic University of Norway, a lake and nature reserve, the city's airport, and even a beach. A network of underground tunnels replaces the need for large highways on the island's surface.

The compact walkable central area has the biggest concentration of original wooden houses north of Trondheim. The central area's main artery is **Storgata.** Although most

the iconic Arctic Cathedral

attractions are located in and around this stretch, the Arctic Cathedral and Cable Car are in the **Tromsdalen** neighborhood on the mainland to the east. This is easy to reach by car, bicycle, local bus, taxi, or even by walking over the Tromsø Bridge, Norway's first cantilever bridge.

SIGHTS
★ Arctic Cathedral
(Ishavskatedralen)

Despite its eye-catching name, the **Arctic Cathedral** (Hans Nilsens vei 41, tel. 47 68 06 68, www.ishavskatedralen.no) is formally known as Tromsdalen Parish Church. It surprises many visitors to learn that the striking modern design of the church was actually completed as long ago as 1965. The tall white triangular structure featuring a large cross and 11 aluminum-coated concrete panels is clearly visible from across the water on Tromsøya island. Thanks to the brave vision of architect Jan Inge Hovig, the church has become far more than a place of worship and is today an internationally recognized icon of Arctic Norway.

The interior is simple, but your attention will be drawn to the prism chandeliers and prominent glass mosaic on the far wall, packed with intricate detail and symbolism. Installed more recently, the French Romantic organ was inspired by the sails on passing ships.

From June to mid-August, the church is open 9am-7pm daily (1pm-7pm Sun.), but opening hours are much shorter the rest of the year, typically 3pm-6pm daily. An entrance fee of 40kr is charged, but you are free to stay in the church for as long as it is open.

CONCERTS

From June to mid-August the church is open every night for a **Midnight Sun Concert** (170kr) at 11:30pm. Originally started as a hobby by local musicians, the concerts quickly became one of the most popular ways to experience the midnight sun, which floods into the church through the stained-glass window.

The same musicians perform both religious and Sami folk music, classical music, and ballads during the late winter. The **Northern Lights Concert** (170kr) starts at 11pm on selected nights during February and early March.

Tromsø Cable Car
(Fjellheisen)

To fully appreciate the spectacular mountainous surroundings of Tromsøya island, take the **Tromsø Cable Car** (Solliveien 12, tel. 92 61 78 37, www.fjellheisen.no, 10am-1am daily mid-May to mid-Aug., 10am-10pm daily rest of year, 170kr, 60kr under age 16) to the Storsteinen mountain summit, 421 meters (1,381 feet) above sea level. An investment of US$8 million in 2016 saw a new suite of gondolas introduced, along with a welcome expansion of the panoramic viewing terrace.

Gondolas depart the Solliveien station every half hour, with the last departure 30 minutes before closing. The station gets especially busy around midnight in the summer, so it's best to arrive a little early and give yourself some time to fully appreciate the views. In the winter, it's a popular place for hunting the northern lights, but make sure you wrap up warm—unlike the relatively mild temperatures of the city below, the winds up here can be bone-chilling. The 350kr family ticket offers a good saving if you are a couple traveling with one or two children.

Located at the summit, the **Fjellstua** restaurant (tel. 92 61 88 39, 10am-10pm daily) serves an à la carte menu of local produce but

The view from the Tromsø Cable Car is unbeatable.

is most popular for its range of light meals, snacks, and beverages, especially during the winter months.

Tromsø University Museum
(Universitetsmuseet)

As an important research center, Tromsø has an ambitious range of museums provided by the **Tromsø University Museum** (tel. 77 64 50 01, www.uit.no/tmu), a research and teaching institute dedicated to natural and cultural sciences. Although the four attractions are spread across various locations on Tromsøya island, a combination ticket for 80kr offers good value if you plan to visit at least two of the three fee-charging attractions. The Botanic Garden is free.

POLAR MUSEUM
(Polarmuseet)

Chronicling the city's rich history as a base for polar exploration, the **Polar Museum** (Søndre Tollbodgt 11, tel. 77 62 33 60, 9am-6pm daily mid-June-mid-Aug., 11am-5pm daily rest of year, 60kr) tells the story of the people and vessels behind the long seafaring tradition. Learn about famous characters such as Willem Barentsz, who discovered the Svalbard archipelago in 1596, and Henry Rudi, who killed hundreds of polar bears, one of the world's most dangerous predators, in the early 20th century. The museum opened in 1978, exactly 50 years to the day after Roald Amundsen left the city on his last expedition north. He never returned, so it seems fitting a large portion of the museum is dedicated to Amundsen, the first man to reach both the North and South Poles. The museum's temporary exhibitions are housed inside an early-19th-century wooden sea warehouse, itself a museum piece. The museum lies at the northern edge of the city center near the base of the bridge to the mainland.

MS POLSTJERNA

Adjacent to the Polaria Aquarium, the former sealing ship **MS Polstjerna** (Hjalmar Johansens gate 10, tel. 77 62 33 60, 10am-5pm daily mid-June to mid-Aug., 40kr) is preserved inside a purpose-built glass building. The 1949 ship's interior fittings are original, as are the rig, small hunting boats, tools, and equipment. The museum does not promote sealing, but it is dedicated to preserving the memory of the importance of hunting to Tromsø over many decades past. In addition to exploring the deck of the 28-meter-long (93-foot-long) ship, you'll also learn about Arctic fauna, polar expeditions, and the lifestyle of the indigenous Sami people.

TROMSØ MUSEUM

Set in a residential area on the south side of Tromsøya island, **Tromsø Museum** (Lars Thørings veg 10, tel. 77 64 50 00, 9am-6pm daily June-Aug., 10am-4pm Mon.-Fri., noon-3pm Sat., 11am-4pm Sun. Sep.-May., 60kr) is a pleasant 30-minute walk or a 10-minute bus ride on line 37 from the central area. The museum is an absolute must-do for aurora hunters, as the permanent The Aurora Explained exhibition reveals the science behind the seemingly magical ribbons of light. A unique plasma chamber recreates the actual phenomenon in front of your eyes, so Tromsø really is the only place on earth that can truly guarantee an aurora sighting!

The other permanent exhibit lets you discover the political struggle for recognition of the Sami people in Norway. The museum calls out other Norwegian institutions who present the Sami as reindeer herders and a cultural quirk, whereas in reality as many as 95 percent are fully integrated into daily Norwegian life.

BOTANIC GARDEN
(Botanisk hage)

Rather than the astonishing array of color presented by many such gardens around the world, the **Botanic Garden** (Yrkesskolevegen, tel. 90 94 17 14, always open, free) focuses on Arctic and Alpine plantlife from across the world. The Tibetan blue poppy from the Himalayas and slipper flowers from the Falkland Islands are just some of the highlights in these peaceful grounds, set against the backdrop of Tromsdalstind mountain.

The garden is on the southern border of the university campus, which is 3.3 kilometers (two miles) north of central Tromsø. A 40-minute walk or 10-minute bus ride on any line marked for the university campus will bring you here. Although the garden is open year-round, a visit between November and April is unlikely to be worthwhile given the likelihood of a snow covering.

Polaria Aquarium

One of the few attractions in Norway open every day of the year, the **Polaria Aquarium** (Hjalmar Johansens gate 12, tel. 77 75 01 00, www.polaria.no, 10am-7pm daily, 125kr) is housed within a distinctive building that represents Arctic ice floes pressed up against land. Before you enter the aquarium, watch the short wordless movies about Svalbard and the northern lights in the panoramic cinema. From here, the Arctic Walkway leads visitors to the aquarium through a series of exhibitions about the fragile nature of the Arctic. Don't miss feeding time for the intelligent bearded seals, the highlight of a visit for any children in your group.

Art Galleries

Take a walk through the history of contemporary Norwegian art from the early 19th century onward at **Northern Norway Art Museum (Nordnorsk Kunstmuseum)** (Sjøgata 1, tel. 77 64 70 20, 10am-4pm daily, free), inside one of the grandest old buildings in Tromsø, just steps away from the Tromsø Tourist Information office. Although there is a broad range of subject matter within the gallery, Arctic landscapes with jagged mountain peaks, raging oceans, and Norse legends are commonplace. Pick up an English-language pamphlet for some minimal guiding.

A gallery designed primarily to make you think, the **Perspective Museum (Perspektivet Museum)** (Storgata 95, tel. 77 60 19 10, 10am-4pm Tues.-Fri., 11am-5pm Sat.-Sun., free) uses photography to tell the stories of different sociocultural perspectives, mostly explained in English. The quality of photography is outstanding, but the social debate and thought-provoking themes are what you'll walk away with.

Tromsø Cathedral
(Tromsø domkirke)

Although not as famous at the Arctic Cathedral across the water, **Tromsø**

feeding time at the Polaria Aquarium

Cathedral (Sjøgata 2, tel. 77 60 50 90, 1pm-5pm Mon.-Wed. and Fri., 1pm-4pm Thurs., free) is still an impressive sight. Built in 1861 in the Gothic Revival style with the entrance under the clock tower, the building is Norway's only wooden cathedral and the northernmost Lutheran cathedral in the world. Its proud position at the center of town means the cathedral's grounds are a popular meeting place for locals. The modest interior is enlivened with golden chandeliers, a Madonna figure believed to be more than 400 years older than the church itself, and a copy of the 19th-century resurrection painting by Adolph Tidemand that hangs above the altar. During the summer concerts are held sporadically within, while during the long winter nights the cathedral is floodlit.

Mack Brewery Tour

Although its claim to be the world's northernmost brewery is disputed by several microbreweries, the Mack Brewery nevertheless has a proud history in Tromsø. These days the beer is brewed outside Tromsø, but the old factory buildings still play host to the **Mack Brewery Tour** (Storgata 4, www.olhallen.no, 170kr), held at 3:30pm Monday-Friday. On the one-hour tour you'll learn about the ingredients and the beer brewing process, and of course the strong relationship Mack has with the city of Tromsø. The tour ends in the adjacent **Ølhallen**, Tromsø's oldest pub, where you'll be given a sample of the latest brew and encouraged to stay to sample the rest of the range. Meet in the Mack shop at least 15 minutes early to guarantee your place.

Science Centre of Northern Norway
(Nordnorsk Vitensenter)

Useful to combine with a trip to the adjacent Botanic Garden, the planetarium at the **Science Centre of Northern Norway** (Hansine Hansens veg 17, tel. 77 62 09 45, www.nordnorsk.vitensenter.no, 10am-5pm daily mid-June to mid-Aug., shorter hours rest of year, 120kr) is a little pricey, but a great introduction to scientific principles for children, who get half-price admission. Short daily subtitled movies include a look at the northern lights or a journey through the solar system and beyond. The associated museum is full of interactive exhibits that demonstrate science in action, and wannabe weather forecasters can even star in their own report and email it to their friends.

SPORTS AND RECREATION
★ Northern Lights Chase

Standing on a chilly beach or some mountaintop miles from civilization, you may struggle to see why your experienced guide is so excited. But then from behind the mountain appears a faint ribbon of light, barely noticeable without your guide's keen eye. Moments later, the sky erupts into a curtain of vivid green jumping from one side of the sky to the other. You notice flecks of pink and purple flickering around the edge of the lights as your brain struggles to equate the connection between the incredible light show in front of your eyes and the total silence in your ears.

A northern lights sighting out in the wild can never be guaranteed, but the Northern Lights Chase from **Tromsø Friluftsenter** (Kvaløyvågvegen 669, tel. 90 75 15 83, www.tromso-friluftsenter.no, 1,050kr) gives you the best possible chance. You'll be picked up from central Tromsø and, depending on cloud cover, taken by minibus to the center's farm out on Kvaløya island or deep into the mountains. On the journey there, your guide will explain all about the myths and legends behind the aurora, and some of the science too. Photography tips will also be given.

If you are taken to the center's farm, you can wait by the roaring fire inside the traditional Sami *lavvu* tent and enjoy hot coffee until the lights appear. If due to cloudy weather the chase takes you elsewhere, expect some fun and games in the snow. Warm clothing is provided as well as coffee and cake. The tour departs from the Scandic Ishavshotel

Chasing the Northern Lights

the northern lights

Many people prefer the DIY option when it comes to hunting the aurora. To increase your chances, it's all about your location. Check the aurora forecast a day or so prior to your trip and be flexible if the forecast is low. Just as important is the weather forecast—although it might seem that you can reach out and touch the lights, any cloud cover will make the aurora impossible to see.

The **Aurora Service** (aurora-service.eu) produces hourly aurora forecasts on its website using real-time solar wind data from NASA, but also daily and three-day advance forecasts. For weather, Norwegian website **YR** (www.yr.no) has a reliable cloud-cover forecast.

The best times of year to see the lights are **September-October** and **February-March.** The winter months tend to be too cloudy, while in the summer it simply doesn't get dark enough. Contrary to popular belief, the lights are "on" year-round but cannot be seen unless it is pitch black. When you have found a good day and a good cloud-free location, head to high ground as far away from city lights as possible.

Tromsø is one of the world's best cities for northern lights spotting. Although good displays can be enjoyed from the **city center,** fainter displays will be harder to see because of the light pollution from the city. Many head to the shores of the **Prestvannet lake** at the top of Tromsøya island, or to the quiet beaches on **Kvaløya** island.

When it comes to **clothing,** pick function over fashion. Layers of thin clothing, preferably at least one wool, with a thick winter coat, are essential, as are gloves, hat, warm socks, and winter boots. You will likely be standing in the snow for several hours, after all.

To **capture the lights on film,** select a long shutter speed and a low aperture. Compact cameras and basic smartphone cameras are unlikely to be good enough to capture the lights, but do check if your device has a fireworks mode, which often helps.

(Fredrik Langes gate 2) at 7pm and you should be back in Tromsø before 1am. Dress warmly, with hats, gloves, and warm boots essential. If in the unfortunate case the lights don't make an appearance, you will be offered a free or discounted trip the following day, subject to availability.

Whale Watching

In addition to their Northern Lights

Chase, the team at **Tromsø Friluftsenter** (Kvaløyvågvegen 669, tel. 90 75 15 83, www.tromso-friluftsenter.no, 1,200kr) also runs a Whale Safari daily from November to mid-January. The waters surrounding Tromsø's neighboring island Kvaløya (which means Whale Island in English) are full of the majestic creatures, who come inland to feed during the winter. You will be guided by a trained marine biologist and with luck spot a whale in the backdrop of the beautiful twilight of an Arctic winter daytime.

The five-hour trip by RIB boat starts at 8:30am outside the Scandic Ishavshotel (Fredrik Langes gate 2) and includes all transportation and safety equipment. You can expect to spend at least a couple of hours out on the water. Book well in advance, because the trip needs a minimum of five confirmed bookings to go ahead.

Fishing

You won't forget a three-hour trip with skipper Chas Walker on British fishing boat *Lady Elsie* (Sjøtunvegen 481, Kvaløya, tel. 47 89 58 64, www.ladyelsietromso.no, May-Sept., 1,000kr) in a hurry. Depending on the time of year, cod, wolffish, coalfish, haddock, plaice, and halibut are just some of the possibilities for a catch in the plentiful waters around Tromsø. Deep-sea fishing for Arctic skrei in March and April is available for groups on request.

Hiking

The mountains surrounding Tromsø offer some of the best hiking opportunities anywhere in Norway, with over 600 peaks above 900 meters (2,952 feet) within easy reach of the city.

Tromsøya island itself is great for recreational walking, with the nature trail around **Prestvannet lake** a particular highlight; the 1.8-kilometer (1.1-mile) trail takes no more than 30 minutes. The highest point on the island, Prestvannet can be reached in just five minutes by bus route 28 from Sjøgata or route 40 from Fredrik Langes gate, if you don't fancy the very steep 1.6-kilometer (one-mile) walk.

Alternatively, the beach at the **Telegrafbutka bay** on the southern tip of the island is a pleasant 3.2-kilometer (two-mile) walk around the coastline from central Tromsø.

For more experienced hikers, several **mountain trails** start from the top of the **Tromsø Cable Car,** although serious hikers

Whale watching by inflatable RIB boat is an exhilarating experience.

will walk up rather than take a gondola! For specific trail advice, consult **Tromsø Tourist Information** (Kirkegata 2, tel. 77 61 00 00, 9am-7pm Mon.-Fri., 10am-6pm Sat.-Sun.) or the information boards at the top of the cable car.

Biking

Bikes are available to rent from **Tromsø Outdoor** (Sjøgata 14, tel. 975 75 875, www.tromsooutdoor.no), from city bikes to tootle around the compact central area to mountain bikes and fat bikes with extra thick tires suitable for winter riding. Rates vary by model, but expect to pay at least 250kr for a day's rental. Book online in advance to guarantee availability.

Running

The novelty of racing through a city in the middle of the night while the sun shines draws participants from as far afield as New Zealand and China to enter the annual **Midnight Sun Marathon** (tel. 77 67 33 63, www.msm.no) in mid-June. Few people set a personal best here, most probably because of the distraction of the incredible scenery on this largely waterside course. A 10k, 4.2k, and children's fun run allow many more people than just serious runners to enjoy the experience.

Unsurprisingly, the corresponding **Polar Night Half Marathon** in early January draws far fewer participants for its 5k, 10k, and half marathon races.

Skiing
ALPINE SKIING

Nine kilometers (5.6 miles) northeast of Tromsøya island in the mountains of the mainland is **Tromsø Alpinpark** (Jadevegen 129, Krokelvdalen, tel. 77 60 66 80, www.tromsoalpinpark.no), where day passes for the four alpine slopes are available at 260kr. A complete package of skis, boots, and poles can be rented for 200kr. Discounts are available on both rates for longer stays. The season is weather dependent but typically December to early April.

CROSS-COUNTRY SKIING

To explore the landscape of Tromsøya island or farther afield, consider renting a cross-country ski package from **Tromsø Outdoor** (Sjøgata 14, tel. 975 75 875, www.tromsooutdoor.no), handily located in the center of town. The package, costing 280kr per day or 910kr for four days, is aimed at beginners and includes a map of suggested trails close to the city. Deals for younger skiers are also available for half price.

Golf

The world's northernmost 18-hole golf course is 47 kilometers (29 miles) east of Tromsø, with a spectacular backdrop of fjord and mountains. **Tromsø Golfklubb** (Breivikeidet, tel. 77 63 32 60, www.tromsogolf.com) offers tee times under the midnight sun, but as members have priority, contact the club well in advance if you wish to play. Greens fees run approximately 400kr plus 200kr club rental.

Soccer

Local professional team **Tromsø IL** has a habit of yo-yoing between the top two divisions of Norwegian soccer. It can be a strange experience watching a game during April or October, when flurries of snow can frequently interrupt play. Home games take place at the compact **Alfheim Stadium** (Stadionvegen 3, tel. 77 60 26 01, www.til.no), and tickets, usually around 200kr, can be bought on the day for all but the biggest games. For schedule and ticket information, check the website.

ENTERTAINMENT AND EVENTS
Nightlife

A small frontage hides one of the most popular bars in the city, the deceptively large **Tromsø Jernbanestasjon** (Strandgata 33, tel. 77 61 23 48, noon-2am Mon.-Thurs. noon-3:30am Fri.-Sat., noon-midnight Sun.), which translates to Tromsø Railroad Station. The interior walls are packed with railroad memorabilia, including genuine conductors' uniforms, made all the more bizarre when you consider the closest railroad is a 249-kilometer (155-mile) drive away in Narvik. One of the pub's rooms contains an impressive collection of scarves donated by visiting soccer fans from all over the world. As the beer flows here all day and all night, you're sure to meet some of Tromsø's more colorful characters.

The city's other famous pub, **Rorbua** (Holmboe-brygga, tel. 77 75 90 86, noon-midnight Sun.-Tues., noon-1:30am Wed.-Sat.), is named after the distinctive red fishing cottages that dot the coastline all over northern Norway. Norwegians hold a special place in their hearts for this pub, which hosted a storytelling television show for 16 seasons (1987-2003). Today you'll meet a diverse range of locals, all of whom will claim they were featured on the show, while you make your way through the selection of local Mack beers on offer.

The city's oldest pub, founded in 1928, **Ølhallen** (Storgata 4, tel. 77 62 45 80, www.olhallen.no, 10am-7pm Mon.-Wed., 10am-midnight Thurs.-Sat.) hosts one of the country's largest selections of tap beers. Founder Lauritz Bredrup spent four years trying to convince the mostly teetotal council that his establishment would help to cut the high levels of drinking on the street before he was finally granted a license. The pub quickly became a regular fixture for the men of the city and is known to this day for its storytelling local regulars.

Festivals and Events

Considering its small size, Tromsø has an astonishing number of festivals throughout the year. While even the biggest cities in Norway fall into a slumber during the long winter nights, the people of Tromsø embrace the dark time and come out to play.

WINTER

One of the city's longest running events and one of the most important film festivals in northern Europe, **Tromsø International Film Festival** (TIFF, tel. 77 75 30 90, www.tiff.no) is an exciting time to be in the city. It's held over a week in mid-January, and the dark, freezing city streets come alive with outdoor screenings for hundreds of schoolchildren alongside more traditional cinema showings. There is a focus on supporting filmmakers from the Arctic region across the globe, not just in Norway.

Hot on the heels of TIFF comes the 10-day-long **Northern Lights Festival (Nordlysfestivalen)** (tel. 77 68 90 70, www.nordlysfestivalen.no), which usually straddles January and February. Since its origins as a classical music event in 1988, the festival has grown to include contemporary music and today presents a wide variety of artists from across many genres. Some concerts are free while others require individual tickets.

Often overlapping with the Northern Lights Festival, **Sami Week** (www.msm.no) centers around the Sami National Day on February 6 and is a celebration of the unique culture of Norway's indigenous people. Highlights for visitors include the reindeer race through the streets of Tromsø, held on the festival's final day, and the Norwegian Lasso Throwing Championships. Storytelling sessions and concerts, many of them free, take place throughout the week in various venues.

SUMMER AND FALL

At the height of July, the people of Tromsø gather on the beach at Telegrafbukta bay at the island's southern tip for the **Bukta Open Air Festival** (www.bukta.no), where rock and metal bands dominate the three-day bill. In the days around the festival there's an increase in the number of live concerts on offer in the city center, so keep an eye on the schedule if you're planning a trip to Tromsø during July.

This part of the world has a surprising reputation for electronic music (Bel Canto and Röyksopp have their roots here), and this is celebrated in the otherwise dreary fall season with the three-day multi-venue **Insomnia Festival** (www.insomniafestival.no), a showcase of emerging electronica and techno artists from across Norway and beyond held every October.

SHOPPING

If you miss the winter festival season, head for **Backbeat** (Vestregata 3, 11am-6pm Wed.-Fri., 11am-4pm Sat.) to get a taste of the Tromsø music scene. This tiny record store stocks many Norwegian favorites and doubles as a coffee shop.

It's impossible to wander past the gorgeous old-fashioned frontage of **Sweet Heart** (Storgata 71, tel. 77 69 54 80, www. sweetheart.no, 9am-6pm Mon.-Fri., 10am-5pm Sat., noon-6pm Sun.) without noticing it, and once you step inside, the sweet aroma makes it difficult to leave without a tempting treat. The intimate store stocks international candies and salty licorice, every Scandinavian's favorite. Boxed chocolates and jars of chocolate-coated licorice make excellent small gifts.

FOOD
Cafés and Light Bites

For the best coffee in town, pastries, and light lunches, the contemporary setting of **Risø** (Strandgata 32, tel. 41 66 45 16, www.risoe-mk.no, 7:30am-5pm Mon.-Fri., 9am-5pm Sat.) fits the bill. Light soups, topped focaccia bread, salads, and cinnamon buns mean it's hard to snag a table around the Norwegian lunchtime (11am-1pm), but takeout coffee is always available. It's worth waiting longer to have your choice of roast drip-brewed on the counter.

Run by the Student Society, **Driv** (Storgata 6, tel. 77 60 07 63, noon-9pm Mon.-Sat.) welcomes all comers to its lively informal café, which serves quick, filling food that's friendly to a student budget. Expect burgers, hot dogs, and nachos for about 120kr, or you can just pop in to play board games over a coffee in the afternoon. Note that Driv is closed from mid-June to mid-August when most students return home for the summer.

Traditional Scandinavian

Somewhat confusingly run by a local lady called Anne Brit, ★ **Emmas** (Kirkegata 8, tel. 77 63 77 30, www.emmasdrommekjokken.

no, bistro 11am-10pm Mon.-Fri., noon-10pm Sat., restaurant 6pm-10pm Mon.-Sat.) is actually two restaurant concepts in one. The downstairs bistro serves relatively inexpensive dishes through the day, with the fish au gratin and sashimi of salmon popular choices. For dinner, choose to eat in the informal bistro setting or from 6pm in the more elegant upstairs restaurant with more attentive service; the menu is the same. Expect to pay around 180kr for lunch while mains on the à la carte menu run 295-365kr. Make reservations for the restaurant (the bistro is drop-in).

Seafood

For the best fish in the city, head to **Fiskekompaniet** (Killengreens gate, tel. 77 68 76 00, www.fiskekompani.no, 4pm-10pm daily) for a contemporary dining experience of seasonal Nordic fish that manages to combine gourmet with simplicity. Expect to pay 335kr for the catch of the day, while something from the wide shellfish bar will set you back 185-235kr. Try the local king crab, dressed simply with a wedge of lemon and a sprig of dill. Ask for a window table for a view across the harbor.

Choose between a charming cottage interior or the airy terrace at **Arctandria** (Strandtorget 1, tel. 77 60 07 20, www.skarven. no, 4pm-11pm Mon.-Sat., 285-350kr), which specializes in dried and salted fish dishes such as *bacalao* along with fresh shellfish. The well-composed meals and delicate presentation are a good choice for foodies but overpriced for those who just want to sample a local fish dish. The small menu limits options for those who don't like seafood to reindeer, whale steak, and fresh pasta.

American

If you grow tired of the endless fish dishes in northern Norway, then head for a touch of 1930s Chicago at **Steakers** (Fredrik Langes gate 13, tel. 77 61 33 30, 3pm-11pm Mon.-Sat., 2pm-10pm Sun., 250-375kr), where T-bone, filet steaks, and ribs are given precedence over a smaller selection of seafood. The outgoing staff and a lively atmosphere are in stark contrast to many more traditional restaurants. As one of the larger restaurants in Tromsø, it's usually a good choice when you haven't booked a table and is great for groups. Modeled on a 1960s American burger bar, the walls of **Burgr** (Skippergata 6a, tel. 41 48 08 88, noon-9pm Sun.-Mon., noon-11pm Tues.-Sat.) are plastered with comic books and video game memorabilia. It gets crowded in the evenings, so head here in the afternoon to enjoy a burger and shake in relative peace. The Smokey Joe burger with cheddar, grilled sweet-and-sour peppers, and smoked paprika aioli is a local favorite.

Italian

Imagine an Italian pizza restaurant set inside a steampunk novel and you might have some idea what to expect at **Casa Inferno** (Vestregata 2, tel. 77 68 22 00, www.casainferno.no, 4pm-10pm Sun.-Tues., 4pm-11pm Wed.-Sat., 158-228kr), where a young crowd fills the intimate tables to enjoy the large pizzas baked in a wood-fired oven. A fast takeaway service is available.

ACCOMMODATIONS
Downtown
500-1,000KR

A rare genuine alternative to a hotel or hostel, the ★ **Tromsø Bed & Books** guesthouse (Strandvegen 45, tel. 77 02 98 00, www.bedandbooks.no, 650kr s, 950kr d) offers five comfortable rooms in a shared writer's home, complete with a well-stocked library that runs a take one, leave one concept. Rooms are small yet comfortable and decorated in a homey style, while the fully equipped kitchen and Scandinvian interior design of the shared lounge encourage you to mingle with the other guests. Free use of the laundry and free parking are some other notable perks. Four rooms are also available in the older, more basic fisher's home a few blocks away overlooking the water.

Since its opening in 2013, **Smarthotel Tromsø** (Vestregata 12, tel. 41 53 65 00, www.

smarthotel.no, 695kr d) has brought some desperately needed budget accommodations to central Tromsø. The 160 rooms are tight, but all feature luxury Scandinavian beds, a work desk, and a private bathroom with shower. The 24-hour reception doubles as a café serving light sandwiches, salads, and coffee throughout the day.

Located up a short but steep hill from the central area, the bed-and-breakfast accommodations offered by the **Ami Hotel** (Skolegata 24, tel. 77 62 10 00, www.amihotel.no) are hard to beat for value. The 17 functional rooms feel rather soulless, but given the building's high elevation, many have terrific views of the central area. Free hot drinks and a shared kitchen are available. Book directly with the hotel for the cheapest rates, which start from 600kr for a simple double and around 850kr for a triple, both with shared bathroom facilities. Rooms with en suite facilities come in around 150kr higher. Discounts are available for stays of two days or more.

Another downtown budget option is the **Viking Hotell** (Grønnegata 18, tel. 77 64 77 30, www.vikinghotell.no, 690kr s, 790kr d, 1,290kr t), which despite the aged exterior appearance has 25 light, modern rooms. Tea and coffee are always available in reception, along with a make-your-own-waffle bar in the early evening. For bigger groups, the hotel owns a selection of luxury self-catered apartments in the immediate neighborhood.

Just a few minutes' drive from the central area, **Tromsø Camping** (Elvestrandvegen 10, tel. 77 63 80 37, www.tromsocamping. no) is a collection of 53 cabins of varying standards plus plenty of space for camping. The most basic cabins start from 590kr and offer simple furniture with bunk beds, but no bathroom or running water. Sauna, shared bathroom facilities, and kitchen are available nearby. Larger cabins equipped to a much higher standard and that sleep up to four start from 1,195kr. Be aware of the high charges for bed linen (100kr per set) and the end-of-stay cleaning (150-450kr); if you're only staying for a single night the cost can really mount up. For a longer stay, the site has a wilderness feel yet with easy access to the city. Central Tromsø is a 35-minute walk over the bridge to the central area, or bus 20 or 24 is a 10-minute walk away.

1,000-1,500KR
The pickup point for many of the city's tours and activities, the **Scandic Ishavshotel** (Fredrik Langes gate 2, tel. 77 66 64 00, www. scandichotels.com, 1,249kr d) has a super convenient location on the quayside. Most of the 214 modern rooms overlook the water, as do the hotel's restaurant and bar. Superior rooms are split over two floors with a lounge that features a floor-to-ceiling wraparound window. A generous breakfast buffet including fresh smoothies, salmon, and pastries is available to all guests.

Contemporary luxury underpins the style of the quayside **The Edge** (Kaigata 6, tel. 77 66 84 00, www.choice.no, 1,285kr d), from the Clarion group. The glitzy high-rise exterior dominates the waterfront, while bright cushions add a splash of color to the modern grayscale decor of the rooms. The city's only sky bar is on the 11th floor, which provides an unbeatable view of the city at any time of year. Guests can use the adjacent gym at a charge of 50kr per visit.

Rental Camper Vans
Designed by backpackers for backpackers, the garish campervans from **Norwagon** (tel. 93 85 32 01, www.norwagon.com) are without doubt a unique way to get around and see northern Norway on a budget. The price you pay, 1,000-1,500kr per day depending on season, includes insurance, and there are no mileage limits, so you just pay for fuel, road tolls, and ferry charges with no further costs for accommodations. The vans sleep two and come complete with double sofa bed, kitchenette, sink, and gas stove. Free pickup and drop-off from the airport or central Tromsø are included in the price. To get your hands on one of these campers you'll need to book at least a few weeks in advance.

INFORMATION AND SERVICES
Visitor Information
Tromsø Tourist Information (Kirkegata 2, tel. 77 61 00 00, 9am-7pm Mon.-Fri., 10am-6pm Sat.-Sun.) is one of the better equipped tourist offices in the region, although it can be extremely busy when a cruise ship has just arrived at the adjacent port. City maps are available, along with an interesting range of local books and souvenirs.

Post Offices and Courier Services
Tromsø Post Office (Tromsø postkontor) (Sjøgata 7, 8am-6pm Mon.-Fri., 10am-3pm Sat.) is between Tromsø Cathedral and the Scandic Ishavshotel. Some supermarkets also offer basic postal services. Look for the Posten sign.

Urgent Health Care
For urgent medical care, call the **Tromsø Emergency Room (Legavakt i Tromsø)** (Sykehusvegen 30, tel. 77 62 80 00, 8am-4pm Mon.-Fri.) to be assigned a time to visit based on the seriousness of your condition. The clinic itself is 4.5 kilometers (2.8 miles) north of central Tromsø on the university campus. Take a cab from central Tromsø, or any bus marked for the university. In a life-threatening emergency, call for an ambulance on 113.

GETTING THERE
Car
Getting to Tromsø might look straightforward on a map, but it's a journey that shouldn't be undertaken without some serious research. From Oslo, the quickest way isn't the E6 highway that links the two cities because of slow speed limits and mountainous terrain on the route. The shortest alternative is the 1,738-kilometer (1,079-mile) drive along the Swedish highways E45 and E8. Factoring in overnight stops and points of interest, the drive will take a minimum of three days. Even from Trondheim, few locals undertake the 1,150-kilometer (715-mile) drive along the E6, preferring instead to fly.

Air

On the western side of Tromsøya island, **Tromsø Airport Langnes** (Flyplassvegen 31, tel. 67 03 46 20) is the biggest airport in northern Norway. Both SAS and Norwegian operate several daily flights to Oslo, while direct flights to Bergen, Trondheim, London, and many Mediterranean destinations are also available. Tromsø Airport is the northern hub for regional airline Widerøe, which operates flights to more than 15 local airports across the region, including Alta, Honningsvåg (for the North Cape), and Stokmarknes (for Lofoten).

To reach the city center, the **Airport Express Coach (Flybussen)** (tel. 48 28 05 00, www.flybussen.no) takes advantage of the island's extensive underground road system to reach the city center in around 10 minutes. The price is on the expensive side at 90kr one-way, 45kr children under 16, but a round-trip ticket offers a saving at 140kr.

Those without bulky luggage should buy a local bus ticket at the kiosk inside the terminal building. The stop for lines 40 and 42 (half-hourly) is directly across the car park from the terminal entrance. Although it takes only a few minutes more than the express coach, the fare is substantially cheaper at just 36kr (18kr child) when bought in advance from the kiosk. If you choose to pay on the bus, the fare is 50kr, with only Norwegian currency (no cards) accepted.

If you are not staying in the city center or you are traveling in a group, taxis are available outside the terminal building. Expect to pay at least 200kr for the 10-minute ride into central Tromsø, more in the evenings and at weekends.

Bus and Rail

Long-distance bus travel is not as extensive in northern Norway as it once was because of the popularity of flights and the motorcar. Today, **Troms Fylketrafikk** (tel. 77 78 87 77, www.tromskortet.no) operates three daily buses to/from Narvik, from where connections are available to Bodø, Lofoten, or by rail into Sweden. The travel time is around 4.5 hours and the fare is 340kr.

It is possible to travel between Oslo and Tromsø by public transit without flying, but be prepared for a journey spanning at least two days. Take the seven-hour **NSB** (www.nsb.no) train service from Oslo to Trondheim to connect to the service toward Fauske or Bodø, which can take up to an additional 10 hours. A daily bus leaves at 8:15am from Fauske or 7:15am from Bodø, arriving at Narvik at 1:30pm. From Narvik, take the bus to Tromsø. The bus journey from Fauske/Bodø to Tromsø will cost around 450kr.

Boat

Tromsø is a major stop for the **Hurtigruten** (tel. 81 03 00 00, www.hurtigruten.com) coastal express ferry that runs between Bergen and Kirkenes. Many northbound travelers from Bergen, Trondheim, or Lofoten choose to spend a few days in Tromsø after several days at sea. The northbound ferry continues on to Hammerfest and Honningsvåg, among other ports. The journey takes approximately 3.5 days from Bergen, 2 days from Trondheim, and 16 hours from Svolvær on Lofoten.

GETTING AROUND

Local Bus

Local buses from **Troms Fylketrafikk** (tel. 81 50 01 63, www.tromskortet.no) run within the city of Tromsø 6am-midnight weekdays, 8am-midnight on weekends. Most lines operate four departures every hour, with a higher frequency during peak weekday hours. Single tickets bought onboard a bus cost 50kr (cash only), whereas pre-bought tickets from the Tromsø Tourist Information office or the MIX or Narvesen convenience stores cost 37kr. Most city bus lines leave from Sjøgata, Fredrik Langes gate, or Havnegata.

Taxi

Tromsø Taxi (Heilovegen 22, tel. 77 60 30 00, www.tromso-taxi.no) is the main taxi company in the town and could be a good, albeit expensive, solution to visit sights such as the

Arctic Cathedral or the Tromsø Cable Car if you are in a group and pushed for time. Rates depend on distance, time taken, and the time of day, so ask your driver for an estimate if you are unsure. A typical eight-kilometer (five-mile) journey will cost 212-286kr.

Car Rental

Aside from the big brand car rental companies at the airport, **Rent-a-Wreck Tromsø Airport** (Flyplassveien 31, tel. 77 67 22 01, 8am-8pm Mon.-Fri.) offers great deals on well-maintained used cars. As a supplemental rate is charged per kilometer, the prices are even more economical if you intend to drive around the immediate area only.

If you decide to rent a car once you've already arrived in Tromsø or if you are arriving by ship, **Hertz** (Fridtjof Nansenplass 3, tel. 40 43 64 81, 8am-4pm Mon.-Fri., 10am-3pm Sat.-Sun.) and **Budget** (Strandskillet 5, tel. 77 50 02 70, 8am-4pm Mon.-Fri., 10am-1pm Sat.) both run city center locations in addition to their airport desks.

Alta

The biggest town in Finnmark county, Alta is the gateway to the vast Finnmarksvidda, which at 22,000 square kilometers (8,500 square miles) is Norway's largest mountain plateau. As it's a functional town made up of several villages dotted along the E6 highway, you could easily pass through Alta without a moment's thought.

There's not a great deal here to keep you occupied beyond a one-day stay, but if you are in the region a trip to the World Heritage Rock Art Centre is an absolute must. The town also serves as an obvious starting point to explore not only the Finnmarksvidda, but also the Sami communities of Kautokeino and Karasjok.

HISTORY

Up to the year 1500, the Sami were mainly fishermen and trappers, and they led a nomadic lifestyle around the migrations of the reindeer. Due to excessive hunting because of tax demands from Norway, Sweden, and Russia, the number of reindeer started to decrease, pushing many Sami to settle along the coastline. A small minority of the Sami then started to tame the reindeer and continued a nomadic existence to this day.

During the occupation of Norway during World War II, Alta was a key strategic location for German forces. The battleship *Tirpitz* was based in the Altafjord for two years and served as one of the main threats against convoys delivering supplies from Western Allies to the Soviet Union.

In the late 1970s and early 1980s, there was a series of protests in Finnmark against the construction of a hydroelectric power plant in the Alta River. Known as the Alta Controversy, it put the rights of the Sami as an indigenous people, with distinct rights over the lands in northern Norway, onto the national political agenda. For the first time since World War II, Norwegians were arrested and charged with violating laws against rioting. The central organizations for the Sami people discontinued all cooperation with the Norwegian government. Two Sami women even traveled to Rome to petition the pope.

The Supreme Court ruled in favor of the government in early 1982, at which point organized opposition to the power plant ceased, and the power plant was built. However, it is considered that, although the Sami lost the battle over this particular issue, they made important long-term gains. Revived Sami interest in their culture and history rolled back efforts of the Norwegian government's Norwegianization policy of assimilation. In 2005, the Finnmark Act was passed, placing much of the land in Finnmark under the

The High North

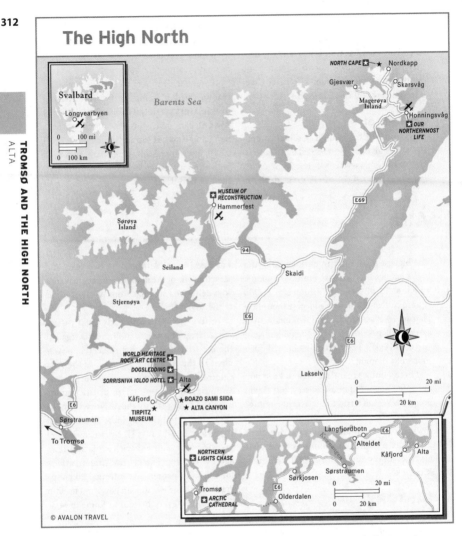

management of the Sami; it was a key milestone in the fight for Sami rights.

SIGHTS
★ World Heritage Rock Art Centre
(Verdensarvsenter for Bergkunst)

Step back into a time when people believed nature possessed a soul at the UNESCO-listed **World Heritage Rock Art Centre** (Altaveien 19, tel. 41 75 63 30, www.alta.

museum.no, 8am-8pm daily June-Aug., 110kr), a four-kilometer (2.5-mile) drive along the E6 southwest from downtown. Outside of summer, hours vary based on weather (typically 9am-3pm Mon.-Fri., 11am-4pm Sat.-Sun.). Made between 2,000 and 7,000 years ago, many of the thousands of carvings indicate that Alta was a religious meeting place in the Stone Age. Artwork depicts scenes from days long gone, specifically hunting and gathering, fishing, rituals, and social occasions.

Many of Alta's famous rock carvings are colored red for better visibility.

Tours are self-guided by way of a map booklet (included in the fee) or an audio guide that costs an additional 20kr. A 45-minute guided tour can be reserved in advance, but the additional 600kr cost means it's best suited only for those with a serious interest in archaeology. You can explore the site in advance using the Digital Rock Art Archive at www.altarockart.no.

The outdoor carvings are accessible during the snow-free season (typically May-Oct.) but the indoor exhibitions are open year-round. Children under 16 get significantly reduced admission (30kr summer, 20kr rest of year), while children under 7 go free throughout the year. The half-hourly city bus 140 run by **Snelandia** (www.snelandia.no) passes the museum in less than 10 minutes from downtown Alta.

Downtown

Downtown Alta is a relatively modern development, little more than a series of parking lots and shopping malls to service the regional population.

NORTHERN LIGHTS CATHEDRAL (Nordlyskatedralen)

An unusual building that at first glance looks more like a crematorium than a church, the **Northern Lights Cathedral** (Markedsgata 30, tel. 78 44 42 70, www.alta.kirken.no, 11am-3pm Mon.-Fri., 10am-3pm Sat.-Sun., 40kr) opened in 2013 after more than 40 years of struggle to get a new church for the parish. The curved titanium exterior and coiling 150-foot spire are designed to reflect the delicate movement of the ribbons of the northern lights, while the simple interior is complemented with beautiful northern lights-inspired lighting.

The 40kr entry fee is designed to restrict the number of visitors inside the church, preserving its primary use as a place of worship. On that note, services in Norwegian take place every Sunday at 11am. From the end of June to mid-August, the church is also open to visitors 6pm-9pm daily in addition to

A wooden pathway several miles long has been constructed to lead visitors around the otherwise boggy ground where the rock carvings are. The pathway is split into two loops; the shorter loop takes approximately 45 minutes, while you should allow 2-3 hours to fully explore the entire site. Many of the older carvings were painted red in the 1970s to make them more visible, which was normal practice at the time. However, this process is now being reversed to preserve the authenticity of the art, even though some of the carvings will be harder to see.

A permanent indoor exhibition tells the story of the inaccessible carvings such as the Kåfjord panel, consisting of around 1,500 carvings including many of bears, suggesting that the animal had a special ritual significance to the local people. The Kåfjord art is carved into basaltic tuff, a very soft rock that is at high risk of erosion, so the carvings are permanently covered and the exhibition at the museum is the only way to see what lies underneath.

Sami Culture in Northern Norway

The Sami people are a very visible characteristic of Finnmark county in northern Norway. The indigenous people are spread over the north of Norway, Sweden, Finland, and Russia. Many visitors are spellbound by the vivid costumes, outdoor lifestyle, and folk songs known as *joik,* compared by some to the traditional chanting of some Native American cultures.

Although visible in Alta, the Sami culture really comes to the forefront in **Kautokeino,** a small town of just a few thousand people 130 kilometers (80 miles) to the south. Here, around four in five people speak Sami as their primary language of everyday life, and throughout Finnmark county you will find road signs and place-names listed in Norwegian, Sami, and possibly a local dialect too. One in three Kautokeino residents work in the reindeer business, which has sustained the Sami people for years and continues to do so today.

The similarly sized village of **Karasjok,** 130 kilometers (80 miles) to the northeast of Kautokeino, is home to the Sami Parliament. Opened in 1989, the Parliament acts as an institution of cultural autonomy for the Sami people, through 39 representatives elected every four years. The responsibilities of the Parliament include the management of the national government's Sami Development Fund, the development of the Sami language, protection of cultural heritage sites, and development of Sami teaching aids.

A total of 14,000 people in Norway are registered in the Sami electoral register. To be eligible for inclusion, you must have at least one great-grandparent who speaks or spoke Sami and you must attest to "feeling" Sami. Set amid the pine forests of Karasjok, the Parliament building is clad in Siberian larch to blend in with its surroundings.

the regular opening hours. Waffles and coffee are usually available to buy inside for a nominal fee.

South of Alta
BOAZO SAMI SIIDA
Immediately adjacent to Alta River Camping, **Boazo Sami Siida** (Steinfossveien 5, tel. 41 47 34 05, www.sami-siida.no, 3pm-midnight daily mid-June to mid-Aug., 50kr) is a Sami reindeer farm, café, pub, and museum all rolled into one. Only open during the summer months because its owners return to Kautokeino with their reindeer during the winter, the museum is really just a traditional *lavvu* tent with various items of clothing, tools, and reindeer skins from Sami life. However, your host, Nils Henrik, will answer all your questions about the nomadic Sami lifestyle, reindeer herding, and the Sami culture, making the 50kr entrance fee a bargain. For a further 50kr you can feed a bag of moss to the reindeer.

Kåfjord
The tiny village of Kåfjord, named after the adjacent fjord, is 15 kilometers (nine miles) west of downtown Alta. The 19th-century wooden **Kåfjord Church (Kåfjord kirke)** seats 300 and was originally built in 1837 to serve the local English-owned Copper Works. Although not generally open to visitors, it's worth a brief stop to look at one of Finnmark's oldest buildings, as almost everything else was destroyed in World War II. The Raller family statue out front commemorates the many migrant workers that were drawn to work at the Copper Works from the north of Sweden and Finland.

TIRPITZ MUSEUM
A little awkward to find, the **Tirpitz Museum** (Crowesvei 3, tel. 92 09 23 70, www.tirpitz-museum.no, 10am-5pm daily mid-June to mid-Aug., 50kr) commemorates the history of the German battleship *Tirpitz,* which was anchored for nearly two years in the Kåfjord before being sunk outside Tromsø.

Park in the area signed off the main road but don't enter the building in front of you. Instead, take the small footbridge over the stream and you will find the small 19th-century timber building that houses the museum dead ahead. Inside, many photographs are displayed, along with original uniforms and personal effects from the crew. A collection of model ships and more general artifacts from the war are also on display. A short movie in English about the ship's history is played upon request.

On your return to Alta, pull over into the parking area on the lefthand side immediately after the impressive Kåfjord Bridge. Take a short stroll along the hill and you'll find a substantial crater left when a Tall Boy bomb missed its target during World War II.

Those with a deeper interest in history should consider a private tour of the Tirpitz Museum given on request by **North Adventure** (Bjørn Wirkolasvei 11, tel. 78 44 50 50, www.northadventure.no, 1,800kr). The guide will take you to both sites and point out many of the scars still visible from the war. The three-hour tour, which includes transport to/from Alta, is offered from June until the weather deteriorates and can start at any time from 9am to 11am.

SPORTS AND RECREATION
★ Dogsledding

There are few more exhilarating experiences throughout Norway than feeling the ice-cold air on your face as you speed through the bright white surroundings of the Finnmarksvidda mountain plateau. With the only sound you hear the rush of the wind and the barking of the Alaskan huskies, you will feel at one with nature in a way you never thought possible.

Alta is arguably the home of dogsledding as a sport, as it serves as the start and end point of the epic 1,000-kilometer (620-mile) **Finnmarksløpet** dogsled race around Finnmark county. For those who just want a taste of the activity, Alta's active dogsled community provides a range of excursions for all ages and experience levels. Trips last from a couple of hours through to multi-day safaris with overnight accommodations at a mountain cabin or in a Sami tent.

WINTER

The best of the tour operators is **Holmen Husky Lodge** (Holmen 48, tel. 78 43 66 45, www.holmenhusky.no). The most popular tour is the 15-kilometer (9.3-mile) trip into the

The dogs at Holmen Husky Lodge await the busy winter season.

forest and along the banks of the Alta river, where moose can frequently be spotted. The 2.5-hour tours run twice daily, at 10am and at 4pm (it's a more atmospheric ride through the twilight). On both tours, participants can drive the sled if they desire.

The 1,250kr fee (625kr for children under 12) includes transport to/from central Alta and thermal suits if required. The experience concludes with warm coffee served inside a traditional Sami *lavvo* tent, where one of the guides will talk about life on a husky farm and the importance of dogsledding to Alta. Day trips from 1,990kr per person are available on request February through April with a minimum group size of four, which can optionally include ice fishing. Weekend trips and multi-day adventures can also be arranged upon request.

SUMMER

Although dogsledding is very much a winter activity, **Holmen Husky Lodge** (Holmen 48, tel. 78 43 66 45, www.holmenhusky.no) also provides activities during the summer months. The dogs love to run, whatever the weather! From May onward, the same 2.5-hour 15-kilometer (9.3-mile) dogsled tour is available using wheeled carts. Each off-road cart is built for two and can be steered by yourself or a guide. Like the winter tour, the summer tour costs 1,250kr (625kr for children under 12) and runs twice daily at 10am and 4pm with transport provided from central Alta. Advance booking is required for all tours.

Alta Canyon

At 9.6 kilometers (six miles) long and up to 410 meters (1,350 feet) deep, Sautso, popularly known as **Alta Canyon,** is northern Europe's largest canyon. One of the lesser-known spots of the Finnmark region among tourists, the canyon is generally accessible from spring through fall and is a popular **hiking** spot for locals.

The most popular starting point for hikes to the canyon is the **Gargia Mountain**

Lodge (Gargia Fjellstue) (Gargiaveien 96, tel. 78 43 33 51, www.gargiafjellstue.no), 24 kilometers (15 miles) south on Route 30, the old post route between Alta and Kautokeino. From the lodge it is a 10-kilometer (six-mile) hike one-way along a marked trail through relatively easy albeit boggy conditions. The end of the hike is a spectacular viewpoint of the canyon more than 300 meters above the river. The trail takes 6-8 hours round-trip—it varies hugely depending on season, weather, and conditions. Take enough food and drink for a full day's hike, and waterproof footwear and outer layers are strongly recommended. The lodge runs occasional guided hikes; contact them in advance for details.

From December to April the lodge runs a twice-daily two-hour **Snowscooter Safari** in the surrounding area. Using this popular form of local transport, you'll be whisked through the silent darkness and perhaps even glimpse the northern lights. The price (1,995 pp, or 1,675kr pp if two share a vehicle) includes all safety equipment, a guide, a warm meal on return to the lodge, and a shuttle to/from central Alta on request.

From June to mid-August, **Sorrisniva** (Sorrisniva 20, tel. 78 43 33 78, www.sorrisniva.no) runs daily guided **riverboat tours** through the canyon. A 2.5-hour tour from Sorrisniva, 16 kilometers (10 miles) south of Alta, to the canyon's most dramatic section costs 1,495kr per person and includes coffee and waffles afterward. A shorter 1.5-hour tour to the river's first major rapids costs 895kr per person. Tours must be booked in advance and are subject to safe river flows.

Tours
SAMI EXPERIENCE

For a true insight into traditional Sami culture, **Sorrisniva** (Sorrisniva 20, tel. 78 43 33 78, www.sorrisniva.no) offers a dogsledding and **Sami Experience** combined with a chance to spot the northern lights from mid-December to mid-March. You will meet a local reindeer herd and even drive your own sled if desired. Afterward, the group gathers in a traditional Sami tent to warm up with hot coffee and homemade cake, listen to folk tales, and hear the unique *joik* style of folk song. Take the opportunity to ask your Sami host about their unique nomadic lifestyle and the challenges they face in the modern day. The 2.5-hour tour runs daily at 9pm, costing 1,895kr (945kr children under 12), and must be booked no later than the day before.

NORTHERN LIGHTS

Alta is ideal northern lights territory—as the town doesn't produce too much light pollution, you don't even need to leave it to catch a glimpse on a good night. To increase your chances, especially if the weather is cloudy above Alta, a northern lights tour from **Glød Explorer** (tel. 99 79 42 56, www.glodexplorer. no) is a good investment.

Participants (maximum eight) are picked up from central Alta at 7pm before being served soup and lent a thermal suit if required. The trip can last up to six hours because the guide studies the forecasts to find the very best spot for the lights. If your camera isn't of a high enough quality to capture the lights, the guide will ensure you have a photo to take home as a souvenir. Tours cost 1,500kr (1,050kr children under 12) and run daily from mid-September to mid-April.

BIKING

Glød Explorer (tel. 99 79 42 56, www.glod-explorer.no) offers tours by fat bike, which are mountain bikes with oversized tires suitable for winter cycling on the snowmobile tracks through the Alta Valley. During the 1.5-hour ride, the guide will stop at a rustic shelter to light a fire and share some coffee and snacks along with some stories from the local area.

A reasonable level of fitness is required for the tour, which runs at 10am daily throughout the year and costs 1,100kr pp, including transport to/from central Alta, and all equipment including a down-filled jacket. For those especially keen to ride on snow, the season runs approximately November through April. For a chance to see the northern lights, try

a headlamp-lit alternative at 10pm daily, for 100kr more.

Fishing

Fishing is among the region's most popular activities thanks to the Alta River, one of Norway's best rivers for salmon fishing. Heavily regulated, fishing in the river requires a permit for the short season that runs from June to August. Permits are notoriously difficult to get, even for the rock stars, royalty, and wealthy investors that flock to the region with the hope of landing a giant salmon or trout.

The **Alta Salmon Fishing Association (Alta Laksefiskeri Interessentskap)** (www.altalaks.no) holds all the rights to fishing in the Alta River and runs two separate licensing systems, one for locals and one for visitors. Despite the lottery costing 400kr to enter, only about 10 percent of applicants are successful and the money is nonrefundable. An open fishing period runs the first two weeks in June, a license for which costs 400kr for non-Norwegians.

Hiking

There are 10 popular hikes around Alta that many locals aim to complete every year.

One of the closest to the city starts from Saga School (Saga skole) on Aspemyra road, eight kilometers (five miles) east of downtown Alta. Look for the red markings of the **People's Trail (Folkestien)** that leads you toward Skogvannet lake. Some picnic benches mark the intersection of the red trail with a tougher blue trail that climbs 359 meters (1,177 feet) to the **Borras Vestre** peak. The latter trail is rocky and leads you over bare mountain, so care should be taken and appropriate footwear worn for the weather conditions. Even if you don't complete the full trail, there are many great locations for a picnic with views across the Altafjord and the valley. To complete the full four-kilometer (2.5-mile) round-trip will take approximately two hours, while the red trail is half that. At the starting point, there is an information board with a map and descriptions in English.

The other popular hike takes you up a former mining road to the 286-meter (938-foot) peak known as **Lille Raipas**. Following the marked blue trail, which can be muddy and steep in parts, takes you past the remains of a former copper mine and eventually to the Alta point of the Struve Geodetic Arc, a chain of measurements that led to the first accurate recording of the curvature of the earth. A bronze plaque commemorates the location at the top of the hike. The full four-kilometer (2.5-mile) round-trip should take less than two hours. The parking lot at the start of the trail is 10 kilometers (six miles) south of Alta via Route 93, the Raipasveien road, and the Stranddalen road. Look for the brown sign marked Struves Meridianbue.

Skiing

For downhill skiing, head to **Sarvesalta Alpinsenter** (Rafsbotnveien, tel. 90 69 97 41, www.altaski.no, 5pm-9pm Tues.-Wed., 11am-5pm Sat.-Sun.), a 20-kilometer (12-mile) drive northeast of Alta. The center is open dependent on snow conditions but usually from early December to early April. Runs range from a gentle 1,200-meter-long (3,937-foot-long) touring slope to a much more challenging 640-meter (2,100-foot) expert run. A children's slope is available, along with facilities for snowboarders.

A day pass costs 315kr (255kr evening) with a full set of equipment available to rent from 250kr (200kr evening). Snowboard equipment is also for rent from 300kr (230kr evening). A café serves basic salads, sandwiches, pizzas, and baked potatoes (100-130kr), along with plenty of warming coffee and hot chocolate.

ENTERTAINMENT AND EVENTS
Finnmarksløpet Dogsled Race
Alta serves as the start and end of the epic 1,000-kilometer (620-mile) **Finnmarksløpet** (www.finnmarkslopet.no) dogsled race that stretches all the way to the Russian border at Kirkenes.

Approximately 150 teams of 1,500 dogs take part in this annual event around the second week of March. The passionate competitors come primarily from northern Norway, Sweden, and Finland, but entries from as far afield as Spain and Italy are regularly accepted. There are no stages in this race; these energetic dogs just run and run, interrupted only by compulsory rest breaks. Teams typically take 5.5-7 days to complete the race.

The race is surprisingly spectator friendly. In addition to the excitement of the start and finish line in Alta, locals come out to cheer on the teams throughout the county. During the event, Alta is transformed into a festival arena showcasing local musical talent, colorful handicrafts, and piping hot bowls of *bidos*, the traditional reindeer stew of the Sami people.

FOOD AND ACCOMMODATIONS
★ Sorrisniva Igloo Hotel
From mid-December to March every year, the **Sorrisniva Igloo Hotel** (Sorrisniva 20, tel. 78 43 33 78, www.sorrisniva.no, 2,300kr pp) stands in beautiful surroundings on the banks of the Alta river like something out of a fairy tale. Located 16 kilometers (10 miles) south of Alta, the hotel is built from scratch from snow and ice every winter, which allows the owners to change theme every season.

A night in one of the approximately 30 rooms is a surprisingly comfortable experience thanks to the insulation provided by the rock-hard snow, natural reindeer hides, and sleeping bags, even though the beds themselves are made of ice! You'll need to bring woolen underwear, socks, gloves, and a hat. If for some reason you can't sleep, wander around the ice sculpture gallery, which of course changes every year.

Adjacent to the igloo is a modern service building, in which you'll find bathrooms, a restaurant, a luggage room, and a place to charge your electronics. There is also a comfortable lounge with a roaring fireplace, in case the cold gets too much for you! Although expensive, a night at the igloo hotel is a unique opportunity, a true fairy-tale experience that you are unlikely to forget. It's no surprise that weddings take place here throughout the winter. Breakfast and transfers to/from Alta are included in the room rates.

If you don't fancy the idea of staying overnight in sub-zero temperatures, consider visiting Sorrisniva on a **day visit**. For 200kr (50kr children aged 3-12), you gain access to the igloo hotel for a look around the sculpture gallery and ice chapel. Sorrisniva is also the base for several outdoor activities and excursions, which can be combined with a night in the igloo hotel.

Throughout the hotel's season, **Restaurant Laksestua** provides high-quality à la carte meals sourced from the fjord, mountains, and rivers around Alta. An on-site bakery and agreements with local farms ensure the restaurant is as local as it's possible to get. Main courses run 395kr, but the carefully constructed three-course (645kr) and four-course (695kr) menus offer the best tasting experience. Hours vary throughout the season so it's best to call ahead.

The hotel is 15 kilometers (9.3 miles) south of central Alta but is not accessible by public transit, so you'll need your own car or to take a taxi.

Central Alta

The best of the chain hotels in the central district is the **Thon Hotel Alta** (Labyrinten 6, tel. 78 49 40 00, www.thonhotels.no, 1,145kr d). The 146 modern rooms are decorated in vivid colors, a welcome change to the typical Scandinavian whites and grays, especially in the winter months. Many rooms have a view of the Northern Lights Cathedral. If you are staying for more than one night, ask for one of the rooms with a kitchenette to save money on eating out. Whichever room you pick, a substantial breakfast with hot options is served in the adjacent pizza restaurant.

On the opposite side of the shopping mall, **Du Verden Matbar** (Markedsgata 21, tel. 45 90 82 13, www.duverden.no, 10am-midnight Mon.-Sat., 1pm-10pm Sun.) is a cozy bistro with reindeer hides in place of cushions.

Seafood features heavily on the casual lunch menu, but salads, burgers, and pasta are also available. The evening tapas menu is a great choice for groups, while the shellfish plate (495kr pp) comprising mussels, shrimp, crab claws, and lobster is ideal for two to share. Expect to pay around 195kr for lunch, while evening mains run 200-350kr.

Take a closer look at ★ **Kokkejævel Hoftepluss** (AMFI Storsenter, tel. 95 73 06 79, www.hoftepluss.no, 79-179kr), which at first glance appears as a simple coffee bar in the shopping mall. It's actually a deli counter that serves a vast flavor-packed menu, including baguettes packed with reindeer meat and lingonberries, hamburgers with hand-cut potatoes, and a homemade salsa that goes well with everything. All dishes are served streetfood style on cardboard plates, so this is a great choice if you are just passing through Alta and looking for a quick lunch.

Bossekop (Western Alta)

Each of the 10 rooms in the distinctive redbrick **Altafjord Gjestegaard & Spa** (Bossekopveien 19, tel. 78 43 19 60, www.altafjordgs.no, 1,095kr) is a curious mix of traditional wooden floors and rugs with contemporary armchairs and accessories. Ask for a fjord-view room, which typically run an extra 200kr. If you can't snag one of those rooms, the communal terrace overlooks the Altafjord and is ideal for a chilled beer in the summer, while the bookable sauna will warm you up in the winter. The restaurant is known for its king crab and arctic char, while lighter meals and a range of drinks are available from the cozy in-house pub.

Consisting of restored farm buildings set in Alta's old town, the **Hotel Vica** (Fogdebakken 6, tel. 78 48 22 22, vica@thonhotels.no, 1,245kr d) presents rustic rooms with wooden floors and a mismatch of furniture. The breakfast buffet included with all room rates is the finest spread in Alta, with hot dishes alongside the usual Scandinavian fare of fresh fruit, cereal, and cold cuts. The à la carte restaurant is the best in Alta; however, it is also a popular stop for cruise visitors and organized trips, so if you see tour buses outside it's best to head elsewhere. The restaurant, which features local ingredients in almost every dish, is open daily (4pm-10pm Mon.-Thurs., 4pm-11pm Sat.-Sun., 1pm-10pm Sun.).

A cheaper alternative option for food just a 20-minute walk away from the Hotel Vica is **Alta Bistro** (Svaneveien 7, tel. 78 43 65 30, 179kr), which serves fish, pizzas, steaks, and cold cut buffets. Not many international visitors find their way here, so you are assured of an authentic local experience inside the wooden barn littered with antique furniture and decor. Opening hours vary throughout the year but are typically 1pm-midnight daily.

South of Alta

Several accommodations are available a few miles south of downtown Alta along Route 93.

In addition to the dogsled tours, the owners of the ★ **Holmen Husky Lodge** (Holmen 48, tel. 78 43 66 45, www.holmen-husky.no, 1,095kr d) have built a series of Sami-style lodgings across their farm. The tent-shaped wooden cabins are carpeted with electric blankets supplied to ensure comfort, while shared bathrooms are just seconds away. Each cabin features a floor-to-ceiling glass window giving guests a rare opportunity to spot the northern lights from inside. In the summer, the window can be covered from the outside to prevent the midnight sun from interrupting your sleep. For groups, the lodge offers a larger tipi that can sleep six in comfort, eight at a stretch, from 1,990kr a night.

Open-air hot tubs, a sauna, and a barbeque pit are all available for hire, while a comfortable lounge in the main building is available for all guests. A generous breakfast buffet is served in the morning for all overnight guests. Combine a stay at the lodge with a dogsledding experience for a true northern Norwegian adventure, year-round.

The cottages, rooms, and camping facilities at **Alta River Camping** (Steinfossveien 5, tel. 78 43 43 53, www.altarivercamping.com) are among the best in the area. Tent pitches along the river start from 120kr (150kr with a car), basic hostel-style private rooms with shared facilities run 500-600kr, while well-equipped two-bed cabins with bath start from 1,200kr. The campsite is popular with Finnish tourists and as such offers a Finnish-style outdoor sauna overlooking the river (50kr) and two shared grill houses.

INFORMATION AND SERVICES
Tourist Information

Located by the bus station in a drab part of central Alta, **Alta Tourist Information** (Bjørn Wirkolas vei 11, tel. 99 10 00 22, 9am-8pm daily June-Aug., 9am-4pm weekdays only rest of year) is the ideal place to check weather reports and collect maps for driving or hiking. General tourist information is also available at the Tirpitz Museum in Kåfjord.

Health Care

For urgent health care, call the **Alta Health Center (Alta Helsesenter)** (Markveien 29-33, tel. 78 45 55 55), which is staffed by a nurse around the clock. Doctors and nurses staff the center 8am-4pm weekdays. Outside these times, including weekends, assessment is stricter as only on-call doctors are available. For serious emergencies, call an ambulance on 113.

GETTING THERE
Car

Although Alta is only a 303-kilometer (188-mile) drive east of Tromsø, the drive takes at least six hours due to the mountainous terrain. Outside the summer season, snowdrifts and high winds can increase that time significantly. Although navigation systems may suggest you take Route 91 east of Tromsø, the road is interrupted by the irregular service of the Svensby-Breivikeidet and Olderdalen-Lyngseidet ferry crossings. Instead, head south for 70 kilometers (43.5 miles) along the E8 to Nordkjosbotn, where you can pick up the E6 eastward to Alta.

Air

Flying is the most popular way to reach the town as **Alta Airport (Alta lufthavn)** (Altagårdsskogen 32, tel. 67 03 49 00) is one of the few airports in Finnmark county to offer regular direct flights to Oslo. Both SAS and Norwegian operate daily flights to the capital, sometimes calling at Tromsø en route. Otherwise, Widerøe operates flights to the northern hub Tromsø and several other airports across Finnmark.

The small fjordside airport is just four kilometers (2.5 miles) east of central Alta, which takes approximately 50 minutes to walk. The local bus company **Snelandia** (www.snelandia.no) operates an airport bus to meet all arrivals. The short route calls at both central Alta and Bossekop (western Alta) within 10 minutes and costs 50kr. Alternatively, taxis are always on hand to meet arriving passengers, although the short ride will cost at least 130kr, more in the evening and on weekends.

Bus

Alta can be reached by bus on route 150 from Tromsø for a fare of 500kr (250kr children and seniors). The daily service operated by **Troms Fylketrafikk** (www.tromskortet.no) leaves Tromsø (Prostneset, by the tourist information office) at 4pm and arrives at Alta Bus Station at 10:20pm. From Hammerfest, route 061 leaves the bus terminal at 11:20am (Mon.-Fri.) or 2pm (Sun.) and takes approximately 2.5 hours to reach Alta Bus Station. The fare is 275kr.

GETTING AROUND
Local Bus

As the city is spread out and most attractions are outside the modern downtown complex, it's useful to locate **Alta Bus Station** opposite the entrance to the Thon Hotel on Labyrinten in downtown Alta. Bus 140, known as the City Bus (ByBuss), links downtown Alta to the Alta Museum. The City Bus runs 6am-11pm Monday-Friday, 9am-11pm Saturday-Sunday, and the fare is 50kr. Operators for the public bus services vary but all the information is gathered under the **Snelandia** (www.snelandia.no) brand.

Taxi

Alta Taxi (tel. 78 43 38 79, www.altataxi.no) is the local taxi service.

Car Rental

Avis, Budget, Europcar, Hertz, and Sixt all operate car rental desks at the airport but are usually closed on weekends, and walk-up rentals are not always available. Because of the remote location, prices are higher than in the rest of Norway, but two cheaper options are available elsewhere in Alta.

The office of locally owned **Alta Bilutleie** (Betongveien 4, tel. 90 82 48 93, www.altabilutleie.no) is a 10-minute walk from the airport, and although **Rent-a-Wreck Alta** (Markveien 53, tel. 78 43 40 88, 8am-4pm Mon.-Fri.) is based in central Alta, they will deliver and collect the car out of hours to a location just five minutes from the terminal building. The latter rents out used cars of reasonable quality, and the overall rental cost can be as little as one-third of the major car rental brands, but be wary of renting such a vehicle during the frigid winter months.

Hammerfest

On arrival at Hammerfest you can't miss the references to the world's northernmost city, but is that really true? It comes down to the definition of a city in the Norwegian language. Originally only places with a population of above 5,000 could be defined as a city, but since that restriction was removed, the fishing village of Honningsvåg has contested the claim.

The city's mascot is a polar bear, which at first thought seems strange given the predators live an hour and a half's flight away across the ocean on the Svalbard archipelago. However, Hammerfest's prosperity in times gone by was based on hunting marine mammals in the Arctic Ocean, and expeditions to Svalbard were commonplace to hunt for seal, walrus, and polar bear, back in the days when the polar ice came much farther south.

One animal that does roam the streets of Hammerfest is the reindeer. During the summer, reindeer herds can be quite the hazard to drivers on approach to Hammerfest as they wander into the roads with little regard for the danger. Despite measures taken by the local council, the animals do on occasion breach the city limits, so care should be taken even when driving around Hammerfest itself.

HISTORY

The history of Hammerfest, one of northern Norway's oldest towns, is littered with tragedy. The city received its first doctor in 1792, but within a couple of decades the population had been ravaged by plague and the Napoleonic wars. In 1890, two-thirds of the town was destroyed by fire, but just one year later electric streetlighting was introduced—the first Norwegian city to get the technology—as part of the rebuilding efforts. It was around this time that the town began to attract wealthy tourists from the United Kingdom and western Europe keen to experience the midnight sun. Kaiser Wilhelm of Germany was an annual visitor in the years leading up to World War I.

Because of its ice-free harbor, Hammerfest was an important naval base throughout the German occupation of Norway in World War II. Parts of the town suffered bomb damage,

Summer days in Hammerfest can be surprisingly warm.

but the most damage was done by German forces themselves at the end of the war. The retreating army systematically burned almost every building in Hammerfest—and across Finnmark county—and forcibly evacuated all residents. The reconstruction efforts are the focus of the Museum of Reconstruction.

The town's fortunes were transformed in 2007 when the Snøhvit natural gas processing plant opened on the island of Melkøya, which is linked to the city by a private underground tunnel. The biggest industrial development in northern Norway, the plant has caused an increase in the number of hotels, restaurant, and shops opening in recent years to serve the increased population.

SIGHTS

★ Museum of Reconstruction
(Gjenreisningsmuseet)

The **Museum of Reconstruction for Finnmark and North Troms** (Kirkegata 21, tel. 78 40 29 30, www.gjenreisningsmuseet.no, 10am-4pm daily June to mid-Aug., shorter hours rest of year, 80kr) commemorates the destruction of the town at the end of World War II through a range of exhibitions, including original film, photographs, and items from the town. Many people buried their valuable or sentimental items in the ground before fleeing, and some of those items are today on display in the museum.

One object prominently displayed in the reception area is the piano of the Feddersen family. Left behind in the family home during the evacuation, the piano was assumed destroyed, but in fact the German army had commandeered it. It was rediscovered years later with a German reference number and returned to the family, who gifted it to the museum.

The exhibition also covers the post-war years, the reconstruction of the town using simple single-dwelling properties, and a gradual increase in the standards of furnishing and living. A walk up to the top of the museum's tower (an elevator is available) is essential to see some of the examples of the reconstruction that still stand today.

As international interest in the museum grows, an increasing number of exhibits are explained in English, and information leaflets in English, German, and Spanish can be borrowed for the remainder. At the back of the museum is a tiny series of rooms chronicling the history of telecommunications in Norway. A small gift shop styled as a 1950s convenience store and a café serving waffles and hot drinks are open during the museum opening hours.

Royal and Ancient Polar Bear Society
(Isbjørnklubben)

Founded in 1963 by a couple of enterprising locals, there is nothing royal nor ancient about the **Royal and Ancient Polar Bear Society** (Havnegata 3, tel. 78 41 31 00, 9am-4pm Mon.-Fri., 10am-2pm Sat.-Sun.). For 200kr, you can join and claim a member's certificate and pin badge. While membership doesn't bring you any real benefits, it does prove you visited this northern outpost, as membership can only be obtained in person, so there is a certain novelty value. If you're wisely not interested in this tourist trap, it's still worth a visit because the society's small museum about Hammerfest culture is free, and it also happens to be co-located with the Hammerfest Tourist Information office, just steps from the Hurtigruten ferry quay.

Hammerfest Church
(Hammerfest kirke)

The triangular design of **Hammerfest Church** (Kirkegata 21, 9am-3pm Mon.-Fri., free) is reminiscent of the Arctic Cathedral in Tromsø, but this landmark of the town is actually inspired by the fish-drying racks found throughout the north of Norway. Built in 1961, the stone and concrete building seats more than 500 people and is the main parish church for the municipality. The eastern wall features a beautiful 15-piece stained-glass window and, combined with the brightly colored pews, helps to create a surprisingly warm interior, in contrast to the cold concrete of the building itself. The wood carvings on the organ gallery detail the town's previous churches, which have been destroyed over the years.

Meridian Monument
(Meridianstøtten)

Hammerfest marks the northernmost point of the Struve Geodetic Arc, a chain of 19th-century survey triangulations stretching down to the Black Sea that yielded the first accurate measurement of a meridian. Modern computerized measurement techniques have shown the original measurement to be just a few hundred feet out. The chain is today a UNESCO World Heritage listed site, so the northernmost point is marked by the Meridian Monument (Meridiangata, free), an obelisk and information plaque.

The monument isn't the most pleasant place to visit as it's sited in the middle of an industrial park on the opposite side of the bay, and any nice view of the central area is obscured by anonymous factory buildings and yards. On a sunny day, the monument is a pleasant 30-minute stroll around the bay from the central area. If the weather isn't so good, ask at the tourist office for details of the city bus service (route 130) that passes close by every 15-30 minutes. The journey takes just five minutes.

SPORTS AND RECREATION
Hiking

The hills around Hammerfest are ideal for hikers of all ages and ability. Start out with Gammelveien, literally The Old Road, a gravel path that circles the town and surrounding hills and lakes. The path is well maintained, and is signed with information boards and maps at regular intervals. The path incorporates SikkSakk-veien, a path that zigzags its way up the sheer cliff that towers over downtown. Despite the height of the cliff,

Hammerfest Church

the path is a gentler slope than you may expect, and the views from the top are spectacular. This section is, however, closed during the winter. The path begins from Salsgata, just a five-minute walk from the tourist information office.

Sørøya island is a popular hiking destination, especially in the summer when the long sandy beaches are the ideal place to wild camp under the midnight sun. A common starting point is the small village of Akkarfjord on Sørøya, which can be reached via a boat from Hammerfest. From here you can hike to the stone navigation marker Kjøttvik beacon, atop the 319-meter (1,046-foot) Mount Kjøttvikfjellet on the north side of the island. The full round-trip from Akkarfjord is 18.2 kilometers (11.3 miles), so it's wise to plan to stay overnight in one of the 12 beds at Akkarfjord Hostel (tel. 78 41 91 34, 100kr), located at the village school.

The express boat from Hammerfest to Akkarfjord runs just twice daily and the timetable varies by season, so check ahead with the tourist information office or directly with operator **Snelandia** (www.177finnmark.no). A one-way ticket for the 25-minute crossing costs 147kr, and you'll likely be sharing the ride with goods and supplies destined for the 100 people who live permanently on the island. As the boat returns immediately to Hammerfest, it's possible to make a round-trip without setting foot on Sørøya.

An alternative hiking tour closer to Hammerfest starts just behind the city's airport in the district known as Prærien. A 2.5-hour round-trip along a marked trail takes you to the summit of **Storfjellet,** near the transmission tower, from where you can get clear views of the city, Sørøya island, and Melkøya island. The trail is suited to inexperienced hikers, although if you are starting from central Hammerfest you should allow around four hours for the full round-trip.

Biking

The tourist information office has electric cycles for hire, ideal to reach the Meridian Monument or just explore the downtown area. The power-assisted bikes allow you to easily explore the Gammelveien paths around the town and reach the viewpoints at the top of the various hills that surround the bay. Rental costs from 150kr for an hour or 360kr for a 24-hour period, and airport pickup can be arranged in advance.

Tours

If your time in Hammerfest is limited or you are without your own transport, consider the daily **Sightseeing Tour** that starts by the tourist information office at 10:45am. The English-speaking tour guide will describe life in the Arctic as you visit the Meridian Monument and various viewpoints around the town. Tickets for the 75-minute minibus tour cost 350kr (175kr children under 12) and should be booked in advance with the tourist information office.

ENTERTAINMENT AND EVENTS

The centerpiece of the modern board-walk, the **Arctic Cultural Center (Arktisk kultursenter)** (Strandgata 30, tel. 78 40 20 99, www.aks.no) is the cultural meeting place for Hammerfest and the surrounding region. The vivid red wooden panels and glass skin of the modern building have created a new architectural icon for the city. Inside, a cinema shows domestic and international movies daily on two screens, with a varied program

Reindeer are more common than cars on the roads around Hammerfest.

of theatrical performances and other events throughout the year.

Held over a week in mid-July, the annual **Hammerfestdagan** (www.hammerfestdagan.no) brings together the city's sports clubs, cultural venues, and businesses for a series of open days, activities, exhibitions, and live entertainment. Centered around a large marquee in the town square, the varied program changes each year but usually includes stand-up comedy, live music, and talks from the local history group. Much of the festival is free, although there is generally a charge for the live music.

FOOD AND ACCOMMODATIONS

The large varied menu along with the enthusiastic team of young staff keeps **Qa Spiseri** (Sjøgata 8, tel. 97 07 00 10, 10am-midnight Mon.-Fri., 11am-1am Sat., 129-249kr) top of the list in Hammerfest. Choose between a table on the large outdoor terrace overlooking the water or inside in contemporary surroundings with a coffee shop vibe. Best value is the large bowl of creamy fish soup served with chunky bread and butter, while the pizzas are big enough to share. A lighter menu including open-faced sandwiches and cakes is available earlier in the day.

The newest addition to Hammerfest's waterfront, the fish counter at **Havørna** (Strandgata 16, tel. 95 93 00 55, www.havorna.com, 1pm-10pm Mon.-Sat., 189kr) does a brisk trade in fresh shrimp throughout the day, but hidden to the side is a superb small restaurant. The menu changes dependent on the catch of the day, so you can be sure you're eating the freshest possible fish. Popular dishes include fish burgers and a large bowl of shrimp served with bread and butter to share on the outside seating.

Even the single rooms at the waterside **Scandic Hammerfest** (Sørøygata 15, tel. 78 42 57 00, hammerfest@scandichotels.com, 1,049kr s, 1,249kr d) are spacious, while for an extra 250kr the superior rooms offer even more space, brighter furnishings,

and a sea view. The hotel's intimate restaurant **Skansen** has an open kitchen, roaring fireplace, and floor-to-ceiling windows with sea views, but with mains at around 289kr the prices are easily the most expensive in the city.

If price is your primary concern, the 120-square-foot rooms at the **Smarthotel Hammerfest** (Strandgata 32, tel. 41 53 65 00, 750kr s, 850kr d) are your best solution. There's very little space for anything beyond a suitcase, but all rooms are clean and minimalist with a work desk, flat-screen TV, and small bathroom with shower. There are 21 larger long-stay rooms are available from 1,500kr with a comfortable lounge area, workstation, and a kitchenette. No cash is accepted at the hotel, so a debit/credit card is essential. A Scandinavian breakfast buffet is served on the ground floor in the quayside **Du Verden** restaurant, which also offers an à la carte menu for lunch and dinner.

There are two ways to reach **Hotell Skytterhuset** (Skytterveien 24, tel. 78 42 20 10, www.skytterhuset.no), perched just behind the cliff that overlooks the city. You can take a six- or seven-minute drive from the central area, or scramble up the zigzag path from the city. The 145 basic rooms are dominated by wood and old-fashioned decor, but unfortunately the curtains aren't thick enough to keep out the summer's midnight sun, so an eye mask is strongly recommended. The in-house restaurant provides a daily serve-yourself menu consisting of two main courses (meat and fish) with vegetables and a salad bar. The environment feels more like an office canteen than a hotel restaurant, but at 155kr for unlimited food it's great value.

Another budget option above the town is **Storvannet Camping** (Storvannsveien 103, tel. 78 41 10 10, storvannet@yahoo.no). The city's most popular campsite opens from mid-May to mid-September, weather permitting. The quiet campsite is situated on the banks of the Storvannet lake, 1.6 kilometers (one mile) southeast of central Hammerfest, and is a good base for hiking. Such campsites are in short supply around Hammerfest, so to secure one of the seven small cabins (450kr) you'll need to call at least a week in advance. Pitches for tents and motorhomes run 100-160kr with basic shared shower facilities available.

INFORMATION AND SERVICES
Tourist Information

Just steps from the Hurtigruten ferry terminal, **Hammerfest Tourist Information** (Hamnegata 3, tel. 78 41 31 00, 9am-4pm Mon.-Fri., 10am-2pm Sat.-Sun.) provides a wealth of information on activities in the local area and hiking trails, offers weather advice, and even rents electric cycles. The small museum of the Royal and Ancient Polar Bear Society is co-located here, and there is a small shop with a great selection of local produce and gifts.

Health Care

For urgent treatment, contact the **Hammerfest Medical Center (Hammerfest legesenter)** (Strandgata 52, tel. 78 40 00 55, 8am-3pm Mon.-Fri.). For treatment after hours, call 78 41 20 00, or 113 in emergencies. The **Apotek1 Pharmacy** (Strandgata 8, tel. 78 40 74 60, 8:30am-5pm Mon.-Fri., 10am-2pm Sat.) is well stocked with basic medical supplies.

GETTING THERE
Car

A worthy detour for road trippers on their way to the North Cape, Hammerfest is 55 kilometers (34 miles) west along Route 94 from the junction with the main E6 highway at Skaidi. Allow around 2.5 hours for the 141-kilometer (87.5-mile) drive from Alta, while about 3.5 hours are needed to reach the North Cape, 206 kilometers (128 miles) away.

Air

The small **Hammerfest Airport (Hammer-** **fest lufthavn)** (Finnmarksveien, tel. 67 03 50 50, www.avinor.no) is across the bay, 2.5 kilometers (1.5 miles) from the central area. Regional airline Widerøe is the only airline providing regular service to the airport, with several departures a day to and from northern Norway's airport hub at Tromsø. Minor regional airports can also be reached, including Honningsvåg (for the North Cape) and Kirkenes.

Downtown Hammerfest is a 45-minute mostly downhill walk from the airport. Alternatively, the short ride with **Hammerfest Taxi** (tel. 78 41 12 34) will cost from 130kr.

Bus

There is a direct public bus connection from Alta and Honningsvåg. Route 061 operated by **Boreal Transport** leaves Alta with 1-2 daily departures to Hammerfest, but other connections are available by changing buses at Skaidi. Check www.177finnmark.no for timetables and price information, as they vary by season. The bus station in Hammerfest is immediately outside the tourist information office, which can help with information.

Boat

The **Hurtigruten** (tel. 77 59 71 81, www. hurtigruten.com) coastal express ferry calls at Hammerfest twice every morning, once southbound and once northbound. The overnight journey from Tromsø takes around 10 hours, and tickets are available from 1,100kr with advance booking.

GETTING AROUND
Car Rental

Avis (tel. 78 40 78 28, hammerfest@avis. no), **Europcar** (tel. 78 42 95 49, hammerfest@europcar.no), and **Hertz** (tel. 90 06 18 22, hammerfest@hertz.no) all operate from Hammerfest Airport, but reservations should be made well in advance.

Magerøya and the North Cape

The ultimate aim of many Arctic road trippers is to make it to the North Cape at the top of Magerøya island. Although it is not actually the northernmost point of Europe, this iconic destination still attracts hundreds of thousands of visitors every year, as the view from the plateau on a clear day really does feel like you are standing on the edge of the world.

Yet the rest of the island offers stunning views and an isolation that you won't find at the North Cape itself given its popularity. Whether you choose to visit the expensive plateau depends on your own desires. If your sole wish is to see the midnight sun, consider whether you would prefer a short hike to the top of a hill where you can enjoy the near-sunset in total isolation, while a visit to the North Cape Museum in Honningsvåg will ensure you don't miss the context or the history of the area.

Magerøya Island itself is a barren, lonely place lacking even a single tree, yet the landscape can still be as beautiful as anything else you'll find in Norway, with rolling hills, mountain lakes, and intriguing rock formations along with a rich population of diverse birdlife.

Facilities this far north are few and far between, so it's wise to plan your visit around the village of Honningsvåg, where you'll find hotels, restaurants, a supermarket, and perhaps most importantly, a gas station.

★ NORTH CAPE
(Nordkapp)

The North Cape may not actually be Europe's northernmost point, but that doesn't stop hundreds of thousands of visitors from descending on the 307-meter (1,007-foot) cliff every summer. Named by an English sailor in the 16th century who discovered it when searching for the northeast passage, the North Cape is the point where the Norwegian Sea meets the Barents Sea.

Given its location at over 71 degrees north latitude, weather can be highly unpredictable, and thick fog can often obscure the otherwise beautiful view across open ocean and make driving the E69 highway difficult and dangerous. For these reasons, planning ahead is essential on any visit to the cape.

A controversial 260kr admission charge is required to drive onto the plateau, with extra charges for additional passengers. Because of this, budget travelers often choose to hitchhike from Honningsvåg or the junction at Skarsvåg and jump out a few hundred feet before the toll booth so they can just walk on through.

The charge is justified in part by the modern visitor center (11am-1am daily mid-May to mid-Aug., 11am-3pm daily mid-Aug. to mid-May), home to a panoramic movie of the weather conditions and birdlife at the North Cape year-round, a gallery, a small chapel, and most importantly in this part of the world, clean public restrooms. The center also contains what has to be one of Norway's largest gift shops, with a wide range of products. You can even send postcards with a Nordkapp postmark from the in-house postbox. Numerous cafés and an à la carte restaurant (6pm-10:30pm daily June-Aug.) are available, but prices are 30 percent higher than anywhere else in northern Norway, so bringing your own picnic and water bottles is a wise move. On the other side of the building is a large viewing platform, where you can watch the midnight sun and enjoy the view of the open ocean. Standing front and center on the platform is the iconic globe sculpture, perfect for that must-have selfie to prove you were here.

The ticket is also valid for 24 hours, meaning a visit in daytime and at midnight is possible. Many people driving large vehicles, campervans, and RVs take advantage of the large parking lot and camp here. There is no

Svalbard, Norway's Arctic Outpost

polar bear on Svalbard

Although you will have read this many times before, Svalbard really is like nowhere else on earth. The landscape is formed by glaciers providing a natural habitat for reindeer, walruses, seals, and even the awe-inspiring polar bear. A few thousand people, mainly miners, researchers, students, and tourism workers, live on Svalbard year-round. Almost everyone lives in **Longyearbyen,** the closest thing to a city on Svalbard with a population of around 2,000. The settlement has a couple of hotels, a general store, and even a couple of pubs. Longyearbyen lies at over 78 degrees north latitude, farther north than many of Canada's Queen Elizabeth Islands. As the crow flies, it is 2,050 kilometers (1,274 miles) north of Norway's capital, Oslo.

Most visitors stop a night or two in Longyearbyen before boating around the islands in search of **polar bears** or riding a snow scooter over the pristine landscape. The midnight sun and polar nights are more extreme at this latitude, so there is a real danger from polar bears during the pitch-black winter months. In fact, you're not permitted to leave the settlement without a rifle. Most people prefer to visit around Easter, as there is still plenty of snow yet the light days have returned, while summers are usually snow-free and surprisingly mild.

Blanketed in permafrost, Svalbard will play a critical role in any post-apocalyptic scenario in which we find ourselves. The main island, **Spitsbergen,** is home to the **Global Seed Vault,** which is secure storage for almost one million types of plant and vegetable seeds from across the planet—the idea being in the event of an apocalyptic global crisis, the human race will have the seeds of life to start over again.

Although Norway has sovereignty over the Svalbard archipelago thanks to the 1920 **Svalbard Treaty** (signed by, among others, the United States, Japan, and Great Britain), other countries have rights to engage in commercial activity. In recent years only Norway and Russia have run commercial mining operations. Under the terms of the treaty, the entire archipelago is a visa-free zone. In practice, however, all travelers must pass through mainland Norway on their way to the islands.

If you are interested in visiting this Arctic archipelago, contact **Svalbard Tourist Information** (tel. 79 02 55 50, www.visitsvalbard.com) for information and advice.

formal campsite, although many people pitch their tents on the grassy areas set back from the cliff.

It's possible to see the midnight sun at the North Cape from mid-May to the end of July, but it can get exceptionally busy around midnight with an incredible number of visitors bused in from cruise ships moored at Honningsvåg. The sun will be at its lowest point around 20 minutes after midnight, creating a stunning golden glow across the plateau.

Transport and Tours

If you are without your own transport, the **North Cape Express** (tel. 78 47 58 40, www. nordkapp.no, 590kr, 295kr children under 16) is a round-trip bus to the plateau from the Visit Nordcapp tourist information center in Honningsvåg. Several departures throughout the day allow you to return on a later departure if you prefer a longer stay at the North Cape. The one-way drive takes around 45 minutes. Trips should be booked in advance, especially if you intend to take a return bus after midnight.

On select days throughout the summer and weather permitting, seeing the North Cape by helicopter with an English-speaking guide from **Helitours** (Honningsvåg Airport, tel. 47 67 71 23, www.helitours.no) is a one-of-a-kind experience. The 20-minute flight from Honningsvåg circles the iconic cliff but also allows you to see the cliff in context with the rest of Magerøya island, including the Gjesværstappan bird cliffs. Optionally, you can land and spend some time at the visitor center. Several daily departures are offered on selected days throughout the summer months, and prices start at 2,250kr, or 1,950kr for children under 12. Transfer to and from the airport from central Honningsvåg is included.

A word of warning to those traveling outside the summer months: The E69 highway north of Honningsvåg and therefore the North Cape can only be accessed via a controlled convoy that runs only a few times per day, weather permitting. With its exposed

The iconic globe sculpture at the North Cape is a popular spot for selfies.

location and lack of trees, the entire island of Magerøya is a windy, snowy, icy hazard in the winter months. Think very carefully before booking an independent winter trip!

HONNINGSVÅG

Rivaling Hammerfest for the title of mainland Norway's northernmost city, Honningsvåg is a great choice to stop overnight on your way to or from the North Cape. Despite its small size (a population of just 2,000), the settlement has everything a traveler needs, including several food and accommodation options, supermarkets, a museum, an ice bar, and a sizable gift shop. It's also the base for tours to the North Cape and, for the more adventurous, king crab fishing and wintertime all-terrain vehicle tours.

The couple of streets that make up the city center get swamped with people several times per day as up to four mammoth cruise ships dock at once. Most visitors head straight for the fleet of buses and off to the North Cape, so it's worth spending some time exploring the otherwise peaceful streets. The locals are super friendly, reliant on the tourist industry as they are.

Sights
ARTICO ICE BAR

Run by Spanish expats José Mijares and Gloria Pamplona, the **Artico Ice Bar** (Sjøgata 1a, tel. 78 47 15 00, www.articoicebar.com) provides a winter arctic experience to those who visit during the summer. Unlike some ice bars that use industrially frozen water, the owners use specialist equipment to cut 800-kilogram (1,800-pound) blocks of ice from the region's lakes in the spring. The blocks are transported to the frozen warehouse in Honningsvåg before being cut and sculpted to create Finnmark's coolest bar, with the help of reindeer hides, hundreds of LED lights, and a screen displaying images and sounds of a Magerøya winter.

While not as visually impressive as the ice sculpture gallery in Svolvær on the Lofoten islands, a drink at Artico is nevertheless a unique opportunity to feel the chill of an Arctic winter and learn more about the tough lifestyle at 71 degrees north. Opening hours vary throughout the season (May-Sept.) but are typically 10am-10pm daily, with hours adjusted to meet cruise ship arrivals. The 139kr entry fee (40kr children under 12) includes a thermal suit and two non-alcoholic drinks. The associated gift shop is worth a look, as it contains a wide range of traditional Scandinavian Christmas decorations, including wooden figurines and snow globes.

NORTH CAPE MUSEUM
(Nordkappmuseet)

Rather than a museum about the North Cape itself, the **North Cape Museum** (Holmen 1, tel. 78 47 72 00, 10am-4pm daily mid-June to mid-Aug., 50kr) chronicles the history of Magerøya island with a special focus on the culture of the island and its fisheries. The ground floor is home to temporary exhibitions of contemporary art from local Honningsvåg artists. The permanent exhibits

are all described in English; while this may not be the case for the temporary exhibitions, the friendly staff can fill in the gaps.

Sports and Recreation
TOURS

Based in the center of Honningsvåg, **Destinasjon 71 Nord** (tel. 47 28 93 20, www.71-nord.no) is an adventure tour company that knows Magerøya inside out and operates year-round. In the summer, you can take a **King Crab Safari** (noon daily mid-May to Sept., 1,490kr, 745kr children under 12) on a raft into the Sarnesfjord. The three-hour trip ends with the experience of cooking and eating the freshly caught king crabs in a Sami-style camp.

During the winter (Nov.-Apr. depending on weather), a guide leads a two-hour tour by **All-Terrain Vehicle** (995kr), for which a driving license is required. The tour group starts in Honningsvåg before making its way up the nearby mountain for excellent views of the ocean, fjord, and snow-covered island. Alternatively, you can explore the wilderness on foot with a **Snowshoe Safari** (595kr), which rewards you for the tough workout with similar outstanding views. The two-hour snowshoe tour ends with coffee brewed over an open fire in a Sami-style camp.

Entertainment and Events
★ OUR NORTHERNMOST LIFE

Despite the vast number of cruise ship visitors that wander inquisitively around Honningsvåg every summer, very few make it to see the amateur production *Our Northernmost Life* at the **Perleporten Culture House (Perleporten Kulturhus)** (Storgata 19, tel. 99 51 58 43, www.perleportenkulturhus.no, mid-June to mid-Aug., 190kr). That's a real shame, because this performance is a real eye-opener to the challenges—and the humor found by the locals—in this remote corner of the world.

Every day at 1pm and 8pm, four talented youngsters bare their lives for all to see. If you've ever wondered what it's like to live at such a high latitude and in such a remote place, or how exactly tourists are perceived in a place like Honningsvåg, you'll find all the answers and more in this hilarious 45-minute musical. Tickets can be purchased on arrival from the café in the Culture House. An extra daily show is often put on during high-season (June-Aug.), and these will be advertised on posters around the town and on the website.

Food and Accommodations

For a true taste of Arctic specialties and not what is usually served to tourists, try the modern and spacious **Corner Spiseri** (Fiskeriveien 2a, tel. 78 47 63 40, www.corner.no, 10am-11pm Mon.-Thurs., 10am-2am Fri.-Sat., noon-11pm Sun., kitchen closes 9pm). This multifunctional restaurant, café, and bar serves such intriguing dishes as deep-fried cod tongue and a stew made from whale meat, alongside less adventurous salads, sandwiches, and pasta dishes. Arctic specialties cost 229kr while smaller dishes, offering the best value lunch choice in Honningsvåg, run 109-139kr.

It should be obvious what the house special is at ★ **King Crab House** (Sjøgata 6, tel. 91 33 08 45, www.kingcrabhouse.no, 11am-10pm daily), but the popular restaurant also serves a flavor-packed fish soup and some great value salads with chicken, shrimp, or brie. Although there's nothing Norwegian about the spicy coconut sauce, it brings out the best in the crab, which is caught all along the region's coastline. Light meals range 115-185kr; king crab costs 295-320kr. Since the restaurant doubles as a bar, the large outdoor terrace is the perfect spot to enjoy the long summer evenings.

The best hotel on Magerøya island by some distance, **Scandic Bryggen** (Vågen 1, tel. 78 47 72 20, www.scandichotels.com, 11am-10pm daily, 1,599kr) offers small but tastefully decorated rooms, many with a view of the town's harbor. Noise can sometimes be an issue with late arrivals or early departures of cruise ships, but thick blackout curtains will at least keep the bright summer nights at bay. Arctic fish and seafood dominate the menu at

the in-house contemporary restaurant (6pm-10pm Mon.-Fri., 179-329kr), while a small lobby bar (noon-2am daily) is a nice option for a nightcap after watching the midnight sun or the northern lights.

Located three kilometers (1.9 miles) out of town on the E69 highway, the HI-affiliated **Nordkapp Vandrerhjem Hostel** (Kobbhullveien 10, tel. 91 82 41 56) is ideal for backpackers, cyclists, and hitchhikers on their way to the North Cape. Despite the positive initial impression with a moose head on the wall, chandeliers overhead, and comfortable TV lounges, the rooms themselves are tight and very basic for the price. However, parking, bed linen, towels, and a reasonable breakfast buffet are all included in the rate. A dorm bed starts from 350kr, with private rooms available at 550-975kr. Bathroom facilities are shared for all but the largest family-sized room.

An eight-kilometer (five-mile) drive north of Honningsvåg is **Nordkapp Camping** (Skipsfjorden, tel. 78 47 33 77, www.nordkappcamping.no, May-Sept.). A terrific deal for small groups or families, well-equipped two-bedroom bungalow cabins with kitchen and bathroom facilities are available for 1,120-1,380kr. More basic cabins with shared facilities range 595-650kr, while camping pitches are available for 160kr. However, there is a 50kr supplement per person with a further 55kr charge for electricity, making this one of the more expensive campsites on the island.

For a more intimate experience, the family-owned **North Cape Cabins** (tel. 91 71 19 64, www.northcapecabins.no) are a short walk from a parking area just a few hundred meters past Nordkapp Camping. Look for the small sign. Each of the three waterside cabins is furnished to a high standard complete with lounge, kitchen, bathroom with shower, and a deck to enjoy a barbecue or simply watch the world go by. Two of the cabins are also available for rent during the winter. Ideal for groups of 2-6 people, the cabins vary in price 600-1,500kr depending on the cabin and number of guests, with additional charges for bed linen and final cleaning.

SKARSVÅG

Mainland Europe's northernmost fishing village is a sight in itself and a mere five-minute detour from the road to the North Cape. It's the last place before the North Cape, but be aware there are very few facilities and no gas station. Even so, the picturesque village's small harbor is worthy of a stroll and is a good starting point for hikes or fishing trips.

Skarsvåg is 23 kilometers (14.3 miles) north of Honningsvåg along the E69 toward the North Cape. The drive should take around 20 minutes. From Skarsvåg, it is just 14 kilometers (nine miles) to the North Cape.

Sports and Recreation
HIKING

For a pleasant alternative place to view the midnight sun, take the short but rocky 25-minute trail to the Kirkeporten rock formation or the beach at Mefjorden. Start at the very edge of Kirkeporten Camping (Storvannsveien 2, on the village side) and follow the white markers over the hill. You can head down to the beach for a great view of the midnight sun and a great place to barbecue, or continue over the hill to Kirkeporten.

About six kilometers (3.7 miles) south of the North Cape is the starting point for the popular 18-kilometer (11.2-mile) round-trip hike to Knivskjellodden, a peninsula that juts out into the ocean about one mile farther north than the famous cliff. The parking lot is well signed from the E69. Although the eight- to nine-hour round-trip is a popular suggestion at the tourist office, the hike is not suitable for beginners due to the inclement weather, high winds, and steep rocky path toward the end. Marked by stone towers, the trail is open to the elements with no trees for cover, so hiking boots and good quality waterproof clothing are essential.

Many hikers choose to camp here in relative isolation, a world away from the crowded North Cape, which is easily visible on clear days. Every year approximately 300,000 travelers visit the North Cape but only 1,000 hike to Knivskjellodden, so be sure to sign the visitors book (inside the wooden box marked T) if you do. There are no facilities and little shelter, so if you plan on camping, be sure to come well prepared.

FISHING

The deep waters around the North Cape are proven fishing grounds, and you're all but guaranteed a catch on this 2.5-hour tour with Nordkapp Safari based at Kirkeporten Camping (Storvannsveien 2, tel. 90 96 06 48, www.kirkeporten.no, May-Sept.). Group sizes in the traditional fishing boat are limited to four to ensure personal attention from the captain. All safety and fishing equipment is included in the 650kr fee, and you could catch arctic cod, halibut, haddock, catfish, and coalfish.

Food and Accommodations

The best of the campsites clustered around Skarsvåg is Kirkeporten Camping (Storvannsveien 2, tel. 90 96 06 48, www.kirkeporten.no, May-Sept.), named after the unique rock formation close by. Ten basic cabins that sleep two are available from 610kr and are just a few seconds' walk from the excellent shared service house with kitchen and bathroom facilities. A few bigger cabins with bathroom and kitchenette are available for 895-970kr, but these book up well in advance. Camping pitches start at 150kr, but if you're wild camping in the area, visitors are permitted to use the shower facilities for a one-off payment of 40kr. A small cafeteria (5pm-10pm, 99-169kr) serves pizza and reindeer steaks, with snacks available from noon. Beer and wine are also available, at surprisingly reasonable prices for Norway.

If Kirkeporten is all booked up, try to snag one of the 30 simply furnished rooms at the neighboring Nordkapp Turisthotell (Storvannsveien 8, tel. 94 20 43 39, www.nordkappturisthotell.no, 840kr s, 1,160kr d). Although the building has the feel of a hostel at hotel prices, all rooms have a private bathroom and present the most comfortable accommodations for miles around. Unlike many of the area's campsites, the hotel is open year-round. The hotel's restaurant (noon-11pm, 169-299kr) serves locally caught fish and seafood, typically king crab and coalfish, alongside meatballs and reindeer stew.

GJESVÆR

The tiny fishing village of Gjesvær has existed since the Viking times, but no building is more than 80 years old because of the destruction during World War II. Less than 100 people call Gjesvær their home, but the population of this isolated community swells during the summer thanks to the holiday cottages and efforts of the tourism authorities.

The main attraction is on an island about five kilometers (3.1 miles) north of the village. **Gjesværstappan nature reserve** is home to some of the most famous bird cliffs in all of Norway. Take to the water for a two-hour boat trip to Europe's largest bird colony with **Bird Safari** (Nygårdsveien 38, tel. 41 61 39 83, www.birdsafari.no, 650kr) to spot puffins, white-tailed eagles, cormorants, and lots more. Daily departures at noon run from mid-April to the end of August, with extra afternoon departures from mid-June to mid-August. Book in advance.

Gjesvær is on the northwest coastline of Magerøya facing out into the open ocean and therefore offers a terrific view of the midnight sun. Leave Honningsvåg toward the North Cape on the E69 and follow the signed road to Gjesvær. The 34-kilometer (21-mile) drive should take around 35 minutes but is subject to convoy driving throughout winter and spring, and when the weather is poor.

Many cabins are privately owned, but **Barents Cabin & Cruise** (tel. 97 70 70 76, www.barentscabincruise.com) rents out spacious, fully equipped wooden cabins, many recently built right on the shoreline. A kitchen with hot water, bathroom with shower, TV, and free Wi-Fi are included in each cabin. Overnight rates vary from 900kr (one person)

up to 2,300kr for a group of six, with all towels and bed linen included. The cabins are available year-round, and discounts are offered from September to April for those hunting the northern lights.

INFORMATION AND SERVICES
Tourist Information

In the harbor of Honningsvåg, the information center of **Visit Nordkapp** (Fiskeriveien 4d, tel. 78 47 70 30, www.nordkapp.no, 9am-6pm Mon.-Fri., 11am-4pm Sat.-Sun., shorter hours outside of summer) provides information on not only the town, but the entire island of Magerøya, including the North Cape, Skarsvåg, and Gjesvær. Hikers and campers should check for the latest weather forecasts and tips on the most suitable trails and camping spots for the current conditions.

Health Care

Medical services are few and far between on the island of Magerøya. In Honningsvåg, the **North Cape Health Center (Nordkapp Legesenter)** (Sykehusveien 16b, tel. 78 47 66 60, 8am-3pm Mon.-Fri.) can administer urgent care, but calling ahead is essential. In all other urgent cases, call 113 for an ambulance. Honningsvåg has one pharmacy, a branch of **Apotek 1** (Storgata 9, tel. 78 47 71 10, 9am-4pm Mon.-Fri., 10am-2pm Sat.) on the main shopping street.

GETTING THERE
Car

Honningsvåg is a 100-kilometer (62-mile) drive northeast along the E69 from the junction with Norway's main E6 highway at Olderfjord. The journey should take around 1.5 hours with no stops, although stops are more or less essential along the narrow picturesque coastal road. From Alta, allow at least three hours to drive the 208 kilometers (129 miles), while the journey time for the 178-kilometer (110-mile) drive from Hammerfest is only 20 minutes less. During the summer months, hitchhikers are a common sight anywhere north of Olderfjord and especially on Magerøya island.

Unlike many road tunnels in Norway, the North Cape tunnel a few miles south of Honningsvåg that links Magerøya to the mainland is open to cyclists. The toll-free 6.9-kilometer (4.3-mile) tunnel reaches a depth of 212 meters (696 feet) and has anti-freezing gates that open automatically when cars approach. Lighting is not great, so exercise caution when using this tunnel. A useful modern rest area with clean restrooms is immediately after the tunnel.

Air

Just 3.5 kilometers (2 miles) north of the town, the tiny **Honningsvåg Airport** (tel. 67 03 51 19) links the town with Tromsø, Hammerfest, and smaller regional airports across Finnmark via the small propeller planes of regional airline Widerøe. A taxi for the drive into Honningsvåg will cost around 130kr. Call (tel. 78 47 22 34) for reservations. Alternatively, the central area of the village is a pleasant 45-minute walk from the airport on a sunny day.

Bus

Line 062 operated by **Boreal Transport Nord** (www.177finnmark.no) links Alta with Honningsvåg via Skaidi and Olderfjord. Expect to pay around 400kr for the four-hour ride. Three daily departures are common, but timetables vary during the year, so verify the timetable for the specific day

you are interested in, or check with the Visit Nordcapp tourist information office.

Boat

Honningsvåg is the northernmost stop on the **Hurtigruten** (tel. 81 03 00 00, www.hurtigruten.com) coastal express ferry that runs between Bergen and Kirkenes. Many travelers disembark and head straight to the North Cape on a bus before returning to the ship, but it's also a useful way for independent travelers to reach Magerøya island. Exact departure and arrival times depend on season, but tickets for the overnight route between Tromsø and Honningsvåg can be booked for 1,000-2,500kr in advance, and you will get a basic cabin for the 16- to 17-hour journey. The journey from the Lofoten islands involves two nights at sea with an advance fare ranging 2,500-5,500kr depending on season.

GETTING AROUND
Car Rental

Other than the organized coach trips to the North Cape, renting your own transport is the only way to get around Magerøya with any speed. **Avis** (tel. 78 47 62 22) has a car rental desk at the airport, but reservations must be made in advance or the service desk will not open. A local alternative with a good range of 4x4 and larger vehicles is **Nordkapp Bilservice** (Nordkappveien, tel. 78 47 60 60). Although based at the town's gas station, they will deliver and pick up from the airport. Rates start at 950kr for 24 hours.

Background

The Landscape

The development of Norway has been influenced to an extraordinary degree by the mountainous terrain and the historic climate of the region. Although known for its iconic fjords, Norway has some of the most diverse terrain in Europe. From immense glaciers, lush forests, and the highest mountains in northern Europe to the plains of Arctic tundra in the High North and an endless string of skerries, islets, and islands, Norway has natural beauty in abundance.

GEOGRAPHY

Even at more than 2,500 kilometers in length, 70 percent of mainland Norway's landmass is covered with mountains, glaciers, and lakes. Just 4 percent of the land is arable, which is one of the reasons Norway's farming industry is heavily subsidized by the government. The elongated country stretches from 58°N to more than 71°N latitude, with Svalbard lying at 81°N. The north of Norway wraps around the top of the Scandinavian peninsula so much that Kirkenes lies farther east than Finland's capital, Helsinki, and on the same longitude as Saint Petersburg, Russia.

Although Norway's total area is given as 385,199 square kilometers, some 16 percent of that is the Svalbard archipelago, high up in the Arctic Ocean. Mainland Norway's landmass consists mostly of igneous and metamorphic rock. There is very little sedimentary rock, so mining was limited to silver and copper rather than coal.

The striking fjords were created thousands of years ago when the ocean flowed into glacial valleys, cutting deep into the landscape. The after-effects can still be seen today at the innermost arms of the immense Sognefjord, where Norway's longest and deepest fjord almost touches the glaciers that remain.

The 1,700-kilometer-long (1,100-mile-long) Scandinavian Mountains line the center of the country and along the Swedish border to the High North. The geography of these mountains bears a striking similarity to those of Scotland, Ireland, and North America's Appalachian Mountains, leading geologists to believe that it was all one single mountain range prior to the breakup of Pangaea about 175 million years ago.

The mountainous heart of the country means nearly all major towns and cities, including Oslo, Bergen, Trondheim, Stavanger, and Tromsø, hug the coastline or the shoreline of a fjord. On the shores of Lake Mjøsa, Lillehammer is one notable exception, but the surrounding Gudbrandsdalen valley is known for its wealth of flora and fauna and acres of cultivated land. Despite the mountains making much of the country uninhabitable, there's plenty of room for everyone, with an astonishing 60,896 kilometers (37,839 miles) of shoreline.

CLIMATE

Heat that the Gulf Stream emits into the atmosphere is vital for the relatively mild climate in Norway. Southern and western coastal areas in particular enjoy warm summers and surprisingly mild, albeit dark and wet, winters. Despite the exposed nature of many Norwegian coastal cities, thousands of small islands off the west coast help to protect the population from the worst of the storms.

Temperature

Were it not for the warming effect of the Gulf Stream, Norway would be up to 25°F colder.

Previous: sea eagle, commonplace along the coastline; the Dalsnibba viewpoint high above the Geirangerfjord.

Fjords and National Parks

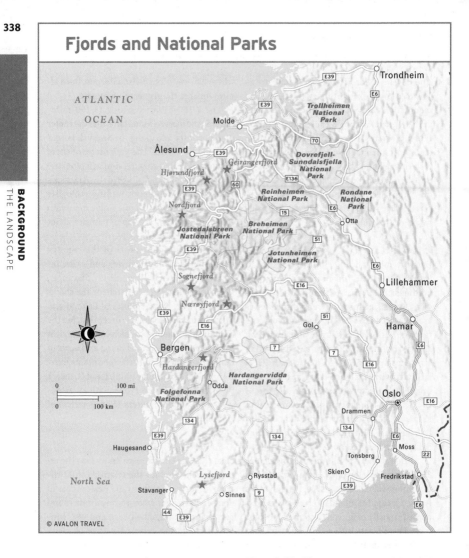

© AVALON TRAVEL

To understand this, head away from the coast and over the mountains into the center of the country. Here, where the climate is much less affected by ocean currents, temperatures plummet. The daily mean temperature for February is 2.1°C (35.8°F) in coastal Bergen, 4°C (24.8°F) in Oslo, and -10.4°C (13.3°F) in Røros, far inland. The summers can reach as high as 30°C (86°F) in the major cities, but an average of 20°C (68°F) is more common.

Precipitation

Although the coastal cities are warmer, they must put up with increased rainfall. Bergen and the surrounding fjords are some of the wettest parts of northern Europe. The city receives rainfall an average of 231 days every year, with Stavanger not far behind with 221 days. In contrast, Oslo receives rainfall on only 160 days per year. September through November is the wettest time of the year in almost all the country, while May through July offers the most pleasant weather.

Winters are surprisingly mild, and some coastal areas receive very little snowfall. Broadly speaking, most Norwegian cities can expect snowfall from November through March, with that period extending the farther inland and the farther north you travel.

ENVIRONMENTAL ISSUES

Arctic Drilling

The chief concern among environmentalists in Norway today is the emerging interest in drilling for natural resources in Arctic waters. It is believed that vast quantities of oil and gas reserves lie under the Arctic Ocean, possibly the last major discoveries still to be made on the planet. On the other hand, campaigners view the Arctic as a delicate ecosystem, one of the world's last great wilderness areas and a safe haven for endangered species.

The great irony is that even thinking about drilling is only possible because manmade climate change has caused the Arctic region to warm twice as fast as anywhere else on earth. Melting ice has exposed more of the ocean, making these huge reserves of natural resources more accessible than ever before.

Climate Change

Norwegians are said to be some of the most concerned about climate change, even though its effects will harm Norway significantly less than many other countries. That said, future climate models predict increased precipitation, which risks landslides and floods. As winters become significantly milder, Arctic sea ice may start to disappear, threatening the polar bear on Svalbard and shifting many species northward. Mackerel and red deer have been recorded farther north than ever before.

Despite acid rain decreasing in recent years as a result of reduced emissions across Europe, its effects have damaged lakes, rivers, and forests. In southern Norway, most populations of wild salmon have disappeared.

Melting Glaciers

Norway's glaciers continue to recede at an alarming rate. Since 1986, the total area covered by glaciers has decreased by 11 percent, and the most pessimistic predictions claim some of Norway's glaciers could disappear completely by 2030. The effect is more marked in the Svalbard archipelago, where glaciers are on average losing 23-27 inches of their thickness every single year.

Plants and Animals

VEGETATION ZONES

Vegetation varies considerably across the country, providing one of the most diverse range of habitats in Europe. Forest covers nearly one-fourth of the Norway's land area, while in highland areas and the High North there are areas of tundra.

A small nemoral vegetation zone runs along the southern coastline and is dominated by oak. Covering 7 percent of the country and mostly located around the Oslofjord and north of Oslo, the hemiboreal zone contains a mix of nemoral and boreal plant species.

Covering the majority of non-Arctic Norway, the diverse boreal zone is home to species that adapt well to long, cold winters. Bogs and lakes are common throughout the zone, and it's dominated by forests of birch and spruce. In high mountain areas and the High North, alpine tundra is common. The area closest to the tree line has continuous plant cover, while mosses and lichens are more prevalent higher up. A considerable number of alpine species in the mountains cannot tolerate long, warm summers, including the glacier buttercup.

Some species of palm grow in the mild coastal areas, while one of the largest remaining linden forests in Europe grows at Stryn, an inland region along the Nordfjord. Wild berries, such as the blueberry and lingonberry, grow in most woodland areas, with the cloudberry found at high altitudes.

TREES

Thick birch forests are common throughout the country, from the coastlines up to the alpine tree line and as far north as Finnmark county. The wood is popular as interior paneling, furniture, and firewood. A relatively recent immigrant, spruce is another common sighting across the country and also commonly used in building materials.

Majestic oak trees dominate the lowland forests, with the oldest tree in Norway believed to be around 1,000 years old. They are dependent on a mild climate and so only grow in the south of the country. Scots pine arrived early to Norway as the ice retreated and can be found across the country.

MAMMALS

Aside from the breathtaking scenery and multitude of outdoor activities, many visitors to the forests and mountains of Norway hope to spot wild animals in their natural habitat. While the country's declining populations of brown bears and wolves remain elusive, some of the country's most iconic animals are surprisingly accessible.

Brown Bear

Very few brown bears are left in Norway's forests. They hibernate all winter and live off berries, plants, and occasionally sheep for the rest of the year. The Øvre Pasvik National Park on the border with Finland and Russia in the extreme northeast of Norway is the last remaining place where these creatures can be commonly sighted.

Polar Bear

Skeletons of polar bears have been found as far south as Stavanger, but today Norway's population is limited to the Arctic archipelago of Svalbard. Closely related to the brown bear, the world's largest land carnivore has evolved quickly to adapt to the harsh Arctic climate, primarily existing on a diet of ringed seal and bearded seal. They roam over huge distances looking for food.

Polar bears pose a genuine risk to humans living on and visiting Svalbard, and it is not permitted to leave a settlement without a firearm. However, it is only permitted to kill a polar bear as a last resort when life is seriously under threat.

Arctic Fox

The chief threat to the critically endangered arctic fox, which numbers just a couple hundred, is the growing population of the larger red fox. Small populations survive in Svalbard, Børgefjell National Park, and Dovrefjell National Park, although sightings in the latter are rare. The arctic fox is superbly adapted to harsh winter climates and can survive temperatures of below -60°C (-76°F) thanks to its thick layer of underfur. Although known for its stunning bright white fur, the fox actually turns gray-brown during the summertime.

Elk

Elk can be found in forests across the country, although reindeer take over the farther north you go. Hunting for elk is a popular activity, but the population remains above 100,000. Elk with antlers are harder to spot. Only the males have them, and they shed them after mating season each year to conserve energy for the cold winter ahead. Elk are herbivores but can still be intimidating if you come across one on a rural road, as an adult can stand over two meters (up to 7.5 feet) tall and weigh up to 725 kilograms (1,600 pounds).

Deer

Identifiable because of their red-brown fur in the summer, deer are found in the forests all across Norway. The herbivores can grow up to 1.2 meters (four feet) tall, while the males have a fine set of antlers. They are notoriously shy animals and can generally only be appreciated from a distance.

Norway's Red List

Some 2,398 species are currently on the Red List, Norway's classification of species that are under threat of extinction. Beetles, fungi, butterflies and moths, vascular plants, and lichens make up the majority of the list, with more than half of those threatened found in a forest environment. The Svalbard archipelago is home to 47 threatened species, including the polar bear.

Of the threatened species, 276 are classified as critically endangered, including the bee *Andrena hattorfiana*. It lives in dry, hot pastures where it collects pollen and has probably declined due to changes in agricultural methods. The basking shark *(Cetorhinus maximus)* is considered endangered due to the strong population decline that resulted from extensive hunting. Deliberate fishing for basking sharks is now forbidden in the Norwegian Economic Zone.

The list was compiled by 26 expert committees with more than 100 members. They evaluated more than 20,000 species, in accordance with criteria and guidelines created by the International Union for Conservation of Nature (IUCN).

Reindeer

Still herded by the Sami people, reindeer graze freely inland during the winter and in coastal areas during the summer. Although naturally shy animals, reindeer happily wander along the rural roads of the north and will not run away when approached. If you are traveling through Finnmark on your way to the North Cape, especially around the Hammerfest area, you are almost guaranteed to spot a few reindeer.

With a population of more than 100,000, reindeer farming is a sustainable industry, and most restaurants in the north will feature the meat in some form on their menu. Whereas the reindeer of the north are all domesticated and owned by the Sami people, wild reindeer do roam Norway's central mountain ranges, including the Hardanger, Dovre, and Rondane National Parks.

Musk Ox

Other than the glaciers of central Norway, the mighty musk ox is the country's most visible link with the last Ice Age. Once close to extinction, the animal was introduced to

Most reindeer in northern Norway are domesticated and belong to Sami herders.

Norway from Greenland around 100 years ago. The herd now living in Dovre National Park south of Trondheim is one of only a handful of places in the world where these animals can be seen. Famed for their thick coat and pungent odor, males can withstand hostile conditions and weigh over 400 kilograms (up to 900 pounds).

Lynx

With an appearance similar to an oversized domestic cat, the secretive lynx lives in forested areas throughout the country. Typically over one meter (three feet) long, lynx are solitary predators and eat birds, hares, rodents, and sheep.

AQUATIC ANIMALS
Freshwater

Good freshwater fishing spots are spread all over Norway, with salmon, brown trout, grayling, common whitefish, and arctic char commonplace. Norway's cold water lakes are well-suited to pike and perch. Some of the better known areas for freshwater fishing include the Hemsedal Valley, the upper reaches of the river Glomma, the rivers of Trondheim and central Norway, and the lakes around Gjøvik, near Lillehammer.

Since wealthy British anglers discovered the quality of the Norwegian rivers in the 1800s, thousands of foreign fishers have come to fish salmon here each year. The short salmon season lasts from June to September, and local knowledge is critical for a successful trip.

Saltwater

Beluga whales, also known as white whales, are found in northern waters and often seen off the coast of Svalbard. They can be up to five meters (16 feet) long and weigh up to 1,500 kilograms (3,300 pounds). Pods of up to 100 individuals have been recorded. Sperm whales can often be seen off the coast of Norway during the summer, while around 3,000 killer whales are thought to be living in the northern waters.

Herring, cod, halibut, haddock, and mackerel are among the species of fish that spawn in coastal waters, while shrimp and king crabs are common catches along the northern coastline.

BIRDS

With snowy owls, golden eagles, and Atlantic puffins among the 470 species of birds found in the country, Norway is a year-round paradise for bird-watchers. White-tailed eagles, also known as sea eagles, nest along the entire coast of Norway. They are the largest bird of prey in Europe, with a wingspan over two meters (up to 7.5 feet).

Seabird Colonies

The very remote islands of Runde (off Ålesund) and Røst (near Lofoten) are known for their seabird colonies. From February through August each year, more than 100,000 birds (including kittiwakes, razorbills, gannets, and guillemots) nest on Runde, while, despite its size of just 10.13 square kilometers (3.91 square miles), Røst is home to one-quarter of the country's seabird population, including many Atlantic puffins. Sadly, due to the difficulties of finding food for their offspring, the local population of these remarkable birds has dwindled from 1.5 million to just 350,000 over the past 35 years.

The Gjesværstappan bird cliffs near the North Cape are also a draw for bird-watchers. The puffin population is in better shape here, and they share one of Norway's biggest bird cliffs with northern fulmars, kittiwakes, guillemots, shags, and arctic skuas.

History

EARLY HISTORY

The land now known as Norway emerged from the Ice Age thanks to the warming effect of the Gulf Stream. The glacial land became habitable from around 12,000 BC, with good conditions for sealing, fishing, and hunting along the coastline attracting immigration. Although it is believed people arrived earlier, the oldest human skeleton found in Norway was carbon dated to 6,600 BC. It was found in the waters of the Sognefjord as recently as 1994.

As people in the north began to travel on basic wooden skis and use slate tools, the Oslofjord region became suitable for farming thanks to technology from farther south. Sometime around 2,500 BC, farming spread quickly northward across the country, with oats, barley, pigs, cattle, sheep, and goats becoming commonplace.

Fertile areas around the Oslofjord, Trondheimsfjord, Lake Mjøsa (near Lillehammer), and Jæren (near Stavanger) began to create wealth for farming communities. Around the advent of the Common Era, speakers of Uralic languages arrived in the north and mixed with the indigenous population, becoming the Sami people.

The Iron Age allowed for easier cultivation, and thus new areas were cleared as the population grew with the increased harvests. A new social structure evolved: When sons married, they would remain in the same house; such an extended family was a clan. They would offer protection from other clans; if conflicts arose, the issue would be decided at a *thing,* a sacred place where all freemen from the surrounding area would assemble and could determine punishments for crimes, such as paying fines in food. The word *thing* is still used today to refer to council chambers. The Norwegian Parliament, Stortinget, literally translates as "The Big Thing."

From the first century AD a cultural influence from the Roman Empire took place. Norwegians created a runic alphabet and began trading furs and skins for luxury items. Some of the most powerful farmers became chieftains, and their power increased during the Migration Period between 400 and 550, as other Germanic tribes migrated northward and local farmers wanted protection.

VIKING ERA

Perhaps the most famous period in Norwegian history, the Viking Age was a period of expansion not just for Norway, but for the whole Nordic region. Far from just barbaric, axe-wielding invaders, the Vikings created complex social institutions, oversaw the coming of Christianity to Scandinavia, and left a major impact on European history through trade, colonization, and far-flung exploration.

The first record of the Vikings was the late 8th-century invasion of Lindisfarne, an island off the northeast coast of England. It was quite the way to announce themselves, as at the time, Lindisfarne monastery was considered one of the great sanctuaries of the Christian church in western Europe.

The *Anglo-Saxon Chronicle* stated: "In this year fierce, foreboding omens came over the land of the Northumbrians, and the wretched people shook; there were excessive whirlwinds, lightning, and fiery dragons were seen flying in the sky. These signs were followed by great famine, and a little after those, that same year on 6th ides of January, the ravaging of wretched heathen people destroyed God's church at Lindisfarne."

Vikings proceeded to raid a monastery at Jarrow in Northumbria. with southern Wales and Ireland falling victim to invasions soon after. Over a thousand Old Norse words influenced modern English, along with more than 1,000 place-names in northeastern England and the Scottish islands. Vikings were well trained, with good weapons and chain-mail

Norway's UNESCO World Heritage Sites

Norway's eight World Heritage Sites are a diverse mix of world-famous sights and little-known gems. Potential new additions include the Svalbard archipelago, the Lofoten islands, the Viking burial mounds of the Oslofjord, and the Laponian area, which stretches across Arctic Norway and Sweden.

- **West Norwegian Fjords:** While the other sites are listed for their cultural value, the Geirangerfjord and Nærøyfjord are listed together for their incredible natural beauty.

- **Bryggen:** The Hanseatic traders of Bergen lived and worked in these colorful wooden wharf buildings at the city's waterfront. The area has suffered from fire on multiple occasions, most recently in 1955, but care has been taken to restore the buildings using traditional material and methods.

- **Røros:** Founded after substantial deposits of copper were found in the area, the town is an incredibly well-preserved example of a remote industrial community.

Alta rock carvings

- **Urnes Stave Church:** On the banks of the Lustrafjord stands this fabulous example of 12th-century architecture, which demonstrates a visible link between Christianity and the pagan beliefs of the Viking era.

- **Alta Rock Carvings:** Thousands of original carvings at the World Heritage Rock Art Centre give insight into the lives of prehistoric hunters and gatherers, with human figures featuring in many of the scenes.

- **Rjukan-Notodden:** Located in a dramatic landscape of mountains, waterfalls, and valleys are the hydroelectric power plant, transmission lines, dams, tunnels, and factories of this remote industrial area in the forested south-central region.

- **Struve Geodetic Arc:** A chain of survey triangulations stretches from Hammerfest in Arctic Norway all the way to the Black Sea. A monument in Hammerfest marks the northernmost point of this extraordinary example of scientific collaboration.

- **Vega Archipelago:** Known for their distinctive eider ducks, these remote islands, off the northwest coast of Norway between Trondheim and Bodø, bear testimony to a distinctive, frugal way of life.

armor, and their belief that being killed in battle resulted in them going to Valhalla gave them a psychological advantage in battle for many years.

Misconceptions about the Vikings remain today. For example, the myth that Vikings wore horned helmets was actually an invention of 19th-century Romanticism. Although many women stayed to look after the household during Viking raids, some women and even children traveled with the men. One of the most fearsome Viking commanders was a woman, known as the Red Maiden.

The raids produced riches and slaves, which the Vikings brought back to Scandinavia to work the farms. As farmland grew scarce and resistance against the invasions grew in England, the Vikings began to look at targets further afield, such as Iceland, Greenland, and Newfoundland.

Inside a Viking Home

The ships found in the Viking burial mounds along the Oslofjord are spectacular, but it's what's inside them that has given us a far greater understanding of what daily life was like.

The Viking apron-dress was worn suspended over the shoulders by paired brooches hooked through narrow looped straps, and worn over a smock or gown. Fewer finds of clothing exist for Viking men than for Viking women because men tended to be cremated, but it seems that the basics of men's clothing in Scandinavia changed little throughout the Viking Age. Materials of trousers, tunics, coats, and cloaks changed from leather to wool to linen, but style changed little. Many textiles were made of carefully woven wool, attractively textured and often dyed in bright colors.

The Vikings ate two meals each day. The first was eaten in the morning, around two hours after the day's work was started (around 8am), while the second was consumed at the end of the day's work, around 7pm. Exact times would vary seasonally. Beef, mutton, lamb, goat, pork, and horsemeat were eaten, along with fish and whale. Root vegetables, plus plentiful plums, apples, and blackberries were common accompaniments.

While alcoholic beverages (most notably ale and mead) played an important role in festivities, the Vikings had an acute awareness of the perils and dangers of drunkenness.

During the 9th century, the largest chieftains began a long period of civil war, until King Harald Fairhair was able to unite the country and create the first Norwegian state.

Early Vikings saw Christianity as a heretical threat to their own pagan beliefs. Christian monks and missionaries were active in Scandinavia throughout the Viking Age, but it took until the era of Olav Tryggvason (963-1000) for the tide to begin to change. He is believed to have built Norway's first church, although information about him is sparse. He did, however, found the city of Trondheim (then called Nidaros), and a statue of him today stands high above the city's main square.

Following Tryggvason's death, it was Olav Haraldsson who began to pass church laws, destroyed pagan temples, build churches, and appoint priests. As many chieftains feared that Christianization would rob them of power, it took centuries for Christianity to be fully accepted. For years many people adopted both religions as an insurance policy in case one didn't work out. Evidence of this can be seen today in the carvings on some of Norway's oldest stave churches, which feature figures from Norse mythology.

MIDDLE AGES

After almost a century of peace, civil war broke out in 1130 because on ambiguous rules of succession. The newly-created Archdiocese of Nidaros attempted to control the appointment of kings, which led to the church taking sides in the various battles. In 1217, Håkon Håkonsson introduced a clear law of succession.

Through the 11th and 12th centuries, population increased drastically and farms began to be subdivided, with many landowners turning over parts of their land to the king or the church in challenging times. Throughout the 13th century a tithe of around twenty percent of a farmer's yield went to the landowners.

Norway's Golden Age—at least until the much more recent discovery of oil—is widely accepted to be the late 13th and early 14th centuries. It was a time of peace and growing international trade with Britain and Germany, most notably the Hanseatic League (a commercial federation of merchant guilds founded in Germany that dominated northern European trade for centuries), which took control of trade through Bergen. However, this time of prosperity came to an abrupt end in 1349 as the Black Death arrived in Norway and killed a third of the population within a year. Many communities were entirely wiped out and the subsequent reduction in tax income weakened the king's position and the church became increasingly powerful.

POLITICAL UNIONS

In 1380 Olav Haakonsson inherited the thrones of both Norway and Denmark and created a union, the start of a long period of political alliances and wars between the Scandinavian countries. Seventeen years later, the Kalmar Union was created between Norway, Denmark, and Sweden. Although the ruling Margaret I pursued a centralizing policy that favored Denmark's greater population, Norway was too weak economically to pull out of the union. Supported by Margaret, the Hanseatic League formed its own state within the city of Bergen, further weakening Norway's status.

Norway continued to play a minor role in the union until Sweden declared independence in the 1520s. This created a Denmark-Norway nation ruled from Copenhagen. Frederick I of Denmark favored Martin Luther's Reformation and initially agreed not to introduce Protestantism to Norway, but in 1529 he proceeded to begin the process.

The Catholic resistance within Norway was led by Olav Engelbrektsson but found little support. Christian III formally introduced Lutheranism, demoted Norway to the status of a Danish province, and introduced the Danish written language, although Norwegian dialects remained in place. During the 17th century, Denmark entered into a series of territorial wars with Sweden, which culminated in the Great Northern War (1700-1721) in which a Russian-led coalition ended the supremacy of the Swedish empire in northern Europe. Toward the end of the war, Swedish forces tried unsuccessfully to invade Trondheim. Norway's economy grew thanks in part to the timber trade, and the population grew from around 150,000 in 1500 to around 900,000 in 1800. Many Norwegians earned a living as sailors in foreign ships, especially the Dutch ships that came for the timber.

To avoid deforestation, a royal decree closed a large number of sawmills in 1688; because this mostly affected farmers with small mills, by the mid-18th century only a handful of merchants controlled the entire lumber industry. Mining, including the Kongsberg silver mines and Røros copper mines; shipping; and fishing became the chief drivers of the economy.

Throughout the period, Bergen was the largest town in the country, twice the size of Christiania (now Oslo) and Trondheim combined.

AN INDEPENDENT NATION

The economy suffered as Denmark-Norway backed France in the Napoleonic Wars, and soon Sweden took an interest in Norway. Following defeat at the Battle of Leipzig in 1813, the Crown Prince of Denmark-Norway and resident viceroy in Norway, Christian Frederik, began a Norwegian independence movement. A national assembly was called at Eidsvoll, but rather than elect Frederik as an absolute monarch the 112 members instead chose to form a constitution. It was written over the course of five weeks and adopted on May 17, 1814, the date celebrated today as Norwegian Constitution Day. The constitution split the nation's power between a king, a position to which Christian Frederik was appointed, and a new parliamentary body.

Just weeks after the signing of the constitution, King Carl Johan of Sweden invaded Norway, and due to economic troubles, Norway accepted Swedish rule, albeit with their constitution intact. Rather than an independence day, May 17 became an important political rally every year. In search of a better life, Norwegians began leaving rural Norway for North America in 1825, with mass emigration occurring over the following 100 years. By 1930, approximately 800,000 people had left Norway, with the majority settling in the American Midwest, where Norwegian heritage and traditions remain strong to this day.

Improvements in agricultural technology and transport infrastructure, notably a railroad that connected Oslo with Trondheim for the first time, helped to grow the economy during the late 19th century. The shipping industry enjoyed a boom, and by 1880 there were 60,000 Norwegian seamen. In 1913, Norway became the second country in Europe after Finland to give women the vote, after years of campaigning from liberal politician Gina Krog.

Although Norway adopted a policy of neutrality from 1905, the Norwegian merchant marine supported the British in World War I. Half the fleet was sunk and thousands of seamen were killed. The interwar period was dominated by economic instability, caused among other things by a succession of short-term governments, strikes, lockouts, and deflation.

OCCUPATION

Forces of Nazi Germany occupied Norway from the beginning to the end of World War II. The German goal was to use Norway to control access to the North Sea and the Atlantic, and to station air and naval forces to prevent convoys traveling between Britain and the USSR.

The government in exile, including the royal family, escaped to London. Politics were suspended and the government coordinated action with the Allies, retained control of a world-wide diplomatic and consular service, and operated the huge Norwegian merchant marine. It organized and supervised the resistance within Norway, which numbered 40,000 by the end of the war. The home front relied on sabotage, raids, clandestine operations, and intelligence gathering to hinder German operations. One of the most successful actions undertaken by the Norwegian resistance was the heavy water sabotage, which crippled the German nuclear energy project and has since been immortalized in several books and TV series.

The economic consequences of the German occupation were severe. Trading partners were lost, and although Germany stepped in, it could not totally replace the lost export business, and in fact confiscated more than half of what was produced within Norway. Because of this, and combined with a drop in productivity, Norwegians were quickly confronted with scarcity of food, so many turned to growing their own crops and keeping livestock.

In the latter years of the war, Hitler's scorched earth policy left a lasting impact on Finnmark. Transport infrastructure and homes were burned to the ground, with populations fleeing to the mountains and living in caves. In early 1945, returning Norwegian forces slowly took back the region and helped the remaining population to deal with the harsh Arctic winter and occasional German air raids.

POST-WAR RECOVERY

The immediate post-war years saw an increase in Nordic collaboration, including the creation of Scandinavian Airlines System (SAS) and the Nordic Council. Norway started negotiations for the creation of a Scandinavian defense union, but instead opted to become a founding member of the North Atlantic Treaty Organization (NATO). The Labour Party retained power throughout this period and enforced a policy of public planning. Construction of new railroads, hydroelectricity plants, aluminum works, and a steel mill helped the country to recover, as did the hosting of the 1952 Winter Olympics in Oslo.

Throughout the post-war period, fishing and agriculture became more mechanized, while agricultural subsidies rose to the third highest in the world. Heavy industry grew in the 1960s, and Norway became Europe's largest exporter of aluminum.

THE OIL ERA

In 1969, oil was discovered in the Ekofisk field, which would eventually become one of the largest oil fields in the world. The emerging industry not only created jobs in production, but a large number of supply and technology companies were established. High petroleum taxes and dividends from state-run Statoil earned the government significant reventues.

Stavanger in particular experienced a boom as an international workforce descended on the city, but the oil boom wasn't all great news. In 1977, Ekofisk experienced a major blowout, and 123 people were killed when the Alexander Kielland accommodation rig capsized in 1980. Regulation increased, and by 1990 Norway was Europe's largest oil producer.

The population rejected EU membership in a 1994 referendum, but the country joined the European Economic Area and the Schengen Area (an area comprising 26 European states that have officially abolished passport and border control at their mutual borders). These decisions contributed to the rise in population from 4.2 million in 1990 to 5.2 million in 2016. Population growth is expected to continue and hit 6 million sometime before 2030.

Government and Economy

POLITICS

Norway is a constitutional monarchy, currently led by King Harald V. In practice the king has very little political power, as all legislative power resides in the elected Parliament led by a prime minister. Despite this, Norway's royal family remains popular throughout the country.

Norway's multi-party system tends to result in coalition governments, although the Labour Party (Arbeiderpartiet) has traditionally seen the most success. Since World War II, Labour Party governments have often relied on the support of other socialist and left-leaning parties to form a government.

However, in 2013 the Conservative (Høyre) leader Erna Solberg was able to form a center-right coalition with the Progress Party (Fremskrittspartiet), even though the Labour Party won 30.8 percent of the popular vote and won the most seats. Currently, eight parties are represented within the Norwegian Parliament.

Generally speaking, Norwegians trust in their political process and therefore turnout at both general and local elections is relatively high.

ECONOMY

Norway consistently tops the standard of living when compared with other European countries, helped by a strong welfare system. The system, along with the country's agricultural and manufacturing systems, relies heavily on a "savings account" created from the oil and gas wealth. The value of the Government Pension Fund of Norway (commonly referred to as the Oil Fund) constantly fluctuates but fund manager Norges Bank maintains a running total on its website (www.norges-bank.no).

The country's workforce is heavily unionized, and most employees, both public and private, are a member of at least one trade body.

Central, regional, and local governments are major employers throughout Norway. Many government departments are located around the country to help with job creation, such as the register of businesses at Brønnøysund, midway between Trondheim and Bodø.

Petroleum and natural gas remain Norway's most important private sector industries. Seafood is a thriving export business, including smoked salmon from the country's turbulent rivers and dried fish products from Lofoten.

Future Economy

Because of the oil boom since the 1970s, there has been little government incentive to help develop and encourage new industries in the private sector, in contrast to other

Nordic countries like Sweden and particularly Finland. However, the government has committed significant cash to the Innovation Norway organization, which is charged with stimulating the future Norwegian economy by helping companies to develop their competitive advantage and enhance innovation.

While the country's tech startup community lags behind Nordic neighbors Sweden and Finland, new business ventures are finding success in the research, development, and commercialization of new processes and technologies for the energy, seafood, and maritime industries.

People and Culture

DEMOGRAPHY AND DIVERSITY

Citizens of Norway are primarily ethnic Norwegians of north Germanic descent. Outside of Norway, the largest concentration of the ethnic group exists in the United States, where an estimated four million ethnic Norwegians live as a result of the mass migration 100-150 years ago. Canada and Brazil also have large numbers of ethnic Norwegians among their populations.

Other than recent economic migrants, the main demographic diversity is provided by the indigenous Sami people, who settled across the north of Scandinavia around 8,000 years ago.

The Sami People

The Sami are an indigenous people known as nomadic reindeer herders, although only a few thousand still participate. The rest make their living through fishing, farming, and hunting, and a great many have moved elsewhere in Norway to work in the modern service sector.

Sami people are known for their colorful knitted dress and the *joik*, a form of song dedicated to a person, animal, or place. Each Sami has their own melody, and traditionally a young Sami boy will compose a unique *yoik* for the girl he is courting. Many traditional melodies are still alive, having been handed down for generations. The lavish outfits resplendent with jewelry used to be in daily use, whereas today the outfits are reserved for special occasions, or to welcome tourists.

Many varieties of the Sami language,

a Uralic language with no connection to Norwegian, are under threat as the number of native speakers continues to drop. To help combat this, national broadcaster NRK runs a Sami-only radio station, while schoolchildren can now choose to continue their studies on to higher education in their native language.

Based upon the Norwegian constitution and the Sami Act of 1987, the Sami are recognized indigenous people of Norway and as such are entitled to special protections and rights. In particular, a national Sami Parliament of 37 elected representatives works with political issues relevant to Sami people and has responsibility for a budget of more than 400 million kroner. Much of the land in Finnmark, Norway's vast northeastern county, is managed by the Parliament.

Before the Sami Parliament was initiated, a political movement began when power company Statkraft planned to dam the Alta River in Finnmark. The case known as the Alta Controversy united the environmental and Sami interest groups, and although the dam was eventually built, the political fallout led to the end of the controversial "Norwegianization" policy of the government and the eventual creation of the Sami Parliament.

RELIGION

The Church of Norway has dominated religion in Norway for around 1,000 years. It has belonged to the Evangelical Lutheran branch of the Christian church since the 16th century, and was until very recently the official church of the Norwegian state.

The separation of the Church of Norway from the Norwegian state began in 2008 and is still ongoing. As a result of the initial changes, Norway now has no formal state religion, the government will not participate in the appointment of church deans and bishops, and there is no longer a requirement that at least half of the government ministers must belong to the Lutheran Church. As of 2017, the Church of Norway is an entirely separate entity from the state.

It is important to note that the constitution still establishes the Church of Norway as "The People's Church" and establishes Norway's values as stemming from "our Christian and Humanist heritance." The constitution also still requires monarchs to swear allegiance to "God the all-knowing and almighty" when they are sworn into office, and they are still obliged to adhere to the Evangelical Lutheran faith of the Church of Norway.

The separation of church and state reflects a broader rise in atheism across Norway. In 2016, a national survey revealed that more Norwegians don't believe in God than do, for the first time.

LANGUAGE

Norwegian is a Scandinavian language, a collection of North Germanic languages closely related to one another. Native speakers of Norwegian, Swedish, and Danish can to a large extent understand one another even though the languages are distinct. Faroese and Icelandic, whilst also being North Germanic, because of their differences are not considered Scandinavian languages.

The heritage of all the North Germanic languages lies in the Old Norse language spoken by the Vikings. Originally the people of what is now Norway spoke a Western Old Norse dialect, which developed into the Icelandic and Faroese of today. A long period of political union with Denmark resulted in Danish being introduced across Norway, eventually splintering to become a distinct language.

The vivid Sami dress is today used for ceremonies and celebrations.

Because of this history, there are actually two forms of written Norwegian, Bokmål and Nynorsk. Bokmål (book language) is the dominant form, taught as standard in 86.5 percent of schools, and is the language of urban Norway. Nynorsk (new Norwegian) was created as an alternative to the Danish-influenced Bokmål in the 19th century. It is used mainly in rural municipalities of western Norway, where you may find spellings of place-names and attractions that differ slightly from those listed in this guide.

Strong dialects are commonplace and more or less fall into four regional variants: North, West, South, and East, but dialects exist right down to a local level. Politicians and TV presenters often use their local dialects, which can make learning and understanding Norwegian more problematic.

In parts of northern Norway, Sami languages are spoken and appear on road signs alongside Norwegian. In Kirkenes, you'll even see road signs in Norwegian and Russian.

Norwegians are some of the best nonnative

speakers of English in the world. Norwegian children learn English from the first year of school. In addition, British and American television is commonplace and almost always subtitled rather than dubbed. Some of the older generation may struggle with speaking English, but 99 percent of Norwegians you meet will understand every word you say.

LITERATURE

Other than original pagan Eddaic poetry from the Viking era, the first significant Norwegian literature came as a result of the learnings from the introduction of Christianity. *Historia Norwegiæ* is a short history of Norway written in Latin by an anonymous monk, while the speculum piece *Konungs skuggsjá* (*King's Mirror*) deals with politics and morality.

The next significant period of Norwegian literature wasn't until the struggle for independence from Denmark. The dramatist Henrik Wergeland was the most influential author of the period, while the works of Henrik Ibsen were consumed around the world. His fairy-tale-inspired five-act play *Peer Gynt* is still performed today.

Crime is the number one fiction genre across Scandinavia today and is characterized by its plain, direct writing style that's high on descriptive setting and low on metaphor. It is especially popular around Easter, when many television channels run detective shows and crime movie marathons. Jo Nesbø, Jørn Lier Horst, and the former Minister of Justice Anne Holt are some of the leading names to look out for.

VISUAL ARTS
Artists

Norwegian art came into its own in the 19th century as the influence of Danish rule began to erode and a new sense of identity gripped the nation. Landscape painting from the era remains one of the best examples of Norwegian art and dominates many of the country's galleries. Johan Christian Dahl (1788-1857) is often said to be the "father of Norwegian landscape painting." His

notable works include *Vinter ved Sognefjorden* (*Winter by the Sognefjord*) and *Skibbrudd ved den norske kyst* (*Shipwreck on the Norwegian coast*), both of which are in the collection of Oslo's National Gallery.

Many keen young painters studied in France and brought back Impressionism and Realism, which gradually became more popular within Norway.

The intense psychological themes in the works of Edvard Munch (1863-1944) are arguably Norway's most famous cultural export. His 1893 painting *The Scream* features a figure with an agonized expression on a bridge with a fiery sky in the backdrop. Four versions of the work exist, which have been targets for numerous theft attempts and the subject of many parodies.

Nikolai Astrup (1880-1928) spent time in France and Germany before returning to Jølster in western Norway, where he became one of the greatest Norwegian artists from the early 20th century. Only recently becoming known outside of Norway, his neo-romantic landscapes are known for their vivid colors.

Film

The dramatic scenery of Norway has become a popular location for TV and movie makers, and the government now offers tax incentives to tempt international studios.

Battle scenes on the ice planet Hoth from the Star Wars movie *The Empire Strikes Back* were filmed around the tiny village of Finse, high up in the mountains between Oslo and Bergen, while parts of Svalbard and Jostedalsbreen National Park were used to film scenes for the James Bond movie *Die Another Day*. Large parts of the science-fiction psychological thriller *Ex Machina* were shot on location at the Juvet Landscape Hotel in Valldalen.

In recent years the Norwegian movie industry has produced some notable works of its own. The horror movie *Død Snø* (*Dead Snow*), dark fantasy mockumentary *Trollhunter*, and disaster movie *Bølgen* (*The Wave*) have all found a cult following outside of Norway.

MUSIC

Composers Edvard Grieg (1843-1907) and Johan Svendsen (1840-1911) were leading composers of the Romantic era and played a pivotal role in forming Norwegian national identity following the end of Danish rule. Both composers added elements of Norwegian folk music to European classical traditions to create a distinctive Norwegian sound.

Many traditional styles of folk music have died out, aside from the traditional Sami *joik,* which has enjoyed something of a revival in recent years. Having said that, Norwegian folk music does still influence the contemporary music of today. The progressive rock band Gåte rearranged traditional folk tunes and performed in a heavy central Norwegian dialect.

The country enjoys a strong choir tradition, especially in smaller rural towns. This tradition can be traced back to the 12th century, with a resurgence during the 19th century around the time of independence.

Contemporary styles from jazz to rap are popular, but artists with international success are limited. Norway is, however, noted for its electronic and dance music scene, with artists like Röyksopp and Bel Canto becoming worldwide names. In the 1980s, Norwegian pop group A-ha achieved meteoric international success when the trio's 1985 debut *Take On Me* shot to number one in the United States and the United Kingdom. The band, led by vocalist Morten Harket, went on to sell more than 80 million records worldwide.

Essentials

Transportation

GETTING THERE
Air

Almost all international visitors to Norway will arrive at the modern **Oslo Airport Gardermoen** (OSL), which is also the main domestic hub for connections to all parts of the country.

If you are connecting onto a domestic flight, you must collect your baggage, clear customs, and recheck your bags. The extra time required for this and the additional security check mean you should allow at least 90 minutes for a connection at Gardermoen. Trials for an expedited process called Connecting Norway are underway for selected flights, although this seems unlikely to be rolled out beyond arrivals from select other Schengen Area nations (26 European states that have officially abolished passport and border control at their mutual borders). Note these rules only apply to those with checked luggage. If you're carrying only hand luggage, you can pass through a separate section of the airport and straight into the domestic terminal.

If you need to transfer onto a domestic flight, check the latest regulations with staff on-site at Oslo Airport. Based on several frustrating experiences, airline staff in other countries and even non-Norwegian cabin crew are unlikely to know the latest process, even if they think they do.

FROM NORTH AMERICA

Scandinavian Airlines (SAS) (www.flysas. com) operates nonstop flights to Oslo from Newark and Miami. SAS also operates services to Stockholm and Copenhagen from Chicago, San Francisco, Los Angeles, and Washington-Dulles. A connecting flight to Oslo is usually included at no extra or little additional cost.

At the time of writing, low-cost airline **Norwegian** (www.norwegian.com) flies to Oslo from Boston, Fort Lauderdale, Las Vegas, Los Angeles, New York JFK, Oakland, and Orlando. The schedules vary seasonally, and due to the limited number of weekly departures (usually one or two per route), delays can have severe knock-on effects across the network.

SAS's Star Alliance partner **United** (www. united.com) offers an additional service between Newark and Oslo, while KLM, Air France, British Airways, Lufthansa, and Icelandair offer connections from many North American airports via Amsterdam, Paris, London, Frankfurt, and Reykjavik, respectively. **Icelandair** (www.icelandair.com) in particular is a popular option because it allows free stopovers to add a night in Reykjavik to your itinerary.

FROM EUROPE

Both SAS and Norwegian offer a vast network of flights to Oslo from European destinations, with connections to the United Kingdom and Spain particularly strong. Along with the major flag-carriers such as British Airways, Lufthansa, and KLM, low-cost airline **Ryanair** (www.ryanair.com) currently flies to Oslo from destinations including London Stansted and Manchester, but the latter along with eight other routes land at Sandefjord Airport Torp, one of the few Norwegian airports not operated by state-run Avinor. Despite the budget airline listing the airport as Oslo, it is almost two hours by bus from the city.

Both SAS and Norwegian also operate

---

flights from select European destinations to Bergen, Stavanger, Trondheim, Ålesund, and Tromsø. SAS tends to run flights to its hubs in Copenhagen and Stockholm, while Norwegian runs flights to London Gatwick and many vacation spots in the Mediterranean.

Car or Motorcycle

Many travelers from northern Europe enter Norway in their own car or a rented vehicle to avoid the relatively high cost of rental within Norway. As Norway and Sweden are both Schengen countries, the multiple border crossings are always open, but occasional customs checks do take place. The busiest border crossing is the Svinesundsbrua bridge on the E6 highway between Oslo and Gotheburg.

In Finnmark there are border crossings with Finland and Russia. Although the Finland crossings are straightforward, crossing to/from Russia requires advance paperwork and often long periods of waiting. Just a few miles from Kirkenes, the Storskog border station is a 220-kilometer (137-mile) drive from Murmansk, from where the Kirov Railway provides a connection to Saint Petersburg.

Driving licenses issued in the EU/EEA are valid for driving in Norway as long as they are valid in the country they were issued. Driving licenses issued outside the EU/EEA are valid for driving in Norway for up to three months.

Bus

Long-distance coach services are available from across northern Europe and are often the cheapest method of transportation. **Oslo Bus Terminal** (Schweigaards gate 6-14) is the arrival point for all international bus routes. **Swebus** (www.swebus.se) runs regular coaches from Stockholm, Gothenburg, and Copenhagen, from where **Eurolines** (tel. +49/6196 2078 501, www.eurolines.de) offers connections from Berlin, Frankfurt, and Hamburg. **Czech Transport** (tel. +420/776 677 890 Mon.-Fri., www.czech-transport. com) runs a weekly service from Prague.

Rail

Oslo Central Station (Jernbanetorget 1, tel. 81 50 08 88, www.oslo-s.no) is linked into the European rail network via Swedish cities Gothenburg and Stockholm. Three daily trains make the four-hour journey from Gothenburg, and tickets can be booked via the Norwegian state railway company **NSB** (tel. 81 50 08 88, www.nsb.no), but to make the five-hour journey from Stockholm, you must book in advance with the Swedish state company **SJ** (tel. +46/771 757575, www.sj.se). Trondheim can also be reached from the central Swedish city Östersund, from where connections to Stockholm and across the Swedish rail network are available.

If you are arriving by rail and plan to continue your journey around Norway by rail, it's worth investigating the European rail passes on offer. Non-Europeans can use **Eurail** (www.eurail.com) and European citizens **Interrail** (interrail.eu). Both passes are especially good value for those under 25 and for families traveling together.

Boat

In addition to the increasing numbers of cruise ships, three international ferry operators service Oslo. **DFDS** (tel. +44/330 333 0245, www.dfdsseaways.co.uk) operates overnight boats from Copenhagen, while **Color Line** (tel. 81 00 08 11, www.colorline. no) runs a daily service to and from Kiel in northern Germany. Finally, **Stena Line** (tel. 23 17 91 30, www.stenaline.no) operates a 24-hour return service to and from Fredrikshavn in northern Denmark, known locally as a "booze cruise"; Oslo locals take advantage of the duty-free regulations on board, often stumbling back into Oslo with crates of beer in tow.

At the time of writing all ferry services linking the United Kingdom with the west of Norway have ceased, but there is an option from Denmark. The daily car ferry service operated by **Fjordline** (tel. 81 53 35 00, www.fjordline.com) links the Danish port of Hirtshals with Stavanger and Bergen. Great deals can be found for those traveling without a car.

GETTING AROUND

Air

Spectacular as it may be, Norway's natural environment of fjords and mountains means that air travel is often the only option for getting somewhere quickly. As such, the domestic air travel network is highly developed.

SAS and Norwegian operate services from Oslo to all parts of the country and between popular cities such as Bergen, Stavanger, and Trondheim multiple times per day, every day. Domestic airline **Widerøe** (www.wideroe.no) is a lifeline for residents of remote towns and villages in northern Norway. They operate small prop planes several times a day from their northern hubs Bodø and Tromsø, and also around the fjord region from Bergen.

Prices on all domestic airlines rise substantially around 48 hours before travel. Book at least one week in advance for the best rates. On weekdays, traveling outside peak times (10am-3pm, after 6pm) offers a further saving.

During the summer, Widerøe offers an **Explore Norway** ticket, which entitles you to unlimited flights within a specified region: South of Trondheim, Trondheim to Tromsø, or East of Tromsø. The fare starts from 3,390kr for one week within one zone, up to 6,590kr for a two-week pass covering the whole of Norway. With some advance planning, savings made can be substantial, making this one of Norway's greatest travel bargains. The ticket is available from mid-June to the end of August.

Bus

Long-distance buses are usually the cheapest but slowest option for moving between Norway's cities. Budget-concious travelers looking to travel between Stavanger, Oslo, and Trondheim should book in advance with **Lavprisekspressen** (www.lavprisekspressen.no) for cheap deals.

For a wider network of destinations across south and central Norway, **NOR-WAY Bussekspress** (tel. 81 54 44 44, www.norway.no) runs a network of well-established routes, including the Fjordekspressen between Bergen and Ålesund, and the Kystbussen between Bergen and Stavanger.

Car

Driving in Norway outside the cities is a relatively pleasurable experience. Roads can be quiet and speed limits are low, so taking your time is strongly recommended given the spectacular scenery on offer. Journeys between towns and especially around the fjord region should be carefully planned to take into account potential ferry crossings. These can add substantial time and cost to your journey.

THE ROAD SYSTEM

Any road designated E (e.g., E6, E18) is part of the European highway system and tends to be better maintained. They are double-lane in the vicinity of cities but can be single-lane in rural areas.

The rest of the road system is split between national roads (Rv) and county roads (Fv). The designation refers to which authority has responsibility for maintenance and is of little relevance to travelers. In fact, most road signs and maps will just reference the route number without the Fv/Rv designation.

ROAD CONDITIONS

Road conditions are generally good, but snow and high winds can cause even major highways to close temporarily during the winter months. The E6 Oslo and Trondheim road around the Dovrefjell National Park is especially prone to problems. Many minor roads and mountain passes are closed throughout the winter, which tends to be from October to April (depending on the weather), or subject to convoy driving at certain points in the day. It's worth checking with the **Norwegian Public Roads Administration (Statens vegvesen)** (tel. 91 50 20 30, www.vegvesen.

no) if you are planning any road trip outside the summer season.

RULES OF THE ROAD

On motorways and some highways, speed limits are 90kph or 100kph. On all other roads outside built-up areas, the limit is 80kph unless otherwise indicated. In built-up areas the speed limit is 50kph unless indicated, but can drop as low as 30kph.

It is compulsory for all drivers of all vehicles, including RVs, cars, motorcycles, and mopeds, to have their headlights on at all times. Headlamp beam deflectors may be required. Warning triangles and reflective jackets are compulsory accessories for all private vehicles, so be sure to check your rental car is properly equipped. Hefty on-the-spot fines can be issued for failing to carry specific items. Drivers and passengers of motorcycles and mopeds must wear a crash helmet, while a vehicle towing a caravan must be equipped with special rearview mirrors.

CAR RENTAL

Car rental is expensive by international standards, with daily rates from most known brands starting from 500kr. Advance booking is wise in the summer and essential if you are planning on driving away from smaller airports, as many rental desks only open based on reservations.

Small cars with engines under 2.0L offer the best value and will easily be enough for a couple with luggage. Both gasoline (petrol) and diesel cars are commonplace. Gasoline prices vary but are typically 11-14kr per liter. Diesel tends to be about 10 percent higher. Prices will be higher for all fuel outside of cities and in the north of the country. Many rental companies offer hybrid cars that will save considerable gasoline costs, especially if you are driving around mountainous terrain. The market for electric cars continues to boom in Norway and they are available from most rental companies. Although the charging infrastructure is generally good across the country, it may be best to ask for a gasoline/diesel model if you are unfamiliar with how the charging process works or if you are planning long road trips.

Your rental company will provide breakdown cover. Alternatively, contact the **Norwegian Automobile Association (Norges Automobil-Forbund)** (tel. 92 60 85 05, naf.no), known as NAF, for advice.

Ferry

One of the most recognizable Norwegian icons, the **Hurtigruten** (www.hurtigruten. com) coastal express ferry has made its way up and down the Norwegian coastline for more than 100 years. It sails almost the entire length of the country between Bergen and the Russian border. The Hurtigruten serves a dual purpose as an informal cruise through stunning scenery and a vital service for tiny coastal communities. Either use the ship as a relaxing cruise with time to explore the major cities on foot, or as a ferry to move between some of Norway's coastal highlights including Bergen, Ålesund, Trondheim, Lofoten, and Tromsø.

Hurtigruten fares vary wildly and depend on two main factors: how far in advance you book and the specific ship in service on the day you choose. The full 12/13-day round-trip from Bergen to Kirkenes and back in high season costs from around 17,000kr up to 45,000kr on the newest ships, but the average cost runs 26,000kr. Trips outside the summer season can drop below 10,000kr. Pricing for shorter hops is a bit more stable and depends mainly on the number of nights you'll be aboard.

Visas and Officialdom

PASSPORTS AND TOURIST VISAS

Immigration paperwork is straightforward for the vast majority of international arrivals who are visiting Norway for tourism. As Norway is a member of the European Schengen Agreement, passport checks are not required for international arrivals from the 25 other members of the Schengen Area. Two notable omissions from the Schengen Area are the United Kingdom and Ireland. This means that if you arrive in Oslo from a connection in Amsterdam, for example, then you will clear immigration into the Schengen Area in Amsterdam, not in Oslo.

Citizens of the United Kingdom and Ireland are free to visit Norway without the need for a visa, as are citizens of the United States, Canada, Mexico, Australia, New Zealand, and many other non-European Union (EU)/European Economic Area (EEA) countries. People who fall into this category are free to stay in Norway (and indeed, the whole Schengen Area) for up to 90 days.

CUSTOMS

Although a member of the Schengen Agreement, Norway's status outside the European Union means it sets its own customs rules. Tourists can bring an unlimited amount of luggage, including clothing, electronics, and jewelry, for use during their stay that they take with them when they leave.

It is forbidden to import any meat and dairy products from outside the EEA. Cash above 25,000kr (or the foreign currency equivalent) must be declared to the Customs Office on arrival.

Tobacco and Alcohol

Alcohol and tobacco quotas are strictly enforced. The amount of alcohol you can bring into the country (which includes purchases at the duty-free stores on arrival) depends on whether you bring tobacco or not. With up to 200 cigarettes or 250 grams of tobacco, you are entitled to bring one liter of spirits, 1.5 liters of wine, and 2 liters of beer. If you forgo the liter of spirits, the quota for beer or wine can increase. Without cigarettes or tobacco, you are permitted to bring 1 liter of spirits, 3 liters of wine, and 2 liters of beer. Again, forgoing the spirit allowance increases the allowance for wine or beer.

You must be at least 18 to bring beer, wine, and tobacco products to Norway, and at least 20 to bring beverages over 22 percent alcohol content. Detailed information on the exact quotas is available from **Norwegian Customs (Toll)** (tel. 22 86 03 12, www.toll. no).

POLICE

Uniformed officers and white squad cars of the **Norwegian Police (Politi)** (www.politi. no) are a regular sight around Norwegian cities. As a general rule, officers are more than happy to give directions to tourists. The emergency number for the police is 112, or 02800 to be put through to the nearest regional police district.

Norwegian police officers are in general respected by the population. In the unlikely event you feel the need to file a complaint, contact the relevant regional police district, where the police chief will consider the complaint within one month. If you disagree with the decision, there is an appeal process overseen by the National Police Directorate.

Food

Abundant fish and seafood, succulent lamb and reindeer, and sharp mountain berries are among the highlights of the Norwegian kitchen. The trend of New Nordic cooking, which combines local seasonal ingredients with an international flair, is rapidly replacing traditional Norwegian dishes from a time when meat and fish had to be preserved by salting and drying.

The same international influence dominates the lower end. You're more likely to find pasta, pizza, hamburgers, and the Norwegian take on a taco rather than traditional favorites such as meatballs or cod. In many restaurants, the menu bears a striking resemblance to what you would find in any western country.

Because of the high cost of wages, prices are high for food across the board. This means that high-end restaurants often represent better value than their cheaper counterparts.

MEALTIMES

Be prepared to adjust your mealtimes. A typical Norwegian lunch is eaten between 11am and 1pm and often consists of bread topped with ham, salami, or cheese. Dinner is taken between 4pm and 7pm and traditionally consists of meat or fish with boiled potatoes and a vegetable, although nowadays pizza is the number one choice in the family home. Restaurants follow these times, and you may struggle to find a kitchen taking orders after 10pm.

The typical Scandinavian breakfast buffet features freshly baked breads with a selection of hams, cheeses, and other cold cuts along with lashings of coffee. The higher-end hotels will offer hot options and fresh juices.

MEAT

Roasted meats are commonplace, although beef tends to be roughly ground with onion and formed into meatcakes *(kjøttkaker)* or meatballs *(kjøttboller)*, typically served with potatoes and a thick brown sauce.

Lamb and mutton are popular around Easter and in the fall. Popular dishes include the national dish, *fårikål* (mutton and cabbage stew), and the traditional Christmas dish *pinnekjøtt* (slow-cooked cured mutton ribs).

Pork roast and chops are popular, as is reindeer, which tends to be served as a steak or in cured sausage form. Reindeer has a distinct, strong taste and is often served with crushed juniper berries and a sour lingonberry jam.

Whale *(hval)* meat is available from high-end restaurants in most parts of Norway. As a traditional food, its consumption is considered less controversial than in many other parts of the world. The lean meat is surprisingly tender and tastes more like beef than anything from the sea.

FISH AND SEAFOOD

After oil, fish and seafood remain Norway's most important exports, and with good reason. The outstanding Norwegian smoked salmon is eaten all around the world, while the fresh variety is a staple feature on Norwegian menus.

Cod is still caught in large numbers along the Norwegian coast, although the most popular variety comes from around the Lofoten islands. Traditionally poached and served with a simple accompaniment of boiled potatoes and carrots, cod is also dried (either by air or salt) and shipped out around the world in vast numbers. The most famous preparation of preserved fish is the traditional Christmas dish lutefisk. Originally prepared before the days of refrigeration, lutefisk is dried cod that is steeped in lye. The gelatinous dish is popular amongst the older generation and at Christmastime but is rarely eaten by the general population.

Fish soup is popular throughout the country and is often one of the cheapest options on a restaurant menu. Recipes vary regionally, but typically the milk-based soup includes 2-3 types of fish with carrots, onions, and potato.

Shrimp is a popular fast food and is prepared simply with a dash of lemon juice, served with bread and butter. Recent decades have seen an explosion of king crabs along the Arctic coast of Norway, increasing the availability of crab legs in Arctic restaurants.

CHEESE

During your travels two types of cheese will dominate breakfast buffets. A mild yellow cheese *(gulost)*, most likely Jarlsberg or Norvegia, is thinly sliced and eaten with bread.

The more curious selection is the peanut-butter colored block of brown cheese *(brunost)*, a tangy, sweet cheese with a fudge-like texture. Unique to Norway and technically not a cheese, brown cheese is made from the whey of cow's milk or goat's milk produced during the cheese-making process. Many variants of brown cheese exist, but the intense, caramelized taste is common to all.

Gamalost is an aged hard cheese made from soured cow's milk. It is grainy in texture, sharp and bitter in flavor, with an extremely pungent aroma.

FRUITS AND DESSERTS

Traditional Norwegian desserts such as the vanilla-cream layered *bløtkake* and the stunning conical *kransekake* are almost always home-baked and rarely found on restaurant menus. Desserts tend to utilize the fruits that grow well in cold climates, such as apples and a wide range of berries.

Strawberries are popular nationwide and can often be bought directly from farmers in stalls at gas stations and town centers. The golden cloudberry *(multe)* grows only in mountain climates and is regarded as a delicacy. They are often eaten at Christmas with whipped cream and sugar.

SNACKS

Spend any time traveling the country and you'll soon come across the staple Norwegian snacks of *pølser* (hot dogs), *boller* (sweet buns), and *lefser* (flatbread, often sweetened). The buns are available in a wide range of forms, from a basic bread roll *(bolle)* to ornate creations flavored with cinnamon *(kanelbolle)*. Such items sustain locals on long hiking trips and are available in abundance at roadside kiosks and gas stations and on many ferries. The budget conscious could easily make a quick lunch out of these items.

Sweet buns flavored with cinnamon or cardamom are a staple feature of all Norwegian cafés.

BEVERAGES
Coffee

Like the other Scandinavian countries, Norway is a nation of coffee drinkers. Strong black filter coffee is preferred to milky drinks, and a consumption of four or five cups a day is not considered unusual. When taking a guided tour or excursion that includes hot drinks, don't be surprised if black coffee is the only option.

Alcohol

The reputation of Norway having some of the highest alcohol taxes in the world is fully deserved. All alcohol is expensive, although the taxes get progressively higher with the alcohol content. Witness the rush to the duty-free store by Norwegians arriving home after an international flight for proof, along with the fact that most locals have the duty-free allowances committed to memory.

It's not just price that makes consumption of alcohol in Norway difficult. Availability can be a problem too. Outside of licensed bars and restaurants, only beer under 4.7 percent alcohol by volume can be bought in supermarkets. All other alcohol, including stronger beers, wines, and spirits, can only be purchased from the state-run off license chain, Vinmopolet. It is not possible to buy alcohol outside of bars and licensed restaurants after 8pm weekdays, 6pm Saturday, or at all on Sunday. Vinmopolet opening hours are shorter, and stores in smaller towns often close at 3pm on Saturday.

A trend for craft beer has swept the country over the past few years, with brewpubs popular in all major cities. Traditionalists prefer *akevitt* (also spelled aquavit), a spirit flavored with caraway or dill. It is a common accompaniment to fish, and is occasionally drunk together with dark beer.

Accommodations

Norway's accommodations vary from international chain hotels to budget campsites, and everything in between. Facilities are rarely poor, but luxury accommodations are not commonplace either. One plus point: Wi-Fi is standard across all types of accommodations, with even most budget hostels and campsites offering a free connection.

HOTELS

Hotel accommodations in cities are generally of a good standard, but expect a more basic level of service in smaller towns and rural areas. In cheaper hotels, rooms advertised as double consist of two single beds pushed together. Even on double beds, two separate duvets are commonplace throughout Scandinavia. Almost all hotels will offer a Scandinavian cold breakfast buffet, more often than not included in the price.

High season for hotels is mid-June to mid-August, but curiously this tends to be when rates are at their cheapest. July is Norway's national holiday month, with most locals taking to their mountain cabin hideaways or traveling overseas for the entire month, freeing up capacity for international tourists. However, hotels in major cities and in popular areas with limited options, such as the Lofoten islands, fill up fast, so advance booking is essential during high season.

Outside of high season, availability is less of a problem, although be aware of any major festivals or conferences, which have been known to book out an entire city. Prices for swish business hotels in Oslo, Bergen, Stavanger, and Trondheim drop substantially at weekends. Expect to pay at least 1,000-1,500kr for an international standard hotel and 750-1,000kr for a budget hotel.

GUESTHOUSES

Somewhere between a basic hotel and a British-style bed-and-breakfast, a Norwegian

The Right to Roam

Throughout Norway, everyone has the unrestricted right to free access to the open countryside, opening up a budget accommodation option to keen campers. Known as "Allemannsretten," the legislation ensures that everyone can enjoy nature on equal terms, even within national parks.

The rules are simple: Be considerate and thoughtful, and leave no trace. The right of access applies to open countryside, which includes most shorelines, bogs, forests, mountains, and national parks. It does not apply to private fenced or cultivated land, and you must keep at least 500 feet away from private cabins or homes.

If you want to stay for more than two nights in the same place, you must ask the landowner's permission, except in the mountains or very remote areas. Picking berries, mushrooms, and wildflowers is permitted, but fires are not allowed in or near woodland between April and August. Places for emptying toilets are signposted, and doing so elsewhere is strictly prohibited.

guesthouse (*gjestehus* or *pensjon*) is a common sight in suburbs and smaller industrial towns. Offering comfortable, clean but basic accommodations, rooms usually share bathroom and kitchen facilities. Rooms typically run 500-750kr per night.

During high season, many householders along popular tourist routes will advertise private lodgings for rent with a simple *rom* sign by the roadside.

CABINS

Anywhere there is a shoreline you will find cabins to rent. Standards vary wildly, from a simple four-walled timber hut to a luxury Swiss-style mountain lodge. In the Lofoten islands, the former fishing cottages known as *rorbuer* are the principal accommodation option outside of Svolvær. Elsewhere in Norway, a timber cabin *(hytte)* is an atmospheric, traditional, and often great value accommodation choice for road trips around the fjords.

Cabins can be rented privately, through hotel booking websites, or as part of a campsite. Typically, private cabins and those on campsites come equipped with electricity, running water, and a small kitchenette. Expect to pay 800-1,200kr for one that sleeps four, depending on location. More basic cabins without any facilities can be snapped up for around 500-700kr. All cabins can be rented nightly, but substantial savings are available for stays of a week or more.

Some of the pricier options have bathrooms, a number of separate bedrooms, and all the mod cons. In and around ski resorts, standards and prices rocket.

Mountain Huts

The **Norwegian Trekking Association (Den Norske Turistforening)** (DNT, tel. 40 00 18 70, www.dnt.no) maintains hundreds of small mountain cabins across their network of hiking and skiing trails. These huts are spaced out so hikers and cross-country skiers have a convenient place to stay overnight on weeklong hikes. The cabins range from tiny unstaffed huts with room for two people through to hostel-style lodges with bathrooms and hot food. DNT members receive preferential rates, and no one is turned away from staffed lodges, even if you have to sleep on the floor.

HOSTELS

Most hostels *(vandrerhjem)* in Norway are only open from May to September, so you'll have to look much harder for budget accommodations if traveling in the wintertime. Dorm rooms typically sleep 4-6 with shared bathroom, kitchen, and lounge facilities. In almost all hostels, guests are required to bring their own bedding or pay a fee (50-100kr) to hire a set. The downside of hosteling in Norway is the price, typically twice what you'd pay elsewhere in Europe. A couple of uncomfortable nights in a cramped 250-350kr dorm bed may make that 600kr guesthouse seem like a steal.

CAMPING

More than a thousand campsites dot the Norwegian countryside, but the majority are only open from May to September, so those open in low season are in high demand. Pitches for RVs and tents are available for around 150-250kr depending on season and the facilities at the campsite. Most campsites have decent kitchen and bathroom facilities, although you should expect to pay 10kr for a shower. Many receptions double as a small kiosk selling bread and other basic groceries at vastly marked-up prices.

Health and Safety

VACCINATIONS AND GENERAL RISKS

Beyond ensuring routine vaccinations are up-to-date, no special preparations are required for travel to Norway. It's a good idea to ensure you are up to date with vaccines for measles-mumps-rubella (MMR), diphtheria-tetanus-pertussis, varicella (chickenpox), polio, and flu. Rabies is present in bats in Norway, but is not a risk to the vast majority of travelers. Only those who plan some serious hiking in remote areas should consider a rabies shot.

The biggest risks to your health in Norway are likely to be weather related. Sunburn and dehydration are possible in the summer but also when the temperatures are below freezing. Long summer days and the sun reflecting off snow in the winter can catch people unaware, so sunscreen and sunglasses are recommended. Blisters are common among inexperienced hikers, and beware of mosquito bites near water. The quality of the tap water is excellent throughout the country.

MEDICAL SERVICES

The Norwegian health care system is founded on the principles of universal access, decentralization, and free choice of provider. This means although health-care policy is handled centrally, the standard of available services can and does vary around the country. Most hospitals in Norway are public hospitals, funded and owned by the state.

Although health care is excellent, it is very expensive, and therefore comprehensive travel insurance is an absolute must. If you intend on taking part in any activities such as skiing, snowboarding, hiking, rock climbing, or motorcycling, be sure it is covered by your travel insurance, as many cheaper policies exclude many forms of outdoor activity that are popular in Norway.

EU/EEA citizens visiting Norway should obtain a free European Health Insurance Card (EHIC) before leaving their country of citizenship. The EHIC isn't a substitute for medical and travel insurance, but it entitles you to the same state-provided medical treatment as Norwegian nationals; you must pay for any treatment out of your own pocket. Reimbursement of these expenses is a matter between you and your national health insurer. For queries on the process within Norway, contact **Helfo** (tel. 33 51 22 80, www.helfo.no). If you misplace your EHIC while in Norway, contact your country's health department for a temporary certificate. The EHIC won't cover repatriation, ongoing medical treatment, or non-urgent treatment, so comprehensive travel insurance is still highly recommended.

Bear in mind that medical facilities in remote areas, especially in Arctic Norway, are spread far apart. Search-and-rescue response will often need to be dispatched from many hundreds of miles away. If traveling through remote regions, talk to a medical professional prior to your trip and develop a contingency plan. Those taking a cruise or boat trip in Arctic Norway should investigate the previous operational experience of operators and consider the on-board medical facilities of the ship in question. Responsible cruise operators should happily provide additional information relevant to the circumstances of the cruise they are offering and address any concerns you may have. Always be sure to have access to funds that will cover the cost of any medical treatment or potential repatriation.

CRIME

Despite the reputation given to the country by its excellent crime novelists, Norway is a safe country in which to travel. Having said that, petty theft has been on the rise in the major cities, so vigilance is still called for.

Drugs are sold openly on the streets near Oslo Central Station. Although the practice is to a certain extent tolerated, it is of course illegal.

Travel Tips

WHAT TO PACK

If you get into conversation with a local during a summer downpour, you'll inevitably hear the Norwegian saying "There's no such thing as bad weather, only bad clothing." (It's actually a lot catchier in Norwegian: *Det finnes ikke dårlig vær, bare dårlige klær.*)

To avoid being subjected to this, packing appropriate clothing is a must. This means waterproofs and plenty of layers at any time of year. Two or three thin layers is better than one thick layer, as you can easily alter your clothing depending on if and when the weather changes. Woolen underwear is an essential component to layering outside the summer, especially if you are traveling to the fjords, mountains, or Arctic region. (Merino wool, while a little expensive, is suitable for most sensitive skin conditions.) Good quality hiking boots or at the very least shoes with good grip are essential if you plan to take any hikes or long walks.

If traveling in the winter, take sunglasses and sunscreen. The reflection of the bright winter sun off the snow February-April can catch many travelers by surprise. Sunburn and dehydration are possible in the summer but also when the temperatures are below freezing.

A basic first-aid kit is recommended for those who plan to hike or travel to any remote parts of the country. Be sure to include mosquito repellent, as bites can be common throughout the summer and into the fall.

BUDGET TRAVEL

Advance planning is the key to avoiding sticker-shock and saving money in one of the world's most expensive travel destinations.

Air travel and train tickets should be booked at least seven days in advance to secure the best deals. Plan your day's itinerary around mealtimes so you are in a place with multiple options when you will want to eat. Being forced to eat at the only restaurant for miles around is a sure-fire way to bust your budget.

Make the most of the generous breakfast buffets offered by hotels and most hostels. Many will allow you to make a packed lunch from the buffet for an additional 50kr, which is much less than buying lunch in a café or restaurant will cost. The quality of tap water is excellent, so invest in a refillable bottle rather than buying expensive bottled water throughout the day.

When it comes to planning your itinerary, look to the Norwegians for inspiration. On their summer vacations, Norwegians young and old tend to stay in basic accommodations, eat simple meals, and spend their time at one with nature in the mountains, fjords, and valleys. Hiking, cycling, and cross-country skiing are all outstanding ways to see the very best Norway has to offer without breaking the bank.

However, when it comes to the cost of travel in Norway, it's best to approach your trip with an open mind. To guarantee a memorable vacation, be prepared to pay for the experiences that you want, and plan to save money in other areas. Advance planning, knowing your priorities, and avoiding the constant urge to calculate the exchange rate is absolutely key to a successful trip.

BUSINESS TRAVEL

Norwegians work to live rather than live to work. Don't expect to take any business meetings on a Friday afternoon, school holidays, or the holiday month of July.

But don't let the short working hours together with the informal attitude to business dress mislead you; Norwegians make the most of their time in the office. Business lunches are short and efficient, generally involving topped open-faced sandwiches and almost never alcohol.

A national attitude toward freedom of information (an individual's tax records are a matter of public record) extends toward business, where honesty trumps a smoke-and-mirrors approach to selling.

ACCESS FOR TRAVELERS WITH DISABILITIES

All trains are adapted for accessibility, and all stations have access ramps and lifts. Some buses, especially within cities, are equipped with ground-level entries to ease the loading of wheelchairs.

In 2014, the Council of Europe awarded the Accessibility Award to Norway for the Oslo Opera House. There is a genuine desire driven by government to improve access for people with disabilities based on equal-access policies. Most modern museums, galleries, and attractions will be equipped with ramps and lifts, while many offer special facilities for the partially sighted and hard of hearing, such as self-guided audio tours and braille information boards.

However, some historical attractions are not so well suited to accessibility because of the difficulty of adapting traditional buildings. Inquire in advance to be sure.

LGBT TRAVEL

Like their Nordic neighbors, Norwegians in general have a liberal attitude toward LGBT people. Norway was among the first countries to introduce anti-discrimination laws against LGBT people. Gays and lesbians have the same rights as heterosexuals in church weddings, adoptions, and assisted pregnancies. Many senior politicians have been openly gay or lesbian, and LGBT people are in general well integrated into society. For this reason, the gay scene is not especially large even in Oslo. The capital is home to several well-established gay bars, nightclubs, and social groups, although Bergen, Stavanger, and Trondheim also have at least one gay venue.

Oslo Pride is the country's primary LGBT festival. Held every summer, the festival provides a very visible recognition of the status of the community within Oslo, with parades, lectures, exhibitions, and political debates alongside the parties. Smaller events take place in Trondheim, Bergen, and Stavanger most years.

A welcome event taking place away from the cities, **Skeive Ski** (www.skeiveski.no) is an annual LGBT ski event. Dubbed "Scandinavian Ski Pride," the event is held every February in Hemsedal, a large ski resort at the very heart of the country, midway between Oslo, Bergen, and Lillehammer.

Skeiv Ungdom (Tollbugata 24, tel. 23 10 39 36, www.skeivungdom.no) is a nationwide youth group for LGBT people under 30. Headquartered in Oslo, the association has branches in most regions.

Although homophobic behavior can and does occur, gay and lesbian travelers should not expect to encounter any problems within Norway.

Information and Services

TOURIST OFFICES

All major cities and many smaller towns will have a well-signposted tourist information center. Opening hours are generally business hours Monday to Friday, although many offices will open daily during the high season. English is spoken at all offices, and English-language publications, maps, and general advice are available.

When offices are closed, and in smaller cities without permanent offices, information boards featuring maps of the local area and including marked hiking trails are readily available and usually signposted.

MONEY

Norway uses the Norwegian krone (plural kroner), commonly written as kr (after the amount) or NOK (before the amount) and often translated by enthusiastic cashiers as the Norwegian crown. Bills are in denominations of 1,000kr, 500kr, 200kr, 100kr, and 50kr. Coins are in denominations of 20kr, 10kr, 5kr, and 1kr. One Norwegian krone is made up of 100 øre, although this subdivision is rarely used now that the smallest coin in circulation is a one-krone coin. A price of 17.90 will be rounded up to 18kr in a store, although the exact amount would be charged to a debit or credit card.

The thousand separator is written as a full stop in Norwegian, with a comma used before any øre amount. For example, 1.000,50 is one-thousand kroner, fifty øre. To prevent confusion, this guide sticks to the English conventions.

The exchange rate has fluctuated wildly between 5.5kr and 8.9kr per US$1 over the past five years. At the time of writing, US$1 bought about 8.5kr.

Changing money can be troublesome, as many bank branches no longer carry cash, and rates on offer at exchange bureaus leave a lot to be desired. The best rates can usually be obtained by simply withdrawing cash from an ATM, but be aware of what your own bank will charge you for this service. Many banks have ATMs inside a vestibule that is open outside of regular banking hours.

Debit and credit cards are the primary form of payment in almost all Norwegian stores, regardless of the amount. Digital solutions are rapidly taking over from cash, so much so that cash is expected to be phased out from everyday transactions in the coming years. It's a good idea nonetheless to keep some cash on you at all times, as some of the cheaper card readers only accept Norwegian debit cards. For all ferries and the vast majority of tourist attractions, international credit cards will work fine.

Tipping

Tipping is not necessary in restaurants because all staff are paid a fair wage. Rounding up the bill is considered a compliment on the service. However, don't be surprised to see extra enthusiasm from your waiter or waitress when they realize you are a foreigner. North Americans are especially well looked after given their reputation for tipping well.

Taxes

If you buy goods priced more than 315kr from stores that display the blue Tax Free logo, you're entitled to a refund of the 25 percent MVA, the Norwegian equivalent of a sales tax that is added to the price of most goods and services. At the point of sale, you must complete a form, which you then present at your point of departure along with the goods to claim your refund. Tourist information offices stock an information leaflet detailing the process, as do all shops displaying the logo.

COMMUNICATIONS
Telephone

The country code for Norway is 47. Norwegian

phone numbers are eight digits long, and there are no area codes. To call a number from within the country, you just dial the eight digits. (Some information services and taxi providers use special shortened five-digit numbers that start with 0; in these cases, you just dial the five digits.) To call Norway from abroad, dial the international access code plus 47 followed by the five- or eight-digit number.

The directory inquiry service at **Gule Sider** (www.gulesider.no) will provide the phone numbers of the majority of businesses and individuals and also allow you to find the owner of a phone number.

MOBILE PHONES

Roaming prices across the European Economic Area (EEA) were slashed in 2016, meaning that most citizens of EEA countries can use their mobile phones in Norway as if they were in their home country; check with your carrier for confirmation and any exceptions. For others, prepaid SIM cards can be purchased in convenience stores and in kiosks in all airports and public transport hubs. **Telenor** (www.telenor.no) and **Telia** (www.telia.no) are the two biggest carriers in Norway and offer cards for 100kr and 200kr suitable for calls and text messages, and up to 500kr for data. Other options include **Chess** (www.chess.no) and **Lycamobile** (www.lyca-mobile.no).

Internet Access

Wireless Internet connectivity is commonplace in Norwegian hotels, shopping centers, and cafés. Most require a simple login procedure with a password that can be obtained from reception or on purchase of an item.

TIME ZONE

All of Norway observes Central European Time (CET), which is one hour ahead of Greenwich Mean Time (GMT) and six hours ahead of the U.S. Eastern time zone. Daylight Saving Time is observed but the exact dates can differ by a week or two from the United States, so double-check if traveling in the spring or fall.

WEIGHTS AND MEASURES

Norway uses the metric system. All road signs are in kilometers and all weights are given in kilograms/grams. Beer is served in liters, with 0.4 and 0.6 used commonly used to indicate 400 ml (small) and 600 ml (large) respectively.

Standard voltage in Norway is 230 V. The power sockets take the rounded two-prong Type F plugs, which are common across much of mainland Europe. Power adapters are available from airports, major train stations, and **Clas Ohlson** (www.clasohlson.com) and **Lefdal** (www.lefdal.com) stores across the country.

Resources

Glossary

In Norwegian (and unlike in English), descriptive words such as lake *(vann, vannet, vatnet)*, mountain *(fjell)*, waterfall *(foss, fossen)*, and so on are incorporated into the place name. This is handy information to know when you are unsure what a place name might mean.

akevitt: a traditional Scandinavian distilled spirit spiced with caraway or dill; also known as aquavit

bacalao: dried and salted cod, typically cooked in a tomato-based sauce; not to be confused with the Spanish word *bacalao* (fresh cod)

bidos: slow-cooked reindeer stew, a traditional Sami dish

bløtkake: a layer cake of vanilla sponge and cream, often decorated with strawberries

brunost: brown cheese, a sweet dairy product and one of Norway's most iconic foods

by: city or town, all places from Oslo down to all but the smallest villages

dal: valley

damer: ladies; may be displayed on a bathroom door as simply "D"

ferge: ferry

fjell: mountain

foss, fossen: waterfall

fylke: county; Norway is split into 19 counties, although that number is set to decrease in the coming years as several counties merge (road numbers sometimes change across county borders)

gamalost/gammelost: extremely strong, firm, sour cheese; hard to find outside Norway

gate: street

gjestehus: guesthouse

gulost: any variety of mild, yellow cheese

herrer: gentlemen; may be displayed on a bathroom door as simply "H"

hval: whale

hytte: cabin

jolk: a traditional Sami folk song

kjøttboller: meatballs

kjøttkaker: larger meatballs (but smaller than a burger patty)

kommune: municipality

kransekake: an eye-catching traditional celebratory cake, made up of donut-like rings piled into a pyramid

kvæfjordkake: a cake of meringue, almond, and vanilla cream

lavvu: a traditional large Sami tent

lefse/lefser: a soft flatbread of varying thickness, commonly served with butter, sugar, and/or cinnamon

lege: doctor

legevakt: emergency room; sometimes, but not always, colocated at a hospital

lutefisk: dried cod treated with lye, a Norwegian speciality of acquired taste

matpakke: a packed lunch, typically consisting of sandwiches

pensjon: guesthouse, bed-and-breakfast

pinnekjøtt: dried and salted lamb

plass: place, typically a public square

pølser: hot dog sausages, typically served in buns or a tortilla-like wrap

risgrøt: rice porridge, often served at Christmas

rom: room

rorbuer: traditional fisherman's cabin, often now used as vacation cabins

sentrum: downtown
stengt: closed
stranda: beach
sykehus: hospital
tannlege: dentist
torsk: cod
ungdom: youth
vandrerhjem: hostel
vann, vannet, vatnet: lake

ABBREVIATIONS

Ca: often precedes a time on a live information board at public transit stops; it indicates an approximate time, usually the time listed on the timetable when live information is unavailable

Fv: *fylkesvei* (county road)

kr: kroner, the currency of Norway, which translates as "crowns"; also occasionally written before the number as NOK (Norwegian kroner)

Mvh: *med vennlig hilsen* (with kind regards); often used as a shorthand way of signing off a letter or email

Rv: *riksvei* (national road)

Norwegian Phrasebook

English is spoken and understood throughout Norway by all but the oldest generation. A little Norwegian goes a long way toward getting a smile, but the person will almost certainly respond to you in English. Don't take offense, as Norwegians absolutely love to practice their English with native speakers.

PRONUNCIATION

Regional dialects are strong throughout Norway, so don't be dismayed if you cannot understand the locals, particularly in Bergen and the rural regions surrounding the fjords. The biggest differences tend to be with pronunciation of prepositions, which can make understanding even basic sentences difficult for beginners.

Almost all Norwegian lessons teach the standard Eastern Norwegian dialect, also known as the Oslo dialect. Most Norwegian words place the emphasis on the first syllable, which results in the sing-song melody the language is known for.

Vowels

Each vowel can be either long or short. As a general rule, a vowel is long if it followed by one consonant and short if it is followed by two. This distinguishes *tak* (roof) from *takk* (thanks). Norwegian has three extra vowels at the end of the alphabet: æ, ø, and å. Although at first confusing, the sounds all exist in English.

a   resembles the a in "tar"
e   resembles the e in "left"
i   resembles the ee in "teeth"
o   resembles the o in "lord" or the oo in "soon" when long
u   resembles the oo in "foot"
y   English speakers have trouble with this vowel; a good approximation is to make an "ee" sound but with pursed lips
æ   resembles the a in "hat"
ø   resembles the u in "burn"
å   resembles the o in "lord"

Consonants

The letters c, q, w, x, and z are rare and only tend to be used in foreign loan words. Notable differences in pronunciation include:

g   like the hard English g, except when used before i or j when it resembles the y in "yes"; also, a g is always silent at the end of a word
j   resembles the y in "yes"
k   like the hard English k, except when used before I or j, when it resembles the soft ch in "loch"
r   a very soft sound, like the "r" in "feather"; some dialects roll the r as in Spanish

BASIC EXPRESSIONS

Norwegian is a simple direct language and can appear abrupt when translated. For example, there is no direct equivalent for please, and using the nearest equivalent, *vær så snill,* is only required in the most formal of scenarios. You can add *takk* (thank you) on to the end of a request to convey politeness. To start a conversation with a Norwegian, a simple *Hei! (hay)* (Hi!) or *Unnskyld? (un-shull)* (Excuse me?) is all that is required.

Hello. *Hallo.*
Hi. *Hei.*
Good morning. *God morgen.*
How are you? *Hvordan går det?*
I'm fine, thank you. *Jeg har det bra, takk.*
Thank you. *Takk.*
Thank you very much. *Tusen takk.*
You're welcome. *Vær så god.*
No problem. *Bare hyggelig.*
Good-bye. *Ha det bra.*
yes *ja*
no *nei*
I don't know. *Jeg vet ikke.*
Just a moment. *Ett øyeblikk.*
Excuse me? *Unnskyld?*
Sorry. *Beklager.*
What is your name? *Hva heter du?*
My name is . . . *Jeg heter . . .*
Pleased to meet you. *Hyggelig å treffe deg.*
Do you speak English? *Snakker du engelsk?*
I don't understand Norwegian. *Jeg forstår ikke norsk.*
Where is the bathroom? *Hvor er toalettet?*
Ladies *Damer*
Gentlemen *Herrer*

TERMS OF ADDRESS

Norwegians often address people using just their surname or simply saying *du* (you).

I *Jeg*
you *du/dere* (singular/plural)
he *han*
she *hun*
we *vi*
they *de*
man *mann*

woman *kvinne*
boy *gutt*
girl *jente*
husband *ektemann*
wife *kone*
friend *venn*
son *sønn*
daughter *datter*
brother *bror*
sister *søster*
father *far*
mother *mor*
grandfather *bestefar*
grandmother *bestemor*

TRANSPORTATION

car *bil*
bus *buss*
train *tog*
boat *båt*
plane *fly*
airport bus *flybuss*
the border *grensen*
customs *toll*
immigration *innvandring*
passport *pass*
insurance *forsikring*
driver's license *førerkort*
Where is . . . ? *Hvor er . . . ?*
How far is it to . . . ? *Jeg vet ikke . . . ?*
(the) bus station *busstasjon(en), bussterminal(en)*
(the) train station *jernbanestasjon(en)*
(the) ferry port *fergelei(et), fergekai(en)*
(the) airport *flyplass(en)*
downtown *sentrum*
Where is the train/bus/ferry to . . . ? *Hvor finner jeg toget/bussen/fergen til . . . ?*
Does this stop at . . . ? *Stopper denne på . . . ?*
How much is a ticket to . . . ? *Hva koster en billett til . . . ?*
I want to go to . . . *Jeg skal til . . .*
one-way *envei*
round-trip *tur/retur* (literally, trip/return)
canceled *kansellert, avlyst*
delayed *forsinket*

north *nord*
south *sør, syd*
east *øst*
west *vest*
left *venstre*
right *høyre*

ACCOMMODATIONS

hotel *hotell*
youth hostel *vandrerhjem*
campsite *camping*
cabin *hytte*
guesthouse *gjestehus/pensjon*
apartment *leilighet*
room *rom*
bathroom *bad*
balcony *balkong*
Is there a single/double room? *Finnes*
   det et enkeltrom/dobbelrom?
How much does it cost per night? *Hva*
   koster det per natt?
Is breakfast included? *Er frokost inkludert?*

FOOD

When ordering food, it is common to simply
state the specific item with no "Can I have ..."
preceding it. Another option is to precede the
item with *Jeg ta ...*, which literally means "I'll
take ..." With no direct equivalent for please,
use *takk* (thanks) after the order to convey politeness.

breakfast *frokost*
lunch *lunsj*
dinner *middag*
a table for two *et bord til to*
menu *meny*
What does it include? *Hva inkluderer det?*
I am allergic to ... *Jeg er allergisk mot ...*
I don't eat meat. *Jeg spiser ikke kjøtt.*
Is there a menu in English? *Finnes det en*
   meny på engelsk?
fork *gaffel*
knife *kniv*
spoon *skje*
the check *regningen*
a glass of water *et glass vann*
a glass of wine *et glass vin*
beer *øl*

coffee *kaffe*
juice *jus*
red wine *rødvin*
soft drink *brus*
tea *te*
white wine *hvitvin*
with/without milk *med/uten melk*
with/without cream *med/uten krem*
with/without sugar *med/uten suker*
meat *kjøtt*
fish *fisk*
seafood *sjømat*
beef *oksekjøtt, storfekjøtt*
chicken *kylling*
cod *torsk*
dried cod *tørrfisk*
dried cod (salted) *klippfisk*
duck *and*
halibut *kveite*
herring *sild*
lamb *lam*
mackerel *makrell*
pork *svinekjøtt*
reindeer *reinsdyr*
salmon *laks*
shellfish *skalldyr*
shrimp *reker*
trout *ørret*
whale *hval*
fruit *frukt*
vegetables *grønnsaker*
apple *eple*
banana *banan*
beans *bønner*
blueberry *blåbær*
carrot *gulrot*
cloudberry *multe*
corn *korn/mais*
orange *appelsin*
pineapple *ananas*
potato *potet*
raspberry *bringebær*
strawberry *jordbær*
tomato *tomat*
nuts *nøtter*
wheat *hvete*
dairy products *melkeprodukter*
butter *smør*

cheese ost
ice cream is
milk melk
pepper pepper
salt salt

SHOPPING

I'm looking for . . . Jeg letter etter . . .
How much does it cost? Hva koster det?
money penger
ATM minibank
credit card kredittkort
shopping mall kjøpesenter

HEALTH

Can you help me? Kan du hjelpe meg?
I am ill. Jeg er syk.
I need a doctor. Jeg trenger en lege.
pharmacy apotek
hospital sykehus
doctor lege
dentist tannlege
emergency room legevakt
pain smerte
fever feber
nausea kvalme
vomiting oppkast

NUMBERS

zero null
one en, ett
two to
three tre
four fire
five fem
six seks
seven sju, syv
eight åtte
nine ni
10 ti
11 elleve
12 tolv
13 tretten
14 fjorten
15 femten
16 seksten
17 sytten
18 atten
19 nitten
20 tjue, tyve
30 tretti
40 førti
50 femti
60 seksti
70 sytti
80 åtti
90 nitti
100 (ett) hundre
101 (ett) hundre og en
200 to hundre
500 fem hundre
1,000 (ett) tusen
2,000 to tusen
1,000,000 en million
half halv
quarter kvart
less mindre
more mer

TIME

Time is usually written using the 24-hour clock, so supermarket opening hours of 8-20 mean 8am-8pm. Stores often put Saturday hours in parentheses, with the assumption it will be closed on Sunday: e.g., 8-20 (10-16).

When time is spoken, it's common to use the 12-hour clock. The biggest difference is how half-hours are treated. Halv fire translates as "half to four" not "half past four" as you would first expect. If in doubt, always ask for written confirmation of times. It's also a good idea never to say "half four" to a Norwegian when you mean 4:30, as it could well be misunderstood.

What time is it? Hva er klokka?
It's one o'clock. Klokka er ett.
It's five past one. Klokka er fem over ett.
It's quarter past eight. Klokka er kvart over åtte.
It's 3:35. Klokka er fem over halv fire.
noon middagstid
midnight midnatt
morning morgen
afternoon ettermiddag
evening kveld
night natt

yesterday *i går*
today *i dag*
tomorrow *i morgen*
an hour *en time*
a day *en dag*
a week *en uke*
a month *en måned*
a year *et år*

DAYS, MONTHS, AND SEASONS

Days, months, and seasons are always written in lowercase. A common way to write the date is the number followed by a dot followed by the first three letters of the month: e.g., 4.jul for July 4.

Monday *mandag*
Tuesday *tirsdag*
Wednesday *onsdag*
Thursday *torsdag*
Friday *fredag*
Saturday *lørdag*
Sunday *søndag*
January *januar*
February *februar*
March *mars*
April *april*
May *mai*
June *juni*
July *juli*
August *august*
September *september*
October *oktober*
November *november*
December *desember*
spring *vår*
summer *sommer*
autumn *vår*
winter *vinter*

Suggested Reading

HISTORY

Hunt, Vincent. *Fire and Ice: The Nazis' Scorched Earth Campaign in Norway.* The History Press, 2014. Norway's grim World War II history is told in thousands of Norwegian language books, but previously little existed in English. British journalist Vincent Hunt traveled across Arctic Norway to uncover the human tales behind the devastation of Finnmark at the end of the war.

Roesdahl, Else. *The Vikings.* Penguin, 1998. Hundreds of books exist profiling the most famous period of Nordic history, but this one can be considered the gold standard. Roesdahl gives the Scandinavian perspective on the art, customs, and daily life of the Viking people, blowing wide open their reputation as a band of savage explorers.

CRIME FICTION

Holt, Anne. *1222.* Scribner, 2012. As the former Norwegian Minister of Justice, Holt brings an air of realism to her detective novels. A classic locked-room mystery, *1222* is set in an atmospheric snowed-in mountain hotel following a train crash on the Oslo to Bergen railway.

MacLean, Alistair. *Bear Island.* Harper, 2009 reissue. A converted fishing trawler carries a production crew across the Barents Sea for some on-location filming, but the script is known only to the producer and screenwriter. On the way to remote Bear Island, members of the crew begin to die under mysterious circumstances. It seems that nearly everyone in the crew had secrets and were not who they claimed to be.

Nesbø, Jo. *The Redbreast.* Harper Perennial, 2008. The former soccer player, financial analyst, and rock star turned his hand to crime novels in 1997 and hasn't looked back since. His series following fictional Oslo sleuth Harry Hole investigating a series of gruesome murders is a worldwide smash. *The Redbreast* is the best introduction and won't spoil the earlier books.

LITERATURE

Gaader, Jostein. *Sophie's World*. Weidenfeld & Nicolson, 1994. One of the most globally successful Norwegian novels, *Sophie's World* is a long, complex tale of teenage Sophie Amundsen, who begins to learn philosophy under the guidance of a middle-aged professor. As Sophie begins to question the world in which she lives, the story takes an unlikely twist. A little heavy on the philosophy it may be, but it's key to developing the story.

Jacobsen, Roy. *Child Wonder*. Graywolf Press, 2011. In this uplifting coming-of-age novel set in 1960s Oslo, eight-year-old Finn lives with his mother, and they just about make ends meet in a working-class suburb. Soon Finn experiences dramatic change as a lodger arrives, followed by a younger sister whom he never knew existed. An intricately worked story, rich in detail and a beautiful exploration of an adult world through the mind of a child.

Kirkwood, Thomas, and Geir Finne. *The Svalbard Passage*. CreateSpace, 2011. Co-written by Norwegian and American authors, this Cold War thriller has a familiar premise—the United States and the United Soviet Socialist Republic on the verge of nuclear war—but with an unfamiliar setting: the Norwegian Arctic territory of Svalbard. Not the most dramatic of thrillers, yet the dramatic descriptions of Svalbard will draw you into the story.

Knausgård, Karl Ove. *A Death in the Family*. Farrar, Straus, and Giroux, 2013. The first in the *My Struggle* autobiographical series that captivated Norwegian readers for years before the books made their international breakthrough, this honest window exposes the fragility of the teenage mind while providing a frank and critical look at those who influenced the author's early years. Odds are you'll want to read the remaining five parts in this epic series.

NATURE AND THE ENVIRONMENT

Francis, Gavin. *True North: Travels in Arctic Europe*. Polygon, 2008. This travelogue sets northern Norway in context with the rest of Arctic Europe, from the windswept Shetland Isles to the indigenous villages of Greenland. It's an engaging narrative that traces the history of polar exploration along with the stories of the locals the author meets on his journey.

Jørgensen, Morten. *Polar Bears on the Edge: Heading for Extinction While Management Fails*. Self-published, 2015. This eye-opening book asks provocative questions about whether enough is being done to protect the remaining population of polar bears on Svalbard and elsewhere in the Arctic. The author painstakingly builds a case to say that human involvement, not climate change, is the biggest threat to the species.

SOCIETY AND CULTURE

Booth, Michael. *The Almost Nearly Perfect People: The Truth About the Nordic Miracle*. Picador, 2015. Loved and criticized in equal measure, British journalist Booth's study of the Nordic people is skewed toward his perceptions of his adopted homeland Denmark, but it contains some interesting observations on Norwegians, in particular their attitude toward their Swedish and Danish siblings.

Mytting, Lars. *Norwegian Wood: Chopping, Stacking and Drying Wood the Scandinavian Way*. MacLehose Press, 2015. Surely one of the most unlikely nonfiction successes ever written, this handbook on the Norwegian relationship with the forest has sold over half a million copies worldwide. Mytting has distilled the chopping, storing, drying, and burning wisdom of professionals and enthusiasts into this truly Scandinavian tome. You'll never look at your firewood in the same way again.

Seierstad, Anne. *One of Us: The Story of Anders Breivik and the Massacre in Norway.* Virago, 2015. When the peaceful Utøya island was scarred forever in 2011, Norwegians were taken aback that the atrocity had been committed by one of their own. Beginning with a powerful narrative from the island, Norwegian journalist Seierstad proceeds to provide a meticulously researched, honest yet compassionate account of the tragedy, as well as the background of the man behind it.

FOOD

Love, Whitney. *Thanks for the Food: The Culinary Adventures of an American in Norway.* Digital Word Norway, 2014. An American expat living in Stavanger, Love turned her popular food blog into a recipe book that combines the traditional national dishes with a modern twist on classic ingredients. She also shares her tips for travelers wanting to make the most of their visits to Norway's famous agricultural, fishing, and dairy regions.

Thorud, Richard A. *Aunt Hildur's Excellent Norwegian Recipes.* Elliot House, 2013. This very small book is reminiscent of the recipes Norwegian grandmothers would have passed around at church decades ago. It's worth it for the traditional methods of making *lefse* and *kransekake* without lots of fancy, modern equipment.

FOR CHILDREN

Brett, Jan. *Trouble with Trolls.* G.P. Putnam's Sons, 2016 reissue. This beautifully illustrated 32-page hardback is the perfect way to get younger children excited about a visit to Norway. The story follows Treva and her dog Tuffi as they set out to climb Mount Baldy. But the mountain is inhabited by a family of trolls who wish for a dog. Every page details a new challenge for Treva and Tuffi as they bid to outwit the trolls.

Preus, Margi. *Shadow on the Mountain.* Amulet Books, 2012. Written by a Minnesota native, this novel captures the atmosphere and danger of living in Norway during World War II. Loosely based on real events, the part spy thriller part coming-of-age tale follows teenager Epsen as he is swept up in the resistance movement, first by delivering underground newsletters and eventually becoming a spy.

Internet Resources

GENERAL INTEREST

**Norwegian Polar Institute
(Norsk Polarinstitutt)
www.npolar.no**
Norway's central governmental institution for scientific research, mapping, and environmental monitoring in the Arctic and the Antarctic.

HIKING

**Norwegian Trekking Association
(Den Norske Turistforening)
www.dnt.no**
Your starting point for planning a hiking trip, DNT provides a wealth of information about the vast network of hiking trails, cross-country skiing routes, and cabins across the country.

UT
www.ut.no

This site offers detailed maps and instructions for hiking trails across the country, from beginner to week-long expeditions. Large maps can be printed or downloaded to a GPS device. It's only available in Norwegian but useful regardless.

NEWS AND MEDIA

Aftenposten
www.aftenposten.no

Aftenposten is a national daily newspaper with a particular focus on Oslo. Occasionally, major breaking news is published in English.

The Local
www.thelocal.no

The Local is the most frequently updated English-language news source.

NRK
www.nrk.no

State broadcaster NRK runs several TV channels, a breaking news website, a radio station, and a vast podcast network. Occasionally, major breaking news is published in English.

SOCIETY

A Frog in the Fjord
www.afroginthefjord.com

The funniest website about Norway, this expat blog written by a French lady living in Oslo since 2010 has been syndicated and translated into Norwegian by major newspapers.

Life in Norway
www.lifeinnorway.net

Expats from all over the world who have made Norway their home contribute to this insider look on Norwegian culture and society.

TRAVEL INFORMATION

Avinor
www.avinor.no

Almost all Norwegian airports are run by state-owned Avinor, whose website provides excellent live departure and arrivals information plus a detailed rundown of facilities available at each airport, all fully translated into English. Their excellent **Avinor Flights** app (download link on website) is a useful way to access the same live information on the move.

Norwegian Public Roads Administration (Statens Vegvesen)
www.vegvesen.no

The place to go for all driving-related information. Of particular interest to travelers is the list of toll roads and the current status of road closures.

Visit Norway
www.visitnorway.com

The country's official travel guide is maintained by Innovation Norway, a body given the responsibility to promote Norway as an attractive travel destination by the Ministry of Trade, Industry, and Fisheries.

Norway Traveller
www.norwaytraveller.com

Destination guides and travel blog about visiting Norway for international tourists. Includes advice on hunting for the northern lights, skiing in Norway, and enjoying the best of Norway on a budget.

WEATHER

Yr
www.yr.no

A joint venture between state broadcaster NRK and the Norwegian Meteorological Institute, Yr provides excellent hyperlocal weather forecasts, including rain and wind. Download the app for weather on the move.

Index

WXYZ

List of Maps

Photo Credits

Acknowledgments

Undertaking research of a guidebook to an entire country is a mammoth task and one which I couldn't have completed without heaps of help and assistance from many people. First and foremost, I thank my partner, Gerardo Alfredo Perez Valdes, and apologize for the months spent on the road and in the air away from our brand-new home, followed by weeks of frantic late-night writing sessions.

Second on the list is the team at Avalon Travel who have worked tirelessly to make this book the best it can possibly be. In particular, I must thank acquisitions editor Elizabeth Hansen for her help in taking the book from idea to final proposal and project editor Kathryn Ettinger for answering a barrage of questions throughout the process and being patient with my constant use of Britishisms.

Thanks must also go to the following people: the pilots and cabin crew of Scandinavian Airlines, Norwegian, and Widerøe and the drivers of NSB for getting me safely around the country; photographer Cody Duncan and Destination Lofoten's Kristian Nashoug for their helpful advice on Lofoten and Vesterålen; Raymond Limstrand Jakobsen for his help in arranging a tour of Bodø; Kyle Parsonage in the Visit Tromsø office and blogger Vanessa Brune for their savvy advice; Trine Risvik for her insights into the northern lights and a memorable evening chasing the tricky lady; food writer Whitney Love for her restaurant and coffee shop recommendations in Stavanger; Wil and Ida Lee-Wright from *The List* magazine for their recommendations of restaurants in Trondheim; Elise Aasen for showing me every corner of Ålesund and making sure I didn't miss the hidden delights of the Giske islands and the Hjørundfjord; Dave Harrison-Fox for sharing his geological expertise; and Tara Kelly Dolgner for her help in getting to grips with the constantly changing restaurant scene of Oslo.

Last but not least, thanks to the readers of *Life in Norway, Norway Traveller, Norway Weekly,* and the *Norwegian American* for their help, support, and suggestions during the course of the research.

Also Available

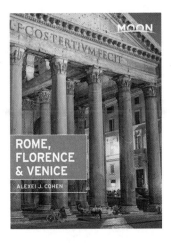

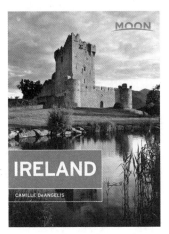

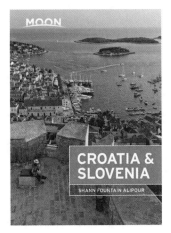

MAP SYMBOLS

≡≡≡ Expressway	○ City/Town	✈ Airport	⚲ Golf Course
═══ Primary Road	◉ State Capital	✗ Airfield	🅿 Parking Area
═══ Secondary Road	⊛ National Capital	▲ Mountain	⬟ Archaeological Site
- - - - Unpaved Road	★ Point of Interest	✛ Unique Natural Feature	⌂ Church
━━━ Feature Trail	• Accommodation		⛽ Gas Station
- - - - - Other Trail	▾ Restaurant/Bar	🐾 Waterfall	Glacier
·········· Ferry	■ Other Location	♠ Park	Mangrove
═══ Pedestrian Walkway		⊓ Trailhead	Reef
▥▥▥ Stairs	Λ Campground	⛷ Skiing Area	Swamp

CONVERSION TABLES

°C = (°F - 32) / 1.8
°F = (°C x 1.8) + 32
1 inch = 2.54 centimeters (cm)
1 foot = 0.304 meters (m)
1 yard = 0.914 meters
1 mile = 1.6093 kilometers (km)
1 km = 0.6214 miles
1 fathom = 1.8288 m
1 chain = 20.1168 m
1 furlong = 201.168 m
1 acre = 0.4047 hectares
1 sq km = 100 hectares
1 sq mile = 2.59 square km
1 ounce = 28.35 grams
1 pound = 0.4536 kilograms
1 short ton = 0.90718 metric ton
1 short ton = 2,000 pounds
1 long ton = 1.016 metric tons
1 long ton = 2,240 pounds
1 metric ton = 1,000 kilograms
1 quart = 0.94635 liters
1 US gallon = 3.7854 liters
1 Imperial gallon = 4.5459 liters
1 nautical mile = 1.852 km

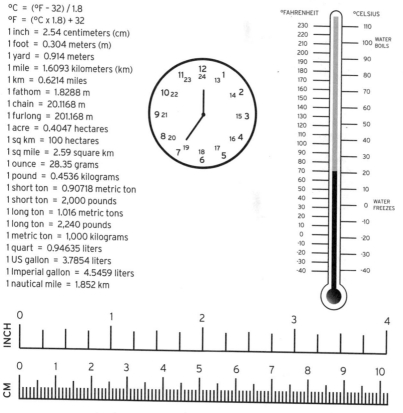

MOON NORWAY

Avalon Travel
Hachette Book Group
1700 Fourth Street
Berkeley, CA 94710, USA
www.moon.com

Editor and Series Manager: Kathryn Ettinger
Copy Editor: Deana Shields
Graphics and Production Coordinator:
  Lucie Ericksen
Cover Design: Faceout Studios, Charles Brock
Interior Design: Domini Dragoone
Moon Logo: Tim McGrath
Map Editor: Kat Bennett
Cartographers: Bart Wright (Lohnes+Wright),
  Kat Bennett
Indexer: Deana Shields

ISBN-13: 978-1-63121-481-3

Printing History
1st Edition — September 2017
5 4 3 2 1

Text © 2017 by David Nikel.
Maps © 2017 by Avalon Travel.

Front cover photo: Geirangerfjord © imageBROKER
  / Alamy Stock Photo
Back cover photo: wooden fishing cabins in Norway
  © Galyna Andrushko/123RF

Printed in Canada by Friesens

Avalon Travel is a division of Hachette Book Group, Inc. Moon and the Moon logo are trademarks of Hachette Book Group, Inc. All other marks and logos depicted are the property of the original owners.